HISTORICAL DICTIONARY
OF
NORTH AMERICAN
ARCHAEOLOGY

Historical Dictionary
of
North American Archaeology

Edward B. Jelks
EDITOR

Juliet C. Jelks
ASSISTANT EDITOR

GREENWOOD PRESS
NEW YORK • WESTPORT, CONNECTICUT • LONDON

Library of Congress Cataloging-in-Publication Data

Historical dictionary of North American archaeology.

Bibliography: p.
Includes index.
1. Indians of North America—Antiquities—Dictionaries.
2. North America—Antiquities—Dictionaries.
3. Archaeology—North America—Dictionaries. I. Jelks,
Edward B. II. Jelks, Juliet C.
E77.9.H57   1988   970.01   87–17581
ISBN 0–313–24307–7 (lib. bdg. : alk. paper)

British Library Cataloguing in Publication Data is available.

Library of Congress Catalog Card Number: 87–17581
ISBN: 0–313–24307–7

First published in 1988

Greenwood Press, Inc.
88 Post Road West, Westport, Connecticut 06881

Printed in the United States of America

The paper used in this book complies with the
Permanent Paper Standard issued by the National
Information Standards Organization (Z39.48–1984).

10 9 8 7 6 5 4 3 2 1

To the memory of
WILLIAM S. WILLIS, JR.

Contents

Editors, Consultants, and Contributors

Editor: Edward B. Jelks, Professor Emeritus, Illinois State University
Assistant Editor: Juliet C. Jelks

REGIONAL CONSULTANTS

California: R. E. Taylor and Louis A. Payen, University of California, Riverside
Eastern Arctic and Subarctic: Moreau S. Maxwell, Michigan State University
Great Basin: Robert L. Bettinger, University of California, Davis
Middle Atlantic: Joffre L. Coe, University of North Carolina, Chapel Hill
Midwest: Charles E. Cleland, Michigan State University
Northeast: James A. Tuck, Memorial University of Newfoundland
Northwest Coast: Donald H. Mitchell, University of Victoria
Plains: Patricia J. O'Brien, Kansas State University
Plateau: Frank C. Leonhardy, University of Idaho
Southeast: John A. Walthall, Illinois Department of Transportation
Southwest: Stewart Peckham, Museum of New Mexico
Western Arctic and Subarctic: Donald W. Clark, Archaeological Survey of
  Canada

CONTRIBUTORS

Robert E. Ackerman, Washington State University
Larry D. Agenbroad, Northern Arizona University
George A. Agogino, Eastern New Mexico University
Stanley A. Ahler, University of North Dakota
C. Melvin Aikens, University of Oregon
Bruce Anderson, National Park Service, Sante Fe, New Mexico

Duane C. Anderson, University of Iowa

David J. W. Archer, University of Calgary

Lawrence E. Aten, National Park Service, Washington, D.C.

Janet R. Balsom, National Park Service, Grand Canyon National Park, Arizona

Larry D. Banks, U.S. Army Corps of Engineers, Dallas

Charles J. Bareis, University of Illinois

William M. Bass, University of Tennessee

Patrick H. Beckett, COAS Publishing & Research, Las Cruces, New Mexico

Donald J. Blakeslee, Wichita State University

David A. Breternitz, University of Colorado

James A. Brown, Northwestern University

David V. Burley, University of Saskatchewan

Robert J. Burton, U.S. Army Corps of Engineers, Dallas

Brian M. Butler, Southern Illinois University, Carbondale

William J. Byrne, Alberta Cultural & Historical Resources, Edmonton

John S. Cable, Pueblo Grande Museum, Phoenix, Arizona

Roy L. Carlson, Simon Fraser University

Jefferson Chapman, University of Tennessee

Gerald H. Clark, U.S. Forest Service, Juneau, Alaska

James E. Corbin, Stephen F. Austin State University

Gary Coupland, University of British Columbia

Darrell G. Creel, Texas A&M University

Patricia L. Crown, Southern Methodist University

Richard D. Daugherty, Washington State University

John Dewhirst, Archaeotech Associates, Victoria, British Columbia

Herbert W. Dick, New Mexico Mining and Milling, Inc., Taos

Roy S. Dickens, Jr., University of North Carolina

David E. Doyel, Pueblo Grande Museum, Phoenix, Arizona

Stephen R. Durand, Desert Research Institute, Reno, Nevada

Frank W. Eddy, University of Colorado

Keith T. Egloff, Virginia Department of Conservation and Historic Resources, Yorktown

Michael L. Elliott, Jemez Mountains Research Center, Albuquerque, New Mexico

Robert G. Elston, Intermountain Research, Silver City, Nevada

Duane Esarey, Dickson Mounds Museum, Lewiston, Illinois

Gloria J. Fenner, National Park Service, Tucson, Arizona

Knut R. Fladmark, Simon Fraser University

Richard G. Forbis, University of Calgary

Andrew C. Fortier, University of Illinois

Richard A. Fox, University of Calgary

Gay Frederick, University of Victoria

George C. Frison, University of Wyoming

Gayle Fritz, Arkansas Archeological Survey, State University

Eugene M. Futato, University of Alabama

Jerry Galm, Eastern Washington University

Roger T. Grange, Jr., University of South Florida

N'omi B. Greber, Cleveland Museum of Natural History

Robert E. Greengo, University of Washington

Roger D. Grosser, Army Corps of Engineers, Kansas City, Missouri

George J. Gumerman, Southern Illinois University, Carbondale

J. N. Gunderson, Wichita State University

Janice A. Guy, University of Texas, Austin

William G. Haag, Louisiana State University

James C. Haggarty, British Columbia Provincial Museum, Victoria, British Columbia

Leonard Ham, Richmond, British Columbia

Margaret Hanna, Museum of Natural History, Regina, Saskatchewan

Alan D. Harn, Dickson Mounds Museum, Lewistown, Illinois

Patricia A. Hicks, Desert Research Institute, Reno, Nevada

Christy Hohman-Caine, U.S. Forest Service, Duluth, Minnesota

Vance T. Holliday, Texas A&M University

Margaret B. Holman, Michigan State University

Margaret Ann Howard, Prewitt and Associates, Austin, Texas

Wesley R. Hurt, Indiana University

Cynthia Irwin-Williams, Desert Research Institute, Reno, Nevada

Eileen Johnson, Texas Tech University

Elden Johnson, University of Minnesota

Thomas F. Kehoe, Milwaukee Public Museum

James H. Kellar, Indiana University

Richard A. Krause, University of Alabama

Richard W. Lang, Sante Fe, New Mexico

Frances Levine, Santa Fe, New Mexico

Alexander J. Lindsay, Jr., Arizona State Museum, Tucson

Christopher Lintz, Albuquerque, New Mexico

William Lipe, Washington State University

Kerry Lippincott, Casper, Wyoming

Susan V. Lisk, Prewitt and Associates, Austin, Texas

John Ludwickson, Nebraska State Historical Society, Lincoln, Nebraska

Margaret M. Lyneis, University of Nevada, Las Vegas

David B. Madsen, Utah State Historical Society, Salt Lake City, Utah

Robert J. Mallouf, Texas Historical Commission, Austin, Texas

Frances Joan Mathien, National Park Service, Sante Fe, New Mexico

R. G. Matson, Northern Arizona University

Charle E. McGimsey, Illinois State Museum, Springfield

Peter J. McKenna, National Park Service, Santa Fe, New Mexico

Jerald T. Milanich, Florida State Museum

Michael J. Moratto, Infotec Research, Inc., Sonora, California

Dan F. Morse, Arkansas Archeological Survey, State University

Phyllis A. Morse, Arkansas Archeological Survey, State University

Robert W. Neuman, Louisiana State University

Larry V. Nordby, National Park Service, Santa Fe, New Mexico

Billy L. Oliver, North Carolina Department of Cultural Resources, Raleigh

David Overstreet, Great Lakes Archaeological Research Center, Inc., Wauwatosa, Wisconsin

Richard A. Pailes, University of Oklahoma

Gordon R. Peters, U.S. Forest Service, Duluth, Minnesota

Leslie D. Peterson, U.S. Forest Service, Duluth, Minnesota

David A. Phillips, Jr., Museum of New Mexico, Santa Fe

Peter J. Pilles, Jr., U.S. Forest Service, Flagstaff, Arizona

Lonnie C. Pippin, Desert Research Institute, Reno, Nevada

Stephen R. Potter, National Park Service, Washington, D.C.

Shirley Powell, Southern Illinois University, Carbondale

Elton R. Prewitt, Prewitt and Associates, Inc., Austin, Texas

Burton L. Purrington, Southwest Missouri State University

J. Jefferson Reid, Arizona State Museum, University of Arizona, Tucson

Kenneth C. Reid, University of Tulsa

John D. Reynolds, Kansas State Historical Society

Richard A. Rogers, University of Kansas

Charles L. Rohrbaugh, Illinois State University

Martha A. Rolingson, Arkansas Archaeological Survey, Scott

Matthew J. Root, University of North Dakota

George Sabo III, Arkansas Archeological Survey, Fayetteville

Frank F. Schambach, Arkansas Archeological Survey, Magnolia

Albert H. Schroeder, National Park Service, Sante Fe, New Mexico

Preface

This dictionary of more than 1800 entries, produced through the collaborative efforts of 151 archaeologists, is intended as a source of basic information on the major prehistoric cultures, archaeological sites, and artifact types of North America. One will not find an entry here for every North American archaeological site, for every artifact type, and for every prehistoric culture that has been described in print. Any such comprehensive coverage would have been hopelessly impractical: At least half a million archaeological sites have been recorded in North America; tens of thousands of these have been tested, partially excavated, or completely excavated; thousands of named artifact types and culture complexes have been described in the literature, many of which were current for a time, then were renamed or replaced by other types and complexes.

One will find here, however, an entry for every site that, in the opinion of the regional consultants who selected the topics, has contributed uniquely to the essential body of information upon which the current major classifications and interpretations of North American prehistory are based. One also will find entries for major artifact types and for major cultures and their phases or other subdivisions. Sources are listed at the end of each entry, through which comprehensive information about that particular topic may be obtained. The sources are mostly published works; but in some cases unpublished reports are cited because they are the only available written sources of information.

A typical site entry includes information on the site's location, who excavated it and when, what was found, the culture or cultures that occupied it, its function, and what it has contributed to archaeological knowledge. Some of these entires are only a sentence or two. A few, dealing with especially important sites, run for a couple of pages.

A typical entry for a culture, tradition, phase, or the like includes information on its geographical and temporal distribution, its distinctive traits, its relationships to other culture units, who defined it, and when. Sites in Greenland, although not in North America proper, have been included because they were occupied by peoples who shared the same cultures with peoples of the eastern North American arctic and subarctic regions.

The sources listed at the end of each entry are not comprehensive. They were selected, rather, to provide an interested reader with references containing basic information about a topic. They also contain additional bibliographical references that should lead the interested reader to exhaustive information on the topic.

The bibliography consists of the references cited in the text. Compiled by more than 150 archaeologists, each a specialist in a particular region, it should be especially useful to those who have need for a single, authoritative, up-tp-date list of basic publications and file reports covering the prehistory of the entire continent. Many of the references are reports on surveys, site excavations, or other field work—often done under contract with federal and state agencies—that were never published; museums, or government agencies where they are available to scholars. In the bibliography, these important unpublished sources of information are listed with the designation "n.d." instead of publication date.

Every effort has been made to make the dictionary an authoritative, up-to-date, and useful compendium of basic information about North American prehistory as perceived by leading scholars in the field. The dictionary's content was organized by the thirteen regional consultants listed in the Editors, Consultants, and Contributors section, each a recognized authority on one of the major culture areas of North America. Each of them prepared a list of archaeological sites, prehistoric cultures, and artifact types, for his or her region that, collectively, would give an overview of basic knowledge about prehistoric peoples who lived in the region. After I approved the list the consultants usually arranged with colleagues to help write the individual entries. Three of the consultants wrote all the entries for their respective regions themselves; for the other regions, the number of contributors per region varied from two to thirty-four. All the contributors have had direct experience with the subjects they wrote about. I edited their drafts to ensure consistency in style, format, and basic content, then returned them to their authors for final corrections.

I am vastly indebted to each of the consultants and to each of the contributors for their efforts, which sometimes bordered on the herculean. I wish also to thank Greenwood Press editors Mary R. Sive, Cynthia Harris, Julie Marothy, and William Neenan for advice and assistance; also Preston A. Hawks, Laboratory Director at the Midwestern Archeological Center, Illinois State University, for library research, and Michael B. Collins of Prewitt and Associates in Austin, Texas, for providing important information about several sites. I owe my wife Juliet, the Assistant Editor, special recognition for her diligent research of source materials, proofreading, and for many suggestions that helped improve the content and style of the book. She also deserves a martyr's medal for her patience and moral support during the three years that I was working on, and sometimes seemed dominated by *The Dictionary*. A very special acknowledgment is due my friend and colleague, the late Dr. William S. Willis, Jr., whose encouragement led to my undertaking this project in the first place.

Edward B. Jelks

HISTORICAL DICTIONARY
OF
NORTH AMERICAN
ARCHAEOLOGY

A

ABAJO PHASE, a phase of the Pueblo I period dating ca. A.D. 700–850, defined by J. O. Brew at the Alkali Ridge Site (q.v.) on the eastern edge of the Cedar Mesa Province (q.v.) in southeastern Utah. Its sites have up to 300 rooms arranged in lines of small, above-ground rooms that face smaller numbers of pithouse proto-kivas. Known for its large amounts of Red-on-Orange (Abajo) pottery, the phase extends westward to Comb Wash in the center of the Cedar Mesa Province. Neither it nor any other Pueblo I material is found significantly west of there.
SOURCE: Brew 1946.

R. G. Matson

ABBOTT FARM SITE, the best-known and by far the largest and most thoroughly studied prehistoric site in the Delaware River Valley, located south of Trenton, New Jersey. It was first investigated before the turn of the 20th century by Charles Abbott, M.D., a well-known antiquarian. In the late 1930s and early 1940s, Dorothy Cross conducted intensive investigations which demonstrated the site's significance. More recently, Louis Berger Associates have devoted thousands of person-hours to the most intensive and extensive archaeological research ever conducted in the northeastern United States.

Abbott Farm contains evidence of intensive occupation, beginning ca. 3000 B.C. in the Late Archaic period and continuing almost unabated until ca. A.D 1600 in the Late Woodland period. Its extensive Middle Woodland occupation initially was thought to have been influenced by the Hopewell Culture (q.v.) of the Midwest, but recent research interprets Abbott Farm as a permanent occupation site of peoples with a local, riverine-oriented economy.
SOURCE: Cross 1956.

Ronald A. Thomas

ABBOTT WARE, a group of several related pottery types defined by Dorothy Cross, who found them associated with Early and Middle Woodland occupations at the Abbott Farm Site (q.v.) south of Trenton on the Delaware

River. Vessels are conical with net- and cord-impressed exteriors. Several types have complex, zoned, incised decorations; rocker-stamped designs appear on other types.
SOURCE: Cross 1956.

Ronald A. Thomas

ABERDEEN SITE, a Pre-Dorset site in the Keewatin Barren Grounds, interior eastern Northwest Territories, excavated by J. V. Wright. It was occupied during a cold period ca. 1000–900 B.C. by Pre-Dorset peoples who had moved there from the coastal area to the north.
SOURCES: J. V. Wright 1972b.

Moreau S. Maxwell

ABO SITE, a site near Mountainair, New Mexico comprising the ruins of the 17th-century Franciscan mission complex of San Gregorio de Abo and ten largely unexcavated house mounds and associated plazas of a Tompiro pueblo of ca. A.D. 1300–1672. Extensive pictograph and petroglyph panels also have been recorded near the ruins. Abo was purchased by the Museum of New Mexico in 1937, became a state monument in 1938, and was transferred to the newly created Salinas National Monument in 1981.

J. H. Toulouse, Jr., excavated and stabilized the church and convento in 1938. B. P. Dutton conducted excavations in the Puebloan remains in 1944, and W. R. Hurt made a study of the rock art in 1939. Recently, several investigators have completed additional rock-art studies and test excavations. Research questions have focused on the cultural and linguistic relationships between Abo's occupants and those of the Piro pueblos on the Rio Grande and the other Salinas pueblos.
SOURCES: Toulouse 1949; Dutton 1981.

Frances Levine

ABVERDJAR SITE, type site for the late Dorset Phase (q.v.), dating ca. A.D. 800–1000, situated at the northern end of Foxe Basin, Northwest Territories. One of the first published Dorset components, this single-occupation site, rich in carved ivory and other artifacts, was excavated by Graham Rowley in 1939.
SOURCES: Rowley 1940; Maxwell 1985: 218–226.

Moreau S. Maxwell

ACASTA PHASE (or COMPLEX), an early (ca. 5000 B.C.) manifestation in the Mackenzie District, distinguished by Kamut points, notched Acasta bipoints, burinated flake tools, and heavy core tools or scraper planes. W. C. Noble, who excavated the type site for the phase (the Acasta Site, q.v.),

places the phase within a northern Plano Tradition (q.v.), although Acasta-type artifacts are also found in the northern Cordilleran region.
    SOURCES: Forbis 1961; W. C. Noble 1971, 1981.

                                                            Donald W. Clark

ACASTA SITE, type site for the Acasta Phase (q.v.) in the Mackenzie District east of Great Bear Lake; radiocarbon dated to ca. 5000 B.C. It comprises a series of flaking stations and hearths surrounding a large glacial erratic that served as a source of quartzite for tool manufacture. Excavated by W. C. Noble in 1960, it produced large, lobate-stemmed Kamut type points; large Acasta bipoints with a pair of small notches near the base; lanceolate points similar to the Agate Basin type (q.v.); transversely burinated flake tools; and many heavy core tools or scraper planes.
    SOURCES: Forbis 1961; W. C. Noble 1971, 1981.

                                                            Donald W. Clark

ACCOKEEK CREEK SITE COMPLEX, a group of four contiguous sites on the Potomac River in southern Maryland: a Late Archaic through Middle Woodland site, an early Late Woodland village, a 16th-century village, and the A.D. 1675 Susquehannock Indian Fort. One of the most important series of sites in the Middle Atlantic states, it was excavated by A. L. L. Ferguson in the 1930s and analyzed by R. L. Stephenson in the 1950s.
    SOURCES: A. L. L. Ferguson 1941: 1–9; Stephenson et al. 1963; Potter 1984: 36–39.

                                                            Stephen R. Potter

ACCOKEEK WARE, a sand-tempered, cord-marked pottery type thought to date 800–300 B.C., associated with Early Woodland sites of in the coastal plain between southern Maryland and the James River, Virginia. Vessels are large to medium-sized and have conical or semiconical bases and straight or slightly everted or inverted rims.
    SOURCES: Stephenson et al. 1963: 96–100; Egloff and Potter 1982: 97–99.

                                                            Stephen R. Potter

ADAMSON MOUND SITE, a Pee Dee mound and village complex of the South Appalachian Mississippian period (ca. A.D. 1250–1350), located near the Wateree River in Kershaw County, South Carolina. First reported by William Blanding in 1948, it has occasionally been visited by archaeologists

since. The larger of the two mounds is rectangular, about 11 meters high, and 52 by 40 meters at the base.
SOURCES: G. E. Stuart 1975; DePratter 1985b; DePratter and Judge 1986.

Michael Trinkley

ADDICKS SITES, a series of sites near Addicks, Texas that, when investigated in 1947 by J. B. Wheat, revealed the outlines of cultural prehistory from Paleoindian to late prehistoric times for the upper Texas coastal region. Wheat's work stood for nearly two decades as the primary documented archaeological record for the region.
SOURCE: Wheat 1953.

Lawrence E. Aten

ADENA CULTURE, an Early Woodland (ca. 1000–100 B.C.) manifestation distributed across eastern North America from the midlands to the coast, identified by early archaeologists from traits found in mounds of the central Ohio River drainage, where the major traditions of the culture are concentrated. Some rockshelters and a very few habitation sites are known.

Formal Adena trait analyses began with E. F. Greenman and continued with W. S. Webb, C. E. Snow, R. S. Baby, and D. W. Dragoo. Limited subsistence information indicates no major changes from preceding complexes. While there was an emphasis upon mound construction in Adena times, other burial customs appear to have been extensions of Late Archaic practices in the lower Great Lakes area. Pottery, tubular pipes, exotic flints, and small numbers of exotic copper, mica, and shell artifacts are among the materials that occur in various Adena complexes.
SOURCES: Mills 1902; Greenman 1932; Webb and Snow 1945; Morgan 1952:86–88; Webb and Baby 1957; Dragoo 1963; Swartz 1971; Kraft 1976; Otto 1979; J. B. Griffin 1983:254–259; Funk 1983:306–307, 334–337; Muller 1983:385–392.

N'omi B. Greber

ADENA MOUND, a two-stage burial mound for which the Adena Culture (q.v.) was named, located at Chillicothe, Ohio and excavated in 1901 by W. C. Mills. The first stage began with the construction of a large, subsurface, bark-lined tomb containing extended and cremated burials, and continued with the addition of log tombs and burials. The second stage—offset from the first stage and composed of distinctly different soil—had been heaped over individual burials without log tombs. Artifacts, probably from the late Adena Culture (ca. 500–100 B.C.), came from both stages.
SOURCE: Mills 1902.

N'omi B. Greber

AGATE BASIN COMPLEX, a Paleoindian complex of eastern Wyoming and northeastern Colorado that has been radiocarbon dated to ca. 8500–8000 B.C. It was first recognized by F. H. H. Roberts, Jr., in 1942 when he worked at the Agate Basin Site (q.v.) in Wyoming, type site of the complex. Other sites producing Agate Basin artifacts are the Hell Gap Site (q.v.) in Wyoming and the Frazier Site in Colorado. The complex's diagnostic trait is the Agate Basin type dart point, a lanceolate point with rounded base and lenticular transverse cross section.

SOURCES: F. H. H. Roberts, Jr. 1943; Frison and Stanford 1982; Wormington 1957: 141–142.

George Frison

AGATE BASIN SITE, a stratified, multicomponent site in east-central Wyoming containing Hell Gap, Agate Basin, and Folsom (qq.v.) components. It was the location of an arroyo bison kill carried out in cold weather so the meat could be preserved by freezing. Type site of the Agate Basin Complex (q.v.), it was investigated by F. H. H. Roberts, Jr., in 1942, by Roberts and W. M. Bass in 1961, and by George Frison between 1972 and 1980.

SOURCES: F. H. H. Roberts, Jr. 1943; Frison and Stanford 1982.

George Frison

AGLU HUNTING (or MAUPOK HUNTING or BREATHING-HOLE HUNTING), a method of hunting seals on the sea ice in winter, whereby seals are harpooned through breathing holes (aglu) maintained in the ice by hunters.

Moreau S. Maxwell

AGUA FRIA–NEW RIVER PROVINCE, a culture area in southwestern Arizona on the immediate northwestern periphery of the Phoenix Basin Province (q.v.), encompassing the drainages of the Agua Fria River and its two main tributary streams, New River and Skunk Creek. The Hassayampa River to the west probably also should be included in the province.

Prehistoric population densities in this area were lower than those of the Phoenix Basin because the streams were intermittent and seasonal. Nevertheless, recent archaeological investigation indicates that similar culture patterns were present in the two provinces. Small-scale, canal-irrigation agriculture was supplemented by various floodwater farming techniques, and the settlement pattern was characterized by dispersed farmsteads and a few large villages. A specialized economic focus upon the production of corn-grinding stone implements for exchange purposes has recently been recognized. Ceramic and architectural styles parallel those of the Phoenix Basin Province, although the presence of rock-lined ball courts, rock-lined buildings, and fortified hill sites hints at some regional variation similar to that in the Gila Bend Province (q.v.).

Hohokam peoples used the area sporadically during the Pioneer Period (ca. A.D. 0–700); more permanent settlement began during the Colonial

Period (ca. A.D. 700–900). After the Sedentary Period (ca. A.D. 900–1100), the province was depopulated the few remaining sites continuing to exhibit affinities with sites in the Phoenix Basin.

SOURCES: Weaver 1974; Bruder 1983; Spoerl and Gumerman 1984; Doyel and Elson 1985.

David E. Doyel and John S. Cable

AGUA FRIA PROVINCE, a poorly reported expression of the Sinagua Division, Hakataya Culture (qq.v.), located in Arizona south of the Prescott Province and west of the Verde Province (qq.v.). Dating ca. A.D. 800–1450, the province is identified by the presence of Alameda Brown Ware (q.v.) pottery, a diagnostic type of the Sinagua Division. No phases have been defined. A pre-A.D. 1125 beginning for the province is indicated by the presence of intrusive Sacaton Red-on-buff pottery at a site with a roasting pit and stone-outlined, oval to rectangular structures with rounded corners, in which notched stones were found.

As elsewhere in the Sinagua provinces, pueblos appeared about or before A.D. 1125. They usually were situated on high elevations overlooking stream valleys with field houses nearby. Many of the large pueblos were enclosed with compound walls reminiscent of late East Verde and Salado Province (qq.v.) architecture. They contain intrusive Jeddito and Gila Polychrome ceramics which date from between A.D. 1325 and 1450.

SOURCES: Schroeder 1954; Gumerman and Weed 1976.

Albert H. Schroeder

AK CHIN AGRICULTURE, a method of farming on alluvial fans of intermittent streams, employed by the Papago and other Southwestern Indians, as well as by their prehistoric predecessors. The fans are created when the water of an intermittent stream spreads out at the point (called "ak chin" in Papago) where the stream's channel ceases to be incised. This spreads soil, brings in high amounts of dissolved or suspended nutrients, and allows water to soak into the ground. The Papago usually install a system of ditches, spreaders, and even reservoirs to help distribute the water to their fields.

SOURCES: Hack 1942; Nabhan 1982, 1983.

David A. Phillips, Jr.

AKMAK COMPLEX, type complex and earlier of two phases of the American Paleo-Arctic Tradition (q.v.), discovered at Onion Portage (q.v.), Alaska, in 1965. The Akmak lithic assemblage is characterized by a blade industry including blade tools, a microblade industry that utilized wedge-

shaped cores, burins on flakes, and large bifaces, some of which may be flake cores.
SOURCE: D. D. Anderson 1970a.

Donald W. Clark

ALABAMA RIVER PHASE, a late (ca. A.D. 1500–1700) culture unit in central Alabama characterized by the unusual mortuary practice of interring infant and adult bundle burials in large pottery jars capped with highly decorated, inverted bowls. Components of the phase probably represent settlements of protohistoric Creek tribes. A few European trade goods, especially glass beads, have been found in some of the urn burials.
SOURCE: Sheldon 1974.

John A. Walthall

ALACHUA TRADITION, a farming culture in north-central Florida ca. A.D. 700–1700 that made distinctive cord- and corncob-impressed pottery. It correlates with historic Potano and Ocale Indians.
SOURCES: Goggin 1949; Milanich 1971a, 1978b; Milanich and Fairbanks 1980:169–180.

Jerald T. Milanich

ALAMEDA BROWN WARE, the major indigenous plain pottery of the prehistoric Sinagua Tradition (q.v.) of the Flagstaff, Chevelon-Chavez, and Verde provinces (qq.v.) in Arizona. The ware comprises a large number of types that represent different phases and time periods, generally distinguished from one another by the tempering materials used and/or by the presence or absence of a red slip, smudging, or polishing.
SOURCES: Colton 1926, 1932b, 1941, 1946, 1958, 1965; Hargrave 1932b; Colton and Hargrave 1937; Reed n.d.; McGregor 1941a; F. R. Peck 1956; Breternitz 1960; J. P. Wilson 1969; Schroeder 1975; Pilles 1976, 1978, 1979; McGuire 1977; Henderson n.d.; Wells 1981; Shutler and Adams, n.d.

Peter J. Pilles, Jr.

ALARNERK SITE, an Early to Late Dorset Phase (q.v.) site near Igloolik at the northern end of Foxe Basin, eastern Northwest Territories, excavated by Jørdan Meldgaard in the late 1950s. It comprised a series of dwellings on raised beach strand lines, from 8 to 22 meters above present sea level, which provided a sequence of data ranging from Early Dorset (ca. 500 B.C.) to Late Dorset (ca. A.D. 1300).
SOURCE: Meldgaard 1962.

Moreau S. Maxwell

ALBA POINT, a late prehistoric (ca. A.D. 700–1300) arrow point with a short, rectangular stem, outflaring barbs, and triangular blade with recurved

edges; associated primarily with Caddoan cultures in eastern Texas and western Louisiana.
  SOURCES: Newell and Krieger 1949; Suhm et al. 1954; Turner and Hester1985.

Elton R. Prewitt

ALBEMARLE POTTERY SERIES, a Middle Woodland, rock-tempered, fabric- or cord-impressed ware in west-central Virginia, mostly undecorated.
  SOURCE: Clifford Evans 1955.

Keith T. Egloff

ALBERTA POINT, a large, stemmed, chipped-stone spear point characteristic of the Plano Culture (q.v.), dated to the period 7700–6650 B.C.
  SOURCES: Wormington and Forbis 1965; Forbis 1968; Agenbroad1978b.

Larry D. Agenbroad

ALDER HILL QUARRY, one of several basalt sources in the Truckee Basin, California that was quarried extensively during the Martis Phase (q.v.) and probably earlier.
  SOURCE: Elston et al. 1982.

Robert G. Elston

ALEUTIAN CORE AND BLADE INDUSTRY (or ANANGULA TRA-DITION), a stone-flaking industry in the Aleutian Islands, dating ca. 6500–6000 B.C., featuring implements made both on blades (including some in the microblade size range) and on blade-like ridged flakes. Transversally burinated flakes and unifacially retouched end scrapers are typical; bifacial projectile points and knives do not appear in the region until later. Probable technological continuity with the succeeding Aleutian Tradition (q.v.) has been noted.
  SOURCES: Laughlin 1951, 1963, 1975; Laughlin and Aigner 1966; McCartney and Turner 1966; Aigner 1974.

Donald W. Clark

ALEUTIAN TRADITION, the distinctive culture of the Aleutian Islanders over approximately the past 4000 years; some authorities would extend the tradition back to include the Aleutian Core and Blade Industry (q.v.), or Anangula Tradition, of more than 8000 years ago. Eastern and western phases as well as various local stages or periods have been recognized. Distinctive traits vary according to time and region but include a great range of harpoons (predominately non-toggling and often decorated), harpoon-darts, harpoon-arrows, bird spears, and fish spears; stone lamps; composite fishhooks; notched or grooved stone fishing weights; prolific flaked-stone scrapers, knives, and weapon tips; mummification (in later times) and cave inhumation; and, especially in the east, a ground-slate industry.

Archaeological research in the Aleutians began with excavations by W. H. Dall in the 1870s, was resumed by Waldemar Jochelson during the first decade of the 20th century, and was continued by E. M. Weyer in 1928 and Aleš Hrdlička in the late 1930s. Since then many others have conducted field studies in the Aleutians, among them W. S. Laughlin, T. P. Bank, A. C. Spaulding, A. P. McCartney, J. S. Aigner, C. G. Turner, II, Douglas Veltre, Glenda Denniston, and John Cook. Important sites (in order from west to east) include Krugloi Point on Agattu Island (western phase), Amchitka sites, historic and prehistoric Korovinski on Atka, mummy caves on the Islands of the Four Mountains, Neo- and Paleo-Aleut Chaluka (q.v.) on Umnak Island, the Amaknak sites near Unalaska, historic and Neo-Aleut Chulka on the easterly Krenitzin Islands, and typologically intergradational Aleut Tradition-Neoeskimo sites at Izembek Lagoon on the Alaska Peninsula, together with the possible Paleo-Aleut and Neo-Aleut Hot Springs Site at Port Moller (q.v.).

SOURCE: McCartney 1984 (this references in detail the extensive literature on Aleutian prehistory).

Donald W. Clark

ALEXANDER CULTURE, a late Early Woodland (ca. 600–100 B.C.) manifestation of the western Tennessee Valley. Components occur at riverine shell middens, at upland open camps, and in rockshelters. Alexander potters produced some of the most elaborate pre-Mississippian ceramics in the eastern United States.

SOURCE: Walthall and Jenkins 1976.

John A. Walthall

ALIBATES FLINT QUARRIES, a series of large quarry excavations in Potter County, Texas, now a National Monument: the source of Alibates "flint," actually an unfossiliferous, fine-grained, mottled or banded chert, whose colors commonly are rich reds, but range to blues and purples. This stone was used extensively from Paleoindian to protohistoric times for making chipped-stone implements.

SOURCE: Schaeffer 1958.

Patricia J. O'Brien

ALKALI PHASE. See Surprise Valley.

ALLEGAN TRADITION, an early Late Woodland ceramic tradition in southwestern lower Michigan comprising two phases: Early Allegan (ca.

A.D. 600–900) and Late Allegan (ca. A.D. 900–1200). Allegan pottery is similar to that of the Wayne Tradition (q.v.).
  SOURCES: M. B. Rogers 1972; Brashler 1973, 1981; Kingsley 1977.

Margaret B. Holman

ALLEN PHASE (or FOCUS), best known of the historic Caddoan culture units in eastern Texas, defined by A. D. Kreiger in the 1940s. Centered on the upper Neches River drainage, the phase is equated with the historic Hasinai or Tejas Indians, for whom Texas was named.
  SOURCES: Suhm et al. 1954: 219–221; Wyckoff 1974:203–204; Nancy Cole 1975; Story and Creel 1982.

James E. Corbin

ALLIGATOR CREEK SITE, one of the few north coastal Refuge Phase sites known in South Carolina. Located on Alligator Creek in Charleston County and dating ca. 800 B.C., it was excavated in 1981 by Michael Trinkley, who collected a large assemblage of Refuge artifacts from it.
  SOURCE: Trinkley 1982.

Michael Trinkley

ALPOWA LOCALITY, a series of ten aboriginal sites at the confluence of Alpowa Creek and the Snake River, near Clarkston, Washington, including the site of the 19th-century Nez Perce village of Alpowayma. At four of the sites, excavated extensively between 1972 and 1975, a culture sequence extending from ca. 3000 B.C. to the 19th century was disclosed. At Timothy's Village, housepits of the late Cascade and Tucannon phases (qq.v.) were discovered for the first time, documenting that a house form previously known only from later contexts was in use by ca. 3000 B.C. That the Nez Perce had adopted horticulture by the mid–19th century was evidenced by the presence of corn.
  SOURCE: Brauner 1976.

Frank C. Leonhardy

ALTA TOQUIMA VILLAGE, a two-component site located at an elevation of 3350 meters above sea level in the Toquima Range, central Nevada, excavated by D. H. Thomas in 1981 and 1983. A pre-A.D. 1000 occupation—which appears to have been largely an all-male, high-altitude outpost used for procuring bighorn sheep—produced several hundred projectile points, mainly of the Elko and Gatecliff series (q.v.). Most of the 31 house rings, of which 18 were excavated, are attributed to a post-A.D. 1000 occupation, whose rich artifact inventory included thousands of Desert Side-notched and Cottonwood (qq.v.) projectile points, Shoshone Ware ceramics, and many grinding stones. Preliminary evidence strongly suggests that this

later component represents a full-blown summer residential base camp for entire Western Shoshone families.
SOURCE: D. H. Thomas 1982.

David Hurst Thomas

ALTO PHASE (or FOCUS), an Early Caddo manifestation in eastern Texas and western Louisiana, dating ca. A.D. 800–1250; defined by H. P. Newell and A. D. Kreiger in 1949. The phase is typified by large villages containing both structural and mortuary mounds. High-status burials indicate that elite members of the society (a chiefdom ?) may have maintained status through elaborate trade networks for exchanging exotic goods with similar societies in the trans-Mississippi South. Diagnostic artifacts include ceramic types Crockett, Pennington, Hickory, and Holly; ceramic bottles with tapering spouts; Alba type arrow points; and long-stemmed clay pipes. Type site is the George C. Davis Site in Cherokee County, Texas.
SOURCES: Newell and Krieger 1949; Wyckoff 1974:41–57; Thomas et al. 1980; Story and Creel 1982.

James E. Corbin

ALTON SITE, a predominantly Paleoindian site located on an Ohio River terrace in Perry County, Indiana; the most productive Paleoindian site known in the state. Private collectors have found a great many fluted and unfluted, early projectile points on the surface. In test excavations in 1984, C. H. Tomak found points in Paleoindian contexts, but the results of this work have not yet been published.
SOURCE: Tomak 1979.

James H. Kellar

AMARGOSA INDUSTRY, a culture unit of the southeastern California deserts, especially in the vicinity of the Amargosa River, identified in 1939 by M. J. Rogers, who recognized two phases (I and II) and dated it between A.D. 200 and 900. Amargosa I was said to be characterized by large seasonal settlements and large corner-notched projectile points, Amargosa II by small seasonal camps and projectile points similar in shape to those of Phase I but either longer or smaller. Subsequent classification schemes of Rogers and of E. W. Haury used the term Amargosa differently and much confused its meaning, but these revisions have largely been ignored, and the term now is used nearly always in the sense of Rogers' original definition.
SOURCES: M. J. Rogers 1939; Haury 1950: 193; C. N. Warren 1984.

Robert L. Bettinger

AMERICAN PALEO-ARCTIC TRADITION, earliest (ca. 9500–4000 B.C.) generally accepted prehistoric tradition in the northwestern Arctic-Subarctic region. The type site is Onion Portage (q.v.) in northwestern Alaska, where

a relatively late phase is defined by the Kobuk Complex and an earlier phase by the Akmak Complex (q.v.). Akmak is characterized by a blade industry and concomitant blade tools, a microblade industry, flake burins, and large bifacial blades or knives. Other early sites of the tradition, found elsewhere in Alaska (see Dry Creek Site), have produced more or less similar assemblages. The term *American* draws attention to the fact that this is part of a broader Siberian-American tradition that evidently originated in Siberia.
SOURCES: D. D. Anderson 1970a, 1970b.

Donald W. Clark

AMMASSALIK (or ANGMAGSSALIK) SITE, a multicomponent settlement on Greenland's inhospitable east coast, occupied from Saqqaq Phase (q.v.) times, ca. 1300 B.C., to the present. Because of the harsh environment, particularly the dangerous East Greenland Current, the locale has remained generally isolated from surrounding cultural developments. The site's original occupants probably came either from the southwestern coast of Greenland or around the top of Greenland during warmer climatic conditions.
SOURCES: Mathiassen 1933; Meldgaard 1960.

Moreau S. Maxwell

ANAHIM OBSIDIAN, the most common type of obsidian used for prehistoric tool production on the Canadian Plateau, where it is widely distributed; distinguishable from other obsidians by X-ray fluorescence. It occurs as glacially redeposited nodules in the till and streambeds near Anahim Peak in the Rainbow Mountains of central British Columbia, the most extensive quarries being along Obsidian Creek. Anahim obsidian was used as early as 7000–5000 B.C. on the central British Columbia coast, but the earliest occurrence yet reported on the Plateau is in the first millennium A.D.
SOURCES: Nelson and Will 1976; Apland 1979.

Arnoud H. Stryd

ANAKTUVUK PASS SITES, a series of sites on the Anaktuvuk Pass caribou migration route through the Brooks Range in northern Alaska. The principal sites and their affiliated complexes and phases—all investigated by J. M. Campbell in the late 1950s—are (from oldest to youngest) as follows:

Kogruk Complex, now regarded as largely a flake industry belonging to one of the following phases.

Tuktu Site and Complex (dating ca. 4500 B.C.?), characterized by sidenotched and oblanceolate points, notched pebble choppers, partially smoothed slate bars (whetstones?), and a microblade industry not based on wedge-shaped cores. Tuktu sometimes is classified with the Northern Archaic Tradition, sometimes with the Northwest Microblade Tradition (qq.v.).

Nayuk Complex (undated), found at the Tuktu Site and possibly part of the Tuktu Complex.

Kayuk Complex (undated), with points flaked in a style suggestive of both late Paleoindian and interior Choris (qq.v.); found associated with probable Ipiutak (q.v.) artifacts.

Kavik Phase, identified with late prehistoric Athapaskan Indians and distinguished by flaked arrow points with small, offset, pointed stems.

Archaeological remains attributed to Neoeskimo, historic Nunamiut, and other groups also have been reported from the pass.

SOURCES: Rausch 1951; Helge Ingstad 1954; J. M. Campbell 1959, 1961, 1962, 1968; Gubser 1965; E. S. Hall, Jr. 1976; Binford 1978.

Donald W. Clark

ANANGULA BLADE SITE, principal locus of the Aleutian Core and Blade Industry (q.v.) on tiny Anangula (Ananiuliak) Island at the entrance to Nikolski Bay, Umnak, Aleutian Islands; initially occupied ca. 6400 B.C. Major excavations there in 1963, 1970, and 1974 by W. S. Laughlin and visiting Soviet archaeologists opened a new perspective on the prehistory of the region and added several millennia time depth to knowledge of regional maritime adaptation.

SOURCES: Laughlin 1951, 1963, 1975; Laughlin and Aigner 1966; McCartney and Turner 1966; Aigner 1970, 1974.

Donald W. Clark

ANANGULA TRADITION, a term sometimes used for the Aleutian Core and Blade Industry (q.v.).

ANASAZI CULTURE, a generic term (derived from a Navajo word meaning "enemy ancestors") for the late prehistoric (ca. A.D. 200–1600 culture occupying the Four Corners area of northwestern New Mexico, northern Arizona, southwestern Colorado, and southern Utah. In general, the Anasazi people are considered ancestors of the modern Pueblo Indian groups in New Mexico and the Hopi Indians of northwestern Arizona. It is likely that some features of the Mogollon Culture (q.v.) merged with those of the Anasazi after A.D. 1200.

The Anasazi (1) were agricultural, growing maize, beans, and squash; (2) built structures, at various times, pithouses, surface dwellings, surface storage rooms, and kivas [q.v.], including great kivas [q.v.] in some areas; (3) made pottery, primarily gray-firing cooking ware and white-, gray-, red-, orange-, and yellow-firing service wares with painted decorations; (4) had, by inference, religious centers (kivas) and a religion devoted to rainmaking, crop fertility, healing, success in hunting, warfare (late), and general well-being of the group. Configurations of these traits distinguish the Anasazi

Culture from the other three principal prehistoric southwestern cultures: Mogollon, Hohokam, and Hakataya (qq.v.).

Sixteen significant regional variations of the Anasazi Culture, termed *provinces*, have been recognized which appear to have risen from geographic separation, differences in natural environment, exposure to influences from different neighbors, and varying rates of adaptation to these factors. The provinces are: Cedar Mesa, Chaco, Chevelon-Chavez, Chuska, Grand Canyon, Jemez, Largo-Gallina, Middle Puerco Valley, Middle Rio Grande, Northern Sinagua, Taos, Tewa Basin, Upper San Juan, Tano Basin, Virgin, and Winslow (qq.v.). At least some of the provinces may correspond to tribal or linguistic divisions.

SOURCES: Kidder 1924, 1936; Gladwin et al. 1938; Haury 1936; Schroeder 1960; Ortiz 1969.

Stewart Peckham

ANDERSON FOCUS, a unit of the Fort Ancient Aspect (q.v.), named for the Anderson Village Site near the Fort Ancient Earthworks in southwestern Ohio.

SOURCES: J. B. Griffin 1943a: 92–118, 1979.

N'omi B. Greber

ANDERSON PHASE (or FOCUS), complex that D. J. Lehmer originally defined on the basis of materials at the Dodd Site (q.v.) in South Dakota, then later subsumed under what is now called the Initial Middle Missouri Variant (q.v.), dating ca. A.D. 900–1400. The Breeden and Fay Tolton sites, both in South Dakota, are other Anderson Phase sites.

SOURCES: Lehmer 1971; W. R. Wood 1976.

Patricia J. O'Brien

ANDREWS LAKE SITE, a late prehistoric (ca. A.D. 1000–1400), two-component hunting camp beside a playa lake in Andrews County, western Texas, excavated between 1964 and 1967 by the Midland Archeological Society and M. B. Collins. The earlier occupation produced triangular arrow points, brownware pottery, and other artifacts typical of southern Plains people. In the later component, ascribed to the Ochoa Phase of the Jornada Branch, Mogollon Culture, were an abundance of bison bones, lesser numbers of deer and antelope bones, triangular arrow points, and Ochoa Phase pottery. There were no storage features in either component, nor any evidence of cultigens, despite thorough fine screening of deposits. Two human burials

that apparently represented the Ochoa Phase were riddled with stemmed arrow points, some sticking in the bones.
SOURCE: M. B. Collins 1966.

Edward B. Jelks

ANDREWS SITE, a burial site of the Red Ocher Culture (q.v.) located in Saginaw County, Michigan, radiocarbon dated to ca. 1220 B.C. It produced red-ocher-covered cremations associated with copper beads, a barbed copper projectile point, corner-notching points of chert, and birdstones.
SOURCES: Papworth 1967; Fitting 1970.

Charles E. Cleland

ANGEL PHASE, a Late Mississippian (ca. A.D. 1200–1450) culture unit in southwestern Indiana and adjacent portions of Kentucky and probably Illinois; defined by M. W. Honerkamp in 1975. The settlement pattern was dominated by the large, complex Angel Site (q.v.), around which were distributed small villages, hamlets, farmsteads, and camps.
SOURCES: Black 1967; Honerkamp 1975; Green and Munson 1978.

James H. Kellar

ANGEL SITE, a large (43-hectare), stockaded, Late Mississippian (ca. A.D. 1200–1450) central town on the Ohio River floodplain about 10 kilometers east of Evansville, Vanderburgh County, Indiana. The easternmost town in the Ohio Valley with major truncated mounds and a plaza, it was purchased by the Indiana Historical Society in 1938 and excavated between then and 1962 by G. A. Black, initially as a Work Projects Administration undertaking and later as an Indiana University field school. With funds provided by Lilly Endowment, Inc., an interpretive center and other on-site interpretive features were constructed in 1972. These now are administered by the Indiana Department of Natural Resources.
SOURCES: Black 1967; Honerkamp 1975; Green and Munson 1978.

James H. Kellar

ANGELL PHASE, the first post-eruptive phase of the Northern Sinagua Tradition (q.v.) in north-central Arizona, dating ca. A.D. 1066–1100. It was contemporaneous with the Winona Focus (q.v.), originally thought to have represented a migration of Hohokam (q.v.) people to the Flagstaff area but now explained in other ways. Angell Phase sites are most numerous in the pinyon-juniper zone east of the San Francisco Peaks. It appears that there was a population expansion or movement from the ponderosa zone along the flanks of the peaks to the lower elevations, perhaps in response to moister climatic conditions.

The phase was defined by J. C. McGregor from his work at Winona Village and Ridge Ruin (q.v.), primarily on the basis of pithouse styles and on the occurrence of Mogollon-like pottery types such as Winona Red, Smudged, and Corrugated. The classic Angell pithouse was large (about 35 square meters in floor area) and subrectangular to oval in shape. It had a large vestibule entry on the east side and roof-support posts set around its periphery, either at ground level or on a shallow bench just below ground level. Walls were lined with clay or stones. Other pithouse forms also are present.

Pottery consists of paddle-and-anvil produced types Winona Brown, Angell Brown, and Sunset Brown, together with their smudged, polished, and redware variants. Most burials are extended, although flexed inhumations and cremations also occur.

SOURCES: McGregor 1941a; Colton 1946:270, 312–314; J. P. Wilson 1969:17–21.

Peter J. Pilles, Jr.

ANGMAGSSALIK SITE. See Ammassalik Site.

ANGOSTURA POINT, a narrow, obliquely flaked, lanceolate, late Paleoindian dart point type, dating ca. 6000–5000 B.C., first found in situ in 1948 by J. T. Hughes at the Ray Long Site, South Dakota, during construction of the Angostura Reservoir. The name Angostura has been applied widely, sometimes to point styles not related culturally or temporally to the original Angostura type.

SOURCES: Hughes 1949; Agogino et al. 1964.

George A. Agogino

ANNAWAK SITE, a single-component Pre-Dorset site in the Lake Harbour region of southern Baffin Island, where excavations by a team from Michigan State University in 1960 produced a lithic assemblage dominated by spalled burins and burin spalls. Radiocarbon dates of ca. 1800 B.C. place it early in the sequence of Pre-Dorset sites of the region.

SOURCE: Maxwell 1973.

Moreau S. Maxwell

ANOKA FOCUS, an early Coalescent (ca. 1480–1500) complex of earth-lodge village sites in extreme northeastern Nebraska and central South Dakota, characteristically built on hilltops in defensible positions. The phase is attributed to Central Plains Tradition (q.v.) peoples who moved into the area from the south.

SOURCE: Witty 1962a.

Thomas A. Witty, Jr.

ANTELOPE CREEK PHASE (or FOCUS), a late prehistoric (A.D. 1200–1500) village adaptation to the southern short-grass plains region in the Texas and Oklahoma panhandles. These semisedentary peoples resided in scattered homesteads and large hamlets along river valleys and depended upon a mixed hunting-gathering-horticultural subsistence. A major departure from other Plains Village complexes is the frequent use of stone masonry architecture, apparently an imitation of construction methods used by the Anasazi (q.v.) to the west. The common use of vertically set stone-slab foundations is a unique local innovation. Cordmarked ceramics, bison-bone horticultural implements, distinctive chipped-stone tools, and human skeletal morphology indicate close ties with other Plains cultures. However, immediate cultural antecedents and continuity with specific historic tribes remain uncertain.

SOURCES: A. D. Krieger 1946; Lintz 1984, 1986; F. E. Green n.d.

Christopher Lintz

ANZICK SITE, the first reported Clovis Culture (q.v.) burial site, located near Wilsall in southwestern Montana, exposed in 1968 by construction operations. It contained two subadult skeletons that were covered with red ocher, accompanied by over 100 stone and bone tools, including Clovis type projectile points (q.v.).

SOURCE: Lahren and Bonnichsen 1974.

Patricia J. O'Brien

APACHE CREEK PUEBLO, a complex of the Mogollon Culture in the Cibola Province (qq.v.) near Reserve, New Mexico, consisting of two masonry surface houseblocks (excavated in 1954 by P. S. Martin and J. B. Rinaldo), seven masonry-lined pithouses (excavated in 1955 by Stewart Peckham), and a great kiva. All but one of the pithouses had been abandoned and then used as refuse dumps by occupants of the surface rooms.

On the basis of the construction sequence and pottery types, an Apache Creek Phase (q.v.) occupation was distinguished. Large dwelling rooms in the surface roomblocks matched the pithouses feature for feature, except that there were subfloor vaults ("floor drums") of probable ceremonial function in two pithouses. Though the pithouses were primarily domiciles, Martin proposed calling them "pithouse kivas" in view of their juxtaposition with surface rooms in the manner of kivas associated with Anasazi pueblos.

SOURCES: Peckham et al. 1956; Martin et al. 1957.

Stewart Peckham

APACHE PHASE. See Casas Grandes Province.

APISHAPA FOCUS, late prehistoric (A.D. 1000–1350) culture whose sites occur along the Apishapa, Purgatoire, and Cucharas rivers in southeastern Colorado and on the Cimarron River in New Mexico. Vertical stone-slab foundations, cordmarked ceramics, side-notched arrow points, and maize horticulture resemble traits of the Antelope Creek Phase, but Apishapa is earlier and lacks bone horticultural tools and other elements of Antelope Creek material culture. Apishapa and Antelope Creek have been grouped together within the Panhandle Aspect (q.v.).

SOURCES: Withers 1954; Robert Campbell 1969, 1976; Nowak and Headington 1983; Eighmy 1984.

Christopher Lintz

AQUA PLANO, term applied by G. I. Quimby in 1960 to late Paleoindian manifestations in Wisconsin and surrounding states, primarily to differentiate them from Paleoindian adaptations to the grassland environment to the west. There is good evidence that the Aqua Plano homeland was a dense spruce parkland with many large postglacial lakes. Typical artifacts are Eden-Scottsbluff projectile points and woodworking tools, including adzes, perhaps for making dugout canoes.

SOURCE: Quimby 1960.

David Overstreet

ARANSAS FOCUS, a poorly known, preceramic culture unit whose shell-midden sites along the central Texas coast have produced a modest assemblage of lithic, conch-shell, and pelecypod-shell tools. Sites are estimated to date between ca. 3000 B.C. and A.D. 1100.

SOURCES: T. N. Campbell 1947; Suhm et al. 1954:121–125; Corbin 1974.

Lawrence E. Aten

ARANT'S FIELD SITE, a site containing components of the Late Archaic (ca. 2500 B.C.) and Middle Woodland (ca. A.D. 500–1000) periods, located on the Congaree River in Calhoun County, South Carolina. G. A. Teague tested the site briefly in 1972 and found features, postmolds, and Camden Ware pottery (q.v.).

SOURCE: Teague 1972.

Michael Trinkley

ARBOLES PHASE, an early (ca. A.D. 950–1050) expression of the Pueblo II Stage of the Pecos Classification (q.v.) in the Upper San Juan Province (q.v.). By this time, Anasazi peoples had gradually withdrawn up the Piedra River Valley and into the uplands where they established pithouse settlements. During the phase, masonry architecture and corrugated pottery appeared at some sites, as did a slip-decorated ware, Arboles Black-on-White, which became the dominant pottery type after A.D. 950.

SOURCES: Jeancon 1922; F. H. H. Roberts, Jr. 1930; Dittert et al. 1961; Sciscenti et al. 1963; Eddy 1966, 1972, 1977; E. C. Adams 1975.

Frank W. Eddy

ARCHAIC, a term that has been widely used in North America to designate, collectively, non-Paleoindian (q.v.) hunting-gathering cultures. W. A. Ritchie first used the term in this sense in 1932 to designate a preceramic, preagricultural level at the Lamoka Lake Site (q.v.) in New York. In 1941, J. A. Ford and G. R. Willey described an Eastern Archaic cultural horizon for the eastern United States. Thereafter, the concept of an Archaic stage, tradition, or period, dating between the earlier Paleoindian and the later Woodland (q.v.) cultures, became solidly entrenched in the prehistoric chronology of eastern North America. Early, Middle, and Late Archaic periods are generally recognized in the different eastern subregions.

More recently, the idea of a continent-wide Archaic stage or tradition comprising non-Paleoindian hunting-gathering cultures has also come into broad, but not universal, usage. However, some western Archaic cultures (for example, Old Cordilleran [q.v.]) were contemporaneous with Paleoindian peoples to the east, and some hunting-gathering societies (for example, the Desert Culture [q.v.]) survived into historic times. Therefore, the western Archaic is generally viewed as a tradition or a stage not confined to a specific time period, as is often the case in the East. Regional expressions of the western Archaic are also usually divided into early, middle, and late periods.

SOURCES: Ritchie 1932:79–134; Ford and Willey 1941; Griffin 1952:352–364; Suhm et al. 1954. Spenser and Jennings et al. 1965:39–56; Caldwell and Henning 1978:120–121; Funk 1978:19–27; Weir 1976; Oliver 1981:12–30; Prewitt 1981.

Edward B. Jelks

ARCTIC SMALL TOOL TRADITION, a series of early (ca. 2500–2000 B.C.) lithic assemblages distributed across nothern North America from southwestern Alaska to Greenland and Newfoundland. First defined by W. N. Irving in 1957 as an inclusive category comprising Denbigh, Pre-Dorset, and other Arctic lithic assemblages, it is characterized by miniaturization of artifact categories. The tradition's tool inventory, which remains remarkably uniform throughout the Arctic, includes spalled burins, burin spalls, microblades, and both side and end scrapers. The term is sometimes used in referring to later Dorset phases where lithic tools remain small.

SOURCES: Irving 1957; McGhee 1978:26–29; Maxwell 1985:40–42.

Moreau S. Maxwell

ARCTIC WOODLAND CULTURE, a term coined by J. L. Giddings, Jr., in the 1940s for the Neoeskimo culture of northwestern interior Alaska (called Thule by most prehistorians), in particular along the forested Kobuk River. Giddings found that this culture, dating from ca. A.D. 1100 into the

20th century, resembled in many way that of the neighboring interior Athapaskan Indians. Distinctive traits, in addition to ones characteristic of the
coastal Thule Phase (q.v.), include well-fired, relatively thin pottery, birchbark containers, expertly made snowshoes of western Athapaskan form,
and a kind of partially open kayak, somewhat like a canoe, covered with
birchbark.
SOURCES: Giddings 1952, 1956.

                                                                Donald W. Clark

ARENOSA SHELTER, a deeply stratified rockshelter near the Rio Grande–
Pecos River confluence in Val Verde County, southwestern Texas, now
beneath the waters of Lake Amistad. Excavated by D. S. Dibble in 1965–
1966, it contained a long sequence of Archaic hunter-gatherer occupations,
beginning ca. 5000 B.C. and extending into the late prehistoric period. Data
from the site contributed substantially to the development of a culture-
history framework for the lower Pecos River region.
SOURCE: Dibble n.d.

                                                                Robert J. Mallouf

ARKANSAS POST, an important trading and military post on the lower
Arkansas River where there was strong interaction between the French
nation and the Quapaw Indians who lived nearby. The first European settlement in the lower Mississippi Valley, it was founded by Henri de Tonti
in 1686 at the Quapaw village of Osotouy, thought to be at the archaeological Menard Site (q.v.) in Arkansas County, Arkansas. The post later
was moved elsewhere.
SOURCES: J. A. Ford 1961; John Walker 1971; Morse and Morse 1983.

                                                                Dan F. Morse

ARLINGTON SPRINGS, a site on the northwestern shore of Santa Rosa
Island, California, where in 1960 P. C. Orr and a team of Quaternary
specialists found human bone fragments buried 11 meters deep in alluvial
sediments of terminal Pleistocene age. There was no evidence of a burial,
and no artifacts were present. Radiocarbon determination on charcoal adjacent to the bones and from organic fraction of a femur yielded values of
about 8000 B.C.
SOURCE: P. C. Orr 1962.

                                                                Michael J. Moratto

ARMIJO PHASE, fourth phase of the Oshara Tradition (q.v.) in the Four
Corners area of the Southwest, dating ca. 1800–800 B.C. During the phase,
maize and squash were added to the diet and limited horticulture began to
provide a reliable, seasonally abundant resource, which in some areas produced a temporary local food surplus that allowed population aggregation

during the fall and perhaps the winter. Base camps used in other seasons continued to be located in places that provided ready access to water and to a wide variety of microenvironments. Hunting camps of the phase also have been recorded.

Tool kits from the fall/winter aggregation sites include a much wider range of tool classes than the kits associated with base camps used in other seasons, in some cases containing artifacts thought to have had magico-religious or ideological importance. Ground-stone items increased in frequency through the phase. In other respects, the tool kits are similar to those of the preceding San Jose Phase (q.v.). Variations in projectile-point form began to increase significantly. The most common point style resembles the serrated San Jose type (q.v.), but with a very short, widely expanding stem and a concave or straight base.

Evidently, as many as 30 to 50 individuals aggregated in the fall in some areas, which created opportunities for maximizing interpersonal interaction, including larger scale social and ceremonial activities than was possible for smaller groups. This social pattern, in turn, may have imparted a year-round seasonal structure to economic and social activities.

SOURCES: Irwin-Williams and Tomkins 1968; Irwin-Williams and Haynes 1970; Irwin-Williams 1973, 1979; Simmons 1986.

Cynthia Irwin-Williams and Patricia A. Hicks

ARNAPIK SITE, an early Pre-Dorset site on Mansel Island in northeastern Hudson Bay, dating ca. 1800 B.C. Excavations by W. E. Taylor, Jr., in 1957–1959 produced a lithic assemblage which, when compared to that of the early Dorset Tyara Site (q.v.) on Sugluk Island, led him to conclude that Pre-Dorset and Dorset were parts of a single cultural continuum. One of the first Pre-Dorset sites published in detail, Arnapik has become recognized as one of the type sites for the phase.

SOURCE: W. E. Taylor, Jr. 1968.

Moreau S. Maxwell

ARROWHEAD RUIN, an Anasazi (q.v.) site dating ca. A.D. 1370–1450, located near Glorieta Pass, New Mexico about 11 kilometers northwest of Pecos Pueblo (q.v.). Between 1933 and 1948, W. C. Holden excavated 79 rooms surrounding a single plaza; another plaza with an unknown number of rooms has not been explored. The regular pattern and room distribution suggest a planned community, although the rooms at the southeastern side of the pueblo were built first. Construction is largely of uncoursed masonry, and the southern part of the rectangular village may have been two stories high. There was a large, circular kiva with a banquette in the southwest corner of the plaza.

The site's lateness is significant because, with the singular exception of Pecos Pueblo, other sites in the Upper Pecos River Valley were abandoned well before A.D. 1400.

SOURCES: Jane Holden 1955; Kidder 1958:49–51.

Larry V. Nordby

ARVILLA BURIAL COMPLEX, a recurring archaeological burial pattern, originally defined by A. E. Jenks in 1932, that includes flexed and disarticulated primary burials and bundled secondary burials in subsoil pits underlying circular and linear burial mounds. Burials are accompanied by grave goods, including shell, bone, antler, and pottery elbow pipes. Stone tools and pottery vessels are uncommon. The suggested dates for Arvilla of A.D. 500–900 may be too early, as the complex probably is coeval with the Blackduck Culture (q.v.) of the Late Woodland Period. While the type site is located at Arvilla, North Dakota, the complex extends from the St. Croix River in east-central Minnesota, through central Minnesota to the Red River Valley, northward into Manitoba, and westward into the Dakotas.

SOURCES: Jenks 1932, 1935; Wilford 1941, 1955; Elden Johnson 1973; R. G. Thompson 1985.

Gordon R. Peters

ARZBERGER SITE, a fortified village site dating ca. A.D. 1400–1550, located in Hughes County, South Dakota on a terrace overlooking the Missouri River. Showing both Upper Republican and Lower Loup phase (qq.v.) affinities, as well as some Oneota and even some Mandan influences, the site probably represents an early stage in the separation of the Arikara from the Pawnee.

SOURCE: Spaulding 1956.

Patricia J. O'Brien

ASH HOLLOW CAVE, a multicomponent, stratified site located across the North Platte River from Lewellen, Nebraska; excavated by A. T. Hill in 1939 and analyzed in detail by J. L. Champe in 1946. Champe's study documents seven strata containing cultural remains from a Dismal River Aspect component dating ca. A.D. 1675–1705 at the top to Upper Republican, Woodland (similar to the Valley Focus), and Archaic components. The Archaic materials are similar to materials from the Signal Butte II Site (q.v.) where many stemmed projectile points were found that now are attributed to Late Archaic peoples of ca. 2000 B.C. One of the first stratified sites on the central Plains to be excavated, Ash Hollow Cave outlined a culture sequence for the area that is still used today. Also, one of the earliest attempts to combine dendrochronology with stratified cultural levels was made there.

SOURCE: Champe 1946.

Patricia J. O'Brien

ATHAPASKAN TRADITION, a term that has been applied by some pre-historians largely to assemblages of the present millennium, but sometimes to a longer period, in the region west of the Mackenzie River. Distinctive traits include large tabular hide-working stones (chithos), large grooved splitting adzes, bone beamers and fleshers, and, in late phases, implements beaten from native copper and crooked knives. In western Alaska, pottery, ground-slate tools, and certain house forms apparently were derived from adjacent Eskimos.

No one has attempted to define a single tradition encompassing all of Athapaskan prehistory. Sites and local phases of the tradition include the Kavik Phase of northern Alaska with its Anaktuvuk Pass (q.v.) and Antigun sites; the Klo-Kut, Rat Indian Creek (qq.v.), and Old Chief sites, along with the Klo-Kut and Old Chief phases, of the northern Yukon; the Kijik Site (q.v.) in southwestern Alaska; the Dixthada, Gulkana series, and Dakah De'nin's Village sites in eastern Alaska; the Aishihik Phase of the southern Yukon Territory; and the upper component at Whirl Lake at the head of the MacKenzie delta. If the tradition is extended to comprise possibly Atha-paskan sites in central British Columbia, it then includes the prehistoric Natalkuz, Punchaw Lake, and Tezli sites and the early historic Chinlac, Ulkatcho Carrier Indian, and Potlatch Chilcotin Indian sites. East of the Mackenzie Valley and in northern Alberta most coeval sites belong to the Taltheilei Tradition (q.v.).

SOURCES: Although the term Athapaskan Tradition is widely used, there is no definitive publication dealing with these sites as a tradition.

Donald W. Clark

AUGUSTINE MOUND, a large earthen burial mound on the Miramichi River, New Brunswick; the northeasternmost known expression of Adena (q.v.), or Adena-like, culture. The burials were accompanied by large numbers of implements, including tubular pipes and chipped-stone from the American Midwest; copper beads; pieces of textiles, skin, and basketry (preserved by contact with the copper beads); and many other artifacts. The age of the mound is not entirely clear, but it appears to have been in use shortly after 500 B.C.

SOURCE: Turnbull 1976.

James A. Tuck

AUGUSTINE PATTERN, previously termed the "Late Horizon" (ca. A.D. 300–1850), a widespread socioeconomic adaptation in central California distinguished by intensive fishing, hunting, and gathering; large, dense pop-

ulations; highly developed exchange systems; social stratification, as indicated by variability in grave furnishings; ceremonialism, with large communal buildings; and preinterment burning of artifacts in grave pits.
SOURCES: Fredrickson 1973; Moratto 1984:211–214.

Michael J. Moratto

AUGUSTINE SITE, one of the sites excavated in the 1930s in the Sacramento portion of the central valley of California, by a team from Sacramento Junior College. Located on the Consumnes River east of Sacramento, it contributed substantially to the definition of the Early, Intermediate, and Late "cultural levels" identified for the region.
SOURCE: Lillard et al. 1939.

Michael J. Moratto

AUSTIN PHASE, a late prehistoric (ca. A.D. 500–1200) entity in central Texas with an economy based primarily on plant gathering and deer hunting. The many sites, both open and in rockshelters, contain basin-shaped hearths, burned-rock scatters, and cemetery areas with both cremated and noncremated burials. Expanding-stem arrow points (Scallorn and related types) are the chief diagnostic. Other artifacts include bifaces, unifaces, grinding stones, painted pebbles, bone awls, deer-ulna flakers, and ornaments of bone and shell. Representative sites are Kyle, Pat Parker, Smith Rockshelter, and Scorpion Cave. The Austin Focus was named and briefly described by J. C. Kelley in 1949 and was more fully defined by E. B. Jelks in 1962. It was designated a phase by E. R. Prewitt in 1981.
SOURCES: J. C. Kelley 1947a; Suhm 1957; Jelks 1962:84–99; Prewitt 1981:82–83; Highley et al. 1978; and Greer and Benfer 1975.

Frank A. Weir

AVAYALIK SITE, a middle Dorset Phase site on Labrador's northern coast, radiocarbon dated to ca. A.D. 450; excavated by the Torngat Project in 1977. Numerous artifacts, many of wood, demonstrated the richness of the latter part of the Middle Dorset, a time when people apparently had abandoned much of the Arctic north of Labrador. Harpoon heads resemble those of earlier Middle Dorset to the north.
SOURCE: Jordan 1980.

Moreau S. Maxwell

AVINGA SITE, a transitional Late Pre-Dorset/Early Dorset (ca. 700–600 B.C.) site on the south coast of Baffin Island at Cape Tanfield, excavated by Michigan State University in 1962, 1963, and 1976. Lithic artifacts exhibit both Pre-Dorset and Early Dorset features. Located approximately 100 meters from an Early Dorset permafrost site, Avinga apparently was occupied at the end of a warm period immediately preceding the onset of permafrost ca. 500 B.C.

SOURCES: Maxwell 1973, 1985:123–125.

Moreau S. Maxwell

AVONLEA COMPLEX (or PHASE), a late prehistoric (ca. A.D. 200–800) culture of the northern Plains associated with the first archers and bison-corral users of the region. Distinctive traits include the Avonlea type arrow point (q.v.), chipped-stone end scrapers and unifaces, hammerstones, a variety of stone tools, and both net-impressed and grooved pottery. Type site of the complex is the Avonlea Site in south-central Saskatchewan, a location where bison were killed or disabled by driving them down a steep declivity.

SOURCES: Kehoe and McCorquodale 1961; Kehoe 1966, 1973.

Thomas F. Kehoe

AVONLEA POINT, earliest of the small, side-notched, projectile-point types in the Northern Plains; a diagnostic trait of the Avonlea Complex (q.v.).

SOURCES: Kehoe and McCorquodale 1961; Kehoe 1966, 1973.

Thomas F. Kehoe

AWATOVI SITE, a 9-hectare complex known to the Hopi Indians as "Place of the Bow Clan People," comprising at least three two-story, stone-built pueblos and an early Spanish Franciscan mission establishment, located on the southeast rim of Antelope Mesa in the Hopi Province (q.v.) in north-eastern Arizona. There were at least 1300 ground-floor rooms, a minimum of 25 rectangular kivas (probably not all in use at once), and a peak population of from 1000 to 2000, or possibly more. The earliest occupation (by Tewa or Keres from the east?) was at the Western Mound, where two two-story pueblos stood between ca. A.D. 1175 and 1450. They were replaced by a large two-story pueblo that was occupied from ca. A.D. 1450 to 1700.

Some of Awatovi's notable archaeological features are (1) elaborate, free-form, polychrome murals on kiva walls that portray kachinas (q.v.), humans, and gods engaged in ceremonial activities, parrots, eagles, reptiles (including the plumed serpent), eagle-man, the sun, stars, clouds, tadpoles, moths, butterflies, and mythical figures; (2) the remains of mid–17th-century Franciscan churches and associated friary, offices, stables, and work areas; (3) good evidence for the prehistoric use of coal in pottery firing and in kiva and house hearths; (4) evidence of contacts with peoples in other areas (Rio Grande, East Puerco, Kayenta, Mesa Verde, the Zuni, the Little Colorado River, and possibly the southern desert and northern Mexico).

The Mindeleff brothers surveyed and mapped Awatovi in 1882; J. W. Fewkes tested and briefly excavated it in 1892 and 1895; Frank Russell dug there in 1900; L. L. Hargrave collected ceramics and tree-ring specimens in

1928; and J. O. Brew, Watson Smith, R. B. Woodbury, and Al Lancaster excavated extensively between 1935 and 1939. Reports on this work were still appearing in 1986.

SOURCES: Montgomery et al. 1949; Watson Smith 1952b, 1971, 1972; Woodbury 1954; Brew 1979.

Michael B. Stanislawski

AWENDAW SHELL MIDDEN, an expression of the Pee Dee Phase overlying a thin Middle Woodland component on Awendaw Creek in Charleston County, South Carolina. Michael Trinkley excavated the site in 1981, giving special attention to the Pee Dee component (estimated to date ca. A.D. 1600), which contained large quantities of shellfish remains that probably had been collected in the late fall or early winter. Few other subsistence items were found.

SOURCE: Trinkley 1981b.

Michael Trinkley

AZTALAN SITE, a combined Middle Mississippian and Late Woodland (Effigy Mound) site on the Crawfish River in southeastern Wisconsin, estimated to date ca. A.D. 1100. Excavated and reported by S. A. Barrett in the early 1930s, it consists of a complex of truncated pyramidal mounds, domestic structures, status burials, and a wattle-and-daub palisade with bastions. Some scholars believe the site represents a site-unit intrusion from the Middle Mississippian site of Cahokia (q.v.) at East St. Louis, Illinois. Others identify it as a primarily Late Woodland site with Middle Mississippian influences grafted onto a local Effigy Mound cultural base. Lack of recent studies hinders resolution of the different interpretations.

SOURCES: Barrett 1933; Baerreis 1958; Baerreis and Freeman 1958:35–61.

David Overstreet

AZTATLAN COMPLEX, a Mesoamerican culture which, ca. A.D. 700/750–1400/1450, briefly extended into northern Sinaloa, previously a part of the Southwestern culture area. At the time of Spanish contact, ca. 1530, the Mesoamerican frontier had retreated and northern Sinaloa was again part of the Southwest.

SOURCES: Kelley and Winters 1960; Di Peso 1974.

David A. Phillips, Jr.

AZTEC (or WEST) RUIN, one of the largest outliers of Chaco Canyon, located on the Animas River in Aztec National Monument, northwestern New Mexico. Occupied during the late Bonito, Intermediate, and Mesa Verde phases (qq.v.), it was a multistory pueblo of about 450 rooms and more than 28 kivas, with an associated great kiva and refuse mounds. Numerous prehistoric dwellings surround the ruin, including two tri-wall structures (q.v.). The pueblo was constructed between A.D. 1110 and 1120, but subsequent occupation by Mesa Verdeans in the 13th century obscured and altered much of the original Chacoan architecture. Earl Morris, who excavated the ruin between 1916 and 1927, reconstructed the great kiva, including the roof. It remains the only intact great kiva today (1988).

SOURCES: E. H. Morris 1919–1928.

Thomas C. Windes

B

BACHE PENINSULA LOCALITY, region of over 100 archaeological sites spanning the period from Paleoeskimo to Neoeskimo (qq.v.), located midway along the east coast of Ellesmere Island in the eastern Canadian Arctic; investigated by Peter Schledermann between 1977 and 1980. Situated near a large polynia (q.v.) close to the northern boundary of the open water of Baffin Bay, the sites probably mark the location of early crossings from the Canadian Arctic to northwestern Greenland.
SOURCE: Schledermann 1978b.

Moreau S. Maxwell

BACKHOE VILLAGE, a Sevier/Fremont site in the Sevier River Valley, central Utah, excavated by D. B. Madsen and L. M. Lindsay in 1976. Heavy reliance on both wild marsh resources and horticulture led Madsen to conclude that the sedentism of Sevier/Fremont sites was largely due to the proximity and productivity of marsh resources.
SOURCE: Madsen and Lindsay 1977.

David B. Madsen

BADIN POTTERY SERIES, the earliest (ca. 1000–400 B.C.) pottery in the southern North Carolina Piedmont. There are two principal types, cord-marked and fabric impressed, although net-impressed and plain varieties occur. Vessel forms include simple bowls and jars with undecorated straight rims and conical or semiconical bases.
SOURCE: Coe 1964:28–29.

Billy L. Oliver

BADIN TRIANGULAR POINT, a large, crudely made, triangular, Early Woodland (ca. 1000–400) B.C. projectile point produced strictly by percussion flaking techniques; a common type of the North Carolina Piedmont, where it co-occurs with Badin Series pottery (q.v.) and Gypsy Stemmed points. Badin and other large triangular varieties are believed to represent the introduction of the bow and arrow to North Carolina, most likely from the Northeast.

SOURCES: Coe 1964:45; Oliver 1981, 1985.

Billy L. Oliver

BAD RIVER PHASE, 17th- and 18th-century archaeological culture ascribed to the Arikara of the northern Plains by D. J. Lehmer, who first defined the phase. Type sites are Dodd A and Phillips Ranch, South Dakota, where domed earth lodges, Stanley pottery ware, and European trade items of iron, brass, and copper occurred. Economy was based upon seasonal changes of residence, with agriculture practiced in river valleys and bison hunting on the open plains.

SOURCES: Lehmer 1954, 1971.

Wesley R. Hurt

BAJADA PHASE, second phase of the Oshara Tradition (q.v.) in the Four Corners area of the southwest, dating ca. 4800–3300 B.C. The climate during this period was exceptionally arid, and subsistence practices, like those of the preceding Jay Phase (q.v.), were based on extensive foraging by small, mobile bands. Base camps continued to be located close to reliable water sources with easy access to a wide range of microenvironments. Campsites remained small but were more numerous than in the Jay Phase, suggesting a slight population increase. Hunting camps and quarries have been identified.

The diagnostic projectile-point style of the Bajada Phase was relatively large with slight shoulders, a straight or slightly contracting stem, and a straight or concave base that was thinned in a characteristic fashion. Late in the phase, shoulders tended to be more prominent, stem length decreased, and bases became more deeply concave. There was a low frequency of bifacial knives but numerous steep-angled scrapers, large chopping tools, and scrapers made from thin flakes. Ground-stone implements may have been present in some tool assemblages.

On the whole, there was considerable continuity from the Jay Phase to the Bajada Phase. The slight population increase has been interpreted as reflecting an increasingly effective adaptation to a broad-spectrum subsistence base.

SOURCES: Irwin-Williams and Haynes 1970; Irwin-Williams 1973, 1979; R. A. Moore 1983.

Cynthia Irwin-Williams and Patricia A. Hicks

BAKER CAVE, a large, deeply stratified rockshelter in Val Verde County, southwestern Texas, containing extensive late Paleoindian, Archaic, and late prehistoric deposits, first excavated by J. H. Word from 1962 to 1966.

Initial occupation has been radiocarbon dated to ca. 7000 B.C. Features included a late Paleoindian hearth associated with a wide range of micro-fauna and plant remains, an Archaic "screen" or partition wall constructed of sotol or lechuguilla stalks, and a series of bowl-shaped, grass-lined pits. Good stratification and excellent preservation of perishable materials at the site have contributed greatly to the reconstruction of regional lifeways over a period of several thousand years.

SOURCES: Word and Douglas 1970; Chadderdon 1981; T. R. Hester 1982:101–120.

Robert J. Mallouf

BAKER LAKE SITE, a Barren Ground, multicomponent site in the Keewatin District, eastern Northwest Territories; excavated by B. H.C. Gordon. The presence of Pre-Dorset Phase (q.v.) artifacts indicated a penetration by northern coastal hunters who were following the Keewatin caribou herd southward during a cold period ca. 1000 B.C., after Indians had abandoned the site.

SOURCE: Gordon 1975.

Moreau S. Maxwell

BAKER PHASE. See Owens Valley Locality.

BAKERS CREEK POINT, a medium to small, stemmed, chipped-stone projectile-point type with a triangular blade, a triangular expanding stem, and a base that often is as wide as the blade. Affiliated with the Middle Woodland of the Tennessee River Valley and adjacent regions, the type dates ca. 100 B.C. to A.D. 500.

SOURCES: Cambron and Hulse 1964:8, 1975:8; Faulkner and McCollough 1974:145–146; Walthall 1973; Futato 1983:239.

Eugene M. Futato

BALDWIN PHASE. See Fraser Canyon Sequence.

BALEEN PERIOD, an early interval in the development of the eastern Thule Phase (q.v.) when baleen whale hunting was of prime importance. Dense layers of baleen occur in house sites of the period.

Moreau S. Maxwell

BALLANTINE SITE, an early Dorset Phase (q.v.) site on the Ekalluk River, southern Victoria Island, excavated by W. E. Taylor, Jr. Fish and caribou dominated the faunal remains, indicating that riverine and lacustrine sources of game were more important than seal hunting. Caribou may have been speared with harpoons in lakes. Close resemblances of Ballantine lithic and

nonlithic artifacts to those from Early Dorset sites to the east led Taylor to hypothesize a westward return of Paleoeskimo to the area.
SOURCE: W. E. Taylor, Jr. 1967.

Moreau S. Maxwell

BALL COURT, a large, elliptical depression with high, crescentic sides, found in major sites of the Hohokam (q.v.) and some neighboring cultures of the American Southwest; thought to be courts for athletic contests played with a rubber ball like those staged in Mesoamerica, or possibly ceremonial dance floors. Known examples are 18 to 83 meters long, 9 to 32 meters wide, and 0.5 to 5.8 meters deep. Two varieties have been recognized: the larger, earlier Snaketown type of the Colonial Period (ca. A.D. 700–900), and the smaller Casa Grande type of the Sedentary and early Classic periods (ca. A.D. 900–1300). Large and important sites often had more than one ball court. Of the more than 200 courts identified in Arizona, about 40 percent are in the Phoenix Basin Province (q.v.).
SOURCES: Gladwin el al. 1937; Ferdon 1967; Haury 1976; Wilcox and Sternberg 1983.

John S. Cable and David E. Doyel

BANDELIER BEND SITE. See Forked Lightning Pueblo.

BANNERSTONE, a type of polished-stone object, bilaterally symmetrical along a long, drilled hole. Examples have been found in numerous Archaic assemblages in a variety of shapes, including tubular, bar shaped, winged, and geniculate. After finding bannerstones in context with atlatl hooks and shafts at the Indian Knoll Site in Kentucky, W. S. Webb concluded that they functioned as atlatl weights.
SOURCES: W. S. Webb 1946:267–271, 319–333; J. B. Griffin 1952: figs. 13, 14, 21, 28, 29, 66, 102, 157, 163, 168.

N'omi B. Greber

BAOLE COMPLEX, a poorly defined, poorly understood complex in the Las Animas area of northwestern Durango that probably dates to the middle of the first millennium A.D. Known traits include agriculture and simple pottery vessels decorated with black and red designs.
SOURCE: Spence 1978.

David A. Phillips, Jr.

BARE CREEK PHASE. See Surprise Valley.

BARNES SITE, a site in southern Midland County, Michigan, thought to date ca. 9200 B.C., which has produced an assemblage of Paleoindian artifacts that includes more than twenty fluted projectile points.

SOURCES: Wright and Roosa 1966; Mason 1981.

Charles E. Cleland

BASKETMAKER. See Pecos Classification System.

BASS POND DAM SITE, a Thom's Creek Phase midden at the south end of Kiawah Island in Charleston County, South Carolina, dating ca. 1500 B.C. When excavated by J. L. Michie in 1978, it produced Thom's Creek pottery, worked bone, faunal remains, and stone tools.
SOURCES: Michie 1979; Trinkley 1980b.

Michael Trinkley

BASS QUARRY SITE, a stone-working station at an exposure of the cherty lower unit of the Galena formation in the uplands of Grant County, Wisconsin. The chert was utilized by late Paleoindian (q.v.) and Early Archaic peoples, after which the site became buried and was preserved by geomorphic processes. Large numbers of Hardin Barbed type projectile points, cores, and debitage were recovered there during excavations by J. B. Stoltman in 1983. One of the very few Early Archaic components known in Wisconsin, it is an important source of information on the technology associated with Hardin Barbed production.
SOURCE: Stoltman et al. 1984.

David Overstreet

BATACOSA BROWN WARE, a pottery ware dating ca. A.D. 200–1530, found in the upper and lower foothills of southern Sonora. The basic type of the Batacosa Phase (q.v.), it also was made during the succeeding Cuchujaqui, Los Camotes, and San Bernardo phases (qq.v.).
SOURCE: Pailes 1972:229–231.

Richard A. Pailes

BATACOSA PHASE, the earlier phase (dating ca. A.D. 200–700) of a two-phase sequence forming an unnamed complex in southern Sonora that is thought to be a foothill version of the Huatabampo Culture (q.v.) of the adjacent coastal plain. Sites of the phase are small, consisting of concentrations of potsherds and lithic debris on terraces and bluffs overlooking the watercourses in the foothills, each within easy walking distance of the nearest arable floodplain land. Pottery is plain Batacosa Brown Ware (q.v.); other artifacts include basin and slab metates used with one- and two-hand manos. No structural remains have been found, and it is presumed that

habitations were made of perishable materials in the manner of the wattled and mat-covered structures recorded in historic times.
SOURCES: Pailes 1972:346–347, 356–371, 1976.

Richard A. Pailes

BATTLE MOUND, the largest and probably the latest Caddoan mound, standing alone amid some 16 hectares of associated middens and cemeteries in the Great Bend Region of the Red River Valley, Arkansas. Occupied between ca. A.D. 1400 and A.D. 1750 or later, the site comprises components of the Bossier, Belcher, and Chakanina phases. Even though its main platform is disproportionately low and narrow, it is one of the biggest mounds in North America, with a volume of about 20,000 cubic meters. Absence of the thick, weather-resistant clay cap found on most Caddoan mounds suggests that the Caddo never "finished" the mound and that the ceremonial structure that presumably stood on its platform was still in use as recently as A.D. 1750–1770. Lynn Howard carried out exploratory excavations at the site in 1949, and F. F. Schambach has been conducting a controlled surface collection program there since 1980.
SOURCES: C. B. Moore 1912:566–573; Schambach 1982b:2–11.

Frank F. Schambach

BATZA TENA SITES, numerous flaking stations around a geologic source of obsidian south of Hughes, Alaska; investigated by A. M. and D. W. Clark in 1969–1971. Although not closely dated, the sites have yielded fluted points apparently related to Paleoindian forms, as well as earlier and later blade and microblade tools. One component, approximately 2000 years old, shows numerous attributes of the Northern Archaic Tradition (q.v.). At least three obsidian types distinguished on the basis of trace elements come from this and other sources in the region. One type is distributed in sites from the Bering Sea to the Mackenzie River, evidently through trade.
SOURCES: Patton and Miller 1970; D. W. Clark 1974c; D. W. Clark and A. M. Clark 1975; Wheeler and Clark 1977.

Donald W. Clark

BAUMER SITE, a large village located in the Black Bottom of the Ohio River in Massac County, Illinois; the type site for the largely Middle Woodland Baumer Focus. Investigated in 1936 and 1939 by University of Chicago archaeologists, the site contained substantial midden deposits and many large storage pits. The Baumer Focus was originally defined for the lower Ohio River Valley but now is generally included within the larger Crab

Orchard Tradition (q.v.), which spans both the Early and Middle Woodland periods (ca. 600 B.C.–A.D. 400).
SOURCES: Cole et al. 1951:184–210; Butler and Jefferies 1986.

Brian M. Butler

BAUM FOCUS, a unit of the Fort Ancient Aspect (q.v.), named for the Baum Village Site (q.v.) near Bainbridge, Ohio.
SOURCES: J. B. Griffin 1943a:36–39, 1979.

N'omi B. Greber

BAUM SITE, a large Colington Phase (q.v.) village situated along Currituck Sound in Currituck County, North Carolina, radiocarbon dated to ca. A.D. 1315. Excavations by D. S. Phelps in 1979–1980 disclosed abundant features, including mass human burials and excellently preserved floral and faunal remains.
SOURCE: Phelps 1983.

Billy L. Oliver

BAUM VILLAGE, a site of the Fort Ancient Tradition (q.v.), located on Paint Creek west of Chillicothe, Ohio; the type site for the Baum Focus of the Fort Ancient Aspect (qq.v.). Cyrus Thomas, W. K. Moorehead, and W. C. Mills, all of whom excavated there between 1888 and 1905, discovered 48 house patterns, a larger oblong structure, many storage pits, and grouped burials. A truncated mound containing burials covered the remains of two superimposed structures. Ceramics from the site were the basis for the Baum Cordmarked series defined by J. B. Griffin. On typological grounds, the site has been placed early (ca. A.D. 900) in the Fort Ancient Tradition.
SOURCES: Squier and Davis 1848:57–58, pl. 21:1; Cyrus Thomas 1984; Mills 1906; J. B. Griffin 1943a, 1979:551–557, 1983:293–294.

N'omi B. Greber

BAYOU LABATRE CULTURE, an Early Woodland culture of the Mobile Bay region, dating ca. 600 B.C.–A.D. 1; defined by S. B. Wimberly in 1960. Bayou LaBatre peoples lived along the bayous and streams of this coastal region gathering shellfish, collecting plant foods, and hunting game. Their pottery, often highly decorative, is thought to have been ancestral to local Hopewell wares. No burials attributed to these peoples have yet been found.
SOURCE: Wimberly 1960.

John A. Walthall

BAYPORT CHERT, a light to dark gray, nodular chert with light gray and white concentric banding, occurring in Bayport limestones of the upper Mississippian Meramec Group. Exposed at several locations around Sagi-

naw Bay, Michigan, this chert was the predominate material used for chipped-stone tools by prehistoric Indians of the eastern and central parts of Michigan's lower peninsula.
SOURCE: Leudtke 1976.

Charles E. Cleland

BAYTOWN SITE, a site covering some 10 hectares and comprising nine earthen mounds, including one 6 meters high, located in eastern Arkansas; type site for the Baytown Phase (dated ca. A.D. 400–800) and for the Baytown period (dated ca. A.D. 400–700). Pottery from the site is grog tempered and plain surfaced, typical of Baytown ware. There has been only minimal investigation of this important site, and the mounds have not been dated precisely.
SOURCES: Phillips et al. 1951:328; Phillips 1970:903, 916; Morse and Morse 1983.

Dan F. Morse

BEACHRIDGE PHASE. See Brooks River-Naknek Drainage Sites.

BEE CAVE CANYON SHELTER, an enormous rockshelter (230 meters long by 33 meters deep) in Brewster County, southern Trans-Pecos Texas, partially excavated by M. R. Harrington in 1928 and shortly thereafter by E. F. Coffin, who concluded that it had been used repeatedly as a summer encampment. Probably occupied ca. 3000 B.C.–A.D. 1500, the site contained at least six stacked-stone enclosures, numerous refuse pits, roasting pits, accumulations of grasses, cache pits, and many hearths. An extremely rich assortment of perishable and nonperishable artifacts was collected, including anthropomorphic figurines of unfired clay, limestone pipes, gourd vessels, atlatls, arrowshafts, and wooden clubs. Three ceramic sherds, a few maize specimens, and several squash and pumpkin seeds were found. While the materials and features are of great interest, their interpretive value is hampered by scanty stratigraphic and provenience data. The site is reported to have been completely destroyed by relic hunters within a few years of Harrington's and Coffin's work there.
SOURCE: Coffin 1932.

Robert J. Mallouf

BELANGER SITE, a terminal Dorset component at Gulf Hazard (q.v.), on the eastern coast of Hudson Bay, excavated by Elmer Harp, Jr. in 1974. A C^{14} date of ca. A.D. 1460 on a wood sample makes this one of the most recent Dorset Phase occupations. Retention of the mid-passage (q.v.) or axial feature in houses points to an extremely conservative factor in Dorset culture.

SOURCE: Harp 1976.

Moreau S. Maxwell

BELCHER FOCUS (or PHASE), a Late Caddoan unit of the 16th and 17th centuries A.D., comprising numerous hamlets or village sites in the Red River Valley, on lateral lakes, and along upland tributaries in northwestern Louisiana, southwestern Arkansas, and northeastern Texas. Definition of the focus rests largely on excavation of the Belcher Mound (q.v.) in Caddo Parish, Louisiana by C. H. Webb in the late 1930s and early 1950s and on a study of surface collections from other Red River sites. Distinguishing culture traits include a ranked societal organization; an economy based on maize and bean agriculture supplemented by intensive hunting, fishing, and gathering; well-developed ceramic and lithic technologies; and elaborate mortuary practices.

SOURCES: Suhm et al. 1954:199–203; C. H. Webb 1959; Schambach and Miller 1984.

Clarence H. Webb

BELCHER ISLANDS SITES, a series of sites on the Belcher Islands in southern Hudson Bay spanning a period from the earliest Dorset Phase to modern Inuit. They were excavated in 1975 by Elmer Harp, Jr.

SOURCE: Harp n.d.

Moreau S. Maxwell

BELCHER MOUND SITE, a single burial mound containing multiple prehistoric Caddoan components in Caddo Parish, northwestern Louisiana. Situated on a relict Red River course about a mile west of the present river channel and some five miles north of the Mounds Plantation Site (q.v.), the mound was excavated by C. H. Webb with the assistance of family and friends during the late 1930s and early 1950s.

After the owner had removed the mound's top, Webb's initial investigation revealed an accretional mound containing a sequence of structures, each of them burned before the next one was built. Strip excavation exposed entire house ruins and associated interments. Eight houses, presumably temples, and 26 burial pits related to five of the houses were correlated with Caddo II, III, and IV and were radiocarbon dated to A.D. 1310–1670. The period of highest ceramic development, with numerous burial placements

and lingering elements of the Southern Cult, was a Belcher Focus manifestation of the 17th century.
SOURCE: C. H. Webb 1959.

Clarence H. Webb

BELCHER POTTERY, one of the distinctive Late Caddo (ca. A.D. 1500–1700) wares centered on the Red River in northwestern Louisiana, southwestern Arkansas, and northeastern Texas, but widely traded. Typical are thin-walled bottles and shallow bowls made of finely ground clay with shell temper or with no detectable temper. On their highly polished brown to black surfaces are engraved decorations, often highlighted with red or white pigment in the lines of the decorations. Bottles are globular with tubular spouts; favored designs on bottles are concentric circles of unbroken and slotted lines quadrating the body, the quadrants centered with sun symbols, swastikas, or triskeles. Bowls commonly have carinated shoulders, node quadration, and flaring rims with horizontal slotted or unbroken lines. Coarser wares range from children's toy bottles, and pots to moderate-sized jars and pots (often carbonized from cooking), to larger ollas for storage. Surfaces of the coarse wares usually are roughened by vertical ridging, zoned brushing, incising, or, occasionally, punctating or stamping, the latter often patterned. Compound or animal effigy vessels are not infrequent.
SOURCES: C. H. Webb 1959:120–123; Suhm and Jelks 1962:9–12; Schambach and Miller 1984:120.

Clarence H. Webb

BELLE GLADE CULTURE, a culture that occupied the Lake Okeechobee basin and portions of the adjacent Caloosahatchee and Kississimmee river valleys from ca. 500 B.C. to A.D. 1700. Typical sites contain mounds, multiple earthworks, ditches, raised fields, and middens.
SOURCES: Willey 1949c; Sears 1971, 1974, 1982; Milanich and Fairbanks 1980:180–189.

Jerald T. Milanich

BELL POINT, an Early Archaic (ca. 4150–3150 B.C.) dart-point type diagnostic of the Jarrell Phase in central Texas. A large triangular blade, mildly expanding stem, and massive, downwardly expanding barbs whose ends are even with the base are typical. Bell, which stylistically and temporally comprises a series with the Calf Creek and Andice types, is associated with a bison-presence period on the Edwards Plateau.
SOURCES: Sorrow et al. 1967; Prewitt 1981, 1983; Turner and Hester 1985.

Elton R. Prewitt

BELL SITE (1), a two-component (Late Dorset and Early Thule) site on southeastern Victoria Island, Northwest Territories. This is one of several known sites occupied by Dorset and Thule peoples at nearly the same time

but with no evidence of contact. When excavated by W. E. Taylor, Jr., the site's two components were not always separable stratigraphically.
SOURCE: W. E. Taylor, Jr. 1967.

Moreau S. Maxwell

BELL SITE (2), a Fox village site occupied between A.D. 1680 and 1730; one of the very few Midwestern sites where a direct historical connection can accurately be made. Excavations by W. L. Wittry in 1959 disclosed that the site was palisaded and that it contained storage and refuse pits, human and dog burials, and domestic dwellings of both wigwam and rectangular wall-trench styles. Artifact assemblages provide an excellent opportunity to study the influence of European trade goods on aboriginal material culture.
SOURCE: Wittry 1963.

David Overstreet

BENTON POINT, a large, thin, stemmed, Middle Archaic (ca. 3700–3000 B.C.), chipped-stone projectile point type found in the middle to lower Tennessee-Cumberland and upper Tombigbee river drainages and adjacent areas.
SOURCES: Kneberg 1956:25–26; Lewis and Kneberg 1951:34; Cambron and Hulse 1964:11, 1975:12–13; Bense 1983; Futato 1983:205–213.

Eugene M. Futato

BENTSEN-CLARK SITE, a buried, multicomponent, Caddoan site on the south bank of the Red River, in Red River County, Texas, where two shaft burials, a buried occupation zone, and several house mounds/middens were exposed by bank sloughing in 1969. Preliminary investigation by L. D. Banks indicated that the buried zone dated to the Caddo I, III, and IV periods. One of the shaft burials showed close similarities to materials from the Harlan and Spiro phases (qq.v.) at the Spiro Site (q.v.), while the midden appeared to be of Caddo III affiliation.
SOURCE: Banks and Winters 1975.

James E. Corbin

BERKELEY PATTERN, previously termed "Middle Horizon," a socioeconomic adaptation in the middle Central Bay, San Francisco Valley, and central coast areas of California, dating ca. 2000 B.C.–A.D. 500. It is marked by intensive use of coastal and marsh resources as well as acorns as a dietary staple; extensive trade; well-developed bone, shell, and ground-stone industries; and flexed burials, sometimes furnished with distinctive shell, bone, and stone artifacts. Named by D. A. Fredrickson for the West Berkeley type

site (Ala–307) in Alameda County, this pattern may represent the spread of Penutian language groups in central California.
SOURCES: Fredrickson 1973; Moratto 1984:207–211.

Michael J. Moratto

BERNHARD HARBOUR SITE, an early Dorset Phase component, dating ca. 400 B.C., on the shore of Dolphin and Union Strait south of the southwest corner of Victoria Island, Northwest Territories. The cultural assemblage has aspects of eastern Early Dorset but no traits attributable to the Western Arctic. This contrasts with the Lagoon Site (q.v.), farther west on Banks Island, which produced elements of both.
SOURCE: W. E. Taylor, Jr. 1972.

Moreau S. Maxwell

BESANT MIDDEN, a name sometimes used in reference to the Mortlach Site (q.v.) in Saskatchewan.

BESANT PHASE, a Late Archaic culture (ca. A.D. 1–600) of the Canadian prairie provinces and the upper Missouri River drainage of the adjacent United States, named and described by Boyd Wettlaufer in the mid–1950s and later amplified by Brian Reeves. Distinctive projectile points are accompanied by knives, scrapers, and other lithic artifacts, often made of Knife River flint (q.v.) from North Dakota. Ceramics are rare. Vertical "uprights" (bison long bones and ribs driven into the earth or packed into holes) are diagnostic. Intensive communal hunting of bison is indicated by numerous jumps and pounds; campsites are often located on low stream terraces. Besant has close relationships with the contemporaneous Sonota Complex (q.v.) of the Dakotas but lacks the abundant Middle Woodland ceramics and burial mounds of Sonota.
SOURCES: Wettlaufer 1956; Neuman 1975; Frison 1978; B. O. K. Reeves 1983.

Richard G. Forbis

BESSEMER SITE (1), a Late Woodland village, northernmost known component of the Dan River Culture, on the upper James River in the mountains of western Virginia. Excavations by C. R. Geier in 1977 exposed a large rectangular longhouse, very unusual for the area, and storage pits, hearths, and a human burial.
SOURCE: Geier and Moldenhauer 1977.

Keith T. Egloff

BESSEMER SITE (2), a major Early Mississippian (ca. A.D. 1000–1200) ceremonial center on a tributary of the Black Warrior River, just south of Birmingham, Alabama. Three earthen mounds and the remains of rectan-

gular timber structures associated with them were excavated there by the
Alabama Museum of Natural History in 1938–1939.
SOURCES: DeJarnette and Wimberly 1941; Walthall 1980.

John A. Walthall

BEZYA SITE, a site in northeastern Alberta with a radiocarbon date of ca.
2000 B.C., where excavations by R. J. Le Blanc and Jack Ives in 1982 and
by Le Blanc in 1983 yielded artifacts related to the production of microblades. This documented the extension of the Northwest Microblade Tradition (q.v.) beyond the Alaskan-Cordilleran core area.
SOURCE: Le Blanc n.d.

Donald W. Clark

BIDWELL PHASE. See Surprise Valley.

BIESTERFELDT SITE, a protohistoric site of the Plains Village Tradition
(q.v.) on the Sheyenne River in Ransom County, North Dakota, dug by
W. D. Strong. Long believed to be of Cheyenne Indian origin, it is also
known as the Sheyenne-Cheyenne site. Euro-American trade goods, the
presence of horse bones, and historical records date the site to the late
1700s.
     More than 60 circular earthlodges on a flat terrace edge were surrounded
on three sides by a curved fortification ditch. Pottery and other artifacts
show strong similarities to contemporary Arikara sites along the Missouri
River, but ethnohistorical data support its identification as a Cheyenne
village, occupied after the Cheyenne left the general area of Minnesota and
before they migrated west of the Missouri. There are, however, no sites in
Minnesota that resemble Biesterfeldt, so its genesis remains cloudy.
SOURCES: Strong 1940; W. R. Wood 1971.

W. Raymond Wood

BIG BEND MOUND GROUP, one of several sites used by W. C. McKern
in his definition of the Waukesha Focus of the Hopewell Culture (qq.v.) in
the 1930s. Excavations there by E. F. Wood in 1934 demonstrated relationships between Middle Woodland populations in southeastern Wisconsin
and those in the Illinois River Valley.
SOURCES: E. F. Wood 1936; McKern 1942.

David Overstreet

BIGGS FORD SITE, a multicomponent site representing several Late Wood-
land complexes dating ca. A.D. 1000–1600, located in the Monocacy River
Valley, Maryland. More than 30 aboriginal features, including 12 Luray
Phase burials, were found during excavations there in 1969 and 1970 by

the Maryland Geological Survey. The predominant occupation contained Keyser Cordmarked ceramics of the Luray Phase (qq.v.).
SOURCE: Kavanagh 1982.

Stephen R. Potter

BIG HAWK VALLEY, a locality some 50 kilometers northeast of Flagstaff, Arizona in Wupatki National Monument containing several Kayenta Anasazi/Singua sites, four of which were excavated by Watson Smith in 1948. Ceramic dated to ca. A.D. 1070–1200, these Pueblo Phases II and III sites shed light on cultural mixing in the area.
SOURCE: Watson Smith 1952a.

Bruce Anderson

BIG HORN MEDICINE WHEEL, the best-known medicine wheel (q.v.), located in Wyoming, dating ca. A.D. 1200. It has a hollowed-out central cairn from which 28 spokes radiate, a number of which are aligned with astronomical phenomena: summer-solstice sunrise and sunset, and the rises of Aldebaran, Rigel, and Sirius.
SOURCE: J. A. Eddy 1975.

Patricia J. O'Brien

BIRCH MOUNTAINS ARCHAEOLOGICAL AREA, an area of northeastern Alberta comprising earlier components of the 5000-year-old Oxbow Complex and later components ascribed to ancestral Athapaskans of the Taltheilei Tradition (q.v.).
SOURCE: Donahue 1976.

Donald W. Clark

BIRDSTONE, a polished-stone object of stylized, birdlike shape. Variations include "popeyed birds" and forms with bar- and disc-shaped bodies. Thought to have been atlatl weights, birdstones have been found most commonly in Late Archaic and Early Woodland sites of the Old Copper, Glacial Kame, Red Ocher, and Meadowood complexes, from southern Michigan through northern sections of Indiana and Ohio into adjoining parts of New York and Ontario.
SOURCES: Moorehead 1899; J. B. Griffin 1952:figs. 16, 28, 30; Ritchie 1969:180–182; Fitting 1975:80–89.

N'omi B. Greber

BIRNIRK PHASE, immediate forerunner and genitor of the Thule Phase (q.v.) in northwestern Alaska. In the second half of the first millenium A.D., Birnirk people occupied the Alaskan coast north of the Bering Strait and the adjacent coasts of the Chukchi Peninsula in Siberia. Their artifacts also are found on St. Lawrence Island, where they may predate the Punuk Phase (q.v.) but principally co-occur with it in what may be a culture-contact situation.

Birnirk was recognized by Clark Wissler in 1916 and its role in Eskimo prehistory was discussed in the 1920s, but comprehensive definition of the phase rests on investigation of the Birnirk Site at Point Barrow by J. A. Ford in 1932 and 1936 and on excavations at the Walakpa Site by D. J. Stanford in 1968–1969. Common artifacts include toggling harpoons, arrow and bird dart heads which, in attributes of style and decoration, distinguish Birnirk from earlier and later phases. Coarse paddled pottery with curvilinear designs appears with Birnirk and continues into early Thule.

SOURCES: J. A. Ford 1959; Stanford 1976.

Donald W. Clark

BIRNIRK SITE, type site for the Birnirk Phase (q.v.), located at Point Barrow, Alaska.

BISCUITWARE, a generally thick, soft, carbon-painted pottery diagnostic of the Classic Period (A.D. 1400–1600) Rio Grande Anasazi in the Tewa Basin Province (qq.v.) of northern New Mexico; so called because of its similarity in appearance to the bisque or biscuit stage (after first firing) in the manufacture of modern glazed pottery. Derived from the Coalition Period type, Wiyo Black-on-white, three types of Biscuitware are recognized: Biscuit A (or Agiquiu Black-on-gray), Biscuit B (or Bandelier Black-on-gray), and Biscuit C (or Cuyamungue Black-on-tan).

SOURCES: Kidder 1915; Mera 1932; Harlow 1973.

Stewart Peckham

BIS SA'ANI SITE, a Chacoan outlier of some 40 rooms and five kivas, located on the narrow crest of a butte just northeast of Chaco Culture National Historical Park, New Mexico. It was occupied during the late Bonito, Intermediate (?), and Mesa Verde phases (qq.v.) in the A.D. 1100s and 1200s. Partially excavated by M. P. Marshall in 1980–1981 for the Navajo Tribe, on whose land it is situated, Bis sa'ani is notable as the subject of the first published, intensive archaeological study of a Chacoan outlier and its surrounding small-house community.

SOURCE: Breternitz et al. 1982.

Thomas C. Windes

BITTERROOT SIDE-NOTCHED POINT, a large, side-notched projectile point with a concave base and deep, comma-shaped notches; thought to be diagnostic of the Bitterroot Culture of Idaho and to date between 7000 and

1000 B.C. The type was first defined in 1961 by Ruth Gruhn. In the Great Basin, similar points are called *Northern Side-Notched*.

SOURCES: Gruhn 1961; Swanson 1966; Heizer and Hester 1978.

Robert G. Elston

BLACKDUCK CULTURE, a Late Woodland manifestation, dating ca. A.D. 800–1400, initially defined by L. A. Wilford from his excavations at the Shocker Site near Blackduck, Minnesota. Blackduck pottery, the chief diagnostic trait, is distributed from northwestern Michigan through the Lake Superior Basin into east-central Saskatchewan. The grit-tempered, globular vessels have constricted necks and flared rims; they usually have cordmarked surfaces, although fabric marking also is common in the Rainy River region. Decorative techniques include cord-wrapped stick impressing, punctating, and combing. Blackduck ceramics show affinities to Clam River ware of northwestern Wisconsin, to St. Croix and Onamia ceramics in central and southern Minnesota, and to Selkirk pottery of northern Minnesota, Ontario, and Manitoba. Other culture traits include burial mounds, copper beads and fishhooks, barbed bone harpoons, small triangular and side-notched projectile points, bone spatulas, and oval and lunate knives. The economy was based on hunting and gathering, with intensive utilization of fish and wild rice.

SOURCES: Wilford 1941, 1945a, n.d.a., n.d.b.; MacNeish 1958a; G. E. Evans 1961a, 1961b; McPherron 1967; Lugenbeal 1976, 1978; Carmichael 1977; Rajnovich 1984.

Gordon R. Peters

BLACK MESA, a term applied to the northern two-thirds of a massive uplift (circumference 440 kilometers) in northeastern Arizona; the locale of episodic human occupation from ca. 6000 B.C. to the 20th century. The uplift's southern third is commonly known as the Hopi Mesas. Black Mesa was virtually unknown archaeologically until, between 1967 and 1983, an extensive program of rescue archaeology was carried out on mining leases by Prescott College, Southern Illinois University, and Fort Lewis College.

The Early Archaic period (ca. 6000 B.C.–A.D. 100) is represented by sparse remains of ephemeral hunting and gathering camps, several of which have been excavated. The lithic assemblages consist mostly of bifacial tools made of both local and exotic stones. The Hisatsinom Phase (ca. 1500–900 B.C.) of the Late Archaic period resembled the earlier period in its material culture, which is consistent with a generalized hunting-gathering adaptation.

The Lolomai Phase of the Basketmaker II period, dating ca. A.D. 100–300, marks the introduction of agriculturally based subsistence to the area. Sites vary from chipped-stone scatters to multistructure pithouse villages. Chipped stone assemblages are dominated by retouched tools made of locally available materials; ground-stone tools include basin and trough metates and one-hand manos. Basketmaker III remains have been found only on the southern edge of the mesa despite surveys in the central and northern areas.

A Puebloan occupation at ca. A.D. 825–1150 comprising three phases (Dinnebito, Lamoki, and Toreva) was agriculturally based but differed from earlier occupations by the presence of ceramics. Most sites are small, although there is considerable variation in site size and configuration, suggesting a correspondingly variable settlement pattern. Ceramic inventories are dominated by Tusayan Gray Wares and Tusayan White Wares; San Juan Red Wares occur in smaller numbers and are replaced by Tsegi Orange Wares between A.D. 1000 and 1050. Chipped-stone tools indicate an expedient flake technology using both local and exotic raw materials. Groundstone tools are dominated by trough metates and two-hand manos.

The northern part of the mesa was abandoned ca. A.D. 1150, but people of the Klethla Phase occupied the central part until ca. A.D. 1300, by which time the mesa was completely unoccupied except for a small area around the Hopi Mesas. Black Mesa was reoccupied by Navajos in the mid–1700s, an occupation that continues today (1987).

SOURCES: Beals et al. 1945; Linford 1982; Gumerman 1984; Christenson and Parry 1985; Powell and Gumerman 1987.

Shirley Powell

BLACK SAND PHASE, an Early Woodland manifestation defined essentially as a ceramic complex of sand-tempered, noded, incised-over-cord-marked pottery. It is distributed throughout western Illinois west of the Illinois River, and variations occur in eastern Missouri, eastern Iowa, and southeastern Wisconsin. The type site is Liverpool (q.v.), where in 1930 archaeologists from the University of Chicago found burials of the phase in a natural black sand stratum sealed by a Middle Woodland mound. The phase is poorly dated but probably existed ca. 400–200 B.C.

SOURCES: Cole and Deuel 1937:132–150; P. J. Munson 1982.

Alan D. Harn

BLACK VERMILLION PHASE, an Archaic manifestation defined by L. J. Schmits on the basis of his work at the Coffey Site (q.v.) in Kansas. Dating ca. 3200–3100 B.C., it is characterized by basally notched projectile points of the Smith and Calf's Creek types, Clear Fork gouges, and polished, asymmetrical knives related to knives of the Munkers Creek Phase (q.v.). The complex appears to have been contemporaneous with the Munkers Creek and Nebo Hill (q.v.) phases in eastern and central Kansas.

SOURCE: Schmits 1978.

Patricia J. O'Brien

BLACKWATER DRAW (or CLOVIS) SITE, a stratified, multicomponent, Paleoindian site near Clovis, New Mexico which has produced artifacts of the Clovis, Folsom, and Plano cultures (qq.v.). E. B. Howard tested the site in 1933 and found several chipped-stone scrapers and other stone artifacts in situ. In 1937, J. L. Cotter found two Clovis points (q.v.) and several other stone and bone artifacts associated with mammoth bones in a layer of sand resting on bedrock, which clearly established the contemporaneity of humans and mammoths in North America.

Later work by E. H. Sellards, G. L. Evans, J. J. Hester, and others revealed several geological strata overlying the basal sand, one of which contained Folsom Culture artifacts, including Folsom points (q.v.), dating ca. 8000 B.C. A more recent stratum contained several projectile points attributed to the Plano Culture of ca. 5000 B.C.

The stratified deposits at Blackwater Draw provided some of the earliest and clearest evidence for the relative and absolute temporal placement of several Paleoindian cultures and artifact types.

SOURCES: E. B. Howard 1935; Cotter 1937, 1938; Sellards 1952:28–31, 54–58, 72–75; J. J. Hester 1972.

Edward B. Jelks

BLOCK LOOKOUT (or SMOKEY BEAR) RUIN, a moderate-sized but very important pueblo site in southeastern New Mexico, a component of the Lincoln Phase (q.v.), Sierra Blanca Sub-Province, Jornada Province, Mogollon Culture. Excavations by J. H. Kelley in 1956 encountered superimposed structures all over the site, but the date of the earliest occupation is uncertain. Occupation seems to have ceased by ca. A.D. 1450.

Architectural forms include roomblocks of small habitation rooms and large, deep, square-to-rectangular, subterranean, ceremonial chambers. Ceramics were dominated by Corona Corrugated and Chupadero Black-on-white; smaller quantities of other types also were present. The site's importance lies in its well-preserved artifacts made of organic materials and in its complex stratigraphy.

SOURCES: Wiseman et al. 1976; J. H. Kelley 1984.

R. N. Wiseman

BLOODY FALLS SITE, a multicomponent site on the Coppermine River, Northwest Territories. Excavations by R. J. McGhee in 1968 disclosed one of the most westerly Pre-Dorset components on the mainland. Although radiocarbon dates suggest that it was occupied too late for the initial eastward migration, there are close typological resemblances to early dated sites to the east.

SOURCE: McGhee 1970.

Moreau S. Maxwell

BLOOM MOUND, a small pueblo near Roswell, New Mexico, that tentatively has been assigned by J. H. Kelley to the Lincoln Phase (q.v.), Sierra Blanca Sub-Province, Jornada Province, Mogollon Culture. It is estimated to date to the early 14th century A.D. The far eastern location with respect to other sites of the phase, the specialized inventory of small artifacts (such as copper bells and hundreds of disc beads), and the pottery types suggest that the site may have been a trading outpost with connections to the Plains and to the El Paso Sub-Province (q.v.) as well as to other Lincoln Phase sites.

SOURCE: J. H. Kelley 1984.

R. N. Wiseman

BLOSSOM SITE, a site in the Sacramento portion of the Central Valley of California from which the oldest (ca. 2500 B.C.) Windmiller or Early Horizon materials were recovered.

SOURCE: Ragir 1972.

Michael J. Moratto

BLUEFISH CAVES, three small rockshelters in the Porcupine River drainage west of Old Crow, northern Yukon Territory, which yielded the oldest radiocarbon-dated archaeological materials from a primary context in northern northwestern North America. Excavations between 1978 and 1985 by Jacques Cinq-Mars disclosed a small number of burins, microblade cores, flakes, and a mammoth bone core, together with numerous altered bones, in a loess layer of Late Pleistocene age. Pollen from the loess reflected the same Late Pleistocene sequence reconstructed and dated elsewhere in Beringia: treeless, herbaceous tundra followed by a rise in *Betula* which, in turn, was succeeded by a boreal spruce forest. Horse and mammoth bones from the loess produced radiocarbon dates of 12,900 ± 100 years and 15,500 ± 1300 years B.P. Other large fauna found in the caves include *Rangifer, Cervus, Ovis, Alces,* and *Bison.*

SOURCES: Cinq-Mars 1979; Morlan and Cinq-Mars 1982.

Donald W. Clark

BLUE RIVER KANSA VILLAGE, a historic (ca. A.D. 1800–1830) village of the Kansa Indians located on the Kansas River just east of its juncture with the Big Blue River in north-central Kansas. It was excavated in 1937 by W. R. Wedel.

SOURCE: Wedel 1959.

Patricia J. O'Brien

BLUFF CREEK COMPLEX, a Middle Ceramic complex of small villages built along the edge of the Bluff Creek Valley in south-central Kansas, radiocarbon dated to an average of A.D. 1050. House types are daub-covered frame structures with square, rectangular, or oval floor plans. There are numerous straight-sided storage pits, both within and without the houses, throughout the village. Ceramics share characteristics with the Washita

River Focus (q.v.) of central Oklahoma and the Central Plains Phase (q.v.) of northern Kansas and Nebraska. Subsistence was based on hunting, gathering, and corn growing.
SOURCES: Witty 1969, 1978b.

Thomas A. Witty, Jr.

BLUFF PHASE. See Brooks River-Naknek Drainage Sites.

BOAS MASTODON, the remains of a mastodon in Richland County, Wisconsin; one of the few possible examples of association between extinct Pleistocene fauna and stone tools in the state. An "association" was reconstructed by H. A. Palmer and J. B. Stoltman on the basis of interviews that had been made with informants who were on the scene when the mastodon remains were unearthed in the late 19th century.
SOURCE: Palmer and Stoltman 1976.

David Overstreet

BOB WILLIAMS SITE, a Late Caddo (ca. A.D. 1500–1700) occupation and mortuary site, apparently a southward extension of the Sam Kaufman Site (q.v.) in Red River County, Texas.
SOURCE: Perino 1983.

James E. Corbin

BOIS BLANC PHASE, a Late Woodland culture unit in the Straits of Mackinac, Michigan, temporally intermediate (ca. A.D. 900–1100) between the Mackinac and Juntunen phases (qq.v.); characterized by pottery with rounded castellations and beaded or braced rims. Punctations over twisted cord decorations suggest affinities with Black Duck Phase (q.v.) ceramics. Bois Blanc is represented at the stratified Juntunen Site (q.v.) on Bois Blanc Island in the straits, where warm-season and fall-spawning fish were primary resources.
SOURCES: Yarnell 1964; Cleland 1966; McPherron 1967.

Margaret B. Holman

BONE BANK SITE, a Late Mississippian site on the Wabash River about two miles above its juncture with the Ohio River in Posey County, Indiana, now all but destroyed by bank erosion. During the 19th century, a great number of pottery vessels associated with burials were exposed by riverbank erosion, making the site a landmark for travelers in the area. The Museum of the American Indian in New York curates the only known large collection from the site, including not only more than 300 typical Mississippian vessels

of forms expected in the area, but also some painted headpots like those of the Caborn-Welborn Phase (q.v.).
SOURCE: W. K. Adams 1949:18–25.

James H. Kellar

BONFIRE SHELTER, a stratified bison jump site with associated butchering floors in Val Verde County, western Texas, where herds of bison were driven over a cliff above the rockshelter by both Paleoindian (q.v.) and Late Archaic peoples. Excavations in 1963–1964 by D. S. Dibble exposed two massive bone beds: the earlier one (radiocarbon dated to ca. 8000 B.C.) containing the remains of an estimated 120 animals (*Bison antiquus* or *occidentalis*) along with associated Plainview points and a single Folsom point (q.q.v.); the second bed containing some 800 modern (*Bison bison*) animals, representing a series of drives ca. 670 B.C., associated with Late Archaic points. There was evidence of only minor occupation in the rockshelter between the two bison-jump episodes.
SOURCES: Dibble and Lorrain 1968; Dibble 1970.

Robert J. Mallouf

BONITO PHASE, an Eastern Anasazi expression in the Chaco Province (q.v.) of northwestern New Mexico that was recently redefined into the Early, Classic, and Late Bonito phases.

In the Early Bonito Phase (ca. A.D. 900–1040/1050), formerly called the Red Mesa Phase, the dramatic change in architecture that earmarks the Chaco phenomenon began, while the social, economic, and ceremonial components became more complex, possibly reflecting a hierarchical social system. Communities of small houses were similar in plan and architecture to those of the earlier White Mound Phase (q.v.), typically consisting of a midden, pitstructure, plaza, living room, and storage room. Houses were small, usually having less than fifteen rooms; domestic activities became centered in the surface dwellings and plazas, as well as in the pitstructures.

Large houses, termed greathouses, dwarfed the small houses. Most were multistoried with huge rooms; a majority of the space was allocated to storage, unlike the use of space in small houses. Masonry construction practices for small surface buildings continued from the White Mound Phase. Pitstructures were large, but great kivas remained rare until the following Classic period.

Subsistence appears to have relied heavily on the horticultural triad of maize, beans, and squash, with some dependence on hunting and gathering. Ceramics were dominated by Red Mesa Black-on-white and narrow neck-banded pottery, the two type markers for the Early Bonito period. Small quantities of Chuskan pottery from the west reflect limited ties with the Chuska Valley; San Juan Redware was the preferred redware of the period.

The Classic Bonito Phase (ca. A.D. 1040/1050–1100), which includes H. S. Gladwin's Wingate Phase in part, embodies all that most investigators have envisioned as the climax period in Chaco Canyon. There were dramatic changes in many aspects of culture; for example, pottery styles, population size, communications, the extent of the cultural system, trade, and the source areas being utilized. Massive building programs were undertaken in Chaco Canyon as new greathouses were erected and existing ones were enlarged. Tens of thousands of roofing timbers were brought into the canyon from the surrounding mountain ranges. Occupation of the greathouses apparently was limited to a few families, but seasonal influxes of people apparently contributed large amounts of trash to the huge greathouse middens. Small sites may have been mostly abandoned, their residents evidently leaving the canyon rather than shifting residence to the greathouses. Some probably moved into small communities which became concentrated to the south and west during the period, perhaps using a widespread road network that connected Chaco Canyon to outlying communities.

Visual communications networks (e.g., shrines), great kivas, and other esoteric features reveal increased emphasis on ceremonialism and social control throughout the Chaco Province and beyond. Dwelling and kiva construction methods were similar to, but more refined than, those in the preceding period, producing some of the finest stonemasonry workmanship in North America. Severe droughts may have been responsible for the increased complexity and spread of interaction and social control during the Classic Phase.

Gallup Black-on-white (q.v.) and overall-indented, corrugated pottery dominated ceramic assemblages. Much of the corrugated ware was made in the Chuska Valley and imported into Chaco Canyon. Chaco Black-on-white (a fine geometric pottery style) and cylinder jars appeared. Stone artifacts and other goods reveal widespread exchange or use of resources far from Chaco Canyon, especially to the west and the Chuska Valley. Mesoamerican goods were imported for the first time. Subsistence was based on horticulture and, to a lesser extent, on small game (especially rabbits) and large game (especially deer and antelope). Canals and terraces were built to increase crop production. Turkeys and raptors were important ceremonially.

The Late Bonito Phase (ca. A.D. 1100–1140/1150), which incorporates H. S. Gladwin's McElmo and Hosta Butte phases, has often been seen as the period of Chaco decline and demise, although it witnessed the largest population of the entire Bonito Phase, as well as other startling changes. It was marked by a dramatic increase in small-house sites, often in close proximity to greathouses, and by the appearance of McElmo-style greathouse sites, characterized by a reduction in room size and by series of roomblocks, each surrounding a Chaco-style kiva. In existing greathouse sites, there were changes in the way space was utilized, in construction styles, in trash-deposition patterns, in ceramics, in source areas, and in the use of roads. Small San Juan-style kivas appeared. Small-house sites mirror many of these same changes. Remodeling of both large and small sites was widespread, although timber procurement from the surrounding mountains dropped sharply. No new great kivas were built, although earlier ones were remodeled.

Overall, influence from the Upper San Juan Province was paramount. An influx of greathouse outliers appeared in that province, starting ca. A.D. 1080, and others were established along roads to the south and west. An abnormally wet period in the early 12th century may have been responsible for the population influx and other changes. A lengthy drought after A.D. 1130 forced massive abandonment of Chaco Canyon and a majority of the outliers.

Ceramic assemblages of the Late Bonito period were dominated by Gallup and Chaco-McElmo Black-on-whites (qq.v.) and by overall-indented, corrugated pottery. The use of sherd temper in culinary wares became important, and White Mountain Redwares appeared for the first time. Chuskan pottery decreased in frequency as San Juan ceramic imports increased. Significant amounts of Jemez obsidian began to appear. Turkeys and prairie dogs became important, but dogs dwindled in numbers. Horticulture dominated the subsistence strategy, but small-game hunting, especially of rabbits and prairie dogs, remained important.

SOURCES: Lekson 1986; McKenna and Truell 1986.

Thomas C. Windes

BONNELL SITE, a pithouse site of four occupations dating between A.D. 1200 and 1400 in southeastern New Mexico; major source of data for J. H. Kelley's description of the late Glencoe Phase (q.v.) of the Sierra Blanca Sub-Province. The ceramic assemblage, certain architectural features, and attributes of various small artifacts show unmistakable influences from the neighboring Lincoln Phase (q.v.) people to the north.

SOURCE: J. H. Kelley 1984.

R. N. Wiseman

BOOTLEGGER TRAIL SITE, the location of bison kills dating between ca. A.D. 1200 and 1400 on the Marias River northwest of Fort Benton, Montana. T. E. Roll's excavations in 1975–1976 disclosed two levels representing spring kills; they document the mass killing techniques used by Indians who probably lived in villages along the Upper Missouri River.

SOURCE: Roll and Deaver 1980.

Patricia J. O'Brien

BORAX LAKE SITE, a stratified site on the edge of a dry lakebed near Clear Lake, northern California, where avocational archaeologist Chester Post in the 1930s found fluted projectile points of obsidian that resembled the Clovis type (q.v.). The site was subsequently excavated by M. R. Harrington between 1938 and 1945, by R. J. Sayles in 1946, and by C. W. Meighan and C. V. Haynes in the late 1960s. This is the type site for both the (Paleoindian) Post Pattern in the North Coast Ranges and for the later (Archaic) Borax Lake Pattern.

SOURCES: M. R. Harrington 1948; Meighan and Haynes 1970; Moratto 1984:82–83.

L. A. Payen

BORDERTOWN SITE, a large, open, multicomponent site on the ridge between White Lake Playa and Long Valley Creek, north of Reno on the California-Nevada state line, where excavations by the Nevada Archaeological Survey in 1976 exposed several housepits, storage features, hearths, earth ovens, and a human burial. Apparently occupied from very early times, the intensity of occupation began increasing ca. 1500 B.C. with the Martis Phase (q.v.), culminated between A.D. 500 and 1200 in the early Kings Beach Phase (q.v.), and declined thereafter in the late Kings Beach Phase and into the protohistoric period. The transition from Martis to Kings Beach is marked at the site by an increased dependence on small game and seed processing.

SOURCE: Elston 1979.

Robert G. Elston

BOSSIER FOCUS (or PHASE), a Caddo II-III (ca. A.D. 1200–1500) culture centered in northwestern Louisiana along the Red River, its lateral lakes and upland tributaries, and extending into eastern Texas and southwestern Arkansas. Originally defined by C. H. Webb in 1948, the focus is divided into two periods: Bossier I and II. The initial Bossier manifestation followed Caddo I in the Red River Valley, then spread into the upland, and finally returned to the valley above Shreveport. These movements possibly were responses to the formation of the Great Raft on the river.

This culture is characterized by diminished ceremonialism; construction of mounds (mostly in Bossier II); the use of mounds for interring destroyed temples; a simple farming-gathering-hunting existence; a settlement pattern comprising hamlets, farmsteads, and small villages; predominantly culinary pottery but with moderate amounts of fine engraved and stamped vessels in Bossier II; and changes through time in ways of decorating pottery. In their terminal phase, the Bossier people may have been the Naguatex mentioned in the De Soto narratives as living east of the Red River.

SOURCES: C. H. Webb 1948, 1983; Suhm et al. 1954:195–199.

Clarence H. Webb

BOTONAPA SITE, a Trincheras Culture (q.v.) site in the upper Rio Sonora Valley of north-central Sonora, consisting of a large rectangular enclosure and several terraces on the edge of a mesa overlooking the floodplain. It was tested by R. A. Pailes in 1978.

SOURCES: Bandelier 1892; Sauer and Brand 1931.

Richard A. Pailes

BOULDER EFFIGIES, representations of humans, animals resembling turtles, and circles outlined on the ground surface with boulders; found in Manitoba, Saskatachewan, and the Dakotas. The circles are believed to be tipi rings (q.v.) or cairns. They are of uncertain age, but some are reputed to be historic.

SOURCES: Wedel 1961; Kehoe 1965.

Patricia J. O'Brien

BOWMAN SITE, a Late Woodland village, probably dating ca. A.D. 1550, on Cedar Creek in the northern Shenandoah Valley, Virginia. Testing by H. A. MacCord in 1964 revealed refuse-filled storage pits, human burials, postmolds, and undisturbed midden. Keyser Cordmarked Ware (q.v.) is the predominant pottery.

SOURCE: MacCord 1964b.

Keith T. Egloff

BRANCHVILLE POTTERY SERIES, a quartz-tempered ceramic found in the interior coastal plain of southern Virginia and dating ca. A.D. 1000–1600. Similar to Cashie Ware in the adjacent section of North Carolina, Branchville vessels may be plain or impressed with a fabric, cord, or simple stamp; occasionally punctations and incised chevrons or bands appear below the lip.

SOURCES: Binford 1964; Egloff and Potter 1982.

Keith T. Egloff

BRAND SITE, an open site in northeastern Arkansas containing a major, stratigraphically intact component of the Dalton Culture (q.v.) at the base of windblown silts capping a knoll. Excavation by D. F. Morse in 1970 produced a variety of artifacts interpreted as task-specific tools for butchering and for bone-tool manufacturing, but no faunal material was recovered due to soil acidity. The artifacts occurred in clusters of from 74 to 89 tools per cluster.

SOURCES: Goodyear 1974; Morse and Morse 1983.

Dan F. Morse

BRANDON SITE, a late prehistoric (ca. A.D. 1000) fortified village of long, narrow lodges overlooking the Big Sioux River near Brandon, South Dakota, excavated by W. H. Over and E. E. Meleen in 1939. Initially, the site was

ascribed to the Over Focus (q.v.), a complex that now is subsumed under the taxon Initial Middle Missouri Variant (q.v.).
SOURCE: Over and Meleen 1941.

Larry J. Zimmerman

BRAVO VALLEY ASPECT, an agriculturally based culture unit that occupied a series of villages around the confluence of the Rio Conchos and the Rio Grande in western Texas and northern Chihuahua ca. A.D. 1200–1900. As defined by J. C. Kelley in the 1940s, the aspect comprised five sequential foci (now termed phases): La Junta, Concepcion, Conchos, Alamito, and Presidio. The La Junta Phase was closely related to the Jornada Branch of the Mogollon (q.v.), whose villages extended up the Rio Grande to the El Paso area. The later phases were restricted more closely to the locality.

Small villages of both pithouses and above-ground dwellings on elevated silt terraces and ridges along the Rio Grande were the primary places of residence, but small rockshelters and open campsites containing hearths and middens (including ring middens, or sotol pits) also have been identified with the aspect. Cultigens included corn, beans, and cucurbits; fishing, hunting, and collecting of various foods also were practiced. Typical artifacts were awls, needles, spatulas, and tubular beads of bone; shell pendants, beads, and gorgets; stone metates, pestles, sinkers, abraders, scrapers, handaxes, knives, perforators, and a variety of finely made arrow points. Several pottery varieties were made locally; other wares were traded from the Jornada area up the Rio Grande and from northern Mexico. Burials usually were tightly flexed and frequently were placed beneath house floors, with or without offerings.
SOURCES: J. C. Kelley et al. 1940; J. C. Kelley 1949:89–114, 1985:149–159.

Robert J. Mallouf

BRECKENRIDGE SITE, a multicomponent, stratified rockshelter on the White River in northwestern Arkansas, now inundated by Beaver Reservoir; investigated briefly by M. R. Harrington in 1922, then by crews from the University of Arkansas Museum in 1932, and excavated extensively by University of Arkansas Museum personnel between 1960 and 1963. The three-meter-thick deposits contained seven cultural zones spanning the period ca. 8000 B.C.–A.D 1500: a transitional Paleoindian/Early Archaic component, followed by three successive Archaic strata, a Late Archaic/Early Woodland occupation, a later Woodland occupation, and, finally, a Mississippian component. This cultural stratigraphy was fundamental to the

development of a prehistoric sequence for the region that related Harrington's Ozark Bluff Dwellers to more recently recognized culture-history frameworks.
SOURCES: W. R. Wood 1963; R. A. Thomas 1969.

George Sabo III

BREWSTER SITE, a Paleoindian occupation comprising Folsom and Agate Basin (qq.v.) components in east-central Wyoming, dug in 1959 by George Agogino and in 1975–1980 by George Frison. It was given separate site status in 1959 before later work proved it to be part of the Agate Basin Site (q.v.).
SOURCE: Agogino and Frankforter 1972.

George Frison

BRITISH MOUNTAIN COMPLEX, a complex of crude, chipped-stone tools found in northwestern Canada, principally at the Engigstciak Site (q.v.) in the northern Yukon; described by R. S. MacNeish in the late 1950s and thought by him to be more than 14,000 years old. Most archaeologists currently do not accept this as a valid complex, although some interpret rough bifaces in younger northern materials as possessing British Mountain attributes.
SOURCES: MacNeish 1959a; MacKay et al. 1961.

Donald W. Clark

BROADSPEAR POINT SERIES, projectile points occurring in the lower Delaware River Valley, often made of nonflinty materials, consisting of three defined types: Susquehanna Broadspear, Lehigh Stemmed, and Perkiomen. The series is identified with the late Archaic period (ca. 2500–1000 B.C.), sometimes referred to in the region as the Terminal Archaic.
SOURCES: Witthoft 1953; Ritchie 1961.

Ronald A. Thomas

BROADSPEAR TRADITION, a terminal Archaic (e.g.) expression in the Middle Atlantic and New England states, comprising several cultures that share certain distinctive traits: broad-bladed notched or stemmed projectile points, drills with the same basal treatment, bifaces, scrapers, ground-stone celts, and soapstone cooking vessels. The tradition appears to have originated in the Southeast and to have spread northward, possibly through a migration, along the Atlantic coast early in the second millennium B.C.
SOURCE: Witthoft 1953.

James A. Tuck

BROOKS RIVER–NAKNEK DRAINAGE SITES, a series of sites at Katmai National Monument on the Alaska Peninsula comprising components of these phases:

Koggiung Phase of the American Paleo-Arctic Tradition (q.v.), presently known only from Kvichak Bay (at the head of Bristol Bay).
Graveyard and Beachridge Phases of the Northern Archaic Tradition (q.v.), at Kvichak and the Brooks River area, respectively.
Strand Phase of the Ocean Bay Tradition (q.v.) in the Brooks River area.
Gravels Phase of the Arctic Small Tool Tradition (q.v.) in the Brooks River area.
Smelt Creek and Weir Phases of the Norton Tradition (q.v.) in the Naknek River and Brooks River areas.
Camp and Bluff Phases of the Thule Tradition (q.v.) in the Brooks River area.
Pavik Phase at the mouth of the Naknek River.

The area was investigated archaeologically for nine seasons between 1960 and 1975 by D. E. Dumond, and additional work was done to develop features at the Katmai Monument interpretation center. Dumond and James VanStone conducted the principal investigation of the Pavik Phase (see Paugvik) in 1984. Artifact assemblages of the Norton and Arctic Small Tool traditions are particularly noteworthy, and the Brooks River area contains the largest reported concentration of Arctic Small Tool Tradition houses.

These sites have produced important information on prehistoric cultures of the Bering Sea region at their southern limits and on the interaction across the Alaska Peninsula between peoples of the Bering Sea and the Gulf of Alaska.

SOURCES: Shields 1977; Dumond 1981.

Donald W. Clark

BROOMAN POINT SITE, an early Thule Phase settlement on the eastern coast of Bathurst Island, radiocarbon dated to the 11th century A.D. R. J. McGhee's investigations there in 1979 exposed semisubterranean Thule houses that cut through an earlier Late Dorset component, virtually obliterating it. There was no indication of contact between the two cultures. Late Dorset art objects found in the refuse of Thule houses were interpreted as intrusive materials that had been fortuitously encapsulated in sod building blocks.

SOURCE: McGhee 1984.

Moreau S. Maxwell

BROWN JOHNSON SITE, a Late Woodland palisaded village, radiocarbon dated to ca. A.D. 1500, located on a tributary of the New River in the mountains of southwestern Virginia. Completely excavated in 1970 by H. A.

MacCord, the site contained circular house patterns, storage pits, hearths, and human burials.
SOURCE: MacCord 1971b.

Keith T. Egloff

BROWNS VALLEY SITE, a late Paleoindian (q.v.) burial in western Minnesota associated with parallel-flaked projectile points and knives, investigated by A. E. Jenks in 1933. The grave had been dug into gravel at the outlet of glacial Lake Agassiz, but, because its geological context was disturbed before it could be examined by an archaeologist or geologist, no firm date can be assigned except on typological grounds. A range of 8000–6000 B.C. has been suggested.
SOURCES: Jenks 1937b; Elden Johnson 1969.

Christy Hohman-Caine

BROWNSVILLE FOCUS, a late prehistoric manifestation, estimated to date from ca. A.D. 1100 to the 18th century, that is known primarily from surface collections in the Rio Grande delta area of the southern Texas coastal plain. The artifact assemblage, one of the most unique and varied on the Texas coast, includes lithic, bone, and shell tools; bone and shell ornaments; and ceramics, some of which evidently originated in the central Texas coast and some in northeastern Mexico.
SOURCES: Suhm et al. 1954:130–133; Prewitt 1974c.

Lawrence E. Aten

BROWNWARE PHASE, informal term for an unnamed eastern Anasazi (q.v.) manifestation dating ca. A.D. 450–550, whose sites occur widely in the Chaco, Mesa Verde (Mancos Canyon), Navajo Reservoir, and Middle Rio Grande provinces (qq.v.). Its distinguishing traits are very shallow pithouses; small, slab-lined storage cists; and brownware pottery similar to that of the early Mogollon Culture (q.v.). Settlement patterns are poorly known but may consist of both large communities (some with great kivas) and scattered, isolated pithouses.
SOURCES: F. H. H. Roberts, Jr. 1929a; McKenna and Truell 1986.

Thomas C. Windes

BRUNSWICK WARE, a kind of pottery made in the 18th century by Indians of the southeastern coastal states (as far north as North Carolina) in imitation of English pottery of the same period. Sometimes called Colono-

Indian pottery, it has a smoothed to heavily burnished, undecorated surface and no visible temper.
SOURCE: South 1976:27–38.

Billy L. Oliver

BRYAN SITE, a Silvernale Phase site of the southern Minnesota Mississippian Tradition, located at the juncture of the Cannon and Mississippi rivers near Red Wing; excavated by L. A. Wilford in the 1950s and Elden Johnson and C. Dobbs in 1983–1984. Radiocarbon dated to ca. A.D. 1100–1400, it is considered to be of Middle Mississippian affinity but with definite Oneota (Blue Earth) connections. Although there is ample evidence of corn agriculture at the site, bison, fish, avifauna, and small mammals also were utilized for food. Site features included hundreds of storage pits, semisubterranean houses, and a palisaded fortification.
SOURCES: Gibbon 1974, 1978; *Minnesota Archaeologist* 1984.

Christy Hohman-Caine

BUCHANAN LAKE SITE, a late Dorset Phase (q.v.) site on Axel Heiberg Island in the High Arctic west of Ellesmere Island; the only Dorset site yet reported from this relatively large but inhospitable island. Excavations by Patricia Sutherland in 1980 contributed important information on the geographic spread of the Dorset culture.
SOURCE: Patricia Sutherland n.d.

Moreau S. Maxwell

BUCHANAN RESERVOIR, a locality at the juncture of the San Joaquin Valley and the Sierra Nevada foothills, in California, where, between 1967 and 1972, T. F. King and M. J. Moratto excavated nearly 30 sites and defined a culture sequence of three phases: Chowchilla (ca. 800 B.C.–A.D. 500), Raymond (ca. A.D. 55–1500), and Madera (ca. A.D. 1500–1850). The Buchanan Reservoir sequence is a major point of comparison for discoveries elsewhere in south-central California.
SOURCES: T. F. King 1976; Moratto 1972.

Michael J. Moratto

BUCHANAN SITE, a two-component (Pre-Dorset and Dorset) site on the Ekalluk River, Victoria Island, Northwest Territories; excavated by W. E. Taylor, Jr. The Pre-Dorset assemblage, with a relatively early radiocarbon date of ca. 960 B.C., resembles earlier Pre-Dorset assemblages to the east as well as assemblages of the Canadian Tundra and Taiga Tradition (q.v.). Unlike at eastern Pre-Dorset sites, microblades are absent and quartzite

tools are large. The Dorset component was early and contained discrete variants of eastern harpoon-head styles.
    SOURCE: W. E. Taylor, Jr. 1967.

                                                                Moreau S. Maxwell

BUENA FE PHASE. See Casas Grandes Province.

BUENA VISTA LAKE SITES, an extensive lakeshore habitation area and an adjacent hilltop cemetery in the southern San Joaquin Valley of central California, first excavated by W. R. Wedel in 1933–1934 with Work Projects Administration crews. Wedel recognized three phases of occupation, the earliest of which was thought to be comparable to coastal Oak Grove assemblages and the final phase dating to protohistoric-historic times. Later excavation in the mid–1960s by D. A. Fredrickson disclosed deeply buried artifacts and burned shell dated to approximately 8200 radiocarbon years.
    SOURCES: Wedel 1941; Fredrickson and Grossman 1977.

                                                                    L. A. Payen

BUFFALO JUMP, a site where hunters stampeded a herd of bison over a cliff or into an arroyo to kill or severely injure them. Jump sites, most commonly of Paleoindian or Archaic (qq.v.) affinity, occur over the Plains from Alberta and Manitoba in the north to Texas in the south. Major sites include Bonfire Shelter in Texas, the Olsen-Chubbuck Site in Colorado (qq.v), and the Old Women's Buffalo Jump in Alberta. Stone spear points and butchering tools are commonly found among the bison bones at such sites.
    SOURCES: Schultz 1943; Forbis 1960; Dibble and Lorrain 1968; Wheat 1972.

                                                                Wesley R. Hurt

BULL BROOK SITE, a large, shallow, Paleoindian (q.v.) site near Ipswich, eastern Massachusetts, investigated by D. S. Byers, who reported small concentrations of artifacts that appeared to mark living areas. Fluted projectile points, scrapers, bifaces, twist drills, and other chipped-stone artifacts are typical of the assemblage at the site. Dating is not entirely satisfactory, but an estimate of 9000–8500 B.C. is not unreasonable.
    SOURCES: Byers 1954, 1956.

                                                                James A. Tuck

BULVERDE POINT, a Middle Archaic dart-point type, diagnostic of the Marshall Ford Phase (ca. 1550–650 B.C.) in central Texas, also occurring in lesser numbers in surrounding areas. Distinctive attributes are a moderately broad, triangular blade, squared or barbed shoulders, and a rectangular to gently contracting stem with straight edges and a straight base. There are stylistic similarities to the preceding Travis and Nolan (qq.v.)

types and to the succeeding Pedernales (q.v.) type. Bulverde occurs very
frequently in burned rock middens on the Edwards Plateau.
    SOURCES: Suhm et al. 1954; Weir 1976; Prewitt 1981, 1983; Turner and Hester
1985.

                                                              Elton R. Prewitt

BURIN, a flint or chert tool formed by driving a spall from one or more
corners of a mitten-shaped preform. Burins were used for grooving wood,
bone, antler, ivory, and soapstone. They occur over much of North America,
but are especially common in the Arctic and Subarctic regions, where they
dominate Independence I and Pre-Dorset (qq.v.) assemblages and are a
characteristic Dorset Phase (q.v.) tool.

                                                              Moreau S. Maxwell

BURIN-LIKE TOOL, a stone tool used like a burin but with a working
surface, and usually both faces, formed by grinding and polishing; characteristic of Dorset Phase (q.v.) assemblages.

                                                              Moreau S. Maxwell

BURIN SPALL, a spall driven from a core to produce a burin and often
retouched for use as a micrograver or sewing awl; especially characteristic
of Arctic Small Tool Tradition (q.v.) assemblages.

                                                              Moreau S. Maxwell

BURTON BAY SITE, a possibly Pre-Dorset house site on Frobisher Bay,
Baffin Island, with a barely indicated mid-passage (q.v.), a dwelling trait
previously known only for the High Arctic, Labrador, and coastal Quebec.
Tests by M. S. Maxwell in 1980 produced no artifacts or other cultural
materials, but the site's height above sea level suggests an early date.
    SOURCE: Jacobs n.d.

                                                              Moreau S. Maxwell

BUSHNELL WARE, a ceramic associated with the Early Woodland period
in the Northern Neck of tidewater Virginia between the Rappahannock and
Potomac rivers, radiocarbon dated to an average of ca. 1100 B.C. The
tempering material is mainly schist, which occurs in combination with grog,
fiber, steatite, and minute particles of shell and bone. Vessels are small,
shallow bowls, either ovoid or rectangular with rounded corners, and having

flat bases impressed with bundled fibers. Lugs were attached by clay rivets passed through holes in the vessel walls.
SOURCES: Waselkov 1982:282–283; Egloff and Potter 1982:95.

Stephen R. Potter

BUTTON POINT SITE, a multicomponent site on Bylot Island off the northern coast of Baffin Island, partly eroded by the sea. First described by Therkel Mathiassen in 1927 and partially excavated by Guy Mary-Rousseliere in 1975, it yielded artifacts of types that span the period from earliest Pre-Dorset to modern Inuit. Their provenience, however, is unreliable owing to displacement by permafrost action. Many magico-religious art objects—including four unique, life-sized, wooden Dorset masks—were found in the very rich deposits.
SOURCES: Mathiassen 1927; Mary-Rousseliere 1976.

Moreau S. Maxwell

BUXHALL SITE, a Groswater Dorset Phase (q.v.) site at Hamilton Inlet on the coast of Labrador, one of the first sites to demonstrate clearly that Groswater Dorset assemblages and settlement systems are distinctively different from those of the Pre-Dorset and Dorset phases (qq.v.). Excavated by W. W. Fitzhugh, the site produced two radiocarbon dates—700 B.C. and 300 B.C., respectively—the earlier overlapping with late Pre-Dorset, the later overlapping with Early Dorset. Fitzhugh favors the later date as the more likely one.
SOURCE: Fitzhugh 1972.

Moreau S. Maxwell

BUZZARD ROCK SITE, a Late Woodland village on the Roanoke River in Roanoke, Virginia, dug in 1977 by W. E. Clark, who found refuse-filled pits, hearths, and one rectangular and two circular house patterns at the site. The storage pits, which contained Dan River pottery, were radiocarbon dated, probably too early, to A.D. 1010–1110.
SOURCES: P. S. Gardner 1980; Clark et al. n.d.

Keith T. Egloff

C

CABIN RUN DISTRICT, a series of sites located along the South Fork of the Shenandoah River, Virginia, occupied from the Early Archaic through the Late Woodland periods. The Habron Site, tested in 1966 by C. L. Rodgers, contained stratified materials dating from the Middle Archaic through A.D. 1600. Four other sites, tested in 1980 by W. M. Gardner, contained features and artifacts of the Early Archaic and the Early, Middle, and Late Woodland periods.

SOURCES: Rodgers 1968; Snyder and Fehr 1984.

Keith T. Egloff

CABORN-WELBORN PHASE, a late prehistoric-protohistoric Mississippian (q.v.) unit in the lower Wabash-Ohio Valley, defined by T. J. Green and C. J. Munson in 1978. The settlement pattern was more dispersed than that of the immediately preceding Angel Phase (q.v.) of the same area, and there seems to have been no social-political-religious center like the one at the Angel Site (q.v.). Though ceramics resemble those of the Angel Phase in many ways, they differ in the presence of incised/punctated decorations and, apparently, of a few painted, human-head effigy vessels. In contrast to Angel, ceramic vessels regularly occur with burials. Small, chipped-stone, thumbnail scrapers are a common artifact; glass beads and brass artifacts attest to contact with Europeans. Probable bison remains have been reported. The phase seems to be most closely related to manifestations in the central Mississippi Valley.

SOURCE: Green and Munson 1978.

James H. Kellar

CACHE CREEK BASALT, a fine-grained, vitreous stone occurring as cobbles in streambeds along the southern flank of the Arrowstone Hills near the town of Cache Creek, British Columbia. The primary deposit whence the cobbles derived has not been identified. This and other basalts were the most commonly used materials for stone-tool production on the Canadian Plateau; more than 95 percent of lithic tools were fashioned from them. Vitreous basalts, used for tools most frequently after ca. 400 B.C., sometimes are referred to collectively as Cache Creek basalt, even though their origin is uncertain.

SOURCE: Teit 1900.

Arnoud H. Stryd

CADDOAN AREA CHRONOLOGY. Since the 1940s several classification schemes have been proposed for temporally ordering the archaeological cultures of the Caddoan area. The earliest scheme, and the one most widely used until recently, was devised by A. D. Krieger in 1946. Using the McKern classification system (q.v.) then in vogue, Krieger defined a Gibson Aspect (ca. A.D. 800–1400) representing the earlier segment of Caddoan prehistory, and a Fulton Aspect (A.D. 1400–1700 +) representing the later segment. At the Eleventh Caddoan Conference in 1968, the archaeologists present reached a consensus that a five-period sequence (designated Caddo I through V) was better suited for ordering data than Krieger's scheme. However, the five-period sequence has not found universal acceptance, and many archaeologists use a three-period chronology: Early Caddo (ca. A.D. 700–1200), Middle Caddo (ca. A.D. 1200–1400), and Late Caddo (ca. A.D. 1400–1700 +).

SOURCES: Krieger 1946; C. H. Webb 1961:136–137; Wyckoff 1974:40–41; E. M. Davis 1970:40.

James E. Corbin

CADDOAN CERAMICS, distinctive wares of the Caddoan cultures in eastern Texas, southeastern Oklahoma, southwestern Arkansas, and northwestern Louisiana, dating ca. A.D. 600–1700. Although some stylistic and technical attributes probably were inspired by flourishing Mississippian base cultures to the east, Caddoan ceramics clearly developed primarily out of antecedent local wares. In its full flower, Caddoan pottery was superior in quality of construction to most full Mississippian ceramics.

Earliest Caddoan pottery was either untempered or tempered with grog. Later, during Middle Caddoan times, bone was used as a tempering agent, either alone or with grog. In the protohistoric and historic periods, vessels frequently were tempered with crushed shell in many areas. Formed by coiling (and paddling?), Caddoan vessels typically occur in bowl form— especially carinated bowls, with or without flaring rims—or as jars or bottles. Tripod bottles, effigy vessels, rattle bowls, and pipes also were produced.

Hard-paste and wet-paste decorations on vessels are common, particularly on the rim and/or upper portions of bowls and jars, and on the bodies of bottles. Incising and punctating predominate on jars; bottles are usually engraved; both techniques occur on bowls. Brushing, punctating, and coarse incising are often present on utilitarian wares. Painting is uncommon in the Caddoan ceramic tradition, but the lines forming engraved or incised designs sometimes were filled with white, red, or occasionally green pigments.

SOURCES: Newell and Krieger 1949; Suhm et al. 1954; Westbrook 1982.

James E. Corbin

CADDO TRADITION, a 1000-year cultural manifestation in the four-state area of northwestern Louisiana, eastern Texas, eastern Oklahoma, and southwestern Arkansas. By ca. A.D. 800, the Caddos were becoming well established throughout this biogeographical area of upland terraces and eroded mountains, transected by the Red and Arkansas rivers and numerous lesser rivers and tributaries. The Caddos combined indigenous gathering, fishing, and bow-and-arrow hunting with maize-squash-bean-sunflower-tobacco agriculture in the fertile stream valleys. The linguistically related Wichita, Pawnee, and Arikara broke away and moved into the Plains, evidently by A.D. 1000, to combine bison hunting with horticulture.

Distinctive Caddoan traits were evidenced in Caddo I (A.D. 800–1000), after which they evolved through Caddo II–V into historic times. Early traits include ceremonial centers consisting of mounds surrounding plazas, situated in the river valleys; hamlets and farmsteads spread around the centers in valleys and uplands; strong sociopolitical organization, with ranking and mortuary ceremonialism featuring deep tomb burials accompanied by massive offerings in mounds, in cemeteries, and, at farmsteads, in shallow individual graves; ceramic dichotomy, with sturdy culinary wares of both indigenous and Lower Mississippi Valley derivation, and fine wares (presumably of Mesoamerican inspiration) in the form of bottles and carinated bowls with polished surfaces and decorations traced with engraved lines that sometimes contain pigments; brisk intergroup and extraneous trading of necessities and exotics.

Well-known Caddo I and II sites include George C. Davis on the Neches River; Gahagan, Mounds Plantation, Crenshaw, Haley, Bowman, and Sanders on Red River; early McCurtain and Mineral Springs in the Little River area; Ozan, Washington, and East mounds toward the Ouachita; and Harlan and Spiro in Oklahoma. Caddo III and IV, with diminished ceremonialism and widespread dispersion of hamlets in the uplands, are represented by the Frankston, Titus, Bossier, McCurtain, Mid-Ouachita, and Ft. Coffee phases (or foci), with the best-known mounds at the Belcher, Hatchel, Battle, Rosebrough, and Werner sites. Caddo V encompasses the Historic Hasinai, Kadohadacho, Natchitoches, Ouachita, Cahinnio, and associated groups, compressed by hostile encroachment and decimated by epidemic diseases.

SOURCES: Suhm et al. 1954:151–228; C. H. Webb 1959; Schambach 1970, 1982b.

Clarence H. Webb

CADES POND CULTURE, a culture in western north-central Florida, dating ca. A.D. 200–700, related to the Weeden Island Culture (q.v.). Village sites, some with single or multiple mounds, are situated adjacent to extensive aquatic resources, especially lakes and wet prairies.

SOURCES: Hemmings 1978; Milanich 1978a; Milanich and Fairbanks 1980:96–111.

Jerald T. Milanich

CAHOKIA SITE, a multicomponent site on the Mississippi River floodplain in the American Bottom of southwestern Illinois, the major component of which is the largest Mississippian (q.v.) mound and temple complex in North America. Designated a World Heritage site in 1982, Cahokia was occupied over many centuries, from the Late Archaic to the Early Historic period (ca. 1000 B.C.–A.D. 1800). Major excavations have been conducted there by the University of Illinois at Urbana-Champaign, the University of Wisconsin-Milwaukee, Beloit College, Southern Illinois University at Carbondale, Southern Illinois University at Edwardsville, and Washington University, St. Louis.

In the primary site area, which covers approximately 5 to 6 square miles, are more than 100 mounds, including the largest prehistoric earthen structure in North America, Monks Mound (q.v.), and a variety of both temple and burial mounds. A large circular arrangement of heavy posts (called *woodhenge* after the circles of stone at Stonehenge, England) is thought to have functioned as a sun calendar. Excavations have indicated an extensive residential area encompassing most of the site.

SOURCES: Bushnell 1904; Moorehead 1929; Wittry 1969; Fowler 1969, 1975; O'Brien 1972a; Fowler and Hall 1972.

Charles J. Bareis and Andrew C. Fortier

CALAVERAS SKULL, a partial human skull and postcranial skeletal fragments purportedly found in 1866 at a depth of 130 feet in a mine shaft dug through Tertiary lava and gravel, at Bald Hill near Angeles Camp, California. The skull was championed by geologist J. D. Whitney as evidence that human remains and extinct fauna were coeval in Pliocene gravels—a contention made infamous by Bret Harte's satirical poem. W. H. Holmes and later W. J. Sinclair concluded that the episode was likely the result of a mining-camp joke.

SOURCES: Brewer 1866; Whitney 1879; W. J. Sinclair 1908.

L. A. Payen

CALDWELL VILLAGE, a Fremont (q.v.) site in the Uinta Basin of northeastern Utah. R. J. Ambler's excavations there in 1964 led to his definition of the Fremont Culture.

SOURCE: Ambler 1966.

David B. Madsen

CALICO SITE, a controversial, alleged preprojectile-point site in the Mohave Desert region of interior southern California, where in the 1960s and 1970s L. S. B. Leakey and R. D. Simpson found numerous flaked-stone specimens in alluvial fan deposits that have been dated by radiocarbon analysis at greater than 40,000 years old and by the uranium-series method at approximately 200,000 years. The controversy revolves round the question of whether the specimens are man-made or were flaked by natural forces.

SOURCES: Haynes 1973; Schuilling 1979; Taylor and Payen 1979.

L. A. Payen

CALIFORNIA PROVINCES, a series of four provinces (Salton, Coastal, Peninsular, and Salada) of the Patayan Division of the Hakataya Culture (qq.v.), located in the basin and range region of southern California, from the Mohave River southward into Baja California, and westward to the coastal region near San Diego. Contacts were primarily with the Laquish Province of southwestern Arizona. Estimated to date between ca. A.D. 600 and the historic period, the provinces are based on the distribution of Tizon Brown Ware pottery. No phases have been defined for any of them.

SOURCES: M. J. Rogers 1945; May 1978.

Albert H. Schroeder

CALLAWASSIE ISLAND BURIAL MOUND, a St. Catherines Phase burial mound, dating ca. A.D. 1100, located on Callawassie Island in Beaufort County, South Carolina. Briefly investigated by C. B. Moore in 1898 and more completely by M. J. Brooks in 1982, it has produced pottery, faunal material, and a number of burials. T. A. Rathbun conducted a thorough osteological study of the human bones.

SOURCES: C. B. Moore 1898; Brooks et al. 1982.

Michael Trinkley

CAL SMOAK SITE, an Archaic and Woodland campsite on the Brier Creek floodplain in Bamberg County, South Carolina, excavated from 1971 to 1973 by S. T. Lee and A. R. Palmer. They exposed distinct occupation-

specific artifact clusters and collected abundant ceramic and lithic artifacts, as well as a small sample of ethnobotanical specimens.
SOURCES: Lee and Parler 1972; D. G. Anderson et al. 1979.

Michael Trinkley

CALVERT POINT, a short, thick, wide, Early Woodland (ca. 1100–400 B.C.) projectile point with slight shoulders, straight stem, and straight or slightly rounded base. Most often made of quartz, the type occurs in the piedmont and coastal plain sections of the Potomac River valley and along most of the western shore of Maryland.
SOURCES: Stephenson et al. 1963:143–144; Steponaitis 1980:15; Waselkov 1982:277, 283–284.

Stephen R. Potter

CAMBRIA PHASE, a unit of the Initial Variant of the Middle Missouri Tradition (q.v.) in southern Minnesota, dating ca. A.D. 1000–1300. Subsistence data show a mixed base including corn agriculture, hunting, gathering, and fishing. Bell-shaped storage pits are numerous at most sites. Pottery vessels are predominantly grit-tempered, globular jars with smoothed-over surfaces decorated with incised or trailed, rectilinear or curvilinear designs. Cambria Village on the Minnesota River in south-central Minnesota is the type site.
SOURCES: Wilford 1945b; Knudson 1967.

Christy Hohman-Caine

CAMDEN DISTRICT, a series of sites along the Rappahannock River in the interior coastal plain of Virginia, first investigated by H. A. MacCord in 1965. Although there were Early and Middle Woodland occupations, the most significant components are dispersed cabin sites, dating ca. 1680, that document acculturation between Native American and European societies.
SOURCE: MacCord 1969.

Keith T. Egloff

CAMDEN WARE (1), an untempered, clayey-paste, undecorated ceramic in the form of bowls with flattened bases, found in the interior coastal plain of northern Virginia, dating ca. A.D. 1660.
SOURCES: MacCord 1969; Egloff and Potter 1982.

Keith T. Egloff

CAMDEN WARE (2), a probable late Middle Woodland and early Late Woodland pottery, estimated to date ca. A.D. 900–1400. Possibly a stylistic descendant of Deptford Culture (q.v.) wares, it is found in the upper and middle coastal plain of South Carolina. The Santee and McClellanville series

are possibly related. All of these wares are distinguished by gritty paste, predominately simple stamping, and globular or conoidal vessel forms. Camden Ware frequently also has a distinctive rim incising.
SOURCES: Stuart 1975; Trinkley 1981a; D. G. Anderson n.d.b.

Michael Trinkley

CAMPBELL TRADITION, a cultural expression dating ca. 3000 B.C.–A.D. 500 along the Santa Barbara Channel and adjacent parts of coastal southern California. Defined by C. N. Warren in 1968, this tradition is distinguished by mortars and pestles, intensive use of marine and littoral resources, shell and bone ornaments, and numerous projectile points. Campbell gave rise to the Chumash Tradition and thus was ancestral to the ethnographic cultures of the Santa Barbara Channel coast.
SOURCES: C. N. Warren 1968; Moratto 1984:160–164.

Michael J. Moratto

CAMP PHASE. See Brooks River-Naknek Drainage Sites.

CAMPUS SITE, a site on the campus of the University of Alaska at Fairbanks that produced the first northern interior assemblage to attract widespread attention. Excavations in the 1930s and 1960s by several archaeologists produced information that figured in definition of the Northwest Microblade Tradition and the Denali Complex (qq.v.) and drew attention to apparent Asian ties of the site's microblade and core industry. Today the contributions of this unstratified, largely undated, and incompletely reported site have been superseded by information from other sites.
SOURCES: N. C. Nelson 1935, 1937; Rainey 1939.

Donald W. Clark

CAMP VERDE PHASE, a phase of the Verde Province of the Sinagua Division, Hakataya Culture (qq.v.) in Arizona, dating ca. A.D. 900–1125 and based on excavations at a number of sites. Pithouses are similar to those of the previous Cloverleaf Phase (q.v.), but the pits form the lower walls of some; others have vertical slabs at the base; and still others have jacal walls from the floor level up. Both two- and four-post roof supports occur. Larger communal structures similar to those of the Cloverleaf Phase also are present.

Verde Brown Ware remains the dominant ceramic, but Tuzigoot Brown and Red both occur late in the phase; Verde Red-on-brown is rare. Other artifacts are similar to Cloverleaf artifacts with the addition of grooved abraders and anvils of pottery and stone. The presence of azurite and copper ore indicates quarrying in the mines near Jerome. Extended burials on the back have been noted. Diagnostic intrusives are the Hohokam (q.v.) type Sacaton Red-on-buff and the Anasazi (q.v.) types Black Mesa Black-on-

white, late Black Mesa, and Tusayan Black-on-red. Hohokam type ball courts and irrigation canals are associated with some sites.
SOURCE: Breternitz 1960.

Albert H. Schroeder

CANADIAN TUNDRA TAIGA TRADITION, a term first used by W. C. Noble in 1971 for an inventory of material from a number of small Barren Ground sites distributed from Great Bear Lake to Hudson Bay. Thought by Noble to represent a cultural hybrid, these are now interpreted as multicomponent sites abandoned by Indians during the second millenium B.C., then reoccupied by Paleoeskimo people.
SOURCES: W. C. Noble 1971; Maxwell 1985:100.

Moreau S. Maxwell

CANALIÑO CULTURE, the most recent (ca. 2000 B.C.–A.D. 1780) of three prehistoric phases proposed by D. B. Rogers in 1929 for the Santa Barbara region of coastal southern California. Now subsumed by the Campbell and Chumash traditions, the Canaliño Culture was characterized by domed thatched houses, flexed burials, and well-developed shell and steatite industries.
SOURCES: D. B. Rogers 1929:367–419; Moratto 1984:124, 132–134.

Michael J. Moratto

CANYON SITE, oldest excavated and dated site in the southwestern Yukon Territory, located at the Aishihik River crossing of the Alaska Highway. Excavations by several archaeologists between 1944 and 1966 revealed an early (ca. 5200 B.C.) occupation and meager traces of subsequent occupations extending to relatively recent time. In the early component were found a hearth, two lanceolate projectile points (one of them burinated) suggestive of the Plano series (q.v.), flakes, and a few other items.
SOURCES: Workman 1974, 1978.

Donald W. Clark

CAPE ALITAK PETROGLYPH SITE, the principal rock-art location in ethnographic Eskimo territory, located at the southwestern end of Kodiak Island, Alaska. Carved into granitic outcrops, the petroglyphs consist of numerous schematic faces and, less commonly, whales and geometric figures. There also are petroglyphs on Afognak Island just north of Kodiak Island.
SOURCES: Heizer 1952; D. W. Clark 1970a.

Donald W. Clark

CAPE FEAR PHASE, a poorly defined Middle Woodland manifestation, dating ca. A.D. 400–1000, extending along the south coastal region of North

Carolina. Diagnostic elements include Cape Fear and Hanover series ceramics (qq.v.) and many low, sand burial mounds.
SOURCE: Phelps 1983:35.

Billy L. Oliver

CAPE FEAR POTTERY SERIES, a sand-tempered ware widely distributed throughout the southern coastal region of North Carolina, thought to date to Middle Woodland times (ca. A.D. 400–1000) and possibly associated with distinctive, low, sand mounds of the area. Surfaces are cordmarked, fabric impressed, or net impressed.
SOURCES:South 1976:18; Phelps 1983.

Billy L. Oliver

CAPE KRUSENSTERN ARCHAEOLOGICAL AREA, a series of beach ridges on the northwestern coast of Alaska where archaeological remains document nearly every prehistoric coastal occupation of the region, beginning more than 4000 years ago. Type sites for the Old Whaling Culture (q.v.) and the Palisades Complex (now considered to belong to the Portage Phase of the Northern Archaic Tradition, q.v.) are there. Beach-ridge chronology, based on a patterned succession in the formation of beach ridges, initially observed by H. B. Collins at the Gambell sites (q.v.) and developed by J. L. Giddings, Jr., during the 1950s, provided an important complement to radiocarbon dating. Because of its archaeological importance, this area has been designated a U.S. National Monument.
SOURCES: Giddings 1962a, 1962b, 1966, 1967; Giddings and Anderson 1985.

Donald W. Clark

CAPE SPARBO SITE, one of the first reported Pre-Dorset Phase (q.v.) sites in the Canadian High Arctic, located on the north shore of Devon Island. Excavations there by G. R. Lowther in 1959 yielded a lithic assemblage dominated by spalled burins.
SOURCE: Lowther 1962.

Moreau S. Maxwell

CAPE TANFIELD SITES, a series of habitation sites (including Closure, Loon, Tanfield/Morrison, Nanook, Kemp, and Shorty, qq.v.) at Cape Tanfield on the southern coast of Baffin Island, Northwest Territories. The sites span the period from earliest Pre-Dorset through Thule phases to modern Inuit.
SOURCE: Maxwell 1973.

Moreau S. Maxwell

CAPE TYSON SITE, one of the northernmost known Dorset sites in Greenland, located on the island's northwestern coast at latitude 81° 10′N. Dis-

covered by the explorer Lauge Koch in 1922, it was reported and identified as Dorset by Therkel Mathiassen in 1929.
SOURCE: Mathiassen 1929.

Moreau S. Maxwell

CARAWAY POTTERY SERIES, the culmination (at ca. A.D. 1700) of the Badin-Yadkin-Uwharrie-Dan River (qq.v.) ceramic tradition in the North Carolina Piedmont. This sand-tempered ware's surface was finished by burnishing, complicated stamping, simple stamping, net impressing, or corncob brushing.
SOURCE: Coe 1964:33–34.

Billy L. Oliver

CARAWAY TRIANGULAR POINT, a medium-sized, straight-sided, generally isosceles-triangular, chipped-stone projectile point with a straight or slightly concave base. The type is widely distributed throughout the southern North Carolina Piedmont.
SOURCE: Coe 1964:49.

Billy L. Oliver

CARCAJOU POINT SITE, a site on the Rock River (Lake Koshkonong) in southeastern Wisconsin containing both early (ca. A.D. 900) and late (ca. A.D. 1400) Oneota (q.v.) components; the type site for the Koshkonong Phase (or Focus). Excavations there by R. L. Hall between 1955 and 1959 produced earlier ceramics that share decorative motif characteristics with Ramey Incised pottery as well as later ceramics with linear/geometric decorations.
SOURCE: R. L. Hall 1962.

David Overstreet

CARPENTER BROOK PHASE, earliest phase (ca. A.D. 1000 to after 1100) of the Owasco Culture (q.v.) in central New York, represented by both fortified and unfortified upland villages and large fishing stations. Uncollared, cord-impressed pottery and an economy based upon hunting, gathering, fishing, and horticulture characterize the phase.
SOURCE: Ritchie 1969:281ff.

James A. Tuck

CARTERET POTTERY SERIES, a clay- or sherd-tempered ware with cord-marked, fabric-impressed, or smoothed surfaces that is distributed over the central coastal region of North Carolina. Dating ca. 300 B.C.–A.D. 800, the type often is subsumed under the Hanover Pottery Series (q.v.), although some perceive it as a distinctive regional variation of the clay- or sherd-tempering mode.

SOURCES: Loftfield 1976:154–158; Phelps 1983.

Billy L. Oliver

CARTER/KERR-MCGEE SITE, a stratified, multicomponent, Paleoindian (q.v.) site in north-central Wyoming comprising Goshen, Folsom, mixed Agate Basin–Hell Gap, Alberta, and Cody (qq.v.) components. The only radiocarbon dated component is Folsom at ca. 8400 B.C. Excavated by George Frison in 1977, the site was a remnant of an arroyo bison kill. A bison-bone bed in the Cody Complex level contained both Eden and Scottsbluff (qq.v.) projectile points.

SOURCE: Frison 1984.

George Frison

CARTERSVILLE CULTURE, an early Middle Woodland (ca. 200 B.C.– A.D. 200) unit in the Piedmont region of northern Georgia and adjacent parts of Alabama and South Carolina. Sites represent camps, seasonal villages with circular houses, and small ceremonial centers with burial mounds containing interments, sometimes associated with early Hopewell ritual artifacts. Typical are pottery jars and bowls with check-stamped, simple-stamped, or plain surfaces; jars with tetrapodal supports; small, stemmed, chipped-stone points; slate hoes; celts and gorgets of ground stone; and several kinds of bone implements.

SOURCES: J. R. Caldwell 1958; Wauchope 1966; Garrow 1975.

Roy S. Dickens, Jr.

CASA DIABLO QUARRY, a massive obsidian outcrop in central-eastern California, source of raw material for the manufacture of many tools in California east of the Sierra Nevada, as well as in areas closer to the quarry. Casa Diablo obsidian, along with that from several other eastern California sources, apparently was the focus of a long-standing trans-Sierran trade system, in which shell beads moved from western to eastern California in exchange for this valued stone.

SOURCES: Bettinger and King 1971; Jack 1976; Ericson 1977.

Robert L. Bettinger

CASA GRANDE, an extensive Hohokam (q.v.) settlement near Coolidge, Arizona on the Gila River in the Phoenix Basin Province (q.v.). Visited by Father Eusibio Kino in the 1690s, the site was described by Adolph Bandelier and Cosmos Mindeleff in the late 19th century and was partially excavated and stabilized by J. W. Fewkes and Harold Gladwin in the early 20th century.

The ruin contains the only standing Hohokam "big house", which is one of an estimated four such structures known to have existed in the region. It is constructed of massive, puddled, caliche-adobe walls standing four stories high and contains numerous rooms. The big house and other associated structures are enclosed by a large, rectangular compound wall like those surrounding most major villages of the Hohokam's Classic Period (q.v.). The big house has been interpreted as a communal granary or a chief's house, and it may have been aligned with celestial phenomena for making astronomical sightings.

The ruin is located at the end of an extensive irrigation network comprising many miles of canals. There are a number of other mounds and compounds at the site, and a small ball court lies between two of the largest compounds. While the massive adobe ruins of the Classic Period (ca. A.D. 1100–1450) are the most visible remains, research has demonstrated that the site also contains earlier (ca. A.D. 700–1100) Colonial through Sedentary period components.

SOURCES: Fewkes 1912; Gladwin 1928; Ambler 1961; Wilcox and Shenk 1977.

David E. Doyel and John S. Cable

CASA RINCONADA, the largest known kiva in Chaco Canyon, located in a small-house community in Chaco Culture National Historical Park, New Mexico. Dating to the Classic and Late Bonito phases (qq.v.), it was built ca. A.D. 1060 and was used into the early 12th century in an area prolific with small-house sites. The round chamber had entries from antechambers on the north and south sides, and a unique underground passage led under the north entry onto the kiva's floor, perhaps to allow performers to enter the kiva secretly during ceremonies. A single window and 34 rectangular niches were located above multiple benches (from remodeling) around the interior wall. A raised firebox, two raised vaults, and four masonry-lined postholes completed the primary features. Excavated in 1931 by Gordon Vivian, the kiva was rebuilt without a roof.

SOURCE: Vivian and Reiter 1960.

Thomas C. Windes

CASAS GRANDES CULTURE, an archaeological manifestation centered in northwestern Chihuahua that was defined by C. C. Di Peso on the basis of extensive excavation and survey. Two periods are recognized: Medio (A.D. 1060–1340) and Tardio (A.D. 1340–1660), both of which are segments of a longer chronological sequence in the Casas Grandes Province (q.v.). Related sites in southeastern Arizona, southwestern New Mexico, and the extreme northeastern corner of Sonora are attributed to the Animas Phase; a "peripheral Casas Grandes" expression occurs in the Rio Sonora area of Sonora. Chihuahua Polychrome pottery (q.v.) is the culture's most definitive and best-known artifact class.

Di Peso thought that the onset of the Casas Grandes Culture was brought about by major contact and influence from the south (probably from the west coast of Mexico), instigated by professional merchants—who sought turquoise, other mineral resources, and possibly peyote and slaves—and effected by practitioners of the Quetzalcoatl Cult of Mesoamerica. The result was a sovereign area of thousands of sites governed from a capital city, the Casas Grandes Site (q.v.), also known as Paquime.

The Medio Period encompassed both the creation and the zenith of the Casas Grandes Culture. At the Casas Grandes Site, it has been divided into three phases on the basis of the architectural sequence: Buena Fé Phase (A.D. 1060–1205), Paquimé Phase (A.D. 1205–1261), and Diablo Phase (A.D. 1261–1340). Di Peso viewed the period as a time when these people lived in villages and hillside fortresses surrounding the capital, practiced well-developed irrigation agriculture, and managed a soil- and water-conservation system of some 12,000 square kilometers. The several million artifacts excavated from the Casas Grandes Site included troves of workshop materials indicating shell, lapidary, and copper craft guilds. Ceremonial artifacts, architectural features, and symbolic representations gave evidence of a resident priesthood and of the worship of at least six Mesoamerican deities. The dead were inhumed in plazas and below the floors of ground-story rooms; the most common grave goods were pottery vessels, jewelry, and other personal items. Strong Mesoamerican influence was reflected in group burials and in sacrificial mutilation (including decapitation) of individuals.

The Buena Fé Phase settlement at Casas Grandes was a planned community of at least 20 one-story, puddled-adobe compounds composed of both domestic and ceremonial rooms and enclosed formal plazas. An acequia system was constructed to bring water into the city from a spring over 3 kilometers away; Chihuahua Polychrome and Ramos Black pottery (qq.v.) came into use; macaw aviculture was initiated.

The high point of the Casas Grandes Culture was reached during the Paquimé Phase, when a vast urban renewal project was carried out at the capital city, whose population is estimated then to have been about 2,200. Apartment complexes were enlarged into multistory buildings, and impressive public and ceremonial features were constructed, including mounds, open parks, at least one open market, two I-shaped ball courts, and a subterranean city well. Specialized equipment and architecture were employed for breeding hundreds of macaws and turkeys. The scarlet macaw, brought from its home far to the south, was used for sacrifices and also probably was traded to the north.

Sometime ca. A.D. 1261, governance of the capital city and of the entire province apparently failed, marking the start of the Diablo Phase. The city of mud buildings began to fall apart, collapsed walls were not removed, roofed public and ceremonial areas were converted into crude living areas, and the dead were hastily buried in water canals. Yet, in spite of the social and political disarray, much of the routine life and craftwork continued until the city was destroyed suddenly and violently, perhaps as the result of a widespread, frontier "Chichimecan Revolt" ca. 1205. Hundreds of men, women, and children were killed and never interred; altars and goods were destroyed and scattered; and, finally, the city was burned.

But even though the capital city had fallen, limited fieldwork has revealed that some Medio Period traits (e.g., Chihuahua Polychrome and Ramos Black pottery) survived into the Tardio Period in peripheral areas. Following the destruction of the capital city, some refugee craftsmen may have found their way northward to the ancestral lands of the Zuni, Hopi, Saline, and other eastern Puebloan groups in Arizona and New Mexico; in the Tres Rios area of easternmost Sonora, other survivors lived in mountain villages of stone and adobe pueblos. Two Tardio phases have been defined: Robles (A.D. 1340–1519) and Sporadic Spanish Contact (A.D. 1519–1660).

SOURCES: Di Peso 1974; Di Peso et al. 1974.

Gloria J. Fenner

CASAS GRANDES PROVINCE, the core area for the Casas Grandes Culture (q.v.), covering almost 88,000 square kilometers, primarily in northwestern Chihuahua. Other cultures occupied the area, however, both before and after Casas Grandes. The entire culture sequence is as follows:

PRECERAMIC HORIZON (?–ca. A.D. 1)
PLAINWARE PERIOD (ca. A.D. 1–700)
VIEJO PERIOD (ca. A.D. 700–1060)
    Convento Phase (ca. A.D. 700–900)
    Pilon Phase (A.D. 900–950)
    Perros Bravos Phase (A.D. 950–1060)
MEDIO PERIOD (A.D. 1060–1340)
    Buena Fé Phase (A.D. 1060–1205)
    Paquimé Phase (A.D. 1205–1261)
    Diablo Phase (A.D. 1261–1340)
TARDIO PERIOD (A.D. 1340–1660)
    Robles Phase (A.D. 1340–1519)
    Sporadic Spanish Contact Phase (A.D. 1519–1660)
ESPAÑOLES PERIOD (A.D. 1660–1821)
    San Antonio de Padua Phase (A.D. 1660–1686)
    Apache Phase (A.D. 1686–1821)

The most distinctive trait of the Viejo Period is the appearance of the first painted pottery in the province, attributed by most authorities to the early Mogollon Culture (q.v.). However, C. C. Di Peso, who did the definitive work there, classified the Viejo as part of a generic culture of the Gran Chichimeca (q.v.). While the basic, indigenous traits of the Viejo Phase were not out of place with those of their contemporaries to the north and west, several traits—sheet copper, a sandstone mirror back, ceramic hand drums,

Mesoamerican pottery types from as far away as Jalisco, and fronto-occipital cranial deformation—gave evidence of contacts to the south. Di Peso interpreted these as indicating the beginning of exploration and manipulation of local peoples by professional merchants (*puchteca*) from Mexico's west coast.

It was during the Medio and Tardio periods that the spectacular Casas Grandes Culture developed, reached a climax, and declined. For an outline of these events, see CASAS GRANDES SITE and CASAS GRANDES CULTURE.

The influence of Spanish missionaries distinguished the Españoles Period. Tenuous archaeological clues suggest that remnant populations of the Casas Grandes Culture, in response to Spanish pressures, slowly abandoned their lands and sedentary way of life to join with mobile Indian groups engaged in guerrilla warfare against the Spanish and, eventually, to amalgamate with the post–1686 Apache.

SOURCES: Di Peso 1974; Di Peso et al. 1974.

Gloria J. Fenner

CASAS GRANDES (or PAQUIME) SITE, the type site for the Medio Period of the Casas Grandes Culture (q.v.), occupying 36 hectares on the west bank of the Rio Casas Grandes in Chihuahua and dating A.D. 1060–1340; also the capital city of the Casas Grandes Province (q.v.). General Francisco Ibarra noted the ruin's presence in the 1560s.

C. C. Di Peso excavated the site from 1959 to 1961 in an attempt to determine the relationships that obtained between the Casas Grandes Culture and such central Arizona sites as Casa Grande, Pueblo Grande, and Los Muertos (qq.v.). He employed a multidisciplinary approach in order to gain a comprehensive view of human activities in an arid zone. Architectural styles at the site were the basis for Di Peso's definition of the Medio Period and its sequence of three phases: Buena Fé, Paquimé, and Diablo.

SOURCES: Di Peso 1974:vols. 1,2; Di Peso et al. 1974:vols. 4,5.

Gloria J. Fenner

CASCADE PHASE, second earliest of the five phases in the Lower Snake River culture sequence (q.v.) of southwestern Washington, dating ca. 6000–2800 B.C. Two subphases, early and late, have been recognized. Distinctive traits are the Cascade point (q.v.), the Cascade technique (q.v.), and the edge-ground cobble. There are close similarities with the Vantage Phase of the Middle Columbia and with the Olcott Phase of Puget Sound. The Cascade Phase is a local manifestation of a widespread population of broad-

spectrum foragers adapted to the many environmental variations found in the Northwest.
SOURCES: Leonhardy and Rice 1970; Bense 1972.

Frank C. Leonhardy

CASCADE POINT, a lanceolate dart point with a convex base, chipped from a blade, dating ca. 6000–3000 B.C. and distributed from the northern Great Basin in Oregon through the southern Plateau in Washington, Oregon, and Idaho. The type was first recognized by B. R. Butler, who considered it a diagnostic trait of the Cascade Phase (q.v.). Similar forms have been reported in British Columbia and southwestern Alberta.
SOURCES: B. R. Butler 1961; C. M. Nelson 1969; Leonhardy 1970.

Frank C. Leonhardy

CASCADE TECHNIQUE, a lithic reduction technique with marked similarities to the Levallois technique of the Old World; associated with the earliest phases of southern Plateau prehistory. Several types of specialized flakes were struck from the top of a prepared core, producing primary and secondary flakes indistinguishable from Levallois flakes. Several kinds of blades, some identical to those produced from a polyhedral core, were also produced from the same core. This contrasts with the Old World Levallois technique, which did not produce flakes and blades from the same core. Commonly used on andesite or andesitic basalt—both very tough tool stones—the technique appeared during the Windust Phase (q.v.) of ca. 8800–6000 B.C. and became a dominant technological element between 6000 and 3000 B.C. A hallmark of the Cascade Phase (q.v.), it also occurs in sites of other contemporary phases (e.g., the Vantage and Olcott phases).
SOURCE: Muto 1976.

Frank C. Leonhardy

CASHIE PHASE, a manifestation identified with the Tuscarora occupations of the Inner Coastal Plain, in North Carolina, at ca. A.D. 800–1815; defined chiefly by the presence of Cashie Series pottery (q.v.). Other traits include Clarksville Triangular and Roanoke Large Triangular points (qq.v.), bone and shell tools, celts, bifacial blades, unifacial scraping tools, milling stones, drills, smoking pipes, and ossuary burials generally containing from two to five individuals deposited as secondary bundles.
SOURCE: Phelps 1983:43–47.

Billy L. Oliver

CASHIE POTTERY SERIES, a ware tempered with small pebbles that is associated with the Tuscarora occupations of ca. A.D. 800–1715 on the Inner Coastal Plain of North Carolina; the major diagnostic of the Cashie Phase (q.v.). Surface finishes include fabric impressing, simple stamping,

incising, and plain; typical vessel shapes are conoidal pots, hemispherical and simple bowls, beakers, ladles, and dippers with long handles. Rims may be decorated with punctations, incisions, or pinches. The Cashie series may be an equivalent of, or have relationships to, the Gaston (q.v.), Branchville, and Sturgeon Head series of North Carolina and Virginia.
SOURCE: Phelps 1983:43–44.

Billy L. Oliver

CASPER SITE, the remains of a bison kill in a parabolic sand dune in central Wyoming along the North Platte River, associated with artifacts of the Hell Gap Complex and dating ca. 8000 B.C. Excavations by George Frison in 1971 and 1976 produced large numbers of extinct, Late Pleistocene bison bones and Hell Gap type projectile points. The partial remains of a *Camelops* is the latest known dated occurrence of this species.
SOURCES: Frison 1974, 1978:168–177; Frison et al. 1978.

George Frison

CASTLE CREEK PHASE, a unit of the Owasco Culture (q.v.) of New York state, immediate precursor of Iroquois culture in the area. Collared ceramics, still decorated by cord-wrapped paddle impressions, foreshadowed Iroquois forms. Large upland villages often were situated in naturally defensible positions. Horticulture may have become the dominant means of food acquisition by Castle Creek times.
SOURCE: Ritchie 1969.

James A. Tuck

CASTROVILLE POINT, a Late Archaic (ca. 850–450 B.C.) dart point diagnostic of the Uvalde Phase (q.v.) in central Texas and of the Cibola Phase (q.v.) in southwestern Texas; characterized by a large triangular blade, strong barbs formed by basal notches that angle inward, and a straight to gently expanding stem. Associated with a period when bison were numerous on the Edwards Plateau, Castroville stylistically and temporally forms a series with the Montell and Marcos types.
SOURCES: Suhm and Jelks 1962; Dillehay 1974; Prewitt 1981; Turner and Hester 1985.

Elton R. Prewitt

CATARACT PHASE, a phase of the Cohonina Province, Patayan Division, Hakataya Culture (qq.v.) in Arizona, dating ca. A.D. 950–1100. It is similar to the preceding Coconino Phase (q.v.) in architecture, in arrow-point styles, in the use of platform metates, in the reuse of structures (suggesting seasonal occupation), and in the presence of local pottery types. It differs from Co-

conino in having corrugated and other intrusive Anasazi pottery of later date. Pittsberg Village (q.v.) is the type site for the phase.
SOURCES: McGregor 1951; Hargrave 1938.

Albert H. Schroeder

CATLINITE, a reddish pipestone argillite whose primary provenance is the vicinity of Pipestone National Monument, Minnesota; highly favored by prehistoric and historic Native Americans for carved tobacco pipes and ornaments. Typically lean in quartz, and containing varying amounts of diaspore, pyrophyllite, and muscovite, along with traces of kaolinite and diagnostic chlorite, catlinite's mineralogy is distinctly different from pipestones quarried at other sites in Minnesota and South Dakota.
SOURCES: Gundersen 1983, 1984.

J. N. Gundersen

CATLOW AND ROARING SPRINGS CAVES, two companion sites in central Oregon, situated on the high strand line of pluvial Lake Catlow, where excavations by L. S. Cressman between 1935 and 1938 yielded rich inventories of Great Basin Desert Culture materials: basketry, matting, sandals woven of sagebrush bark and tule, atlatls and darts, bows and arrows, and various lithic specimens. In both caves, animal bones and plant remains, as well as projectile points and milling stones, indicated the importance of hunting and gathering to the early people who lived there. Current interpretations indicate that Catlow Cave was first occupied ca. 6000 B.C., Roaring Springs Cave ca. 5000 B.C. Among the first Desert Culture (q.v.) sites excavated in the northern Great Basin, these caves indicated a much greater age for that lifeway than was generally accepted at the time. Because they provided detailed information about Desert Culture technology, the sites remain of first-rank importance today for synthetic studies.
SOURCES: Cressman et al. 1940, 1942; Wilde 1985.

C. Melvin Aikens

CATLOW TWINE BASKETRY, a distinctive, Z-twined basketry common in the northwestern Great Basin, particularly in the region around Fort Rock Basin, Oregon. In 1942, L. S. Cressman identified Catlow Twine as one of the earliest types of basketry in the area, but C. E. Rozaire later dated it by radiocarbon analysis as no more than 1000 years old.
SOURCES: Cressman 1942; Rozaire 1974.

Robert G. Elston

CATTLE POINT SITE, a large site in the San Juan Islands, Washington, probably occupied from ca. 2000 B.C. to the historic period, excavated by A. R. King in 1946–1947. The four components identified by King have not been reported elsewhere, and King's proposed phase sequence has seen little use.

SOURCES: A. R. King 1950; R. L. Carlson 1960.

Roy L. Carlson

CAVATE ROOM, a dwelling room dug into the soft, volcanic-tuff cliffs of mesas and canyons on the eastern flanks of the Jemez Mountains in the Tewa Basin and Middle Rio Grande provinces of nothern New Mexico. Masonry rooms were built against the cliffs in front of the cavate rooms. Probably dating to the Coalition and Classic Anasazi periods (qq.v.) between ca. A.D. 1125 and 1600, the best examples are at the Tyuonyi and Puye sites.

SOURCES: Hendron 1940; Hewett and Dutton 1953.

Stewart Peckham

CAYUSE PHASE, the final phase (ca. 500 B.C.–A.D. 1750) of the Mid-Columbia culture sequence in Oregon and Washington; characterized by winter pithouse villages, a presumed dependence on salmon fishing, and a variety of small projectile points. Initially defined by E. J. Swanson Jr., redefined by C. M. Nelson, and elaborated by J. R. Galm and others, it has been variously divided into two or three phases.

SOURCES: Swanson 1962; C. M. Nelson 1969; Galm et al. 1981.

Frank C. Leonhardy

CEDAR CREEK POINT, a small- to medium-size projectile-point type with a straight or corner-notched stem, defined by J. L. Benthall in 1979 from a sample found at Daugherty's Cave (q.v.) in southwestern Virginia. Recovered from stratified context and radiocarbon dated to 3740 B.C., the type closely resembles Jefferson Chapman's categories 6 and 7 from the Icehouse Bottom Site (q.v.) on the Little Tennessee River.

SOURCES: Benthall n.d.; Jefferson Chapman 1977.

Keith T. Egloff

CEDAR MESA PROVINCE, a culture area defined by F. T. Plog that comprises the highlands surrounding the San Juan River as it passes through southeastern Utah. It is bounded by the Mesa Verde Province (q.v.) on the east, by the Navajo Mountain and Black Mesa provinces (qq.v.) on the south, and by the Colorado River on the west. Its archaeologial remains grade and fit securely into the cultures of the Mesa Verde Province on the east, while in the western and lower areas a less dense occupation reflects Kayenta influences.

Intensive work in the province has revealed a pattern of short occupations alternating with periods of abandonment. The relatively well-known western third of the province, called the Red Rock Plateau, was first occupied by White Dog Phase peoples of the Basketmaker II period (ca. A.D. 200–400). Then, after a period of abandonment, it was reoccupied by Kayenta Klethla Phase peoples ca. A.D. 1100–1150, only to be abandoned again until Horsefly Hollow Phase (q.v.) peoples utilized it ca. 1210–1260.

At Cedar Mesa proper, in the center of province, a heavy Basketmaker II occupation ca. A.D. 200–400 was followed by a hiatus and then, ca. A.D. 650–750, by a short but intensive highland Basketmaker III occupation, apparently the westward limit of this culture's expansion. After 300 more years of abandonment, Pueblo II carriers of the Windgate Phase (q.v.) of the Mesa Verde tradition appeared ca. A.D. 1070, to be followed by a Clay Hills Phase (q.v.), Kayenta tradition occupation, and then, in Pueblo III times (ca. A.D. 1170), by Woodenshoe and Redhouse phases (qq.v.) peoples of the Mesa Verde tradition. After a terminal occupation emphasizing canyons and cliff dwellings, the area was finally abandoned for good by A.D. 1270.

The Pueblo I period is not represented west of Comb Wash, located in the middle of the province, but it is well known on the eastern border because of J. O. Brew's pioneering work at the Alkali Ridge Site (q.v.), where the Abajo Phase (q.v.) was defined. The eastern part of the province also includes large Pueblo III period sites and other elements typical of the Mesa Verde Province, which probably would lead most workers to include this eastern area in the adjacent Mesa Verde Province proper.

SOURCES: Brew 1946; Lipe 1970; Matson and Lipe 1978; Plog 1979a.

R. G. Matson

CENTRAL COAST SEQUENCE, the known sequence of cultures on the central coast of British Columbia, extending from ca. 8000 B.C. to the historic period. The Early Period (ca. 8000–3500 B.C.) is best represented at the Namu (q.v.) and Bear Cove sites, which contained chipped-stone assemblages but lacked bone preservation and shellfish remains. Middle Period (ca. 3500 B.C.–A.D. 500) components, with shell middens and bone hunting and fishing tools, are known at several sites. By the beginning of the Late Period (ca. A.D. 500), the full ethnographic pattern of historic times was probably present.

The only substantial break in the sequence was between ca. 3500 and 2500 B.C., when large shell middens started to accumulate, the chipped-stone industry declined, and the microblade industry disappeared.

SOURCES: Catherine Carlson 1979; D. H. Mitchell 1980–1981; Hobler 1982; R. L. Carlson 1983a, 1983b.

Roy L. Carlson

CENTRAL LITTLE COLORADO PROVINCE, a regional division of the Western Anasazi Culture in northeastern Arizona, extending westward from Holbrook to Grand Falls, and from a few miles south of the Little Colorado

River northward to the foot of Black Mesa. The province was defined by G.J. Gumerman as an arid physiographic and cultural sink where Anasazi and Mogollon (qq.v.) peoples from wetter zones to the north and south, respectively, amalgamated. Gumerman expanded the Winslow Branch (q.v.) to include this Anasazi/Mogollon culture complex and renamed the whole the Central Little Colorado Province.

SOURCES: Gumerman and Skinner 1968; Gumerman 1969.

Donald E. Weaver, Jr.

CENTRAL PLAINS TRADITION, a term referring collectively to those post-A.D.–1000 but precontact complexes in Nebraska and Kansas variously identified as Upper Republican, Smoky Hill, or Nebraska (qq.v.) foci, aspects, phases, variants, or cultures. Elements of culture content shared by these complexes include a subsistence farming lifestyle featuring maize, beans, squash, tobacco, and perhaps sunflower cultivation; hunting of herd and solitary Plains animals, chiefly bison, deer, antelope and elk; square, semisubterranean, timber-framed, earth-covered houses with rectangular entranceways; sand-, grit-, grog-, or shell-tempered, globular pots with straight, outflaring, or collared rims, featuring surface smoothing, cord roughing, incising, finger impressing, and/or cord impressing; and a variety of farming, hunting, and domestic tools made of bone and stone.

SOURCES: Lehmer 1954; L. A. Brown 1966:294–301; Krause 1969:82–96.

Richard A. Krause

CERBAT PROVINCE, a regional expression of the Patayan Division of the Hakataya Culture (qq.v.) occupying northwestern Arizona between the Coconino Plateau and the Colorado River north of Bill Williams River. It has been dated at pre-A.D. 700–1200± through intrusive pottery types, some of which appear to have survived into historic times among the Walapais. H. S. Colton's definition of the province in 1939 was based on the distribution of Tizon Brown Ware pottery at campsites near springs. There was little evidence of agriculture, but contacts are indicated with the Laquish Division (q.v.) in southwestern Arizona and with southern California.

SOURCE: Colton 1939a.

Albert H. Schroeder

CERRITO SITE, a Gallina Phase (q.v.) village about 8 kilometers west of Llaves in the Largo-Gallina Province (q.v.) of north-central New Mexico. It consists of three groups of surface houses and pithouses on a ridge spur on the north side of the Gallina River. The middle group contained eight

burned, contiguous, surface houses, of which five were excavated by F. C. Hibben in 1937. They dendrodated between A.D. 1235 and 1241.
SOURCES: Hibben 1940; Blumenthal 1940:10–13.

Herbert W. Dick

CERRO DE LOS GENTILES SITE, an unexcavated site in southern Sonora, located atop a mountain with limited access. Its location, its pottery, and its twelve structures of crude stone masonry are typical of the Los Camotes Phase (q.v.) of ca. A.D. 700–1150.
SOURCE: Pailes 1972.

Richard A. Pailes

CERROS DE TRINCHERAS, prehistoric terraced hills in Sonora, Chihuahua, and Arizona that are not associated with any one archaeological culture. Terraces up to 2 meters high were built at the bases or on the crests of the hills, and fill was placed behind them to create flat living surfaces; sometimes circular or elliptical rock walls up to a meter high are also present. The best-known examples, including the type site of Cerros de Trincheras, are in the Altar-Concepcion-Magdalena River Basin and date ca. A.D. 1300–1450.
SOURCES: Sauer and Brand 1931; Bowen 1976b.

David A. Phillips, Jr.

CERVENKA SITE, a deeply stratified site on the San Gabriel River in east-central Texas, dug in 1978–1979 by O. F. McCormick and D. E. Peter, containing a succession of occupations beginning ca. 6550 B.C. with the Early Archaic Circleville Phase (q.v.) and extending through the Twin Sisters Phase (q.v.) until ca. A.D. 500. Cervenka clarified relationships between central Texas and east-central Texas cultures.
SOURCE: Hays 1982.

Elton R. Prewitt

CHACOAN HUMAN EFFIGY PITCHER, a kind of pottery vessel in the form of a complete male or female human figure, diagnostic of the Bonito Phase of the Chaco Province (qq.v.) in northwestern New Mexico. Done in the Cibola ceramic tradition and usually associated with greathouses, these figurines are anatomically complete and show a variety of facial decorations, hair styles, personal ornamentation, and stylized geometric designs on the body. The majority are from Pueblo Bonito, although others are

known from Salmon Ruin, the Bis Sa'ani community, and other places throughout the province.
SOURCES: Pepper 1906; Judd 1954.

Peter J. McKenna

CHACOAN PITCHER, a distinctive pottery vessel form diagnostic of the Bonito Phase (ca. A.D. 1050–1150) of the Chaco Province (qq.v.) in northwestern New Mexico. The form has a tall, cylindrical upper body or neck that is set off from a small, bowl-shaped lower body by a sharp shoulder. A wide, vertical, strap handle extends the length of the neck, terminating just above the shoulder. Earlier pitchers have a globular body lacking angularity in profile. The form is most often expressed in the Gallup, Chaco, and Chaco-McElmo Black-on white types.
SOURCES: Judd 1954; Toll and McKenna 1987.

Peter J. McKenna

CHACOAN ROADS, engineered, carefully constructed roadways that connected major Bonito Phase (q.v.) pueblos in the Chaco Province (q.v.) in northwestern New Mexico ca. A.D. 900–1140. Usually 9 to 10 meters wide (but wider as they approached a greathouse), they were made by excavating down to a compact substrate and piling the excavated soil in rows along their margins. Minor, esoteric architectural features were associated with the roads between greathouses.

The limits of the road system have not yet been determined, but they may have extended hundreds of kilometers beyond Pueblo Bonito (q.v.), which seems to have been a hub to the system. Several major roads have been recognized, e.g., the great North Road extending from Pueblo Alto (q.v.) to the San Juan River Valley near Bloomfield, New Mexico; the South Road, running from Pueblo Bonito to Kin Ya'a near Crown Point, New Mexico; and the Coyote Canyon Road that extends the South Road from Kin Ya'a to the west an unknown distance into Arizona.

The roads may have served as transportation arteries, but massive movement of goods over them is not clearly indicated. Although their function remains uncertain, studies have shown that their use was highly structured.
SOURCES: Kincaid 1983; Nials et al. 1983.

John R. Stein

CHACOAN SHRINES, walled, semicircular or rectangular areas open to the east, or unroofed circular structures, situated on isolated high points throughout the Chaco Province (q.v.) of northwestern New Mexico. Termed shrines, these are believed to have been stations for a visual communication network between major pueblos that operated during the Bonito Phase (q.v.), ca. A.D. 900–1140. Occasionally, there are "caches" of small rocks

on a shrine's east side, and sometimes pieces of turquoise are scattered all about. Very few other items are associated with these features.
SOURCE: Hayes and Windes 1975.

Peter J. McKenna

CHACO-MCELMO BLACK-ON-WHITE POTTERY, the diagnostic ceramic of the late Bonito Phase in the Chaco Province (qq.v.) of northwestern New Mexico, dating ca. A.D. 1090–1150. Most commonly associated with greathouses, the series marks critical changes in the Chacoan socioreligious and sociopolitical systems. The series is a continuation of the Cibola whiteware tradition, but it is distinguished by the use of carbon paint and by a change in decorative motifs from running hachuring to paneled, wide-lined designs, checkerboards, opposed contiguous triangles, interlocked key figures, and dot groups used as space fillers. Vessels usually are highly polished and have a band of slip just below the rim on bowl exteriors that provides a ground for painting the decorations. The extremely fine temper is predominately grog mixed with lesser amounts of crushed rock of regional derivation.
SOURCES: Judd 1959; Windes 1986.

Peter J. McKenna

CHACO PROVINCE, an Eastern Anasazi (q.v.) culture area covering the entire San Juan Basin of northwestern New Mexico at a minimum, but traditionally focused upon Bonito Phase (q.v.) settlements in Chaco Canyon, dating ca. A.D. 900–1140, that comprised many large, multistoried pueblos built of the finest masonry, as well as numerous small pueblos. The province is known for a high degree of interaction that is evident in the continuity of architectural forms, masonry style, trade goods, and ceremonialism, and in a regional, prehistoric road system and a visual communication network. The major Chacoan-type sites, many of which occur beyond the boundaries of the province, have architecturally distinctive structures known as greathouses.

Chacoan Anasazi occupation before A.D. 900 cannot be distinguished from coeval occupations by Eastern and Western Anasazi peoples in surrounding provinces; and during the following two centuries the Chacoan system, or *Chacoan Phenomenon*, as it sometimes is called, spread over the continguous provinces. Peoples of the Chuska and Mesa Verde provinces (qq.v.), in particular, shared many culture traits with Chacoan peoples. Mesoamerican influence has been seen by some as the prime mover of the Bonito Phase; others suggest that developments were wrought internally by responses to an unpredictable environment and to population pressures.

The nine Anasazi phases recognized in the Chaco Province are listed in the following table (all dates are A.D.).

Chaco Province Phase Sequence

Phase Name	A.D. *Time Span*	*Pecos Classification*	*Associated Ceramics*
Unnamed	450–550	Late BM II–Early BM III	Brownwares, Obelisk Gray
La Plata	550–700	Late BM III	Lino Gray, La Plata B/W
White Mound	700–800	Early P I	Lino Gray, Whitemound B/W
Kiatuthlanna	800–900	Late P I	Lino Gray, Kana'a Gray Kiatuthlanna B/W, Piedra B/W
Early Bonito	900–1040/1050	Early & Mid P II	Narrow neckbanded, Lino Gray, Red Mesa B/W
Classic Bonito	1040/1050–1100	Late P II	Indented corrugated, Gallup B/W
Late Bonito	1100–1140	Early P III	Indented corrugated, Chaco-McElmo B/W, Gallup B/W
Intermediate	1140–1200	Mid P III	Indented corrugated, (San Juan) McElmo B/W
Mesa Verde	1200–1300	Late P III	Indented corrugated, Mesa Verde B/W

SOURCE: Frazier, 1986.

Thomas C. Windes

CHALCHIHUITES CULTURE, a Mesoamerican culture which, ca. A.D. 500, expanded into portions of Durango that previously had been part of the Southwestern culture area; ca. 1350, it retreated southward. The culture may have served as a point of indirect or direct contact between Mesoamerica and Southwestern centers such as Casas Grandes (q.v.).

SOURCES: Kelley and Abbott 1966; J. C. Kelley 1971; Di Peso 1979.

David A. Phillips, Jr.

CHALUKA SITE, a large, deep village midden of the Aleutian Tradition (q.v.) on Umnak Island, Alaska; earlier location of present-day Nikolski village. Some 4000 years of Paleo- and Neo-Aleut prehistory plus contact-period occupation at the site have been documented by the investigations of numerous researchers between 1911 and the 1970s, including Waldemar

Jochelson (who worked at an adjacent area), Aleš Hrdlička, W. S. Laughlin, J. S. Aigner, and Robert Black. Concomitant with the archaeology were multidisciplinary studies in the human biology, linguistics, and ethnography of the area.

SOURCES: Hrdlička 1945; Laughlin and Reeder 1966; Aigner 1974; Turner et al. 1974.

Donald W. Clark

CHANCE PHASE, earliest (ca. A.D. 1300–1400) manifestation of the Iroquois culture in New York state, typified by palisaded villages, often located in naturally defensible positions, comprising numbers of longhouses that varied greatly in length. Ceramics foreshadow later Iroquois forms but retain vestiges of their Owasco ancestry; smoking pipes often occur in effigy forms or as precursors of the Iroquois trumpet form. Chance Phase people made extensive use of corn, beans, and squash as well as of the products of hunting, fishing, and gathering.

SOURCES: Ritchie 1980; Tuck 1978.

James A. Tuck

CHARLES TOWNE SITE, a now-destroyed, moundless ceremonial center of the South Appalachian Mississippian period (ca. A.D. 1300), formerly located on the Ashley River in Charleston County, South Carolina. Stanley South explored the site in 1970 and discovered Pee Dee Phase materials, including pottery and structural remains, as well as earlier Woodland features.

SOURCES: Stephenson 1969; South 1970, 1971.

Michael Trinkley

CHARLIE LAKE CAVE, a deeply stratified site near Ft. Saint John, northeastern British Columbia, excavated in 1983 by K. R. Fladmark after preliminary testing in 1974–1975. Its lowest layers, radiocarbon dated to an average of ca. 8500 B.C., yielded the first well-dated Paleoindian fluted point from northwestern Canada plus a few other artifacts. Later strata are characterized by medium to large corner-notched points, commencing before 3000 B.C., and small corner- and side-notched points dating within the present millennium.

SOURCE: Fladmark et al. n.d.

Donald W. Clark

CHARMSTONE, a spindle-, plumb bob-, ovoid-, or phallus-shaped, polished-stone artifact, sometimes having a groove or drilled perforation at one end; made of various stones including amphibolite schist, granite, and calcite. A common item in central California Early Horizon burials, charm-

stones also occur at later sites in both central and other regions of the state. Their purpose is unknown.
SOURCES: Yates 1889; Heizer 1949.

L. A. Payen

CHASE BURIAL SITE, type site of the Kamloops Phase (q.v.); a mound on the South Thompson River near the town of Chase, British Columbia, partially dug in 1960 by David Sanger and C. E. Borden. They found five late prehistoric, flexed human interments associated with elaborate necrolia, including small stone carvings that were the first evidence of a prehistoric stone-carving tradition in the area. The carvings led Sanger to postulate that late prehistoric status differentiation may have been more pronounced than was reported ethnographically.
SOURCE: Sanger 1968a.

Arnoud H. Stryd

CHAUGA SITE, a multicomponent mound and village site on the Tugalo River in Oconee County, South Carolina, occupied from the early Mississippian (q.v.) period (ca. A.D. 1100) through historic Cherokee times. Excavations by R. S. Neitzel in 1958–1959 revealed ten mound stages—the earliest dating to the 12th century A.D.—and uncovered a number of burials in the mound and village areas.
SOURCES: Kelly and Neitzel 1961; D. G. Anderson et al. 1986:34–35.

Paul A. Webb

CHAVEZ PASS RUINS, a multicomponent village site 60 kilometers southeast of Flagstaff on Anderson Mesa in northern Arizona, occupied between A.D. 1100 and 1400. Chavez Pass North is a large roomblock of from 60 to 100 rooms on a prominent hill. Chavez Pass South, on a flat-topped hill to the southwest, consists of two large roomblocks: one rectangular with about 180 rooms, the other consisting of from 300 to 400 rooms arranged around a large, enclosed plaza. Both roomblocks contain possible kivas and may have been two or three stories high in places.

Associated with the three large roomblocks are numerous extended burials (on the slopes north of Chavez Pass South), extensive agricultural fields and terraces, possible reservoirs, a possible ball court, borrow pits where clay was dug for mortar, numerous petroglyphs, check dams, and scattered field houses.

J. W. Fewkes excavated a few rooms and a number of burials at Chavez Pass South in 1896. Subsequently, for many years, professional workers merely collected artifacts from the surface and described the site surficially while pothunters severely damaged the burial area and the roomblocks. Between 1975 and 1983, intensive studies were conducted at the site by archaeologists from Arizona State University and the University of Chicago, and by members of the Arizona Archaeological Society.

Historically, Chavez Pass Ruins has been ascribed to the Sinagua Branch of the Mogollon Root, occupied during the Turkey Hill and Clear Creek foci, but, more recently, the site has been considered part of the Anderson Mesa settlement cluster and of the Chevelon-Chavez Province (q.v.) of the Western Anasazi.

Chavez Pass Ruins is significant because of its size and complexity, its status as a regional trade center, and its importance as an ancestral Hopi village. It has gained additional importance because it is one of the few large sites in the region that has been intensively investigated in modern times.
SOURCES: Fewkes 1898b, 1904; Upham 1982.

Donald E. Weaver, Jr.

CHECK DAM, a small barrier, usually made of rocks, placed across a small rill or drainage way to trap water and silt during rainy periods. The increased moisture and soil concentration thus provided permitted the establishment of small garden plots in areas where plants otherwise could not be grown. Check dams were used by many prehistoric peoples in the Southwest including the Anasazi, Mogollon, and Hohokam (qq.v.).

David A. Phillips, Jr.

CHELSEA PHASE, earliest of the Late Archaic phases defined by R. D. Grosser at the Snyder site in south-central Kansas. Dating there between 2800 and 2200 B.C., the phase is characterized by the exploitation of diverse biotic resources, the use of semipermanent structures and settlements, and small side- or corner-notched projectile points similar to types of the Simonsen-Logan Creek complex.
SOURCES: Grosser 1973, 1977.

Roger D. Grosser

CHEROKEE SEWER SITE, a stratified, multicomponent site incorporated in an alluvial fan in the Little Sioux River valley near Cherokee, Iowa, excavated by Richard Shutler, Jr., Duane Anderson, and Holmes Semken, Jr., in 1973 and 1976. The earliest components, representing two separate late Paleoindian (q.v.) bison-processing camps dating to ca. 6500 B.C., contained projectile points reminiscent of the Agate Basin and Hell Gap types (qq.v.).

Two Archaic (q.v.) occupations also were present, dating respectively ca. 5300 and 4450 B.C. Each contained choppers fashioned from bison lower limb bones, together with milling stones and chipped-stone projectile points, choppers, scrapers, bifaces, and flake tools. At each camp, bison were dis-

articulated and stripped of meat, then their bones were fragmented to obtain marrow and to facilitate rendering of bone grease.
SOURCE: Anderson and Semken 1980.

Duane C. Anderson

CHERRY VALLEY SITE, a grouping of five mounds in northeastern Arkansas, type site for the Cherry Valley Phase, dating ca. A.D. 1050–1150. Excavations by Gregory Perino in 1958 disclosed remnants of a circular "council house" with an extended entryway at the base of one mound. Within the mound were bundle burials accompanied by characteristic pottery vessels—handled beakers, bottles, and small jars—that possibly were used for a libation ceremony. Such mortuary/ceremonial centers, usually not associated with villages, served a dispersed population in the early developmental stages of the Mississippian Culture (q.v.). By the end of the 12th century, more and more villages became established beside mound groups.
SOURCES: Perino 1967; Morse and Morse 1983.

Dan F. Morse

CHESTER FIELD SHELL RING, a Thom's Creek Phase component, dating ca. 1500 B.C., that also contained some Stallings pottery; located on Port Royal Island in Beaufort County, South Carolina. It was extensively tested in 1932–1933 by Woldemar Ritter, who found features, postmolds, pottery, worked bone, and stone tools.
SOURCES: Flannery 1943; J. B. Griffin 1943b; Trinkley 1980a.

Michael Trinkley

CHETRO KETL, the second largest Chacoan greathouse in the Chaco Province (q.v.), located just east of Pueblo Bonito (q.v.) in Chaco Culture National Historical Park, New Mexico. Dating to the Classic, Late Bonito, Intermediate, and Mesa Verde phases (qq.v.), Chetro Ketl was built by A.D. 1030 or earlier and was extensively renovated and enlarged in the late 11th and early 12th centuries. A number of roads led from it to other communities, including Pueblo Alto (q.v.) on the mesa to the north. The four-story pueblo of Chetro Ketl contained some 580 rooms and more than sixteen kivas. Two great kivas and a huge refuse mound were associated. Between one third and one half of the buildings were excavated by E. L. Hewett and Paul Reiter in 1920–1921 and 1929–1934.

A remarkable collection of painted wood was excavated from Room 93 by Gordon Vivian in 1947; Kiva F has yielded the most extensive ceramics sample to date (1987) of the Intermediate Phase (ca. A.D. 1150–1200) in the Chaco Province. Chetro Ketl also is notable for having produced the largest number of tree-ring-dated specimens of any site in the world, owing to the pioneering dendrochonological studies of Florence Hawley (Ellis).

The sequence of ceramic types from the refuse mound enabled Hawley to assemble the first ceramic typology for the province.

SOURCES: Vivian et al. 1978; Lekson 1983.

Thomas C. Windes

CHEVELON-CHAVEZ PROVINCE, a regional division of the western Anasazi (q.v.) in northeastern Arizona, bounded by the Hopi Buttes on the north, the Mogollon Rim on the south, Silver Creek on the east, and Canyon Diablo on the west. Formulated by F. T. Plog, who based it on a theoretical hexagonal grid system, this designation combines the southern portion of the Winslow Branch of the Anasazi with the southeastern portion of the Sinagua Branch of the Mogollon (q.v.) as originally defined by H. S. Colton. This forced combination of two very different archaeological regions is generally not accepted by scholars working in the area. Plog's definition was intended to encompass the period ca. A.D. 900–1455, but it is considered most applicable to the period A.D. 1100–1300.

The province as defined by Plog is characterized by early pithouse architecture, followed by U-shaped surface structures, and, finally, by true Pueblo units with enclosed plazas and kivas, circular and square great kivas, and a very mixed ceramic assemblage comprising Mogollon and Alameda brownwares, Tusayan and Little Colorado graywares and whitewares, Cibola whitewares, and ancestral Hopi wares.

SOURCES: Colton 1939a; Plog 1979a, 1979b, 1983.

Donald E. Weaver, Jr.

CHEVELON RUIN, a large village overlooking the confluence of Chevelon Creek and the Little Colorado River 20 kilometers east of Winslow, in northeastern Arizona. It contains from 300 to 400 rooms in seven roomblocks that may have been two or three stories high in places, three plazas, and at least three possible kivas. The main occupation was ca. A.D. 1300–1425, but there is some evidence of a much earlier pithouse village dating to late Basketmaker III or Pueblo I times. Formerly identified with the Homolovi Focus of the Winslow Branch (q.v.), Anasazi Root, the site now is considered part of the Chevelon-Chavez Province (q.v.) of the Western Anasazi.

Chevelon Ruin is significant because of its size, its status as a regional center for long-distance trade, and its importance in Hopi oral migration traditions. Even so, it has received little professional study. In 1896 J. W. Fewkes spent two weeks excavating trash deposits north of the roomblocks where he removed from 60 to 100 burials—many of apparently high-status individuals—along with associated artifacts. For many years thereafter, researchers examined the site only superficially while pothunters damaged large portions of it. Between 1982 and 1984, Northern Arizona University evaluated the site for inclusion in a regional state park, carried out minor stabilization measures, and filled more than 400 potholes.

SOURCES: Fewkes 1898b, 1904; Plog et al. 1976; Andrews n.d.

Donald E. Weaver, Jr.

CHICKAHOMINY POTTERY SERIES, a catchall term formerly used for all shell-tempered pottery in the Virginia coastal plain, now broken down into wares (e.g., Mockley, Townsend, Roanoke, Yeocomico).

SOURCES: Clifford Evans 1955; Egloff and Potter 1982.

Keith T. Egloff

CHIEF JOSEPH DAM LOCALITY, the reservoir area behind Chief Joseph Dam on the Upper Columbia River in Washington; focus of a massive rescue archaeology project by the University of Washington from 1978 to 1981. Three phases were defined for the area as a result of this work: Kartar (ca. 4500–2000 B.C.), Hudnut (ca. 2000–1 B.C.), and Coyote Creek (ca. A.D. 1–1930).

SOURCE: S. N. Campbell 1985.

Frank C. Leonhardy

CHIHUAHUA POLYCHROME POTTERY, a ware having red and black painted decorations and comprising eight defined types, probably the best-known feature of the Casas Grandes Culture (q.v.) of northwestern Chihuahua. E. B. Sayles published the first type descriptions in 1936; the definitive descriptions, based on over 200,000 sherds and several hundred vessels, were produced by C. C. Di Peso, J. B. Rinaldo, and G. J. Fenner in 1974.

Decorations usually occur in bands; common figures include triangles, barbed motifs, and stepped designs. Macaws, almost a hallmark of Casas Grandes, appear on virtually all the types in either stylized or realistic form. Vessel shapes include bowls, jars, bottles, eccentrics, hand drums, and various human, bird, and animal effigies including the distinctive hooded effigy. A tendency for the types to blend into one another is characteristic.

Chihuahua polychromes persisted, along with unpainted wares, from the 11th to the 17th century A.D., and some designs—e.g., the macaw motif—may have survived in the work of later Puebloan potters of the southwestern United States, perhaps introduced to them by refugees from Casas Grandes. Recently, Casas Grandes pottery designs have been revived in the work of Juan Quezada and other Chihuahuan potters of Mata Ortiz.

SOURCES: Sayles 1936; Di Peso et al. 1974: vol. 6.

Gloria J. Fenner

CHIMNEY ROCK PHASE, a late (ca. A.D. 925–1125) manifestation of the Pueblo II Stage, localized in southern Colorado at the northern border of the Upper San Juan Province (q.v.). Most of the phase's sites lie within a

15-square-kilometer area of the San Juan National Forest, where they are protected from commercial exploitation and are reserved for their scientific and scenic values. On and immediately around Chimney Rock Mesa are hundreds of rubble-covered mounds—the ruins of surface masonry houses— that cluster into eight named site groups that are interpreted to represent coeval prehistoric communities. Because of its Chacoan-style architecture, one site group is thought to be an outlier of the Chaco Canyon community, some 150 kilometers to the southwest. Upon the surface of the mesa, the structures tend to have round rooms linked in pretzel fashion, while down along the Piedra River the buildings, which are arranged around open plazas, tend toward gridded patterns with kivas and towers.

SOURCES: Jeancon 1922; Truell 1975; Tucker 1981; L. D. Webster n.d.; R. P. Powers et al. 1983; Eddy 1975, 1977, 1983; Eddy and O'Sullivan 1986.

Frank W. Eddy

CHIMNEY ROCK PUEBLO, a Late Bonito Phase (q.v.), classic Chacoan outlier in the San Juan National Forest, Colorado, situated on Chimney Rock Mesa. Nearby are two prominent rock pinnacles that have served historically as Puebloan shrines and probably also did so in the past. The pueblo contains about 55 rooms, including some that are two stories high, and two Chaco-style kivas. Tree-ring dates indicate that it was constructed ca. A.D. 1093; it had been abandoned by the mid-A.D. 1100s.

Chimney Rock is unusual because it may have served as a community and religious center for nearby sites in an area distinctly within the Mesa Verde Province. J. A. Jeançon and F. H. H. Roberts, Jr., investigated the site in 1921–1922; F. W. Eddy conducted additional studies there in 1970–1971.

SOURCE: Eddy 1977.

Thomas C. Windes

CHINDADN COMPLEX, an early (ca. 9000–7000 B.C.) complex, based on finds in the lower levels of the Village Site at Healy Lake (q.v.), that comprises bifacial knives, teardrop-shaped points, basally thinned lanceolate points, and, late in the complex, a microblade industry. Many archaeologists subsume Chindadn under the American Paleo-Arctic Tradition (q.v.), although materials from the type site of that tradition, Akmak (q.v.), differ from Chindadn in several attributes. Chindadn also differs from contemporary Paleoindian industries farther south. Very tentative evidence for Chindadn exists at other sites in components predating Dry Creek II (q.v.).

SOURCES: McKennan and Cook 1970; Dixon 1985.

Donald W. Clark

CHINO PHASE, a phase of the Prescott Province, Patayan Division, Hakataya Culture (qq.v.) that occupied the upper Verde Valley and the Aquarius Plateau in Arizona ca. A.D. 1025–1200. The dates are based on intrusive

Anasazi black-on-white and polychrome pottery, which occurs in association with a local type, Verde Black-on-gray. Pueblo-like structures with walls of river cobbles and mud mortar replaced the jacales of the preceding Prescott Phase (q.v.). Burials, some with green face paint, were extended with heads to the east. Distinctive artifacts include trough metates, shell ornaments, 3/4-groove axes, unnotched obsibian arrow points, vesicular basalt balls and cylinders, bone awls, turquoise jewelry, painted wood, and matting.

SOURCE: Spicer and Caywood 1936.

Albert H. Schroeder

CHIRICAHUA STAGE. See Cochise Culture.

CHISOS PHASE, an essentially hunting-gathering unit of the Late Archaic period (ca. 500 B.C.-A.D. 1000) in Trans-Pecos Texas, originally defined by J. C. Kelley as the Chisos Focus. Material culture from rockshelters and open camps includes fiber basketry, sandals, matting, and netting; wooden firetongs, cane and wooden shafts; sewed and painted skins; stone scrapers, dart points, and disc beads; and, occasionally, corn cobs (8- to 10-row varieties), squash seeds, and beans. Although similarities with assemblages in the lower Pecos River and El Paso regions have been noted, cultural antecedents and successive adaptive mechanisms of the phase remain unclear.

SOURCES: J. C. Kelley et al. 1940; Mallouf 1985.

Robert J. Mallouf

CHIVAS COMPLEX, an early (ca. A.D. 200–620) complex in the Las Animas area of northwestern Durango, poorly understood but possibly an inspiration for the development of pottery in other Southwestern cultures. Known characteristics include rockshelter sites containing storage chambers, corn agriculture, simple blackware pottery, and a lithic technology reminiscent of that of the Cochise Culture.

SOURCE: Spence 1978.

David A. Phillips, Jr.

CHODISTAAS SITE, an 18-room pueblo ruin located about 1.5 kilometers north of the Grasshopper Site (q.v.) on the Fort Apache Indian Reservation in east-central Arizona. A small farming community existing during the Great Drought of A.D. 1276–1299, it probably was similar to the first settlement at Grasshopper. Its archaeological significance derives from its complete burning, which provided a clear picture of human behavior through the 269 whole vessels and other domestic artifacts preserved on

room floors, and also permitted accurate dating of room construction, which began in A.D. 1263 and continued through the mid–1280s.
SOURCE: Crown 1981.

J. Jefferson Reid

CHOKE CANYON SITES, a series of sites in Live Oak and McMullen counties on the southern Texas coastal plain that were investigated by several archaeologists between the late 1960s and the mid–1980s. These sites produced extensive data on the technology, chronology, subsistence, and other aspects of the culture history of the nomadic hunter-gatherers of southern Texas from the Middlle Archaic (ca. 3400 B.C.) to the 19th century.
SOURCE: Hall et al. 1986.

Lawrence E. Aten

CHORIS PHASE, a culture unit of northwestern Alaska, dating ca. 1100–600 B.C., noteworthy for its Asia-derived ceramics. It is known primarily from J. L. Gidding's excavations in 1956 and 1958 of ovoid houses on the south shore of the Chukchi Sea near the Choris Peninsula, but also from other sites, both coastal and inland. Early inland components show a relationship to the Denbigh Flint Complex (q.v.); later coastal sites may be an early form of Norton (q.v.).
SOURCES: Giddings 1957, 1967; Giddings and Anderson 1985.

Donald W. Clark

CHOTA-TANASEE SITE, location of two adjacent, historic, Overhill Cherokee towns in eastern Tennessee, identified and partially excavated by the University of Tennessee in the 1970s. Chota emerged as the principal Overhill town in the mid–18th century and was pivotal in southern colonial history. The excavations provided data on Cherokee culture and acculturation.
SOURCE: Schroedl 1982.

Jefferson Chapman

CHOUTEAU ASPECT, a term applied by R. L. Stephenson in 1954 to a group of 17th-century, precontact villages of circular earthlodges, formerly called the Meyer-LaRoche by D. J. Lehmer, distributed all along the Missouri River from northeastern Nebraska upstream at least as far as the Cheyenne River. Subsequently, the Shannon Focus (q.v.) emerged as the dominant expression of the Chouteau complex in the Big Bend and Fort Randall reservoirs in prehistoric times The seriation of several components and the definition of the sequent Felicia Phase (Smith 1960, 1963; Smith and Johnson 1968) carried the complex into the protohistoric period. The term Chouteau was dropped by Lehmer (1971), who expanded the definition and geographic range of the complex, limited it to the prehistoric period, and renamed it the Extended Coalescent Variant (q.v.).

SOURCES: Lehmer 1954, 1971; Stephenson 1954; Smith and Grange 1958; C. S. Smith 1960, 1963; Smith and Johnson 1968.

Carlyle S. Smith

CHUCALISSA SITE, a Mississippian (q.v.) mound and village in southwestern Tennessee, partially excavated by Charles N. Nash in the 1950s, with continuing investigations by Memphis State University.

SOURCE: Nash 1972.

Jefferson Chapman

CHULA SOAPSTONE QUARRY, a localized outcrop of soapstone in the south-central Piedmont of Virginia, having two associated large pit features where prehistoric peoples procured soapstone for the manufacture of bowls and other objects. F. H. Cushing dug at the site before 1878 and prepared a model of the exposed quarry surface, illustrating the various phases of cutting out soapstone bowls. In 1948 C. G. Holland revisited the quarry and included it in his 1981 analysis of soapstone distribution.

SOURCES: W. H. Holmes 1897; Holland et al. 1981.

Keith T. Egloff

CHUPADERO BLACK-ON-WHITE POTTERY, a whiteware decorated with black designs executed with mineral paint; manufactured in the southern part of the Salina Province (q.v.) in New Mexico, ca. A.D. 1175–1545, and traded widely to the southern and eastern parts of the Jornada Province (q.v.) of the Mogollon Culture. The most common design elements are scrolled, hatched, or checkered panels and solid triangles arranged in serrated motifs. Vessel forms are either flat-bottomed bowls or, more frequently, closed jars. Bowl exteriors and jar interiors usually are brushed or striated.

SOURCE: Hayes et al. 1981.

Frances Levine

CHUSKAN POTTERY SERIES, the diagnostic ceramic of the Chuskan Anasazi culture in the overlapping Chuska and Chaco provinces (qq.v.) of northwestern New Mexico. Produced along the eastern slopes of the Chuska Mountains between Gallup and Shiprock, this series of decorated and utility wares correlates roughly with the stylistic development of the Chacoan Cibola Series, but it is distinctive in its thick, creamy-white slip, in the use of carbon paint for decorating, and in its abundant trachyte (a dark, igneous rock) temper. Chuskan wares became the primary ceramic import into Chaco Canyon during the Bonito Phase (q.v.).

SOURCES: Windes 1977; Toll 1985.

Peter J. McKenna

CHUSKA PROVINCE, a regional expression of the Anasazi Culture (q.v.), primarily in the western San Juan Basin of New Mexico, between the foothills of the Chuska Mountains and the northward-flowing segment of the Chaco River. Most knowledge of the province came from an extensive survey in 1962–1963 by Stewart Peckham and J. P. Wilson, who developed a chronological sequence based on pottery associations and changes. They found that the province lay within an undifferentiated Chaco/Zuni province until late Basketmaker III times (ca. A.D. 700–750), after which the Chaco presence became limited to several Chaco outliers, while influences from Anasazi provinces to the west (Chinle and Kayenta) and to the north (Mesa Verde) brought about marked changes in ceramics typology: (1) adoption of trachyte (a local igneous rock) for tempering and (2) production of pottery types decorated with both iron and carbon paint whose decorative styles varied periodically, depending on the strength of outside influences.

Natural resources from the mountains and food from the rich agricultural lands probably made the Chuska Province the breadbasket for the settlements at Chaco Canyon, where Chuska wares often comprise from 60 percent to 70 percent of the ceramic assemblages. The Chaco outlier sites were abandoned at the same time that the other Chaco communities collapsed, between A.D. 1130 and 1200, following or coinciding with increased influence—and settlement—from the Mesa Verde Province (q.v.). Total abandonment of the Chuska Province coincided with the Great Drought of A.D. 1276–1299.

SOURCES: E. A. Morris 1959; Sciscenti and Greminger 1962; C.R. Johnson, Jr. 1963; Peckham and Wilson n.d.; Reher 1977.

Stewart Peckham

CIBOLA PROVINCE, a manifestation of the Mogollon Culture (q.v.) in west-central New Mexico, from near Quemado to south of Reserve, with a slight extension into adjacent Arizona. Intensive investigations by a number of researchers between 1903 and the 1970s significantly increased knowledge of the Mogollon people and their way of life. Research reports were largely descriptive until the 1950s, when multidisciplinary studies (botany, geology, paleoclimatology) began to seek environmental explanations of culture change.

Sites of the Cochise Culture of the Archaic tradition (qq.v.) have been studied in the province, particularly those associated with the introduction of agriculture. However, most work has focused on the almost 1100-year tenure of Mogollon peoples in the region between A.D. 300 and 1350, during which time pottery making was introduced and elaborated, settlements grew from scattered pithouses to large pueblos, and the Mogollon great kiva evolved. At first an apparent northward extension of the Mimbres Phase the province by A.D. 1000 had lost much contact from that direction while increasing its interaction with the Anasazi of the Zuni Province (q.v.) and with the Little Colorado region. As a Mogollon entity, the Cibola Province had ceased to exist by A.D. 1350.

SOURCES: P. S. Martin 1940, 1943; Martin and Rinaldo 1947, 1950a, 1950b, Martin et al. 1949; Martin et al. 1952, 1956; Peckham et al. 1956; Martin, et al. 1957; Rinaldo 1959.

Stewart Peckham

CICUYE PUEBLO. See Pecos Pueblo.

CIELO PHASE, a late prehistoric-protohistoric (ca. A.D. 1200–1600) hunting-gathering manifestation in the Big Bend region of western Texas and northern Mexico, defined by R. J. Mallouf in 1981. Sites contain from 1 to 45 circular, stacked-stone, often semisubterranean, house enclosures approximately 3 meters in diameter, with well-defined entranceways oriented to the northwest or south. Evidently occupied repeatedly by nomadic peoples during their seasonal rounds, the sites usually occur on elevated landforms in foothills or on freestanding mesas and saddles. Material assemblages include several forms of arrow points, scraping and perforating tools, hammerstones, cores, bifacial knives, manos, slab metates, quartz crystals, stone disc beads, ovate stone pendants, and, at the most recent sites, possibly spherical blue glass trade beads. Cultural affiliations are uncertain but may involve early historic-period Chisos, Jumano, Tobosos, or, less likely, Apachean groups and their ancestors. They appear to have carried on trade relationships with agriculturalists of the La Junta Phase (q.v.) along the Rio Grande in the vicinity of Presidio, Texas.

SOURCE: Mallouf 1985.

Robert J. Mallouf

CINDER PARK PHASE, the earliest phase of the Northern Sinagua Tradition (q.v.) in north-central Arizona, coeval with the late Basketmaker III period, ca. A.D. 600–700. It was named after Cinder Park, a large alluvial basin 21 kilometers east of Flagstaff where sites of the phase are relatively common. Small to moderately sized pithouse villages, each probably occupied by an extended family group, also are widely scattered throughout the southern and eastern parts of Northern Sinaguan territory.

The houses are round to subsquare, 4 to 4.5 meters in maximum dimension, with central firepits and long, sloping ramp entries on their east sides. Some have peripheral posthole patterns, suggesting a tipi-like superstructure.

One community room 8.5 meters in diameter has been reported, implying intervillage organization from the beginning of the Sinagua sequence. The type site, located on the margin of Cinder Park, was partly excavated in 1941 by Frederica de Laguna.

Pottery is the Rio de Flag Brown type, produced by the paddle-and-anvil technique, with forms similar to those in the Mogollon (q.v.) area. The ceramics indicate trade with Hohokam (q.v.) people to the south and with the Kayenta Anasazi (q.v.) to the north. Typical burials are semiflexed or extended inhumations with little or no occipital deformation.

SOURCES: Colton 1946:243–247, 268–269, 312–314; Breternitz 1957a, 1957b, 1959.

Peter J. Pilles, Jr.

CITADEL PUEBLO/NALAKIHU, two closely related Pueblo III Phase, Kayenta Anasazi sites in Wupatki National Monument approximately 55 kilometers northeast of Flagstaff, Arizona. Citadel Ruin, consisting of some 30 rooms and possibly a kiva, covers the top of a small, round, basalt butte. Nalakihu, at the foot of the butte on the flat Antelope Prairie, comprises ten ground-floor rooms and three or four more in a second story. Dating ca. A.D. 1125–1200, Citadel is one of the larger sites on Antelope Prairie and, because of its elevated position, one of the most visible. A burial area to the northeast was excavated by pothunters before the monument was established.

Nalakihu, excavated in 1933–1934 by D. S. King, has been partially restored. It contained a high percentage of Prescott (q.v.) ceramics, a cremation, and Koishi ovens.

SOURCES: Barrett 1927; Colton 1946:52–54; D. S. King 1949.

Bruce Anderson

CIVANO PHASE. See Classic Period (Hohokam).

CLACHAN SITE, a Thule Phase (q.v.) settlement on western Coronation Gulf, Northwest Territories, occupied ca. A.D. 1100–1400, where between 1970 and 1981 D. A. Morrison unearthed stylistic variants of Thule artifacts that are affiliated primarily with western rather than with eastern Thule. Aglu hunting (q.v.) evidently had not yet developed.

SOURCE: D. A. Morrison 1983.

Moreau S. Maxwell

CLAM RIVER FOCUS, a unit defined by W. C. McKern in 1963 to characterize terminal Woodland-protohistoric manifestations in northwestern

Wisconsin, dating ca. A.D. 1100–1400 and thought to be the archaeological culture of the Santee Sioux.
SOURCE: McKern 1963.

David Overstreet

CLARKSVILLE POTTERY SERIES, a sand-tempered ware of the southeast Piedmont of Virginia, dating ca. A.D. 1300–1650. It may be either plain or impressed with a net, cord, simple stamp, or corncob and decorated with punctations, notches, gashes, or finger-pinches.
SOURCE: Clifford Evans 1955.

Keith T. Egloff

CLARKSVILLE TRIANGULAR POINT, a very small, triangular (usually equilateral), chipped-stone projectile point associated with the Siouan occupations of the Late Woodland and early historic periods (ca. 1600–1715) in the Piedmont of southern Virginia and northern North Carolina.
SOURCE: Coe 1964:112.

Billy L. Oliver

CLASSIC PERIOD, ANASAZI CULTURE, the final period (A.D. 1325/ 1360–1600) of the prehistoric Rio Grande Anasazi, marked by the establishment or expansion of more than 100 pueblos throughout the region and by the subsequent abandonment of many. The pueblos, apparently designed for defense, were invariably built around single or multiple plazas in locations with limited access. Differentiation of the major provinces (Northern Rio Grande, Tewa Basin, Galisteo Basin, Pecos, Middle Rio Grande, Jemez, Salinas, and Rio Abajo [qq.v.]) became more pronounced, as many adopted distinctive pottery-making styles, e.g., the Biscuitwares of the Tewa Basin Province, Jemez Whiteware in the Jemez Province, Taos-Picuris Whiteware in the Northern Rio Grande Province, and Rio Grande Glazewares in the remaining provinces.

Small subterranean kivas, many with multicolored murals, were common throughout the region: rectangular ones near and south of Bernalillo, round ones elsewhere. Major pueblos had Rio Grande "big kivas." Thousands of acres of garden plots were developed on marginal land to provide food for the many pueblos. Water control devices—reservoirs, check dams, and probably irrigation ditches—maximized the use of land for agriculture. Formalized warfare evidently became more widespread as competition for land and water increased.

SOURCES: Hewett 1906, 1909; Morley 1910; N.C. Nelson 1914, 1916; Kidder 1915, 1958; Reiter 1938; Reiter et al. 1940; Wendorf 1953; Lambert 1954; Wendorf and Reed 1955; Peckham 1979; A. H. Warren 1979; Hayes et al. 1981; Hewitt and Dutton 1953.

Stewart Peckham

CLASSIC PERIOD, HOHOKAM CULTURE, the final stage of the Hohokam Culture (q.v.) in southern Arizona and northern Sonora, dating ca. A.D. 1100–1450 and comprising two phases, Soho and Civano. During the Soho Phase (ca. A.D. 1100–1300), red-on-buff pottery diminished markedly in popularity, while polished redwares with blackened interiors became common. Above-ground, rectangular houses made of caliche-adobe, wood, and stone outnumbered pithouses. The compound, consisting of houses and plazas enclosed with a surrounding wall, appeared in most areas. Massive platform mounds were elaborated; more than 40 were built in the Phoenix Basin Province (q.v.). Mortuary practices varied from cremation to extended or flexed inhumation with associated grave goods. The elaborate stonework of earlier periods died out, while shell and turquoise inlay continued.

During the Civano Phase (ca. A.D. 1300–1450), massive, walled, multi-storied roomblocks appeared, along with "big houses" such as those at Casa Grande Ruins National Monument. Roomblocks made of solid caliche-adobe were built on mounds. Red-on-buff pottery continued to decline, while polished redwares and Salado Polychrome (a redware with black-on-white designs) became common.

The Classic Period Hohokam cultural pattern is fully expressed only in the Phoenix Basin Province, although weaker versions are known in the Tucson Basin and Papagueria provinces (qq.v.). The period was a time of rapidly fluctuating, unpredictable climatic conditions. Some places, such as Snaketown (q.v.), were all but abandoned, while full occupation continued at other villages, such as Pueblo Grande and Casa Grande ruins. New settlements (e.g., the Los Muertos Site [q.v.]) also were established.

SOURCES: Haury 1945; J. D. Hayden 1957; Doyel 1974, 1981; Wilcox and Shenk 1977.

David E. Doyel and John S. Cable

CLAY FUNERAL MASKS, rather unique anthropomorphic masks occurring in burials of the Red Cedar River Focus (q.v.) in northwestern Wisconsin. They are thought to represent a local interpretation of Havana Tradition, Middle Woodland mortuary practices.

SOURCE: Cooper 1933.

David Overstreet

CLAY HILLS PHASE, a late Pueblo II period phase of the Kayenta tradition whose sites occur on Cedar Mesa in the center of the Cedar Mesa Province (q.v.) in southeastern Utah. The easternmost expression of the Kayenta tradition north of the San Juan River, the phase dates ca. A.D. 1100–1150 and consists of small, scattered, highland sites containing Kayenta ceramics. There was also a cliff-dwelling episode in the Cedar Mesa canyons at about the same time that may belong to the phase. The Klethla Phase (q.v.) in the Red Rock Plateau may be equivalent to Clay Hills.

SOURCES: Lipe 1970; Matson and Lipe 1978.

R. G. Matson

CLEAR CREEK PHASE, the final phase of the Northern Sinagua Tradition (q.v.) in north-central Arizona. It dates ca. A.D. 1300–1400, after which the Sinagua can no longer be recognized in the archaeological record. By the beginning of the phase, Sinaguan peoples had abandoned their former homeland in the Flagstaff Province (q.v.) save for one pueblo, Old Caves, and had relocated their main center of occupation on Anderson Mesa in the Chevelon-Chavez Province (q.v.). The major settlements there were at Grapevine Pueblo, Kinnikinnick Ruin, the Pollock Site, and Chavez Ruins.

Clear Creek sites consist exclusively of large pueblos of from twenty to several hundred rooms arranged in blocks or linear tiers, reflecting a final aggregation of the Sinaguans into a few towns. Some of the larger pueblos had a companion pueblo, usually smaller, in close proximity, a pattern that first appeared during the earlier Elden Phase (q.v.). Community architecture is represented by a few plazas, community rooms, ball courts, and rectangular, benched kivas. Chavez Pass and Old Caves represent the final examples of primary, central villages in the Sinagua settlement hierarchy, with plazas, hilltop locations, community rooms, and ball courts.

Local Sinaguan pottery is the same as in the preceding Turkey Hill Phase, with trade wares indicating major contacts with the Hopi in the Little Colorado River Valley and Hopi Mesas, as well as with groups in the White Mountain and Zuni areas. The presence of shell jewelry, macaws, and copper bells indicates that trade with southern Arizona and Mexico continued.

There are extensive agricultural systems around all of the Anderson Mesa pueblos, including linear borders, grid borders, and terracing. Many fields appear to have been fertilized by purposeful addition of trash to the soil. Burials are extended, wrapped in reed matting, and placed in branch-covered cists that sometimes are lined with stones. Some burials have copper-based mineral pigment sprinkled on the face or over the entire body of the deceased.

After A.D. 1400, the Sinagua Tradition appears to have been absorbed into the culture of the Hopi, whose traditions suggest that the inhabitants of the last Sinaguan pueblos on Anderson Mesa abandoned them and joined Hopi people in the Little Colorado River Valley.

H. S. Gladwin published phase names for the archaeological remains in the Flagstaff Province in 1934. H. S. Colton, in his definitive work of 1939, created his own phase names for the most part but retained Gladwin's name for the Clear Creek Phase.

SOURCES: Gladwin 1934:25; Colton 1939b:43–44, 1946:273, 312–314; McGregor 1965:420–421; J. P. Wilson; 1969:27–28; Upham n.d., 1982.

Peter J. Pilles, Jr.

CLEAR FORK PHASE, earliest (ca. 3000–2000 B.C.) Middle Archaic phase in central Texas. Sites typically contain massive burned-rock middens; diagnostic artifacts are the weak-shouldered dart-point types Nolan and Travis. Gouges, carried over from the Early Archaic, continued in use, and increased specialization in resource utilization is apparent. Representative excavated sites include Williams, Crumley, and McGann. C. N. Ray's Clear Fork Culture of the 1930s and 1940s and J. C. Kelley's Clear Fork Focus of the 1940s represent early efforts to formulate an accurate definition of this phase when only scanty stratigraphic, conjunctive, and temporal data were available. F. A. Weir defined the phase more completely in 1976.

SOURCES: C. N. Ray 1938, 1948; J. C. Kelley 1947b; Suhm 1959:226–234; T. C. Kelley 1961:252–255; N. E. Preston 1969:172–191; Weir 1976:124–128.

Frank A. Weir

CLEAR LAKE PERIOD. See Galveston Bay Focus.

CLEAR LAKE SITE, a multicomponent habitation and burial complex on the east bluff of the Illinois River between the mouths of the Spoon and Mackinaw rivers. Stratified with deep aeolian sand deposits, the site has components dating from Early Woodland (ca. 600 B.C.) through late Oneota (ca. A.D. 1500) times. Its principal Middle Woodland mound was excavated by the University of Chicago in 1932; portions of the associated village were excavated by the Peoria Academy of Science in the 1940s and by the Illinois State Museum in 1950. Most pottery types known to occur in the central Illinois River Valley are represented at Clear Lake.

SOURCES: Cole and Deuel 1937:181–191; Schoenbeck 1940, 1941, 1942, 1943, 1944, 1946, 1949; Fowler 1952.

Alan D. Harn

CLEAR MOUNT SITE, a multicomponent Woodland site, dating ca. 1800 B.C.–A.D. 1550, located on a sand ridge rising above the Savannah River floodplain in the Groton Plantation locality (q.v.), Hampton County, South Carolina. Excavations there by J. B. Stoltman in 1974 and by Drexel Peterson in 1969 produced abundant ceramics and lithics, as well as several burials.

SOURCES: Drexel Peterson 1971; Stoltman 1974a.

Michael Trinkley

CLEMENTS POTTERY SERIES, a well-made, thin-walled, sand-tempered ware distributed over the northern Piedmont. Vessel rims tend to flare and occasionally are notched along the lip. Interiors are smoothed; surfaces usually are cordmarked or fabric impressed. Dating ca. A.D 400–1200, Clements ware appears to have developed out of the preceding Vincent Series (q.v.).

SOURCES: Coe 1964:102–105; Ward 1983.

Billy L. Oliver

CLOSURE SITE, an early (ca. 200–1700 B.C.), single-component, Pre-Dorset Phase (q.v.) site on the southern coast of Baffin Island at Cape Tanfield, dug by A. A. Dekin in 1966. The artifact assemblage was dominated by spalled burins and burin spalls, but also contained items missing from most Pre-Dorset assemblages: slate knives, soapstone lamps, side-notched end blades, and rare burin-like tools (q.v.). As dwelling remains were not apparent, the occupants may have lived in tents or snow houses.

SOURCES: Dekin 1975; Maxwell 1973.

Moreau S. Maxwell

CLOUD BLOWER, a stemless pipe of either pottery or stone, used in historic times to produce clouds of smoke symbolic of rain clouds and thought to have functioned similarly prehistorically.

David A. Phillips, Jr.

CLOVERLEAF PHASE, a phase of the Verde Province of the Sinagua Division, Hakataya Culture (qq.v.) in Arizona, dating ca. A.D. 800–900. Houses of the phase were surface jacales—either rectangular with rounded ends or roughly oval—having two center-post roof supports and a ramp entry with a step. Some had a raised floor supported by notched stones or wooden blocks. A larger communal structure of similar plan with a ramp to the east has been reported.

These structures and the materials associated with them exhibit considerable Hohokam (q.v.) influence or presence. Artifacts included trough metates and grinding slabs, rectangular and round manos, pounder pestles, hammerstones, stone bowls, vesicular basalt cylinders with an encircling groove, stone rings, paint palettes, hematite, scrapers, choppers, hoes, utilized flakes, and, rarely, ornaments of slate and shell. Intrusive ceramics

were Santa Cruz Red-on-buff of the Hohokam Culture, Kana'a Black-on-white of the Anasazi Culture (q.v.), and related types.
SOURCE: Breternitz 1960.

Albert H. Schroeder

CLOVIS (or LLANO) CULTURE, earliest of the major Paleoindian (q.v.) cultures, dating ca. 11,000 to 9000 B.C., whose artifacts (termed the Llano Complex [q.v.]) occur widely, from the Rocky Mountains to the Atlantic and from southern Canada to northern Mexico. Archaeological evidence of the culture has been found almost entirely at hunting stations and at surface sites; however one component at the Mockingbird Gap Site in central New Mexico was a Clovis campsite, and a Clovis burial in Montana has been reported.

Clovis type projectile points (q.v.), considered diagnostic of the culture, have been recorded in association with mammoth bones in undisturbed geological contexts at the Blackwater Draw Site in eastern New Mexico, the Naco and Lehner sites in southern Arizona, the Dent Site in Colorado, and the Miami Site (qq.v.) in the Texas panhandle.

Clovis people are thought to have derived much of their food from mammoths, bison, horses, camels, and other large Pleistocene fauna, although they surely exploited other food sources as well. They probably were organized into typical hunter-gatherer bands, each of which moved about a sizable home territory, following game herds and foraging for seeds, nuts, berries, and roots as they became seasonably harvestable. By ca. 10,000 B.C. such bands apparently occupied much of the continent from the western fringes of the Plains to the Atlantic.
SOURCES: Sellards 1952:17–46; Wormington 1957:43–84; J. J. Hester 1972; Jennings 1978:23–30; Weber 1973; Weber and Agogino n.d.a., n.d.b.

Edward B. Jelks

CLOVIS POINT, a large, lanceolate, fluted, chipped-stone Paleoindian (q.v.) projectile point, dating ca. 11,000–9000 B.C., the diagnostic artifact of the Clovis Culture (q.v.). Widely but thinly distributed from the Rocky Mountains to the Atlantic and from Canada's southern provinces to northeastern Mexico, it has been found at kill sites of Pleistocene elephants at several sites in Arizona, New Mexico, Colorado, Texas, and Oklahoma.
SOURCES: E. B. Howard 1935; Sellards 1952:17–42; Suhm et al. 1954; Wormington 1957:42–84; J. J. Hester 1972.

Edward B. Jelks

CLUNY COMPLEX, a ceramic complex derived from the Middle Missouri River region that intruded into southern and central Alberta between A.D. 1700 and 1750. Markedly different from the indigenous pottery of Alberta, this ware features squat bodies with complex, frequently S-shaped profiles, and collared or braced rims. Vessel exteriors display smoothed-over check and simple stamps and some instances of vertical brushing; decoration generally consists of linear dentate stamping or very fine cord-wrapped or stick impressions. Although it occurs as a minor element in other Alberta sites, the largest collection of this pottery came from the Cluny Site (q.v.) east of Calgary.

SOURCES: Byrne 1973; Forbis 1977.

William J. Byrne

CLUNY SITE, a fortified earthlodge village dating to the 16th century, situated on the Bow River in Alberta east of Calgary. Excavated by the Glenbow Foundation in 1960, it produced distinctive pottery, termed Cluny Complex (q.v.) ceramics, as well as bone, stone, and shell artifacts that serve to link the site with the Coalescent Period (q.v.) of the Missouri River in North and South Dakota. Horse bones were present; bison bones were common. No comparable site has as yet been found in the prairie provinces of Canada. Cluny may represent a transient occupation of the Crow or another Hidatsa-related group that moved to Canada from the Dakotas during the early protohistoric period.

SOURCES: Byrne 1973; Forbis 1977.

Richard G. Forbis

CLYDE PHASE. See Owens Valley Locality.

COAHUILA SEQUENCE, a culture classification system worked out between the late 1930s and the early 1960s by W. W. Taylor for Coahuila, based primarily on his excavations in the vicinity of Cuatro Cienegas, at Frightful, Fat Burro, and Nopal caves, plus investigations at Candelaria Cave by Pablo Martinez del Rio in 1953. Taylor classified the prehistoric cultures of Coahuila into four complexes: Cienegas (ca. 10,000 to 5000/4000 B.C.), Coahuila (ca. 8000 B.C. to A.D. 1550), Jora (ca. A.D. 1 to an unknown termination date), and Mayran (ca. 1 A.D. to the early 1600s). All were hunting-gathering, nonagricultural peoples without pottery. Except for Martinez del Rio's work at Candelaria, Taylor's is the only substantial field research carried out to date in Coahuila, and his published descriptions are brief. Coahuila's prehistory remains poorly known.

SOURCES: W. W. Taylor 1948, 1956, 1966.

Edward B. Jelks

COALESCENT PERIOD, a time in Plains culture history, from ca. A.D. 1450 into the 19th century, when the respective traditions of the Central

Plains and the Middle Missouri area were in the process of fusing into a homogeneous culture.

SOURCE: Lehmer and Caldwell 1966.

Patricia J. O'Brien

COALITION PERIOD, ANASAZI CULTURE, the middle period (A.D. 1150/1175–1325/1360) of the Rio Grande Anasazi, a period of adjustment for thousands of arriving migrants who had fled a series of droughts, including the Great Drought of A.D. 1276–1299 in western New Mexico. Early in the period, hundreds of family-size dwelling sites were constructed on the Pajarito Plateau and elsewhere. In the 1300s—during the Pindi and Galisteo phases and into the Classic Period (qq.v.)—the population became consolidated into fewer (though there still were many) large pueblos. Kivas in many provinces were built into houseblocks at ground level. Potters switched from an iron oxide to a carbon or vegetal paint for decorating pottery. Almost all of the modern Rio Grande pueblos were established at this time.

SOURCES: Hibben 1937; Stubbs and Stallings 1953; Kidder 1958; McNutt 1969; Worman 1967; Schwartz and Lang 1973; Steen 1977, 1982; Skinner et al. 1980; Poore 1981; Peckham 1981.

Stewart Peckham

COAL-OIL CANYON SITE, a multicomponent (Woodland, Upper Republican, Dismal River, and maybe historic Pawnee), specialized, limited-activity site in Logan County, western Kansas, that was excavated in 1956 by members of the Kansas Anthropological Association. The site documents the temporary use of this semiarid High Plains region by hunters, for only several days at a time, over a period of some 800 to 900 years (ca. A.D. 800–1700).

SOURCE: Bowman 1960.

Patricia J. O'Brien

COCHISE CULTURE, a generic name for the Archaic (q.v.) hunters and gatherers who occupied northwestern Mexico, southeastern Arizona, and southwestern New Mexico ca. 10,500–1 B.C.; a regional manifestation of the Desert Culture (q.v.) of the semiarid desert West. Three Cochise stages have been recognized: Sulphur Spring (ca. 10,500–6000 B.C.), Chiricahua (ca. 6000–1500 B.C.), and San Pedro (ca. 1500–1 B.C.).

Sulphur Spring, least understood of the stages, is known from only a few sites where artifacts reportedly were associated stratigraphically with Pleistocene fauna (horse, bison, pronghorn antelope, dire wolf, coyote, and mammoth).

Major components of the Chiricahua Stage, best defined stage of the three, have been excavated by E. W. Haury at Ventana Cave, Arizona, by H. W.

Dick at Bat Cave, New Mexico, and by P. S. Martin and J. B. Rinaldo in the Reserve area, New Mexico. Maize and squash were found in these sites, along with grinding stones and projectile-point types Pelona (leaf-shaped), Chiricahua (side-notched), Augustin (contracting stemmed), and Bat Cave (lanceolate).

In the San Pedro Stage, grinding tools continued in wide usage and plant foods were used extensively, perhaps one reason for the addition of the mortar and pestle to the artifact inventory. A broad range of projectile points consisted generally of variations on shallow corner- and side-notched types. With the addition of pottery and pithouses, the San Pedro Stage evolved into the Hohokam and Mogollon cultures (qq.v.).

SOURCES: Sayles and Antevs 1941; Martin et al. 1949; Dick 1965a; N. B. Whalen 1971; Sayles 1983.

Patrick H. Beckett

COCONINO PHASE, a manifestation of the Cohonina Province of the Patayan Division, Hakataya Culture (qq.v.) in Arizona, dating ca. A.D. 750–900. Settlements contain oval, round, and irregularly shaped jacales, along with more or less rectangular single rooms (or sometimes clusters of contiguous rooms) having low stone foundations topped with pole-and-mud superstructures. Much reuse of buildings suggests seasonal occupation. The ceramic inventory includes the Deadman's Gray and Fugitive Red types, both continued from the preceding Naylier Phase (q.v.), with the addition of local type Floyd Black-on-gray and intrusive Anasazi type Black Mesa Black-on-white. Other common artifacts are platform metates; core choppers; and long, unstemmed, unnotched, obsidian arrow points. Ornaments are rare.

SOURCE: McGregor 1967.

Albert H. Schroeder

CODY COMPLEX, a group of stone artifact types and forms that have been found in association with one another at several sites in the Plains. Diagnostics are Scottsbluff and Eden projectile points and Code knives (qq.v.), commonly found with scrapers, gravers, perforators, choppers, pounders, and rubbing stones. R. Johnson first recognized the association and named it the Little Gem complex. G. L. Jepsen labeled it the Cody Complex on the basis of finds at the Horner Site (q.v.) near Cody, Wyoming.

SOURCES: Agenbroad 1978a; Forbis 1968; Huckell 1978; Jepsen 1951; Wormington and Forbis 1965.

Larry D. Agenbroad

COFFEY SITE, a major Archaic (q.v.) site near Blue Rapids, Kansas, with eleven stratified layers, the best known of which, Horizon III (with radiocarbon dates averaging from between 3200 and 3100 B.C.), was the focus

of specialized seasonal activities between late August and late September by the hunters-gatherers of the Black Vermillion Phase (q.v.). Coffey was one of the first Archaic sites on the Plains where soil from fireplaces was floated, a technique that produced detailed information on plant and small mammal utilization. C. Johnson and L. J. Schmits excavated the site between 1970 and 1975.
SOURCE: Schmits 1978.

Patricia J. O'Brien

COGGED STONE, a round to ovoid ground-stone disk characteristic of the La Jolla Complex (q.v.) in southwestern California and Baja California between 4000 and 1000 B.C. Averaging about 10 centimeters in diameter, these disks have smooth, flat to slightly convex faces, and regularly spaced grooves along their edges which give them the appearance of cogwheels or gears. In some cases, there is a central perforation.
SOURCE: Eberhart 1961.

L. A. Payen

COHONINA PROVINCE, an expression of the Patayan Division of the Hakataya Culture (qq.v.) on the Coconino Plateau near Flagstaff, Arizona. It was named by L. L. Hargrave, defined by H. S. Colton, and revised by J. C. McGregor, who identified the province's territory with the distribution of San Francisco Mountain Gray Ware pottery. Estimated to date from before A.D. 700 to ca. 1200, the province's settlements were small and evidently occupied seasonally. There were major contacts with the Anasazi Culture (q.v.), whose pottery designs the Cohonino people freely adopted. However, they failed to borrow the idea of pueblos from the Anasazi, instead constructing thick, low-walled buildings of a few rooms, some of which have been labeled forts.
SOURCES: Hargrave 1938; Colton 1939a; McGregor 1967.

Albert H. Schroeder

COLBY SITE, a mammoth kill site in the Big Horn Basin of northern Wyoming where parts of at least seven mammoths were found in the channel of an old arroyo by George Frison in 1973, 1975, and 1978. Two bone piles may represent the remains of frozen meat caches. Associated projectile points are slightly different morphologically from those at other mammoth kill sites.
SOURCES: Frison 1976a, 1978; Frison and Todd 1986.

George Frison

COLD SITE. See PORT REFUGE LOCALITY.

COLD SPRINGS SIDE-NOTCHED POINT, a large, chipped-stone, dart-point type, almost invariably made from andesite or andesitic basalt, dating ca. 4700–2500 B.C.; first found between 1947 and 1952 at sites in the

McNary Reservoir area on the middle course of the Columbia River in Washington and Oregon. The blade is triangular with convex sides; there are semicircular side notches about 1/4 of the blade length above the slightly convex to concave base; the edges constrict below the notches. Cold Springs is distinguished from the similar Bitterroot Side-Notched type by its broad, semicircular notches.
SOURCES: B. R. Butler 1961; Shiner 1961.

Frank C. Leonhardy

COLES CREEK CULTURE, the most widespread prehistoric manifestation in southern Louisiana, radiocarbon dated to ca. A.D. 400–1250. Coles Creek mounds—truncated pyramids or temple mounds with ramps—occur in groups clustered around plazas, extending from the Gulf Coast to northern Louisiana and beyond. Extensive habitation areas usually are associated with the mound groups. Distinctive pottery, incised and stamped, appears in abundance. The bow and arrow evidently was in use by this time, and maize was probably known but not yet economically important.
SOURCES: J. A. Ford 1951; Belmont 1967.

William G. Haag

COLINGTON PHASE, a manifestation thought to be the archaeological equivalent of the Algonkian peoples of the Albemarle Sound area of North Carolina between ca. A.D. 800 and 1650. The phase is characterized by Colington Series pottery, Clarksville Triangular and Roanoke Large Triangular projectile points (qq.v.), bifacial blades, polished-stone celts, gorgets, pipes, and communal ossuaries.
SOURCE: Phelps 1983:36.

Billy L. Oliver

COLINGTON POTTERY SERIES, a shell-tempered ceramic with predominantly fabric-impressed, but sometimes simple-stamped, plain or incised, surface treatment; considered characteristic of the Tidewater Algonkian cultures of North Carolina ca. A.D. 800–1650, and of their archaeological equivalent, the Colington Phase (q.v.). Vessel shapes include conoidal pots, hemispherical bowls, and a small beaker form with an everted rim. Equivalent series in southeastern Virginia are the Townsend and Roanoke simple-stamped wares.
SOURCE: Phelps 1983:36.

Billy L. Oliver

COLONIAL PERIOD, the second of the Hohokam Culture's (q.v.) periods, thought to date ca. A.D. 700–900. It comprises two phases: Gila Butte and Santa Cruz.

The Gila Butte Phase (ca. A.D. 700–775) is characterized by ball courts, stone palettes, grave goods with cremations, and Gila Butte Red-on-buff pottery bowls with trailed exterior lines, conventionalized scrolls, life-forms, and small, repeated elements. Carved stone and shell decorative styles were elaborated, irrigation systems were well established, and villages were common throughout the Hohokam provinces.

During the Santa Cruz Phase (ca. A.D. 775–900), trench cremations were replaced by pit cremations, stone and shell carving reached a peak, and stone palettes were often adorned with carved effigies around their borders. Santa Cruz Red-on-buff pottery has high-quality brushwork, band and sectional design patterns, a variety of line-work styles, a wide range of life-forms including human figures, and an emphasis on repeated, solid elements. Shallow, square, or rectangular pithouses with rounded corners were similar to dwellings of the Gila Butte Phase. Trash and artifical mounds are abundant at larger sites.

SOURCES: Woodward 1931; Haury 1932, 1976.

David E. Doyel and John S. Cable

COLONO WARE, a shell-tempered, refined-paste ceramic with plain or burnished surface, distributed mainly in the estuarine coastal plain of Virginia and dating from ca. 1680 well into the 19th century. Vessel shapes, patterned after European forms, include bowls, jars, plates, chamber pots, pipkins, and porringers. This ware is thought to have been made either by Blacks or by Native Americans.

SOURCES: Noël Hume 1962; Egloff and Potter 1982.

Keith T. Egloff

COLTON CLASSIFICATION SYSTEM. See Southwestern Classification Systems.

COLUMBIA PLATEAU (or COLUMBIA INTERMONTANE PLATEAU), a physiographic province in eastern Washington and northwestern Idaho. Because it partially coincides with the southern subarea of the Plateau culture area, the cultural term *Southern Plateau* and the physiographic term *Columbia Plateau* often are used interchangeably.

SOURCES: V. F. Ray 1939; McKee 1972.

Frank C. Leonhardy

COMER'S MIDDEN, a deep cultural deposit near the present settlement of Thule (Uummanaq), in northwestern Greenland, containing late Dorset Phase and early, classic, and later Thule Phase (qq.v.) materials, although not in stratified sequence. Partially excavated by the whaling-ship captain,

George Comer, early in the 20th century, it was dug more systematically by Erik Holtved in the 1940s.

SOURCE: Holtved 1944.

Moreau S. Maxwell

CONCEPCION PHASE, a late prehistoric-early historic (ca. A.D. 1400–1700) phase of the Bravo Valley Aspect (q.v.), comprising a series of villages in western Texas and northern Chihuahua around the confluence of the Rio Grande and the Rio Conchos; defined in the 1940s by J. C. Kelley as the Concepcion Focus, primarily on the basis of architectural details of jacal and masonry dwellings at five sites. Clay-lined storage pits and flexed burials in middens are common features; characteristic artifacts include plain and red-on-brown pottery of several types, stone abraders, manos, metates, plain stone bowls, polishing stones, and ceramic discs. Influences of the Jornada branch of the Mogollon culture (q.v.) up the Rio Grande have been noted, as has the possibilty of trade in pottery with Caddoan peoples of eastern Texas.

SOURCES: J. C. Kelley et al. 1940; J. C. Kelley 1949:89–114, 1985:149–159.

Robert J. Mallouf

CONCHOS PHASE, a historic (ca. A.D. 1700–1800), agriculturally based unit of the Bravo Valley Aspect (q.v.) consisting of small settlements clustered on elevated silt terraces along the Rio Grande in the vicinity of Presidio, in western Texas; defined as the Conchos Focus by J. C. Kelley in the 1940s. Features include surface houses of both adobe and jacal construction, Spanish mission buildings of adobe, and middens at the edges of village areas. Indigenous red-on-brown pottery occurs along with items introduced by the Spanish, including majolica pottery, glazed olive jars, metal tools, and European plants.

SOURCES: J. C. Kelley et al. 1940; J. C. Kelley 1985:149–159.

Robert J. Mallouf

CONNESTEE PHASE, the latest (ca. A.D. 300–1000) Woodland (q.v.) manifestation in the mountain region of North Carolina; believed to be an outgrowth of the preceding Pigeon and Swannanoa phases and a predecessor to the Pisgah Phase (qq.v.). Although most artifact assemblages contain Connestee Series pottery (q.v.) and locally manufactured stone and bone tools, they also include items imported from Hopewell centers to the north; e.g., prismatic blades, polyhedral cores, copper ornaments, and triangular knives or cache blades.

SOURCE: Keel 1976:219–226.

Billy L. Oliver

CONNESTEE POTTERY SERIES, a thin-walled, sand-tempered ware with surfaces that usually are plain, brushed, or simple stamped, but occasionally are cordmarked, fabric marked, check stamped, or complicated stamped.

Forms include both conoidal and hemispherical vessels with constricted necks and flaring rims, flat-based conoidal jars, and (early in the phase) footed vessels. Lips were decorated with punctations, notches, or incisions. Connestee pottery occurs in Connestee Phase (q.v.) sites in the mountainous region of North Carolina and dates ca. A.D. 300–1000.

SOURCES: P. P. Holden 1966; Keel 1976:219–226; Dickens 1976.

Billy L. Oliver

CONNLEY CAVES. See Fort Rock Cave.

CONOWINGO SITE, one of the largest multicomponent sites in Maryland, located on the right bank of the Susquehanna River; locus of seasonal fishing camps from Late Archaic through Middle Woodland times and also a Late Woodland village. Total occupation spanned the period ca. 3000 B.C.–A.D. 1600. R. E. Stearns made surface collections at the site in the 1930s, and the Archeological Society of Maryland, under supervision of the Maryland Geological Survey, conducted excavations there in 1981 and 1982.

SOURCES: Stearns 1943:12–17; McNamara 1982, 1983.

Stephen R. Potter

CONVENT KNOLL SITE, a Red Ocher (q.v.) cemetery in southeastern Wisconsin dating ca. 1000 B.C., where excavations by David Overstreet in 1980 disclosed the graves of seven individuals who had met traumatic deaths and had been dismembered. This was the only controlled excavation of a Red Ocher cemetery in the area.

SOURCES: Ritzenthaler and Quimby 1962; Overstreet 1980.

David Overstreet

CONVENTO PHASE. See Casas Grandes Province.

CONVENTO SITE, the type site for the Viejo Period of the Casas Grandes Province (q.v.), also site of the 17th-century Spanish mission of San Antonio de Padua de Casas Grandes; located in Chihuahua on the west bank of the Rio Casas Grandes about 5.2 kilometers north and downstream from the prehistoric Casas Grandes Site (q.v.). C. C. Di Peso excavated the site in 1959 in the hope of recovering wood samples that would bridge the gap between the historic period and the floating tree-ring chronology then being established for Casas Grandes. Instead, he discovered three stratified village components that predated Casas Grandes and that became the bases, respectively, for the three phases of the Viejo Period. Historic remains at this site served to define the San Antonio de Padua Phase of the Españoles Period of the Casas Grandes Province.

SOURCES: Di Peso 1974, vol. 1; Di Peso et al. 1974, vols. 4, 5.

Gloria J. Fenner

COOPER SITE, a major, multicomponent site located in the Middle Quachita region of south-central Arkansas, occupied from Archaic through Middle Woodland times (ca. 7000 B.C.–A.D. 500); kingpin of the pre-Caddoan cultural sequence in southwestern Arkansas, northwestern Louisiana, and eastern Texas. Extensively excavated in 1939 by a Works Progress Administration crew, then ignored for many years, the site eventually was analyzed by F. F. Schambach in 1970.

SOURCE: Schambach 1970; Schambach et al. 1982.

Frank F. Schambach

COPENA COMPLEX, a regional Middle Woodland mortuary complex of ca. A.D. 1–500 in the Tennessee Valley region of northern Alabama, dating to the first five centuries A.D.; associated with burial mounds and, rarely, with burial caves. The approximately 50 Copena mounds that have been investigated typically are low conoidal structures made of sand or clay, built over subsoil primary burial pits, and usually with secondary burials in the mound fill. The most characteristic offerings accompanying the burials are copper ornaments and celts, ground galena nodules, marine shell cups, steatite elbow pipes, and greenstone celts and slab hoes. The name *Copena* is derived from the first three letters of copper and the last three letters of galena.

SOURCES: W. S. Webb 1939; Walthall 1973, 1979.

John A. Walthall

COPENA POINT, one variety of numerous medium-sized, trianguloid, chipped-stone projectile-point or knife forms associated with Early and Middle Woodland cultures of the interior Southeast, where they occasionally occur in caches in mortuary mounds. Distinguished by recurvate, lanceolate blades and straight or excurvate bases, Copena points date ca. 400 B.C. to A.D. 500.

SOURCES: Larson 1959; Cambron and Hulse 1964:25, 1975:31; Faulkner and McCollough 1974:146–148; Walthall 1973; G. G. Cole 1981.

Eugene M. Futato

CORAL SNAKE MOUND, a Woodland (q.v.) burial mound in western Louisiana, dating ca. 200–300 A.D., identified with the Marksville Culture (q.v.). Excavations by H. P. Jensen, Jr. in 1965 and 1967 exposed burials, fire basins, artifact caches, and a submound cremation pit. The association of typical Caddoan pottery with Marksville material, together with a similar

association at the Jonas Short Mound (about 65 kilometers to the west in Texas), helped clarify relationships between the Caddoan and lower Mississippi River Valley areas.
SOURCES: Jensen 1968; McClurkan et al. 1980.

Edward B. Jelks

CORDOVA CAVE. See Tularosa and Cordova Caves.

CORE AND VENEER MASONRY, a method of wall construction used ca. A.D. 920–1140 by Anasazi (q.v.) people for building greathouses and small houses in the Bonito Phase of the Chaco Province (qq.v.) in northwestern New Mexico. A Chacoan hallmark, the method involved the laying, with minimal exposed mortar, of two masonry walls separated by a core of variable width that was composed either of solid rubble or of dirt, rock, and trash. Pressure of the core on the interior wall faces acted vertically on the stone joints, giving the compound wall great stability and permitting the construction of massive, multistoried greathouses.

Five veneer styles using stones of different sizes and shapes have been recognized: Types I through IV and the McElmo style (earliest to latest). These have proven useful for relative dating of construction units.
SOURCES: Judd 1964; Lekson 1986.

Peter J. McKenna

CORNER DOORWAY, a very rare but famous architectural feature of Bonito Phase (q.v.) Anasazi greathouses in the Chaco Province (qq.v.) of northwestern New Mexico. Such doorways connect two rooms—usually interior rooms—on the same story through the intersection of two walls. Pueblo Bonito (q.v.) has seven corner doorways, Chetro Ketl and Aztec Ruin (qq.v.) have three each, and Pueblo Pintado has one.
SOURCE: Lekson 1986.

Peter J. McKenna

CORNETT SITE, a large, Late Woodland village on the New River in southwestern Virginia, where Wythe Series pottery (q.v.) is the dominant ceramic. Clifford Evans described the site in 1955 and discussed the significance of the occurrence of curvilinear, complicated-stamped sherds there in greater frequency than at any other site in Virginia east of the Tennessee River drainage.
SOURCE: Clifford Evans 1955.

Keith T. Egloff

CORNFIELD TAOS, a coursed adobe pueblo located 0.4 kilometers northeast of the church at the modern pueblo of Taos, New Mexico, to which it is thought to be ancestral. A trench excavated there in 1961 by F. H. Ellis and J. J. Brody suggested occupation ca. A.D. 1350–1450.

SOURCE: Ellis and Brody 1964.

Patricia L. Crown

CORONA PHASE, the earlier of two phases in the northern sector of the Sierra Blanca Sub-Province, Jornada Province, Mogollon Culture (qq.v.) in central New Mexico, dating ca. A.D. 1100–1200. Corona sites give all appearances of short-term occupation of readily constructed structures, which implies mobile populations. They are very similar to sites of the Claunch Focus of the Salinas Province, Anasazi Culture (qq.v.), to the northwest and could be merely a geographical extension of that focus.

Corona sites consist of one or more small pueblo structures—evidently jacals (q.v.)—with rooms outlined by rows of cobbles set on edge. The ceramic assemblage is dominated by Jornada Brown; small amounts of Chupadero Black-on-white also are present. Intrusive types are few in number and sporadic in occurrence. Details about artifacts and subsistence practices are virtually unknown for lack of excavated sites and paucity of all but projectile points on site surfaces.

SOURCE: J. H. Kelley 1984.

R. N. Wiseman

CORRECTIONVILLE-BLUE EARTH PHASE, an Oneota expression of the Mississippian tradition (q.v.) dating ca. A.D. 900–1600, distributed across southern Minnesota, western Wisconsin, Iowa, northern Missouri, and eastern Nebraska. Important sites for phase definition include Humphrey and Vosberg in Minnesota and Correctionville in Iowa. Houses were semisubterranean; subsistence was based largely on bison, deer, small mammals, fish, and corn agriculture. Associated Blue Earth ceramics were first defined by L. A. Wilford in southern Minnesota, but Correctionville ceramics from Iowa, subsequently analyzed by D. R. Henning, are similar. Vessels from both areas have smooth, shell-tempered, globular bodies with constricted necks, flared rims, and rectilinear trailed decorations on the shoulder.

SOURCES: Wilford 1941; Henning 1961, 1970.

Christy Hohman-Caine

COSO LOCALITY, a large area in the southern end of the Coso Range between Owens Valley and China Lake, in California, in which are located a distinctive rock-art area (see Coso Petroglyphs), the Stahl Site (q.v.), major

villages of the Panamint Shoshone, and an important obsidian source, the Sugarloaf Quarry (q.v.).
SOURCES: Grant 1981; Steward 1938.

Robert G. Elston

COSO PETROGLYPHS, designs pecked into the walls of basalt canyons in the Coso Range at the extreme northern edge of the Mojave Desert, in southern California; said to be the largest concentration of rock art in western North America. Designs include representations of bighorn sheep, elaborately costumed anthropomorphs, dogs, quails, atlatls, and "medicine bags." Dating of the petroglyphs is uncertain, but the oldest are thought to have been made over 3000 years ago.
SOURCE: Grant et al. 1968.

L. A. Payen

COTTONWOOD CREEK RUIN, a Western Anasazi village of an estimated 50 rooms overlooking lower Cottonwood Wash 12 kilometers east of Winslow, in northern Arizona, in the Chevelon-Chavez Province (q.v.). Some roomblocks may have been two stories high. Occupied between A.D. 1250 and 1400, it formerly was considered a Homolovi Focus site of the Winslow Branch (qq.v.). There are numerous petroglyphs around the village.

Early researchers described the site and made surface artifact collections, but excavation by professionals has not been undertaken. Much of the site has been destroyed by vandals and by the construction of a now-abandoned Masonic temple. Before it was incorporated into a regional state park in 1986, the site's condition and research potential were evaluated by Soil Systems.
SOURCE: Soil Systems n.d.

Donald E. Weaver, Jr.

COTTONWOOD CREEK SITE, a protohistoric village in Owens Valley, in eastern California, apparently occupied from ca. A.D. 600 until historic times; excavated and reported by H. S. Riddell in 1951. It consisted of a shallow midden deposit, bedrock mortars, grinding slicks, and several shallow depressions marking the locations of former dwellings and possibly a sweathouse. Plant macrofossils collected during excavation include pinyon pine and acorns.
SOURCES: Riddell 1951; Lanning 1963.

Robert L. Bettinger

COTTONWOOD TRIANGULAR POINT, a small, unnotched, thin, triangular projectile-point type found throughout the desert West, dating from ca. A.D. 1300 to historic times.

SOURCES: Lanning 1963; D.H. Thomas 1981.

David Hurst Thomas

COUNCIL CIRCLE, a name applied by W. R. Wedel to a kind of roughly circular structure formed of four elongated pithouses arranged in a quadrilateral plan; found at protohistoric (ca. A.D. 1300–1600) sites of the Great Bend Aspect (q.v.) in Kansas. At the Tobias (q.v.), Thompson, and Hayes sites they were aligned with either the sunrise or sunset of the summer or winter solstice.
SOURCE: Wedel 1967.

Patricia J. O'Brien

COURSED ADOBE CONSTRUCTION, a house-building method often used in areas of the Southwest lacking suitable stone for masonry walls, especially in the lowland areas of the Rio Grande drainage, the Tularosa Basin, the Gila-Salt Basin, and the Casas Grandes Province (q.v.) in northwestern Chihuahua. Walls were built up of a series of courses from 30 to 40 centimeters high; each course was formed with the hands from a mixture of adobe clay and water, sometimes with wood ashes added as a binder. Wooden forms may have been used at Casas Grandes. When one course had dried and set, another course was added to its top, and the process was repeated until a freestanding wall of desired height was attained. The technique also was used to line the walls of subterranean kivas in the Rio Grande region. With the introduction of adobe brickmaking by the Spanish in the 17th century, the Pueblo Indians abandoned the technique.
SOURCES: Stubbs and Stallings 1953; Di Peso 1974.

Stewart Peckham

COURTLAND WARE, a ceramic with a fine-textured, clayey paste and a plain or burnished surface, found in the interior coastal plain of southern Virginia and dating ca. A.D. 1660–1760. Courtland possesses a combination of aboriginal and late 17th- and 18th-century European traits.
SOURCES: Binford 1964, 1965; Egloff and Potter 1982.

Keith T. Egloff

COWBOY CAVE, a dry, stratified cave on the northern Colorado Plateau of eastern Utah containing cultural deposits attributed to early Archaic (ca. 6700–4400 ± B.C.) and late Archaic/Basketmaker (ca. 1500 B.C.–A.D. 500) occupations; excavated by J. D. Jennings in 1975. An underlying dung layer

deposited by a variety of Pleistocene megafauna, which dated ca. 11,000–9000 B.C., produced a possible Paleoindian bone tool.
SOURCE: Jennings et al. 1980.

David B. Madsen

COWEETA CREEK SITE, a Qualla Phase (q.v.) mound and village site in Macon County, North Carolina; excavated by J. L. Coe between 1965 and 1971. Attributed to Cherokee people of the 16th to 18th century, the site consisted of a small village clustered tightly around a plaza, which had a structure standing on a mound at one end and a secondary ceremonial structure at the opposite end.
SOURCES: Keel 1976; Dickens 1976.

Billy L. Oliver

COWHORN PHASE. See Owens Valley Locality.

COYOTE CREEK PHASE. See Chief Joseph Dam Locality.

CRABAPPLE POINT SITE, ostensible location of a historic Winnebago village on the shores of Lake Koshkonong in southeastern Wisconsin, excavated in the early 1970s by Janet Spector. She used data from the site to reconstruct the Winnebagos' material culture of the late 19th century, their involvement in early lead-mining activities, and the disintegration of their traditional institutions.
SOURCE: Spector 1975.

David Overstreet

CRABLE SITE, a typical town of the Spoon River Tradition (q.v.), dating ca. A.D. 1400, comprising a platform mound on an open plaza flanked by rows of structures. It is situated on the western bluff of the central Illinois River Valley above Anderson Lake. Crable was first documented in 1879, and the University of Chicago conducted limited excavations there in 1933, as did the University of Illinois-Chicago Circle in the late 1960s. One of the latest sites known in central Illinois, Crable has not only late Spoon River Mississippian but also intrusive Oneota Tradition (q.v.) cultural elements.
SOURCES: *History of Fulton County, Illinois,* 1879; H. G. Smith 1951b; Morse 1969; Harn 1978.

Duane Esarey

CRAB ORCHARD DISTRICT, a section along the upper Clinch River in southwestern Virginia where there are three related sites: a palisaded village dating ca. A.D. 1600, a rockshelter, and a vertical burial cave. The village site, excavated by H. A. MacCord in 1971 and by K. T. Egloff in 1978, had evidence of three palisade lines, a large semisubterranean structure, circular house patterns, storage pits, and human burials.

SOURCES: MacCord and Buchanan 1980; Egloff and Reed 1980; K. T. Egloff n.d.b.

Keith T. Egloff

CRAB ORCHARD TRADITION, a term variously applied to one or more archaeological cultures and/or to a ceramic tradition centered in extreme southern Illinois and extending slightly into adjacent parts of Missouri, Indiana, and Kentucky. The term derives ultimately from the Crab Orchard Focus in the Big Muddy River drainage, described in 1951 by M. S. Maxwell. As a ceramic tradition, Crab Orchard occurs in both the Early and Middle Woodland periods (ca. 600 B.C.–A.D. 400), but as a relatively distinct regional expression it is affiliated strictly with the Middle Woodland period (ca. 100 B.C.–A.D. 400). The ceramics typically are deep, grit- and/or clay-tempered, conoidal vessels with flat bases; vessel surfaces are cord marked and fabric impressed (actually impressed with cord-wrapped dowels).

SOURCES: Maxwell 1951; Struever and Houart 1972; Butler and Jefferies 1986.

Brian M. Butler

CRACK-IN-ROCK PUEBLO, a Kayenta Anasazi (q.v.) site about 70 kilometers northeast of Flagstaff, Arizona in the northernmost part of Wupatki National Monument, consisting of a sandstone-slab structure on a small mesa top, a series of contiguous rooms around the mesa's base, and sixteen petroglyph panels along the mesa's edge. Ceramic dates indicate that this Pueblo III Phase site was occupied ca. A.D. 1150–1200. When Watson Smith excavated a kiva and one room in 1948, he found a resonator (foot-drum) in the kiva floor and a heavy accumulation of trash, including several perishable items, in the room.

SOURCES: Colton 1946: 68–69; Watson Smith 1952a:70–76, 146–147.

Bruce Anderson

CRAIG MOUNTAIN PHASE, the earliest phase at the Weis Rockshelter (q.v.) in Idaho; associated with the Cascade type projectile point, the most diagnostic trait of the Old Cordilleran Culture (q.v.). B. R. Butler, who defined the phase, dated it at ca. 5500–1500 B.C., a date range inconsistent with similar assemblages of the region. Butler's dates are generally not accepted, and the Craig Mountain Phase is considered the equivalent of, and contemporary with, the Cascade, Vantage (qq.v.), and other similar phases in the southern Plateau.

SOURCES: B. R. Butler 1962; Ruebelmann 1978.

Frank C. Leonhardy

CRANE FLAT SITE, type site for the Crane Flat Complex, located on the west slope of the Sierra Nevada in Yosemite Valley, in California; excavated in 1964 by J. A. Bennyhoff. The complex is marked by manos and metates

for seed processing and by large dart points similar to Martis points for hunting. On the basis of a single radiocarbon date, R. N. Fitzwater proposed a date for the complex between A.D. 1 and A.D. 1000, but this has not been synchronized with the region at large.
SOURCES: Bennyhoff 1956; Fitzwater 1962.

Robert G. Elston

CRENSHAW SITE, earliest known Caddo ceremonial center, located in the Great Bend region of the Red River Valley in southwestern Arkansas. Ca. A.D. 700–900, it was a major Fourche Maline (q.v.) village with at least three mounds, four cemeteries, and several large midden areas. By A.D. 900–1100, it had evolved into a "vacant" Caddo I ceremonial center with six or more mounds and an "antler temple" containing a deposit of 2,042 antlers, indicating a major interest in deer ceremonialism in Caddo I times. Most major events in the genesis of Caddo culture probably are recorded archaeologically at Crenshaw.
SOURCE: Schambach 1982a:150–158.

Frank F. Schambach

CRIB MOUND, a well-known, multicomponent site buried in a bank of the Ohio River in Spencer County, in Indiana; first recorded in 1884, now largely destroyed by cutting action of the river. The most obvious feature was a Late Archaic shell mound, but later cultural deposits also were exposed in the nearly mile-long section of caving riverbank. A mecca for collectors, who came from the entire north-central United States area, Crib Mound produced many finds that were noted in amateur publications.
SOURCES: Kellar 1956; Scheidegger 1962, 1965, 1968; Gerber 1965, 1970; Meek 1969.

James H. Kellar

CROAKER LANDING SITE, a stratified site on the York River in the interior coastal plain of Virginia, containing artifacts and faunal remains from throughout the Woodland period. Excavated by W. E. Clark and K. T. Egloff in 1978, this is the type site for Croaker Landing Ware (q.v.)
SOURCE: Egloff, Norrisey Hodges, and McFaden n.d.

Keith T. Egloff

CROAKER LANDING WARE, a clay-tempered ceramic, either plain or cordmarked, with a flat rectanguloid or round base reminiscent of carved

Southeastern and Mid-Atlantic soapstone vessels; found in the southern coastal plain of Virginia and dating ca. 1200–800 B.C.

SOURCES: Egloff and Potter 1982; Egloff, Norrissey Hodges, and McFaden n.d.

Keith T. Egloff

CROSBY PHASE, the earlier of two phases belonging to the incompletely defined southern sector of the Middle Pecos Sub-Province of the Jornada Province, Mogollon Culture (qq.v.), in eastern New Mexico. As no sites have been excavated, the phase's distinguishing criteria are based upon surface ceramics and similarities with the Mesita Negra Phase (q.v.) of the northern sector. Thus, estimated dates of ca. A.D 1000–1200 are appropriate.

The Crosby ceramic assemblage is dominated by Roswell Brown (a Jornada Brown cognate) and Crosby Black-on-gray (a Chupadero Black-on-white cognate). Two types common to the subprovince's northern sector—Chupadero Black-on-white and Alma Plain—occur in small numbers.

SOURCE: Jelinek 1967.

R. N. Wiseman

CROW CREEK SITE, a two-component site in central South Dakota, excavated by the Nebraska Historical Society in the 1950s and by the University of South Dakota in 1978. The earlier component is an Initial Middle Missouri (q.v.) occupation dating ca. A.D. 1100; the later is an Initial Coalescent (q.v.) component dating ca. A.D. 1325. Visible on the surface is a bastioned fortification ditch nearly 400 meters long that protected the more than 50 earthlodges constituting the village. The 1978 excavations unearthed the remains of nearly 500 people, almost all of them scalped and mutilated, who had been thrown into one end of the fortification ditch. Radiocarbon dates and ceramics link the massacre to the Initial Coalescent occupation in the 14th century. Evidences of nutritional stress in the skeletons suggest that malnutrition and competition for scarce garden lands may have contributed to the massacre.

SOURCES: Kivett and Jensen 1976; Zimmerman et al. 1981.

Larry J. Zimmerman

CRYSTAL RIVER SITE, a multicomponent mound site lying just inland from the Gulf beach in Citrus County, Florida; excavated by C. B. Moore in 1903, 1906, and 1917 and by R. P. Bullen in 1951, 1960, 1964, and 1965. Major features include two burial mounds (one with a surrounding platform and embankment), two ramped mounds, possible plazas, two limestone stelae, shell mounds, and middens. Artifacts from the larger burial mound and its platform include Crystal River Pottery and objects of mica, copper, greenstone, and cut crystal. One stele was erected ca. A.D. 440; the date of the other stele is uncertain. The ramped mounds and the second burial mound date to the early Safety Harbor (q.v.) period (A.D. 1000–1200). The site probably was occupied continuously from A.D. 1 or earlier to ca. A.D. 1200.

SOURCES: C. B. Moore 1903:397–413, 1907:406–425, 1918:571–73; Willey 1949b; H. G. Smith 1951a; Bullen 1951a, 1953, 1966; Sears 1962:5–11.

Jerald T. Milanich

CRYSTAL II SITE, a two-component (late Dorset Phase and early Thule Phase [qq.v.]) settlement on the Sylvia Grinnell River near the present town of Frobisher Bay, Northwest Territories; partially excavated by H. B. Collins in 1950 and completed by a Michigan State University team in 1971. It was there that Collins first demonstrated the stratigraphic precedence of Dorset over Thule. In the Dorset component, 6 percent of the artifacts were spalled burins, a kind of tool that is not present in most Late Dorset assemblages. Typologically, the Thule component appears to be one of the earliest south of Lancaster Sound.

SOURCES: Collins 1950; Maxwell 1976b.

Moreau S. Maxwell

CUCHUJAQUI PHASE, the later phase (dating ca. A.D. 700–1530) of a two-phase sequence forming an unnamed complex in southern Sonora that is thought to be a foothill version of the Huatabampo Culture (q.v.) of the adjacent coastal plain. Sites of the phase are small, consisting of concentrations of sherds and lithic debris on terraces and bluffs overlooking the watercourses, each within easy reach of a portion of arable floodplain. No structural remains have been found, and it is presumed that dwellings were constructed of perishable material in the manner of houses recorded in the area in historic times, the most common type consisting of a wooden frame covered with mats.

Batacosa Brown and Cuchujaqui Red wares (qq.v.) are the dominant pottery types; intrusive sherds from Mesoamerican Sinaloa are found occasionally. Overhanging manos and both basin and flat-slab metates occur, reflecting both coastal and southern affiliations. Other artifacts include cutting implements of slaty shale, occasional stone axes and celts, shell ornaments, and a few stone blades and projectile points. Both inhumed and cremated burials occur.

SOURCES: Pailes 1972:330–338, 356–371, 1976.

Richard A. Pailes

CUCHUJAQUI RED WARE, a pottery type dating ca. A.D. 700–1530, diagnostic of the Cuchujaqui Phase (q.v.) of the lower foothills in southern

Sonora, where it is associated with intrusive ceramic types of the Mesoamerican Aztatlan Complex in Sinaloa.
SOURCE: Pailes 1972:221–224.

Richard A. Pailes

CUESTA PHASE, a Middle Woodland (ca. A.D. 500–1000), Hopewell-influenced cultural entity in the Osage Cuestas and Chautauqua Hills of southeastern Kansas. Type site is the Infinity Site (q.v.) in Montgomery County. Primarily hunters-gatherers (corn has been found at only one site), Cuesta people had contact with peoples of both the Cooper Hopewell to the south and the Kansas City Hopewell to the north. Large populations congregated in nucleated villages along major rivers; more dispersed populations lived in extended communities spread along smaller creek drainages.
SOURCES: J. O. Marshall 1972; Rowlison n.d.a., n.d.b.; Brogan 1981; Thies n.d.

Thomas A. Witty, Jr.

CUEVA DE LA ZONA DE DERRUMBES, a multicomponent site in southeastern Nuevo Leon containing stratified deposits spanning the period ca. 3000 B.C. to A.D. 1500. B. B. McClurkan's work there in the early 1960s resulted in a chronology of projectile points and other artifacts representative of local Archaic (q.v.) hunting-gathering peoples.
SOURCE: McClurkan 1966.

Edward B. Jelks

CULPEPPER SITE, a multicomponent site in Hopkins County, Texas comprising habitation areas and cemeteries of both the La Harpe Aspect (q.v.), dating ca. 2000–200 B.C., and Late Caddo (q.v.) peoples of ca. A.D 1400–1500. It was partially dug by A. T. Jackson in 1931.
SOURCE: Scurlock 1962.

James E. Corbin

CUMBERLAND POINT, a large, lanceolate, fluted, chipped-stone, Paleoindian projectile-point type with ears at the basal corners, dating ca. 9000–8000 B.C. and concentrated in the Ohio and Tennessee river drainages. It is thought to postdate the Clovis (q.v.) type.
SOURCES: Lewis and Kneberg 1951; Kneberg 1956:22; Bell 1960:22–23; Cambron and Hulse 1961, 1964:30, 1975:36.

Jefferson Chapman and Eugene M. Futato

CUMBERLAND SOUND SITES, a sequence of sites at Cumberland Sound on the southeastern coast of Baffin Island, Northwest Territories, where excavations by Peter Schledermann in 1970 demonstrated cultural differ-

ences between the Baleen Period (q.v.) and the post-Baleen Period of the Thule Phase.
SOURCE: Schledermann 1975.

Moreau S. Maxwell

CURRY SITE, a multicomponent site in the Verdigris River valley of eastern Kansas comprising a deeply buried Archaic component, a Pomona Focus (q.v.) component, and a large Greenwood Phase (q.v.) village of Plains Woodland affinity. Excavations at the latter in 1963 and 1966 by T. A. Witty, Jr., revealed part of an oval house structure and a small cemetery complex with grave goods including marine gastropod beads. A radiocarbon sample from the burials dated A.D. 380 ± 230.
SOURCES: Calabrese 1967; Witty 1982.

Thomas A. Witty, Jr.

CUSTER PHASE, an early (ca. A.D. 800–1100) Plains Village complex centered around southwestern Oklahoma that developed from southern Woodland complexes and was ancestral to the historic Wichita or a related tribe. Diagnostic artifacts are Stafford Cordmarked and Stafford Plain pottery and Scallorn, Fresno, and Washita projectile points.
SOURCE: Hofman 1984.

Patricia J. O'Brien

CUTLER MOUND AND VILLAGE SITE, type site of the Waukesha Focus (q.v.) that, when first reported by Increase Lapham in 1854, comprised fourteen large, conical mounds with submound chambers and associated rock features. Artifacts from the mounds included dentate-stamped pottery and a stone pipe. Later work at related sites by W. C. McKern and by R. J. Salzer helped establish a framework of Havana-related and post-Havana Middle Woodland cultures in southern Wisconsin.
SOURCES: Lapham 1854; McKern 1942:153–169, 1945; Salzer n.d.a.

David Overstreet

C. W. HARRIS SITE, a stratified, multicomponent site in southwestern California containing key units of the region's archaeological sequence: a San Dieguito unit (ca. 7000 B.C.), a La Jolla unit (ca. 4350 B.C.), and a Diegueño unit (ca. A.D. 1770).
SOURCES: C. N. Warren 1966; Moratto 1984:97–99.

Michael J. Moratto

CYLINDER JAR, a rare pottery vessel form diagnostic of the Bonito Phase of the Chaco Province (qq.v.) in northwestern New Mexico, most examples of which have been found at Pueblo Bonito (q.v.) in Chaco Canyon. Averaging 24 centimeters high and 10 centimeters in diameter, these vessels have small lugs near their rims, show considerable variation in details of construction and firing, and, when decorated, exhibit a variety of geometric designs painted with mineral or organic pigments, e.g., simple concentric bands, running panels of hachuring, and broad solid-line patterns. They have been interpreted as grave goods, as ceremonial paraphernalia, and as cached symbols of participation in the Chacoan system.

SOURCES: Pepper 1920; Judd 1954.

Peter J. McKenna

D

DALLAS CULTURE, a late (ca. A.D. 1300–1600) Mississippian (q.v.) manifestation in eastern Tennessee, defined from excavations in the Tennessee River Valley, especially at the Dallas, Hixon, and Hiwassee Island sites.
SOURCES: Lewis and Kneberg 1946; Polhemus 1985.

Jefferson Chapman

DALLES SEQUENCE, a temporally ordered series of cultures based on excavations at several sites at The Dalles, a five-mile stretch of rapids on the Columbia River where it cuts through the Cascade Range, about 180 miles from the Pacific coast. For thousands of years, Native Americans visited The Dalles seasonally to harvest the salmon that congest there in vast quantities during their annual upstream migration.

Tens of thousands of salmon bones were found at the earliest known (ca. 8000–6000 B.C.) component, in the basal level of the Roadcut Site, along with a rich mammal and bird fauna; large, lanceolate, chipped-stone projectile points; a variety of other chipped- and ground-stone tools; and a bone/antler industry that includes atlatl spurs and barbed spear points. The next occupation of record, probably dating ca. 6000–4000 B.C. is the early component at the Indian Well Site, which yielded a variety of chipped-stone tools, including large, lanceolate, projectile points.

The period 4000–500 B.C. is poorly known because no components of that age have been scientifically excavated; however, several components with large and remarkably varied inventories of flaked and ground-stone artifacts probably date in this interval. For later occupation of The Dalles region, Richard Pettigrew, in 1981, postulated a Merrybell phase (ca. 600 B.C.–A.D. 200) and a Multnomah phase (ca. A.D. 200–1830). Energized by the prodigious supply of salmon (and other food resources), networks of diffusion and trade already established were further enhanced during the Multnomah phase. Well-documented ethnohistorically, the cultural vigor and widespread relationships of The Dalles region are attested archaeologically in both the artifact types and the distinctive art style. The latter apparently owed much of its inspiration to the Northwest coast, but the media on which it occurred and the forms which it took were characteristically Lower Columbian and were epitomized at The Dalles.

The outstanding Multnomah site was Wakemap, an artificial mound some 30 feet high which was occupied by Chinookan-speaking people living in wood-plank houses when visited by Lewis and Clark in 1805. Archaeological excavations there have revealed the following sequence:

Wakemap I (mid–9th to early 14th century) with rectangular, wood-framed, mat-sided houses; well-developed fishing equipment; and carvings of stone and antler.

Wakemap II (early 14th to mid–18th century), a continuation of Wakemap I with additions such as a dice game borrowed from the Southwest; modelled and incised clay bowls and clay figurines, sometimes fired; and cremation burials, often richly furnished. It was during this period that antler and stone carving reached its apogee—as characterized by such motifs as the grinning face, rib, and nucleated joint—skillfully executed on small objects of antler and stone. Thereafter, the sites reveal intrusion of European goods, a decline in the art, and eventual abandonment.

SOURCES: Strong et al. 1940; B. R. Butler 1957, 1959, 1965a; Cressman et al. 1960; Pettigrew 1981.

Robert E. Greengo

DALTON CULTURE, an Early Archaic culture of the southeastern United States during ca. 8500–7500 B.C. Its diagnostic trait is the Dalton-type dart point (q.v.), which occurs in association with end scrapers and other unifacial stone tools, as well as with a variety of battered and abraded cobble tools and woodworking adzes of chipped stone. Dalton components have been excavated at Graham Cave and Rodgers Shelter in Missouri, at the Brand and Sloan sites in Arkansas, and at the Stanfield-Worley Rockshelter in Alabama (qq.v.).

SOURCES: C. H. Chapman 1948; Logan 1952; De Jarnette et al. 1962; Goodyear 1974; Wood and McMillan 1976; Morse and Morse 1983.

Dan F. Morse

DALTON POINT, an Early Archaic (ca. 8500–7500 B.C.), medium-sized, lanceolate, chipped-stone projectile-point type with a heavily ground, rectangular or auriculate haft element. The blade often exhibits reduction, serration, and/or beveling from extensive rejuvenation. Dalton occurs over most of the central and lower Mississippi valley and the Southeast.

SOURCES: DeJarnette et al. 1962; Coe 1964; Goodyear 1974; C. H. Chapman 1975; Wood and McMillan 1976; Brookes 1979.

Eugene M. Futato

DANGER CAVE, a dry, stratified cave on the western margin of the Great Salt Lake Desert in Utah, containing Paleoindian, Archaic, Sevier/Fremont (qq.v.), and protohistoric components. First investigated by Elmer Smith in the early 1940s, it was excavated extensively by J. D. Jennings in the early 1950s. Radiocarbon dates of 10,000–9000 B.C. on the earliest cultural strata were, at the time, some of the earliest dates on cultural deposits in the New World. Danger Cave served as the basis for Jennings' definition of the Desert Culture (q.v.). The early dates on some artifact types originally were controversial, as was Jennings' conclusion that all the occupants of the site, over many millenia, maintained the same adaptive hunting/gathering subsistence strategy; both the early dates and Jennings' interpretation have since been confirmed.
SOURCE: Jennings 1957.

David B. Madsen

DAN RIVER POTTERY SERIES, a ceramic complex originally identified with the 17th-century Sara Indians along the Virginia–North Carolina boundary, but now known to have a wide distribution in the central Piedmont. It is estimated to date ca. A.D. 1000–1725. Net-impressed surface finishes predominate, although plain, corncob-roughened, cordmarked, brushed, and complicated-stamped treatments occur. Vessel forms include globular jars and bowls with slightly everted rims, conoidal or rounded bases, and, sometimes, strap handles. Decorations may appear as notching or incising at the lip or as a horizontal band of incised or punctated elements on a smoothed or scraped area of the neck. A gradual transition is evinced from the Uwharrie Series (q.v.) to the Dan River Series.
SOURCE: Coe and Lewis 1952.

Billy L. Oliver

DARL POINT. See Mahomet Point.

DAUGHERTY'S CAVE, a deeply stratified site in the Clinch River drainage of southwestern Virginia, tested in 1967 by J. L. Benthall and in 1982–1983 by P. S. Gardner. The eight feet of deposits contained well-preserved faunal and charred floral remains. The lowest level, radiocarbon dated to 7840 B.C., contained a Kirk Corner-Notched point (q.v.); the higher levels

produced a sequence of Archaic and Woodland materials dating up to A.D. 1000.
SOURCES: Benthall n.d.; K. T. Egloff n.d.b.

Keith T. Egloff

DAWS ISLAND SITE, a location in Port Royal Sound, Beaufort County, South Carolina where large quantities of pottery, lithics, worked bone, and baked clay balls are eroding onto the beach from a buried, inundated midden. Surface collections and several salvaged, Late Archaic–Early Woodland burials indicate affiliation with the Stallings and Thom's Creek phases (qq.v.).
SOURCES: Hemmings 1969; Brockington 1971a; Michie 1973, 1974; Trinkley 1980a.

Michael Trinkley

DAXATKANADA, an early historic Tlingit fort near Angoon, Alaska, tested in 1949 and 1950 by Frederica de Laguna as part of a coordinated archaeological/ethnological research program among the northern Tlingit. These earliest controlled archaeological excavations in southeastern Alaska produced a wide variety of bone dart or harpoon heads, heavy woodworking implements, and a scattering of chipped- and ground-stone artifacts.
SOURCE: de Laguna 1960.

Gerald H. Clark

DEBERT SITE, a large Paleoindian (q.v.) site in southwestern Nova Scotia, dating ca. 8600 B.C.. Artifacts from the site include peculiar fluted points with deeply indented bases; bifacially flaked knives, scrapers, drills, pieces esquilles (wedges?), and other chipped-stone tools. These materials were clustered in a number of discrete loci believed to be dwelling sites and in an area where lithic "tempering" was an important activity. Debert is believed to have been a late fall/winter station situated to take advantage of migrating caribou.
SOURCE: MacDonald 1968.

James A. Tuck

DEEP BOTTOM SITE, a site on the James River in the interior coastal plain of Virginia, occupied from the Middle Archaic through the Woodland period. Tested in 1967 by W. T. Buchanan and again in 1970 by J. Harper, it yielded especially important information on Late Archaic and Middle Woodland cultures.
SOURCES: Buchanan 1969; Mouer 1984.

Keith T. Egloff

DEEP CREEK PHASE, an Early Woodland expression on the northern coastal plain of North Carolina dating ca. 1000–300 B.C. and characterized by Deep Creek pottery series (q.v.). This poorly understood phase may be

associated with Stallings Plain fiber-tempered and Marcey Creek Plain (qq.v.) steatite-tempered wares, and with Roanoke Large Triangular (q.v.) and Gypsy Stemmed projectile points.
SOURCE: Phelps 1983:29–30.

Billy L. Oliver

DEEP CREEK POTTERY SERIES, a coarse, sand-tempered ware dating ca. 1000–300 B.C. that is distributed over the north coastal region of North Carolina, where it is the main pottery of the Deep Creek Phase (q.v.). Surfaces are cordmarked, net impressed, fabric impressed, or, rarely, plain; vessels are conoidal or, occasionally, flat-bottomed. The series may correlate with Stony Creek Ware of southeastern Virginia.
SOURCE: Phelps 1983:29–30.

Billy L. Oliver

DEL MAR SKELETON, portions of a human skeleton of controversial age unearthed by M. J. Rogers in 1929 at Del Mar, near San Diego, California. Attention was drawn to the skeleton in 1973 when it was assigned an age of 41,000–48,000 years on the basis of amino acid racemization data. Later, it was dated by radiocarbon analysis to ca. 3500 B.C.
SOURCES: S. L. Rogers 1974; Bada et al. 1974; Taylor et al. 1985.

R. E. Taylor and L. A. Payen

DELMARVA-ADENA PHASE, an Early Woodland (ca. A.D. 200) manifestation in the Delaware and Chesapeake river drainages, characterized by an exotic mortuary complex involving a wide variety of interment types, including cremation, bundling, and a multiple curation procedure. A diagnostic trait of the phase is the burial of grave goods acquired from the Adena Culture (q.v.) of the Midwest.
SOURCES: R. A. Thomas 1970; Custer 1984:113–130.

Ronald A. Thomas

DENALI COMPLEX, a classifactory construct proposed by Frederick Hadleigh West in the 1960s for interior Alaskan blade and microblade industries with wedge-shaped cores, dating between 1,500 and 11,000 years ago. Present usage differs among archaeologists: E. J. Dixon, for example, sees Denali as a regional form of the Paleo-Arctic Tradition but also recognizes a "Late Denali" of ca. 1500 B.C.–A.D. 500 that is separated from Denali by the Northern Archaic Tradition (q.v.). Related constructs include the Northwest Microblade and the American Paleo-Arctic traditions (qq.v.). In a broad frame of reference, Hadleigh West interpreted Denali as part of an

early Beringian tradition tying together the Asian and North American continents (see Northwest Microblade Tradition).
SOURCES: Hadleigh West 1967, 1975, 1981; Dixon 1985.

Donald W. Clark

DENBIGH FLINT COMPLEX, a regional manifestation of the Arctic Small Tool Tradition (q.v.), dating ca. 2200–1600 B.C., found in numerous coastal and interior components in northwestern Alaska. It was discovered in 1948 by J. L. Giddings beneath Norton Phase occupation levels at the Iyatayet Site (q.v.) on Cape Denbigh. Consisting of a microblade industry, burins, and exquisitely flaked, tiny points (end blades) and lateral insets (side blades), the complex is considered ancestral Eskimo by most archaeologists. Similar but not identical artifacts, from which Denbigh technology may have derived, occur in northeastern Asia.
SOURCES: Giddings 1951, 1964, 1967.

Donald W. Clark

DENETASIRO TRADITION, a now little-used term, introduced in 1964 by R. S. MacNeish, that is largely equivalent to the northern Athapaskan Tradition (q.v.).
SOURCE: MacNeish 1964.

Donald W. Clark

DENT SITE, the location, near Dent, Colorado, of the first unmistakable, generally accepted association of a fluted projectile point (Clovis type [q.v.]) with articulated mammoth bones, discovered in 1932 by J. D. Figgins. Ultimately, the remains of twelve individual mammoths were unearthed, mostly females and immature animals. Later analyses revealed that the animals died naturally and, therefore, that the site was not a kill site. Thus, some of the mammoths must have escaped after being wounded by hunters, carrying off the spear points in their bodies.
SOURCES: Wormington 1957; Cassells 1983.

Patricia J. O'Brien

DEPTFORD CULTURE, an Early to Middle Woodland (ca. 500 B.C.–A.D. 500) expression found throughout the coastal plain and into the lower Piedmont of Georgia and South Carolina. Defined in the 1930s by Preston Holder, A. J. Waring, and J. R. Caldwell, the culture has been studied more recently by J. T. Milanich, D. H. Thomas, and C. S. Larsen. Associated artifacts include sand- and grit-tempered pottery (often check stamped), triangular and small-stemmed projectile points, and poorly developed shell and bone industries. Small camps, probable base camps, and large coastal shell middens are the common site types.

SOURCES: J. R. Caldwell 1943; Milanich 1971b; Thomas and Larsen 1979.

Michael Trinkley

DEPTFORD POTTERY SERIES, a sand-tempered ware distributed along the coastal plain of Georgia, northern Florida, and southern Alabama, dating to Early and Middle Woodland times (ca. 400 B.C.-A.D. 100). It often took the form of conoidal jars, frequently with tetrapodal supports. Carved wooden paddles were used to impress the vessels' exterior surfaces with simple- or check-stamped patterns.

SOURCE: Griffin and Sears 1950.

John A. Walthall

DESERT CULTURE, a widespread, long-lived expression of the Archaic tradition in the Great Basin, defined by J. D. Jennings in the 1950s, largely on the basis of his excavations at Danger (q.v.) and Juke Box caves on the Utah-Nevada border. Jennings proposed that the prehistory of the Great Basin was dominated by this single culture which, with minor exceptions, remained stable and virtually unchanged from ca. 8000 B.C. to the 20th century, despite small-scale differences in local environments and changes in climate. He viewed the culture as the archaeological expression of the same basic lifeway that J. H. Steward and others had observed ethnographically among modern groups of the region, the twin material hallmarks of the culture being basketry and milling stones. Later Jennings redefined the Desert Culture as the western expression of a continent-wide Archaic stage in which a broad subsistence base and adaptive efficiency are central themes. The specifics of the older Dessert Culture concept have largely been discarded, but many still accept the idea that Great Basin adaptation was stable over long periods and that seasonal transhumance was basic to this adaptation.

SOURCES: Jennings 1957, 1964; Jennings and Norbeck 1955.

Robert L. Bettinger

DESERT SIDE-NOTCHED POINT, a type of small, triangular, chipped-stone projectile point with side notches found throughout the Desert West, dating from ca. A.D. 1300 to the historic period.

SOURCES: Baumhoff and Byrne 1959; D. H. Thomas 1981.

David Hurst Thomas

DE SHAZO SITE, a multicomponent site in Nacogdoches County, Texas, excavated by D. A. Story in 1975–1976. A small Early Ceramic Period (q.v.) occupation, dating ca. A.D. 600 preceded a very late (ca. A.D. 1500) Caddoan (Allen Phase, q.v.) village and adjacent cemetery. The village contained at

least ten structures and three burials; at the cemetery, nine burials were discovered, four of them containing European trade goods.
SOURCE: Story and Creel 1982.

James E. Corbin

DESHAZO SITE, a late prehistoric—early historic village of the Algonkian-speaking Cuttawomen II chiefdom, on the left bank of the Rappahannock River, in Virginia. Probably one of the villages documented by Captain John Smith in A.D. 1609, the site was visited by D. I. Bushnell in the 1930s and was tested by H. A. MacCord in 1964 and 1972.
SOURCES: Bushnell 1937:60–62; MacCord 1965:98–104.

Stephen R. Potter

DEVELOPMENTAL PERIOD, ANASAZI CULTURE, the earliest (A.D. 500–1150/1200) of the three main periods of the Rio Grande Anasazi, characterized by sparse population and scattered, small pithouse sites on terraces overlooking the Rio Grande and its major tributaries in New Mexico. The earliest pottery in the Albuquerque area was a brownware in the Mogollon (q.v.) tradition, but iron-paint black-on-white and plain gray culinary pottery in the San Juan Anasazi tradition had gained dominance by A.D. 800.

By the middle of the Developmental Period, strong Chacoan influence was present at the Pojoaque Grant Site (q.v.) north of Santa Fe, where surface dwellings with coursed-adobe or jacal walls were being built. In the peripheral Northern Rio Grande Province, pithouses seem to have survived longer, perhaps because of the harsher winters. The Pajarito Plateau and lower Rio Chama Valley were largely vacant at this time. Late Developmental sites have been noted in the Albuquerque area which show strong influence from the Rio Abajo (q.v.) and Acoma provinces.
SOURCES: Mera 1935; Stubbs 1954; Allen and McNutt 1955; Peckham 1954; 1957; Peckham and Reed 1963; Schorsch 1962; S. A. Skinner 1965; Frisbie 1967; Bussey 1968; Ferg 1983.

Stewart Peckham

DEVIL BLISS BRIDGE SITE, a Late Woodland village on the Monocacy River, Maryland, dating to the 12th century A.D. Tests in 1976 by D.W. Peck and T. Bastian revealed that the major occupation was by people of the Montgomery Complex (q.v.).
SOURCES: Peck and Bastian 1977:1–10; Kavanagh 1982.

Stephen R. Potter

DEVILS MOUTH SITE, a deeply stratified campsite buried in an alluvial terrace at the confluence of the Devils River and the Rio Grande in Val Verde County, in western Texas, now under the waters of Lake Amistad.

Excavations there by LeRoy Johnson, Jr., and W. M. Sorrow in the 1960s exposed 24 distinct strata containing many artifacts along with hearths, scatters of burned limestone rocks, bedrock mortars, and other features. Occupied from terminal Paleoindian (q.v.) through late prehistoric times (ca. 6000 B.C.–A.D. 1200), the site produced abundant information that was critical to the development of a regional culture history and to the clarification of relationships between the lower Pecos River, central Texas, and eastern Trans-Pecos regions.

SOURCES: LeRoy Johnson, Jr. 1964; Sorrow 1968:1–70.

Robert J. Mallouf

DEVILS ROCKSHELTER, a small, stratified shelter on the Rio Grande near the mouth of the Devils River in western Texas, where excavations by E. R. Prewitt exposed successive Early Archaic occupations spanning the period ca. 6000–4000 B.C.

SOURCES: Prewitt 1966; Dibble and Prewitt 1967.

Elton R. Prewitt

DIABLO CANYON SITES, a series of coastal archaeological sites in San Luis Obispo County, in California that span nearly 9000 years of prehistory and document the evolution of coastal cultural adaptations in south-central California. The sites were excavated by R. S. Greenwood in 1968 and 1969.

SOURCES: Greenwood 1972; Moratto 1984:107–109, 162–163.

Michael J. Moratto

DIABLO PHASE. See Casas Grandes Province.

DIAMOND BLUFF SITE, a large mound group and village situated atop a high terrace overlooking the Mississippi River near Diamond Bluff, Wisconsin where in 1943 M. S. Maxwell found Mississippian/Oneota ceramics within the fill of a panther-effigy mound. Excavations by R. Alex in 1976 established the presence of both Silvernale and Orr phase occupations at the site.

SOURCES: Maxwell 1950; R. L. Hall 1962.

David Overstreet

DIANA BAY SITES, a group of sites on the northern coast of Ungava, Quebec, excavated in the 1970s by the Tuvaaluk Project (q.v.), which demonstrated a late persistence of the Dorset Phase at that locality to the 15th

century A.D. The occurrence in single houses of both Dorset and Thule traits suggests contact between the two cultures.
SOURCE: Plumet 1979.

                                                                    Moreau S. Maxwell

DICKSON MOUNDS SITE, a large, late prehistoric burial complex in the central Illinois River Valley near the confluence of the Illinois and Spoon rivers that has an estimated burial population of 3,000 individuals. Partially excavated by the Dickson family in 1927 and displayed commercially to the public for many years, the mounds are now a branch of the Illinois State Museum. The site was used as a burial ground for centuries, beginning before A.D. 800 in the early Late Woodland period and continuing through Larson Phase Mississippian after A.D. 1250. Recent excavations at Dickson in the late 1960s by Illinois State Museum archaeologists have led to the development of a cultural framework for assessing indigenous Late Woodland and intrusive early Mississippian relationships pertaining to the emergence of Mississippian culture on the northern Cahokian frontier. The framework weighs culture changes and continuities at the site against sociopolitical adjustments, nutrition, and stress.
SOURCES: Blakely 1973; Harn 1975:414–434, 1980; Lallo et al. 1980; Goodman and Armelagos 1985.

                                                                    Alan D. Harn

DILLINGER FOCUS, a terminal Late Woodland/Emergent Mississippian manifestation, estimated to date ca. A.D. 800–1000, in western areas of extreme southern Illinois and in the Mississippi River floodplain and adjacent upland fringes of eastern Missouri. It was defined by Moreau Maxwell in 1951. Dillinger ceramics are grog tempered and predominantly cordmarked. Particularly characteristic are thick rimfolds and peaked and castellated rims with small lugs. The type site for the focus is the Dillinger Site, located just north of Carbonale, Illinois.
SOURCE: Maxwell 1951.

                                                                    Brian M. Butler

DIRTY SHAME ROCKSHELTER, a dry shelter in extreme southeastern Oregon that was occupied between 7500 B.C. and A.D. 1800; excavated by D. L. Cole in 1973. Abandoned during a mid-postglacial interval of decreased effective moisture, the shelter was reoccupied after some 3000 years by people of the same cultural tradition as before, as indicated by distinctive types of basketry, sandals, and other artifacts. Detailed studies of the artifactual, faunal, and floral remains indicate that the shelter served as a hunting-gathering station—and, in late prehistoric times, possibly as a winter encampment—for groups of people who ranged widely in the region where the modern states of Oregon, Idaho, and Nevada come together.

Throughout the period of record, the natural environment in the site's vicinity was dry and desertlike, as it is today, and subsistence was based on small game, occasional large game (including antelope and deer), and wild plant foods.

SOURCES: Aikens et al. 1977; Hanes 1980; Sanford 1983; Andrews et al. 1986.

C. Melvin Aikens

DISMAL RIVER ASPECT, a culture complex defined by J. H. Gunnerson, consisting of the Stinking Water Focus in western Nebraska and an undefined focus in western Kansas associated with the El Cuartelejo Site. The aspect dates to a 50-year period around A.D. 1700 and is associated with the historic Plains Apache.

SOURCE: Gunnerson 1960.

Patricia J. O'Brien

DISMAL II SITE, the most westerly known Dorset Phase site of the mainland, located on Dismal Lake 80 kilometers inland and 32 kilometers west of the Coppermine River, Northwest Territories. A small assemblage of lithic tools unearthed there by Elmer Harp, Jr., was typologically attributable to the initial eastward Pre-Dorset migration.

SOURCE: Harp 1958.

Moreau S. Maxwell

DODEMANSBUKGT SITE, a single-house complex on Clavering Island, eastern Greenland, where excavations by H.-G. Bandi and Jørgen Meldgaard produced a peculiar assemblage of artifacts suggesting contact between local Late Dorset residents and Thule people coming around the northern Greenland coast.

SOURCE: Bandi and Meldgaard 1952.

Moreau S. Maxwell

DODGE ISLAND SITE, a multi-occupation shell midden on Dodge Island, a short distance from Digby Island in Prince Rupert Harbour, in northern British Columbia. Excavated by G. F. MacDonald in 1967, the site produced a wide range of lithic and organic artifacts, a variety of vertebrate and invertebrate fauna, and human burials representing at least twenty individuals. Evidently, there were two prehistoric components at the site, spanning Period III (3000–1500 B.C.) and most of Period II (1500 B.C.–A.D. 500) of the Prince Rupert Harbour sequence (q.v.).

SOURCE: P. D. Sutherland n.d.

Patricia D. Sutherland

DOERSCHUK SITE, a deeply stratified, multicomponent site on the Yadkin River in Montgomery County, in North Carolina, excavated by J. L. Coe in 1948–1949. The culture chronology at the site, when combined with that at the nearby Hardaway Site (q.v.), provided an unbroken sequence of more than 12,000 years. The Stanly, Morrow Mountain, Guilford, Savannah River, Badin, Yadkin, Pee Dee, and Caraway complexes were all represented at Doerschuk. The earliest occurrence to date (1987) of a semilunar atlatl weight in the eastern United States was in the Stanly component. The site appeared to have functioned as a camp and lithic quarry during all occupations.

SOURCES: Coe 1964; Oliver 1981.

Billy L. Oliver

DOG BIGHT SITE, one of the earliest (ca. 1860 B.C.) radiocarbon dated (on wood) Pre-Dorset (q.v.) sites, located near Nain on the central Labrador coast. Excavations by the Torngat Project revealed dwellings with mid-passages, suggesting an Independence I (q.v.) relationship.

SOURCE: Cox 1978.

Moreau S. Maxwell

DOMEBO SITE, a mammoth kill in southwestern Oklahoma, excavated in 1962 by an interdisciplinary team of archaeologists, zoologists, geologists, and soil scientists. It is not clear whether the Clovis projectile points (q.v.) found with the animal caused its death, but it was obvious that the 11,200-year-old mammoth had been butchered. The site produced significant information about the late Pleistocene environment of the locality, as well as about the hunting activities of the Clovis Culture (q.v.).

SOURCE: Leonhardy 1966.

Patricia J. O'Brien

DONA ANA PHASE, the second phase, following the Mesilla Phase, of the El Paso Sub-Province of the Jornada Province, Mogollon Culture (qq.v.), dating ca. A.D. 1100–1200 and occupying south-central New Mexico and adjacent parts of Texas and Chihuahua. During the phase, there was a transition from pithouses to pueblos as the principal form of dwelling; both pithouses and small clusters of surface or pueblo rooms sometimes occurred in the same site.

Very little is known about the phase because few sites have been recorded; however, Dona Ana sites are more common in some areas (e.g., the southern Tularosa Basin) than in others. Painted, locally made pottery (El Paso Black-on-brown, El Paso Red-on-brown, and early varieties of El Paso Poly-chrome) became more common. Intrusive pottery from the Mimbres Province to the west and from areas to the north and east appear frequently but never in large numbers. Subsistence practices are assumed to have continued from the preceding late Mesilla Phase.

SOURCES: Lehmer 1948; LeBlanc and Whalen 1980.

R. N. Wiseman

DONNAHA SITE, a stratified site on the Yadkin River in Yadkin County, North Carolina, containing components of the Uwharrie and Dan River phases and dating ca. A.D. 1000–1500. J. N. Woodall's excavations there between 1974 and 1983 exposed numerous features, burials, and excellently preserved floral and faunal remains.

SOURCE: Woodall 1984.

Billy L. Oliver

DORSET PHASE, a distinctive phase of the Canadian Arctic region, distributed from Banks Island on the west to Newfoundland and parts of both coasts of Greenland on the east; viewed by many as a continuum from the Pre-Dorset Phase, but with distinctive adaptive changes, possibly to increasingly cold climates. The phase appeared ca. 600 B.C. and had disappeared by ca. A.D. 1000 except in coastal Quebec and Labrador, where it remained a viable entity until the 15th century. Dwellings were shallow pithouses, sod houses, and surface tents. Lithic tools were small, with some continuation of Pre-Dorset styles. Polished burin-like tools and tip-fluted end blades were new, typically Dorset lithic implements. The phase is noted for its small-scale, magico-religious art forms. A sequence of toggling harpoon-head types differentiates the following temporal sequences.

Early Dorset (ca. 600–300 B.C.), defined by distinctive harpoon heads with narrow slices in the dorsal surfaces of their sockets. During this period, ice-hunting gear (sled shoes, snow knives, ice creepers) appear while such Pre-Dorset traits as bows and arrows and drills disappear.

Middle Dorset (ca. 300 B.C.–A.D. 400), marked by the complete closing of harpoon-head sockets. There were other distinctive changes in the material culture, including pithouses with tunnel entries on North Baffin Island, Melville Peninsula, and Labrador. An unstable climatic sequence of alternately colder and warmer periods may have led to a population decrease over much of the eastern Arctic during this period, even though there was an increase on coastal Labrador and Newfoundland.

Late Dorset (ca. A.D. 400–1000), distinguished by double-line-hole harpoon heads and other attributes. During this "Golden Age," which came to a close with the Thule Phase (q.v.) invasion, Dorset peoples spread out over a wide geographic area, particularly into the High Arctic region, and they increased their production of magico-religious objects.

Terminal Dorset (ca. A.D. 1000–1450, with vestiges possibly continuing into the 20th century). Archaeological evidence of Terminal Dorset is restricted to Labrador and coastal Quebec where populations may have been

large enough to resist Thule settlement. This part of the phase, although not well defined, includes dwellings with both Dorset and Thule features. There is weak evidence of Norse contact.
SOURCES: McGhee 1978:52–73; Maxwell 1985: 127–245.

Moreau S. Maxwell

DOVER CHERT, a distinctive, homogeneous, cryptocrystalline stone, non-lustrous and gray to dun in color, with subglobular and streaked black or gray vitreous inclusions. Deriving from the lower St. Louis geological formation, it was quarried extensively by aboriginal peoples near Dover, Tennessee and made into ceremonial chipped-stone eccentrics (bipointed swords, maces, batons, hooks, etc.) that were distributed among the elite at Mississippian mound centers throughout the Southeast.
SOURCES: Thruston 1897; C. K. Peacock 1954; Kellberg 1963.

Jefferson Chapman

DOX PHASE. See Unkar Chronology.

DRAGOON CULTURE. See San Pedro Province.

DRIFTWOOD PHASE, terminal Archaic (q.v.) phase in central Texas, dating ca. A.D. 550–700; defined by E. R. Prewitt in 1981. Most components are in rockshelters, but there are some open sites on stream terraces. Basin-shaped hearths, burned-clay lenses, various forms of pits, scatters of burned stones, and isolated flexed burials are common features. The Darl-type projectile point—renamed Mahomet (q.v.) by Prewitt—is the principal diagnostic. Some Darl (or Mahomet) points are small enough to suggest use on arrows instead of spears. Other frequently found artifacts are various kinds of bifaces and unifaces, gravers, grinding stones, bone tools of several forms, and ornaments of shell and bone. Major excavated sites include Loeve-Fox (q.v.), Williams, and Hoxie Bridge.
SOURCES: Suhm 1959:227–234; Bond 1978:154–157; Prewitt 1981:82, 1982a:230–263.

Frank A. Weir

DRY CREEK SITE, a multicomponent site in central Alaska discovered by C. E. Holmes in 1974 and excavated by W. R. Powers in 1974 and 1976–1977. Occupied ca. 9200–1500 B.C., Dry Creek placed on a more certain basis the knowledge of early peoples in interior Alaska. Dry Creek I (radiocarbon dated to ca. 9200 B.C.) is characterized by small bifaces (probably projectile points), microblades being absent. In the principal occupation, Dry Creek II (radiocarbon dated to ca. 8800 B.C.), microblades are common, as are leaf-shaped points (which analysis of wear marks indicates were used as knives) and other bifacial implements. An overlying minor Northern

Archaic occupation dating ca. 2800–1400 B.C. is distinguished by waisted points.

SOURCES: Powers and Hamilton 1978; Powers et al. n.d.

Donald W. Clark

DUBAWNT SITE, a multi-occupation site containing a rare interior component of the Canadian Tundra Taiga Tradition (q.v.); situated on Dubawnt Lake, west of Baker Lake in the District of Keewatin, Northwest Territories.

SOURCE: Gordon 1975.

Moreau S. Maxwell

DUMAW CREEK SITE, a protohistoric Peninsular Woodland (q.v.) site located along the shore of Lake Michigan in Oceana County, in Michigan. Probably occupied by Potawatomi, it has produced a large collection of early 17th-century Terminal Late Woodland artifacts, including organic materials.

SOURCE: Quimby 1966a.

Charles E. Cleland

DUNLAP SITE, a multicomponent site on a cutoff of the Pee Dee River in Darlington County, in South Carolina, explored briefly by Chester DePratter in 1985. The major component appears to be a Yadkin Phase village, although a small Pee Dee hamlet may also be present. DePratter recorded a large number of postholes and intact features, including a burial.

SOURCE: DePratter 1985a.

Michael Trinkley

DURST ROCKSHELTER, one of several stratified rockshelters in central Wisconsin excavated by W. L. Wittry in the 1950s; the basis for Archaic and Woodland (qq.v.) sequences in the region. Lithics from the site include the type sample for the Durst Stemmed type projectile point.

SOURCE: Wittry 1959b.

David Overstreet

E

EARLY BOREAL, a name applied by C. E. Borden to the earliest known cultural tradition in the northern Northwest Coast-Arctic region, distinguished by a microblade technology; called the Microblade Tradition by R. L. Carlson, the Northwest Microblade Tradition by R. S. MacNeish, and the Early Coast Microblade Complex by K. R. Fladmark. It contrasts with the earliest southern Northwest Coast cultural tradition—referred to by Borden as the Protowestern and by others as the Old Cordilleran (B. R. Butler in part; R. G. Matson), Lithic (D. H. Mitchell), or Pebble Tool Tradition (R. L. Carlson)—in which microblade technology is absent. D. E. Dumond and other Arctic specialists use the name Paleo-Arctic Tradition, identified by the presence of wedge-shaped microblade cores, for the northern part of Early Boreal.
    SOURCES: B. R. Butler 1961; MacNeish 1964; Mitchell 1971; Fladmark 1975; Dumond 1977; Borden 1979; R. L. Carlson 1983b; Matson 1976.

Roy L. Carlson

EARLY CERAMIC PERIOD, a pre-Caddoan, Late Archaic ceramic complex in the Caddoan area dating ca. 300 B.C.–A.D. 700, whose earliest wares are coeval with and related to Tchefuncte Phase (q.v.) wares in the Lower Mississippi Valley, and its latest wares with Late Woodland complexes in general. In the northern part of the Caddoan area, the grog-tempered Williams Plain type is most common; in the central and southern parts, the sandy-paste Bear Creek Plain type predominates.
    SOURCES: Shafer 1975; Story 1981.

James E. Corbin

EARLY HORIZON, the oldest (ca. 2500–500 B.C.) of three cultural expressions (Early, Middle, and Late horizons) identified in the Delta locality of Central California during the 1930s by Jeremiah Lillard, R. F. Heizer, and Franklin Fenenga; characterized by ventrally extended burials and distinc-

tive funerary artifacts. After ca. 1975, the term "Early Horizon" was largely supplanted by "Windmiller Pattern" (q.v.).
SOURCE: Moratto 1984:181–185, 199–207.

Michael J. Moratto

EARTHLODGE, a common type of structure used for both domestic and ceremonial purposes on the Plains, especially in villages along the Missouri River in the Dakotas and in the central Plains. The typical early form, which was in use by ca. A.D. 1000, was square and had four main interior roof supports. The later protohistoric and historic type (common well into the 19th century) was round and generally had either four or eight interior roof supports. All forms had a fireplace in the center.
SOURCES: Wedel 1979; W. R. Wood 1961.

Patricia J. O'Brien

EASTERN EXTENSION SUB-PROVINCE, a division of the Jornada Province, Mogollon Culture (qq.v.), in eastern New Mexico, that was proposed on the basis of survey and excavations undertaken by members of the Lea County Archaeologial Society. Estimated to date from ca. A.D. 950 to 1450, it has a sequence of three phases: Querecho, Maljamar, and Ochoa (qq.v.).

The sub-province is thought to have evolved out of an Archaic base, the Hueco Phase. Locally made ceramics were inspired mainly by similar types in the Sierra Blanca and Middle Pecos Sub-Provinces (qq.v.), and most imported pottery came from the same areas. Presumably, the various architectural forms also were borrowed from those sub-provinces, though direct correspondence in details, particularly of pithouses, cannot be demonstrated on present evidence. The salient feature of the subsistence strategies is that they always were based upon hunting and gathering. Evidently, agriculture was never practiced, for cultigens have not been found at any Eastern Extension site to date.
SOURCES: Corley 1970; Leslie 1979.

R. N. Wiseman

EAST VERDE PROVINCE, a province of the Sinagua Division, Hakataya Culture (qq.v.) that occupied the drainage of the East Verde River in Arizona between ca. A.D. 900 and 1350. In 1975, a research team at Arizona State University implemented a program of systematic survey and excavation of small sites in the Payson Basin, in Tonto National Forest. They also excavated the large Shoofly Village in 1984. This work resulted in the tentative definition of four phases—Union Park, Star Valley, Payson, and Round Valley (qq.v.)—based on the distribution of the Payson Series of Alameda Brown Ware (q.v.) pottery and associated traits. The local plainware closely resembles that of the Verde and Salado provinces (qq.v.). The early presence of Hohokam elements also mirrors developments in those two neighboring

provinces, as does the appearance of pueblo-like structures and redware in the 1100s in the Verde Province.
SOURCE: Redman and Hohmann 1986.

Albert H. Schroeder

EAYEM PHASE. See Fraser Canyon Sequence.

EDEN POINT, a long, slender, lanceolate, Paleoindian (q.v.) projectile point of wide distribution in the High Plains. While sharing some characteristics with the Scottsbluff type (q.v.), with which it sometimes is associated, Eden is narrower than Scottsbluff and has a less strongly indented stem. Eden points most often have collateral, horizontal flake scars which produce a diamond-shaped cross section. The first Eden points found in situ were at the Finley Site near Eden, Wyoming, where they were associated with extinct bison. This discovery was made by O. M. Finley in 1940.
SOURCE: Wormington 1957.

Patricia J. O'Brien

EDENWOOD SITE, an Early Archaic site on the Congaree River floodplain in Lexington County, in South Carolina, where excavations by James Michie in 1978 produced Palmer and Kirk artifact assemblages, as well as some evidence of Middle and Late Archaic occupations. This appears to have been a specialized-activity site, probably related to food procurement.
SOURCE: Michie 1978.

Michael Trinkley

EDGEFIELD SCRAPER, a large, side-notched scraper with an oblique working edge; first recognized by James Michie. Dating from the Paleoindian or Early Archaic period (qq.v.), it occurs in Florida, Georgia, South Carolina, and North Carolina. Although specimens of the type resemble reworked, broken projectile points, they were made directly from raw materials, not from broken points.
SOURCE: Michie 1972.

Michael Trinkley

EDWIN HARNESS MOUND, a large, multistage, Ohio Hopewell (q.v.) mound on a second terrace of the Scioto River south of Chillicothe; one of at least fourteen mounds associated with the Liberty geometric earthwork. Intermittent but extensive excavations since the early 19th century by several investigators have revealed that activities at the site began with the erection of a large, four-sectioned, civic-ceremonial structure that subsequently was partly dismantled and burned, then each section was covered with a small mound. At some later time, these were incorporated into one large mound.

Remains from a variety of social and ritual activities were unearthed within and beside the structure, including a small amount of corn found in likely ceremonial context. Hopewell artifacts were associated with at least one of the later additions. Radiocarbon dates, which generally follow the stratigraphic sequence, indicate site use during the period ca. A.D. 300–800. The Harness Site is unusual in that it has a number of similarities in both embankment design and artifact distribution to the Seip Site (q.v.).

SOURCES: Squier and Davis 1848:56–57, 178–181, pl. 20; Putnam 1885; Cyrus Thomas 1889; Moorehead 1897; Mills 1907; Smart and Ford 1983; Greber 1979a, 1979b, 1983; Seeman and Soday 1980.

N'omi B. Greber

EFFIGY MOUND TRADITION, a Late Woodland expression in Wisconsin and surrounding environs, dating ca. A.D. 800–1100 and noted for its earthen tumuli shaped like various animals or forming geometric patterns, some containing burials, altars, or other internal structures. Often unassociated with habitation sites, effigy mounds were not exclusively for mortuary purposes. Some archaeologists interpret them as markers of social structure, perhaps lineage or clan markers. Information from related villages and camps indicates a mixed hunting, gathering, and horticultural subsistence base.

SOURCES: Hurley 1975; Mallam 1976.

David Overstreet

EIGHTEEN MILE PHASE, the earliest (ca. A.D. 800–1000) phase of the Middle Pecos Sub-Province (q.v.), Jornada Province, Mogollon Culture, in eastern New Mexico. Formally divided into early and late periods, the phase marks the first appearance of agriculturally based, sedentary people along the middle Pecos River.

The few sites recorded for the early Eighteen Mile Phase are reminiscent of the contemporary pithouse villages of the Claunch Focus of the Salinas Province, Anasazi Culture to the west and of the early Glencoe Phase (q.v.) and as yet undefined remains in the Sierra Blanca Sub-Province, Jornada Province, Mogollon Culture to the southwest. The impetus for adopting agriculture, ceramics, and a sedentary lifeway is thought to have come from those areas. Excavations at one site, P 14, revealed a very small pit or pit structure and associated lithics, bone, corner- and base-notched arrow points, and a few brownware pottery sherds thought to be imports from the Sierra Blanca Sub-Province. Subsistence was based upon maize agriculture, hunting, and gathering.

The late Eighteen Mile Phase dates ca A.D. 900–1000. As represented at Site P 4A, it saw the first well-established, small, sedentary communities with shallow, slab-lined pithouses, small pueblos of rectangular rooms, and storage cists. The ceramic assemblage includes locally made cognates of

Jornada Brown and Red Mesa Black-on-white pottery imported from the west. Corner-notched arrow points were used. The subsistence strategy was a continuation from the Early Eighteen Mile Phase.

SOURCE: Jelinek 1967.

R. N. Wiseman

ELDEN PHASE, the best-known phase of the Northern Sinagua Tradition of the Flagstaff Province (qq.v.) in north-central Arizona. More sites of this phase have been excavated than of any other Sinagua phase. Dating ca. A.D. 1150–1200/1225, it marks the beginning of population aggregation into pueblos larger than those of preceding phases.

An architectural and settlement hierarchy can be defined for the phase that suggests the development of a chiefdomlike organization in the region. At the top of the hierarchy are cultural centers such as Ridge Ruin, Juniper Terrace, and Wupatki Pueblo, with ball courts, plazas, and other unique features. Pueblos of similar size (twenty or more rooms) but lacking ball courts and plazas constitute the next level, followed by pueblos of decreasing size down to those of only one to three rooms. The occupants of the large pueblos apparently dispersed at certain seasons of the year to take advantage of various farming opportunities. In addition to open sites, there were cliff dwellings such as those in Walnut Canyon National Monument (q.v.).

Building styles of the preceding Padre Phase (q.v.) continued: masonry-lined pithouses, rectangular benched kivas, and community rooms such as the "amphitheater" at Wupatki. Wing walls extended from the sides of many pueblos to partially enclosed outside work areas. Some sites display defensive characteristics such as being located on hilltops or at the ends of peninusulas extending into canyons, with walls to control site access. There also may be a relationship between site locations and transportation or trade routes through the region. Water- and soil-control devices include grid borders, linear borders, check dams, irrigation ditches, terraces, and reservoirs.

Pottery is dominantly Sunset Brown, Winona Brown, and their redware, smudged, and polished varieties. Elden Corrugated—a Mogollon-style vertical and obliterated corrugated type—was made during the latter part of the phase. Trade is represented by pottery from the Kayenta area, with a shift during the phase to the Winslow Anasazi and Cibola Anasazi/Western Pueblo areas. Some trade with Hohokam (q.v.) people is indicated by copper bells, macaws, and Hohokam-style vessels made of local materials.

Burials are predominantly extended, although some cremations occur. The Magician's Burial (q.v.) at Ridge Ruin exemplifies the elaborate burials accorded high-status persons. Unusual artifacts such as nose plugs, carved bone hairpins, and painted wooden wands and staffs have been interpreted as symbols of authority.

SOURCES: Colton 1939b:40–42, 1946:271–273, 312–314; Schroeder 1961c, 1977; J. P. Wilson 1969:23–25; Pilles 1978, 1979; Fish et al. 1980; Hohmann 1982.

Peter J. Pilles, Jr.

ELDEN PUEBLO, a pueblo of from 60 to 70 rooms at the edge of Flagstaff, Arizona containing burials, mounds, smaller pueblos, pithouses, and other features. Dating ca. A.D. 1100–1275, it is the type site for the Elden Phase of the Northern Sinagua Tradition (qq.v.), as well as for the pottery type Elden Corrugated. It is listed in the National Register of Historic Places.

Elden was partly excavated in 1926 by J. W. Fewkes and J. P. Harrington. The first excavation of consequence in the Flagstaff area, this attracted considerable public attention and was one stimulus that led to the formation of the Museum of Northern Arizona in 1927. It also prompted Byron Cummings to excavate Turkey Hill Pueblo (q.v.) in 1927–1928.

Fewkes and Harrington dug 33 rooms and over 150 burials. They discovered a community room which identified the site as a major regional center, and they found a number of unique artifacts, including an antelope-effigy jar, a copper bell, carved bone hairpins, and pottery vessels. Later reanalysis of the burials and artifacts suggested the presence of craft specialists and a hereditary, hierarchical society. The burials produced the first data on Sinaguan dietary deficiencies and other health conditions, including the identification of intestinal parasites and rickets.

In the 1980s, the site has been the focus of a cooperative project of the Coconino National Forest, the Arizona Archaeological Society, and the Museum of Northern Arizona to re-excavate and stabilize rooms as an educational program to teach children and the general public about archaeology and cultural values.

SOURCES: Fewkes 1927; Hough 1932; R.E. Kelly 1970; Hohmann 1982.

Peter J. Pilles, Jr.

EL DORADO PHASE, a semisedentary, Archaic (1900–1300 B.C.) culture, originally defined by R. D. Grosser on the basis of excavations at the Snyder Site (q.v.), Kansas, and subsequently demonstrated to exist at other sites in the central Plains, including Williamson, Coffey (qq.v.), and the Matter Mound. Projectile point types diagnostic of the phase include Dustin, Duncan, and Table Rock Stemmed. Significant characteristics are intensive exploitation of biotic resources and mound burials containing offerings. The earliest Woodland occupants of the central Plains may have descended from indigenous Archaic populations, such as the El Dorado Phase, rather than from eastern Woodland migrants.

SOURCES: Grosser 1973; Schmits 1980a.

Roger D. Grosser

ELK ISLAND DISTRICT, a large island in the James River where it crosses the central Piedmont of Virginia, on which are 35 recorded archaeological sites dating from Middle Archaic through Late Woodland. L. D. Mouer conducted a systematic survey of the island from 1978 to 1980. A number of deeply stratified sites on the island and nearby document the development of Woodland cultures on the James.

SOURCES: Fowke 1894; Mouer et al. 1981.

Keith T. Egloff

ELK ISLAND TRADITION, an Early Woodland (ca. 900–500 B.C.) manifestation, defined in 1981 by L. D. Mouer on the basis of materials found on and near Elk Island, located in the James River where it crosses the Virginia Piedmont. Diagnostic traits are Elk Island Ware pottery, small side-notched points, and lobate points made of quartz. Sedentism is suggested by pit features and large sites.

SOURCE: Mouer et al. 1981.

Keith T. Egloff

ELK ISLAND WARE, a sandy-paste, friable ceramic, radiocarbon dated to ca. 900 B.C., defined by L. D. Mouer in 1981 from plain, cordmarked, and net-impressed sherds found in stratified context at the Stoneman West Site on the James River in the Piedmont of Virginia.

SOURCE: Mouer et al. 1981.

Keith T. Egloff

ELKO POINT SERIES, a series of large, corner-notched, chipped-stone projectile points distributed throughout the desert West, encompassing two different types: Elko Eared and Elko Corner-notched. Dating ca. 1300 B.C.–A.D. 700 in the western and central Great Basin, the series is thought to date at least as early as 5500 B.C. in the eastern Great Basin.

SOURCES: O'Connell 1967; Aikens 1970; D. H. Thomas 1981.

David Hurst Thomas

ELLIS LANDING SITE, a stratified shell midden in the northeastern part of San Francisco Bay, investigated by N. C. Nelson in the first decade of the 20th century. The site provided early evidence of prehistoric culture change in the region, a concept that contrasted with the prevailing view that California culture had remained static over long periods of time.

SOURCE: N. C. Nelson 1910.

Michael J. Moratto

ELLIS POINT, a Late Archaic dart-point type with a triangular blade, barbed shoulders, an expanding stem, and a straight to mildly convex base, dating ca. 600 B.C. to A.D. 700. Its distribution centers in north-central and northeastern Texas and extends into surrounding areas.

SOURCES: Suhm et al. 1954; Bell 1960; Suhm and Jelks 1962; Turner and Hester 1985.

Elton R. Prewitt

ELM HILL SITE, a stratified midden on the Roanoke River in the southeastern Piedmont of Virginia which contained principally Late Woodland, but also Late Archaic and Middle Woodland, cultural materials. In 1955 Clifford Evans analyzed sherds from Elm Hill; in 1964, H. A. MacCord tested the site and discovered its features and strata.
SOURCES: Clifford Evans 1955; MacCord 1968.

Keith T. Egloff

EL PASO BROWN POTTERY, the major locally made ceramic in the early phases of the El Paso Sub-Province of the Jornada Province, Mogollon Culture (qq.v.). Apparently being made by the A.D. 400s or earlier, it has brown paste, prominent quartz and feldspar temper, and scraped exterior-surface finish. There was a general trend from early tapered rims to late parallel-sided, rounded rims. By ca. A.D. 1100, it had evolved into El Paso Polychrome (q.v.), a type on which simple designs were painted with black and red pigments.
SOURCES: Lehmer 1948; Whalen 1981.

R. N. Wiseman

El PASO PHASE, the final phase of the El Paso Sub-Province of the Jornada Province, Mogollon Culture (qq.v.), dating ca. A.D. 1200–1400 and occupying central New Mexico and adjoining parts of Texas and Chihuahua. It has been divided into early and late periods, mainly on the basis of early and late rim styles of El Paso Polychrome pottery.

Characteristic dwellings were adobe pueblos of the linear and enclosed-plaza forms, plus some rectangular pithouses. Very large ceremonial structures are almost always present within roomblocks. Unlike the previous Mesilla Phase (q.v.), settlement centered in the relatively well-watered mountain/basin juncture zone.

Most pottery is El Paso Polychrome but a vast array of intrusive types representing the adjacent regions is always present in very small quantities in site artifact inventories: various types from the Casas Grandes Province, the Salado Culture, the Zuni region, and the Middle Rio Grande Province (qq.v.). Trade in these and other items such as copper bells and beads of shell and stone gave rise to apparent specialized trading centers such as the Brutton Site.

Subsistence relied on maize agriculture supplemented with rabbits, deer, mesquite, cacti, yucca, and other wild foods. Similarities in architecture, village layout, and pottery types to those of the Animas and Black Mountain phases of southwestern New Mexico and northern Mexico suggest that the

El Paso Phase was part of a panregional culture guided or controlled from the Casas Grandes Province in northern Mexico. During the phase, the religious pantheon headed by the Plumed Serpent and the Kachina Cult spread from Mexico into the American Southwest. Many rock-art sites in the Hueco Mountains and elsewhere in the El Paso region depict these figures in striking petroglyphs and polychrome pictographs.

Why sedentary villagers abandoned the region ca. A.D. 1400 remains elusive. Drought, soil exhaustion, and other causes have been suggested, but hard data confirming any of these conjectures are lacking. Even where the people went is the subject of debate. Some may have moved down the Rio Grande, where peoples of the historic period such as the Mansos and Sumas could have been their descendants. Others may have joined the Piro, Tompiro, and/or Jumano pueblos along the Rio Grande to the northwest and in the Salinas Province to the north. Some may simply have remained in the El Paso region and abandoned agriculture for a hunting-gathering existence.

SOURCES: Scholes and Mera 1940; Lehmer 1948; LeBlanc and Whalen 1980.

R. N. Wiseman

EL PASO POLYCHROME POTTERY, the hallmark of the El Paso Phase of the El Paso Sub-Province, Jornada Province, Mogollon Culture (qq.v.), fashioned by painting black and red designs on El Paso Brown pottery (q.v.). It dates ca. A.D. 1100–1400/1450. The designs are frequently quite simple in composition and sloppy in application, but very well-executed designs are also known, particularly those of a simplified Casas Grandes style. Jar rim shapes changed through time, starting as simple, direct, tapered forms and gradually evolving into increasingly everted and thickened forms. Vessel walls are extremely thin; those of some very large jars are only 4 to 5 millimeters thick.

SOURCES: Stallings 1931; M. E. Whalen 1981.

R. N. Wiseman

EL PASO SUB-PROVINCE, a division of the Jornada Province (q.v.) in south-central New Mexico and adjoining parts of Texas and Chihuahua, centered around El Paso. Dating ca. A.D. 1–1400, it consists of three phases—Mesilla, Dona Ana, and El Paso (qq.v.)—that were named and defined by D. J. Lehmer in 1948. The phases evolved out of an indigenous Archaic base, the Hueco Phase.

The architecture and ceramics of the Mesilla Phase, earliest of the three, shows clear ties with the Mimbres Sub-Province of the Mogollon Culture to the west and to the Rio Abajo Province to the northwest. The Dona Ana and El Paso phases are viewed by most researchers as local developments modified by occasional outside influences. Recently, some have focused upon the similarities of El Paso Phase traits to those of more widespread phenomena such as the Animas and Black Mountain phases of the Mimbres Province and the Medio Period of the Casas Grandes Province (q.v.).

The general trend in architecture was from a few scattered pithouses in earlier times to small and large adobe-walled pueblos. Ceramics evolved from the utility pottery type El Paso Brown (q.v.) made as early as the A.D. 400s, into a distinctive black-and-red-on-brown type, El Paso Polychrome (q.v.); many other pottery types from surrounding areas also are found, especially in later times.

Subsistence appears to have included maize agriculture in all three phases, its importance increasing through time. Hunting, especially of rabbits, was common, and a variety of wild plants was important in each phase. Riverine resources such as fish and waterfowl were prominent in sites along the Rio Grande.

Early settlements were more or less evenly distributed throughout the basins and along mountain outwash fans. Later, as agriculture became more important, settlement along the edges of outwash fans became favored. Settlement populations increased through time; the final size of many pueblos reached 100 rooms or more.

SOURCES: Lehmer 1948; LeBlanc and Whalen 1980.

R. N. Wiseman

ELY MOUND, a 19-foot-high Mississippian substructure mound located adjacent to Indian Creek in extreme southwestern Virginia. It is significant in the history of American archaeology because, on the basis of his explorations there in the 1870s, Lucien Carr emphatically rejected the "Lost Race" hypothesis for mound builders in eastern North America.

SOURCES: Carr 1877; K. T. Egloff n.d.b.

Keith T. Egloff

EMERSON PHASE. See Surprise Valley.

EMERY PHASE. See Fraser Canyon Sequence.

EMERYVILLE SITE, one of the largest shell-midden sites in the San Francisco Bay area of California, with deposits almost 10 meters thick. It was first excavated in 1902 by Max Uhle who identified two components, each comprising five strata. In 1924, W. E. Schenk dug the site extensively before it was leveled. A radiocarbon date of ca. 500 B.C. was later obtained from charcoal that he collected from the basal level.

SOURCES: Uhle 1907; Moratto 1984.

Michael J. Moratto

ENCINITAS TRADITION, a culture unit in the valleys of southern California, first recognized and defined by C. N. Warren in 1968. Dating ca. 6000–1000 B.C., the tradition incorporates the La Jolla, Oak Grove, Topanga, and related Millingstone (qq.v.) complexes and is characterized by millingstones, crude chopping and cutting tools, and the relatively rare occurrence of projectile points.

SOURCES: C. N. Warren 1968; Moratto 1984:160–164.

Michael J. Moratto

ENGIGSTCIAK SITE, a location on a caribou migration route, adjacent to the Firth River on the northern Yukon coastal plain, which was occupied intermittently by hunting groups over the course of several thousand years. The richest portions of the site, which covers several acres, were excavated by R. S. MacNeish in the late 1950s. MacNeish assimilated materials from Engigstciak and adjacent coastal sites into nine phases, the earliest of which—British Mountain (q.v.) and Flint Creek—have remained controversial ever since.

SOURCES: MacNeish 1959a; MacKay et al. 1961.

Donald W. Clark

ENGRAVED SHELL GORGETS, large pendants made from the outer walls of marine conchs (Busycon sp.), associated with the Southeastern Ceremonial Complex (q.v.) of the Late Mississippian period (ca. A.D. 1300–1550), in the southeastern United States. Certain iconographic motifs (rattlesnakes, birdmen, sun circles, crosses, etc.) were engraved on the exterior surfaces of the circular gorgets.

SOURCES: Moorehead 1932; Kneberg 1959.

Jefferson Chapman

EN MEDIO PHASE, the last phase, dating ca. 800 B.C.–A.D. 400, of the Oshara Tradition (q.v.) in the Four Corners area of the Southwest, in which the earliest recognizable Anasazi (q.v.) traits, generally termed Basketmaker II, appeared. Horticultural practices evidently increased during this phase, and fall-winter aggregation of the population also intensified in some places. Base camps used in other seasons cover large areas and exhibit evidence of repeated use. Well-made, sometimes slab-lined, storage pits are present at virtually all base camps. The population apparently increased throughout the phase.

In some areas, environments that were rarely exploited in previous phases became heavily utilized. Tool kits contain a wider range of tool classes. Projectile points exhibit a variety of stem forms and show a trend through time of increased barb length. Bifacial, chipped-stone knives and drills—rare early in the phase—increase in frequency through time. Deep-basin metates and cobble manos are present throughout the phase; trough metates and flat manos appear late. The rest of the tool kit remains relatively unchanged from previous phases. Perishable items such as basketry, fiber, leather, and wooden artifacts are sometimes found in dry rockshelters.

As a whole, the evidence indicates that the En Medio people followed a strongly seasonal annual economic cycle. There also are indications of a well-developed socio-ceremonial cycle. After the end of the phase, the importance of horticulture increased over the centuries, culminating in the sedentary, agriculturally based Anasazi lifestyle.

SOURCES: Irwin-Williams and Tomkins 1968; Irwin-Williams and Haynes 1970; Irwin-Williams 1973, 1979.

Cynthia Irwin-Williams and Patricia A. Hicks

ENSOR POINT, a Late Archaic (ca. A.D. 150–550) dart point type of wide distribution in central and southwestern Texas; characterized by a triangular blade, prominent shoulders, and a strongly expanding stem formed by side or corner notches. A prototype of several later point types including Ellis (q.v.), Ensor is considered a diagnostic trait of the Twin Sisters (q.v.) and Blue Hills phases of central and southwestern Texas, respectively.

SOURCES: Suhm and Jelks 1962; Leroy Johnson, Jr., et al. 1962; Turner and Hester 1985.

Elton R. Prewitt

EQUIPAJE SPRING SITE, a large multicomponent site in Brewster County, in western Texas, excavated by R. J. Mallouf in 1980; type site for the late prehistoric (ca. A.D. 1200–1600) Cielo Phase (q.v.), which is represented by a series of refuse concentrations and nine circular to oval, stacked-stone house enclosures. There also are hearths, middens, and bedrock mortars associated with an earlier occupation by Late Archaic peoples.

SOURCE: Mallouf 1985:47–49.

Robert J. Mallouf

ESILAO PHASE. See Fraser Canyon Sequence.

ESPAÑOLES PERIOD. See Casas Grandes Province.

ESTRELLA PHASE. See Pioneer Period.

ETOWAH SITE, a Mississippian (q.v.) mound center covering about 21 hectares on the Etowah River in northwestern Georgia, containing three large mounds, several small mounds, a plaza, and a habitation area, all enclosed by a ditch and palisade. It was occupied ca. A.D. 1000–1550. There have been numerous excavations at the site—including work by J. Rogan in 1883, W. K. Moorehead in 1925–1927, and L. H. Larson, Jr., in 1954–1956—much of it at Mound C, where numerous burials have been exposed, many containing Southeastern Ceremonial Complex artifacts.

SOURCES: Cyrus Thomas 1894:292–311; Moorehead 1932; Wauchope 1966:251–259; Larson 1971, 1972.

Paul A. Webb

EUREKA SOUND SITES, a series of Independence I Phase (q.v.) sites on the northwestern coast of Ellesmere Island, Northwest Territories, investigated by Eigil Knuth and Patricia Sutherland between 1965 and 1980. The sites document the western distribution of Independence I, dated here at ca. 2000 B.C.
SOURCES: Knuth 1967; Patricia Sutherland n.d.

Moreau S. Maxwell

EVANS SITE, a Gallina Phase (q.v.) site in the Largo-Gallina Province (q.v.), approximately 3 kilometers south of Llaves in north-central New Mexico, dating to the mid–13th century A.D. Excavated by C. H. Lange, Jr., in 1941, it consisted of two contiguous surface houses of typical Gallina Phase style, with an unusual association of six surface storage rooms of wattle-and-daub construction.
SOURCES: Lange 1941, 1956:72–92.

Herbert W. Dick

EVA SITE, principally a Middle and Late Archaic site near the Tennessee River in western Tennessee, partially excavated by Douglas Osborne in 1940; pivotal to the definition of Archaic cultures in the western Tennessee Valley. Three components—Big Sandy, Three Mile, and Eva—were defined.
SOURCES: Lewis and Kneberg 1959; Lewis and Lewis 1961.

Jefferson Chapman

EVELAND PHASE, the initial unit of the Spoon River Tradition (q.v.), dating ca. A.D. 1050–1175, characterized by a small intrusion into the central Illinois River Valley of emigrants from Cahokia (q.v.) to the south, who introduced distinctive elements of the Stirling Phase (q.v.) to the local indigenous lifeway. Purely Cahokia-derived elements of material culture, particularly the ceramic types Powell Plain and Ramey Incised, distinguish early contact sites from late acculturated sites of the phase. Eveland differed from later Spoon River phases in having only small, short-term settlements and by the apparent absence of an interregional political network involving complex town construction and temple-mound ceremonialism.
SOURCES: Harn 1975, 1980.

Alan D. Harn

F

FALCON HILL CAVES, a complex of caves overlooking the dessicated lakebed of Winnemucca Lake in northern Nevada that appears to have been used intermittently as cache sites, among other things, from ca. 7500 B.C. to ca. A.D. 1550. Kramer Cave, the largest, has been radiocarbon dated to ca. 1900–1600 B.C. Artifacts from the caves include basketry, Gatecliff and Humboldt series points (qq.v.), dart foreshafts, juniper-seed and marine-shell beads, and other ornaments. The caves were discovered and investigated in the 1950s by W. C. Shinners of Reno.
SOURCE: Hattori 1982.

David Hurst Thomas

FANNING SITE, a site in Doniphan County, in Kansas where W. R. Wedel's excavations in 1937 disclosed a round house with four interior roof-support posts, small triangular projectile points, and both Fanning Plain and Fanning Trailed pottery. Wedel assigned the site to the Oneota Aspect and suggested that the Kansas Indians may have established it some time after A.D. 1500 during their early movement into the area.
SOURCE: Wedel 1959.

Patricia J. O'Brien

FARMINGTON COMPLEX, an assemblage of uncertain age distinguished by core tools and large, reworked flakes, first identified in the Farmington Reservoir area near Stockton, California by A. E. Treganza in 1952. Estimates of its age have ranged from terminal Pleistocene to late Holocene, but the preponderance of current evidence suggests an early Holocene date of ca. 10,000–5000 B.C.
SOURCES: Treganza and Heizer 1953; Ritter et al. 1976; Moratto 1984:62–64.

R. E. Taylor and L. A. Payen

FAST ICE, the sheet of sea ice in the Arctic region frozen to the shore in winter, or separated from shore only by a tidal crack. Large areas of fast ice were used for aglu hunting (q.v.) and for winter snow-house settlements.

Moreau S. Maxwell

FATE BELL SHELTER, one of the largest rockshelters in the southwestern United States, located in Val Verde County, Texas; excavated by several archaeologists between the 1930s and the 1960s. By the 1920s or earlier, its deep, rich cultural deposits had attracted relic hunters, who severely damaged the site over the years until it was given protected-site status by the state in 1978.

The scientific excavations revealed sotol pits, both group and individual burials, bedrock mortars, and a host of artifacts, representing a sequence of Archaic and post-Archaic occupations extending over many thousands of years. Like other rockshelters of the region, Fate Bell contained many well-preserved vegetal food remains and artifacts made of wood and fiber (e.g., spear shafts, digging sticks, basketry, netting, and fiber sandals). There is an extensive gallery of pictographs painted on the wall, most of them done in the distinctive Lower Pecos Archaic (q.v.) style, although some Red Linear motifs typical of the late prehistoric period also are present.

SOURCES: Pearce and Jackson 1933; Kirkland and Newcomb 1967:37–98; S. A. Turpin 1982:64–69.

Robert J. Mallouf

FEEHELEY SITE, a predominately Late Archaic habitation and burial site in Michigan's Saginaw Valley with a radiocarbon date of 1180 B.C. ± 150; excavated in 1960 by University of Michigan archaeologists. Abundant fish bones of several species together with a high frequency of chipped-stone drills for woodworking and of unifaces for processing fish are considered indicative of warm-season occupation. The validity of a radiocarbon date of A.D. 255 ± 120 from a possible Middle Woodland component at the site is questionable.

SOURCES: Yarnell 1964; Cleland 1966; Taggart 1967.

Margaret B. Holman

FERGUSON LAKE SITE, a settlement at the head of Ekalluk River, on Victoria Island, Northwest Territories, excavated by W. E. Taylor, Jr., who found cultural material from both the Early and the Middle Dorset periods, demonstrating a probable indigenous development of regional Dorset culture variants.

SOURCE: W. E. Taylor, Jr. 1967.

Moreau S. Maxwell

FEURT FOCUS, a unit of the Fort Ancient Aspect (q.v.), named for the Feurt Village Site near Portsmouth, Ohio.
SOURCES: J. B. Griffin 1943b:70–91, n.d.

N'omi B. Greber

FIBROLITE AXE, a ground-stone axe made of fibrolite, with a spiral groove (rather than a circular groove or notches) for hafting; a diagnostic trait of the Classic Period of the Rio Grande Anasazi Culture in the Tewa Basin Province (qq.v.), in northern New Mexico. Fibrolite is the popular name for sillimanite, an exceptionally hard rock found near the Truchas Peaks in the Sangre de Cristo Mountains in New Mexico.
SOURCES: Kidder 1932; Arthur Montgomery 1963.

Stewart Peckham

FIG ISLAND SHELL RINGS, an Early Woodland, Thom's Creek Phase (q.v.) site dating ca. 1200 B.C., located at the mouth of Ocella Creek on the north end of Edisto Island, in South Carolina. It was briefly excavated in 1970 by E. T. Hemmings, who identified features and made a large collection of pottery and faunal remains.
SOURCES: Hemmings 1970a, 1970b; Trinkley 1976a.

Michael Trinkley

FIRSTVIEW COMPLEX, a Paleoindian unit (q.v.) estimated to date ca. 8200 B.C., defined by J. B. Wheat in 1972 on the basis of lithic materials found at the Olsen-Chubock Site (q.v.), type site for the complex, located in east-central Colorado. Its diagnostic artifact is the Firstview-type projectile point.
SOURCE: Wheat 1972.

Patricia J. O'Brien

FISHERMAN LAKE SITES, a group of sites in the extreme southwestern district of Mackenzie, excavated by R. S. MacNeish in 1952 and by J. F. V. Millar in 1967 and later. Phases and complexes proposed by Millar in 1981 include the Codille and Klondike complexes of the Northern Plano Tradition, for which there are radiometric dates ranging from 6770 ± 180 to 2835 B.C. (a few unlikely dates excluded), and the Pointed Mountain Complex of the Northwest Microblade Tradition (qq.v.), with radiocarbon dates clustering between 1000 B.C. and A.D. 100. The Julian Complex, succeeding Pointed Mountain, is distinguished by the rough reduction of chert pebbles to produce implements.
SOURCE: Millar 1981.

Donald W. Clark

FISH HAUL SITE, a multicomponent site on Fish Haul Creek on Hilton Head Island, in Beaufort County, South Carolina; excavated by Michael Trinkley in 1982 and 1986. A significant Stallings Island Phase (q.v.) sea-

sonal encampment, dating ca. A.D. 1500, it yielded abundant pottery, lithics, baked-clay objects, worked shell, and faunal and floral remains. A number of Stallings Island postmolds and features, including a typical D-shaped structure, were identified. Components of the Thom's Creek, Deptford, Mount Pleasant, St. Catherines, and Irene phases also were present.
SOURCES: Trinkley et al. 1983; Trinkley 1986.

Michael Trinkley

FISH SPRINGS CAVES, a series of caves on the southern margin of the Great Salt Lake Desert in Utah that contained Late Archaic and Sevier/ Fremont components (q.v.). Excavated in 1978 by D. B. Madsen, the caves produced the first direct evidence of a seasonal round in the Great Basin, apparently having been occupied during the winter after a fall pinenut harvest in the nearby Deep Creek Mountains.
SOURCE: Madsen 1982b.

David B. Madsen

FIVE MILE RAPIDS, anglicized name for The Dalles, a section of great rapids on the middle course of the Columbia River on the Washington-Oregon border, where important salmon fishing and trade centers were concentrated from 8000 B.C. or earlier to historic times. See Dalles Sequence.
SOURCES: B. R. Butler 1957, 1959; Cressman et al. 1960; Pettigrew 1981.

Frank C. Leonhardy

FLAGSTAFF PROVINCE, the homeland of the Sinagua (q.v.) Tradition in north-central Arizona, divided into northern and southern archaeological regions by the Mogollon Rim, a huge geologic uplift. The southern region occupies the Verde Valley south of Flagstaff; the northern region extends from the San Francisco Peaks to East Clear Creek and from the Wupatki Basin to the forest zone of the Mogollon Rim. The Flagstaff Province partly overlaps the Chevelon-Chavez Province (q.v.).

The affinities of the Sinagua Culture with the major Southwestern cultures (Hohokam, Mogollon, and Anasazi [qq.v.]) have long been in dispute. Early researcher H. S. Colton viewed the Sinagua as a regional version of the Mogollon; H. S. Gladwin regarded it as a montane variety of the Anasazi. In the past, most authorities have attributed Sinagua development to migrations of people into the Flagstaff area from neighboring areas to exploit farmlands created through regional ashfall from an eruption of Sunset Crater (q.v.) in A.D. 1064–1066. A. H. Schroeder, who assigned the pre–1064 inhabitants of the area to his Hakataya Culture (q.v.), does not recognize Sinagua as an entity until after 1064, when the new immigrant farmers and resident Hakataya peoples merged to become the Sinagua. Most researchers believe that the Sinagua people merged with the Hopi after A.D. 1400.

H. S. Colton and his associates—L. L. Hargrave, J. C. McGregor, and Katherine Bartlett—did most of the definitive work in the Flagstaff Province between the 1920s and the 1940s. Local interest in archaeology was stimulated in the 1920s by J. W. Fewkes' and Byron Cummings' excavations at Elden Pueblo (q.v.). Four research objectives were the driving force behind most of this work: (1) collecting tree-ring specimens to complete the tree-ring calendar being developed by A. E. Douglass, (2) dating the eruption of Sunset Crater, (3) defining the Cohonina Culture (q.v.), and (4) finding evidence in the Flagstaff area of the then newly identified Hohokam Culture. Ceramics taxonomy was a fifth objective, particularly for Colton and Hargrave, who viewed pottery typology as the single most important means of distinguishing cultural groups and for dating archaeological sites.

In the 1950s, D.A. Breternitz and A. H. Schroeder made major contributions to Sinagua prehistory. Following salvage archaeology projects in the 1950s and 1960s and extensive surveys since 1975, re-evaluation has brought into question many of the traditional concepts about the Sinagua. Rather than explaining their development by migrations of farmers into the area following the eruption of Sunset Crater, new interpretions regard the Sinagua as a fundamentally indigenous phenomenon due to the adoption of specialized agricultural techniques and the growth of regional exchange systems.

As treated here, the Sinagua tradition is considered to have lasted from ca. A.D. 600 to 1400. It is divided into two periods (pre-eruptive and post-eruptive) and a number of phases. In the earlier literature on Sinagua archaeology, the terms *focus* and *phase* were used interchangeably, but since the 1960s *phase* has been increasingly favored. The periods and phases are as follows (all dates are A.D.).

Pre-eruptive Period
  Cinder Park Phase (ca. 600–700)
  Sunset Phase (ca. 700–900)
  Rio de Flag Phase (ca. 900–1064)
Post-eruptive Period
  Angell/Winona phases (ca. 1064–1100)
  Padre Phase (ca. 1100–1150)
  Elden Phase (ca. 1150–1200)
  Turkey Hill Phase (ca. 1200–1300)
  Clear Creek Phase (ca. 1300–1400)

Through the years, archaeologists have disagreed on the nature and intensity of the relationships between the Sinagua and peoples of neighboring provinces, and even on the characteristics that distinguish the Sinagua from other traditions. Few individual traits characterize the Sinagua; rather, it is an *assemblage* of traits that gives the tradition its distinctiveness.

Ceramics are predominantly plainwares of the Alameda Brown Ware series (q.v.), produced by the paddle-and-anvil technique, although coil-and-scrape, corrugated vessels classified as Mogollon Brown Ware appeared during the Elden Phase. Typological distinctions between the plainware types are based upon tempering materials, occasionally on surface texturing, and on the occurrence of red-slipped, smudged, and polished varieties of the plainwares. The Sinagua had no tradition of pottery with painted decorations, although there were occasional attempts to copy painted Hohokam and Anasazi designs during the Post-eruptive Period.

Pithouses of various forms were common throughout the sequence but were most common prior to the Padre Phase. Mogollon-style pithouses were typical of the Pre-eruptive Period; the uses of masonry-lined walls increased through time. Certain pithouses are recognizable as kivas during the Rio de Flag Phase by their relatively large size and by a raised bench across one end, a central firepit, and a ventilator. Extremely large pithouses and rooms, which occur at major villages during all phases, are interpreted as community rooms, or great kivas (q.v.).

Burial patterns are complex. Although extended inhumation is always most typical, flexed inhumations, semiflexed inhumations, primary cremations, and secondary cremations also occur, particularly during the A.D. 1064–1150 period. Formal cemeteries of the Post-eruptive Period have separate areas for cremations and inhumations. Infant subfloor burials became common by the Elden Phase. Skull deformation, usually vertical occipital flattening, was common.

SOURCES: Colton 1932b, 1939b, 1946, 1960; Gladwin 1943; Schroeder 1961c, 1977; J. P. Wilson 1969; Pilles 1978, 1979; Fish et al. 1980.

Peter J. Pilles, Jr.

FLANARY SITE, a palisaded village site, dating ca. A.D. 1400–1700, on a natural levee of the Clinch River in southwestern Virginia. Tests there by H. A. MacCord in 1977 revealed Mississippian artifacts in the midden deposits and burials as well as earlier Archaic materials.

SOURCES: MacCord 1979; K. T. Egloff n.d.b.

Keith T. Egloff

FLETCHER SITE, a large Ottawa cemetery dating to the mid–18th century in Bay County, Michigan, investigated in 1968 by Moreau Maxwell. Analysis of variability in the distribution of grave goods gave insights into rank and status within an Indian community of the fur-trade era.

SOURCES: Mainfort 1979, 1985.

Charles E. Cleland

FLINT HILLS CHERT. See Florence Chert.

FLINT RIDGE, an especially conspicuous outcrop of Vanport flint in western Muskingum and southeastern Licking counties, in Ohio. Numerous quarry areas can still be seen from which high-quality bedded flint was obtained from prehistoric times to the present.

SOURCES: W. H. Holmes 1919; Stout and Schoenlaub 1946:71–92; Celnar 1978.

N'omi B. Greber

FLINT RUN DISTRICT, an area along the South Fork of the Shenandoah River in northwestern Virginia which encompasses six Early Middle Woodland stone burial mounds and many important Paleoindian, Archaic, and Woodland (qq.v.) stratified sites. Since 1971 W. M. Gardner has exposed features and strata at several of the Paleoindian sites.
SOURCES: W. M. Gardner 1974, 1983.

Keith T. Egloff

FLOE EDGE (or SINA), the interface between fast ice (q.v.) and open seawater in the Arctic region. This was a particularly good hunting location for walrus, bearded seal, beluga, narwhal, and subadult ring seal.

Moreau S. Maxwell

FLORENCE (or FLINT HILLS) CHERT, a fine-grained, blue-grey chert utilized prehistorically for making chipped-stone tools, occurring as flat beds in the Permian limestone that forms the Flint Hills, predominately in east-central Kansas but extending into southern Nebraska and northern Oklahoma. In Oklahoma these deposits are called Kay County Chert.
SOURCE: Wedel 1959.

Patricia J. O'Brien

FLOWERDEW HUNDRED, a site on the James River in the interior coastal plain of Virginia that was occupied from the Early Archaic period up to the early 17th century. In excavating there from 1972 to 1978, N. F. Barka identified three major components: one Late Archaic, one Late Woodland, and one protohistoric. Excavated features include two palisades and three probable oval house patterns.
SOURCE: Hodges n.d.

Keith T. Egloff

FLUTED AXE, a distinctive type of ground-stone axe found in Wisconsin, characterized by grooves, or flutes, pecked into its blade, poll, or face. It has been suggested that these implements are a product of the Effigy Mound Culture (q.v.); however, no fluted axes have been found in stratigraphic contexts that would either confirm or deny this hypothesis.
SOURCE: Barrett 1933.

David Overstreet

FOLSOM CULTURE, a Paleoindian (q.v.) expression, dating ca. 9000–7000 B.C., whose hunting stations and campsites are distributed over much of North America east of the Rocky Mountains between southern Canada and Northern Mexico. Hunting stations where late Pleistocene animals, especially *Bison antiquus*, were killed include Folsom (the type site) and Blackwater Draw in eastern New Mexico, Lubbock Lake in the Texas panhandle, and Bonfire Cave (qq.v.) in southwestern Texas. Among the best known campsites are Lindenmeier in northeastern Colorado, MacHaffie (qq.v.) in western Montana, Adair-Steadman in the Texas panhandle, and the Hanson and Agate Basin sites in eastern Wyoming.

The Folsom point with its distinctive flutes is a marker of the culture; other tools include small chipped-stone end scrapers, tiny graver points, and beveled bone tools that probably were used for fleshing animal hides. Although thought of primarily as big-game hunters, Folsom people also hunted small animals and foraged for vegetal foods. They probably were organized into small territorial bands that followed game herds and moved about periodically to gather seeds, roots, nuts, and berries as they became available seasonally.

SOURCES: F. H. H. Roberts, Jr. 1937, 1940; Wormington 1957:23–42; Tunnell 1977; Wilmsen and Roberts 1978; Frison and Bradley 1980; Frison and Stanford 1982.

Edward B. Jelks

FOLSOM POINT, a distinctive chipped-stone projectile point type diagnostic of the Folsom Culture (q.v.), dating ca. 9000-7000 B.C., distributed thinly from southern Canada to northeastern Mexico between the eastern flanks of the Rocky Mountains and the Atlantic coast. This relatively small, carefully crafted, lanceolate point with a concave base has a large flute, or flake scar, on each face and delicate retouching along the edges. The base and the blade edges just above the base are smoothed.

Edward B. Jelks

FOLSOM SITE, a Paleoindian (q.v.) bison kill station near Folsom, New Mexico, dating ca. 8000 B.C.; the type site for the Folsom Culture (q.v.) where, in 1926 and 1927, J. D. Figgins found nineteen Folsom type projectile points (q.v.) associated with the remains of the extinct *Bison antiquus* in an undisturbed geological context. This find established beyond question the presence of people in North America in the late Pleistocene and spurred a successful search for other Pleistocene archaeological sites in various parts of the continent.

SOURCES: Figgins 1927; Sellards 1952:47–49; Wormington 1957:21.

Edward B. Jelks

FOOTE CANYON PUEBLO, a masonry, possibly two-story pueblo of from 30 to 35 ground-floor rooms, with a small, roofed plaza and a nearby great kiva, located on the Blue River in the Cibola Province (q.v.), east-central Arizona. Excavated in 1955 by J. B. Rinaldo, it is the type site for the Foote Creek Phase, dating ca. A.D. 1250–1350, of the Mogollon Culture (q.v.). Almost all painted pottery at the site appears to have been imported from

provinces to the west and north, which supports the hypothesis that Cibola potters made no painted pottery.
SOURCE: Rinaldo 1959.

Stewart Peckham

FORD'S SKULL CREEK SHELL RING, a transitional Stallings Island–Thom's Creek Phase (qq.v.) site on Skull Creek, Hilton Head Island, in Beaufort County, South Carolina, consisting of two shell rings—one superimposed on the other—and scattered materials in adjacent fields. A. R. Calmes' brief excavations in 1966 produced abundant pottery, lithic artifacts, clay balls, bone tools, and two radiocarbon dates: 1635 ± 115 B.C. and 1170 ± 110 B.C.
SOURCES: Calmes n.d.; Trinkley 1980a.

Michael Trinkley

FORKED LIGHTNING PUEBLO (or BANDELIER BEND SITE), the earliest known pueblo in the Upper Pecos River Valley, located at Pecos National Monument, in New Mexico. Occupied between A.D. 1200–1225 and 1300, it comprises an aggregation of unplanned roomblocks, some of which may have been two stories high, loosely arrayed around several plazas. Of the approximately 100 rooms excavated between 1926 and 1929 by A. V. Kidder, most were built of puddled adobe laid in contiguous courses, but a few walls were composed of masonry. Of the seven kivas, two were round subterranean structures; the other five (two rectangular, three D-shaped "corner kivas") were incorporated into surface roomblocks. Kidder used data from Forked Lightning and from contemporaneous sites to define a "Black-on-white pottery period" that preceded the development of the Rio Grande glazeware industry.
SOURCE: Kidder 1958:5–46.

Larry V. Nordby

FORT ANCIENT ASPECT, a formalized description of the Fort Ancient Tradition (q.v.) of the middle Ohio River Valley, made in 1943 by J. B. Griffin in a classic application of the Midwestern Taxonomic System (q.v.). Four foci were identified as units of the aspect: Anderson, Baum, Feurt, and Madisonville (qq.v.). This seminal definition became a basis for Griffin's initial chronological and cultural interpretations within the tradition, and for later extensions and revisions by Griffin and others.
SOURCES: J. B. Griffin 1943a, n.d.; Prufer and Shane 1970; Essenpreis 1978; Graybill 1984.

N'omi B. Greber

FORT ANCIENT SITE, an extensive set of earthern embankments which generally follow the edges of a high terrace above the Little Miami River in Warren County, Ohio, consisting of two sections that are joined (or separated) by a narrow, walled ridge enclosing two mounds and cross walls. Average wall height originally was about 3 meters; the maximum height reached approximately 6 meters near a few of the more than 70 openings. Caches of Hopewell Culture (q.v.) artifacts have been found at the foot of the terrace, where there are several mounds and a long, narrow enclosure. The site's major occupation is attributed to social and ritual uses by Hopewell groups; there are some burials of the Fort Ancient Tradition (q.v.) within the walls.

SOURCES: Moorehead 1890, 1891, 1896, 1908; Mills 1906:135; Morgan 1946.

N'omi B. Greber

FORT ANCIENT TRADITION, a culture unit that occupied the Middle Ohio River Valley from eastern Indiana to western West Virginia ca. A.D. 900–1650; recognized by pioneer archaeologists, including F. W. Putnam, W. K. Moorehead, and W. C. Mills. It was characterized by village settlements; subsistence use of maize and other cultigens; hunting of deer, turkey, and other fauna; distinctive ceramics; and, at least for the later complexes, stylistic connections with widespread Mississippian elements. The Fort Ancient Site (q.v.) is not typical of, nor a major component of, the tradition.

In 1943, J. B. Griffin, in a classic application of the Midwestern Taxonomic System (q.v.), defined a Fort Ancient Aspect (q.v.) comprising four foci as an aid in interpreting the culture. Various geographic and temporal sequences have been proposed for the foci by Griffin and by others; also, "phases" have been defined to replace the foci as subunits of the tradition.

SOURCES: Mills 1904:134–136; J. B. Griffin 1943a, 1979, 1983:293–294; Prufer and Shane 1970; Essenpreis 1978; Graybill 1984.

N'omi B. Greber

FORT CENTER SITE, a complex of earthen mounds, embankments, ditches, and raised fields affiliated with the Belle Glade Culture (q.v.), in Glades County, Florida just west of Lake Okeechobee, dating from ca. 500 B.C. to A.D. 1700. W. H. Sears' excavations in the 1960s produced evidence for maize cultivation by ca. 450 B.C. Carved wooden animal figurines, many larger than life, were collected from a unique charnel pond where they had been preserved in muck.

SOURCES: Sears 1971, 1974, 1982; Sears and Sears 1976.

Jerald T. Milanich

FORT COFFEE FOCUS, an obsolete term for the late prehistoric Fulton Aspect (q.v.) in the Arkansas River region of the Caddoan Area in east-central Oklahoma, now superseded by the Fort Coffee Phase (q.v.).

SOURCES: K. G. Orr 1946; Bell and Baerreis 1951.

Charles L. Rohrbaugh

FORT COFFEE PHASE, the terminal phase of the Caddo Tradition in the Arkansas River region, dating from the end of the Spiro Phase (q.v.), ca. A.D. 1450, to the end of the 16th century. The type site is the Lymon Moore site in east central Oklahoma, excavated by W.P.A.-sponsored crews in 1941 and by the Oklahoma Archaeological Survey in 1969.

Mound construction and burial in mounds had ended by the beginning of the phase, and there is no evidence of the social stratification so apparent in the mound and cemetery burials of the antecedent Spiro Phase. Also, dependence on bison as a food source increased. The material culture of the phase shows continuity with the Caddo Tradition and is distinguished by the overwhelming abundance of plain shell-tempered pottery and small, unnotched arrow points.

SOURCES: Rohrbaugh 1982, 1984; J. A. Brown 1984b.

Charles L. Rohrbaugh

FORT OUIATENON, a military and trading post on the Wabash River near present-day West Lafayette, Indiana; established by France in 1717 and occupied by the British from 1761 to 1763, when it was captured by the Wea Indians. It was a focal point around which Wea, Miami, Kickapoo, and other Native American groups settled in the 18th century. Ouiatenon has been investigated intensively by Indiana and Michigan State universities.

SOURCES: Krauskopf 1955; Kellar, 1970; V. E. Noble 1983; Tordoff 1983.

James H. Kellar

FORT ROCK CAVE, a site in south-central Oregon where, in 1938, L. S. Cressman found a large number of sandals woven from sagebrush bark beneath a thick layer of volcanic ash, later determined to be from the eruption of Mount Mazama in the Oregon Cascades ca. 5000 B.C. In 1952, in an early test of the radiocarbon dating method, W. F. Libby dated a sandal from the cave at ca. 7000 B.C. Cressman and S. F. Bedwell worked further at the site in 1966–1967 and obtained a radiocarbon determination of ca. 11,250 B.C. for charcoal found on lake gravels in the cave.

The Connley Caves (q.v.), a series of small shelters a few miles to the south, also excavated in 1966–1967, produced a rich assemblage of stone artifacts and faunal remains, including waterfowl from nearby Paulina Marsh. These finds, dating between 9000 and 5000 B.C., provided the stimulus for Bedwell's subsequent definition of the Western Pluvial Lakes Tradition (q.v.). D. K. Grayson's study of the faunal remains from the Connley Caves showed that the climate became significantly warmer and drier after 5000 B.C.; concordant with this climatic shift, artifactual evidence from the sites became scarce, suggesting that environmental change brought about a reduction in the intensity of human occupation in the Fort Rock Valley.

SOURCES: Cressman et al. 1942; Bedwell 1973; Grayson 1979.

C. Melvin Aikens

FORT WALTON CULTURE, a unit of the Mississippian Tradition (q.v.) that occupied northwestern Florida ca. A.D. 1000–1500. Politically and socially, the culture was organized into chiefdoms; sites range from large, multimound towns to small, single-family farmsteads.

SOURCES: Willey and Woodbury 1942:244–246; Willey 1949a:452–470, 512–513; Brose and Percy 1980; Milanich and Fairbanks 1980:193–204; Scarry 1980, 1981, 1984; Brose 1984.

Jerald T. Milanich

FORT WALTON SITE, a large, pyramidal, ramped, temple mound and adjacent shell middens, located in downtown Fort Walton Beach, near Santa Rosa Sound in the Florida panhandle. Numerous excavations since the late 19th century have revealed that the sand-and-shell mound served as the base for ceremonial structures during an occupation by the Fort Walton Culture after A.D. 1000, and that the middens were occupied by Deptford, Santa Rosa–Swift Creek, Weeden Island, and Fort Walton (qq.v.) peoples from ca. 500 B.C. to A.D. 1500.

SOURCES: S. T. Walker 1885; Moore 1901:435–454; Willey 1949a:72–88, 213–214; Fairbanks 1965; Lazarus 1970; Lazarus and Fornaro 1975.

Jerald T. Milanich

FOUR BEAR SITE, a fortified earthlodge village dating ca. A.D. 1770–1778 overlooking the Missouri River at its juncture with Buffalo Skin Creek in Dewey County, South Dakota. It was excavated in 1958–1959 by W. R. Hurt. A component of the Four Bear Focus, this probably was the Arikara village visited by Lewis and Clark on 6 October 1804.

SOURCE: Hurt et al. 1962.

Patricia J. O'Brien

FOURCHE MALINE PHASE, the earliest ceramic-producing culture in eastern Oklahoma, of Woodland affiliation (ca. 200 B.C.–A.D. 800), defined primarily on the basis of excavations conducted by J. R. Galm between 1976 and 1978 in the Wister Valley. Distinctive artifacts include contracting- and expanding-stem projectile points/knives, double-bitted axes, and Williams Plain pottery. Fourche Maline appears to be related to Early Woodland development in the lower Mississippi Valley, particularly within the Tchefuncte Culture (q.v.).

SOURCES: Bell 1980; Galm 1984.

Jerry R. Galm

FOX VALLEY TRUNCATED BARB POINT, a type of projectile point, known to collectors as the clipped-wing point, that is common in southern Wisconsin and northern Illinois. The type's age has not been firmly established; some researchers ascribe it to Early Archaic and others to late prehistoric times.

SOURCE: Mason 1966.

David Overstreet

FRANKLIN TANKS SITE, a site at the outlet of Great Bear Lake, Northwest Territories, excavated by R. S. MacNeish in 1952; for decades one of the few excavated sites in the western boreal forest region. The small collection of artifacts garnered by MacNeish, together with material from the nearby Great Bear River Site, initially were given a prominent part in interpretations of northern interior prehistory. Some of these early interpretations are no longer current.

SOURCE: MacNeish 1955.

Donald W. Clark

FRANKSTON PHASE (or FOCUS), a late prehistoric (ca. A.D. 1400–1500) Caddoan culture unit on the upper Neches and Angelina river drainages in eastern Texas, probably ancestral to the historic Allen Phase (q.v.).

SOURCES: Krieger 1946:206–207; Suhm et al. 1954:184–189; Wyckoff 1974:181–185; Story and Creel 1982.

James E. Corbin

FRASER CANYON SEQUENCE, a chronological ordering of prehistoric phases in British Columbia's Fraser River Canyon, developed by C. E. Borden on the basis of excavations at the adjacent Milliken (q.v.) and Esilao sites. While Borden attributed many of the phase differences to the influx of new peoples, recent workers have tended to view the sequence as evidence of changing ways of life among descendant populations. The phases, their approximate ages, and their definitive traits follow.

Milliken: (7000–6000 B.C.) large leaf-shaped, flaked-stone points; pebble tools; unifacially retouched flakes; hammerstones.

Mazama: (6000–4500 B.C.) large leaf-shaped, flaked-stone points; pebble tools; microblades; crude flake tools of various sizes and degrees of retouching or use.

Eayem: (3500–1500 B.C.) stemmed, flaked-stone points; drills; ground slate knives; flaked and partially ground slate points. Eayem probably belongs in the St. Mungo Culture type (q.v.).

Baldwin: (1000–200 B.C.) small, stemmed, flaked-stone points; microblades; mortars and pestles; nephrite celts; disc beads; pendants; rings; earspools; labrets; small, carved animal figures. Baldwin seems most closely allied to the coeval Locarno Beach Culture type (q.v.) of the Gulf of Georgia.

Skamel: (200 B.C.–A.D. 150) barbed, flaked-stone points with expanding stems; many small specialized tools; pithouses; use of cryptocrystalline stone for tool manufacture.

Emery: (A.D. 150–1150) many objects made of steatite and phyllite (including plain and zoomorphic vessels, tubular effigy pipes, and various small carvings).

Esilao: (A.D. 1150–historic contact) small, side-notched, flaked-stone points; endscrapers; abraders; thin ground-slate knives; plain, tubular stone pipes; pithouses.

There is little to distinguish between Milliken and Mazama, both of which are similar to the Old Cordilleran Culture (q.v.); perhaps they should be combined into a single unit.

SOURCES: Borden 1968a, 1975.

Donald H. Mitchell

FRAZIER SITE, the first single-component site of the Agate Basin Complex (q.v.) to be excavated—by H. M. Wormington in 1966–1967. Located about 12 kilometers east of Greeley, Colorado, it contained the remains of 43 bison (either *B. occidentalis* or *B. antiquus*), among which were found five complete and five broken Agate Basin projectile points. The site was radiocarbon dated to ca. 7500 B.C.

SOURCE: Cassells 1983.

Patricia J. O'Brien

FREDERICK COMPLEX, a Paleoindian manifestation dating ca. 6400–6000 B.C. associated with Hell Gap Valley, Wyoming. Its most distinctive trait is a kind of lanceolate projectile point with a markedly concave base but no distinguishable shoulders or stem. These points have narrow, oblique, parallel fake scars across their faces that bear a close resemblance to the flaking on Jimmy Allen type points. Other artifacts of the complex are knives made from the points, raclette scrapers, spur perforators, and other tools similar to those from earlier Paleoindian sites.

SOURCE: Irwin-Williams et al. 1973.

Patricia J. O'Brien

FREMONT CULTURE, a poorly defined complex, first recognized in 1931 by Noel Morss, that occupied an area north of Anasazi (q.v.) territory in Utah, western Colorado, and eastern Nevada. Fremont appears to have developed out of an Archaic (q.v.) base and to have crystallized as a recognizable entity between A.D. 400 and 700. It disappeared between A.D. 1300 and 1600 and was replaced, apparently with no population integration, by protohistoric groups. The culture is characterized by variation, ranging from mobile, full-time hunter-gatherers who did some farming to sedentary, full-time farmers who also hunted and collected wild plants. As there is corresponding variation in settlement location, house construction, and tools, the culture is difficult to define typologically.

Most archaeologists see a basic distinction between Fremont sites on the Colorado Plateau (called Sevier, Sevier/Fremont, or Basin Fremont) and sites in the eastern Great Basin. The Promontory Culture (q.v.)—sometimes identified with Fremont in the northern areas—is more properly considered an early phase of the late prehistoric groups that followed Fremont. Local and regional variants also have been recognized.

Distinctive Fremont artifacts are one-rod-and bundle basketry, several Desert Gray Ware ceramic types, a variety of bone tools, clay figurines, and several arrow-point types. Pithouse dwellings and associated storage structures range from deep clay-lined structures in the south to shallow saucer-shaped depressions in the north, to masonry structures in the east. In the Great Basin, storage structures are usually one- or two-room freestanding adobe buildings, or occasionally adobe-walled rock-niches in cliff faces; on the plateau, similarly shaped structures were built of stone. A wide range of caves, rockshelters, and open brush structures also were used by mobile Fremont groups.

Important Fremont sites include Median Village and O'Malley Shelter (qq.v.) to the south; Backhoe Village (q.v.), Five Finger Ridge, Nawthis, Pharo Village, and the Nephi Mounds in the central Sevier River drainage; and Danger Cave, Hogup Cave (qq.v.), Bear River sites 1, 2, and 3, and the Injun Creek Site near Great Salt Lake to the north. On the Colorado Plateau, important Fremont sites include Caldwell Village (q.v.), Boundry Village, Cub Creek sites, and Deluge Shelter in the Uinat Basin area, with the Turner Look Site (q.v.), Innocents Ridge, and Pint-size Shelter to the south.

SOURCES: Morss 1931; Wormington 1955; Marwitt 1970; Madsen 1979.

David B. Madsen

FRENCH LICK PHASE, a Late Archaic (ca. 3000–1500 B.C.) cultural expression, originally defined by C. A. Munson on the basis of sites in the Patoka River reservoir area of south-central Indiana. It encompasses a range of habitation types in the southwestern quadrant of the state, including shell middens, food-processing stations, and camps. Chief diagnostics are Matanzas, Big Sandy II, and Karnak projectile points.

SOURCE: C. A. Munson 1980.

James H. Kellar

FRENCHMAN SPRINGS PHASE, a culture unit of the mid-Columbia River region of Washington, dating ca. 2500–500 B.C.; initially defined by E. H. Swanson, Jr. Projectile points, the phase's most distinctive artifact class, include lanceolate and triangular forms, together with a stemmed form, the Rabbit Island type. Microblades and microcores also have been found in components of the phase.

SOURCES: Swanson 1962; C. M. Nelson 1969; Galm et al. 1981.

Frank C. Leonhardy

FRESNO POINT, an arrow point of simple triangular shape that is distributed over much of Texas and adjoining areas, associated with a variety of cultures during the period A.D. 1400–1750.

SOURCES: J. C. Kelley 1947a; Suhm and Jelks 1962.

Elton R. Prewitt

FRIO POINT, a Late Archaic (ca. A.D. 150–550) dart point with a triangular blade, short barbs formed by corner notches, and a flaring stem accentuated by a sharp basal indentation or U-notch; widely distributed in and near the

Edwards Plateau, especially the lower Pecos River region; diagnostic of the Blue Hills Phase of southwestern Texas, less common in the Twin Sisters Phase (q.v.) of central Texas.
SOURCES: Suhm and Jelks 1962; Prewitt 1985; Turner and Hester 1985.

Elton R. Prewitt

FRONTENAC ISLAND SITE, type site for the Frontenac Phase (q.v.) located on an island in Cayuga Lake, in central New York. Dug by W. A. Ritchie in 1939–1940, it comprised a large cemetery, in which were more than 300 well-preserved human skeletons, and an area containing refuse from domestic activities. Since the burials contained materials pertaining to both the Lamoka and Laurentian cultures (qq.v.), Ritchie postulated a culture-contact situation between those two groups.
SOURCES: Ritchie 1945, 1965, 1969.

James A. Tuck

FROST ISLAND PHASE, an expression of the Transitional period in parts of the Northeast, dating to the middle of the second millenium B.C. Its defining characteristics include the use of steatite bowls and, in places, steatite-tempered Marcey Creek Ware (q.v.) pottery. Other traits are broad-bladed projectile points (Susquehanna type), polished-stone celts, and a hunting, fishing, and gathering economy.
SOURCE: Ritchie 1969.

James A. Tuck

FULTON ASPECT, a generally outmoded term devised by A. D. Krieger in 1946 to designate those archaeological manifestations in the Caddoan area dating to the period A.D. 1200–1800. Following the Midwestern classification system then current, he defined the aspect as comprising a number of foci. The A.D. 1200–1800 period now is ascribed to Caddoan Periods III, IV, and V; the terms Middle and Late Caddo have superseded the term Fulton Aspect.
SOURCES: Krieger 1946:205–216; Suhm et al. 1954:151–161, 184–227.

James E. Corbin

G

GAHAGAN MOUND SITE, a Caddo I period plaza-and-mound complex on the west bank of Red River in Red River Parish, Louisiana. First described by C. B. Moore in 1912 as a burial mound 11 feet high and 80 by 100 feet at the base, it was judged to be the center of a considerable population because of the many mound remnants seen. A large central burial shaft with five interments contained numerous offerings, including flaked-stone blades (later termed Gahagan blades), other flint objects, copper-plated ornaments, galena, fine-engraved pottery with red pigment in the lines, and a ceramic human effigy "cloud-blower" pipe.

In 1939, C. H. Webb and M. E. Dodd, Jr., reported two additional large shaft tombs with multiple interments, exotic lithics, Holly Fine Engraved ceramics, copper-plated ear ornaments, sheet-copper plaques, bear-claw effigies, hand cutouts, and two Long-Nosed God masks. ᵗ ᵗer exotics were human and frog effigy stone pipes of bauxite, greenstone celts (including some of spatulate form), and *Marginella* shell beads. They found Coles Creek and early Caddoan sherds along the plaza margins. Relationships to other Caddo I ceremonial centers of the 9th to 11th centuries A.D. have been established. In 1965, Stephen Williams and J. M. Goggin included the Gahagan finds in their description of a widespread Long-Nosed God ceremonial cult, antecedent to the Southern Ceremonial Complex (q.v.).

In the 1940s the Red River ravaged the site, destroying the burial mound, the plaza, and all but two possible mound fragments.

SOURCES: C. B. Moore 1912:511–522; C. H. Webb and Dodd 1939; Williams and Goggin 1965.

Clarence H. Webb

GALISTEO BLACK-ON-WHITE POTTERY, a carbon-paint type dating between the late 1200s and the middle 1400s A.D., found commonly in the northern Rio Grande region of north-central New Mexico, where intruding San Juan peoples are thought to have introduced it in the years bracketing

A.D. 1300. Derived from the McElmo and Mesa Verde Black-on-white types (qq.v.), its area of manufacture appears to have included the southern Pajarito Plateau and the Jemez, northern Rio Abajo, and Tano provinces. Over time, Galisto designs and other attributes were influenced by the Santa Fe and Rio Grande glaze types; in turn, Galisteo influenced other carbon-paint types such as Wiyo Black-on-white of the Pajariot and Tewa basins.
SOURCES: Bice and Sundt 1972; Lang 1982.

Richard W. Lang

GALISTEO PHASE, a late Coalition phase of the Tano Province (q.v.) in north-central New Mexico, dating ca. A.D. 1300–1350 and corresponding to the primary production span of the pottery type Galisteo Black-on-white. During the phase, several villages either were founded or saw substantial growth, and both Tano- and Keres-speaking peoples may have occupied portions of the province. Arroyo Hondo Pueblo, a large town of between 1,000 and 2,000 occupants with the only quasi-great kiva (q.v.) known for the phase, appears to have dominated the province. Some large communities had the two small—one large kiva system, together with intra-roomblock ceremonial rooms, all of which seem to reflect a dual moiety division with lineages and multiple religious society groupings.

Mortuary practice suggests a social organization based on both age and position in the ceremonial heirarchy. There is direct evidence of ditch irrigation, impoundment dams, and check dams. An active trade network focused on exchange both within the province and with peoples of adjacent provinces. The Galisteo Phase closed with the drought of the 1340s and attendant abandonment of settlements, warfare, and disruption of exchange systems.
SOURCES: Lang 1977; Lang and Harris 1984.

Richard W. Lang

GALLAGHER FLINT SITE, a flaking station on the north flank of Alaska's Brooks Range, excavated by E. J. Dixon, Jr., in 1971; noteworthy because of an early radiometric date of 10,540 ±150 years for a core and blade industry.
SOURCE: Dixon 1975.

Donald W. Clark

GALLINA PHASE, a prehistorical (ca. A.D. 1100–1275) manifestation most evident in the southern half of the Largo-Gallina Province (q.v.) in north-central New Mexico. The phase shares most of its traits with the Rosa Phase (q.v.), but has two distinctive types of dwellings that do not occur in Rosa sites: rectangular surface houses with thick masonry walls and deep pithouses, both round and rectangular. The houses of both types contain benches and large ventilator-area partition bins; floors covered with fitted stone slabs; deep, slab-lined fire pits; U-shaped adobe air deflectors; four vertical roof-support posts; and geometric wall frescoes. Pithouses sometimes are connected to surface houses by tunnels.

Most pithouses and surface houses are dispersed and are situated on ridges or in rincons, but some surface houses are in cliff overhangs, and occasionally there are villages of from three to twenty contiguous surface houses. Associated features included dams and ponds for water storage, occasional tower-like granaries, and both terraced and linear stone-edged gardens. Typical artifacts are Gallina Black-on-white pottery, Gallina Gray pointed-bottom culinary ware, painted bird-shaped pots, flat metates, comb-shaped arrow polishers, large elk antler abraders, and tri-notched axes.

Five unnamed, classic Rosa Phase sites—two excavated by H. P. Mera in 1938 and three by E. T. Hall, Jr., in 1941—are located within the Largo-Gallina Province near Gobernador, New Mexico. Dendrodated between A.D. 710 and 866, they provide incontrovertible evidence that the Rosa Phase was directly ancestral to the Gallina Phase.

SOURCES: Hibben 1938:131–136; Dick 1976.

Herbert W. Dick

GALLUP BLACK-ON-WHITE POTTERY, the diagnostic Cibola white-ware of the Bonito Phase in the Chaco Province (qq.v.) of northwestern New Mexico, dating ca. A.D. 1040–1150. It is first and foremost a hachured type, with hachures that usually are narrower than, and at an angle to, the framing lines. Counterposed solid elements occur infrequently. The most common design layouts are non-band elements in running panels and quartered fields.

The hard, thin vessel walls are covered with a thin, chalky slip; decorated surfaces are polished; temper typically is a mixture of grog and either sand or crushed sandstone. Common vessel forms are bowls, ollas, pitchers, and ladles; decorations are executed in a black mineral paint. Chaco Black-on-white is a variety of Gallup Black-on-white, differing from it in details of decoration.

SOURCES: Vivian 1959; Windes 1984; Toll and McKenna, 1987.

Peter J. McKenna

GALVESTON BAY FOCUS, an outmoded term orginally defined to encompass all archaeological assemblages containing pottery and arrow points in the greater Galveston Bay—Houston, Texas area. Sites include riverine and estuarine shell middens, earth middens in the interior, and cemeteries. Extensive excavations in recent years have revealed considerable temporal differentiation within these sites, and a sequence of six ceramic periods for the area has been recognized, extending from ca. A.D. 100 to the early 19th century: Clear Lake (A.D. 100–425), Mayes Island (A.D. 425–650), Turtle Bay (A.D. 650–1000), Round Lake (A.D. 1000–1350), Old River (A.D. 1350–

1725?), and Orcoquisac (A.D. 1725?–1810). This sequence of named periods has largely superseded the concept of the Galveston Bay Focus as a classificatory device.
SOURCES: Suhm et al 1954:128–130; Aten 1983:282–290, 1984.

Lawrence E. Aten

GAMBELL SITES, a series of sites near Gambell Village, St. Lawrence Island, Alaska, a number of which were excavated by H. B. Collins and others in the 1930s. Arranged from oldest to youngest (though some have more than one component), the sites are as follows: Hillside sites (components of early and late Old Bering Sea Phase), Miyowagh (late Old Bering Sea), Ievoghiyog (Punuk Phase), Seklowayaget, and Old Gambell (progressively Punuk into modern). Together with the Punuk Site they form the primary basis for the St. Lawrence Island, or Asian Aspect of the Bering Strait regional sequence.
SOURCES: Collins 1937, 1961.

Donald W. Clark

GARDEN BEDS, raised sandy ridges constructed by Oneota (q.v.) farmers in Wisconsin and Michigan which have been demonstrated to be effective frost drainage systems that enhance corn production.
SOURCE: Moffat 1979.

David Overstreet

GARDEN CREEK SITES, a complex of three mounds and two associated villages on the Pigeon River near Canton, North Carolina, where excavations by J. L. Coe in 1965–67 produced evidence for establishing a sequence of Woodland and Mississipian culture phases in the Appalachian Summit area. Components of the Pigeon, Swannanoa, Connestee, Pisgah, and Qualla phases (qq.v.) were represented, spanning the period ca. 800 B.C.–A.D. 1800. Also, clear evidence of contact between the Connestee Phase and the Hopewell Culture of Ohio (qq.v.) during the Middle Hopewell period was found. The Valentine Museum (in 1880) and G. G. Heye (in 1915) conducted early investigations at the sites.
SOURCES: Keel 1976; Dickens 1976.

Billy L. Oliver

GARGAMELLE COVE SITE, a cave in Newfoundland containing several infant and adult burials with associated artifacts of typical Newfoundland

Dorset styles. Located by amateurs, this is one of the very few known Dorset Phase (q.v.) mortuary sites.
SOURCE: Harp and Hughes 1968.

Moreau S. Maxwell

GAROGA PHASE, the last prehistoric Iroquois culture unit in New York state, dating to the 16th and 17th centuries and manifested by large, heavily fortified villages located in easily defended positions. Scraps of European materials sometimes are found at the sites although, by definition, Europeans did not actually visit them. By, or during, the Garoga Phase, tribal divisions were established and the Iroquois political system evolved to the form recorded by Europeans.
SOURCE: Ritchie 1980:317–324.

James A. Tuck

GARY POINT, a Late Archaic–Early Woodland projectile-point type of wide distribution in the southeastern United States. It has a triangular blade, squared shoulders, a contracting stem, and a rounded or sometimes pointed base. Gary is especially common in the Caddoan area.
SOURCES: Newell and Krieger 1949; Bell 1958; Suhm and Jelks 1962; Leroy Johnson, Jr., 1962.

Elton R. Prewitt

GASTON POTTERY SERIES, a quartz-tempered ware characterized by folded, thickened rims which are often notched along the lip and decorated with circular punctuations or pinches. Surfaces are simple stamped save for rare cordmarking, corncob roughening, or check stamping. Some archaeologists consider the Gaston and Cashie (q.v.) series to be equivalent, but their respective temporal distributions differ.
SOURCES: Coe 1964:105–106; Phelps 1983.

Billy L. Oliver

GASTON SITE, a stratified, multicomponent site near Roanoke Rapids, North Carolina, occupied over a span of some 6000 years (ca. 4000 B.C.–A.D. 1700); excavated by J. L. Coe in 1955. The type site for the Halifax Side-Notched point (q.v.) and for the Vincent, Clements, and Gaston complexes (qq.v.), it also contained components of the Guilford, Halifax, and Savannah River complexes (qq.v.).
SOURCE: Coe 1964.

Billy L. Oliver

GATECLIFF POINT SERIES, a range of medium to large, contracting-stem, chipped-stone projectile points found throughout the desert West, dating ca. 3000–1300 B.C. Gatecliff comprises two separate types: Gatecliff

Split Stem and Gatecliff Contracting Stem. The former were previously termed Pinto points, the latter, Gypsum Cave or Elko Contracting Stem points.
SOURCES: D. H. Thomas 1981, 1983.

David Hurst Thomas

GATECLIFF SHELTER, a deeply stratified, multicomponent rockshelter in central Nevada where the American Museum of Natural History conducted full-scale excavations for seven field seasons between 1970 and 1978. The remarkably well-defined stratigraphic column, more than 10 meters deep, comprised 56 geological strata—including a layer of 6900-year-old Mazama volcanic ash (q.v.)—and sixteen cultural horizons, the oldest evidence of human utilization appearing at ca. 3500 B.C., the latest at ca A.D. 1300. The pattern of artifact and ecofact distribution was heavily size sorted, smaller debris occurring in a distinct drop zone throughout the deposits, save in Horizon 2 which contained the remains of 24 bighorn sheep that had been butchered inside the shelter.

More than 400 typable projectile points found in tight stratigraphic sequence ranged from the Gatecliff series through the Desert series (qq.v.) The shelter also produced roughly 400 incised stones. Male extraction and fabrication activities dominated the archaeological record at Gatecliff; only limited evidence of female extraction, and perhaps maintenance, was present. Gatecliff probably was a short-term field camp used by single-sex groups exploiting a logistic radius some distance from their base camp.
SOURCE: D. H. Thomas 1983.

David Hurst Thomas

GATHRIGHT DAM/LAKE MOOMAW DISTRICT, a narrow valley in the mountains of western Virginia, containing numerous sites dating from the Early Archaic through the Woodland periods. Several researchers have conducted surveys and testing there since 1965, including H. A. MacCord, J. L. Benthall, C. R. Geier, W. P. Boyer, and the Iroquois Research Institute. Of the total known 244 sites, 33 have been tested and 10 have been extensively excavated, research which has led to a four-part division of the Late Woodland and protohistoric periods into the Hidden Valley, Huffman, Noahs Ark, and Perkins Point phases.
SOURCES: Benthall 1969b; Iroquois Research Institute 1978; Geier and Boyer 1982.

Keith T. Egloff

GEORGE C. DAVIS SITE, a major Early Caddoan (ca. A.D. 780–1260) mound and village complex on the Neches River in Cherokee County, in Texas. Mound A, a structural mound, was dug by H. P. Newell in 1939–41 and later was described and interpreted by A. D. Krieger, who designated

Davis the type site for his Alto Focus (q.v.). Later excavations by D. A. Story into Mound B (a structural mound), Mound C (a mortuary mound), and a barrow pit established close similarities between Davis and the Gahagan Site in northwestern Louisiana. Story's excavations also revealed the presence of a large village associated with the mound complex. Artifact distribution patterns suggest two high-status "inner" villages directly associated with the two structural mounds and the mortuary mound. Cultural discontinuities between the Davis Site and components of the Early Ceramic Period (q.v.) in the area suggest that Davis represents a Caddoan expansion from the Red River area.

SOURCES: Newell and Krieger 1949; Story and Valastro 1977, Story 1981.

James E. Corbin

GIBSON ASPECT, a generally outmoded term devised by A. D. Krieger in 1946 to designate those archaeological manifestations in the Caddoan area dating to the period A.D. 800–1200. Following the Midwestern Classification System (q.v.) then current, he defined the aspect as comprising a number of foci. The A.D. 800–1200 period now is ascribed to the Caddoan Periods I and II, or is simply termed Early Caddo (q.v.).

SOURCES: Krieger 1946:205–216; Newell and Krieger 1949:193–224; Suhm et al. 1954:151–184.

James E. Corbin

GILA BEND PROVINCE, the far western peripheral region of the Hohokam Culture's (q.v.) territory, below the confluence of the Salt and Gila rivers at Gila Bend in southern Arizona. Archaeological survey and excavation indicate that prehistoric culture patterns in the province, with some differences, were similar to the patterns in the Phoenix Basin Province (q.v.). The pottery sequence is the same, and village locations a kilometer or more away from the Gila River channel suggest that canal irrigation was an important agricultural practice. Some regional differentiation is evidenced by the presence of fortified hill forts, rock-lined ball courts, and other structures. Typical pithouses and earth-walled ball courts are also present, and a late Sedentary Period (q.v.) platform mound was recorded at the Gatlin Site. Occupation of the province began as early as the Pioneer Period (q.v.), ca. A.D. 1–700, and continued into the Classic Period (q.v.), ca. A.D. 1100–1450. Interaction with Yuman/Patayan populations farther to the west is strongly suspected.

SOURCES: Schroeder 1961a; Wasley and Johnson 1965; Greenleaf 1975a; McGuire and Schiffer 1982.

John S. Cable and David E. Doyel

GILA BUTTE PHASE. See Colonial Period.

GILA PHASE, a phase of the Salado Province of the Southern Sinagua Province, Sinagua Division, Hakataya Culture (qq.v.) in Arizon, dating ca. A.D. 1300–1450. The phase, which marks the end of prehistoric occupation in the Salado Province, combines and replaces two phases—Middle Gila and Tonto—of previous classification schemes. Gila Phase settlements consist of cobblestone buildings, sometimes enclosed with a compound wall, and exhibit a range of site plans. Dwellings are noncontiguous one- and two-room structures. Gila Polychrome is the dominant decorated pottery type. The phase marks the end of recognized prehistoric occupation in the Salado Province.

SOURCES: Doyel 1976a, 1976b.

Albert H. Schroeder

GILA-SALT PROVINCE, a regional manifestation of the Hakataya Culture (q.v.) in southern Arizona, dating ca. A.D. 200–600, which usually has been referred to as the Pioneer Period of the Hohokam Culture (q.v.). The earliest paddle-and-anvil pottery in the Southwest appeared there at the beginning of the Pioneer Period (ca. A.D. 200) along with a small roster of other traits, many of which are found in the earliest phases of adjoining and more distant Hakataya provinces. Hakataya elements—e.g., paddle-and-anvil pottery, incised pottery, four-post roof supports, roasting pits, and notched stones—continued for a while into the Hohokam's Colonial Period (after A.D. 700) in the Gila-Salt Province.

SOURCE: Schroeder 1985.

Albert H. Schroeder

GILBERT SITE, a Norteño Focus (q.v.) village site dating to the third quarter of the 18th century A.D., located on the upper Sabine River in northeastern Texas. Excavations there by members of the Texas Archeological Society in 1962 disclosed seventeen clay-capped midden features, eight of which were excavated or tested. Gilbert produced the largest array of Norteño artifacts known at the time, as well as the largest sample of late 18th-century French trade goods in the southern Plains.

SOURCE: Jelks 1967.

Edward B. Jelks

GLADSTONE SITE, a multicomponent site on Kluane Lake in the southwest Yukon, type site for the former Gladstone Phase (now merged into the Taye Lake Phase [q.v.]) and for a purportedly early "Kluane Complex" of the Cordilleran Tradition that remains to be validated. It was tested by Frederick Johnson and H. M. Raup in 1948, and it was more thoroughly excavated by R. S. MacNeish in 1960 and by R. E. Morlan in 1973.

SOURCE: MacNeish 1964.

Donald W. Clark

GLADWIN CLASSIFICATION SYSTEM. See Southwestern Classification Systems.

GLENCOE PHASE, the single phase of the southern sector of the Sierra Blanca Sub-Province, Jornada Province, Mogollon Culture (qq.v.). Occupying a small area in southeastern New Mexico, the phase dates ca. A.D. 1100–1450. Early Glencoe sites such as the Mayhill sites along the Rio Penasco in the south have five to ten round and square pithouses scattered about terraces or ridges along major mountain streams. The ceramic assemblage is dominated by Jornada Brown, but minor quantities of other types are also present. Corner-notched arrow points and through-trough metates are characteristic. Subsistence was based on hunting and gathering, with agriculture playing a poorly understood but minor role. The southern part of the Glencoe region (the Rio Penasco area) was abandoned during late Pueblo III times, ca. A.D. 1300.

The Bonnell Site (q.v.) on the Rio Ruidoso in the northern part of the Glencoe region has been ascribed to the later part of the Glencoe Phase. During one period at Bonnell, square and rectangular pithouses were arranged in two parallel rows, with the houses in each row placed side by side in quasi-pueblo style. The ceramic assemblage was still dominated by Jornada Brown but also included significant quantities of Chupadero Black-on-white, Three Rivers Red-on-terracotta, Lincoln Black-on-red, and El Paso Polychrome. The presence of other exotic pottery types attests to widened contacts and exchange.

Side-notched arrow points, one-end-closed trough metates, bone gaming pieces, and freshwater mussel-shell ornaments are characteristic. Maize agriculture was practiced, but wild plants and animals were also important food items and may have constituted the dietary mainstays. Cultural influences from Lincoln Phase (q.v.) peoples, who shared a common boundary along the Rio Bonito to the north, were marked during the late Glencoe Phase.

SOURCE: J. H. Kelley 1984.

R. N. Wiseman

GLEN ELDER FOCUS, a rather poorly known complex that, together with materials formerly assigned to the Blue Stone Focus, constitute the White Rock Aspect (q.v.). The type site, Glen Elder, is in Mitchell County, in Kansas. The focus may be related to an early (ca. A.D. 1500) intrusion of Siouan speakers into north-central Kansas. Its most diagnostic trait is Walnut Decorated Lip pottery, a ware with strap handles and trailed or incised decorations similar to pottery of the Oneota Tradition (q.v.).

SOURCE: J. O. Marshall 1969.

Patricia J. O'Brien

GLENROSE CANNERY SITE, a deeply stratified site on the Fraser River in southwestern British Columbia, about 20 kilometers from the sea, but at or near the river's mouth at the time of first occupation, ca. 6500 B.C.

There have been several excavations at the site; the principal work is that of R. G. Matson in the early 1970s. The site's significance lies in its stratigraphic evidence for temporal ordering of the Old Cordilleran, St. Mungo, and Marpole culture types. It also contained an Old Cordilleran artifact assemblage that indicated a rudimentary woodworking industry and use of land, riverine, and marine resources before 6000 years B.C.
SOURCE: R. G. Matson 1976.

Donald H. Mitchell

GLENWOOD PHASE, the easternmost expression of the Central Plains Tradition (q.v.), concentrated in a 40-square-mile area of the Horse and Pony creek drainages along the Missouri River loess bluffs in southwestern Iowa. Dating ca. A.D. 900–1100, Glenwood is closely related to the Nebraska Phase (q.v.) of eastern Nebraska. Glenwood people grew corn, beans, and squash; they lived in isolated, square earthlodges strung along ridgelines or in small clusters in stream valleys.
SOURCE: Zimmerman 1977.

Larry J. Zimmerman

GLYCYMERIS BRACELET, a type of jewelry widely traded in the Southwest, made by chipping and grinding a large valve of the seashell *Glycymeris* into a usually simple, but sometimes elaborately carved and even painted bracelet. They were manufactured by the Hohokam and Trincheras cultures (qq.v.) and possibly by others. Smaller *Glycymeris* shells were also worked into necklaces, ear dangles, and rings.
SOURCE: Haury 1976.

David A. Phillips, Jr.

GOBERNADOR PHASE, a term for the archaeological remains of the Navajo occupation of the Upper San Juan Province (q.v.) in northern New Mexico and southern Colorado between A.D. 1700 and 1775. Thousands of 18th-century Navajo hogan sites have been recorded within the greater Four Corners region, centering in northwestern New Mexico and southwestern Colorado. They express an episode of intense acculturation through co-residence and intermarriage with Pueblo Indians and through contacts with Spanish colonists.
SOURCE: Farmer 1942; Keur 1944; Dittert et al., 1961; J. J. Hester 1962; Hester and Shiner 1963; Schaafsma 1963; R. L. Carlson 1965; Eddy et al. 1983.

Frank W. Eddy

GO-KART NORTH SITE, a large Late Archaic, Titterington Phase (q.v.) base settlement on the Mississippi River floodplain in southwestern Illinois. Excavations in 1978 by a team from the University of Illinois at Urbana-Champaign exposed 124 pits distributed in a linear pattern along the outer cut bank of an abandoned channel of the Mississippi River. An extensive diagnostic artifact assemblage was coincident with the distribution of pits. Go-Kart North was the first site in the region to exhibit a complete community site plan dating to the Titterington Phase, and it also produced the first series of radiocarbon dates for the phase in the Midwest—seven dates clustering around 2100 B.C..

SOURCES: Fortier and Emerson 1984; Bareis and Porter 1984.

Andrew C. Fortier

GOLD MINE SITE, a low mound with included burial platforms and bathtub-shaped fire pits; the only Troyville Culture (q.v.) site dug in recent years. J. S. Belmont's excavations there in 1980 yielded two polychrome human effigy vessels and disclosed a number of dog burials.

SOURCE: Belmont 1982.

William G. Haag

GOODALL FOCUS, a culture unit defined in the 1940s by G. I. Quimby as the regional expression of Middle Woodland Hopewell culture in western and southwestern Michigan. Sites constituting the focus were associated with major river systems including the St. Joseph, the Grand, and the Muskegon. Mounds at these sites have been excavated at various times beginning in the 19th century and continuing into the 1980s. The structure of the mounds and the artifacts in them indicate a strong connection with Illinois Havana Middle Woodland culture. The Norton mound group (q.v.) in Grand Rapids, excavated by the University of Michigan in 1963–1964, in particular exhibited detailed similarities to Illinois Hopewell sites.

SOURCE: Quimby 1941a, 1941b, 1943, 1944; J. A. Brown 1964; Flanders 1965; Prahl 1966, 1970; Griffin et al. 1970.

Margaret B. Holman

GOODEN MOUND GROUP. See Maples Mill Site.

GOOSE CREEK WARE, a series of four sandy-paste pottery types (Goose Creek Plain, Goose Creek Incised, Goose Creek Red-Filmed, and Goose Creek Stamped), dating between 100 B.C. and the early 19th century, found widely over coastal and interior southwestern Louisiana and southeastern Texas in both earth and shell middens. Vessels are of typical Woodland (q.v.) shapes and are decorated with achromatic designs closely related to those of Tchefuncte and Coles Creek (qq.v.) ceramics of the lower Mississippi River Valley. The respective types and their varieties, singly or in combination, are diagnostic of particular time periods and are the primary basis for culture chronology in their principal geographic range. The ware appears to have been made by the historical Atakapa and eastern Karankawa tribes and their ancestors.

SOURCE: Wheat 1953:184–190, figs. 19–21, pls. 31–33; Suhm et al. 1954:378–382; Aten 1983:206–237.

Lawerence E. Aten

GORDON CREEK BURIAL, a tightly flexed, 25- to 30-year-old female in a pit coated with red ocher, found in Roosevelt National Forest, Colorado, in 1963. Accompanied by bifaces, a hammerstone, flaked tools, incised animal ribs, and elk incisors, it is thought to be of Early Archaic or Late Paleoindian origin. The left ilium produced a radiocarbon date of 7750 B.C. ±250 years and some charcoal from the grave was dated 7470 B.C. ±120 years.

SOURCES: D. C. Anderson 1966; Gillio 1970; Breternitz et al. 1971.

David A. Breternitz

GORDON SITE, a Mississippian period site in Jefferson County, Mississippi, that originally contained two flat-topped, conical, or pyramidal mounds. It was judged to be the type site for the Coles Creek Culture (q.v.) before J. L. Cotter excavated it completely in 1950 and discovered that it actually was occupied from Late Coles Creek time through most of the following Plaquemine period (ca. A.D. 1000–1500).

SOURCE: Cotter 1952.

William G. Haag

GOSHEN COMPLEX, the immediate predecessor of the Folsom Culture (q.v.) on the Northwestern High Plains; defined in 1973 from the Hell Gap Site (q.v.) in southeastern Wyoming, and further defined in 1985 from the Mill Iron Site, probably a small bison kill, in southeastern Montana. Three radiocarbon dates from Mill Iron average 9,280 B.C.

The projectile points of the complex are basally thinned but, even though they fall short of being fluted like Folsom points, they demonstrate well-developed pressure-flaking techniques that are necessary preconditions for successful fluting. Because these points are reminiscent of Plainview (q.v.) points of the southern Plains, surface finds of Goshen points in the past often have been identified as Plainview and therefore ascribed a post-Folsom age. However, the total Goshen tool assemblage at Mill Iron strongly resembles the Clovis Culture's (q.v.) tool assemblage, which predates Folsom in the Plains.

The Mill Iron Site has not yet been published. The lowest level at the Carter-Kerr/McGee Site (q.v.) in the Powder River Basin, initially identified as a Clovis occupation, is now recognized as a Goshen component.

SOURCES: Irwin-Williams et al. 1973; Frison 1984.

George C. Frison

GOTTSCHALL ROCKSHELTER, a small site in Iowa County, in southwestern Wisconsin, noted for pictographs of animals, humans, and unidentified subjects. One set likely depicts the Ioway myth of Red Horn. Deposits

in the shelter, estimated to date ca. A.D. 1100–1200, include both Effigy Mound and Oneota (qq.v.) occupations. Smashed and cut human remains in the trash midden provide ample testimony to late prehistoric cannibalism.
SOURCE: Salzer n.d.b.

David Overstreet

GOVERNMENT MOUNTAIN, a prominent mountain about 30 kilometers northwest of Flagstaff, Arizona, that was a source of the obsidian traded throughout Arizona in prehistoric times.
SOURCES: Granger 1960; Jack 1971; Schreiber and Breed 1971.

Peter J. Pilles, Jr.

GOWER POINT, an Early Archaic dart-point type, dating ca. 7000–4000 B.C., a definitive trait of both the San Geronimo Phase (q.v.) of central Texas and the Viejo Phase of southwestern Texas. It has a triangular blade, shoulders that range from squared to rounded, a parallel-sided to mildly expanding stem (often smoothed along the edges), and a deeply concave base.
SOURCES: Shafer 1963; Crawford 1965; Prewitt 1981.

Elton R. Prewitt

GRAHAM TRADITION, a manifestation of the Developmental Stage of the British Columbia coastal sequence in the Queen Charlotte Islands; comprising all shell-midden sites dating within the last 5000 years that contain organic and ground/polished stone artifacts. Two Graham Tradition components have been excavated: the Blue Jackets Creek and Honna River sites.
SOURCES: P. D. Sutherland 1974; Fladmark 1975.

Knut R. Fladmark

GRAN CHICHIMECA, a term for a vast North American culture area that, as defined by C. C. Di Peso, comprises some 170 million square kilometers, extending from the Pacific Ocean on the west to 97° west longitude on the east, and from the Tropic of Cancer (23° 27′ north latitude) on the south to the 38th parallel on the north. Thus, it encompasses all of northern Mexico, New Mexico, and Arizona, the western three-fourths of Texas, the southern portions of California, Nevada, Utah, and Colorado, western Oklahoma, and most of southern Kansas.

The name originated in prehistoric Mesoamerica, was used by early Spanish explorers, and was revived by Di Peso in conjunction with his work at Casas Grandes (q.v.) to define the context of the systemic/historical relationships between Mesoamerica, the southwestern United States, the southern Plains, and adjacent areas. Di Peso perceived a broad, encompassing Chichimecan cultural pattern that included a number of indigenous "basic cultures"—e.g., Mogollon, Anasazi, and Desert Hohokam (qq.v.)—which evolved from an early, shared Paleoindian/Archaic (qq.v.) foundation through a series of generally similar sequences in geographically definable subareas.

SOURCE: Di Peso 1968, 1974; vol. 1.

Gloria J. Fenner

GRAND CANYON PROVINCE, the inner canyon and rims of the Grand Canyon of the Colorado River, occupied by western Anasazi (q.v.) people, mainly between A.D. 950 and 1150. There is some evidence of light earlier utilization, as well as of limited later occupation until ca. A.D. 1200–1225. Unlike most of their more sedentary neighbors, the people of the province moved regularly with the seasons to exploit the wide range of plants and animals that had adapted to the respective environmental niches afforded by the rims and inner canyon. This lifestyle tended to produce small, seasonal habitation sites and isolated granaries. Thus, while typical western Anasazi sites average from six to seven rooms, those in the canyon usually have only from two to four. Some, however, both on the rims and in the inner canyon, have up to twenty.

SOURCES: Plog 1979a:108; Effland et al. 1981.

Janet R. Balsom

GRAND RIVER PHASE. See Oneota Tradition.

GRAN QUIVIRA SITE, a location in Salinas National Monument, in New Mexico containing remains of the Tompiro Pueblos (ca. A.D.1375–1672), the Franciscan chapel of the San Ysidro (A.D. 1627–1659), and the mission complex of San Buenaventura (ca. A.D. 1659–1672). The site contains 21 Pueblo house mounds, 10 kivas, and a graveyard associated with the late prehistoric and Spanish Colonial occupations. E. L. Hewett and others excavated the church complexes from 1923 to 1927, and J. H. Toulouse, Jr., stabilized the churches and convento rooms between 1940 and 1942. Gordon Vivian conducted additional excavations in the churches and in the pueblo house mounds and kivas in 1951; A. C. Hayes dug the largest of the house mounds between 1965 and 1967.

An important gateway to the Plains, Gran Quivira played a major role in Plains-Pueblo interregional trade throughout the late prehistoric and Spanish Colonial periods. A large burial population from the site has contributed significantly to knowledge of protohistoric Puebloan demography.

SOURCES: Vivian 1964; A. C. Hayes 1981.

Frances Levine

GRAPEVINE PUEBLO, an unexcavated village of at least 50 ground-floor rooms on Anderson Mesa in northern Arizona; the type site for the Clear Creek Focus (q.v.) of the Sinagua Branch of the Mogollon Root, dating ca. A.D. 1300–1400. Crudely constructed of basalt cobbles and some slab ma-

sonry, the buildings may have been two stories high. The layout is basically linear, three to five tiers wide, with possible plaza areas and kivas.
SOURCES: Colton 1939a, 1946.

Donald E. Weaver, Jr.

GRASSHOPPER FALLS PHASE, a late prehistoric (ca. A.D. 500–1000) hunting-gathering, Plains Woodland culture in northeastern Kansas. Excavated sites contained remains of oval house structures of less than 100 square meters, with external limestone hearths and both external and internal shallow, trash-filled pits. The houses occur in small clusters scattered on alluvial terraces adjacent to secondary drainages.
SOURCES: J. D.Reynolds 1979, 1981.

John D. Reynolds

GRASSHOPPER SITE, a 500-room Pueblo ruin on the Fort Apache Indian Reservation in the mountains of east-central Arizona, occupied ca. A.D. 1300–1400 by at least two ethnic groups: Mogollon (the larger group) and Anasazi (qq.v.). Dry farming techniques produced maize, beans, squash, and cotton; the diet was heavily supplemented by hunting and gathering. Community organizations began with households related by kinship and religious ties expressed in the joint use of ceremonial rooms. Four to six societies provided community leadership.

Since 1963, the University of Arizona Archaeological Field School—the longest, continuous archaeological project in North America—has uncovered 100 rooms and 674 burials and has produced twelve dissertations and numerous journal articles.
SOURCES: J. J. Reid 1974; Longacre et al. 1982; Reid and Whittlesey 1982:687–703.

J. Jefferson Reid

GRAVE CREEK PHASE, second earliest of five phases at the Weis Rockshelter (q.v.) in Idaho, named by B. R. Butler and now estimated to date from between 4700 and 3000 B.C. to ca. 2500 B.C.. Large side-notched and lanceolate projectile points are the chief diagnostics of the phase, which is closely comparable to the later stages of the Cascade and Vantage phases (qq.v.).
SOURCE: B. R. Butler 1962.

Frank C. Leonardy

GRAVELS PHASE. See Brooks River-Naknek Drainage Sites.

GRAVEYARD PHASE. See Brooks River-Naknek Drainage Sites.

GRAYSON POTTERY SERIES, a Middle Woodland, quartz-tempered ceramic decorated with net, cord, fabric, or check-stamp impressions, found in southwestern Virginia on both sides of the Blue Ridge escarpment. It is

similar to the Albemarle Series (q.v.) to the north and to the Yadkin-Uwhar-
rie series (qq.v.) to the south.
SOURCE: Holland 1970.

Keith T. Egloff

GREAT BEND ASPECT, a protohistoric culture complex in the Great Bend
area of the Arkansas River in south-central Kansas that comprises two foci:
Lower Walnut and Little River. Defined by W. R. Wedel, the complex is
attributed to the ancestral Wichita Indians and dates from ca. A.D. 1300
into the 19th century. Many of its sites are quite large and often have storage
pits over two meters deep. Its diagnostic traits are council circles (q.v.) and
shell-tempered, sometimes first-bottomed pottery.
SOURCE: Wedel 1959.

Patricia J. O'Brien

GREAT KIVA, a very large (ca. 16–25 meters in diameter), usually round,
subterranean, ceremonial chamber, examples of which occur along with
small kivas at major San Juan Anasazi (q.v.) communities. Thought to have
been used for community-wide ceremonial activities, they may have an
encircling bench, post, or coursed-masonry roof supports; a masonry firebox; multiple wall niches; paired subfloor vaults ("floor drums"); peripheral
ground-level rooms; and a "northern annex." Great kivas apparently developed from large Basketmaker III communal structures and are most
common in Anasazi areas exposed to Chacoan influence. After the major
Chacoan sites were abandoned ca. A.D. 1130, great kivas survived in the
Zuni area until at least the end of the Pueblo III period (ca. 1325). Pueblo
IV (Classic Period) "big kivas" in Rio Grande Anasazi provinces bore some
resemblance to the earlier great kivas but were appreciably smaller.
    Large, rectangular, ceremonial structures in Mogollon provinces which
may have been used for communal religious activities often are called "Mogollon great kivas." These generally have a broad ramp entry, sometimes
paired subfloor vaults, and, occasionally, a square enclosure of logs set in
the floor around the central hearth; however, they usually lack the other
features of Anasazi great kivas.
SOURCES: E. H. Morris 1919; F. H. H. Roberts, Jr. 1932; Martin et al. 1936;
Hawley 1950; Martin et al. 1957; Bluhm 1957; Judd 1964; Vivian and Reiter 1965;
Peckham 1979; Cattanach 1980; M. P. Marshall 1982.

Stewart Peckham

GREAT NECK DISTRICT, an area at the northern end of Pungo Ridge in
lower tidewater Virginia containing extensive remains of Middle and Late
Woodland cultures. Components in the district have been studied by Floyd

Painter, P. R. Green, C. R. Geier, and the Virginia Research Center for Archaeology.
SOURCES: Painter 1967, 1979; Egloff and Turner 1984.

Keith T. Egloff

GREAT OASIS COMPLEX, a manifestation of the Initial Variant of the Middle Missouri Tradition (q.v.), dating ca. A.D. 800–1100, centered in northwestern Iowa and extending over parts of Minnesota, North and South Dakota, and Nebraska. Villages contain rectangular, semisubterranean houses and numerous storage/trash pits. Subsistence was based on corn agriculture supplemented with bison, deer, small mammals, fish, and migratory birds. Two pottery types are considered diagnostic: Great Oasis High Rim and Great Oasis Wedge Lip, both occurring as grit-tempered, globular vessels with smoothed-over bodies that are decorated with bands or panels of trailed rectilinear motifs.
SOURCES: Henning 1971; Henning and Henning 1978.

Christy Hohman-Caine

GREAT OASIS CULTURE, an archaeological manifestation defined by L. A. Wilford in 1942, distributed over northwestern Iowa and extending up the Missouri River to Mobridge, South Dakota. Possibly related to the Initial Middle Missouri Variant, it dates ca. A.D. 900–1300 and is distinguished by grit-tempered pottery without handles that has polished-over, cord-wrapped, paddle-marked exterior surfaces. Its Mississippian affinities are reflected in its triangular projectile points with and without notches.
SOURCES: Johnston 1967; Henning 1971.

Patricia J. O'Brien

GREAT SALT LAKE MARSH SITES, a series of open sites containing structures, dating to the Sevier/Fremont and late prehistoric periods, located on the marshy deltas of the Weber, Ogden, Jordan, and Bear rivers that feed the Great Salt Lake in Utah. Site density there is by far the highest in the eastern Great Basin. Subsistence data are sketchy, but there was an apparent focus on marsh resources with little evidence of horticulture.
SOURCES: Marwitt 1970; Madsen 1982a.

David B. Madsen

GREAT SALT SPRINGS SITE, a large Mississippian (q.v.) salt-processing site on the lower Saline River in Gallatin County, in Illinois, that also was the locus of an extensive early 19th-century Euroamerican salt works. Although noted in early archaeological literature, the site received no systematic professional treatment until 1981–1982, when John Muller conducted small-scale excavations and mapped the site in detail. He discovered thick

deposits of fire-cracked rock and other pyrolithic products, as well as large quantities of shell-tempered panware and numerous small fired-clay basins.
SOURCES: Sellars 1877; Muller 1984.

Brian M. Butler

GREEN BAY PHASE. See Oneota Tradition.

GREENHILL MOUND, an extensive South Appalachian Mississippian village site situated on a natural sand ridge in the Congaree Swamp, in Richland County, in South Carolina, estimated to date ca. A.D. 1600. Pee Dee (q.v.) urn burials, shell artifacts, and celts have been reported from the site.
SOURCE: Anonymous n.d.

Michael Trinkley

GREEN'S SHELL ENCLOSURE, a shell midden (not actually an enclosure) on Hilton Head Island, in Beaufort County, in South Carolina. Briefly examined by Alan Calmes in 1967, it dates to the Irene Phase (ca. A.D. 1500) of the South Appalachian Mississippian period (qq.v.).
SOURCE: Calmes n.d.b.

Michael Trinkley

GREENWOOD PHASE, a Plaines Woodland cultural manifestation in the Flint Hills and western Osage Plains of eastern Kansas, consisting of villages and small camps in floodplain locations, dating ca. A.D. 400–1000. Distinctive traits include pottery types Verdigris and Greenwood, lithic artifacts typical of this Woodland period, and medium to large daub-covered, oval houses. Curry and Two Dog (qq.v.) are type sites of the phase.
SOURCE: Witty 1982.

Thomas A. Witty, Jr.

GRIESMER SITE, a predominantly Upper Mississippian, early summer camp located north of the Kankakee River in northwestern Lake County, in Indiana. Huber and Fisher phase occupations are present. After excavating there in 1962, C. H. Faulkner concluded that it probably was occupied by Central Algonkian peoples, perhaps the Miami or Illinois.
SOURCE: Faulkner 1972.

James H. Kellar

GROSWATER DORSET PHASE, a cultural manifestation dating ca. 700–350 B.C., centering on the Hamilton Inlet region of Labrador. Distinctive artifacts and settlement systems distinguish it from both the terminal Pre-Dorset Phase and the early Dorset Phase (qq.v.), both of which it overlaps. Its apparently unique response to the environment is thought to have led

to the transition between Pre-Dorset and Dorset. Isolated traits of the phase appear on the Belcher Islands, the Melville Peninsula, and Baffin Island.
    SOURCES: Fitzhugh 1972; Maxwell 1985:115–117.

                                                              Moreau S. Maxwell

GROTON PLANTATION LOCALITY, an area adjacent to the Savannah River in Allendale and Hampton counties, in South Carolina which contains a nearly complete culture sequence from the Early Archaic through the South Appalachian Mississippian period (ca. 8000 B.C.–A.D. 1550). J. B. Stoltman in 1964 and Drexel Peterson in 1969 conducted extensive studies at a variety of sites in the locality, most notably Rabbit Mount and Clear Mount (qq.v.).
    SOURCES: Stoltman 1974a; Drexel Peterson 1971.

                                                              Michael Trinkley

GROUND HOG BAY 2 SITE, a multicomponent site on the north shore of Icy Strait, Alaska, which, when excavated in 1965, extended Northwest coast culture history by several thousand years. The four components span the time from ca. 7200 B.C. to the historic period. Components IV and III contained an early lithic assemblage with both microblade and macroblade industries, bifaces, choppers, scrapers, and flakes. Component II was characterized by ground-stone tools and plank houses. Component I was a surficial historic occupation.
    SOURCES: Ackerman 1968, 1974, 1980; Ackerman et al. 1979.

                                                              Robert E. Ackerman

GROVE FOCUS, a Middle to Late Archaic (ca. 6000–600 B.C.), nonceramic cultural/technological tradition of the prairie-forest border in the northeastern Oklahoma Ozarks. Three sequential complexes (Grove A, B, and C) have been defined, primarily on the basis of shifts through time in projectile point and knife forms. The inferred way of life is that of small-scale, semisedentary groups using diverse forest, prarie, and riverine resources.
    SOURCES: Baerreis 1951; Purrington 1971:522–531.

                                                              Burton L. Purrington

GUADALUPE RUIN, a single-story, 50-room, stone-masonry pueblo situated on an isolated mesa in the middle Rio Puerco Valley, in southwestern Sandoval County, in New Mexico. L. C. Pippin excavated a 40 percent sample of the site between 1972 and 1975. During its initial occupation, ca. A.D. 900–1200, Guadalupe was one of several pueblos in northwestern New Mexico and southwestern Colorado that displayed an architectural form characteristic of "towns" in Chaco Canyon, in New Mexico. The inhabitants of these outlying pueblos communicated with the Chaco Canyon communities along well-defined roads. However, despite the architectural similarities and connecting roads, they had a material culture like that of the local, regionally differentiated, village populations rather than like that at Chaco Canyon.

After having been abandoned by its original inhabitants, Guadalupe was reoccupied in the late 13th century by people with a San Juan/Mesa Verde-like culture, but their stay was short lived, and they abandoned the site in the early 14th century. This second occupation probably reflects the acculturation of San Juan Anasazi migrants into the newly developing Rio Grande cultural sphere.

SOURCE: Pippin 1979.

Lonnie C. Pippin

GUERNSEY SITE, a location on an island in the Wateree River in Kershaw County, in South Carolina where cultural materials that eroded from sites upriver have been redeposited. These materials span the period ca. A.D. 500–1400 and include the type collection from Camden Ware (q.v.) pottery.

SOURCES: J. B. Griffin 1945; Stuart 1975.

Michael Trinkley

GUILFORD LANCEOLATE POINT, a long, slender, relatively thick, leaf-shaped projectile point with a straight, convex, or concave base. The distal edges and base often are smoothed. Dating ca. 4000 B.C., the type is widely distributed throughout the North Carolina Piedmont and occurs less commonly in adjacent mountain and coastal areas. Thought to represent an intrusive technological tradition (most likely from the west), Guilford points may have some relationship to the Nebo Hill points of the southern Plains (see Nebo Hill Phase).

SOURCES: Coe 1964:43; Oliver 1985.

Billy L. Oliver

GULF HAZARD SITES, several late (15th century A.D.) Dorset Phase settlements near Richmond Gulf on the southeastern coast of Hudson Bay, excavated by Elmer Harp, Jr., in 1974. Many earlier Dorset traits had been retained; a copper amulet of European metal was found in a house.

SOURCE: Harp 1976.

Moreau S. Maxwell

GULF OF GEORGIA CULTURE TYPE (or DEVELOPED COAST SALISH), a late unit in the Northwest Coast's southern Gulf of Georgia region, dating from ca. A.D. 400 to historic contact, characterized by small, triangular, flaked-basalt points; thin, triangular, ground-slate points; thin, ground-slate knives; flat-topped hand mauls (q.v.); celts; unilaterally barbed bone points; numerous single- and double-pointed bone artifacts; composite, toggling harpoon valves; geometrically decorated pins and combs; antler wedges and hafts. Flaked-stone artifacts are scarce; bone implements occur frequently.

Virtually all authorities agree that components of the Gulf of Georgia culture type represent Coast Salish occupation.

SOURCES: Borden 1970; Ham 1982; D. H. Mitchell 1971.

Donald H. Mitchell

GULL CLIFF SITE, a settlement of clustered tent rings at Port Refuge, on northwestern Devon Island, Northwest Territories; excavated between 1972 and 1977 by R. J. McGhee, who identified it as Pre-Dorset instead of Independence I because of discrete characteristics of lithic artifacts and because toggling harpoon heads with open sockets were present. The site is some 3 meters closer to sea level than the nearby Cold and Upper Beaches sites, both ascribed to the Independence I Phase, where the dwellings were in linear rather than in clustered arrangements.

SOURCE: McGhee 1979.

Moreau S. Maxwell

GUNTHER ISLAND SITE, the late prehistoric/historic village site of Tolowot, home of the Athapascan-speaking Wiyot people, on Humboldt Bay in northern coastal California. L. L. Loud excavated the site in 1918 and recovered artifacts reflecting late prehistoric influences from Northwest Coast cultures.

SOURCE: Moratto 1984:484–487, 564–565.

Michael J. Moratto

H

HACKBERRY PHASE, a phase of the Verde Province of the Sinagua Division, Hakataya Culture (qq.v.) in Arizona, dating ca. A.D. 700–800. It was originally described on the basis of a partially excavated, slab-lined pithouse containing Verde Brown pottery, round to oval manos, and irregular, thick blades similar to specimens of the Snaketown Phase of the Gila-Salt Province (q.v.). Intrusive Hohokam influences appeared during the Hackberry Phase, including Snaketown Red-on-gray and Gila Butte Red-on-buff pottery, found in association with the Anasazi (q.v.) type Lino Black-on-gray.
SOURCES: Shutler 1951; Breternitz 1960.

Albert H. Schroeder

HAGEN SITE, a village of the A.D. 1780s on the Lower Yellowstone River in Montana, representative of the late horticultural traditions of the Plains. Its artifacts are similar to those of the Mandan and Hidatsa of the Middle Missouri River area, suggesting that this may have been a village of the related Crow people, who occupied the territory in protohistoric times.
SOURCE: Mulloy 1942.

Patricia J. O'Brien

HAKATAYA CULTURE, a prehistoric, pottery-making culture that occupied parts of southwestern Arizona, southern California, and northern Baja California after ca. A.D. 200; formerly sometimes called the Yuman Culture. Three Hakataya divisions have been recognized: the Laquish Division (q.v.) along the lower Colorado and Gila rivers in Arizona; the Patayan Division (q.v.) of upper Baja California, southern Californina, and western Arizona; and the Sinagua Division (q.v.) in the area extending southward from Flagstaff, Arizona, into the drainages of the Verde, East Verde, Tonto, and Agua Fria rivers.

The Hakataya Culture originated in the Gila-Salt Province (q.v.) in south-western Arizona ca. A.D. 200 with the appearance of paddle-and-anvil pottery. From there, it diffused northward to just below the Mogollon Rim and westward to the Pacific coast, arriving there ca. 1300. The Hohokam Culture (q.v.) is thought to have entered the Gila-Salt area from the south ca. A.D. 600 and to have established colonies among adjoining Hakatayan people to the north. (This interpretation has been challenged by some.) Early attributes and briefly occupied sites suggest a mobile or seasonal type of existence with some agriculture. After A.D. 1100–1150, Hohokam elements disappeared from the northern Hakataya region as the number of Anasazi and Mogollon (qq.v.) traits increased.

SOURCES: Schroeder 1960, 1979, (in press).

Albert H. Schroeder

HALE MOUND SITE, one of the westernmost Caddoan mound complexes, located on a high terrace overlooking Blundell Creek in western Titus County, in Texas. It consists of one conical mound, one platform mound, three or more natural knolls overlain by midden debris, a borrow pit, and an artifact deposit around and between the mounds. A. T. Jackson tested the site in 1934 with a Works Progress Administration crew, and O. F. McCormick, III made a surface collection of artifacts there in 1971. Reanalysis of ceramics from the mounds by J. P. Thurmond, II in 1981 led him to conclude that they date to the Early Caddoan Period (ca. A.D. 800–1200). Artifacts from the intervening areas are attributed to the Titus Phase (q.v.) of the Late Caddoan Period (ca. A.D. 1600–1700).

SOURCES: Jackson n.d.b.; McCormick 1973:106; Thurmond 1981:346–353.

Susan V. Lisk and Margaret Ann Howard

HALIFAX SIDE-NOTCHED POINT, a shallowly side-notched, generally slender projectile point with smoothed notches and base, distributed north and east of the lower Roanoke River in northeastern North Carolina. Examples were found at the Gaston Site (q.v.) sandwiched between occupation zones of the Guilford and Savannah River phases, in a stratum radiocarbon dated to ca. 3500 B.C.

SOURCE: Coe 1964: 108–110.

Billy L. Oliver

HAMILTON INLET LOCALITY, locus of major concentrations of Groswater Dorset Phase (q.v.) sites on the east coast of Labrador.

SOURCE: Fitzhugh 1972.

Moreau S. Maxwell

HAMILTON POINT, a variety of the late prehistoric, small, triangular, chipped-stone arrow point, distinguished by incurvate blade and base. Associated with Late Woodland and Early Mississippian cultures of Central Tennessee and northeastern Alabama, it dates ca. A.D. 800–1100.

SOURCES: Lewis and Kneberg 1946:110–111; Kneberg 1956:24; B. M. Butler 1971:30–32; Faulkner 1968; Futato 1977; McCollough and Faulkner 1978.

Eugene M. Futato

HAND MAUL, a kind of hand-held stone hammer known from the Northwest coast and the interior Plateau areas. On the south and central coast and in the adjacent interior occur tapering, spool-shaped forms with broad, flaring striking heads. Northern forms have similar striking heads but are T-shaped to provide a transverse grip at the proximal end. Mauls were probably multipurpose tools used for a variety of pounding or crushing tasks. In woodworking, they were used to drive splitting wedges and chisels.
SOURCE: Hilary Stewart 1973.

Donald H. Mitchell

HAND SITE, a Late Woodland to protohistoric palisaded village located on the Nottoway River in the interior coastal plain of southern Virginia, thought to have been occupied by ancestors of the historic Nottoway Indians. G. P. Smith excavated the site in 1965–1966 and found many features including hearths, storage pits, house patterns, and human and dog burials.
SOURCES: G. P. Smith 1971, 1984.

Keith T. Egloff

HANO (or TEWA VILLAGE) SITE, a village at the north end of First Mesa in northeastern Arizona that was settled in A.D. 1700–1701 by about 300 southern Tewa (or Tano) refugees from the Galisteo Basin, New Mexico, who had fled the Spanish reconquest of their homeland. It was of the hollow-square, central-plaza form typical of the Rio Grande area, with two rectangular, near-surface kivas (one inside, one outside the plaza) and stone-built houses one to four stories high. It probably never held more than 300 people. T. B. Birkedal, Barbara Holmes, and others excavated there between 1980 and 1985 and discovered ceramic evidence of a Pueblo III village on the same site as ca. A.D. 1250–1300.

Hano is particularly known for (1) its proven Rio Grande Tano, or southern Tewa, origins in the midst of the western Hopi Province (q.v.), (2) its role as one of the principal places where the non-Hopi pottery style known as Payupki Polychrome was introduced to the province, and (3) the revival of traditional Hopi pottery by local potters ca. 1895–1900.
SOURCES: Fewkes 1906; Dozier 1954, 1966; Stanislawski 1978, 1979; Holmes and Stanislawski 1986.

Michael B. Stanislawski

HANOVER POTTERY SERIES, a sherd- or clay-tempered ware with fabric-impressed or cord-marked surface finish, dating ca. 300 B.C.–A.D. 400

and distributed across the Tidewater and Coastal Plain regions, from north-eastern North Carolina to the vicinity of Charleston, South Carolina.
SOURCES: South 1976:16–17; Phelps 1983.

Billy L. Oliver

HANOVER WARE. See Wilmington Ware.

HANSON SITE, a campsite of the Folsom Culture (q.v.) in the Big Horn Basin of northern Wyoming that produced a large tool assemblage plus enough debitage to allow the formulation of a complete manufacturing sequence for Folsom type projectile points (q.v.). It was dug in 1973 and 1975 by George Frison.
SOURCES: Frison 1978; Frison and Bradley 1980.

George Frison

HANSONVILLE SITE, a Late Woodland village on the upper drainage of the North Fork of the Holston River in southwestern Virginia. C. G. Holland identified the site in the 1960s; K. E. Bott tested it in 1979, discovering human burials, hearths, and postmolds. The village's upland location led to the hypothesis that in prehistoric times some colluvial upland soils may have been more productive agriculturally than were floodplain soils.
SOURCES: Holland 1970; Bott 1981.

Keith T. Egloff

HARDAWAY-DALTON POINT (or BLADE), a broad, thin projectile point with a deeply concave base and shallow side notches, estimated to date ca. 11,000–10,000 B.C.. Base and notches are smoothed; edges are frequently serrated. Originally identified at the Hardaway Site (q.v.) in North Carolina and widely distributed in the southeastern United States, the type is considered a direct descendant of the Hardaway Point (q.v.) and a predecessor of the Hardaway Side-Notched type (q.v.).
SOURCES: Coe 1964:65; Oliver 1985.

Billy L. Oliver

HARDAWAY POINT (or BLADE), a broad, thin, chipped-stone projectile point with a concave, thinned base, estimated to date ca. 12,000–10,000 B.C.. Basal grinding occurs only rarely. Examples were found in the lowest levels of the Hardaway Site (q.v.) in North Carolina. Similar in form to the Quad type point (q.v.) of Alabama and Tennessee, Hardaway is considered to represent a regionalized technological modification of the Paleoindian projectile-point style in the North Carolina area.

SOURCES: Coe:1964:64; Ward 1983; Olvier 1985.

Billy L. Oliver

HARDAWAY SIDE-NOTCHED POINT (or BLADE), a small, broad, thin projectile point with narrow, U-shaped side notches and a recurvate, concave, smoothed base. Notches are occasionally smoothed. Estimated to date ca. 10,000–9000 B.C. and distributed through much of North Carolina, South Carolina, and Virginia, the type was originally identified by J. L. Coe at the Hardaway Site (q.v.) in North Carolina.

SOURCES: Coe 1964:67; Ward 1983; Oliver 1985.

Billy L. Oliver

HARDAWAY SITE, a multicomponent site on a point overlooking the Yadkin River near Badin, North Carolina, containing intact deposits attributed to Kirk, Palmer, and Hardaway (qq.v.) occupations beneath mixed plowzone deposits of Stanby, Guilford, Morrow Mountain, Savannah River (qq.v.), and various Woodland complexes. Data from the site extended the concept of the Archaic and Paloindian cultures (qq.v.) in the Piedmont and in much of the eastern United States.

The Hardaway Complex in its earliest form is considered at least as old as the Clovis fluted-point tradition in the eastern United States; the succeeding Palmer complex is considered least as old as the Folsom Culture (q.v.). Both are thought to represent regionalized technological modifications of the basic Paleoindian complexes. More than 7 metric tons of artifactual material, including over 5000 projectile points, were collected from the site during intermittent excavations directed by J. L. Coe between 1948 and 1981.

SOURCES: Coe 1964; Ward 1983; Oliver 1985.

Billy L. Oliver

HARDER PHASE, a unit in the Lower Snake River Culture (q.v.) sequence of southeastern Washington, dating ca. 500 B.C.–A.D. 1750. It is divided into two sequential subphases on the basis of changes in house size and projectile-point styles. Sites in the river canyon are principally winter settlements with multiple semisubterranean houses; upland sites are seasonal base camps. Typical artifacts are corner-notched and base-notched projectile points, chipped-stone knives of several forms, digging stick handles, mortars and pestles, and fishing tools.

SOURCES: Leonhardy and Rice 1970; Yent 1976.

Frank C. Leonhardy

HARLAN MILL STEATITE QUARRY, a steatite deposit in Cecil County, in Maryland that was quarried by Late Archaic peoples. Investigated in the

1950s and 1960s by E. S. Wilkins, Jr., it has produced a radiocarbon date of 1380 B.C. +160 years.
SOURCES: Wilkins 1962, 1964, 1970.

                                                                                Stephen R. Potter

HARLAN PHASE, a culture unit dating ca. A.D. 800–1250 that represents the full establishment of the Caddo Tradition (q.v.) in eastern Oklahoma and northwestern Arkansas. Small settlements of sedentary agriculturalists, who supplemented their diet with wild plant food, supported civic-ceremonial centers of different sizes within neighborhoods of habitation sites. A typical center consisted of a platform mound with a ceremonial structure on top, an accretional mound containing layers of burials, and a nearby cluster of mound-covered structures thought to be dismantled mortuaries. Grave goods included with elite burials indicate trade with, and emulation of, Mississippian peoples in the Mississippi River Valley. Dwellings were square with clay-daubed walls and peaked, thatched roofs.
SOURCES: Bell 1972, 1984; Brown et al. 1978.

                                                                                James A Brown

HARPOON HEAD, an artifact of antler or ivory (rarely bone or wood) used for hunting sea mammals and swimming caribou, of common occurrence in the Arctic region. Throughout the 4,000-year prehistory of that region, stylistic changes in harpoon-head attributes provide many temporal clues comparable to clues provided by ceramic types in archeological contexts to the south.

                                                                                Moreau S. Maxwell

HARROUN SITE, a Late Caddo (ca. A.D. 1500) site on Cypress Creek in Upshur County, Texas, comprising four small mounds, all of which were completely excavated by E. B. Jelks and C. D. Tunnell in 1958. One mound contained a single human burial; the others had been heaped over the remains of burned circular structures. The paucity of domestic artifacts and the apparent ritual burning of the structures suggest that the site had primarily a ceremonial rather than a domestic function.
SOURCE: Jelks and Tunnell 1959.

                                                                                James E. Corbin

HASKET POINT, a large projectile point with sloping shoulders and long, edge-ground stems, found in Idaho and the Great Basin; estimated to date ca. 8000–6000 B.C.

SOURCES: B. R. Butler 1965c; A. L. Bryan 1980.

Robert G. Elston

HATCHEL-MITCHELL SITE, a large Middle and Late Caddoan (ca. A.D. 1200–1720) site originally comprising at least three mounds, village areas, and cemeteries, located on Red River in northeastern Texas; excavated by William Beatty, Jr., Glenn Martin, and A. M. Woolsey in 1938–1939, following less extensive excavations by several people in 1931, 1932, and 1935. At the largest mound, several superimposed building levels attributable to the Middle, Late, and possibly the Historic Caddo were exposed during the excavations, scores of burials were dug in the cemeteries, and the village middens were explored, making this one of the most extensively investigated Caddo sites. On the basis of this work and the artifacts it produced, A. D. Krieger defined the Texarkana Focus (q.v.) in 1944.

SOURCES: Krieger 1944, 1946:205–214; Suhm et al. 1954:203–209; E. M. Davis 1970:25–67.

Darrell Creel

HATCH SITE, a site near the James River in the interior coastal plain of Virginia that was utilized by Early Archaic, Late Archaic, Early Woodland, Middle Woodland, and protohistoric peoples. The last occupants may have been Weyanoke Indians. More than 80 dog burials have been found at the site, which was investigated by L. B. Gregory in 1975.

SOURCE: Gregory 1980.

Keith T. Egloff

HATWAI SITE, a site at the confluence of Hatwai Creek and the Clearwater River near Lewiston, Idaho, where excavations revealed four components radiocarbon dated to earlier than 1150 B.C. Hatwai I (ca. 8850–7850 B.C.) is the earliest known Windust Phase (q.v.) component. Hatwai III (ca. 3100–1150 B.C.), a Tucannon Phase village of ten pithouses, established an early date for winter population aggregation in pithouse villages. Hatwai II and IV were light, relatively insignificant occupations.

SOURCE: Ames et al. 1981.

Frank C. Leonhardy

HAVANA SITE, an extensive Middle Woodland mound group and associated habitation area overlooking the Illinois River at Havana, Illinois, dating ca. 200 B.C.–A.D. 250. It is the type site for the Havana Tradition, represented here by the Fulton, Ogden, and Steuben phases. W. K. Moore-

head and J. L. B. Taylor in 1927 and R. S. MacNeish in 1945 excavated in several of the mounds. Since then, a majority of the site has been destroyed by a power plant.
SOURCES: Cochrane 1878; Moorehead 1928; Baker et al. 1941; McGregor 1952.

Alan D. Harn

HAW RIVER SITES, a series of sites along the Haw River in Chatham County, in North Carolina which contained a complete stratigraphic record from Paleoindian (q.v.) through protohistoric times (ca. 12,000 B.C.–A.D. 1700). S. R. Claggett's and J. S. Cable's excavations there in 1979 largely reaffirmed the culture sequence established at the Hardaway, Doerschuk, and Gaston sites (qq.v.) and also identified the Bifurcate Tradition, a complex dating ca. 6000 B.C. that has birfurcated-stem projectile points as its chief diagnostic trait.
SOURCE: Claggett and Cable n.d.

Billy L. Oliver

HAYES' CREEK MOUND, a burial mound on Hayes Creek, a tributary of the James River in the mountains of west-central Virginia, probably dating ca. A.D. 950–1450. In 1904, E. P. Valentine dug the mound competely and found therein more than 400 human burials and eight dog burials.
SOURCE: Valentine 1903.

Keith T. Egloff

HEALY LAKE LOCALITY, a place in eastern interior Alaska where the Village and Garden sites, occupied recurrently during the past 11,000 years, were excavated between 1967 and 1970 by J. P. Cook and R. A. McKennan. Although deposits were relatively thin and poorly stratified, an early (ca. 9000–7000 B.C.) component, designated the Chindadn Complex (q.v.), produced important new information about early cultures of the region.
SOURCES: J. P. Cook 1969; McKennan and Cook 1970.

Donald W. Clark

HEART RIVER PHASE, a protohistoric complex of ca. A.D. 1600–1800 that directly preceded the historic Mandan Indians in the Heart River area of North Dakota.
SOURCE: W. R. Wood 1967.

Patricia J. O'Brien

HEINS CREEK SITE, one of the two stratified sites on the Door County Peninsula, in northeastern Wisconsin, where excavations by R. J. Mason in the 1960s established a regional Middle to Late Woodland sequence and

led to the definition of typologies for both Heins Creek and North Bay ceramic wares (qq.v.).
SOURCE: Mason 1967.

David Overstreet

HEINS CREEK WARE, a type of cordmarked pottery associated with the Heins Creek Culture and dating ca. A.D. 1200, found on the Door County Peninsula, in Wisconsin. Defined by R. J. Mason on the basis of a sample from a single unmixed component, it is decorated with patterns of impressions produced by varied applications of cord-wrapped sticks.
SOURCE: Mason 1966.

David Overstreet

HELENA MOUNDS, a cluster of five mounds and an associated village area in eastern Arkansas; the type site of the Helena Phase, dating ca. A.D. 1–200. When J. A. Ford dug two of the mounds in 1960, he discovered typical Illinois Hopewell (q.v.) log-roofed tombs and other features associated with typical Marksville (q.v.) and Illinois Hopewell artifacts, including a silver- and copper-covered cane panpipe. Helena is the only major site of the Marksville period that has been excavated in eastern Arkansas.
SOURCES: J. A. Ford 1963; Morse and Morse 1983.

Dan F. Morse

HELLEBAEK SITE, one of a number of Independence II Phase components on the northeastern coast of Greenland having dwellings with mid-passages (q.v.). It was excavated by Eigil Knuth in 1954. A radiocarbon date of ca. 560 B.C. suggests a return of people to northern Greenland after a hiatus of more than 1000 years.
SOURCE: Knuth 1967.

Moreau S. Maxwell

HELL GAP COMPLEX, a Paleoindian (q.v.) complex dating ca. 8000–7500 B.C. that followed the Agate Basin Complex (q.v.) in Wyoming and Colorado; first recognized by G. A. Agogino at the Hell Gap Site (q.v.) in southeastern Wyoming. Other important sites of the complex are Casper (q.v.) in Wyoming and Jones-Miller (q.v.) in Colorado.
SOURCE: Irwin-Williams et al., 1973.

George Frison

HELL GAP SITE, a stratified, multicomponent campsite in southeastern Wyoming that contained Paleoindian occupation levels of the Goshen, Folsom, Agate Basin, Hell Gap, Cody, Frederick (qq.v.), Alberta, and Midland complexes, plus overlying Archaic and post-Archaic levels. The site was excavated between 1959 and 1966 by Cynthia Irwin-Williams and H. J. Irwin.

SOURCE: Irwin-Williams et al. 1973.

George Frison

HELTON PHASE, a Middle Archaic (ca. 3500–3000 B.C.), nonceramic, cultural/technological horizon of the southern Prairie Peninsula border in west-central Illinois and central Missouri. Diagnostic artifacts include Karnak Stemmed and Matansas Side-notched bifaces and incised bone pins. Helton Phase settlements include hunting and gathering stations, mortuary sites, and extensive year-round villages containing shelters and large pits. Subsistence remains from village sites indicate intensive exploitation of aquatic resources (fish and mussels), deer, and nuts.

SOURCES: T. G. Cook 1976:106–108; Wiant et al. 1983; Brown and Vierra 1983:165–195.

Michael D. Wiant

HENRIETTA FOCUS, a late prehistoric (ca. A.D. 1300–1600) manifestation in the upper drainage of the Red, Trinity, and Brazos rivers in north-central Texas and south-central Oklahoma; defined by A. D. Krieger in 1946 largely on the basis of the M. D. Harrell Site in Young County, Texas. Other excavated sites are Coyote and Glass, both in Montague County, Texas. Settlements are small agricultural villages containing pithouses and storage pits; common artifacts include shell-tempered Nocona Plain type pottery, metates, and arrow-point types Scallorn and Perdiz. Typical Plains artifacts also are present, most notably chipped-stone, four-edged, alternatively beveled knives (Harahey type) and hoes made from bison scapulas and skulls. Quantities of their bones indicate that bison were hunted regularly.

SOURCES: Krieger 1946; Suhm et al. 1954:80–87; Lorrain 1967.

Edward B. Jelks

HERCULES WARE, a kind of pottery tempered with crushed granite or gneiss and decorated with fabric or cord impressions, occurring in the southern half of Virginia's interior coastal plain and dating ca. A.D. 900.

SOURCES: G. P. Smith 1971, 1984; Egloff and Potter 1982.

Keith T. Egloff

HESQUIAT HARBOUR SEQUENCE, a late prehistoric culture sequence on the west coast of Vancouver Island, in British Columbia, comprising two periods: Hesquiat Harbour I (ca. A.D. 100–400) and Hesquiat Harbour II

(ca. A.D. 700–1774). The periods differ primarily in the relative frequencies of several artifact classes and use categories.
SOURCES: Calvert 1980; Haggarty 1982.

James C. Haggarty

HIDDEN CAVE, a site in Western Nevada which contained a geological record spanning the last 21,000 years and cultural strata that have been radiocarbon dated from ca. 3685 B.C. to ca. A.D. 1140. Several archaeologists have excavated there: S. M. and G. N. Wheeler in 1940; N. L. Roust and G. L. Grosscup (in collaboration with R. B. Morrisson) in 1951; and D. H. Thomas in 1979 and 1980. The cave was utilized from spring through fall—primarily for storing personal items that had temporally and temporarily passed into a "passive" state—but also as a burial site, a diurnal way station, and a resource cache.
SOURCES: R. B. Morrison 1964; D. H. Thomas 1985.

David Hurst Thomas

HIDDEN FALLS SITE, a stratified, multicomponent site at the head of Kasnyku Bay, in southeastern Alaska, where excavations by S. D. Davis in 1978 and 1979 revealed three prehistoric components underlying a 20th-century industrial occupation. Component I, dating around 7500 B.C., yielded a small sample of artifacts representing a unifacial tool industry with microblades and wedge-shaped microblade cores. These resemble materials of a somewhat later date from the Ground Hog Bay 2 Site (q.v.), about 70 miles to the north. From Component II (ca. 2600–1200 B.C.) came chipped-stone, ground-stone, and bone implements with formal similarities to materials of similar age from the Alaska Peninsula and Kodiak Island, as well as to St. Mungo (q.v.) and Mayne phase tools from the southern British Columbia coast. Chipped-stone, ground-stone, bone, and shell tools were found in Component III (ca. 1000 B.C. to A.D. 700), but diagnostic specimens were too few to permit close comparisons with nearby cultures.

One of only two sites in southeastern Alaska with well-documented Holocene occupations, Hidden Falls has provided significant data on human culture and adaptations during the last 10,000 years. A unique feature is the evidence of a local glacial advance that overrode Holocene cultural deposits.
SOURCE: S. D. Davis 1984.

Gerald H. Clark

HIGGINS FLAT PUEBLO, a Mogollon masonry-walled pueblo of at least 30 rooms, with two great kivas nearby (one superimposed over the other), in the Cibola Province (q.v.) near Reserve, New Mexico. It was excavated by P. S. Martin and J. B. Rinaldo in 1953–1954 and has been dated by dendrochronology to the late Tularosa (q.v.) Phase, ca. A.D. 1250. A ma-

sonry-lined pithouse or "pithouse-kiva" close to the pueblo shows possible use in the early 12th century during the Apache Creek Phase.
SOURCES: Martin et al. 1956; Martin et al. 1957.

Stewart Peckham

HINDS CAVE, a large, deeply stratified rockshelter in the lower Pecos River region of southwestern Texas, containing deposits spanning the Archaic and extending into the late prehistoric period (ca. 6500 B.C.–A.D. ?). Perishable materials are well preserved in the dry deposits; investigated features include an Early Archaic floor of prickly-pear pads, burned-rock middens, lenses of dense fiber material, and numerous pits, some of them lined with grass. Recent investigations have emphasized environmental reconstruction, techniques specially developed for exploiting local resources, clarification of subsistence strategies, demographic patterning, and other adaptive mechanisms through time. Analysis continues on over 1000 human coprolites dating from throughout the Archaic period.
SOURCES: Shafer and Bryant 1977; Williams–Dean 1978; Dering 1979.

Robert J. Mallouf

HIRSH MOUND SITE, a site with two mounds, located on the Jackson River in the mountains of west-central Virginia. In 1962, C. G. Holland tested the larger mound and uncovered bundle burials, layers of stones, and a large, shallow pit at the mound's base. The mound was radiocarbon dated to ca. A.D. 1070.
SOURCE: Holland 1963.

Keith T. Egloff

HIRUNDO SITE, a site near Old Town, Maine occupied mainly during the Late Archaic (between 4000 and 1700 B.C.), although there was an earlier light occupation by Middle Archaic people. Excavated by an interdisciplinary team from the University of Maine, it is the most thoroughly studied Late Archaic site of interior New England.
SOURCES: Sanger et al. 1977; D. R. Snow 1980:173-200.

Edward B. Jelks

HIWASSEE ISLAND CULTURE, an early Mississippian (ca. A.D.1100–1300) manifestation in eastern Tennessee, defined on the basis of excavations in the Tennessee River valley, especially at the Hiwassee Island site (q.v.).
SOURCES: Lewis and Kneberg 1946, 1958; Schroedl et al. 1985.

Jefferson Chapman

HIWASSEE ISLAND SITE, a multicomponent site on the Tennesse River in eastern Tennessee, dug by C. H. Nash in 1937–1939. Work there and at other Chickamauga Reservoir sites led to the definition of the Hamilton,

Hiwassee Island, and Dallas cultures (qq.v.), respectively affiliated with the Late Woodland, Early Mississippian, and Late Mississippian traditions.
SOURCE: Lewis and Kneberg 1946.

Jefferson Chapman

HIXTON (or SILVER MOUND) SITE, a major quarry in west-central Wisconsin; the source of a metamorphosed sandstone, Hixton Silicified Sandstone (often called Hixton Quartzite or Sugar Quartz), that was mined by prehistoric peoples for more than 10,000 years, beginning as early as ca. 9400 B.C. This material was distributed widely throughout the western Great Lakes area.
SOURCES: Porter 1961; C. E. Brown n.d.; Overstreet n.d.a.

David Overstreet

HOCHELAGA, an early 16th-century St. Lawrence Iroquoian village visited by Jacques Cartier in 1535. Remains possibly from this village have been recovered in the present city of Montreal, Quebec, from time to time, beginning in the late 19th century with the discoveries of Sir J. W. Dawson. B. G. Trigger's and J. F. Pendergast's most recent analysis of these remains led them to conclude that they date from the early 16th century but were not necessarily from the site visited by Cartier.
SOURCE: Pendergast and Trigger 1972.

James A. Tuck

HOGE SITE, a Late Woodland palisaded village site at Burke Garden in the mountains of southwestern Virginia, first described by R. D. Wainwright in 1914. E. E. Jones, who relocated the site and excavated there from 1976 to 1985, found human burials, storage pits, hearths, and circular house patterns associated with Radford pottery (q.v.).
SOURCES: Holland 1970; E. E. Jones n.d.; Wainwright n.d.

Keith T. Egloff

HOGUP CAVE, a dry, stratified cave on the northern margin of the Great Salt Lake Desert in Utah, whose deposits spanned the last 8600 years and included all Archaic, Sevier/Fremont (q.v.), and late prehistoric phases of the region. Excavated in 1967–1968 by C. M. Aikens, Hogup Cave confirmed the early artifact dates reported earlier at Danger Cove (q.v.).
SOURCE: Aikens 1970.

David B. Madsen

HOHOKAM CULTURE, a long-lived (ca. A.D. 1–1450) cultural tradition centering on the lush river valleys of central and south-central Arizona, generally correlated with the Sonoran Desert biotic province. Subsistence during earlier phases was based upon hunting of large and small game, aquatic resources, gathered produce (e.g., mesquite beans, cactus fruit, and annual grasses), and limited floodwater agriculture. In later phases, there was extensive irrigation and nonirrigation farming of maize, beans, squash, cotton, tobacco, and other crops.

Four distinctive periods of the culture have been recognized: Pioneer (ca. A.D. 0–700), Colonial (ca. A.D. 700–900), Sedentary (ca. A.D. 900–1100), and Classic (ca. A.D. 1100–1450) (qq.v.). Each of the periods has been divided into two or more phases except the Sedentary Period, which consists of a single phase.

The Pioneer Period is characterized by small to large, shallow, square to rectangular pithouse architecture; simple incised and red geometric designs on gray pottery; polished redware; ornate and stylized clay figurines; stone axes; shaped metates; simple, carved-shell jewelry; and stone sculpture and mosaic work.

During the Colonial and Sedentary periods, cultural florescence is reflected in these innovations: ball courts; platform mounds; extensive shell and stone industries; copper bells; an elaborate cremation burial complex; sophisticated geometric and anthropomorphic designs on a wide variety of red-on-buff pottery; square to elongated, large to small pithouse architecture; village plazas; increased village size; geographic expansion; enlargement of irrigation systems in river valleys; and substantial local and regional trade.

In the Classic Period, there were marked changes: elaboration of massive platform mounds with surface rooms surrounded by enclosing compound walls; discontinuation of ball courts; a shift to above-ground structures made of puddled caliche-adobe, wood, and stone; multistoried architecture by A.D. 1300; a decrease in red-on-buff pottery and a predominance of polished redwares; the appearance of Salado Polychrome pottery by A.D. 1300; variable mortuary practices, shifting from cremation to inhumation; turquoise mosaic and inlay; concentration of settlements along major rivers; large communities; villages composed of numerous compounds; expansion of irrigation systems in some areas, abandonment in others; extensive trading systems after A.D. 1300; and disappearance of the pattern by A.D. 1450.

Currently, it is held that the Hohokam Culture originated either by emigration to the Phoenix Basin of peoples from Mexico, or by in-place development of an indigenous Archaic population. Once in place, it occupied the basin continuously until ca. A.D. 1450, at which time its traces seem to disappear from the archaeological record. Explanations for its disappearance include (1) salination and waterlogging of agricultural fields, (2) disease, (3) invasion by other peoples, (4) drought, (5) cessation of trade, (6) collapse of the sociopolitical system, and (7) combinations of the above. A reduction in cultural complexity is thought to have occurred between A.D. 1400 and 1500, with a return to single-unit houses while mounds and

compounds disappeared. A continuum from Hohokam to the historic Pima Indians has been proposed, but it has not been thoroughly demonstrated.
SOURCES: Gladwin et al. 1937; Haury 1976; Doyel 1979; Doyel and Plog 1980.

David E. Doyel and John S. Cable

HOLBROOK FOCUS, the earliest division of the Winslow Branch (q.v.) of the Anasazi Culture (q.v.), located in northeastern Arizona; originally formulated in 1939 by H. S. Colton. According to the interpretations of G. J. Gumerman, who later revised Colton's definition, the focus dates ca. A.D. 1075–1100 and is characterized by small villages with shallow, rectangular pithouses associated with small rectangular surface structures and Holbrook Black-on-white pottery, a Little Colorado type.
SOURCES: Colton 1939a:66–67, 1955; Gumerman, 1969:328–331; Gumerman and Skinner 1968.

Donald E. Weaver, Jr.

HOLCOMBE SITE, a series of small Paleoindian (q.v.) camping stations along a fossil beach of glacial Lake Algonquian in Macomb County, in Michigan, dating ca. 9000 B.C. Remains of caribou and a high frequency of projectile-point bases relative to unreworked points indicate the refurbishing of broken spears at a temporary campsite.
SOURCES: Cleland 1965; Fitting et al. 1966.

Charles E. Cleland

HOLIDAY SITE, a multicomponent site on the edge of a freshwater swamp near Gallivants Ferry in Horry County, in South Carolina. T. A. Rathbun excavated there in 1984–85 and found a Middle Woodland ossuary dating ca. A.D. 800, together with a number of features, including 42 inhumations of uncertain cultural affiliation.
SOURCES: Rathbun 1984a, 1984b, 1985.

Michael Trinkley

HOLLYWOOD SITE, a poorly known Mississippian (q.v.) site dating ca. A.D. 1200–1300 that contains two burial mounds but evidently no associated village; located in the Savannah River floodplain south of August, Georgia. In 1891 H. Reynolds found Southern Ceremonial Complex artifacts associated with burials in the smaller mound. In 1965 Clemens de Baillou tested the site and found ceramics showing similarities to materials from Mississppian sites in North and South Carolina.
SOURCE: Cyrus Thomas 1894:317–326; de Baillou 1965; J. J. Reid 1965.

Paul A. Webb

HOLMAN SHELTER, a rockshelter in northwestern Arkansas whose dry sediments yielded a wide variety of plant remains brought there between ca. A.D. 700 and 1500 by Woodland and Mississippian peoples. University

of Arkansas Museum personnel excavated the site in 1932. Recently, Gayle Fritz described specimens of pale-seeded cultigen amaranth (*Amaranthus Hypochondriacus* L.) and cultigen chenopodium (*Chenopodium berlandieri* spp. *nuttalliae*). Both may be Mesoamerican domesticates, but the chenopod is possibly a product of indigenous North American husbandry.
SOURCE: Fritz 1984.

Gayle J. Fritz

HOMOLOVI FOCUS, the last division of the Winslow Branch (q.v.) of the Anasazi Culture (q.v.) in northeastern Arizona, spanning the period from ca. A.D. 1300 to 1400. Focus characteristics include medium to large stone and adobe pueblos with enclosed plazas and kivas, extended inhumations, and both Homolovi Orange Ware and Winslow Orange Ware (qq.v.) pottery.
SOURCES: Fewkes 1904; Colton 1939a:69, 1956.

Donald E. Weaver, Jr.

HOMOLOVI ORANGE WARE, the major utility pottery along the Little Colorado River and its tributaries in northeastern Arizona between A.D. 1300 and 1400. As defined by H. S. Colton and L. L. Hargrave, this ware includes two types, Homolovi Plain and Homolovi Corrugated, and it is distinguished from other similar wares primarily by its quartz-sand temper, consisting of angular red, black, white, and orange fragments.
SOURCES: Hargrave 1932b:24–25; Colton and Hargrave 1937:132–134; Colton 1956.

Donald E. Weaver, Jr.

HOMOLOVI SITES, a group of ancestral Hopi village sites located near Winslow in northern Arizona. Occupied between A.D. 1100 and 1450, they figure prominently in Hopi oral traditions.

Homolovi I, containing an estimated 250 rooms, is on the east side of the Little Colorado River 3 kilometers northeast of Winslow. It comprises a massive roomblock two stories high, to which is appended a U-shaped, one-story roomblock enclosing a large plaza. There are two extensive, adjacent burial areas. Ceramic cross-dating indicates occupation between A.D. 1275 and 1425.

Homolovi II, containing more than 1000 rooms, is on a large, flat-topped mesa on the east side of the Little Colorado River, 8 kilometers northeast of Winslow. It consists of three linearly aligned plazas, two completely surrounded by blocks of rooms, the other enclosed on three sides. In some areas, the roomblocks were two stories high. There are subterranean kivas in all three plazas; the areas around the roomblocks, especially to the south and east, were used as cemeteries. Ceramics indicate occupation from ca. A.D. 1275 to 1450. In the immediate vicinity are many petroglyphs.

Homolovi III is a rectangular, 30-room pueblo, with at least one possible kiva, located on the west floodplain of the Little Colorado River about 7 kilometers north of Winslow. It was occupied between A.D. 1250 and 1325.

Homolovi IV, dating ca. A.D. 1100–1250 and containing at least 100 rooms, occupies the top and slopes of a small butte on the west side of the Little Colorado River, about 8 kilometers north of Winslow. There are numerous petroglyphs around the site.

In 1896 and 1897, J. W. Fewkes conducted extensive excavations at Homolovi I and tested the burial area at Homolovi II. H. S. Colton made surface investigations at the Homolovi sites in 1937, and G. G. Pond dug a painted kiva in the west plaza at Homolovi II in 1962. In 1979, archaeologists from the Museum of Northern Arizona initiated long-term studies that resulted, in 1986, in the establishment of a regional state park, including the Homolovi sites and the Chevelon and Cottonwood Creek ruins (qq.v.). Arizona State Museum archaeologists excavated five rooms at Homolovi II and a large portion of Homolovi III between 1984 and 1987. Long-term studies of Homolovi rock art by Museum of Northern Arizona researchers are ongoing.

Formerly, the Homolovi sites were considered part of the Winslow Branch (q.v.) of the Anasazi Root, with Homolovi IV designated the type site for the Tuwiuca Focus (q.v.) and Homolovi I and II the type sites for the Homolovi Focus (q.v.). More recently, the sites have been reclassified as part of the Chevelon-Chavez Province (q.v.) of the western Anasazi Culture.

SOURCES: Fewkes 1898b, 1904; Pond 1966; W. K. Adams n.d.; Andrews n.d.; Hays and Adams n.d.; Soil Systems n.d.; Weaver et al. n.d.

Donald E. Weaver, Jr.

HONANKI PHASE, a phase of the Verde Province of the Sinagua Division, Hakataya Culture (qq.v.), dating ca. A.D. 1125–1300, based on surveys and excavations at Tuzigoot Pueblo and Montezuma Castle (qq.v.). An influx of Flagstaff Province Sinagua people introduced pueblo architecture to the Verde Valley at the beginning of the phase, when the evidence of Hohokam (q.v.) influence seen in the preceding Camp Verde Phase disappeared. The pueblo walls are of rock and mud, rarely coursed; kivas are lacking. In addition to open sites, there are cliff dwellings. Extended burials like those of the Verde Phase continued, some with occipital deformation, as did painted cotton textiles and other traits. Irrigation was still practiced; field houses and rock-outlined garden plots have been reported.

Intrusive Anasazi pottery occurs in association with Tuzigoot Brown, Red, and Smudged wares, indicating a shift in trade or contacts, those prior to A.D. 1200 originating in the Kayenta Province northeast of Wupatki Pueblo (q.v.), those after 1200 coming from the Winslow Province (q.v.) on the middle Little Colorado River. Hopi tradition holds that a number of Sinagua migrated to the Winslow area and eventually joined the Hopis ca. A.D. 1450.

SOURCES: Caywood and Spicer 1935; Jackson and Van Valkenburgh 1954.

Albert H. Schroeder

HOPEWELL AIRPORT (or JORDAN POINT) SITE, a large site on the James River in the interior coastal plain of Virginia that was occupied during the Archaic, Woodland, protohistoric, and early Colonial periods. In 1955 Clifford Evans analyzed sherds from the site; in 1965, H. A. MacCord tested it and found Woodland hearths, refuse-filled pits, and a wide variety of ceramics.

SOURCES: Clifford Evans 1955; MacCord 1967.

Keith T. Egloff

HOPEWELL CULTURE, a range of behavioral patterns practiced by groups within the Eastern Woodlands from ca. 100 B.C. to ca. A.D. 400, consisting of several traditions, the two major ones being the Havana Hopewell, centered in the Illinois River Valley, and the Ohio Hopewell of southern Ohio. Although their social and political elements probably varied, all traditions appear to have shared in a continuation of earlier subsistence patterns, which included the use of Eastern Agriculture Complex seeds. Common, but variably expressed ideas included the use of fire in public ritual areas; emphasis upon group and individual social identifications in clothing and display objects; the construction of mounds; and the interment of nonutilitarian objects in graves or in caches. A distinctive art style was expressed in different media, both within and among the traditions. Numerous theoretical frameworks have been proposed to interpret this culture, including "cult" (O. H. Prufer), "interaction sphere" (J. R. Caldwell), and "regional transaction centers" (Stuart Struever and G. L. Houart).

SOURCES: Mills 1906:135; Shetrone 1920; Ford and Willey 1940; Deuel 1952; Morgan 1952:88–93, figs. 32, 33; Quimby 1952:102–104, fig. 37; J. B.Griffin 1967, 1983:260–272; Caldwell and Hall 1964; Brose and Greber 1979.

N'omi B. Greber

HOPEWELL SITE (called CLARK'S WORKS in 1848), the type site for the Hopewell Culture (q.v.), located on the North Fork of Paint Creek northwest of Chillicothe, Ohio. It contained at least 38 mounds, the majority of which were within an extensive, low, earthen embankment that followed the natural topography. A partial square was conjoined, and two smaller enclosures were within. Beginning early in the 19th century, several major excavations uncovered a range of features and vast quantities of artifacts that showed a high level of craftsmanship.

Mound 25, the largest of the Hopewell Culture (over 140 meters long), consisted of three linearly connected elements, the middle one covering a number of small mounds heaped over separate structures, the outer two covering extensive plazas. A similar pattern was found under Mound 23, which was about 45 meters long. All the other mounds were considerably smaller. Some covered imposing deposits of exotic materials (e.g., worked obsidian, mica, or flint); others covered only more utilitarian remains (e.g., burned matting, potsherds, and unworked bone). On typological grounds, it is estimated that the site was in use from ca. 100 B.C. to ca. A.D. 300.

SOURCES: Squier and Davis 1848:26–29, pl. 10, 186–287 passim; Moorehead 1892, 1922a; Shetrone 1926; Seeman 1979.

N'omi B. Greber

HOPI BUTTES DISTRICT, a subarea of the Winslow Province (q.v.) located in the dessicated zone between the Little Colorado River and the Hopi Mesas in northern Arizona—a place characterized by localized sand dunes, eroded badland, and volcanic plugs and dikes. There is no primary drainage, and dendritic systems are rare.

Archaeological sites are small and scattered owing to the dispersed pattern of agriculturally suitable land and productive areas for wild plants. The history of human occupation seems to have followed that of the Winslow Province generally, except that the Hopi Buttes subarea appears to have been abandoned as a place of permanent habitation ca. A.D. 1250 and thereafter used only for specialized and limited purposes. The artifact inventory is similar to that in other subareas of the province.

SOURCE: Gumerman and Skinner 1968.

George J. Gumerman

HOPI (or TUSAYAN) PROVINCE, the heartland of the Hopi people, centered around the rocky, southern extensions of Black Mesa (q.v.) in northeastern Arizona. At maximum expansion, the province reached as far south as the upper Little Colorado River near Winslow, as far north as the west Grand Canyon and Navajo Mountain, and as far east as Canyon de Chelly. Before A.D. 1200, it is difficult to separate the province from the contiguous Sinagua (q.v.), Kayenta, and Tsegi provinces, but it became a culturally distinct area after large-scale migrations of Kayenta, Mesa Verde, Zuni, Sinagua, and Rio Grande peoples ca. A.D. 1150–1250 produced a new cultural fusion that led to the development of the Hopi tradition.

SOURCES: Montgomery et al. 1949; Ellis 1961; James 1974.

Michael B. Stanislawski

HOPI (or TUSAYAN) TRADITION, a culture unit dating from ca. A.D. 1200 to the present, the resident culture of the Hopi Province (q.v.) of northeastern Arizona. Along with the Zuni Tradition, it forms the Western Pueblo Culture. On the west, pueblos consisted of contiguous surface rooms arranged in parallel rows; to the east, they were placed around single or multiple plazas in the Rio Grande–Upper Colorado style. Construction was of masonry, and buildings were one to four stories high with from 40 to 1000 rooms that housed up to 2000 people. Semisubterranean, rectangular kivas of stone masonry, located between house rows or in plazas, had a raised bench across the south end and multiple layers of wall plaster with polychrome Sikyatki-style murals that frequently portrayed Kachina figures engaging in ceremonies.

A sequence of pottery styles correlates with different periods of the tradition: first (ca. A.D. 1300–1700), polished, unslipped orange and yellow wares with curvilinear, free-form designs on low, broad jars and bowls (Jeddito and Sikyatki series); next, a century (1700–1800) of Tewa-style, large jars and bowls painted with densely packed geometric designs in black- and red-on-orange (Payupki Polychrome series); then, a Zuni series of black- and red-on-white wares (Polacca Polychrome, ca. A.D. 1800–1900); and, finally, a revival of unslipped but polished orange, yellow, red, and white wares painted in black and/or white (Hano polychromes, ca. 1900–present).

Archaeology and recorded clan legends suggest that the distinctive Hopi tradition formed only after people came to the mesa from other areas (Rio Grande, Keres, Tewa, Jemez, Sinagua, Kayenta, Mesa Verde, Upper Colorado, and perhaps the southern deserts of Arizona and northern Mexico) between ca. A.D. 1150 and the 1300s. Ethnographic/ethnohistoric data suggest that land, produce, housing, springs, shrines, and ceremonies were controlled through a matrilineal/matrilocal clan system, which cross cut the controls exercised by Kachina and Horn/Flute societies, which were responsible for performing religious ceremonies.

SOURCES: Colton 1939a; Watson Smith 1952b, 1971, 1972; Woodbury 1954; Ellis 1961; E. C. Adams 1982.

Michael B. Stanislawski

HORICON SITE, a Late Woodland site located adjacent to the Horicon Marsh in east-central Wisconsin, investigated by R. O. Keslin in 1958 and by G. R. Peters in 1978. The site is notable for having produced large quantities of ceramics (including Madison Ware types) and many storage and cooking features, but few lithics (there was a 14 to 1 ratio of potsherds to lithic specimens).

SOURCES: Keslin 1958; Peters 1978; Overstreet 1978.

David Overstreet

HORNER SITE, the type site of the Cody Complex (q.v.) in northwestern Wyoming, investigated by Glenn Jepsen in 1949, by Jepsen and W. R. Wedel in 1951–1952, and by George Frison in 1977–1978. The 1949–1952 investigations produced a large assemblage of Cody Complex tools and projectile points (types Eden and Scottsbluff, qq.v.) from what probably are two separate bison-bone beds near the surface that date ca. 7000 B.C. The

1977–1978 excavations were in an earlier (ca. 8000 B.C.) bone bed ascribed to an Alberta/Cody occupation that was buried under nearly two meters of alluvial material.

SOURCES: Jepsen 1953; Wormington 1957:127–128; Frison 1978:181–182. Frison and Todd 1987.

George Frison

HORSEFLY HOLLOW PHASE, a phase of the Pueblo III period dating ca. A.D. 1210–1260 that was defined by W. D. Lipe for the Red Rock Plateau portion of the Cedar Mesa Province (q.v.) in southeastern Utah. It seemingly possesses a mixture of Kayenta and Mesa Verde ceramics and architectural styles, sometimes at the same site. Although the phase's settlement pattern is the densest on the plateau, it is still one of small, sparsely spread sites located in the canyons leading into the San Juan and Colorado rivers. These well-preserved sites are coeval with other terminal cliff-dwelling episodes elsewhere in the Anasazi culture area.

SOURCE: Lipe 1970.

R. G. Matson

HORSE ISLAND SHELL RING, a Thom's Creek Phase site dating ca. 1500 B.C. on Horse Island near the mouth of North Edisto Creek in Charleston, South Carolina. In the late 1940s, both J. R. Caldwell and Antonio Waring conducted extensive excavations at the site, which later was largely destroyed.

SOURCES: J. R. Caldwell 1952; Trinkley 1980a.

Michael Trinkley

HOSTA BUTTE PHASE, an outmoded term for a phase of the Anasazi Culture in the Chaco Province (qq.v.) of northwestern New Mexico, now subsumed under the Bonito Phase (q.v.) It was defined originally by H. S. Gladwin in 1945 and was redefined by Gordon Vivian and T. W. Mathews in 1965.

SOURCES: Gladwin 1945; Vivian and Mathews 1965.

Peter J. McKenna

HOT SPRINGS VILLAGE SITE, formal name for a site on the Alaska Peninsula more commonly known as the Port Moller Site (q.v.).

HOWARD LAKE PHASE, a Middle Woodland complex defined from excavations by A. E. Jenks in 1932 and 1934 at the Anderson Site and by L. A. Wilford in 1950 at the Howard Lake Mounds on Howard Lake, approximately 25 miles northeast of Minneapolis. Diagnostic of the phase are its ceramics, which bear similarities to the Havana and Havana-like wares of Wisconsin, Illinois, and eastern Iowa. Aside from ceramics and a

few burial mounds, the Howard Lake Phase has little in common with Middle Woodland complexes to the south and east.
SOURCES: Wilford 1937, 1955, n.d.c.; Flaskerd 1943.

Gordon R. Peters

HOXIE POINT, an Early Archaic (ca. 4850–4150 B.C.) dart point, diagnostic of the San Geronimo Phase (q.v.) of central Texas. It has a long, slender blade with alternately beveled edges, squared shoulders, a rectangular stem with dulled edges, and a mildly concave base. Hoxie formerly was included within the Darl (q.v.) type.
SOURCES: Prewitt 1981, 1982b; Turner and Hester 1985.

Elton R. Prewitt

HUATABAMPO BROWN WARE, a generic, plain, brown pottery associated with the Huatabampo Culture (q.v.) in southern Sonora.
SOURCE: Pailes 1972:238–240.

Richard A. Pailes

HUATABAMPO CULTURE, an archaeological manifestation on the coastal plain of southern Sonora and northern Sinaloa identified by Gordon Ekholm in 1939. It remains undated but may have been present as early as the second or third century A.D. and apparently lasted until protohistoric times, which would identify it as ancestral Cahita. Ekholm postulated that the Huatabampo Culture blended with an intrusive Mixteca-Puebla complex, known in Sinaloa as the Aztatlan complex, to produce the northern-most extension of the Mesoamerican frontier at Guasave, Sinaloa, ca. A.D. 1200–1350.

Huatabampo sites on the Rio Mayo in southern Sonora appear as large sherd scatters along old river channels and are characterized by a fine red-ware pottery, abundant use of marine shell, and figurine fragments similar to those found at Snaketown, Arizona, a site of the Hohokam Culture (q.v.). Nothing is known of architectural forms.

Similarities with both Southwestern traditions to the north and Mesoamerican traditions to the south have suggested that Huatabampo served as a link between cultures of those two regions.
SOURCES: Ekholm 1939, 1940, 1942; Haury 1950; Pailes 1972.

Richard A. Pailes

HUATABAMPO RED WARE, a type of pottery associated with the Huatabampo Culture (q.v.) of southern Sonora: a fine, hard, redware that occurs in the form of hemispherical bowls and swollen-neck jugs. The bowls typically have rims that are either scalloped or extended to form tabular handles. The jugs have necks expanded to as much as half the diameter of the body, forming a bi-lobed silhouette. This ware includes both Mesoamerican and

Southwestern vessel forms and has been compared to Vahki Red, San Fran-
ciso Red, and Valshni Red of the Mogollon and Hohokam cultures.
    SOURCES: Ekholm 1939, 1940, 1942:75–77, fig. 12.

Richard A. Pailes

HUDNUT PHASE. See Chief Joseph Dam Locality.

HUDSON-MENG SITE, an arroyo bison jump and associated butchering
floor in Nebraska, with a radiocarbon date of 7870 B.C., where more than
600 bison were killed in one or several hunting episodes by the makers of
Alberta points (q.v.) and Cody knives. The first definitive lithic analysis of
the Alberta type was carried out on the large sample of points and debitage
collected from the butchering floor between 1968 and 1977.
    SOURCE: Agenbroad 1978b.

Larry D. Agenbroad

HUERFANO MESA VILLAGE, a group of structures scattered over a 21-
hectare mesa about 5 kilometers north-northeast of Llaves, New Mexico,
in the Largo-Gallina Province (q.v.). It consisted of ten pithouses, four with
extensive outbuildings, and seven surface houses of stone with mud mortar.
H. W. Dick's excavations there from 1972 to 1978 revealed a late (ca. A.D.
700–1100) Rosa Phase (q.v.) occupation, followed by a Gallina Phase (q.v.)
occupation of ca. A.D. 1100–1275. By dividing the village chronology into
early (ca. A.D. 1000–1100), intermediate (ca. A.D. 1100–1200), and late
(ca. A.D. 1200–1275) periods on the basis of house styles, Dick estimated
that the population reached its apogee of 40 persons during the late period.
    SOURCES: Dick 1976, 1985:31–42.

Herbert W. Dick

HUFF PHASE, a phase of the Middle Missouri Tradition (q.v.), dating ca.
A.D. 1550–1675, whose villages are concentrated along a 50-mile stretch
of the Missouri River in southern North Dakota. Two sites have been
excavated: Huff and Shermer (qq.v.). Continuity in material culture indicates that the historic Mandan Indians are the direct descendants of the
phase.
    SOURCE: W. R. Wood 1967.

W. Raymond Wood

HUFF SITE, a large (8.5 acre), fortified village of the Middle Missouri
Tradition (q.v.), on the west bank of the Missouri River in Morton County,

North Dakota. The type site for the Huff Phase (q.v.), it is believed to have been occupied ca. A.D. 1550–1675 by ancestors of the Mandan.
SOURCE: W. R. Wood 1967.

W. Raymond Wood

HULL PHASE, a phase of the Cohonina Province, Patayan Division, Hakataya Culture (qq.v.), dating ca. A.D. 1130–1220. Distributed along the border between the Cohonina Province and the Northern Sinagua Division (q.v.), sites of the phase contain mixed elements of both. Masonry pueblos are the typical house type along this frontier.
SOURCE: Colton 1946.

Albert H. Schroeder

HUMBOLDT LAKEBED SITE, a complex of house rings, various other rock alignments, rock cairns, human skeletal remains, numerous grinding stones, and a wide variety of projectile points and other chipped-stone artifacts, located in western Nevada. It is the type site for the Humboldt projectile-point series, which has not been firmly dated. Although investigated by several different researchers beginning in the 1920s, there is no comprehensive report on the site.
SOURCES: M. R. Harrington 1927; Loud and Harrington 1929; Clewlow 1967; Reed 1967; Heizer and Clewlow 1968; Hester and Busby 1977.

David Hurst Thomas

HUNTER'S HOME PHASE, terminal phase of the Middle Woodland period, or Point Peninsula continuum, in New York state. Collarless, cord-wrapped, paddle-impressed ceramics; obtuse-angle and straight smoking pipes; Levanna type arrow points; and small, upland sites with oblong communal houses characterize the phase, which dates ca. A.D. 800–1000.
SOURCE: Ritchie 1969:253–266.

James A. Tuck

HUNTSVILLE SITE, a Mississippian (q.v.) mound center on War Eagle Creek in the Arkansas Ozarks comprising four mounds, so arranged that one pair is closely aligned with the summer solstice sunrise, while another pair is aligned with the summer solstice sunset. Excavations in the largest mound by George Sabo III in 1980–1981 and by Marvin Kay in 1986 revealed that it had been constructed in four major stages. Radiocarbon and archeomagnetic dates indicate that construction began before A.D. 1065 and terminated after A.D. 1350. At each stage, one or more flat-topped surfaces was prepared, several of which supported structures. The absence of associated habitation debris suggests that the structures were used for special—probably ceremonial—purposes.

Huntsville and several other sites like it in northwestern Arkansas, southwestern Missouri, and northeastern Oklahoma are believed to represent an extension of Arkansas River Valley Caddoan culture into the western Ozarks.

SOURCES: J. A. Brown 1984b; Sabo 1986.

George Sabo III

I

ICEHOUSE BOTTOM SITE, a multicomponent, stratified site in eastern Tennessee excavated in the 1970s by Jefferson Chapman. Four meters of alluvial deposits contained a sequence of occupational levels, providing an assemblage chronology for the Early and Middle Archaic periods (ca. 7500–4500 B.C.). An extensive Middle Woodland component produced Ohio Hopewellian (q.v.) ceramic and lithic artifacts.

SOURCES: Jefferson Chapman 1973, 1977; Chapman and Keel 1978; Cridlebaugh 1982.

Jefferson Chapman

I. C. FEW SITE, a probable Connestee-Pisgah Phase (qq.v.) village site now under Keowee Reservoir in Pickens County, in South Carolina, excavated by R. T. Grange, Jr., in 1967. Grange collected ceramics, stone tools, shell items, and numerous other artifacts from the site; he also recorded several burials, postmolds, and other features. Four radiocarbon dates averaged A.D. 944.

SOURCE: Grange n.d.

Michael Trinkley

IGLOOLIK LOCALITY, location of an Inuit settlement at northern Foxe Basin on northeastern Melville Peninsula, Northwest Territories, comprising a number of sites excavated by Jørgen Meldgaard in the 1950s and 1960s. They provided a framework for regional Paleoeskimo and Neoeskimo developmental sequences.

SOURCE: Meldgaard 1962.

Moreau S. Maxwell

INCINERATOR SITE, a village of the Anderson Focus of the Fort Ancient Tradition (qq.v.), located adjacent to the floodplain of the Great Miami River in the outskirts of Dayton, Ohio. Excavations by the Dayton Museum

of Natural History since 1969 have revealed concentric rings of houses, storage/trash pits, and burials around a central plaza, the whole surrounded by a circular stockade. Excellent floral and faunal preservation have enabled the identification of cultivated and wild food resources, including corn, beans, squash, sunflowers, nuts, fruits, deer, and turkey. A suite of radiocarbon dates places the site at near the end of the 12th century A.D.
    SOURCES: Heilman and Hoefer 1981; Robertson 1986.

                                                                N'omi B. Greber

INDEPENDENCE FJORD SITES, a series of Independence I (q.v.) and II sites on a large fjord penetrating inland from the northeastern corner of Greenland. Excavations there by Eigil Knuth in the 1950s and 1960s provided data for the establishment of the two Independence phases of the Paleoeskimo (q.v.) Tradition.
    SOURCE: Knuth 1954.

                                                                Moreau S. Maxwell

INDEPENDENCE I PHASE, a distinctive phase of the eastern Arctic, radiocarbon dated to ca. 2000–1600 B.C., whose sites lie mostly north of Lancaster Sound, spreading from Bathurst Island northward to northeastern Greenland and down its east coast to Dove Bay. Characteristic traits include dwellings (probably tents) marked by rock-slab mid-passages (q.v.); lithic artifacts related to, but larger than, those of the Arctic Small Tool Tradition (q.v.); end-hafted stone tools, many of which are multinotched on tapering proximal stems; and nontoggling harpoon heads with tapering stems for socketing. None of the lithic artifacts are ground or polished. Some investigators see cultural linkage to coastal Labrador.
    SOURCES: McGhee 1978:29–37; Maxwell 1985:60–72.

                                                                Moreau S. Maxwell

INDIAN KNOLL SITE, an Archaic (q.v.) shell midden in Ohio County, Kentucky, dated ca. 4000 to 2000 B.C. More than 1100 burials were exposed there during two periods of excavation: C. B. Moore's in 1915 and W. S. Webb's in the late 1930s. Webb's detailed report on Indian Kroll was one of the first comprehensive descriptions of eastern Archaic culture.
    SOURCES: C. B. Moore 1916; W. S. Webb 1946.

                                                                Edward B. Jelks

INFIERNO CAMP, the type site of the Infierno Phase (q.v.), located on a high divide between canyon systems in the lower Pecos River region of southwestern Texas. Dating ca. A.D. 1400–1600, it contains more than 100 stone circles formed of paired limestone blocks which may be pole supports for grass- or hide-covered huts. A relatively homogeneous artifact assemblage consisting of triangular arrow points, beveled end scrapers, prismatic

blades, and plain brownware potsherds is indicative of a discrete occupation by an intrusive, Plains-affiliated group.
SOURCES: D. S. Dibble n.d.b.; Turpin 1982:109.

Robert J. Mallouf

INFIERNO PHASE, a late prehistoric (ca. A.D. 1400–1600) hunting-gathering culture of the lower Pecos River region of Texas, defined by D. S. Dibble in 1978. Typically located on elevated ridgelines overlooking canyon systems, the sites contain surficial circles of stones, usually consisting of six or eight paired limestone boulders, which probably supported pole frameworks of grass- or hide-covered huts. The artifact assemblage comprises four primary classes: small triangular arrow points, beveled end scrapers, prismatic blades, and plain brownware potsherds. Current interpretation holds that the Infierno people probably were Apachean intruders into the region.
SOURCES: Turpin 1982:164–167.

Robert J. Mallouf

INFINITY SITE, a multicomponent site in southeastern Kansas at Elk City Lake, where excavations by J. O. Marshall in the mid–1960s discovered an early component of indeterminate cultural affiliation, a Pomona Focus (q.v.) component, and a Cuesta Phase (q.v.) village. The latter, where the remains of at least five houses and a large midden were found, is the type component of the phase.
SOURCE: J. O. Marshall 1972.

Thomas A. Witty, Jr.

INGLES BOTTOM, a series of Archaic and Woodland (qq.v.) sites along the New River in southwestern Virginia, first described in 1948 by C. G. Holland, who collected ceramics there which Clifford Evans analyzed in 1955. In 1970 C. G. Holland discussed the site's importance as a source of valuable information on local culture development.
SOURCES: C. G. Holland 1948, 1970; Clifford Evans, 1955.

Keith T. Egloff

INKSTER SITE, a Woodland (q.v.) cemetery in a natural mound overlooking the Forest River in northwestern North Dakota, where in 1980 J. A. Williams unearthed the remains of 28 individuals, most of them secondary interments. In general, they reflect egalitarian burial customs and a high rate of infant and early childhood mortality.
SOURCE: J. A. Williams 1982.

Patricia J. O'Brien

INTERMEDIATE INDIAN, a term used to denote Indian cultures of the Labrador coast between the disappearance of diagnostic Maritime Archaic artifacts about 3,500 years ago and the emergence of Recent Indian cultures

about 2,000 years ago. Their economy apparently was oriented more toward the interior than was that of their Archaic predecessors. To date, only chipped-stone tools have been found in Intermediate Indian sites.
SOURCES: Fitzhugh 1972; Nagle 1978.

James A. Tuck

INTERMEDIATE PHASE, informal term for an unnamed, poorly known Eastern Anasazi (q.v.) period (ca. A.D. 1140/1150–1200) in the Chaco Province (q.v.) of northwestern New Mexico. The phase was identified at the Salmon Ruin (q.v.), but elsewhere there is little evidence of significant residence in the province at this time. Also, no tree-ring cutting dates have been reported for the period. Thus, occupation seems limited to a few older greathouses such as Salmon with no new construction.

At the time, the San Juan Basin apparently had been abandoned because of a lengthy drought and a concomitant collapse of the Chaco Canyon settlements. The subsistence strategy for this period is uncertain, but a return to hunting and gathering may be inferred because the drought conditions made horticulture undependable. Classic San Juan McElmo Black-on-white and indented, corrugated ceramics are time markers for the phase.
SOURCE: Irwin-Williams and Shelley n.d.

Thomas C. Windes

INTERMONTANE WESTERN TRADITION, a now-obsolete term coined by R. D. Daugherty in 1962 in an early attempt to synthesize Plateau prehistory. The tradition was perceived as a basic hunting-gathering culture that endured as an entity from ca. 9000 B.C. to historic times throughout an area extending from southern British Columbia to northern Mexico. New cultural elements were added by gradual accretion with little loss or replacement of earlier elements. Significant regional diversification did not appear until late prehistoric times. Within the tradition, Daugherty recognized five periods correlated with changing climatic and economic conditions.
SOURCE: Daugherty 1962.

Frank C. Leonhardy

INTERSTATE PARK SITE, one of a few sites in Wisconsin where extinct fauna have been found in association with tools—in this instance, big-horned bison with both copper and stone artifacts. Excavated by Alonzo Pond in 1936, the site probably represents a bison kill in late Paleoindian or Early Archaic times. It documents the use of copper at a very early date.
SOURCES: A. W. Pond 1937; Palmer 1954.

David Overstreet

INTRUSIVE MOUND CULTURE, a Late Woodland expression in central and southern Ohio, dating ca. A.D. 500–800; known mainly from burial contexts. Although there are single-component burial-mound sites, the culture was named from burials that were interred in mounds of earlier cultures. Typical artifacts placed in the burials were bone tools; platform pipes; marine-shell beads; and pentagonal, chipped-stone points.

SOURCES: Mills 1922:563–584; Morgan 1952:93, fig. 34; J. B. Griffin 1983:274.

N'omi B. Greber

INUARFISSUAQ (or INUARFIGSSUAQ) SITE, a site excavated by Erik Holtved in 1950 that contained both Late Dorset and Early Thule (qq.v.) materials. It was interpreted by Holtved as the earliest Neoeskimo site in the eastern Arctic; however, R. H. Jordan views it as early but postdating Ruin Island (q.v.).

SOURCES: Holtved 1954; Jordan 1979.

Moreau S. Maxwell

INUGSUK PHASE, a unit of prehistoric Greenlandic culture proposed by Therkel Mathiassen for Thule Phase (q.v.) occupations strongly influenced by Norse Vikings. R. H. Jordan, on the basis of later work, has questioned Inugsuk's validity as a phase.

SOURCE: Jordan 1979.

Moreau S. Maxwell

INUKSUK, a line of stone fences between which wild caribou were driven for a communal autumnal kill. The term also is used for prehistoric, manlike piles of boulders set up as navigational aids along complex shorelines in the eastern Arctic region.

Moreau S. Maxwell

IPIUTAK PHASE, an Alaskan culture unit dating ca. A.D. 150–650, generally interpreted as a late phase of the Norton Tradition (q.v.) and as essentially a North American entity, but with Siberian ties in its artistic and presumably its ceremonial aspects. Spectacularly carved ivory, primarily from burials at coastal sites, is especially noteworthy. The type site is the Ipiutak Site (q.v.). At the Deering Site in coastal northwestern Alaska, excavations by Helge Larsen in 1950 yielded a series of well-preserved wooden artifacts that extended the documented time depth of artifacts such as built-up sleds.

SOURCES: Larsen and Rainey 1948; H. E. Larsen 1951; Giddings 1967; Rainey 1971; D. W. Clark 1977; C. E. Holmes 1982.

Donald W. Clark

IPIUTAK SITE, the type site of the Ipiutak Phase (q.v.) at Point Hope, Alaska, dating ca. A.D. 200–500; discovered by Helge Larson and F. G. Rainey in 1939 and excavated by them in 1939–41. Their finds opened a new vista of Alaskan prehistory featuring rich animal art and fine Paleo-eskimo lithic technology and contributed significant knowledge of prehistoric architecture and maritime adaptations of the region. Later excavations at both coastal and interior Alaskan sites demonstrated that the culture represented at the Ipiutak Site was much more widespread than had been originally thought.

SOURCES: Larsen and Rainey 1948; H. E. Larsen 1951; Giddings 1967; Rainey 1971; D. W. Clark 1977; C. E. Holmes 1982.

Donald W. Clark

IRENE SITE, a Mississippian (q.v.) site near the mouth of the Savannah River in Chatham County, Georgia, dating ca. A.D. 1150–1400. It consisted of a substructure mound, an adjacent burial mound, and, surrounding them, several large, special-purpose structures and enclosures with a few houses. J. R. Caldwell excavated the site in 1937–40 with Works Progress Administration crews.

SOURCE: Caldwell and McCann 1941.

Paul A. Webb

IROQUOIS CULTURE, a major culture of New York state that developed out of the earlier Owasco Culture (q.v.) ca. A.D. 1300. Dwelling in palisaded villages of longhouses, the Iroquois people depended upon agriculture, as well as upon hunting, fishing, and collecting, for subsistence. This prehistoric culture emerged in the historic period as the Five Nations—Seneca, Cayuga, Onandaga, Oneida, and Mohawk—that formed the League of the Iroquois. The term should not not be confused with *Iroquoian*, a language family to which other Northeastern peoples (e.g., the Huron, Erie, Petun, and Neutral) belonged.

James A. Tuck

IRWIN SITE, a site on the Appomattox River just east of the fall line in Virginia where tests by H. A. MacCord in 1964 and W. C. Johnson in 1984 revealed Late Archaic hearths and Woodland refuse-filled pits. A wide variety of ceramics from the site illustrates the complex pattern of cultural interaction along and across the fall line.

SOURCE: MacCord 1964c.

Keith T. Egloff

ISLAND FIELD SITE, an extensive Webb Phase (q.v.) mortuary complex on the west side of Delaware Bay containing over 250 burials and exhibiting nonlocal influences. Excavations there by R. A. Thomas from 1966 to 1974 disclosed numerous mortuary practices, including single and multiple interments; individual and communal graves; grave furnishings; and such corpse treatments as bone scraping, disarticulation, bundling, and cremation

(both in the flesh and after scraping). Radiocarbon dates and culture traits dated elsewhere suggest a temporal range of ca. A.D. 600–1000.
SOURCE: Thomas and Warren 1970:1–33.

Ronald A. Thomas

ITASCA SITE, an early postglacial (ca. 6000–5000 B.C.) bison kill-butchering station and associated camping area, located adjacent to Lake Itasca in northwestern Minnesota. Initialy testing in 1937 by A. E. Jenks demonstrated human association with the extinct *Bison occidentalis*. C. T. Shay, after further excavations in 1963–1964, reconstructed the paleoenvironment and developed a model of ecological adaptation by Early Archaic hunters/gatherers of the locality.
SOURCES: Jenks 1937a; Shay 1971.

Gordon R. Peters

ITINNERA (or ITIVNERA), an inner fjord, middle to late Saqqaq Phase (q.v.) site in western Greenland, probably occupied seasonally in autumn; excavated by Meldgaard and others. Dwellings were round with central rock-slab hearths; caribou was the predominant prey. Radiocarbon dated to ca. 1150 B.C., it has been published in more detail than any other Saqqaq component.
SOURCE: Meldgaard 1977.

Moreau S. Maxwell

ITSKARI PHASE (previously called the LOUP RIVER PHASE), a late prehistoric (A.D. 1100–1500) manifestation of the Plains Village Tradition in the Loup River drainage and vicinity in central Nebraska. Settlements consisted of solitary rectangular earthlodges, or small villages, along major streams and their tributaries, on flood-free alluvial terraces or upland spurs. Bison hunting alternated seasonally with spring and autumn planting and harvesting of maize. Secondary burial in communal ossuaries on high hills above dwelling areas was practiced. Simple sand-tempered pottery jars with collared and unthickened rims are typical. Interaction with peoples of the Middle Missouri Tradition to the north suggests that the Itskari Phase was pivotal in the emergence of the Coalescent Tradition and ultimately of the historic Pawnee and Arikara.
SOURCES: Ludwickson 1978; Ludwickson and Holen (in press).

John Ludwickson

IVUGIVIK SITES, a group of small Pre-Dorset Phase (q.v.) sites at the northeastern corner of Hudson Bay whose lithic assemblages led W. E.

Taylor, Jr., who excavated them in 1958, to conclude that there was an unbroken cultural continuum bridging the Pre-Dorset and Dorset phases.
SOURCE: W. E. Taylor, Jr. 1962.

Moreau S. Maxwell

IYATAYET SITE, the type site for both the Denbigh Flint Complex and the Norton Tradition (qq.v.), located on Norton Sound near Cape Denbigh, Alaska. Excavated by J. L. Giddings, Jr., in 1948–1950 and in 1952, the site also was occupied by peoples of the Nukleet Phase of the Thule Tradition.
SOURCE: Giddings 1964.

Donald W. Clark

J

JACAL, a term of Spanish origin for a common building technique in the prehistoric and historic Southwest whereby a house's walls were constructed by setting closely spaced, vertical poles in a trench, then plastering them with mud. A one-room structure made by this method may be called a jacal (plural *jacales*).

Stewart Peckham

JACKSON SITE, a Neoeskimo settlement on Cape Parry, Northwest Territories, excavated by W. E. Taylor, Jr., to test his theory that the development of the eastern Thule Phase (q.v.) began not in the Birnick Phase (q.v.) of Alaska but in a phase further east. His finds did not support his hypothesis: Artifacts in the wooden-floored houses were related to Alaskan cultures and were too late; radiocarbon dates, which he rejected, were too early.
SOURCE: W. E. Taylor, Jr. 1972.

Moreau S. Maxwell

JAKE MARTIN SITE, a preceramic Archaic (q.v.) site on Cypress Creek in Upshur County, in northeastern Texas, dug by E. M. Davis in 1959. Projectile-point styles indicate a predominantly Early to Middle Archaic (La Harpe Aspect, q.v.) occupation dating ca. 4000–2000 B.C. The presence of Meserve and San Patrice type points (qq.v.) may represent an earlier occupation.
SOURCE: Davis and Davis 1960.

James E. Corbin

JAMES YOUNKIN MOUND, a site with a single mound located just northwest of the juncture of the Kansas and Republican rivers in north-central Kansas, excavated in 1931 by Floyd Schultz. In the mound was a round, stone-lined feature containing a deposit of fragmented human bone asso-

ciated with Woodland and Hopewell artifacts, including a Kansas City Hopewell (q.v.) cross-hatched pottery rimsherd and a platform pipe (q.v.). An extended human skeleton in the same feature may have been an intrusive Smoky Hill Phase (q.v.) burial.
SOURCE: Schultz and Spaulding 1948.

Patricia J. O'Brien

JARRELL PHASE, a Middle Archaic (ca. 4000–3000 B.C.) culture unit in central Texas, defined by E. R. Prewitt in 1981. Typical features at the usually small, but occasionally large sites are hearths lined with flat stones and burned-rock scatters. Diagnostic artifacts are Andice, Bandy, Bell (q.v.), Martindale, and Uvalde (q.v.) dart-point types. Other characteristic artifacts are millingstones and a variety of chipped-stone tools including gouges, denticulates, bifaces, and unifaces. Major components of the phase have been dug at the Wilson-Leonard, Landslide, La Jita, and Wounded Eye sites.
SOURCES: T. R. Hester 1971:71–74; Luke 1980:40–45; Prewitt 1981:78; Sorrow et al. 1967:3–43.

Frank A. Weir

JAY PHASE, the earliest phase of the Archaic Oshara Tradition (q.v.) in the Four Corners area of the Southwest, dating ca. 5500–4800 B.C. It bears little resemblance to the preceding Paleoindian Cody Complex in subsistence practices, settlement patterns, artifact assemblages, or projectile-point forms. Its artifacts, instead, resemble artifacts of the San Dieguito and Lake Mojave complexes (qq.v.) of California, Arizona, and Nevada, suggesting a western origin. The diagnostic Jay type projectile point is large and has slight shoulders, a straight to mildly contracting stem, and a base that is either straight or convex. Lanceolate, bifacial knives and numerous large, steep-angled scrapers are other typical chipped-stone tools. Ground-stone implements may also have been used.

The climate during the phase was considerably more arid than during the previous Paleoindian period. The population consisted of mobile bands that subsisted by foraging for a variety of plants and animals while following a relatively unstructured seasonal round. Some researchers have argued that the large-animal hunting adaptation of the preceding Paleoindian peoples continued into the Jay Phase.

Base camps tended to be small (around 50 square meters) and generally were located close to a water source. Special activity sites, including hunting camps and quarries, also have been identified. A mixed spectrum of subsistence activities is implied by the tool kit, limited faunal remains, and repeated reoccupation of favorable localities with easy access to a wide variety of microenvironments.

SOURCES: Irwin-William and Haynes 1970; Irwin-Williams 1973, 1979; Judge 1979.

Cynthia Irwin-Williams and Patricia A. Hicks

JEDDITO 264 SITE, a Basketmaker III–Pueblo I (qq.v.) period site in the Kayenta/Tsegi cultural area of northeastern Arizona that is particularly significant because it documents the transition from pithouse to surface architecture at ca. A.D. 650–800. It consisted of six randomly situated pithouses; sixteen isolated, slab-lined, round storage cists; ten contiguous, rectanguloid, near-surface storage chambers; six isolated firepits; and one later, Pueblo II, semsubterranean, rectanguloid structure thought to be a kiva. Ceramics and architectural styles relate the site to both the Mogollon and the Anasazi traditions (qq.v.).
SOURCE: Daifuku 1961.

Michael B. Stanislawski

JEFFERSON'S MOUND, a burial mound somewhere on the Rivanna River east of Charlottesville, Virginia, excavated by Thomas Jefferson in 1784 and considered by many people to be the first archaeological site in North America dug and documented scientifically. Beginning with Gerard Fowke in 1894, many have tried to relocate the mound by testing the floodplain where it supposedly stood, but all attempts have failed.
SOURCES: Jefferson 1954; Fowke 1894; Bushnell 1930; Boyer n.d.

Keith T. Egloff

JEMEZ PROVINCE, part of the southern Jemez Plateau in New Mexico defined by the distribution of Anasazi (q.v.) sites containing significant amounts of Jemez Black-on-white ceramics. Its boundaries are marked approximately by San Ysidro on the south, La Cueva on the north, the Nacimiento Range on the west, and Bear Springs Peak on the east.

After some earlier, largely unreported work by various people, most archaeological investigations in the Jemez Province were carried out from 1928 to 1938 by School of American Research and University of New Mexico field schools. They excavated several Classic Period (q.v.) sites including Giusewa, Unshagi, and Nanishagi. No substantive excavations have been conducted in the area since World War II.

No Paleoindian (q.v.) sites are known in the province. The most significant of the very few Archaic sites is Jemez Cave, excavated in the 1930s by University of New Mexico field schools and reinvestigated in 1965 by R. I. Ford. It produced the earliest (ca. 500 B.C.) evidence of maize utilization in the province.

The Jemez Province's sequence of occupations by Anasazi peoples was very much like that of the other Upper Rio Grande provinces until ca. 1250, when Vallecitos Black-on-white pottery began to be made locally, marking the beginning of the Vallecitos (or Late Coalition) Phase, which lasted until ca. 1325.

Migrants from other areas of the Southwest appeared at this time, including Gallina peoples from the north and west who introduced new architectural features and ceramic styles. Population, site size, and site frequency reached their peak in the Rio Grande Classic Period (q.v.) (ca. A.D. 1325–1600). At least nine very large pueblos, as well as the earliest great kivas in the province, were built then, all of them, paradoxically, on high mesas away from permanent water sources.

SOURCES: Bandelier 1892; W. H. Holmes 1905; Reiter 1938; R. I. Ford 1975; Sando 1979, 1982; Elliott 1982.

                                                                    Michael L. Elliott

JEREMY ISLAND MIDDEN, a site on Jeremy Island in Charleston, South Carolina, comprising a Pee Dee Phase (q.v.) component of ca. A.D. 1500 and an earlier component, estimated to date ca. A.D. 1200, characterized by complicated-stamped pottery of the Jeremy Series. The Pee Dee occupation has yielded a large quantity of pottery, including several intact vessels, primarily of the Pee Dee series. The site was investigated by Stuart Mackintosh in the 1960s and by Michael Trinkley in 1979.

SOURCE: Trinkley 1980b.

                                                                    Michael Trinkley

JEWELL SITE, a Mississippian (q.v.) village and mound complex in Barren County, Kentucky, surveyed by R. B. Evans in 1881, tested by R. B. Clay in 1962, and extensively excavated by Clay and L. H. Hanson, Jr. in 1963. The remains of 28 houses revealed details of the village's architectural styles. The platform mound was excavated sufficiently to determine its structural history; a sizeable sample of artifacts provided information on the villager's technology. Radiometric and ceramic dating indicate that the site was first occupied before A.D. 1000 and was abandoned between 1450 and 1600.

SOURCE: Hanson 1970.

                                                                    Edward B. Jelks

JOHN EAST MOUND, a burial mound on the Middle River in west-central Virginia, radiocarbon dated to ca. A.D. 950–1350, which produced numerous human burials. First described by Gerard Fowke in 1894, it was tested by C. G. Holland, Clifford Evans, and B. J. Meggers in 1952, and it was completely excavated by the Archaeological Society of Virginia in 1965.

SOURCES: Fowke 1894; Holland et al. 1953.

                                                                    Keith T. Egloff

JOHN GREEN SITE, a village dating to A.D. 1680–1730 on the Meherrin River in the southern coastal plain of Virginia. In 1968 H. A. MacCord found refuse-filled pits, house patterns, and human burials there. The wide

range of ceramics—Colono, Clarksville, and Courtland (qq.v.)—together with other artifacts from the site document the acculturation of Indian groups, possibly the Weyanoke, Nottoway, and Meherrin.
SOURCE: MacCord 1970.

Keith T. Egloff

JOHN PEARCE SITE, a multicomponent, late Paleoindian–Archaic (qq.v.) site in Caddo Parish, northwestern Louisiana south of Shreveport. Excavated by Wayne Roberts and C. H. Webb between 1966 and 1969, this stratified site produced Archaic lithic artifacts from the disturbed sand overburden and the first pure assemblage of San Patrice Culture (q.v.) artifacts from two occupational clusters in the subsurface clay. The 62 San Patrice type points from the excavations and surrounding surface included both *Hope* and *St. Johns* varieties. Also from the San Patrice clusters came Keithville side-notched points, Albany beveled side scrapers, and a variety of small flaked tools, all made of local tan-brown cherts. No directly dateable material, distinctive features, or ground-stone tools were found.
SOURCES: Webb et al. 1971.

Clarence H. Webb

JONAS SHORT SITE, a conical burial mound surrounded by a habitation area on the Angelina River in San Augustine County, in eastern Texas, estimated to date A.D. 100–800. Partially excavated in 1956 by E. B. Jelks, it contained a human cremation in a submound pit and caches of artifacts in the mound fill. Copper reel-shaped gorgets, boat stones, and other artifacts from the mound are of Hopewell-Marksville (qq.v.) affinity; also in the mound fill, as well as in the habitation area, were locally typical dart points and potsherds. The mound was similar in form and content to the Coral Snake Mound (q.v.) in Sabine Parish, Louisiana.
SOURCES: Jelks 1965; McClurkan et al. 1980.

Edward B. Jelks

JONES-MILLER SITE, a Hell Gap Complex (q.v.) mass-kill site near Wray, Colorado, that was excavated by D. J. Stanford from 1973 to 1975. Remains of nearly 300 disarticulated animals (*Bison antiquus*)—representing several kill episodes in fall, winter, and spring—were exposed, along with 130 stone and 200 bone artifacts. Among the stone tools were 31 complete and 73 broken Hell Gap type projectile points, some of which, with weak shoulders, bear some resemblance to the Agate Basin type. The site is estimated to date ca. 8000 B.C.
SOURCE: Stanford 1978.

Patricia J. O'Brien

JORDAN'S LANDING SITE, a small farming village of the Cashie Phase (q.v.), radiocarbon dated to ca. A.D. 1425, on the Roanoke River in Bertie County, in North Carolina; the type site for the Cashie Phase and for Cashie

Pottery Series (q.v.). Excavations in 1976–1977 by D. S. Phelps disclosed numerous features, burials, and structures identified with the prehistoric antecedents of the historic Tuscarora Indians.
SOURCE: Phelps 1983.

Billy L. Oliver

JORNADA BROWN WARE, the major utility pottery of the Sierra Blanca Sub-Province, Jornada Province, Mogollon Culture (qq.v.) of southeastern New Mexico: a plain, highly polished, thick ware that is strongly reminiscent of its presumed ancestral type, Alma Plain of the Mimbres Province, Mogollon Culture. Its major affiliation is with the Glencoe and Corona phases (qq.v.). Of uncertain beginning date, it was made until ca. A.D. 1400–1500.
SOURCES: Jennings 1940; Mera 1943.

R. N. Wiseman

JORNADA PROVINCE (or BRANCH), an expression of the Mogollon Culture (q.v.), dating ca. A.D. 1–1450, in south-central and southeastern New Mexico and adjacent sections of Chihuahua, and extending down the Rio Grande Valley about 200 kilometers below El Paso. As originally defined by D. J. Lehmer in 1948, it comprised two sequences of phases: one for the northern part of the province and one for the southern part, both presumed to have derived from a common ancestral base, the Hueco Phase.

Later research by M. E Whalen expanded Lehmer's conception of the Jornada Province, increasing its geographical domain, adding three additional phase sequences, and subsuming the respective sequences under named subprovinces. Thus, under this scheme, the Jornada Province consists of the El Paso, Sierra Blanca, Middle Pecos (qq.v.), Brantley-Guadalupe, and Southeast Extension sub-provinces, within each of which is a sequence of phases. A number of important sites in the Roswell area also belong to the province, but the research on them has not progressed to the point of phase definition. The research forming the basis for these sub-provinces and phases varies in depth but is minimal for most of them.

Brownware pottery is a common denominator of the various sub-provinces and is the major link to the Mogollon Culture. While several types (e.g., Jornada Brown and El Paso Brown [qq.v.]) were made and used over vast areas, the ceramic histories of the respective sub-provinces are unique and, to greater or lesser extent, reflect developments of adjacent regions as well. For instance, the artifact inventory of the El Paso Sub-Province is more like that of the Casas Grandes Province (q.v.) than it is like that of the Middle Pecos Sub-Province.

Remains of buildings occur in all the sub-provinces except Brantley-Guadalupe. As with ceramics, the histories of architectural forms are generally similar over most of the Jornada Province, although specific sizes, shapes, construction materials, and intrasettlement patterns vary widely.

The mode of subsistence, in part reflecting the great physiographic diversity encompassed by the province, also varied among the sub-provinces. Agriculture was practiced in most of them, but it appears to have been lacking entirely in both the Brantley-Guadalupe and Eastern Extension sub-provinces. Hunting and gathering were important in all; the major species exploited simply reflect species availability. Thus, bison were important along the Plains margin, as were deer in the mountains and rabbits in the intermountain basins. Fish and fresh-water mollusks were important along the Pecos River and perhaps the Rio Grande. Dogs, turkeys, or other domesticated animals were never prominent on a large scale.

Its vast territory and great variety of archaeological remains make the Jornada Province unique among Southwestern provinces. When more research has been completed, perhaps it will be subjected to greater taxonomic refinement comparable to that of the Anasazi Culture (q.v.) and the rest of the Mogollon Culture.

SOURCES: Mera 1943; Lehmer 1948.

R. N. Wiseman

JOSS SITE, a middle Dorset Phase (q.v.) component at Prince Albert Sound on the western coast of Victoria Island, Northwest Territories, radiocarbon dated to the 1st century A.D.; excavated by R. J. McGhee. One of the farthest west Dorset occupations, it produced an artifact assemblage, closely related to Dorset Phase assemblages farther east, but containing antler arrowheads of western Alaskan (Norton Phase [q.v.]) styles. Arrows do not occur in eastern Dorset sites.

SOURCE: McGhee 1971.

Moreau S. Maxwell

JUHLE SITE, a complex of three 16th-century ossuaries and a probable habitation area on Nanjemoy Creek in southern Maryland, excavated in 1953–1955 by T. D. Stewart and in 1971 and 1980 by D. H. Ubelaker. The ossuaries provided valuable data for reconstructing population profiles of a southeastern Algonkian group.

SOURCE: Ubelaker 1974.

Stephen R. Potter

JULIANEHAB SITE, a city in southern Greenland established by Eric the Red in A.D. 985, where extensive excavations by Danish and other archaeologists have furnished a wealth of data on the development and ultimate collapse of the Viking settlement.

SOURCE: McGovern 1980.

Moreau S. Maxwell

JUNTUNEN PHASE, a well-defined Late Woodland (ca. A.D. 1200–1400) expression centered in the Saint Mary River and Straits of Mackinac region of northern Michigan and adjacent Ontario, defined by Alan McPherron

in 1967. The chief diagnostic trait is collared, sometimes castellated, pottery vessels decorated with rows of horizontal or diagonal stamping made with cord-wrapped sticks, with simple cord markings, or, more frequently, with stab-and-drag lines. Juntunen Phase sites are usually large lakeshore fishing villages.
SOURCE: McPherron 1967.

Charles E. Cleland

JUNTUNEN SITE, a large, stratified, Late Woodland village site on Bois Blanc Island in the Straits of Mackinac, Mackinac County, Michigan; occupied ca. A.D. 800–1350 by proto-Chippewa fishermen. Excavated in the early 1960s by Alan McPherron, it is the type site for the Mackinac, Bois Blanc, and Juntunen phases (qq.v.).
SOURCE: McPherron 1967.

Charles E. Cleland

JURGENS SITE, a Cody Complex, Paleoindian (qq.v.) site in Colorado, excavated by J. B. Wheat and H. M. Wormington in 1968 and 1970. It had three distinct areas: (1) a habitation locus with the remains of fish, small mammals, deer, elk, moose, pronghorn, and at least 31 bison; (2) a concentration of bison and pronghorn bones interpreted as a short-term, meat-procurement camp; and (3) a small kill site with articulated and disarticulated remains of 35 bison and at least two pronghorn antelope.
SOURCE: Wheat 1979.

Patricia J. O'Brien

K

KACHEMAK SITES, a group of sites on Kachemak Bay, an arm of Cook Inlet on the Gulf of Alaska, constituting one of the richer archaeological areas of the region. Frederica de Laguna's excavations in 1931–1932 at the Cottonwood Creek, Yukon Island, and Fox Farm sites led to her definition of the Kachemak Bay stages, now termed the Kachemak Tradition (q.v.). Karen and William Workman and others investigated several Kachemak Bay sites in the 1970s and 1980s.

SOURCES: de Laguna 1934, 1975; Workman and Lobdell 1980.

Donald W. Clark

KACHEMAK TRADITION, an archaeological manifestation distributed over much of the Gulf of Alaska region between 1500 B.C. and A.D. 1100; originally defined by Frederica de Laguna in the 1930s as a series of stages, relating the archaeology of Cook Inlet to the broader domain of Eskimo prehistory, but showing ties with the Northwest Coast. De Laguna's interpretations were based largely on a group of sites at Kachemak Bay (q.v.). The earliest Kachemak people had a simple tool kit comprising both flaked-stone and ground-slate tools plus many composite hooks and weights for fishing in the sea. Later Kachemak people produced a variety of personal ornaments—labrets, pendants, beads, and so on—and massive stone lamps with figures of humans and sea mammals carved into the bowls. Cut and drilled human bones, trophy heads, and artificial eyes in burials are common.

SOURCES: de Laguna 1934, 1975; D. W. Clark 1970b; Dumond 1977; Workman et al. 1980.

Donald W. Clark

K'AERSUT SITE, a settlement near the Igloolik Locality (q.v.) marking the terminal Dorset Phase manifestation in the Foxe Basin, Northwest Terri-

tories. On a strand line standing 8 meters above sea level, it was excavated by Jørgen Meldgaard in 1956.
SOURCE: Meldgaard 1962.

Moreau S. Maxwell

KALERUSERK SITE, an early Pre-Dorset Phase (q.v.) site, radiocarbon dated to ca. 1900 B.C., situated on the strand line 60 meters above sea level near Igloolik on the Melville Peninsula, Northwest Territories. Excavations there in the late 1950s by Jørgen Meldgaard yielded the evidence for his initial definition of the early Pre-Dorset of the eastern Arctic, which he originally called the Sarqaq Phase.
SOURCE: Meldgaard 1962.

Moreau S. Maxwell

KAMLOOPS PHASE (or HORIZON), a late prehistoric (ca. A.D. 800–1800) manifestation of the mid-Fraser and Thompson river drainages in British Columbia, defined in 1968 by David Sanger. The type site is the Chase Burial Site (q.v.) near the town of Chase. Distinctive artifacts are triangular, side-notched arrow points (called Kamloops Side-Notched); variously sized lanceolate, pentagonal, and triangular knives; thumbnail scrapers; a florescent ground-stone industry with nephrite adze blades; seated human-figure bowls; oval, circular, rectangular, and square pithouses; many small food-storage pits; burials that are predominantly primary flexed interments, usually accompanied by artifacts; status and wealth differentiation; and well-developed exchange systems.

Local variants of the phase have been defined by A. H. Stryd, Robert Wilson, Thomas Richards, and Michael Rousseau. Richards and Rousseau have suggested that this unit be renamed the Kamloops Horizon to reflect its broad compass.
SOURCES: Sanger 1968a:86–185; Rousseau and Richards 1986.

Arnoud H. Stryd

KANGEK SITE, a late Thule Phase (Inugsuk, q.v.) site near the Viking western settlement in western Greenland. A radiocarbon date of A.D. 1350–1450 may date an Eskimo occupation during or slightly after the collapse of the Norse settlement.
SOURCES: Gulløv 1982; Jordan 1984.

Moreau S. Maxwell

KANSAS CITY HOPEWELL PHASE, a cultural tradition dating ca. A.D. 1–500 that spread, probably by migration, from the central Illinois River Valley up the Missouri River to just inside Nebraska and, especially, up the Kansas River into central Kansas. It had a settlement pattern of large, permanent camps at major creek mouths; stone-vaulted burial mounds on

nearby bluffs; and ancillary, specialized subsistence-activity sites scattered up the creek's drainage. Defined by W. R. Wedel in 1943, the phase was the subject of much research during the 1970s.
SOURCES: A. E. Johnson 1976; O'Brien 1984b.

Patricia J. O'Brien

KANSAS MONUMENT SITE, a historic Republican Pawnee earthlodge village on the Republican River in north-central Kansas where Jedediah Smith wintered in 1825–1826. After intensive archaeological work by the Kansas State Historical Society, the Pawnee Indian Village Museum was constructed there in 1967.
SOURCES: Wedel 1936; C. S. Smith 1950; Witty 1968.

Thomas A. Witty, Jr.

KAPUIVIK SITE, a site near Igloolik, Northwest Territories, on a strand line 24 meters above sea level, where the earliest known appearance of Dorset culture (ca. 700–600 B.C.) was reported by Jørgen Meldgaard, who excavated there in the late 1950s. Kapuivik has been variously interpreted as representing a continuum from Pre-Dorset to Dorset, as an intrusive culture from the South, and as the result of influences from a distinct transitional culture phase, Groswater Dorset (q.v.).
SOURCE: Meldgaard 1962.

Moreau S. Maxwell

KARLO SITE, a large, multicomponent midden site in the Great Basin portion of northeastern California, excavated by F. A. Riddell in the 1950s. He found numerous artifacts including a variety of ground-stone milling and pounding implements, bone items, and flaked-stone tools. Some 600 projectile points represent many of the principal Great Basin types; e.g., Humboldt, Pinto, Northern Side Notched, Elko, Rose Spring, and Desert Side-Notched (qq.v.). Burials and cremations were encountered throughout the midden, and several graves contained shell beads of types affiliated with central California's Early and Middle horizons, indicating an antiquity around 2000 B.C.
SOURCE: Riddell 1960.

R. E. Taylor and L. A. Payen

KARLUK ISLAND SITES, a series of early Dorset Phase (q.v.) sites between Little Cornwallis and Bathurst islands, Northwest Territories. J. W. Hel-

mer's report of his work there was the first detailed description of Early
Dorset sites in the High Arctic.
SOURCE: Helmer 1980.

                                                                    Moreau S. Maxwell

KARTAR PHASE. See Chief Joseph Dam Locality.

KATHIO PHASE, a culture unit of central Minnesota dated by stratigraphy
and typology to ca. A.D. 800–1200. Typical grit-tempered, globular Kathio
pots have constricted necks, moderate to pronounced rim flare, and cord-
wrapped dowel impressions on the rim and lip. Their similarity to Clam
River (q.v.) ceramics in Wisconsin and to some Blackduck (q.v.) ceramics
in northern Minnesota is pronounced, and the three wares may constitute
a geographical continuum. The phase is characterized not only by the ceramic series, but also by triangular side-notched projectile points, and by
round burial mounds containing secondary bundle burials.
SOURCES: Elden Johnson 1971; Gibbon and Caine 1980; Caine 1983.

                                                                Christy Hohman-Caine

KAVIK PHASE. See Anaktuvuk Pass Sites.

KAWUMKAN SPRINGS MIDDEN, a site in the southeastern foothills of
the Oregon Cascades, just beyond the western rim of the Great Basin, studied
by L. S. Cressman from 1947 through 1951. Originally, the site was thought
to span the last 7500 years, but subsequent obsidian hydration measurements suggest instead a beginning date of ca. 3000 B.C. Hunting of small
and large game is attested throughout by faunal remains associated with
projectile points and processing tools. Cressman postulated that the 2-meter-
deep midden accumulation reflected in situ development of the ethnographically known Klamath culture from its early beginnings in the Great Basin
Desert Culture, as known from caves in south-central Oregon.
SOURCES: Cressman 1956; Aikens and Minor 1978.

                                                                    C. Melvin Aikens

KAY COUNTY CHERT. See Florence Chert.

KAYUK COMPLEX. See Anaktuvuk Pass Sites.

KEITH FOCUS, a Plains Woodland manifestation dating ca. A.D. 400–800,
focused on the Republican River drainage and its major tributaries in northwestern Kansas and southwestern Nebraska. Defined by M. F. Kivett in
1952 on the basis of several habitation and burial sites, it is characterized
by calcite-tempered Harlan Cord-Roughened pottery and by Scallorn arrow
points (q.v.). Burial patterns involve the use of ossuaries like the Woodruff

Ossuary (q.v.), in which are found disarticulated skeletal parts as well as disk beads and both triangular and crescent-shaped pendants, all made from mussel shells.

SOURCES: Kivett 1952:5–32, 1953; Wedel 1959:535–556.

Patricia J. O'Brien

KEMP SITE, an early Middle Dorset settlement on Cape Tanfield, on Baffin Island's southern coast, Northwest Territories, where excavations by a Michigan State University field team in 1962 demonstrated a developmental continuum from Early to Middle Dorset, during an increasingly colder period.

SOURCE: Mawell 1973.

Moreau S. Maxwell

KEOWEE TOWN, the governing town of the Lower Creek people in the 18th century; site of the English Fort Prince George, built in 1753; now inundated by Keowee Reservoir. William Edwards explored the site archaeologically in 1968, at which time he collected probably Qualla pottery (q.v.) and abundant European trade goods.

SOURCES: Harmon 1986; Beuschel n.d.

Michael Trinkley

KESHENA FOCUS, a Woodland (q.v.) manifestation comprising Early, Middle, and Late Woodland habitation sites, single mounds, and mound groups in Shawano and Oconto counties, in Wisconsin, defined by S. A. Barrett and Alanson Skinner in 1932. This northernmost unit of Effigy Mound (q.v.) development represents most of what is known of the archaeology of the Wolf River basin in northeastern Wisconsin, including some historic Menominee occupations.

SOURCE: Barrett and Skinner 1932.

David Overstreet

KETTLE FALLS, a waterfall on the upper Columbia River in northeastern Washington that was second only to The Dalles (q.v.) as a salmon fishery and trading center in aboriginal times. After excavating several sites there in the early 1970s, D. H. Chance defined a six-phase culture sequence for the locality, extending from ca. 7400 B.C. to the 19th century A.D. The artifact assemblages of the respective phases are markedly different from those of the southern Plateau; their affiliations lie rather with cultures of the northern Plateau and the Subarctic.

SOURCE: Chance et al. 1977.

Frank C. Leonhardy

KEYAUWEE SITE, a site near Asheboro, North Carolina, believed to have been occupied by the prehistoric and historic Siouan-speaking Keyauwee Indians. Excavations there in 1935–1936 directed by J. L. Coe led to the

identification of the Uwharrie and Caraway complexes. John Lawson is thought to have visited a Keywauwee village at the site in 1701.
SOURCE: Ward 1983.

Billy L. Oliver

KEY MARCO SITE, a late prehistoric (ca. A.D. 1200–1500) site on the northern end of Marco Island on the southwest Florida Gulf coast. Cushing's 1895 excavation of a mucky part of the site yielded fiber and wooden artifacts, including netting, cordage, bowls, mortars, boxes, tool hafts, atlatl parts, toy canoes, masks, figurines, and net floats.
SOURCES: Cushing 1897; Gilliland 1975.

Jerald T. Milanich

KEYSER CORDMARKED WARE, a shell-tempered, cordmarked, Late Woodland pottery first described by J. B. Griffin in 1944 on the basis of sherds from the Keyser Farm Site (q.v.). There are four equally spaced, cordmarked or incised lugs around the outer edge of the slightly flaring rim. Keyser is distributed from the Shenandoah valley of Northwestern Virginia southward to the headwaters of the James River.
SOURCES: Manson et al. 1944; Geier and Boyer 1982.

Keith T. Egloff

KEYSER FARM SITE, a Late Woodland village at the foot of Massanutten Mountain, Virginia. Tests in 1939 by C. P. Manson and H. A. MacCord uncovered human burials, storage pits, postmolds, and many artifacts, including samples of ceramics which were used in defining Keyser Cordmarked, Page Cordmarked, and Potomac Creek (qq.v.) wares.
SOURCE: Manson et al. 1944

Keith T. Egloff

KIATUTHLANNA PHASE, a poorly known eastern Anasazi manifestation of the Pueblo I period (ca. A.D. 800–900) in the Chaco and Upper Little Colorado provinces. Dwellings were mainly large, deep pithouses occurring in clusters that apparently were occupied by several families, probably related. The lack of surface rooms contrasts sharply with both the preceding and the following phases.

Subsistence was by hunting, gathering, and horticulture. Sites of the phase contain Kiatuthlanna Black-on-white and Kana'a Gray pottery, along with ceramic types carried over from the preceding White Mound Phase (q.v.).
SOURCES: F. H. H. Roberts, Jr. 1931; McKenna and Truell 1986.

Thomas C. Windes

KIJIK SITE, a historic Tanaina Athapaskan site of uncertain calendrical date, located near Lake Clark at the base of the Alaska Peninsula, excavated in 1966 by J. B. Townsend and J. W. VanStone. It yielded a large collection

of American trade goods from the last decades of the 19th century and a small number of earlier Russian trade goods. The few traditional artifacts found there derived from various historic, and possibly prehistoric, occupations. The collections document culture change, especially during the later history of the site.
SOURCE: VanStone and Townsend 1970.

Donald W. Clark

KILLIKTEE SITE, a late Dorset Phase (q.v.) settlement on Itivirk Bay near Lake Harbour, Baffin Island, Northwest Territories; representative of a regional continuum from early Pre-Dorset to modern Inuit. Radiocarbon dated to ca. A.D. 750, the site demonstrates the spread of Late Dorset into inner bays from earlier Dorset sites on the exposed coast. It was excavated by a Michigan State University field team in 1963.
SOURCE: Maxwell 1973.

Moreau S. Maxwell

KILLILUGAK SITE, a transitional Pre-Dorset/Dorset (qq.v.) site on McKellar Bay, Baffin Island, Northwest Territories; radiocarbon dated to ca. 600 B.C. Excavations there by a Michigan State University field team in 1960 demonstrated a typological linkage between the Pre-Dorset and Dorset phases, even though there were discrete differences from both. Typological similarities to the Groswater Dorset Phase and to the Kapuivik Site (qq.v.) also were noted.
SOURCE: Maxwell 1973.

Moreau S. Maxwell

KINCAID SITE, a large Mississippian (q.v.) mound center located in the Ohio River floodplain in Pope and Massac counties, in Illinois, occupying over 100 acres and containing two major mound groups, a palisade, and large areas of village deposits. Major Middle and Late Woodland components are also present. The site was extensively investigated by University of Chicago archaeologists in the 1930s and 1940s; more recent work in the locality has focused on numerous small settlements throughout the bottoms that represent the center's support population. The Mississippian occupation has been radiocarbon dated to ca. A.D. 900–1400.
SOURCES: Cole at al. 1951; B. M. Butler 1977; Muller 1978, 1986.

Brian M. Butler

KINGAALUK SITE, a late Dorset Phase (q.v.) site on the Belcher Islands in Southern Hudson Bay, marking the apparent reoccupation of these iso-

lated islands following their abandonment at the end of the Early Dorset period. The site was excavated by Elmer Harp, Jr., in 1975.
SOURCE: Harp n.d.

Moreau S. Mawell

KINGS BEACH COMPLEX, a term originally defined in 1953 by R. F. Heizer and A. B. Elsasser on the basis of their work at the Kings Beach Site (q.v.); now used collectively for the Late Archaic phases of the eastern slope of the northern Sierra Nevada and the adjacent western great Basin area; Early Kings Beach Phase (ca. A.D. 500–1200) having Rosegate Series points (q.v.) as the principal diagnostic, and Late Kings Beach Phase (ca. 1200–historic) associated with Desert Side-Notched points (q.v.). The transition from Martis to Early Kings Beach is marked by a number of changes, including population growth, intensification of resource exploitation (more use of fish, plant foods, and small mammals), introduction of the bow and arrow, and use of bedrock mortars. Late Kings Beach is poorly known archaeologically; either the population dropped abruptly or changes in material culture caused a decrease in archaeological visibility.
SOURCES: Heizer and Elsasser 1953; Elsasser 1960; Elston 1971, 1982; Elston et al. 1977.

Robert G. Elston

KINGS BEACH SITE, the type site for the Kings Beach Complex (q.v.), located in the Sierra Nevada on the northeastern shore of Lake Tahoe, Nevada; excavated by R. F. Heizer and A. B. Elsasser in 1952.
SOURCE: Heizer and Elsasser 1953.

Robert G. Elston

KING SITE, a palisaded early historic period village site covering about 1.6 hectares, located on the Coosa River in northwestern Georgia. In 1973–1974, D. J. Hally and P. H. Garrow excavated approximately two-thirds of the site, revealing at least 27 structures and over 200 burials, some containing mid–16th-century European iron artifacts. The village may have been visited by the DeSoto entrada in 1540.
SOURCES: Hally 1975; Hudson et al. 1985.

Paul A. Webb

KING'S RUIN, a multicomponent site on the east bank of Chino Creek northwest of Prescott, Arizona, in the Prescott Province of the Patayan Division, Hakataya Culture (qq.v.). Partly excavated by E. H. Spicer in 1932, the site provided stratigraphic evidence of jacal architecture underlyng

a pueblo, as well as data on what now (1988 are known as the Prescott and Chino phases (qq.v.).
SOURCE: Spicer 1936.

Albert H. Schroeder

KIN KLETSO, a late Bonito Phase (q.v.) site representative of a small number of single-component, multistory pueblos without courtyards or great kivas built after A.D. 1100 in Chaco Culture National Historical Park, New Mexico. The three-story pueblo of 135 rooms tightly arranged around one of the site's five kivas is located within the core of Chacoan greathouse development near Pueblo del Arroyo, Pueblo Bonito, and Chetro Ketl (qq.v.). Built in the classic McElmo masonry style (blocks of soft sandstone dressed by pecking and grinding), it is the only excavated site of its type in Chaco Canyon. After partial excavation by E. N. Ferdon, Jr., in 1934, it was completely excavated by Gordon Vivian and T. W. Mathews between 1950 and 1953.
SOURCE: Vivian and Mathews 1965.

Thomas C. Windes

KINNIKINNICK RUIN, a cluster of pueblo structures on the rim of Kinnikinnick Canyon, on Anderson Mesa in northern Arizona. There are two rectangular roomblocks: one, originally two to three stories high, comprises about 75 ground-floor rooms; the other has an estimated 13 ground-floor rooms. There are possible agricultural terraces north of the roomblocks. Surrounding burials and some rooms have been rather extensively vandalized.

In 1940 Milton Wetherill and Sydney Connor excavated one of the rooms to obtain tree-ring samples for bridging a gap in the regional chronology. Ceramic dates from their excavation are A.D. 1200–1325; tree-ring dates are 1269–1308.
SOURCES: Connor 1943; Colton 1946.

Donald E. Weaver, Jr.

KIRK CORNER-NOTCHED POINT, a small to large, corner-notched, Early Archaic (ca. 7500–6500 B.C.), chipped-stone projectile-point type, highly variable in size, base shape, blade shape, and presence or absence of beveling and/ or serrating. Numerous names have been applied to variations of this type, which is found over most of the eastern United States from New York south.
SOURCES: Coe 1964:69–70; Broyles 1966:19–21, 1971; J. W. Griffin 1974; Jefferson Chapman 1975:114–115, 1977.

Eugene M. Futato

KIRK SERRATED POINT (or BLADE), a long, narrow projectile point with deep serrations and a broad, square stem, which distinguishes it from the Kirk Stemmed type (q.v.) with its mildly expanding stem. Estimated to

date ca. 8000–6000 B.C., this type is widely distributed over the eastern United States.
SOURCE: Coe 1964:72.

Billy L. Oliver

KIRK STEMMED POINT (or BLADE), a long, daggerlike projectile point with deeply serrated blade edges, wide corner notches, and a broad, mildly expanding stem with a straight or slightly convex base. The shoulders project backward. Dating ca. 8000–6000 B.C. and distributed over much of the eastern United States, Kirk Stemmed evolved into the Kirk Serrated type (q.v.), as the blade became narrower and the notches broadened to produce a nearly square stem.
SOURCE: Coe 1964:70.

Billy L. Oliver

KITSELAS CANYON SEQUENCE, a culture sequence on the lower Skeena River in northwestern British Columbia comprising five temporally discrete units. The earliest, the Bornite Phase, dating ca. 3000–2300 B.C., is characterized by cobble, flake, and microblade tools. Rare abraders and chipped-stone points occur at ca. 2000 B.C. in the Gitaus Phase, but microblades are absent. Chipped-stone artifacts predominate in the undated middle unit, the Skeena Phase. The Paul Mason Phase is distinguished by cobble, ground-slate, and bone tools. Rectangular house floors of this phase at the Paul Mason site, dated to ca. 1000 B.C., constitute the earliest known evidence of formalized villages on the northern Northwest coast. The latest unit, the Kleanza Phase, dated ca. 400 B.C., has numerous items of personal adornment, which may be related to the evolution of status differentiation.
SOURCES: Allaire 1978; Inglis and MacDonald 1979; Coupland 1985.

Gary Coupland

KITTIGAZUIT SITE, a location on the east side of the Mackenzie delta, Northwest Territories, that was occupied by the Thule-derived Mackenzie Eskimo during most of the second millennium A.D., including the early historic contact period. Partially excavated by Robert McGhee in 1969–70, it is located strategically at a "natural trap" where herds of beluga whales were driven into shallow water and slaughtered for food.
SOURCE: McGhee 1974.

Donald W. Clark

KIVA, a general term (adopted from a Hopi Indian word) for a specialized, usually subterranean room found in sites of the Anasazi Culture (q.v.) and, less frequently, of the Mogollon Culture (q.v.), where men are thought to have performed religious rituals and boys to have received religious instruction. The Anasazi kiva apparently developed out of the Basketmaker III residential pithouse when it was replaced in the Pueblo I period (ca. A.D. 800–900) by surface dwellings and storage rooms. Kivas are still used by Pueblo Indians in New Mexico and Arizona.

Most Anasazi kivas had a series of aligned floor features: ventilator ducts, ladder sockets, deflector, ashpit, hearth, and a *sipapu* (a small hole in the floor symbolic of the place where the earth's first people emerged from the underworld, as related in Pueblo creation legends). Interior features varied in different provinces and at different periods. Features that often were present include a bench built into the base of the wall around the room; peripheral pilasters or vertical posts to support a roof; wall niches; "floor drums" (rectangular subfloor vaults); sockets for a vertical loom (weaving of cotton still is a Pueblo man's task); and multicolor, esoteric murals (mainly during the Pueblo IV period, ca. 1325–1600).

SOURCES: Hawley 1950; Smiley 1952; Kidder 1958; Dutton 1963; Judd 1964; Peckham 1979; Cattanach 1980.

                                                                  Stewart Peckham

KLETHLA PHASE, a manifestion of late Pueblo II culture in the Red Rock Plateau region of the Cedar Mesa Province (q.v.) of southeastern Utah, as well as in the Kayenta area generally. Dating ca. A.D. 1100–1150, the phase's small, well-preserved sites, which are located in canyons, characteristically contain a preponderance of Kayenta ceramics. The Klethla Phase may be equivalent to the Clay Hills Phase (q.v.) on Cedar Mesa.

SOURCES: Colton 1939b; Lipe 1970.

                                                                  R. G. Matson

KLO-KUT SITE, a deeply stratified, Athapaskan Tradition (q.v.) campsite in the boreal forest near the village of Old Crow, northern Yukon Territory, that was occupied over the past twelve centuries. Examined initially by G. R. Lowther, tested in 1965 and 1967 by W. N. Irving and R. E. Morlan, and excavated extensively by Morlan in 1968, the site appears to have been a seasonal base camp for harvesting northwardly migrating caribou in the late spring and early summer.

SOURCE: Morlan 1973.

                                                                  Donald W. Clark

KLONDIKE PHASE. See Owens Valley Locality.

KLUNK-GIBSON MOUNDS, a series of 28 burial mounds in three separate groups on the western bluffs of the lower Illinois River Valley in Calhoun County, in Illinois; excavated in the 1960s nd 1970s by Gregory Perino and Jane Buikstra. Late Archaic (ca. 3000–500 B.C.), Middle Woodland (Havana-Hopewell and Pike Phase) (ca. 150 B.C.–A.D. 400), and Late Woodland (Jersey Bluff) (ca. A.D. 650–900) mortuary components were present. Numerous studies have used data on the 528 individuals buried in the mounds to model Middle and Late Woodland social organization and population dynamics.

SOURCES: Perino 1968:9–124, 1973a:58–89, 1973b:211–213; Tainter 1975, 1977:67–98; Buikstra 1976; Braun 1977, 1979:66–79.

Charles R. McGimsey

KNIFE RIVER FLINT, a uniform, fine-grained, dark-brown, translucent stone occurring naturally over a broad area in western North Dakota. Thought to be of Eocene age, it occurs as cobbles and boulders in secondary deposits. It has excellent flaking properties in raw or heat-treated form and was heavily utilized for chipped-stone tool manufacture for at least 10,500 years. A complex of quarry pits, workshops, and campsites covering at least 4,000 hectares in Dunn and Mercer counties, in North Dakota comprises one of the most extensive prehistoric quarry operations in North America. Artifacts of Knife River flint, widely distributed through prehistoric trade systems, occur from Saskatchewan and Ontario on the north to Ohio, Nebraska, and Colorado on the east and south.

SOURCES: Clayton et al. 1970; Loendorf et al 1984; Ahler and Christensen n.d.

Stanley A. Ahler

KNIGHT ISLAND SITE (also known as the Old Town Site) , a late prehistoric village near Yakutat, Alaska, excavated by Frederica de Laguna in 1952–1953 as part of a program of archaeological, ethnological, and acculturation studies among the northern Tlingit. A diverse artifact sample was recovered from refuse mounds, cache pits, and several large, semisubterranean, rectangular, plank dwellings. Included were heavy woodworking tools, stone lamps, several forms of unilaterally barbed harpoon and arrow heads of bone and a miscellany of ulos, unbarbed arrow points, and knives of chipped stone, polished stone, native copper, and bone. Many of the artifact styles have wide distribution among the protohistoric and early historic Koniag and Chugach Eskimo and northern Northwest Coast cultures.

SOURCE: de Laguna et al. 1964.

Gerald H. Clark

KNIGHT MOUND SITE, a group of sixteen Middle and Late Woodland mounds and an adjacent village area located on terraces along the eastern margin of the Mississippi River floodplain in Calhoun County, in Illinois. Excavated in the 1940s and 1950s by P. F. Titterington and amateur archaeologists, many of the mounds were mortuary structures of the Middle Woodland Pike Phase, dating ca. A.D. 150–400, to which Fox Creek and

Jersey Bluff peoples of Late Woodland times (ca. A.D. 400–900) later added cemeteries. Limited excavations also were conducted in the village area.

SOURCES: McKern et al. 1945:295–302; Flanders 1965; Griffin et al. 1970.

Charles R. McGimsey

KNIGHT'S BLUFF SITE, primarily an early Texarkana Focus (q.v.) (Middle Caddo) village on the Sulphur River in Cass County, in Texas, where excavations by E. B. Jelks in 1952 exposed a number of burials and part of a circular house floor. There also was a small, Early Ceramic period (q.v.) occupation typified by Williams Plain pottery and Gary dart (q.v.) points.

SOURCE: Jelks 1961:11–41.

James E. Corbin

KOEHLER SITE, a Late Woodland village on the Smith River in the southwestern Piedmont of Virginia. Tests by J. P. Gravely in 1960 and excavations by W. E. Clark in 1976 located human burials, hearths, and refuse-filled pits that were radiocarbon dated, perhaps too early, to A.D. 1305–1405.

SOURCE: Coleman n.d.

Keith T. Egloff

KOENS-CRISPIN POINT, a large, contracting-stem projectile point form first described in 1916 in a report on excavations at a Late Archaic cremation cemetery in New Jersey. It is the Delaware River Valley equivalent of the Savannah River type (q.v.).

SOURCE: Hawkes and Linton 1916.

Ronald A. Thomas

KOGGIUNG PHASE. See Brooks River-Naknek Drainage Sites.

KOLIKTALIK SITE, a Middle Dorset settlement near Nain, Labrador, radiocarbon dated to the 1st century A.D. Excavations by the Torngat Project (q.v.) in the 1970s exposed semisubterranean houses with tunnel entryways—a surprising discovery, as such features usually are thought to be restricted to Thule houses of the 2nd century A.D.

SOURCE: Cox 1978.

Moreau S. Maxwell

KOLNAES SITE, a location at the northeastern corner of Greenland, where in 1949 Eigil Knuth unearthed a complete umiak (whale-hunting boat) and other late Thule Phase (q.v.) artifacts of the 14th century A.D. The umiak demonstrates that the northern coast of Greenland was open to navigation

in the 14th century, although it has remained icebound from early in the 15th century to the present.
SOURCE: Knuth 1952.

Moreau S. Maxwell

KOGRUK COMPLEX. See Anaktuvuk Pass Sites.

KOLOMOKI SITE, a multicomponent mound complex located on a small tributary of the Chattahoochee River in southwestern Georgia. The primary occupation and at least some of the mounds appear to date to the late Swift Creek–Weeden Island early cultures (qq.v), ca. A.D. 100–500. Excavations by W. H. Sears in 1948–1952 disclosed indications of elaborate mortuary practices which, along with other evidence, suggest a chiefdom-level society.
SOURCES: Sears 1956; Milanich et al. 1984:19–21.

Paul A. Webb

KONIAG PHASE, the archaeological equivalent of the Koniag Eskimo and their direct antecedents, from ca. A.D. 1100 into the historic contact period. Sites and components include the aceramic Uyak upper levels excavated by Alĕs Hrdlička in the 1930s; the ceramic Rolling Bay and Kiavak sites excavated by W. S. Laughlin in 1961–1963; the historic sites at Karluk tested by F. A. Milan in 1953 and excavated by R. H. Jordan in 1982–1985; and Kukak, on the Alaska Peninsula, excavated by Wilbur Davis in 1953 and by D. E. Dumond in 1963–1965. The Camp Phase of the Brooks River–Naknek drainage (q.v.) is closely related. There are both continuities and discontinuities between Koniag and the antecedent Kachemak Tradition (q.v.), and there are ties with Aleut, Bering Sea Eskimo, and West Coast Indian cultures. Many Koniag implements are like those of the Kachemak Tradition, but plainer. Developed or introduced during the Koniag Phase were petroglyph production, incised pebble figurines for ritual use, the vapor sweat bath, coarse pottery, heavy grooved splitting adzes, whaling with very long slate-tipped darts (not harpoons), and lambdoidal head flattening.
SOURCES: Hrdlicka 1944; Heizer 1956; D. W. Clark 1974a, 1974b, 1975; G. H. Clark 1977.

Donald W. Clark

KOSHKONONG PHASE. See Oneota Tradition.

KOSTER SITE, a deeply stratified, multicomponent site buried in colluvial deposits at the margin of the Illinois River Valley in Greene County, in Illinois. Field-school crews under the direction of Stuart Struever and J. A. Brown excavated there between 1969 and 1978 and exposed 23 stratigraphically distinct components, ranging in age from ca. 7000 B.C. to ca. A.D. 1100. Enormous quantities of lithic, faunal, and floral remains collected

from the long sequence of hunter-gatherer occupations provided the framework for regional Archaic period culture history, evidence for major shifts in subsistence, and insights into the evolution of sedentism. Later Woodland and Mississippian components represent agricultural adaptations to the local setting.
SOURCES: Houart 1971; Brown and Vierra 1983:165–195.

Michael D. Wiant

KUAUA PUEBLO, a Classic Period, Rio Grande Anasazi (q.v.) pueblo near Bernalillo, New Mexico that has been restored as Coronado State Monument. It was excavated between 1934 and 1939 by teams from the University of New Mexico, the Museum of New Mexico, and the School of American Research. Occupied by Tiwa-speaking Pueblo Indians between ca. A.D. 1350 and 1550, the L-shaped site had three plazas surrounded by adobe-walled roomblocks containing a total of approximately 750 rooms. The village had five subterranean kivas in the plazas and three ground-level kiva-like rooms within the houseblocks. Two kivas had multicolored murals (one with 85 layers of paintings) depicting ceremonial figures.
SOURCES: J. L. Sinclair 1951; Dutton 1963.

Stewart Peckham

KUKULIK SITE, an abandoned, 2000-year-old Eskimo village on St. Lawrence Island, Alaska, where excavations from 1931 to 1935 by O. W. Geist and in 1937 by F. G. Rainey revealed an occupational sequence commencing with the Old Bering Sea Phase (q.v.) and extending through the Birnirk and Punuk phases (qq.v.) into modern times, terminating with charnel houses resulting from a winter of starvation and possibly an epidemic in 1878. Specimens from Geist's work there and at Gambell (q.v.) formed the nucleus of extensive Eskimo collections now housed at the University of Alaska, in Fairbanks.
SOURCE: Geist and Rainey 1936.

Donald W. Clark

KWAHE'E BLACK-ON-WHITE POTTERY, a type decorated with mineral paint that was made in north-central New Mexico north of the Rio Abajo Province (q.v.) ca. A.D. 1050–1220/1250. Antecedents were Red Mesa, Gallup, and Puerco Black-on-white wares. Other black-on-white types that influenced Kwahe'e's form, finish, and design, were Socorro, Mancos, McElmo, Mesa Verde, and Gallina. Taos Black-on-white is a northern variety of Kwahe'e.
SOURCES: Mera 1935; Lang 1982.

Richard W. Lang

KWAIKA'A SITE, a pueblo on the southeast edge of Antelope Mesa about 6 kilometers north of the Awatovi Site (q.v.) that was occupied ca. A.D. 1200–1580. Covering more than 8 hectares, it had hundreds of rooms in a series of one- and two-story buildings grouped around several plazas, a minimum of fifteen semisubterranean, rectangular, stone-built kivas, and a population of perhaps from 1000 to 2000. It has been hypothesized that the site initially may have been a Rio Grande Tewa or Keres settlement that later was joined by Zuni and Upper Colorado clans; it may have been the first town in the Hopi Province (q.v.) visited by the Coronado expedition in 1540 and possibly was attacked by the Spaniards.

Kwaika'a is particularly known for Sikyatki style, polychrome murals on its kiva walls that emphasize kachina ceremonies, beasts, birds, and mythical forms (see Sikyatki and Awatovi sites), and for evidence that coal was used ca. A.D. 1200 and after for firing pottery and heataing houses and kivas.

Cosmos and Victor Mindeleff brothers surveyed the site in 1883; Frank Russell and Walter Hough dug there in 1900 and 1901, respectively; L. L. Hargrave collected tree-ring samples in 1928; Earl Morris tested part of the site in 1935; and J. O. Brew, Watson Smith, R. B. Woodbury, Al Lancaster, and others worked there between 1935 and 1939.

SOURCES: Victor Mindeleff 1891; Hargrave 1935; Reed 1942; Watson Smith 1952b, 1972.

Michael B. Stanislawski

KYLE SITE, a stratified rockshelter in Hill County, Texas; partially excavated in 1959 and 1960 by E. B. Jelks. The six major strata of the site, spanning the period ca. A.D. 550–1550, firmly established a clear temporal separation between the Austin and Toyah phases (qq.v.) and provided much of the data for the first definitive description of those two phases.

SOURCE: Jelks 1962.

Edward B. Jelks

L

LA BREA SKELETON, a woman's skull, mandible, and postcranial bones excavated in 1914 by L. E. Wyman from the Rancho La Brea asphalt deposit in Los Angeles, California. Radiating fractures around an irregular hole in the skull suggested that a depressed skull fracture was the cause of death. A mano was found about 10 centimeters above the skull. An age of ca. 7000 B.C. was obtained through radiocarbon analysis of an amino acid fraction from a femur.

SOURCES: Merriam 1914; Kroeber 1962; Berger 1975.

R. E. Taylor and L. A. Payen

LAGOON SITE, the farthest west Dorset Phase (q.v.) site reported to date, located on the southwestern coast of Banks Island, Northwest Territories. Excavations by C. D. Arnold in 1979 unearthed a structure and an artifact assemblage possessing attributes of the Pre-Dorset Phase, the early Dorset Phase, and the western Paleoeskimo Tradition (Norton Phase) (q.q.v.). A radiocarbon date of 450–350 B.C. was obtained. Lagoon provides the best current illustration of contact between western and Dorset peoples.

SOURCE: Arnold 1981.

Moreau S. Maxwell

LAGUNA BEACH SKELETON, a human skull and long-bone fragments of controversial age, dug out of a road cut by teenagers in 1933 in Laguna Beach, California. An initial radiocarbon analysis indicated that the bones were at least 15,000 years old, after which the radiocarbon value for the skull was used as the calibration standard for dating a number of other human bones from southern California by the amino acid racemization method. In 1984, a more reliable data of ca. 3000

B.C. was obtained through radiocarbon analysis of an amino acid fraction, using accelerator mass spectrometry.
SOURCES: Berger 1974; Bada et al. 1984; Taylor et al. 1985.

R. E. Taylor and L.A. Payen.

LAHARPE ASPECT, an inclusive category encompassing the Archaic (q.v.) cultures of eastern Texas and eastern Oklahoma, defined by LeRoy Johnson, Jr. in 1962. Chipped-stone projectile points, scrapers, and knives, plus abundant milling stones, attest to a balanced, hunting-gathering economy that efficiently exploited the animal and plant food resources of the region.
SOURCE: LeRoy Johnson, Jr. 1962.

Edward B. Jelks

LA JOLLA TRADITION, an archaeological manifestation in southwestern California and Baja California, dating ca. 6000–1000 B.C. First described in 1939 by M. Rogers who termed it the *Shell Midden Culture*, the tradition is characterized by milling, discoidal, and cogged stones. Many La Jollan sites are shell middens situated around lagoons.
SOURCE: Moratto 1984:126, 149–152.

Michael J. Moratto

LA JUNTA PHASE, a late prehistoric (ca. A.D. 1200–1400) unit of the Bravo Valley Aspect (q.v.) occupying the lower reaches of the Rio Conchos in Chihuahua and extending along the Rio Grande from the Ojinago-Presidio area to the vicinity of Ciudad Juarez and El Paso; defined as the La Junta Focus by J. C. Kelley and D. J. Lehmer in the 1940s. Villages were concentrated in the river valleys where soils suitable for farming were readily available. Influences from the Jornada branch of the Mogollon Culture (qq.v.) farther up the Rio Grande have been noted.

Dwellings included both above-ground, adobe-walled room blocks and jacal-like pithouses. Typical interior house features were adobe altars, low adobe curbs, and raised adobe hearths; flexed burials were placed in shallow pits beneath prepared house floors. Characteristic artifacts were carved stone bowls, El Paso and Chihuahua polychrome (qq.v.) wares, a variety of decorated wares traded from the Southwestern region, locally made brownwares, pierced and unpierced ceramic discs, several types of arrow points, manos, grinding slabs, and stone pipes.
SOURCES: J. C. Kelley et al. 1940; J. C. Kelley 1949:89–114, 1985:149–159.

Robert J. Mallouf

LAKE ATHABASKA SITES, a series of sites in Alberta affiliated with the Canadian Tundra Taiga Tradition (q.v.) and containing artifacts of Pre-Dorset (q.v.) types. Investigated by W. C. Noble in the late 1960s, these sites represent the most southerly penetration of Pre-Dorset people into the

Barren Grounds and below the present treeline. This movement took place ca. 1000–900 B.C. during a cold period when the treeline retreated several hundred kilometers south of its present location.
SOURCE: W. C. Noble 1971; J. V. Wright 1972b.

Moreau S. Maxwell

LAKE HARBOUR LOCALITY, an Inuit settlement area on the middle southern coast of Baffin Island, Northwest Territories, where a series of archaeological sites was studied between 1960 and 1980 by Michigan State University researchers.
SOURCE: Maxwell 1985.

Moreau S. Maxwell

LAKE HAZEN LOCALITY, a place on northern Ellesmere Island, Northwest Territories, at latitude 81° north, where sites of the Independence I and II, late Dorset, and late Thule phases (qq.v.) have been excavated by A. W. Greeley, in 1881; M. S. Maxwell, in 1958; and P. D. Sutherland, in 1980 and 1981. This is on the migration route from Alaska to Greenland proposed by H. P. Steensby.
SOURCES: Steensby 1917; Maxwell 1960; Sutherland n.d.

Moreau S. Maxwell

LAKE JACKSON SITE, a major mound and village complex of the Fort Walton Culture (q.v.) in Leon County, in Florida, partially excavated by Gordon Willey in 1940, by John Griffin in 1947, by Hale Smith and Charles Fairbanks in the 1950s, and by Calvin Jones in 1975–1976. Dating ca. A.D. 1250–1500, it comprises seven mounds (six of them pyramidal), a plaza, and village middens. One mound contained copper and other Southern Ceremonial Complex (q.v.) paraphernalia associated with high-status burials.
SOURCES: Willey and Woodbury 1942:247; Willey 1949a:95–101, 284; B. C. Jones 1982.

Jerald T. Milanich

LAKE MANIX INDUSTRY, an assemblage of large, ovate bifaces and other flaked chalcedony objects found on desert pavement surfaces above the shore of Pleistocene Lake Manix in the Mojave Desert of southern California. Resemblances to "Paleolithic" implements and apparent correlation with the maximum stand of Lake Manix during the late Pleistocene constitute the basis for suggesting an antiquity of at least 20,000 years. Alternate explanations maintain that the specimens represent quarry-shop refuse of a much later date.

SOURCES: Simpson 1958; Glennan 1976.

L. A. Payen

LAKE MOJAVE, one of the pluvial lakes in the interior desert area of southern California whose name has been variously employed by different authors to identify a complex/culture/phase/pattern and a period, as well as a distinctive projectile-point type that was used in the western Great Basin between about 8000 and 6000 B.C.

SOURCE: Moratto 1984:93–97.

L. A. Payen

LAKE MOJAVE POINT, a type of large, lozenge-shaped projectile point with a short blade and a long stem, found on sites associated with fossil water channels and lake shorelines in the Mojave and Colorado deserts of southeastern California. The type is estimated to date ca. 9000–7000 B.C.

SOURCE: Campbell et al. 1937.

L. A. Payen

LAKES PHASE, a term applied to Late Woodland cultures in north-central Wisconsin. Sites of the phase, which date between A.D. 1000 and 1200, manifest great variation, ranging from small temporary camps to large villages. They share certain characteristics with the Mero and Hein's Creek (q.v.) sites on the Door County peninsula, but they appear to be unrelated to the Effigy Mound Tradition.

SOURCE: Salzer 1969.

David Overstreet

LAKE WINNEBAGO PHASE. See Oneota Tradition.

LAMAR CULTURE (or PHASE), a late prehistoric and protohistoric (ca. A.D. 1400–1700) culture in the northern Coastal Plain and Piedmont of Georgia, eastern Alabama, and western South Carolina. Villages and hamlets seem to be distributed around ceremonial-civic centers with platform mounds, plazas, and palisades. Because the characteristic bold-complicated-stamped and burnished-plain, incised pottery resembles ceramics of other cultures, this other pottery often has been incorrectly identified as Lamar. Recently, there has been a trend to use a taxonomy that more accurately

reflects the variations in all of the late pottery of the southern Piedmont, including Lamar.
SOURCES: A. R. Kelly 1938; L. G. Ferguson 1971.

Roy S. Dickens, Jr.

LAMOKA LAKE SITE, the type site for the Lamoka Culture, located in western New York and dating to the Late Archaic period. Excavations by W. A. Ritchie in the 1920s and again in the 1960s produced an artifact assemblage that is unique in northeastern prehistory: narrow-stemmed projectile points, beveled stone adzes, and a rich variety of organic implements and decorative objects.
SOURCES: Ritchie 1932, 1969.

James A. Tuck

LA MORA SITE, a middle-sized site of the Rio Sonora Culture (q.v.) in north-central Sonora on the upper Rio Sonora. Its significance lies in the presence of a Mesoamerican-style, T-shaped ball court. The unexcavated site has not been dated but probably was occupied between A.D. 1250 and 1500.
SOURCES: Pailes, 1980, 1984.

Richard A. Pailes

LA MOTTE CULTURE, a probable late Middle Woodland (ca. A.D. 200–500) cultural expression concentrated primarily in the Wabash-Embarrass river drainages in Illinois and Indiana; defined by H. D. Winters in 1963 as a close relative of another unit, the Allison Culture. More recent work, however, suggests that the two constitute a single culture and that separation is not warranted. Diagnostic elements include the Lowe Flared Base projectile-point type and varieties of simple and checked-stamped pottery. Evidence of burial ceremonialism is absent.
SOURCES: Winters 1963:61–71; Binford et al. 1970; Pace and Apfelstadt 1980.

James H. Kellar

LANGTRY POINT, a Middle Archaic dart-point type, dating ca. 1950–1250 B.C., diagnostic of the San Felipe Phase of the lower Pecos River region of southwestern Texas; characterized by a triangular blade, squared to mildly barbed shoulders, a contracting stem, and a straight to mildly concave base.
SOURCES: Suhm and Jelks 1962; Ross 1965; Dibble n.d.; Turner and Hester 1985.

Elton R. Prewitt

L'ANSE AUX MEADOWS, a site on the northern tip of Newfoundland's Great Northern Peninsula that is the only documented Norse settlement in North America. Excavations by Anne Stine and Helge Ingstad in the 1960s

and by Parks Canada in the 1970s revealed the presence of large sod houses, a smithy, and other structures. These features, together with associated artifacts and radiocarbon dates, confirm an occupation in the early 11th century A.D. Current interpretation suggests that the site served as a staging area for exploiting the Gulf of St. Lawrence.
SOURCES: A. S. Ingstad 1977.

James A. Tuck

LANSING MAN, a term applied to the partial remains of two human skeletons (an adult male and a six- or seven-year-old child) found in 1902 in loess deposits near the Missouri River in northeastern Kansas. Originally thought by some researchers to be of great antiquity, the bones were later dated to 2660–5020 B.C., placing them in the Middle Archaic period. The bones are the oldest dated human skeletal remains found to date in Kansas.
SOURCE: Bass 1973.

Richard A. Rogers

LA PLATA PHASE, a widespread Eastern Anasazi expression dating ca. A.D. 550–700, distributed throughout the Chaco Province of northwestern New Mexico and adjoining regions, including Mesa Verde, the Chuska Valley, and the Red Mesa Valley. The phase's principal architectural form was a shallow pithouse with four roof-support posts, a large entry antechamber, and associated storage cists. Settlements consisted of from a few to many pithouses; some large communities had a great kiva. Varieties of Lino Gray pottery occur abundantly in the sites, along with small amounts of La Plata Black-on-white, occasional redwares, and some Lino Black-on-gray. Site utilization may have been seasonally oriented; the chief subsistence practices were hunting, gathering, and horticulture.
SOURCES: F. H. H. Roberts, Jr. 1929b; McKenna and Truell 1986.

Thomas C. Windes

LA PLAYA SITE, the best-known site of the Trincheras Culture (q.v.), located in Sonora; apparently occupied before A.D. 800 and abandoned before 1300. As the site was marshy in prehistoric times, the inhabitants built low platforms on which to work and live. One of their main economic activities probably was the manufacture of shell bracelets from *Glycymeris* valves.
SOURCE: A. E. Johnson 1963.

David A. Phillips, Jr.

LAQUISH DIVISION, a division of the Hakataya Culture (q.v.) that was defined by M. J. Rogers, named by H. S. Colton, and revised by A. H. Schroeder to encompass the lower Gila and lower Colorado rivers in southwestern Arizona. It has been dated through intrusive pottery from ca. A.D.

700 or earlier to historic times. No Laquish phases have been defined aside from Rogers' Yuman (q.v.) periods I, II, and III, which were based on excavation of a rock cairn. Laquish contacts were primarily with the Hohokam Culture (q.v.) and with western Arizona peoples. Amacava type red-on-buff pottery, which occurs on sites of the division, survived into historic times among the Mohaves.

SOURCES: Colton, 1946; M. J. Rogers 1945; Schroeder 1952; Kroeber and Harner 1955.

Albert H. Schroeder

LARGO-GALLINA PHASE, an expression of Pueblo II–III culture, dating between A.D. 950/1000 and 1300, which straddles the continental divide in northwestern New Mexico. It represents the southern arm of the Pueblo Tradition in the Upper San Juan Province (q.v.), at a time when the Rosa Phase (q.v.) population had split into two segments.

Sites consist of from one to four thick-walled, masonry surface houses and/or pithouses, either round or rectangular. Both house types have interior ventilators, fire basins, hollow partition walls, hollow deflectors, vertical roof-support posts, and occasional benches; floors and roofs may be covered with flagstones. Agricultural terraces sometimes are associated with the sites.

Typical artifacts are pottery decorated with black carbon paint, tri-notched stone axes, elk-antler fleshers, clay elbow pipes, chipped-stone knives, arrow-shaft straighteners, flat metates with companion manos, twilled yucca sandals, feather cloth, twined bags, and coiled basketry. Large quantities of both eight- and twelve-row maize have been found in Largo-Gallina sites.

J. C. Mackey and S. J. Holbrook have concluded that the Largo-Gallina people abandoned their homeland because of climatic deterioration during the Great Drought of A.D. 1250–1300.

SOURCES: Hibben 1938; Mera 1938; Eddy 1966; R. I. Ford et al. 1972; Mackey and Holbrook 1978.

Frank W. Eddy

LARGO-GALLINA PROVINCE, a culture area comprising 11,750 square kilometers straddling the Continental Divide in the western half of north-central New Mexico. It was settled by emigrant Anasazi (Rosa Phase) (qq.v.) peoples from the Upper San Juan Province (q.v.) to the north and west ca. A.D. 850. Arbitrarily assigned archaeological regions within the Largo-Gallina Province are, from north to south: Dulce, Gobernador, Ojitos, Stone Lake, Llaves, and Cuba.

Prehistorically, two conservative, long-lived phases dominated the province: Rosa (ca. A.D. 700–1100) and Gallina (ca. A.D. 1100–1275) (qq.v.). The Anasazi abandoned the province; then, after a cultural hiatus of over two centuries, Navajo peoples occupied it. Their culture is represented archaeologically by three phases: the Dinetah Phase (ca. A.D. 1500–1710), distinguished by forked-stick hogans, Dinetah Utility pottery, and Jemez Black-on-white trade pottery; the Gobernador Phase (q.v.) (ca. A.D. 1710–1775), characterized by defensive sites with towers, Gobernador Polychrome pottery, general Puebloan trade pottery of the period, and European trade goods; and the Cabezon Phase (ca. A.D. 1775–1850), typified by stone-wall hogans, Navajo Polychrome and Navajo Utility pottery, and greater reliance on a herding economy.

SOURCES: E. T. Hall, Jr. 1944; J. J. Hester 1962; Dick 1976.

Herbert W. Dick

LA ROCHE SITES, a group of several sites on the Missouri River in South Dakota affiliated with the Initial Middle Missouri Variant (q.v.) as defined by D. J. Lehmer. Excavated by G. H. Smith and R. E. Jensen in 1963, they probably were occupied by ancestors of the Arikara and Pawnee. Included are the La Roche Village proper and nearby sites identified as components A through C, all dating after A.D. 1400. The latter phases of occupation are ascribed to the Extended Coalescent horizon.

SOURCES: J. J. Hoffman 1968; Lehmer 1971.

Patricia J. O'Brien

LARSON PHASE, a unit of the Spoon River Tradition (q.v.), dating ca. A.D. 1225–1300. Although sites of the phase are most numerous in the vicinity of the type site, Larson (q.v.), at the mouth of Spoon River, they also occur all along the central Illinois River Valley from the Sangamon River northward to Peoria Lake. Larson Phase settlements—diverse with respect to size, physiographic location, and function—included large fortified temple towns that served as centers, small satellite villages clustered around the towns, and dispersed special-activity sites, often of seasonal occupation. Sociopolitical and sociotechnic ties with the Cahokia Site (q.v.) to the south were strong. A mixed economy is indicated, stressing intensive exploitation of the natural environment in conjunction with corn and bean horticulture.

SOURCES: Harn 1975, 1978, 1980.

Alan D. Harn

LARSON SITE, a large temple-mound center dating to the 13th century A.D., located at the confluence of the Illinois and Spoon rivers in central Illinois. Numerous excavations by several different archaeologists since 1964 revealed that this highly structured, fortified center comprised a truncated pyramidal mound and plaza, around which were residential areas, burial precincts, and borrow pits where earth was obtained for mound construction. The type site for the Larson Phase of the Spoon River variant of the Mississippian tradition (qq.v.), the site also contains a major Marion

Phase component of the Early Woodland Tradition. Data from Larson and related area sites contributed substantially to the development of a socio-settlement framework for the Spoon River variant.
SOURCES: Munson and Hall 1966; Harn 1978:233–268.

Alan D. Harn

LASANEN SITE, a late 17th-century burial locale on the north shore of the Straits of Mackinac, Mackinac County, in Michigan, where in 1967 Charles Cleland found large quantities of French trade goods with artifacts of aboriginal manufacture in small ossuary burials.
SOURCE: Cleland 1971.

Charles E. Cleland

LAS DELICIAS DEL SUR SITE, a large village of the Rio Sonora Culture (q.v.) in north-central Sonora on the upper Rio Sonora, estimated to date ca. A.D. 1000–1500. Excavated in 1978 by R. A. Pailes, it has numerous pithouses, rectangular surface structures, and a large rectangular enclosure.
SOURCES: Pailes 1980, 1984.

Richard A. Pailes

LASLEY'S POINT SITE, the type site for the Lake Winnebago Phase of the Oneota Tradition (q.v.) and one of many large settlements of the phase in the middle Fox River passage in Wisconsin. House mounds, garden beds, cemeteries, refuse/storage pits, and numerous other features were exposed there during excavations by A. Kannenberg in the 1940s. A remnant of the site survives and is protected in a Winnebago County park.
SOURCES: Overstreet 1978.

David Overstreet

LAS TRINCHERAS SITE, the type site of the Trincheras Culture (q.v.) in north-central Sonora. On various parts of the site are from 15 to 30 terraces extending from the base to the top of a hill. There is a rock-wall enclosure on the hilltop and another partway down the slope. Along the terraces are numerous house remains and an amount of trash sufficient to suggest an extended occupation.
SOURCE: A. E. Johnson 1966.

Richard A. Pailes

LATE HORIZON, the most recent (ca. A.D. 300–1850) of three cultural expressions (Early, Middle, and Late horizons), first identified in the Sacramento–San Joaquin Delta locality during the 1930s by Jeremiah Lillard, R. F. Heizer, and Franklin Fenenga, and subsequently recognized throughout much of central California. The horizon is characterized by ceremonial houses, cremation as well as burial of the dead, and distinctive types of

shell and stone artifacts. After ca. 1975, the term "Late Horizon" was largely supplanted by "Augustine Pattern" (q.v.).
SOURCE: Moratto 1984:183–185, 211–214.

Michael J. Moratto

LATE PREHISTORIC PERIOD, a standard term in Plains archaeology for the period (ca. A.D. 500–1500) that encompassed the last stages of the prehistoric communal bison procurement system as it was manifested in Wyoming, Montana, and the northwestern part of the Canadian Plains. The Glenrock Buffalo Jump on the North Platte River and the Avonlea projectile point (q.v.) typify the period.
SOURCE: Frison 1978.

Patricia J. O'Brien

LAUDERDALE CULTURE, a Late Archaic (3000–1000 B.C.) manifestation along the Tennessee River in northwestern Alabama, named and defined by W. S. Webb in 1942. Extensive excavation of riverbank shell middens and upland rockshelters has yielded tremendous amounts of information about these hunting-gathering peoples. Their material culture is typified by large chipped-stone dart points, stone bowls, a variety of stone tools, and burial offerings including red stone beads, copper, and marine shell.
SOURCE: Walthall 1980:68–76.

John A. Walthall

LAUREL CULTURE, an Initial Woodland culture, dating ca. 200 B.C.–A.D. 700, distributed from northern Michigan through northwestern Ontario, northern Minnesota, and south-central Manitoba, to east-central Saskatchewan. Named for its type site, the Laurel Site (currently called the Smith Site (q.v.), the culture appears to be related to the North Bay (Wisconsin), Saugeen (southern Ontario) (qq.v.), and Point Peninsula (New York) cultures. It is characterized by a seminomadic fishing, hunting, and gathering life-style and by a material culture that is dominated by conoidal, grit-tempered vessels with smoothed surfaces, decorated with various forms of stamping, punctating, bossing, and incising, usually confined to the neck and upper rim. Other Laurel characteristics include togglehead antler harpoons, cut beaver incisors, copper implements, copper beads, and burial mounds. Aside from the type site, important Laurel sites are McKinstry, Nett Lake, Pike Bay, and River Point.
SOURCES: Jenks 1935; Wilford 1937, 1941, 1950a, 1950b, 1955; MacNeish 1958a; Stoltman 1962, 1973, 1974b; Lukens 1963; D. L. Webster 1967; J. V. Wright 1967; D. E. Janzen 1968; Mason 1969; Lugenbeal 1976; Peters et al. n.d.

Gordon R. Peters

LAURENTIAN TRADITION, a Late Archaic (ca. 4000–1500 B.C.) unit in New York, Quebec, Ontario, and adjacent New England comprising cultures adapted to the lake forest zone of the continental interior. Typical

traits are broad-bladed, notched projectile points; bifaces; scrapers; and polished-stone tools including celts, gouges, and slate knives or points which appear to have originated on the Atlantic coast.
SOURCE: Ritchie 1969.

James A. Tuck

LAWN POINT SITE, a stratified site in the Queen Charlotte Islands, British Columbia, excavated by K. R. Fladmark in 1970, containing six components ranging in age between ca. 6000 B.C. and A.D. 100. The four oldest components, affiliated with the Moresby Tradition (q.v.), were associated with beach deposits from 10 to 15 meters above present sea level and are dominated by microblade manufacture and flakes produced from cobble cores. The two latest components are of Transitional Complex (q.v.) affinity.
SOURCES: Fladmark 1970, 1979a.

Knut R. Fladmark

LEAVENWORTH SITE, an early 19th-century Arikara settlement consisting of two earthlodge villages and associated cemeteries, on the west bank of the Missouri River near the mouth of the Grand River in northern South Dakota, now submerged by the waters of Oahe Reservoir. Excavations were conducted in both village areas and in the cemeteries by several archaeologists in the 1910s, 1920s, 1930s, and 1960s. The disintegration of Arikara culture in the first three decades of the 19th century is reflected in the burial pattern of the 285 individuals recovered from 223 graves in the main cemetery.
SOURCES: Bass et al. 1971; Krause 1972.

William M. Bass and Richard A. Krause

LECROY POINT, a type name originally applied to all Early Archaic bifurcated, chipped-stone projectile points in the Southeast, but now restricted to small- or medium-sized, straight-stemmed points, usually with short, triangular blades and narrow shoulders. Dated ca. 6500–6000 B.C., the type is found over the Ohio and Tennessee river drainages, thence north to the Great Lakes and east to the Atlantic coast.
SOURCES: Lewis and Kneberg 1955:78–81; Broyles 1966:26–27, 1971; Jefferson Chapman 1975.

Eugene M. Futato

LEE POTTERY SERIES, a sand-tempered ceramic with a thickened rim that is highly decorated with parallel rows of short, diagonal punctations; bodies sometimes bear rectilinear, check-stamped impressions. Found in extreme southwestern Virginia and dating ca. A.D. 1200–1450, the Lee

Series is identical to the Pisgah Pottery Series (q.v.) of western North Carolina.

SOURCES: Holland 1970; K. T. Egloff n.d.b.

Keith T. Egloff

LEGGETT SITE, a Late Woodland hamlet on the Dan River in the south-central Piedmont of Virginia, excavated by W. E. Clark in 1976. Refuse-filled pits contained Dan River pottery (q.v.) and well-preserved faunal remains that yielded radiocarbon dates of A.D. 1150 and 1500.

SOURCES: P. S. Gardner 1980; K. T. Egloff et al. n.d.b.

Keith T. Egloff

LEHMAN PHASE, a culture unit of north-central British Columbia, beginning about 4000 B.C. and terminating between 2000 and 1500 B.C.; defined by S. Lawhead and A. H. Stryd as an alternate culture-historical construct to at least part of Sanger's Nesikep Tradition (q.v.). The seventeen Lehman sites so far identified in the mid-Fraser and Thompson river drainages are characterized by lanceolate projectile points with wide side notches, heavy basal grinding, and pointed or convex bases; thin, pentagonal projectile points with oblique V-shaped notches; elliptical knives with prominent striking platforms; and the apparent absence of microblades and pithouses. Deer and elk were hunted, and freshwater mollusks were collected in large numbers in the Thompson Valley. Lehman appears to have developed out of earlier cultures of the area, but its relationship to subsequent cultures is not clear at present. The Lehman Phase and the Lochnore Complex (q.v.) seem to have coexisted, at least in part, in the same region.

SOURCE: Lawhead and Stryd n.d.

Arnoud H. Stryd

LEHNER SITE, a large bone bed in southern Arizona where, in 1955, E. W. Haury discovered 13 Clovis type projectile points (q.v.) and several stone cutting or scraping tools associated with the remains of extinct Pleistocene animal species, including mammoth, bison, and tapir. Two hearths were also found.

SOURCES: Haury et al. 1959.

Edward B. Jelks

LEIMBACH SITE, a multicomponent site on the western bluff of the Vermillion River Valley in Lorain County, in Ohio, where in 1965, O. C. Shane excavated undisturbed Early Woodland hearths, refuse pits, and part of a living floor. Ceramics constitute the type assemblages for the Leimbach Cordmarked and Leimbach Thick types; the latter is distinguished by cord-

wrapped paddle impressions and massive rectangular lugs. Radiocarbon dates place the Early Woodland occupation ca. 800–200 B.C.
SOURCE: Shane 1975:98–120, 358.

N'omi B. Greber

LEONARD ROCKSHELTER, a small site near Lovelock Cave (q.v.) on the shore gravels of Pleistocene Lake Lahontan in western Nevada, discovered in 1936 by Thomas Derby while mining bat guano. Derby collected many perishable artifacts from the guano layer, which has been radiocarbon dated to ca. 6800–5000 B.C. The oldest sample of cultural refuse, however, dated to only ca. 500 B.C. An infant burial and some shell beads also were found. Curvilinear and rectilinear petroglyphs on the cliff face over the site are believed to be associated with the Lovelock Culture, which dates ca. 5000–3000 B.C.
SOURCE: Heizer 1951.

David Hurst Thomas

LEWIS CENTRAL SCHOOL SITE, an ossuary located on the south edge of Council Bluffs, Iowa, where 25 fragmentary human skeletons were collected from a deposit buried 3 meters below the ground surface. Associated with the skeletons were chipped-stone projectile points, bifaces, and end scrapers, along with bone awls and worked shell. A radiocarbon date of 865 ± 80 B.C. indicates affiliation with the Late Archaic period.
SOURCE: D. C. Anderson et al. 1978.

Duane C. Anderson

LEWIS CREEK MOUND, a burial mound on the Middle River in the southern Shenandoah Valley, in Virginia, radiocarbon dated to A.D. 1100–1370. The type site for the Lewis Creek Mound Culture (q.v.), it was completely excavated by H. A. MacCord in 1964 after previous excavations by C. G. Holland, Clifford Evans, and P. C. Manley. The mound is estimated to have held from 200 to 300 human burials.
SOURCES: Holland 1960a; Manley 1963; MacCord and Valliere 1965.

Keith T. Egloff

LEWIS CREEK MOUND CULTURE, a cultural unit associated with a group of accretional soil and rock mounds in the upper James and Shenandoah river drainages near Staunton, Virginia, defined by H. A. MacCord and radiocarbon dated to ca. A.D. 950–1450. The mounds, each containing from 50 to 1,000 human burials, ranged from 40 to 70 feet across and up to 12 feet high. Secondary bundle burials were most frequent, but extended and flexed primary burials, and occasionally cremations, also were present. Associated with the burials were large and medium triangular projectile points, celts, shell beads, and pipes of both clay and stone.

SOURCES: Fowke 1894; MacCord and Valliere 1965.

Keith T. Egloff

LEWIS FOCUS, a vaguely defined Late Woodland construct developed in the 1940s for the lower Ohio River Valley by University of Chicago archaeologists working in the Black Bottom, in Pope and Massac counties, in Illinois. Since little subsequent work has been done at Late Woodland sites in the area, the term still applies to the entire Late Woodland sequence (ca. A.D. 400–900) there, even though it is not clear whether these materials are sufficiently distinct to warrant terminological separation from other Late Woodland complexes of the region. Lewis ceramics consist of grog-tempered plain and cordmarked vessels. Small, bluff-top, stone burial mounds also have been reported.
SOURCES: Cole et al. 1951:165–183; Muller 1986.

Brian M. Butler

LEWISVILLE SITE, a controversial, probably Paleoindian site of disputed age, consisting of 21 hearth-like burned places buried deeply in Shuler clay deposits on the Elm Fork of the Trinity River about 50 kilometers northwest of Dallas, Texas. The site was discovered in 1951 by paleontologist T. E. White, who noticed several of the burned spots while unearthing Pleistocene fossils in a borrow pit excavated for construction of Lewisville Reservoir. White, G. L. Evans, and E. B. Jelks briefly tested some of the "hearths" at that time, after which the site was monitored by members of the Dallas Archaeological Society until 1956–1957, when they excavated several of the hearths under the direction of R. K. Harris and W. W. Crook, Jr., and collected faunal specimens representing some 30 species, including extinct peccary, horse, camel, mammoth, glyptodon, tortoise, and box turtle, along with baked mud-dauber nests, egg shells, and hackberry seeds. Seven artifacts were found at the site between 1951 and 1957, most of them on the exposed surface of the borrow pit, the only diagnostic one being a Clovis type dart point (q.v.) that was discovered in situ in one of the hearths. Radiocarbon dates on apparent charcoal from some of the hearths indicated an age of from at least 37,000 to 63,000 years, or possibly more—far earlier than the 10,000- to 12,000–year age ascribed to the Clovis Culture (q.v.).

The site has been under 15 feet of water in Lake Lewisville since 1957, save for a period in 1978–1980 when drought conditions lowered the lake level and exposed the burned places. At that time, archaeologists and other scientists from several institutions working under the codirection of Dennis Stanford, R. J. Burton, and L. D. Banks reexamined them and subjected them to numerous tests. Geochemists determined that the supposed charcoal used for the radiocarbon dates actually was lignite. Because of lignite contamination and other factors, refined absolute dates were still unobtainable.

Though not conclusive, the new evidence strongly suggests that Lewisville was a Clovis Culture campsite dating from between 10,000 and 9000 B.C.
   SOURCES: Crook and Harris 1957, 1958; Heizer and Brooks 1965.

                                          Larry D. Banks and Robert J. Burton

LIGHTHOUSE POINT SHELL RING, a Thom's Creek (q.v.) Phase site on James Island in Charleston County, in South Carolina, where Michael Trinkley's extensive excavations in 1976 and 1979 produced important subsistence data, disclosed the ring's form, and revealed that it consisted of village midden deposits. Numerous features and postmolds were recorded; pottery, lithics, worked bone, worked shell, coprolites, and both faunal and floral specimens were collected. Five radiocarbon dates averaged ca. 1225 B.C.
   SOURCES: Trinkley 1980b, 1985.

                                                          Michael Trinkley

LIKE-A-FISHHOOK VILLAGE, a mid to late 19th-century community of Mandan-Hidatsa and Arikara Indians consisting of several earthlodge villages, at Like-A-Fishhook Bend of the Missouri River in central North Dakota. During several field seasons in the early 1950s, Glen Kleinsasser, James Howard, and others partially excavated the site, which now is covered by Garrison Reservoir.
   SOURCES: Metcalf 1963; G. H. Smith 1972.

                                                        Richard A. Krause

LIME CREEK SITE, a Paleoindian (q.v.) site in southwestern Nebraska comprising three cultural layers. Excavated in 1947–1950 by E. M. Davis, it was radiocarbon dated to ca. 7400 B.C. Layer I, the oldest, produced a Scottsbluff point (q.v.) and a Milnesand point plus seventeen Lime Creek knives. No diagnostic artifacts were found in Layer II. From Layer III came a Plainview point and a Milnesand point. There were bones of the extinct *Bison antiquus* both in Layer I, which apparently was a campsite, and in Layer III, probably a small kill site.
   SOURCE: E. M. Davis 1962.

                                                        Patricia J. O'Brien

LINCOLN PHASE, the later of two phases in the northern sector of the Sierra Blanca Sub-Province, Jornada Province, Mogollon Culture (qq.v.) in central New Mexico, dating ca. A.D. 1200–1450. It succeeded and extended farther to the southeast than the Corona Phase (q.v.). Sites are similar to contemporary sites of the Arroya Seco and Gran Quivira foci of the Salinas Province, Anasazi Culture (qq.v.) to the northwest and may represent an extension of that culture.

Lincoln sites are small to large pueblos composed of either coursed adobe or stone masonry rooms arranged in lines or in enclosed plaza configurations. Ceremonial rooms are large, rectangular or square, subterranean structures, located east of the linear roomblocks or, at larger sites, within the central plazas.

The ceramic assemblage is dominated by Corona Corrugated, Chupadero Black-on-white (q.v.), and Jornada Brown (q.v.). There are lesser quantities of Lincoln Black-on-red, Three Rivers Red-on-terracotta, El Paso Polychrome (q.v.), and various distant imports. Other artifacts include both slab and one-end-closed trough metates, side-notched and corner-notched arrow points, full-grooved axes, arrow-shaft straighteners, conical clay pipes, deer- and antelope-rib awls, *Olivella*-shell beads, freshwater mussel-shell pendants, and nonstandardized drill, scraper, and knife forms. Bloom Mound (q.v.) produced large quantities of disc beads, *Oliva*-shell tinklers, and copper bells, suggesting specialized trading with Plains people.

High frequencies of projectile points and bones indicate that hunting of deer, antelope, and rabbits provided a major part of the diet. Also, maize was grown and wild plants were collected.
SOURCE: J. H. Kelley 1984.

R. N. Wiseman

LIND COULEE POINT, a variety of the Windust Point (q.v.) with a long, narrow, straight-sided stem and a rounded base. It takes its name from the Lind Coulee Site (q.v.) where it was first found.
SOURCE: Daugherty 1956.

Frank C. Leonhardy

LIND COULEE SITE, an early (ca. 7500–6500 B.C.) upland campsite in the Columbia River basin near Warden, Washington, excavated by R. D. Daugherty and others in the early 1950s and early 1970s. It is notable for a distinctive type of chipped-stone projectile point, informally called the Lind Coulee point, and for elaborate bone tools, including cylindrical foreshafts and serrated points resembling harpoon points. The artifacts closely resemble those of the Windust Phase (q.v.). The site also contained bison remains. Lind Coulee and the Pilcher Creek Site (q.v.) in Oregon are the only sites of this antiquity yet found outside the river canyons of the interior plateau.
SOURCES: Daugherty 1956; Irwin and Moody 1978.

Frank C. Leonhardy

LINDENMEIER SITE, the first recognized and investigated Paleoindian (q.v.) campsite in the United States, containing Folsom type projectile points as the principal diagnostic; located in the Colorado foothills. F. H. H. Roberts, Jr., dug the site between 1934 and 1940, but the major analysis of the

materials that he collected was carried out much later by E. N. Wilmsen, who concluded that the Folsom materials were contemporaneous with the Clovis Culture (q.v.) and therefore did not evolve from Clovis antecedents. He also suggested that several semiautonomous Paleoindian groups whose respective territories overlapped the site used it alternately as a camping place.
SOURCES: F. H. H. Roberts, Jr. 1935a, 1939; Wilmsen and Roberts 1978.

Edward B. Jelks

LINEAR MOUNDS, low, elongated, earthen mounds once found by the hundreds throughout the upper Mississippi River valley and into the plains as far west as the Missouri River in North Dakota, but now mostly destroyed by farming. Occurring either singly or in groups of up to seven mounds, most were a few hundred feet long although some in North Dakota reached a length of 1500 feet. Low, dome-shaped mounds, some containing human burials, occasionally were attached to either end or stood separately nearby. Most linear mounds are believed to be of Woodland (q.v.) origin.
SOURCE: Chomko and Wood 1973.

W. Raymond Wood

LITTLE ARM PHASE, a southwestern Yukon culture unit with a microblade industry, the earliest (ca. 4000–2000 B.C.) dated phase in the Yukon with a substantial artifact representation; seen by some archaeologists as part of a Northwest Microblade Tradition (q.v.). Components have been reported at the Little Arm Site at Kluane Lake and elsewhere.
SOURCES: MacNeish 1964; Workman 1978.

Donald W. Clark

LITTLE COLORADO GRAY WARE, the major utility pottery along the Little Colorado River and its tributaries in northeastern Arizona between A.D. 700 and 1200. As defined by H. S. Colton and L. L. Hargrave, the ware includes only one type, Little Colorado Corrugated.
SOURCES: Colton and Hargrave 1937:232–233; Colton 1955.

Donald E. Weaver, Jr.

LITTLE COLORADO WHITE WARE, the major decorated pottery along the Little Colorado River and its tributaries in northeastern Arizona. As first defined by H. S. Colton and L. L. Hargrave, this ware was estimated to date ca. A.D. 750–1375 and to include six additional black-on-white types: Dead River, Holbrook, Padre, Walnut, Tularosa, Pinedale, and Klageto. Colton subsequently revised the ware's description to include black-on-white types St. Joseph, Holbrook, Padre, Chevelon, Walnut, and Leupp, and he narrowed its period of use to A.D. 1000–1375.

SOURCES: Hargrave 1932b:20; Colton and Hargrave 1937:233–244; Colton 1955.

Donald E. Weaver, Jr.

LITTLE HARBOR SITE, a location on Santa Catalina Island off the coast of southern California where C. W. Meighan excavated between 1953 and 1955 and found figurine-like, fired-clay objects in levels dated about 2000 B.C. This and similar occurrences in mainland southern California confirm an early indigenous ceramic tradition that was separate from the later introduction of pottery, ca. A.D. 900, from the southern Great Basin and Colorado River areas.
SOURCES: Meighan 1959:383–405; Moratto 1984:149.

Michael J. Moratto

LITTLE LAKE SITE. See STAHL SITE.

LITTLE SALT SPRING SITE, a cenote (large sinkhole in the limestone bedrock) in Sarasota County, in Florida, containing underwater Paleoindian (q.v.) burials and artifacts (10,000–7000 B.C.); also Middle Archaic artifacts and a human burial with preserved brain (ca. 4000 B.C.). There is a Middle Archaic village site adjacent to the cenote. Carl Clausen investigated the Little Salt Spring site in the 1970s.
SOURCE: Clausen et al. 1979.

Jerald T. Milanich

LIVERMORE CACHE, a group of 2,112 complete and fragmentary arrow points found in 1895 beneath a rock cairn on top of Baldy Peak, a cathedral-like pinnacle that forms the crest of Mount Livermore in the Davis Mountains of western Texas. Type collection for the Livermore point type (q.v.), the cache appears to have been an isolated, ceremonial-related phenomenon, there being no occupational debris, burials, or other cultural remains on the narrow, rocky promontory.
SOURCES: Janes 1930:8–9; J. C. Kelley et al. 1940; J. C. Kelley 1957:44–52; Mallouf 1985.

Robert J. Mallouf

LIVERMORE FOCUS, a late prehistoric (ca. A.D. 900–1200) hunting-gathering manifestation in western Texas and southeastern New Mexico, defined in 1940 by J. C. Kelley, who considered it an intrusion from the Plains area to the north. Sites include rockshelters, open camps, and mountain-top caches (cf. Livermore Cache). Typical artifacts are Livermore, Toyah, and Fresno type arrow points (q.v.), beveled knives, snub-nosed scrapers, drills,

disc-based gravers, abraders, oval-bowl metates, manos, and wooden fire tongs. Late in the focus a little El Paso Polychrome pottery (q.v.) appears.
SOURCES: Kelley et al. 1940; J. C. Kelley 1957:44–52.

Robert J. Mallouf

LIVERPOOL SITE, a multicomponent mortuary and habitation site on the Illinois River in central Illinois. The rich and varied materials from log tombs at Liverpool were first reported in 1928 by W. C. Moorehead, who recognized that they represented a modification of the Hopewell (q.v.) Culture. Later investigations by University of Chicago archaeologists produced stratigraphic evidence of Middle Woodland mortuary remains superposed over an Early Woodland occupation, which was designated the Black Sand Culture (q.v.). Grave goods from the Liverpool mounds, along with data from other nearby Middle Woodland sites, contributed to the definition of the Havana Tradition.
SOURCES: Cole and Deuel 1937:132–150; Moorehead 1928.

Duane Esarey

LLANO COMPLEX, a complex of Paleoindian (q.v.) artifacts found in association with mammoth bones at several sites in the southern High Plains and attributed to the Clovis Culture (q.v.). Included are the Clovis type projectile point (q.v.), long lamellar blades, flake scrapers, and rod-like or spatulate bone tools with beveled or pointed ends.
SOURCES: Sellards 1952:17–42; Wormington 1957:43–57; Hester 1972.

Edward B. Jelks

LLANO CULTURE. See Clovis Culture.

LLANO SITE, a multicomponent, coursed adobe pueblo near the town of Llano, New Mexico, where in 1920 J. A. Jeançon excavated 25 rooms and one kiva in a Pot Creek (q.v.) Phase occupation that was tree-ring dated to between A.D. 1207 and 1239. This, the largest excavated Pot Creek Phase component in the Northern Rio Grande Province, overlay an earlier pueblo that was exposed at only a few locations.
SOURCE: Jeancon 1929.

Patricia L. Crown

LOCARNO BEACH CULTURE TYPE, a unit in the southern Gulf of Georgia area of the Northwest coast, dating ca. 1500–500 B.C., first identified by C. E. Borden. It was preceded by the St. Mungo culture (q.v.) type and succeeded by the Marpole culture type (q.v.).
Locarno Beach assemblages characteristically include flaked-basalt projectile points with contracting stems; microblades (mainly of quartz crystal); crude pebble and boulder spall implements; large, faceted, ground-slate

points; small celts; Gulf Islands complex artifacts (carefully fashioned and highly polished objects of soft stone and coal of varying shapes and unknown use); grooved or notched stone sinkers; shaped abrading stones; toggling harpoon heads; foreshafts; celts made of sea mussel shells. Distinctive features include boxes and trenches lined with stone slabs and depressions lined with clay. From such sites as Musqueam Northeast and Hoko River, where perishable materials are preserved, cone-shaped baskets of several complex weaves, woven hats, wooden wedges, and cordage have been found. Faunal remains include wapiti, deer, sea lion, harbor seal, porpoise, birds, fish, a wide variety of shellfish, and domestic dogs of various sizes.
    SOURCES: Mitchell 1971; W. R. B. Peacock n.d.; Trace 1981.

Donald H. Mitchell

LOCARNO BEACH SITE, the type site for the Locarno Beach culture type (q.v.), situated in Vancouver on the south shore of Burrard Inlet; excavated by C. E. Borden in the late 1940s.
    SOURCE: C. E. Borden 1951.

Donald H. Mitchell

LOCHNORE COMPLEX, an early, major archaeological unit in the mid-Fraser and Thompson river drainages of the Canadian Plateau, defined by David Sanger in 1965 and dated by him at ca. 7000–3000 B.C. It is characterized by leaf-shaped projectile points similar to the Cascade type (q.v.), leaf-shaped and ovate bifacial knives, cobble choppers, edge-battered cobbles, heavy flake cores, a weakly developed macroblade industry, and the absence of microblades. Sanger concluded that the complex was introduced into interior British Columbia by people of the Old Cordilleran Culture (q.v.) moving northward from the Southern Plateau region. Recently, K. R. Fladmark, S. Lawhead, and A. H. Stryd have argued that Lochnore is more recent than was proposed by Sanger and that is origins remain to be determined.
    It appears that the mid-Fraser and Thompson drainages were home to two contemporaneous cultures—the Lochnore Complex (or late Canadian Plateau Old Cordilleran) and the Lehman Phase (q.v.)—with neither group having exclusive control of the resources of the region. The presence of Oregon obsidian in some Lochnore (or Old Cordilleran) assemblages indicates an extensive trade network.
    SOURCES: Sanger 1969; Fladmark 1982b; Lawhead and Stryd n.d.

Arnoud H. Stryd

LOCHNORE-NESIKEP LOCALITY, a section of the Fraser River Valley about halfway between Lillooet and Lytton, British Columbia, where ten archaeological sites containing house pits, burial grounds, and summer (?) fishing camps were investigated by David Sanger between 1961 and 1965.

On the basis of this work, Sanger defined the Lochnore Complex and the Nesikep Tradition (qq.v.), which together constituted the first culture-historical model for the Canadian Plateau. Although their validity has been questioned in the 1980s, the evidence from the Lochnore-Nesikep locality is still widely used as the basis for culture-historical reconstructions in interior British Columbia.

SOURCE: Sanger 1970.

Arnoud H. Stryd

LOEVE-FOX SITE, a deeply stratified site on the San Gabriel River in east-central Texas, excavated from 1972 to 1978 by E. R. Prewitt and D. A. Story. Twenty-four strata revealed successive occupations, beginning with the Middle Archaic Round Rock Phase (q.v.) ca. 1550–650 B.C. and terminating with the Late Archaic Toyah Phase (q.v.) ca. A.D. 1300–1750. The site documented camp patterns in the Round Rock and Twin Sisters (q.v.) (ca. A.D. 150–550) phases; marine-shell artifacts indicate trade with coastal peoples 250 kilometers to the southeast during the San Marcos (q.v.), Twin Sisters, and Austin (q.v.) phases. An Austin Phase cemetery contained non-cremated interments surrounded by cremations. Human aggression was evidenced by arrow points lodged in apparently fatal positions in six skeletons.

SOURCES: Prewitt 1974b, 1982a.

Elton R. Prewitt

LOEVE SITE, a deeply stratified site on the San Gabriel River in east-central Texas containing manifestations of the Circleville Phase (Early Archaic, ca. 6550–4850 B.C.) and of Late Archaic peoples (ca. A.D. 150–1750); tested by F. W. Eddy in 1968 and by E. R. Prewitt in 1978.

SOURCES: Eddy n.d.; Prewitt 1982a.

Elton R. Prewitt

LOGAN CREEK SITE, a multicomponent site in Burt County, in eastern Nebraska, excavated by M. F. Kivett in the late 1950s, whose four different occupations are similar to one another in many respects and seem to represent the same way of life. The medium to large projectile points with wide, shallow notches are similar to points from the Simonsen Site (q.v.), where they were associated with a *Bison bison occidentalis* kill. Simonsen has been radiocarbon dated to ca. 6500 B.C., while Logan Creek has a radiocarbon date of ca. 4700 B.C. Culturally, Logan Creek is either of very late Paleoindian or of very early Archaic affiliation.

SOURCE: Wedel 1961:87, 283.

Patricia J. O'Brien

LOGANDALE GRAY WARE, a limestone-tempered pottery distinctive of the lower Virgin and Moapa valleys of southern Nevada in the Virgin

Province (q.v.) of the Western Anasazi Culture; common from ca. A.D. 500 to ca. 950 and virtually absent later. Jars are the most common vessel form, bowls are rare, and there are a few painted vessels.

SOURCES: Colton 1952; Myhrer and Lyneis 1985.

Margaret M. Lyneis

LOHMANN PHASE, an Initial Mississippian expression in the American Bottom of the Mississippi River Valley in southwestern Illinois, dating ca. A.D. 1000–1050, the time of initial mound building at the Cahokia Site (q.v.) and elsewhere in the region. The phase is characterized by post and wall-trench structures, by limestone-tempered pottery, and, in the Cahokia area, by shell-tempered pottery. Vessels include a wide variety of forms: jars, bowls, pans, beakers, bottles, juice presses, and some stumpware. An ordered system of mound centers extending from the Cahokia Site to the mouth of the Kaskaskia River was established during the Lohmann Phase.

SOURCES: Bareis and Porter 1984; Finney and Fortier 1985.

Andrew C. Fortier and Charles J. Bareis

LOMA SAN GABRIEL CULTURE, an early (ca. A.D. 1–1500) culture on the flanks of the Sierra Madre in Durango, possibly the first culture in southwestern North America to use pottery. It is characterized by nonintensive agriculture and small, semipermanent villages, each of which usually contained up to a dozen rectangular houses. Burial, at least sometimes, was in caves.

Typical artifacts include basin metates, one-hand manos, and simple brownware vessels that sometimes were slipped or decorated with red paint. Cueva de los Muertos Chiquitos produced agave(?)-fiber cloth, plaited matting, shell and turquoise ornaments, a wooden batten, wooden shuttles, basketry, and remains of maize, beans, squash, acorns, pinyon nuts, walnuts, and prickly pear fruit. Cotton cloth was present, probably as a trade item.

SOURCES: J. C. Kelley 1971; Foster 1978.

David A. Phillips, Jr.

LONESOME CREEK SITE, a two-component (late Thule and Independence II) site on Coneybeare Bay, Ellesmere Island, Northwest Territories. Excavations by M. S. Maxwell in 1958 disclosed evidence of a penetration in the 13th and 14th centuries A.D. by late Thule (q.v.) people from Greenland; they later abandoned the site, probably because of increasing cold weather. An Independence II dwelling located by Maxwell was dug by Eigil Knuth in 1965.

SOURCES: Maxwell 1960; Knuth 1967.

Moreau S. Maxwell

LONG CREEK SITE, a deeply stratified site in the Long Creek valley of southeastern Saskatchewan where excavations in 1957 revealed nine occupation zones in deposits up to 14 feet thick. Spanning the period from

ca. 3000 B.C. to very late prehistoric times, the identified cultures, in chronological order, are Long Creek (now considered part of the Mummy Cave series [q.v.]), Oxbow, Wood End, Hanna, Pelican Lake (q.v.), Besant (q.v.), Avonlea (q.v.), and Hidatsa—Fall River.
SOURCE: Wettlaufer and Mayer-Oakes 1960.

Margaret Hanna

LONGHOUSE SITE, a late Dorset Phase (q.v.) site on Knud Peninsula, Ellesmere Island, Northwest Territories, excavated in 1980 by Peter Schledermann. He found four boulder enclosures, each 45 meters long by 5 meters wide and each bordered by a row of from three to eighteen hearths. Presumably Late Dorset people of ca. A.D. 800—850 gathered in spring at these structures to renew social and religious obligations. Similar "longhouse" enclosures characterize Late Dorset from Victoria Island eastward and northward.
SOURCE: Schledermann 1981.

Moreau S. Maxwell

LOON SITE, a late Pre-Dorset Phase (q.v.) component on Cape Tanfield, radiocarbon dated to ca. 1150 B.C.; one of a series of sites in a local continuum extending from Pre-Dorset to Dorset. Excavated in 1962 by a Michigan State University field team, the site produced a Pre-Dorset assemblage with some attributes demonstrating a trend toward Dorset styles.
SOURCE: Maxwell 1973.

Moreau S. Maxwell

LOS ANGELES (or BALDWIN HILLS) SKELETON, portions of a human skeleton of controversial age unearthed in 1936 by workmen digging a storm drain in the Baldwin Hills section of Los Angeles, California, from sediments identified as Pleistocene in age. No evidence of a burial was observed, and no artifacts were found. Initial radiocarbon determinations indicated an age in excess of 20,000 years, but a more reliable radiocarbon date of ca. 1500 B.C. was obtained later.
SOURCES: Berger 1975; Taylor et al. 1985.

R. E. Taylor and L. A. Payen

LOS CAMOTES INCISED POTTERY, a type found in the upper foothills of southern Sonora in sites of the Los Camotes Phase (q.v.), dating ca. A.D. 700—1050/1250. Decoration consists of panels of crosshatched incising ap-

pearing above a vessel's shoulder. The type appears to be a southern variant of the textured pottery characteristic of the Rio Sonora Culture (q.v.).
SOURCE: Pailes 1972:212–215, pl. 4.

Richard A. Pailes

LOS CAMOTES PHASE, the earlier of the Rio Sonora Culture's (q.v.) two phases in southern Sonora. It replaced the Batacosa Phase (q.v.) ca. A.D. 700 and terminated sometime between A.D. 1150 and 1250. Sites are in locations of difficult access—on mountaintops, or in saddles, or on benches high up the mountain sides—and consist of either single, isolated structures or a scatter of structures 50 meters or more apart. At least one site, Cerro de los Gentiles (q.v.), has a cluster of twelve houses on top of a mountain. The diagnostic pottery is Los Camotes Incised (q.v.), a southern variant of the textured pottery characteristic of the Rio Sonora Culture.
SOURCE: Pailes 1972:371–382.

Richard A. Pailes

LOSEKE CREEK FOCUS, an expression of what is often called Plains Woodland, probably dating ca. A.D. 500–900, distributed widely in northeastern Nebraska, northwestern Iowa, and southern South Dakota. Defined in 1952 by M. F. Kivett, its distinctive traits are crude Scallorn-like arrow points (q.v.) and Feye Cord Impressed and Feye Cord Roughened pottery. Sites are usually small and inconspicuous, but there is some evidence of corn horticulture.
SOURCE: Kivett 1952:42–58, 67–70.

Patricia J. O'Brien

LOS MADRONOS COMPLEX, a late (ca. A.D. 660–950) complex in the Las Animas area of northwestern Durango, known from its sites located on ridge spurs, on low hills, and in rockshelters. Light brownware and redware pottery are common; blackware is present but rare. A spindle whorl, a cylinder stamp, a sherd disk, and a figurine have been reported from sites of the complex.
SOURCE: Spence 1978.

David A. Phillips, Jr.

LOS PINOS PHASE, a local expression of the Basketmaker (q.v.) II Stage, dating ca. A.D. 1–400, in the Upper San Juan Province (q.v.) of northern New Mexico and southern Colorado. Most sites are along the Pine River, from the Vallecitos Reservoir downstream to the confluence of the Pine with the San Juan.

There are two styles of houses—ring (q.v.) and nonring—that occur either as isolated farmstead structures or as village clusters of from two or three to as many as a dozen. Many houses and sites contain no pottery whereas others have one or a few sherds. The interpretation of these sporadic associations is that the phase was nonceramic until ca. A.D. 300, when pottery began to be manufactured in limited quantities.

SOURCES: Eddy 1961; Dittert et al. 1961, 1963.

Frank W. Eddy

LOST CITY LOCALITY (or PUEBLO GRANDE DE NEVADA), a zone of intensive Anasazi (q.v.) occupation in the Virgin Province (q.v.) along the eastern edge of the lower Moapa Valley in southern Nevada; the type location for the Lost City Phase (q.v.), the local Pueblo I and II analog dating ca. A.D. 700–1100. The Main Ridge location, studied intensively by M. R. Harrington, comprised some 46 houses, each made up of one or several habitation units plus adjacent storage units, all built of mud and poles, brush, or cobbles. Conjoined storage units were arranged in rows, arcs, or blocks; habitation units were sometimes attached, sometimes freestanding.

SOURCES: Shutler 1961; Lyneis 1986.

Margaret M. Lyneis

LOST CITY PHASE, the analog of Pueblo I and II in the Virgin Province (q.v.) of the Western Anasazi Culture, dating ca. A.D. 700–1100. Some sites consist of pithouses associated with rows of surface rooms; at other sites, both living and storage rooms are all on the surface. In the southwestern part of the province, construction was of adobe stretched with cobbles, either haphazardly or in courses, or of wattle and daub. Rooms were arranged in straight or curved rows, or, rarely, in blocks. Habitation rooms were sometimes attached to storage rooms and sometimes situated nearby. Screwbeans and other gathered foods supplemented maize, beans, and squash from the fields. Deer, mountain sheep, antelope, rabbit, and desert tortoise provided meat. Cotton was grown and woven into cloth.

Ceramic indicators of the earlier part of the phase are present but rare. Later, corrugated pottery was added to the utility wares, while black-on-gray pottery designs followed the fashion to the east: Black Mesa (q.v.) designs were common for a time, only to be replaced with Sosi and Dogoszhi designs.

Lost City Phase peoples mined salt and turquoise in the Moapa Valley of southern Nevada, and they participated in trade networks that linked them to the Pacific coast of California for shells, and to the redware-producing areas of northeastern Arizona and southeastern Utah. Olivine for

tempering Moapa Gray Ware (q.v.) may have come from the Arizona strip or the Toroweap area.
SOURCE: Shutler 1961; Aikens 1965.

Margaret M. Lyneis

LOUP RIVER PHASE, a term now replaced by Itskari Phase (q.v.).

LOVELOCK CAVE, an oft-excavated site on the eastern shore of Humboldt Lake in western Nevada, noted for its magnificent specimens of perishable artifacts (e.g., duck decoys, nets, cordage, and basketry). University of California, Berkeley archaeologists worked there over many years: L. L. Loud in 1912; Loud and M. R. Harrington in 1924; R. F. Heizer, L. K. Napton, and others in the 1950s. The earlier work was designed to fill museum cases; the later considered dietary factors, disease, parasites, and functional analyses.

The rich artifact inventory from Lovelock Cave included shell beads from the Pacific coast, bighorn sheep ornaments, mummies, hunting snares, discoidals, feathered duck decoys, and hafted bifaces. Projectile points range from a few Desert Series (q.v.) specimens dating after A.D. 1300, backward in time through the Gatecliff Series (q.v.) of ca. 3000–1300 B.C. Both radiocarbon dates and point types suggest primary occupation was about 2000 years ago.
SOURCES: Loud and Harrington 1929; Grosscup 1960; Heizer and Napton 1970.

David Hurst Thomas

LOVELOCK WICKER WARE BASKETRY, a distinctive plaited basketry found at Lovelock Cave (q.v.), Nevada, and at many other archaeological sites around the lakes and sinks of the western Great Basin. Appearing at ca. 1000 B.C. and declining in use after A.D. 1, the type has been considered an adaptation to the lake and marsh environment of the area and a diagnostic of the Lovelock Culture.
SOURCES: Grosscup 1960; Adovasio 1974.

Robert G. Elston

LOVE SITE, an important Late Archaic–Early Woodland (ca. 2000–1500 B.C.) upland hamlet in Allendale County, in South Carolina that comprises components of the Stallings and Thom's Creek phases. Excavations by S. T. Lee and Thomas Hemmings in 1971 and by Michael Trinkley in 1974 produced abundant pottery, lithic artifacts, and ethnobotanical remains.
SOURCES: S. T. Lee 1971; Trinkley 1974.

Michael Trinkley

LOWDER'S FERRY SITE, the first buried, stratified site excavated in North Carolina, situated at Morrow Mountain State Park in Stanly County. J. L.

Coe's excavations there in 1948 resulted in the identification of the Guilford, Savannah River, Uwharrie, and Pee Dee complexes (qq.v.).
SOURCE: Coe 1964.

Billy L. Oliver

LOWER LOUP PHASE, the archaeological manifestation of protohistoric (A.D. 1500–1750) Pawnee culture in Nebraska. The phase was identified by William D. Strong in 1935, and its affinity with the historic Pawnee was set forth in detail by W. R. Wedel and M. L. Dunlevy the following year. Local sequences subsequently were correlated with the Skiri Pawnee and South Band Pawnee by Roger T. Grange, Jr. Prehistoric forerunners of the phase are to be found within the Central Plains Tradition (q.v.), most specifically among the Loup River Phase, Upper Republican, and Smoky Hill cultures (qq.v.) of Nebraska and Kansas.
SOURCES: Strong 1935; Dunlevy 1936; Wedel 1936; Ludwickson 1978; Grange 1968, 1979, 1984.

Roger T. Grange, Jr.

LOWER PECOS ARCHAIC, a regional variety of the widespread Archaic Tradition (q.v.), dating ca. 7000 B.C.–A.D. 700, situated in the Rio Grande drainage of Val Verde and Terrell counties, in Texas and northern Coahuila. First defined as the Pecos River Focus by J. C. Kelley in 1940, the culture was researched intensively in the 1950s and 1960s during investigations of sites endangered by construction of the Amistad Dam and Reservoir on the Rio Grande. This led to the development of detailed local culture histories and reconstruction of lifeways.

Site types include small to massive rockshelters, many containing deep cultural deposits, well-preserved perishable materials, and spectacular panels of pictographs; sinkholes; open camps with a variety of midden and hearth features; quarries; and a wide range of special-activity locations, including a bison jump (Bonfire Shelter, q.v.). The sites contain a variety of tools fashioned from stone, bone, shell, wood, bark, and plant fibers, all adapted to hunting and gathering techniques in a desert environment.

The Lower Pecos Archaic comprised a long succession of relatively entrenched and stable populations having strong territorial ties, similar material assemblages, and complex rock-art traditions reflecting social structure, ritual behavior, and cultural affiliations.
SOURCES: J. C. Kelley et al. 1940; LeRoy Johnson, Jr. 1964; Dibble and Lorrain 1968; Shafer 1977:228–230; Turpin 1982.

Robert J. Mallouf

LOWER SALMON RIVER REGION, an archaeological region in the southern Plateau, extending along Idaho's Salmon River from its confluence with the Little Salmon to its confluence with the Snake.

                                                      Frank C. Leonhardy

LOWER SNAKE RIVER CULTURE TYPOLOGY, a sequence of archaeological phases in the Lower Snake River region (q.v.) of southeastern Washington, defined in 1970 by F. C. Leonhardy and D. G. Rice. The phases are Windust (q.v.), 8800–6000 B.C.; Cascade (q.v.), 6000–3000 B.C.; Tucannon, 2800–500 B.C.; and Harder (q.v.), 500 B.C.–A.D. 1750.
     SOURCE: Leonhardy and Rice 1970.

                                                      Frank C. Leonhardy

LOWER SNAKE RIVER REGION, an archaeological region in the southern Plateau, extending along the Snake River between its confluence with the Clearwater River at Lewiston, Idaho, and its confluence with the Columbia River at Pasco, Washington.

                                                      Frank C. Leonhardy

LUBBOCK LAKE SITE, a deep, well-stratified site containing a detailed cultural, geological, faunal, and floral record covering the past 11,500 years, located on the Southern High Plains in Yellowhouse Draw, an ephemeral tributary of the Brazos River, in Lubbock County, Texas. One of the major Paleoindian (q.v.) sites, it has contributed much to the chronological ordering of early North American cultures. A 300-acre archaeological preserve encompassing the site has been designated both a National Historic Landmark and a State Archeological Landmark. Several archaeologists have conducted excavations at Lubbock Lake at various times since 1950.
     There are five major stratigraphic units. Stratum 1 (laid down by a meandering stream) and Stratum 2 (lake/pond/marsh deposits) contain the Paleoindian materials: Clovis (q.v.), dated ca. 9100 B.C., in Stratum 1; Folsom (q.v.) ca. 8500 B.C., Plainview (q.v.), ca. 8000 B.C., and Firstview, ca. 6600 B.C., in Stratum 2 (qq.v.). Substratum 2e (aeolian) and Strata 3 and 4 (of lacrustine and aeolian origin), contain Early, Middle, and Late Archaic (qq.v.) cultural materials spanning the period from ca. 6500 B.C. to A.D. 100. Stratum 5, of lacustrine/aeolian derivation, contains artifacts dating between A.D. 970 and 1900, including some from the Garza complex, early Apache, probable late Apache/Comanche, and Euroamerican. A sequence of geological/climatic cycles and attendant changes in the local fauna and flora recorded in the strata have made possible a detailed reconstruction of the ancient landscape, climate, and populations of plants and animals in the vicinity of the site.

SOURCES: Eileen Johnson 1976, 1983; Holliday 1982, 1983; Holliday et al. 1983; Eileen Johnson et al. 1977; Holliday and Johnson 1986.

Eileen Johnson and Vance T. Holliday

LUNSFORD-PULCHER SITE, a major mound center located on the Mississippi River floodplain in the American Bottom, in southwestern Illinois, covering an area of approximately 300 acres and consisting of from twelve to sixteen mounds and associated residential areas. First identified by General Collet and George Rogers Clark during their late 18th-century explorations, the site has remained virtually unknown archaeologically, although the University of Michigan, Ann Arbor and Southern Illinois University, Carbondale have tested it. Presumably occupied from Emergent Mississippian times (ca. A.D. 900) through the Mississippian period to ca. A.D. 1250, it appears to have been flourishing by A.D. 900, coincident with the developmental mound-building phases at the Cahokia Site (q.v.) some 50 kilometers to the north. Lunsford-Pulcher probably was part of a chain of pre-Mississippian mound centers distributed between Cahokia and the mouth of the Kaskaskia River.

SOURCES: Fowler 1969; Griffin and Spaulding 1951; J. B. Griffin 1977.

Charles J. Bareis and Andrew C. Fortier

LURAY PHASE, a Late Woodland unit based on studies by Karl Schmitt, Jr., in 1952 of material from the Keyser Farm Site (q.v.) near Luray, Virginia, and from the Hughes Site in Montgomery County, Maryland. Keyser Cord-marked Ware (q.v.) is the diagnostic artifact type.

SOURCES: Stearns 1940; Manson et al. 1944; Schmitt 1952.

Keith T. Egloff

M

MCCOLLUM MOUND SITE, a South Appalachian Mississippian temple mound on Broad River in Chester County, in South Carolina, dating ca. A.D. 1300. Brief testing by T. M. Ryan in 1971 disclosed features, postholes, and a burial.

SOURCES: J. R. Caldwell 1952; L. G. Ferguson 1971; Ryan 1972b.

Michael Trinkley

MCDONALD FOCUS, a division of the Winslow Branch of the Anasazi Culture (qq.v.) in northeastern Arizona, originally defined by H. S. Colton on the basis of his survey work and of excavations carried out by Walter Hough in McDonald Canyon. G. J. Gumerman's later revision of Colton's definition dated the focus to the period A.D. 1100–1250 and emphasized small pithouse villages with associated surface dwellings, small pueblos, and kivas as its most diagnostic traits. There are both shallow, rectangular pithouses and square, deep ones; the latter variety is the more common. Enclosed plazas and great kivas are associated with rectangular surface rooms. Walnut Black-on-white, a Little Colorado White Ware (q.v.), is the characteristic decorated pottery type.

SOURCES: Hough 1903; Colton 1939a:68, 1955; Gumerman 1969:331–338; Gumerman and Skinner 1968:191–195.

Donald E. Weaver, Jr.

MCGRAW SITE, a midden attributed to the Hopewell Culture (q.v.) located on the edge of a natural levee near Chillicothe, Ohio. It has been radiocarbon dated to ca. A.D. 150–450. O. H. Prufer's excavations there in 1963 produced considerable amounts of local ceramics, lithics, and both faunal and floral material, along with quantities of such exotic substances as mica, limonite, white quartz, and fossils. The McGraw, Chillicothe Rocker Stamped, and Chillicothe Incised pottery types were defined from the ceramic assemblage. Maize that at first was thought to go with the Hopewell occupation later was determined to be modern; the remainder of the floral materials are consistent with those from other Midwestern Middle Woodland sites and indicate a subsistence based on the use of both wild resources and cultigens of the Eastern Agricultural Complex.

SOURCES: Prufer et al. 1965; Prufer 1968; R. I. Ford 1979; Asch et al. 1979.

N'omi B. Greber

MACHAFFIE SITE, a multicomponent, stratified site on a tributary of the Missouri River near Helena, Montana, containing occupation levels of the Paleoindian Folsom and Plano cultures (qq.v.) and of an Archaic (q.v.) culture typical of those living in the mountains and foothills of the area ca. 4000–3000 B.C. Excavations in 1951 produced, in addition to cultural materials, scant faunal remains suggesting the big-game hunters relied primarily on bison in all components. The stratigraphy established the temporal priority of Folsom over Plano in the Northern Plains, as had been earlier demonstrated for the Southern Plains at San Jon and at Blackwater Draw (q.v.); the relationship has since been confirmed at other sites on the Great Plains and in the Bighorn Mountains of Wyoming.

SOURCES: Forbis and Sperry 1952; Forbis 1955.

Richard G. Forbis

MCKEAN COMPLEX, a Middle Plains Archaic complex, dating ca. 5000–3000 B.C., occupying parts of the northwestern Plains periphery. Its type site, the McKean Site in northeastern Wyoming, was investigated by W. B. Mulloy in the early 1950s. The diagnostic trait of the complex is the McKean type projectile point: a stemmed, lanceolate form. The complex is thought to represent people who specialized in plant-food exploitation as part of a multifocused subsistence strategy.

SOURCES: Frison 1978; Keyser 1986.

Patricia J. O'Brien

MCKEITHEN SITE, an early Weeden Island (q.v.) village/plaza/mound complex, dating ca. A.D. 200–750, in inland northern Florida, excavated by J. T. Milanich in 1976–1979. The evidence indicates that ca. A.D. 350–500 a society with incipient social ranking and a big man-type political-social system occupied the site.

SOURCE: Milanich et al. 1984.

Jerald T. Milanich

MCKENZIE PHASE, the third phase, following the Mesita Negra Phase, in the Middle Pecos Sub-Province of the Jornada Province, Mogollon Culture (qq.v.), in eastern New Mexico. Dating ca. A.D. 1200–1300, it is divided into early and late periods.

The early McKenzie Phase is characterized by small blocks of rectangular, slab-based surface rooms, essentially a continuation of the earlier pueblo form. No pithouses have been reported. Ceramics are very similar to the Mesita Negra assemblages except that McKenzie Brown and Middle Pecos Black-on-white (another Chupadero Black-on-white cognate) are better represented, and the incidence of painted wares imported from great distances continues to decline. Arrow points are dominated by side-notched forms, rather than by the corner-notched forms typical of the Mesita Negra Phase. Presumably, maize agriculture, hunting, and wild-plant gathering formed the economic base.

The late McKenzie Phase is represented by only one relatively large site, P 4C, and a few very small sites. The architecture apparently is a continuation from preceding phases (i.e., small pueblos but no pithouses) plus bell-shaped extramural pits. The ceramic assemblage underwent rather drastic changes: Middle Pecos Black-on-white became dominant, plain brownwares were relegated to a minor status, Roswell Brown disappeared altogether, grayware ollas increased in importance, corrugated brownware increased significantly, and Chupadero Black-on-white became more common. Intrusives from afar continued in low frequencies.

Side-notched arrow points continued to dominate, and a small, distinctive end scraper was very common. Subsistence activities witnessed dramatic changes: There was less maize cultivation and much stronger emphasis on hunting, particularly of bison. These changes were evidently encouraged by environmental shifts favoring the spread of grassland and concomitant increases in bison availability.

SOURCE: Jelinek 1967.

R. N. Wiseman

MACKINAC PHASE, a Late Woodland phase of the northern portions of the Lake Michigan, Lake Huron, and eastern Lake Superior basins, dating A.D. 800–1000. Distinctive pottery, originally described by Alan McPherron in 1967, features globular vessels with slightly flaring rims that are decorated with complex cordmarking, often applied in bands. Mackinac Phase sites are usually large, lakeside, fishing villages.

SOURCES: McPherron 1967; Holman 1978; Cleland 1982.

Charles E. Cleland

MCKERN TAXONOMIC SYSTEM. See Midwestern Taxonomic System.

MACKIN SITE, an early (ca. A.D. 900–1000) Caddoan mound and village complex on the upper reaches of Big Pine Creek, a small tributary of the Red River in Lamar County, in Texas. The site comprises two structural mounds: a large, rectangular mound and a smaller mound of undetermined shape. When the larger mound was excavated by R. J. Mallouf in 1974,

charred logs and other evidence of a substantial, partially burned structure were exposed near the mound's base.
Source: Mallouf 1976.

James E. Corbin

MCKINSTRY SITE, a multicomponent, stratified habitation and burial site on Minnesota's northern border which has yielded the state's largest Laurel Culture (q.v.) artifact sample. Excavations in the site's two burial mounds by L. A. Wilford in 1939 and by J. B. Stoltman in 1970, coupled with L. D. Peterson's and W. J. Yourd's work in the habitation areas, resulted in the recognition and definition of an Archaic component, a Laurel (Initial Woodland) component, and a Blackduck (q.v.) (Terminal Woodland) component.
SOURCES: Wilford 1950b; Stoltman 1973, 1974b; Peterson and Yourd n.d.; Yourd n.d.

Leslie D. Peterson

MADISONVILLE FOCUS, a unit of the Fort Ancient Aspect (q.v.), named for the Madisonville Site (q.v.); a large, protohistoric village near Cincinnati, Ohio.
SOURCES: J. B. Griffin 1943a:119–194, 1978.

N'omi B. Greber

MADISONVILLE SITE, a village of the Fort Ancient Tradition (q.v.) near Cincinnati, Ohio, that has been excavated intermittently since 1876. Intensive occupation is indicated by more than 1,200 refuse pits and 1,500 burials, some of which crosscut others. A few items of European manufacture found in burials and pits indicate site use into the protohistoric period.
SOURCES: Hooton and Willoughby 1920; J. B. Griffin 1943a.

N'omi B. Greber

MAGICIAN'S BURIAL, an important burial, dating ca. A.D. 1150–1200, found in 1939 by J. C. McGregor and M. A. Wetherill at Ridge Ruin (q.v.), a Sinaguan (q.v.) pueblo in the Flagstaff Province (q.v.), in Arizona. The burial was in a pit about a meter deep in the floor of a partly subterranean kiva or pithouse that may have predated the pueblo. Two macaw skeletons were in one corner of the room, which evidently was abandoned and filled with trash following the interment.
A wide variety of artifacts was found at several levels within the pit, including many that originated outside the Flagstaff area, from California to southern Arizona and northern New Mexico. Some of the more unique items were painted baskets, a stone-and-shell-beaded cap, 420 chipped-stone projectile points, numerous shell artifacts, a shell trumpet, miniature bows and arrows, painted mountain-lion teeth and claws, and a series of painted wooden wands, some topped with a shell- or turquoise-encrusted crescent.

The main group of wands consisted of four sets of three wands, each of whose ends were carved, respectively, into the form of a human hand, a deer or antelope hoof, and an elongated wedge with serrated edges.

Hopi informants identified these materials as the paraphernalia of a *Qaleetaga*, or important person, of the *Motswimi*, or Warrior Society. This indicates the existence of a Hopi-like society in a Sinaguan community in the 13th century, which strengthens the likelihood that the prehistoric Sinagua were one group that contributed to the development of the Hopi.

J. E. Reyman has suggested that the Magician was a Mexico *Pochteca*, or emmissary, residing at the pueblo. However, physical anthropologists have found no significant difference, save his unusually large size, between the Magician and other Sinaguan individuals.

SOURCES: McGregor 1943; Reyman 1978.

Peter J. Pilles, Jr.

MAHOMET POINT, a type of dart point having a long, slender blade with alternately beveled edges and frequent collateral flaking, squared shoulders, and a rectangular to gently expanding stem with a straight to mildly concave base. A diagnostic trait of the Driftwood Phase (q.v.) in east-central Texas, dating ca. A.D. 550–700, Mahomet marks the terminal Archaic within its localized distribution. It formerly was included within the Darl type.

SOURCES: Prewitt 1981, 1982a.

Elton R. Prewitt

MALAGA COVE SITE, a stratified midden at the south end of Santa Monica Bay in coastal southern California, investigated by Edwin Walker in 1936–1937. Four major levels were present; the earliest was probably older than 4500 B.C. The site was occupied intermittently (with a major interruption) until historic times.

SOURCES: E. F. Walker 1951; Moratto 1984:130–133.

Michael J. Moratto

MALERUALIK SITE, a Thule Phase (q.v.) component on King William Island, Northwest Territories; excavated by Therkel Mathiassen in the 1920s. Dating ca. A.D. 1400—later than the Classic Thule occupation at the Naujan Site (q.v.)—Malerualik lies outside the range of baleen whale and walrus and is an early example of later ecological adaptations by Thule people.

SOURCE: Mathiassen 1927.

Moreau S. Maxwell

MALJAMAR PHASE, the second phase of the Eastern Extension Sub-Province, Jornada Province, Mogollon Culture, which followed the Querecho Phase ca. A.D. 1100/1150–1300 in the southeastern corner of New Mexico.

The village sites have as many as 20 to 30 small, rectangular pithouses. The ceramic assemblage is dominated by various Jornada Brown cognates and Chupadero Black-on-white (qq.v.). Many contemporary pottery types from the neighboring Middle Pecos Sub-Province (q.v.) also are present. Late in the phase, a number of widely traded intrusives appear, e.g., Gila Polychrome, Ramos Polychrome, and Rio Grande Glazes A Red and A Yellow. There was a shift from corner-notched to side-notched arrow points; basin metates and one-hand, oval manos are typical. Hunting and gathering provided sustenance. The exact relationship of Maljamar to the succeeding Ochoa Phase (q.v.) remains to be clarified.
    SOURCE: Leslie 1979.

R. N. Wiseman

MALMO FOCUS, a Middle Woodland complex distributed from Mille Lacs to Gull Lake in north-central Minnesota. It has been dated ca. 800 B.C.–A.D. 200, although a 200 B.C. initial date is probably more realistic. Characteristic of the focus are round mortuary mounds containing secondary burials (usually in shallow pits), stemmed and notched projectile points, and conical vessels with smoothed surfaces. Ceramics exhibit both Havana and Laurel traits.
    SOURCES: Wilford 1941, 1944, 1955; Wilford et al. 1969; Gibbon 1975.

Gordon R. Peters

MALONE SITE, the type site of the Little River Focus of the Great Bend Aspect (q.v.), dating ca. A.D. 1300–1600; located on Cow Creek, a tributary of the Arkansas River in Kansas. Excavated by W. R. Wedel in 1940, it has a possible council circle (q.v.). Its most common pottery belongs to the Geneseo Series: Geneseo Plain, Simple Stamped, and Red Filmed.
    SOURCE: Wedel 1959.

Patricia J. O'Brien

MALPAIS COMPLEX, an artifact assemblage consisting of simple flake and core tools, often displaying desert varnish, found at surface sites in the lower Colorado desert region of southern California. It was originally defined by M. J. Rogers, who concluded that the complex simply represented the earliest phase of his San Dieguito Tradition (q.v.). Recently, several investigators have retained Malpais to distinguish sites they believe precede San Dieguito, although dating of the complex is controversial.
    SOURCES: M. J. Rogers 1939; J. D. Hayden 1976.

R. E. Taylor and L. A. Payen

MANDEVILLE SITE, two mounds and an associated village area about 16 hectares in extent near the Chattahoochee River in southwestern Georgia, attributed predominatly to the Middle Woodland, Swift Creek Culture (q.v.)

of ca. A.D. 1–500. Excavations by A. R. Kelly and others between 1959 and 1962 produced ceramic and lithic assemblages bearing strong similarities to Santa Rosa–Swift Creek materials of northern Florida. Copper earspools and panpipes from mortuary contexts suggest contact with Ohio Hopewell (q.v.).
   SOURCES: Kellar et al. 1962; B. A. Smith 1979.

                                                                    Paul A. Webb

MANN SITE, a large, multicomponent site on a high terrace adjacent to the Ohio River floodplain in Posey County, in extreme southwestern Indiana, excavated in the 1960s and 1970s by J. H. Kellar. Most recognized cultures of the region, from Paleoindian through Mississippian (qq.v.), are represented; most striking is an extensive Middle Woodland village component—more than 80 hectares in area with geometric enclosures, burial mounds, and other earthwork features—that may be the largest ceremonial/village complex of the period in eastern North America. The Mann Site is known for its "high church" artifacts, e.g., numerous terra cotta figurines and ceramics influenced by cultures of the southeastern United States.
   SOURCES: W. K. Adams 1949:47–66; Kellar 1979.

                                                                  James H. Kellar

MAPLES MILLS SITE, a cluster of small burial mounds (Gooden Mound Group) on the bluff top of the central Illinois River Valley near Liverpool; the type site for the Maples Mills Phase (ca. A.D. 900–1150) of the Late Woodland Tradition, as well as for related ceramic and arrow-point styles. The landowner exposed burials in one mound and displayed them commercially from 1928 to the early 1950s, and the University of Chicago dug another mound in 1931. It remains one of the few Maples Mills sites excavated in Illinois.
   SOURCE: Cole and Deuel 1937:191–198.

                                                                    Alan D. Harn

MARCEY CREEK SITE, a stratified, Late Archaic and Early Woodland site dating ca. 2000–750 B.C., overlooking the Little Falls of the Potomac River in northern Virginia. Excavated by C. P. Manson in the 1940s, it is the type site for Marcey Creek Ware (q.v.).
   SOURCE: Manson 1948:223–227.

                                                                Stephen R. Potter

MARCEY CREEK WARE, a type of plain pottery, heavily tempered with particles of crushed steatite, dating ca. 1000 B.C. and found in small quantities in Early Woodland sites throughout Maryland, Delaware, and northern Virginia. Vessels are medium to large rectangular or oval bowls, often with molded lug handles, and having flat bases, protruding heels, and curved to straight sides.

SOURCES: Manson 1948:225; Stephenson et al. 1963:89–92; Egloff and Potter 1982:95–97.

Stephen R. Potter

MARCIA'S RINCON COMMUNITY, a group of eight prehistoric sites in Marcia's Rincon and its environs in Chaco Canyon Culture National Historic Park, New Mexico. One site was dug by Gordon Vivian in 1939; the others were dug by several different archaeologists between 1973 and 1976 as a special project to study the developmental sequence of vernacular sites up to, and contemporary with, the Anasazi greathouses of the Bonito Phase in the Chaco Province (qq.v.).

They discovered components spanning the period ca. A.D. 550–1140 that were attributed to (from early to late) the La Plata, White Mound, Kiatuthlanna, and Bonito phases (qq.v.). Focusing on early and classic period Bonito Phase occupations, the researchers found a patterned variety of surface house forms, room arrangements, and shapes, as well as functional changes in pithouse and kiva design. The knowledge gained from excavating these sites established an archaeological sequence in Chaco Canyon and provided essential data for modeling Anasazi adaptations within the Chaco phenomenon.

SOURCES: McKenna 1984; McKenna and Truell 1986.

Peter J. McKenna

MARIETTA EARTHWORKS, a set of earthworks at the juncture of the Muskingum and Ohio rivers near Marietta, Ohio; one of the first earthworks described in European writings and the subject of much long-standing public interest. The works consist of four flat-topped mounds within a nearly square enclosure, a "graded way," a square with small adjoining mounds, a conical mound encircled by an embankment and a ditch, and a number of other small mounds and embankments. Hopewell Culture (q.v.) artifacts have been found outside the works in nearby open areas and in at least one mound, but no diagnostic artifacts have been found at the works themselves, and consequently their cultural affiliations have not been established. Although usually associated with the Mississippian Period, flat-topped mounds have reliably been reported in Middle Woodland contexts in Ohio and Tennessee.

SOURCES: Livingston 1791; Atwater 1820:133–140; Hildreth 1843; Squier and Davis 1848:73–77, pl. 26; Graybill 1980; Mainfort 1986.

N'omi B. Greber

MARITIME ARCHAIC TRADITION, a coastally adapted culture in Newfoundland and Labrador, dating ca. 6000–1200 B.C. Living sites indicate heavy exploitation of marine resources; burials have yielded evidence of

sophisticated sea-hunting technology. Whether coastal Late Archaic cultures of Maine and the Maritimes should be included within a generalized Maritime Archaic tradition remains a matter of dispute, although common elements exist both north and south of the Gulf of St. Lawrence.
SOURCE: Tuck 1976.

James A. Tuck

MARKSVILLE CULTURE, a distinctive culture dating ca. 100 B.C.–A.D. 300 whose villages are distributed throughout the Gulf coastal area from Texas to Florida. Marksville patently grew out of the preceding Tchefuncte Culture (q.v.) but was strongly modified by Hopewellian influences from the north. At the ceremonial Marksville Site (q.v.) in Louisiana, select personages were buried in log tombs in mounds. Special artifacts include many copper ornaments, zoomorphic pipes, and items made of slate and other exotic materials. Pottery included with burials displays Hopewellian birds and vessel shapes.
SOURCES: Ford and Willey 1940; Toth 1974.

William G. Haag

MARKSVILLE SITE, the type site for the Marksville Culture (q.v.) in east-central Louisiana, consisting of a complex cluster of five mounds enclosed by a low, semicircular, earthen wall, plus at least portions of two other enclosures and seven other mounds. Both conical and flat-topped mounds are present, and numerous circular house sites are in the immediate vicinity. The pottery from excavations by F. M. Setzler in 1933 clearly shows a relationship with other Hopewellian sites in the Lower Mississippi Valley. Protected as a Louisiana Commemorative Area, the site now is open to the public.
SOURCES: Fowke 1928; Toth 1974.

William G. Haag

MARMES ROCKSHELTER, a shelter in the Palouse River Canyon of southeastern Washington where, in 1969, R. D. Daugherty and R. F. Fryxell found skeletal remains representing at least ten human individuals in strata dating between 7000 and 8000 B.C.
SOURCE: Fryxell et al. 1968.

Frank C. Leonhardy

MARPOLE CULTURE TYPE, an archaeological complex in the Gulf of Georgia region on the Northwest coast, dating ca. 500 B.C. to A.D. 1500. The Marpole Site (q.v.) at the mouth of the Fraser River provided the information on which C. E. Borden, in the early 1950s, based his original definition of the culture type.

Distinctive traits include a broad variety of flaked-stone points; micro-blades; ground-slate points; ground-slate fish knives; disc beads of shell and shale; labrets; nipple-top stone hand mauls; stone sculpture; large bone needles; a preponderant use of antler in barbed point and harpoon manu-facture; midden burials, some with plentiful grave goods; artificial skull deformation; and use of large, probably multifamily plank houses.

Most authorities interpret Marpole as an in situ development out of the earlier Locarno Beach culture type (q.v.), as well as a cultural ancestor of both the Gulf of Georgia culture type (q.v.) and the historic Coast Salish Indians. Marpole communities were semisedentary, with winter nucleation into major villages. A focus of their subsistence was an intensive use of the five species of Pacific salmon, which required a mobile settlement pattern and considerable population interaction. There was a high level of artistic achievement, ascribed social ranking—presumably into noble and com-moner classes—and an emphasis on accumulating wealth.

SOURCES: Mitchell 1971; Burley 1980.

David V. Burley

MARPOLE SITE (also known as the Eburne Mound and the Great Fraser Midden), the type site for the Marpole culture type (q.v.), situated near the mouth of the Fraser River in British Columbia. Now completely destroyed by urban development, the original site consisted of 1.9 hectares of shell midden up to 4.5 meters thick. Several researchers dug at the site between the late 19th and mid–20th centuries. C. E. Borden's work there in the 1940s and 1950s led to his definition of the Marpole culture type.

SOURCES: Vancouver Art, Historical and Scientific Association 1948; Burley 1979.

David V. Burley

MARQUETTE MISSION SITE, location of a mission established in 1671 by Father Jacques Marquette for a large village of Huron/Ottawa Indians at present-day St. Ignace in Mackinac County, in Michigan. Extensive ex-cavations at the village by Charles Cleland and Sue Branstner between 1983 and 1986 produced significant information on the nature of early French and Indian contact.

SOURCES: Stone 1972; Fitting 1976; Branstner n.d.

Charles E. Cleland

MARSHALL FORD PHASE, a tentative phase of the Middle Archaic in central Texas, proposed by E. R. Prewitt for the makers of the distinctive barbed and rectangular-stemmed Bulverde type projectile point. Prewitt argues that this is a distinct entity that follows the Clear Fork Phase and

precedes the Round Rock Phase (qq.v.); however, no discrete Marshall Ford component has as yet been reported.
SOURCE: Prewitt 1981:79

Frank A. Weir

MARSHALL POINT, a Middle Archaic dart point in central and south-western Texas dating ca. 1250–300 B.C., diagnostic of the San Marcos Phase (q.v.); characterized by a broad, triangular blade with strong barbs and a parallel-sided to gently expanding stem with a mildly convex to mildly concave base. Stylistically, Marshall grades into the preceding Pedernales (q.v.) and the succeeding Castroville (q.v.) types.
SOURCES: Suhm and Jelks 1962; Denton 1976; Prewitt 1981; Turner and Hester 1985.

Elton R. Prewitt

MARTINS POND SITE, a small but deeply stratified midden located on the Severn River, in Maryland, comprising several components dating from Early through Late Woodland (ca. 750 B.C.–A.D. 1100). Excavated by H. T. Wright in 1958 and 1964, the site provided useful data for establishing a Woodland chronology along the western shore of Chesapeake Bay.
SOURCE: H. T. Wright 1973.

Stephen R. Potter

MARTIS PHASE, a Middle Archaic manifestation occurring along the eastern slope of the northern Sierra Nevada and adjacent western Great Basin in California. The relatively small population subsisted on seed gathering and large-game hunting. Sites of the phase contain large dart points made of basalt which vary a great deal in style, although most are homologous with other Great Basin types, particularly the Elko Series (q.v.).
SOURCES: Heizer and Elsasser 1953; Elsasser 1960; Elston 1971, 1982; Elston et al. 1977.

Robert G. Elston

MARTIS SITE, the type site for the Martis Phase (q.v.) near Truckee, California.

MARY'S HILL SITE, an early pre-Dorset (q.v.) settlement on Pelly Bay, Northwest Territories, excavated by Guy Mary-Rousseliere. Although not radiocarbon dated, its artifact assemblage is typologically early enough that

this site could have been on the initial eastward migration of Pre-Dorset people.
SOURCE: Mary-Rousseliere 1964.

Moreau S. Maxwell

MASON-QUIMBY LINE, an east-west line across the northern tier of the eastern United States and Canada marking the northernmost distribution of fluted projectile points in eastern North America. It is an extension of a line across Michigan's southern peninsula, initially plotted by Ronald Mason and G. I. Quimby, that is coterminous with the northern distribution of mammoth and mastodon fossil remains.
SOURCE: Quimby 1960:30.

Charles E. Cleland

MATTASSEE LAKE SITES, a series of sites occupied intermittently by small groups through much of the Archaic and Woodland (qq.v.) periods (ca. 5000 B.C.–A.D. 1300), located on a terrace overlooking Mattassee Lake and the Santee River in Berkeley County, in South Carolina. Excavations in 1979 by D. G. Anderson produced major stratified artifact assemblages. A posited Late Woodland ceramic type, Santee, similar to the McClellanville Series was defined on the basis of sherds from the site.
SOURCE: D. G. Anderson n.d.b.

Michael Trinkley

MAUPOK HUNTING. See AGLU HUNTING.

MAURY STREET SITE, a stratified site below the falls of the James River in Richmond, Virginia. Tests there by S. M. Perlman in 1979 yielded Early and Middle Woodland artifacts; lower water-logged strata may contain still older cultural material and possibly well-preserved fauna and flora.
SOURCES: Perlman 1983; Mouer 1984.

Keith T. Egloff

MAYCOCKS POINT SITE, a stratified shell midden on the James River in the interior coastal plain of Virginia, where tests by N. F. Barka and B. C. McCary in 1970–1971 led to a date of ca. A.D. 460–875 for Mockley Ware. F. A. Opperman investigated the site further in 1980.
SOURCES: Barka and McCary 1976; Opperman 1980, 1985.

Keith T. Egloff

MAYES ISLAND PERIOD. See Galveston Bay Focus.

MAYHEW SITE, a small, historic Caddoan site on Bayou Loco near Nacogdoches in eastern Texas, excavated in 1975 by E. R. Prewitt. French

glass trade beads, trade gun parts, and other items provided data on mission-era aboriginal cultures in the region ca. A.D. 1725–1775.
SOURCE: Prewitt n.d.

Elton R. Prewitt

MAYHILL SITES, a group of three sites in southeastern New Mexico that provided the excavated data for J. H. Kelley's definition of the early Glencoe Phase (q.v.) of the Sierra Blanca Sub-Province, Jornada Province, Mogollon Culture. Finds included remnants of squarish and rounded pithouses and Jornada Brown (q.v.) type pottery. The sites are estimated to have been occupied from ca. A.D. 1100 to 1200.
SOURCES: R. C. Green 1956; J. H. Kelley 1984.

R. N. Wiseman

MAZAMA PHASE. See Fraser Canyon Sequence.

MAZAMA VOLCANIC ASH, a widely distributed tephra deposit that blankets an area from central Nevada to British Columbia, with detectable deposits as far east as the Rocky Mountain system in Montana and Utah. It was deposited ca. 4700 B.C. when a cataclysmic eruption of Mount Mazama spewed out an estimated 30 cubic kilometers of tephra and created modern Crater Lake in the southern Oregon Cascades. Identifiable by mineralogical analysis, Mazama tephra has been radiocarbon dated at many archaeological sites, as well as from lake sediment cores and other geological contexts. In the northern Great Basin especially, and more broadly throughout the Northwest, this deposit of volcanic ash serves as a valuable time marker for correlating archaeological and paleoenvironmental events. Mazama ash was first put to archaeological use by L. S. Cressman and geologist Howel Williams during the 1930s, when it served as evidence of the extreme antiquity of desert cave sites in south-central Oregon.
SOURCES: Cressman et al. 1940; Kittleman 1973.

C. Melvin Aikens

MEADOWCROFT ROCKSHELTER, a stratified site on a tributary of the Ohio River in extreme eastern Ohio containing cultural materials spanning the entire Archaic and Woodland (qq.v.) periods, as well as deeply buried artifacts from Stratum IIa, the earliest cultural level. Excavated between 1973 and 1978 by J. M. Adovasio, Meadowcroft produced a series of radiocarbon dates for Stratum IIa that range from 17,600 ± 2400 to 6060 ± 110 B.C. Some authorities are skeptical about the validity of these dates.
SOURCES: Adovasio et al. 1977, 1983; Mead 1980; Stanford 1983:70–71.

Edward B. Jelks

MEDIAN VILLAGE, a horticulturally based Sevier/Fremont (q.v.) site in the Parowan Valley, in southwestern Utah, dating ca. A.D. 900–1000. It

was excavated in 1968 by J. P. Marwitt, who used it as the basis for his definition of Fremont regional variation.
    SOURCE: Marwitt 1970.

David B. Madsen

MEDICINE LODGE CREEK SITE, a stratified rockshelter in the Big Horn Basin of Wyoming with components dating from ca. 8000 B.C. to historic times, including a record of the "mountain-oriented" late Paleoindian (q.v.) groups of the High Plains and central Rocky Mountains.
    SOURCES: Frison 1976, 1978.

George Frison

MEDICINE VALLEY PHASE, a unit of the Cohonina Province, Patayan Division, Hakataya Culture (qq.v.), whose sites are distributed along the eastern limits of the province, bordering on territory of the Northern Sinagua Division (q.v.) of the same culture. Dating ca. A.D. 900–1100, Medicine Valley shares basic Cohonina traits with the Cataract Phase (q.v.) to the west, but it is distinguished from Cataract by the presence of Northern Sinagua elements.
    SOURCE: McGregor 1967.

Albert H. Schroeder

MEDICINE WHEEL, a kind of surface site in the northeastern Plains area, especially along the foothills of the Rocky Mountains, that consists of cairns and radiating lines of stones arranged into large figures resembling spoked wheels. The spokes appear to have astronomically significant alignments. These sites date between A.D. 1200 and 1700.
    SOURCE: J. A. Eddy 1975.

Patricia J. O'Brien

MEDIO PERIOD. See Casas Grandes Province.

MELITA FOCUS, an archaeological unit defined by MacNeish in 1958 solely on the basis of the presence of burial mounds in southeastern Manitoba, northeastern North Dakota, and southeastern Saskatchewan. The term is rarely used today. Wedel referred to Melita Focus mounds in southwestern Manitoba; like MacNeish, he considered them related to the Manitoba and Blackduck (q.v.) foci which were thought to be ancestral to the historic Assiniboine. There have been no investigations of Melita Focus mounds in recent years, which may have contributed to the reluctance of regional archaeologists to accept the focus as a valid concept. Ossenberg identified Melita as a phase and cautiously suggested that it, along with other phases, is ancestral to the Assiniboine.

SOURCES: H. Montgomery 1908; MacNeish 1958a:77, 82; Wedel 1961:237–238; Capes 1963; Syms 1977; Ossenberg 1974.

Richard A. Fox

MENARD SITE. See Arkansas Post.

MENLO BAH PHASE. See Surprise Valley.

MESA HOUSE, the type site for the Mesa House Phase (q.v.), the final Anasazi phase in the lower Virgin Province (q.v.). Located in the lower Moapa Valley of southern Nevada and thought to date about A.D. 1100–1150, it was excavated in 1929 by Irwin Hayden. Several arcs of small storage rooms, each conjoined to a large habitation room, surrounded a roundish plaza; like other Anasazi sites in southern Nevada, it lacked a kiva. There was a high percentage (more than 60 percent) of corrugated pottery.

In 1926 Louis Schellbach III excavated a rather extraordinary burial in one of the rooms. Placed in the grave with the body were maize, squash, pine nuts, and sunflower seeds, as well as antler clubs, bone gaming dice, abalone and turquoise artifacts, and 24 well-made arrow points.

SOURCES: Schellbach 1926; Irwin Hayden 1930.

Margaret M. Lyneis

MESA HOUSE PHASE, a manifestation of the Western Anasazi Culture in the Virgin Province (q.v.), known primarily from its type site, Mesa House (q.v.), in the lower Moapa Valley of southern Nevada, which was excavated by Irwin Hayden in 1929. Marking the final occupation of the Virgin Province by Anasazi peoples, the phase is thought to date ca. A.D. 1100–1150.

Maize, beans, and squash were dietary staples, but at Mesa House they were supplemented by such gathered foods as screwbeans, sunflower seeds, and pine nuts. Meat came from desert tortoise, deer, mountain sheep, and antelope.

Architecture and site plans changed subtly from the preceding Lost City Phase (q.v.). At Mesa House and Three Mile Ruin, arcs of rooms are arranged around roundish plazas so as virtually to enclose them. In the lower Moapa Valley, sand-tempered pottery almost completely replaced the olivine-tempered Moapa Gray Ware (q.v.), while corrugated pottery reached its peak of popularity, making up 40 percent or more of the ceramic inventory.

SOURCES: Shutler 1961; Aikens 1965.

Margaret M. Lyneis

MESA SITE, a location on Alaska's north slope, excavated in 1978 by a joint team of the U.S. Geological Survey and the Bureau of Land Management, which yielded lanceolate projectile points almost exclusively. A radiocarbon

date of 7620 B.C. ± 95 years from associated hearths is especially significant
because few lanceolate points from the north have been dated closely.
SOURCE: Kunz 1982.

Donald W. Clark

MESA VERDE PHASE, the final Eastern Anasazi phase of the Chaco Province (q.v.) in northwestern New Mexico, dating ca. A.D. 1200–1300. Except
for the absence of large cliff ruins, the sites of this period resemble those
throughout the Four Corners region. Continuity with the Bonito Phase (q.v.)
is seen in the continued use of roads, reuse of great kivas, and resumed use of
sources utilized earlier. Both large and small sites were reoccupied, but new
settlements also were established, some in the open (often in locations of difficult access) and others in cliffs. Many outliers were fully reoccupied, but
greathouses in Chaco Canyon received only limited use, primarily in the kivas.
Some sites had abundant kivas and storage rooms but no visible living rooms.

The basic settlement pattern was of small homesteads housing a few
families each, with small rooms and kivas like those of the early 12th
century. In the heart of the province, sparse trash deposits indicate short-
lived occupation, most of which probably was between A.D. 1240 and 1260,
a period of increased rainfall. Little is known of subsistence practices in this
period save that beans, squash, and large-cob maize were staples. Hunting
probably was limited to small animals.

McElmo and Mesa Verde Black-on-white bowls and overall-indented,
corrugated pottery dominated ceramic assemblages. Painted pottery was of
both local and northern (San Juan area) varieties; redwares were limited to
White Mountain Redware. Sherd- and sand-tempered wares were the norm.
SOURCES: Pippin 1979; Irwin-Williams and Shelley n.d.

Thomas C. Windes

MESERVE POINT, an early (ca. 7700–6800 B.C.) style of projectile point
widely distributed in the Plains region, having a concave base, prominent
basal thinning, basal grinding, unifacial beveling, and its maximum breadth
at midsection. The beveling is on the right when a specimen is viewed from
its tip. Similar points with serrated edges, named for the Dalton Site in
Missouri, are called Dalton points (q.v.).
SOURCE: Wormington 1957.

Patricia J. O'Brien

MESERVE SITE, a locatioin near Grand Island, Nebraska, where in 1923
F. G. Meserve found the remains of *Bison Occidentalis* associated with a
distinctive projectile point now called the Meserve point (q.v.).

SOURCE: Wormington 1957.

Patricia J. O'Brien

MESILLA PHASE, the earliest phase of the El Paso Sub-Province of the Jornada Province, Mogollon Culture, occupying south-central New Mexico and adjacent parts of Texas and Chihuahua. Dating ca. A.D. 1–1100, the phase has been divided into early and late subphases.

The early Mesilla Phase (ca. A.D. 1–600) is characterized by shallow, round pithouses, early rim variants of El Paso Brown pottery (q.v.), and occasional sherds of San Francisco Red and Alma Plain from the Mimbres Province to the west. Subsistence relied mainly on mesquite, sunflower, cactus fruits, yucca, and other plants, supplemented with rabbits and, in the Rio Grande Valley, fish, ducks, and turtles. Maize was grown but evidently did not constitute a major dietary item. The small villages, consisting of one or several randomly placed pithouses, were scattered over the basin floors, along the mountain margins, and along the Rio Grande, with no preference shown for any particular environmental zone.

The late Mesilla Phase (ca. A.D. 600–1100) saw an increase in village size but no difference in distribution relative to environmental zone. In the Rio Grande Valley villages, some structures were rounded and others rectangular; the latter apparently reflect influences from the Mimbres Province. Ceramics were dominated by late rim forms of El Paso Brown, occasionally with simple black or red designs, and there is some intrusive Mimbres pottery of several types. Early Mesilla Phase subsistence practices continued, and maize became a little more important.

SOURCES: LeBlanc and Whalen 1980; Lehmer 1948.

R. N. Wiseman

MESITA NEGRA PHASE, the second phase of the Middle Pecos Sub-Province of the Jornada Province, Mogollon Culture (qq.v.), in eastern New Mexico. Dating ca. A.D. 1000–1200, it succeeded the Eighteen Mile Phase (q.v.) and saw the most intensive prehistoric use of the sub-province's northern sector.

The early Mesita Negra Phase is characterized by relatively large communities, but architectural details are poorly known. The ceramic assemblage, continuing from the previous phase, is dominated by Jornada Brown (q.v.) cognate, Middle Pecos Micaceous. A locally made Chupadero Black-on-white (q.v.) cognate called Crosby Black-on-gray appears, and pottery imports from the far west and the southwest are present, along with the holdover, Red Mesa Black-on-white. Corner-notched arrow points continue to dominate, and a subsistence strategy of maize agriculture, hunting, and gathering continues as well.

The late Mesita Negra Phase, also poorly known architecturally, saw a decline in Middle Pecos Micaceous pottery in favor of McKenzie Brown

(also a cognate of Jornada Brown) and a marked rise in the popularity of Crosby Black-on-gray. Intrusives from the far west and the northwest are present, but in small quantities. Corner-notched arrow points are more varied in size and shape than before. Animal bones indicate greater use of jackrabbit and bison, but otherwise there is a basic continuation of the former subsistence pattern.
SOURCE: Jelinek 1967.

R. N. Wiseman

MIAMI PHASE, a phase of the Salado Province of the Sinagua Division, Hakataya Culture (qq.v.) in Arizona, dating ca. A.D. 1150–1200. The phase is marked by the appearance of small communities consisting of individual surface houses with cobblestone walls; each community was enclosed with a wall, also of cobblestones. Redware pottery appears in the sites, along with intrusive St. Johns Polychrome, San Carlos Red-on-brown, and both black-on-white and corrugated wares from the Mogollon (q.v.) area to the east and north. Some Little Colorado White Ware from the Winslow Province of the Anasazi Culture (qq.v.) also has been noted. The almost complete dominance of Tonto Brown at some sites, the lack of Gila Plain at others, and a mixture of plainwares at still others indicates that the local ceramics tradition continued through the phase. Extended inhumations and one flexed burial (probably of a non-Saladoan) have been reported.
SOURCES: Brandes 1957; Doyel 1976b.

Albert H. Schroeder

MIAMI SITE, a site in the Texas panhandle, estimated to date between 11,000 and 9,000 B.C., where three Clovis projectile points (q.v.) and a stone scraper were found in a bone bed containing the remains of at least five mammoths. One of the points was discovered by J. A. Mead in 1934; G. L. Evans unearthed the other artifacts in 1937.
SOURCES: Sellards 1938, 1952:18–29.

Edward B. Jelks

MICROBLADE, a parallel-sided blade of flint, chert, or quartz crystal, driven or pressed from a prepared core; a characteristic artifact of the Paleoeskimo and Arctic Small Tool (qq.v.) traditions. By convention, the term is used only for bladelets 10 millimeters or less in width.

Moreau S. Maxwell

MICROBLADE TRADITIONS, various taxonomic constructs at different levels of abstraction that have been advanced for classifying northwestern North American artifact assemblages that include microblade industries. These often encompass whole culture traditions, although focusing on a single stone-working technique. They account for specific regional distributions, interior distributions, all North American microblades, or all occurrences of microblades exclusive of the Arctic Small Tool Tradition. For specific examples, see American Paleo-Arctic Tradition, Denali Complex, Northwest Microblade Tradition, Northern Archaic Tradition, and Aleutian Core and Blade Industry.

Donald W. Clark

MIDDLE COLUMBIA RIVER REGION, an archaeological region in the southern Plateau, extending along the Columbia River between The Dalles, Oregon, and the Okanagan River in Washington.

Frank C. Leonhardy

MIDDLE CUMBERLAND CULTURE, a late Mississippian (q.v.) manifestation in eastern Tennessee, dating ca. A.D. 1100–1300, characterized by stone box-burials and elaborate effigy ceramics.
SOURCE: C. H. Nash 1972.

Jefferson Chapman

MIDDLE HORIZON, the chronologically intermediate (ca. 2000 B.C.–A.D. 500) of three cultural expressions (Early, Middle, and Late horizons) first identified in the Sacramento–San Joaquin Delta locality during the 1930s by Jeremiah Lillard, R. F. Heizer, and Franklin Fenenga, and, in 1948, recognized by R. K. Beardsley in many districts in west-central California. It is characterized by flexed burials and distinctive types of bone and shell artifacts. After ca. 1975, the term "Middle Horizon" was largely supplanted by "Berkeley Pattern" (q.v.).
SOURCE: Moratto 1984:183–185, 207–211.

Michael J. Moratto

MIDDLE MISSOURI TRADITION, one of the three broad cultural traditions—along with the Central Plains and Coalescent traditions (qq.v.)—which constitute the Plains Village Pattern of ca. A.D. 1000–1500. It is represented by a great many permanent farming village sites that line the central Missouri River trench in North and South Dakota.
SOURCE: Lehmer 1971.

Patricia J. O'Brien

MIDDLE PECOS SUB-PROVINCE, an expression of the Jornada Province, Mogollon Culture (qq.v.), that occupied the middle reaches of the Pecos River in eastern New Mexico ca. A.D. 800–1300. As defined by A. J. Jelinek, the sub-province comprised a northern sector and a southern sector, each with its sequence of phases: Eighteen Mile, Mesita Negra, and McKenzie (qq.v.) for the northern sector, Crosby and Roswell (qq.v.) for the southern sector.

After developing out of an Archaic (q.v.) base, the peoples of the northern sector eventually gave up an agriculturally based, ceramic-producing, sedentary lifeway for a bison-hunting strategy. They maintained contacts throughout with both the Salinas Province (q.v.) of the Anasazi Culture and the Sierra Blanca Sub-Province (q.v.) of the Jornada Province, Mogollon Culture, to the west and southwest respectively. The Crosby and Roswell phases are predicated upon survey data and upon ceramic similarities with equivalent northern-sector phases. These Middle Pecos River inhabitants, Jelinek believes, eventually abandoned the river and became the historic Kiowa Indians of the Plains.

SOURCE: Jelinek 1967.

R. N. Wiseman

MIDDLE RIO GRANDE PROVINCE, a culture area in New Mexico occupying the drainage of the Rio Grande and its major tributaries from Bandelier National Monument southward to near Belen, excluding the upper Jemez River Valley near Jemez Pueblo. The Sandia Site (q.v.), the earliest known site in the province, was dug by F. C. Hibben between 1936 and 1940. Other Paleoindian and Archaic period (qq.v.) sites have been recorded.

A number of Developmental Period (q.v.) pithouse sites in the province have been excavated, including Sedillo, Artificial Leg, St. Joseph's, Spearhead, and Denison. Several Coalition Period (q.v.) sites also have been dug. The earliest excavations at Classic Period (q.v.) sites were conducted by N. C. Nelson between 1912 and 1915 at Kotyiti, Tonque, La Bajada, Los Aguajes, Paa-ko, and Ojito Canyoncito. Other sites of the period, investigated by various archaeologists, are Kuaua, Puaray, Pueblo del Encierro (q.v.), San Antonio Pueblo, and Tijeras Pueblo.

SOURCES: Hibben 1941; Campbell and Ellis 1952; Agogino and Hester 1953; Lambert 1954; Peckham 1957; Allen and McNutt 1955; S. A. Skinner 1965; Frisbie 1967; Reinhart 1967a, 1967b; Lange 1968; Bice and Sundt 1972; Judge 1973; L. S. Cordell 1980.

Stewart Peckham

MIDDLE RIO PUERCO VALLEY PROVINCE, a culture area of the Eastern Anasazi, located along the southeastern margin of the San Juan Basin in northwestern New Mexico. The region was occupied from Paleoindian through Pueblo III times (ca. 8500 B.C.–A.D. 1300), but the major occupation was by Anasazi peoples from ca. A.D. 500 to 1300.

The period A.D. 500–900 (Basketmaker III-Pueblo I) was characterized by moderate-sized Eastern Anasazi pithouse villages situated on the uplands above the valley floor. Beginning ca. A.D. 900, sites became increasingly located along the Rio Puerco and its major tributaries. Guadalupe Ruin (q.v.), a Chaco Canyon outlier, was constructed in the mid–900s amidst a sizable, already existing community.

From A.D. 850 to 1150 the material culture of the region was characterized by Cibola Series ceramics and by cultural influences apparently derived from the north and from Chaco Canyon to the northwest. After A.D. 1150, the primary ceramic influences came from the Rio Grande to the east and the Socorro region to the south. There also was a late (ca. A.D. 1200–1300) Mesa Verde influence on local ceramic styles. After ca. A.D. 1300, the province was abandoned until Navajo and Spaniards established settlements there in historic times.

SOURCES: Keur 1941; Washburn 1974; Irwin-Williams n.d.a., n.d.b.; Pippin 1979; Tainter and Gillio 1980; Stuart and Gauthier 1981.

Stephen R. Durand

MIDDLE SNAKE RIVER REGION, an archaeological region in the southern Plateau, extending along the Snake River in Idaho between Weiser and Lewiston.

Frank C. Leonhardy

MIDLAND MAN. See Scharbauer Site.

MIDLAND POINT. See Scharbauer Site.

MID-PASSAGE (or AXIAL) FEATURE, a characteristic structural element of Independence I and II, Middle Dorset, and some Late Dorset (qq.v.) dwellings in the eastern Arctic region. Not a true passage but an area in the center of the dwelling delimited by parallel rows of vertical rock slabs and sometimes paved, this feature was probably used for storage and food preparation. Mid-passages in North American archaeological sites are strikingly similar to features in modern Lapp tents.

Moreau S. Maxwell

MIDWAY VILLAGE SITE, an Oneota (q.v.) manifestation excavated by W. C. McKern in 1944 and by Guy Gibbon in 1968, one of several late Orr Phase-related sites on the La Crosse terrace adjacent to the Mississippi River in western Wisconsin. Subsistence analyses indicate a mixed horticulture, hunting, and gathering economy.

SOURCES: McKern 1945; Gibbon 1970.

David Overstreet

MIDWESTERN (or MCKERN) TAXONOMIC SYSTEM, a scheme devised by W. C. McKern and others in the early 1930s for ordering archaeological cultures into a hierarchical system based on the degree of similarity between the traits of the different cultures. One occupational unit of a particular culture—that is, a site occupied by only one group, or a discrete occupational unit within a site occupied by two or more groups—was called a component. Related components were grouped into a focus, representing a culture unit approximating a tribe. Related foci constituted an aspect, related aspects constituted a phase, related phases constituted a pattern, and related patterns constituted a base, the highest level in the system. Classification was based strictly on similarities between compared units without regard to their respective ages.

During the 1930s, 1940s, and 1950s, the Midwestern system was used by at least some archaeologists in virtually every part of North America, but now other classification systems are used everywhere. Vestiges of the system have survived, however, in the names of cultures that are still called foci and in the standard definition of a component as a single unit of occupation, whether in a single-component or in a multicomponent site. Most units formerly called foci are now called phases, which have temporal as well as descriptive meaning.

SOURCES: McKern 1939.

Edward B. Jelks

MIGOD SITE, a multicomponent Barren Ground site in the Keewatin District, excavated by B. H. C. Gordon in the 1970s. After use for several millennia by prehistoric Indians, the site was occupied by Pre-Dorset (q.v.) peoples during their cold-period invasion of the area ca. 900 B.C. According to Gordon, a Migod radiocarbon date of ca. 835 B.C. marks the end of this Pre-Dorset invasion and the return of the invaders to their former homeland on the northern coasts.

SOURCE: Gordon 1976.

Moreau S. Maxwell

MILBOURN SITE, a series of repeatedly occupied, Late Archaic, warm-season base camps along Durechen Creek, a small tributary of the Walnut River in the Flint Hills of south-central Kansas; they served as focal points in the exploitation of bison, pronghorn, wapiti, and deer. A radiocarbon date of 2485 B.C. ± 100 was obtained on charcoal from the bottom of the cultural horizon. Large bifacial points with deep basal and corner notches evidently were multifunctional, having been used both as projectile points and for cutting and scraping.

The majority of recovered stone tools were for procuring and processing large game animals, but some were used in stoneworking, woodworking, and plant processing. Features include three subterranean roasting ovens and one small hearth. The Milbourn stone-tool assemblage shares techno-

logical characteristics with the Chelsea Phase component at the nearby Snyder site (qq.v.).
SOURCE: Root 1981.

Matthew J. Root

MILEY SITE, a palisaded village on the North Fork of the Shenandoah River in northwestern Virginia, dating to the last half of the Late Woodland period. H. A. MacCord tested the site in 1965 and found house patterns, burials, storage pits, rock hearths, and well-preserved floral and faunal remains. Keyser Cordmarked Ware (q.v.) was the predominant ceramic.
SOURCE: MacCord and Rodgers 1966.

Keith T. Egloff

MILL CREEK CULTURE, the easternmost extension of the Initial Variant of the Middle Missouri Tradition (q.v.), located in northwestern Iowa and composed of coeval Little Sioux and Big Sioux phases (A.D. 900–1300). Defined in 1927 by Charles R. Keyes, Mill Creek is best known from research conducted by the University of Wisconsin to evaluate the effects of climatic change on culture. Compact villages with deep midden accumulations are typical. A defining characteristic distinguishing Mill Creek from other Initial Variant cultures is differing frequencies of major shared ceramic types.
SOURCES: Fugle 1962; Henning 1968; D. C. Anderson 1981; Tiffany 1982.

Joseph A. Tiffany

MILLER CULTURE, the local Woodland (q.v.) sequence of the Upper Tombigbee River drainage area in western Alabama and eastern Mississippi, dating ca. 100 B.C.–A.D. 900. It was defined by J. D. Jennings in 1941. Changes in ceramics over time have led researchers to divide the culture into three sequential phases. Miller I peoples participated in the Hopewell (q.v.) exchange system and constructed burial mounds. Miller II and III peoples practiced maize agriculture and gradually developed a Mississippian (q.v.) lifeway closely associated with the great ceremonial center at Moundville (q.v.) to the east.
SOURCES: Jennings 1941; Cotter and Corbett 1951; Jenkins 1979.

John A. Walthall

MILLER SITE, a multicomponent site on the floodplain of the Sulphur River in Delta County, in Texas, excavated by LeRoy Johnson, Jr., in 1959. There was a strong Middle and Late Archaic component dating ca. 4000 B.C.–A.D. 700 that complemented the Yarbrough Site (q.v.) in the formulation of the La Harpe Aspect (q.v.). A later, Early Caddo

component dating ca. A.D. 800 demonstrated a rather abrupt break between the ceramic-using Late Archaic and the Caddoan populations in much of eastern Texas.
SOURCE: LeRoy Johnson, Jr. 1962.

James E. Corbin

MILLIKEN PHASE. See Fraser Canyon Sequence.

MILLIKEN SITE, a deeply stratified site in the Fraser Canyon, British Columbia, whose earliest occupation began about 7000 B.C. Excavations there between 1959 and 1961 by C. E. Borden contributed significantly to the recognition of a Fraser Canyon Sequence (q.v.).
SOURCES: Borden 1960, 1961, 1975.

Donald H. Mitchell

MILLINGSTONE HORIZON, a widespread cultural tradition in coastal southern California defined by W. J. Wallace in 1955. His Horizon II, or Millingstone Assemblage, was characterized by the use of millingstones and core tools, along with a relative scarcity of chipped-stone projectile points and artifacts of bone and shell. The horizon appears to have begun before 5000 B.C. and to have lasted four or five millennia.
SOURCE: Wallace 1955.

Michael J. Moratto

MILLINGTON SITE, a major agriculture-based, late prehistoric and historic (ca. A.D. 1200–1800) village on the Rio Grande near Presidio in western Texas, comprising components of the La Junta, Concepcion, and Conchos phases (qq.v.), and identified with the historic site of San Cristobal of the Cholomes Indians. During investigations there in 1939, J. C. Kelley found 31 circular and rectangular pithouses, both solitary and contiguous, and excavated 22 of them.
SOURCES: J. C. Kelley 1939:221–234, 1985:149–159; J. C. Kelley et al. 1940.

Robert J. Mallouf

MILL ISLAND SITE, a location on Hudson Strait south of Cape Dorset where excavations by Deric O'Bryan in 1951 revealed a single, Thule-style house within which was a combination of Late Dorset and Thule traits (qq.v.). This has been interpreted variously as (1) an example of contact between Dorset and Thule people, (2) later use of a Thule house by Dorset

people, and (3) a Thule semisubterranean house that was dug through an earlier Dorset midden.
SOURCE: O'Bryan 1953.

Moreau S. Maxwell

MILLVILLE PHASE, a post-Havana, Middle Woodland expression dating ca. A.D. 300–600 in southwestern Wisconsin, defined by J. B. Stoltman in 1979 as a local development subsequent to the demise of the Hopewell (q.v.) interaction sphere.
SOURCE: Stoltman 1979.

David Overstreet

MILLVILLE SITE, a post-Havana, Middle Woodland village; the type site for the Millville Phase as defined by J. B. Stoltman. Excavations by J. E. Freeman in 1968 revealed the remains of numerous houses with associated hearths, refuse/storage pits, and burials.
SOURCES: Freeman 1969; Stoltman 1979.

David Overstreet

MINIM ISLAND SHELL MIDDEN, a multicomponent Early Woodland site on Duck Creek in Georgetown County, in South Carolina. Excavations in 1982 by Lesley Drucker revealed a Thom's Creek (q.v.) Phase component (radiocarbon dated to 1040 + 500 B.C.) and a Deptford (q.v.) Phase component (radiocarbon dated to A.D. 160 ± 80).
SOURCE: Drucker and Jackson n.d.

Michael Trinkley

MINNESOTA WOMAN, a female human skeleton accidentally uncovered in 1931 near Pelican Rapids in western Minnesota; sometimes referred to as Minnesota Man. An elk-antler tool and a marine-shell pendant were in association. Possibly coeval with glacial Lake Pelican, the remains have been variously dated from 25,000 years ago to early historic times. Radiocarbon dates—unreliable because the samples were contaminated—place the remains within the Archaic period, sometime between 5000 and 1000 B.C.
SOURCES: Jenks 1936; Elden Johnson 1964.

Christy Hohman-Caine

MISHONGNAVI SITE, a guard village of the nearby Shungopavi Sites (q.v.), established ca. A.D. 1200 at the base of the eastern finger of Second Mesa in northeastern Arizona. Traditionally, it is said to have been founded by Sinagua Crow Clan members. The Spanish reported a village there in 1583, and they built a chapel nearby during the Spanish mission period of 1629–1680. Following the Pueblo Revolt of 1680, the village was abandoned, and Mishongnavi II, which survives today (1988), was established on the mesa top nearby. Built in the Western Hopi parallel-row style, the second village has one- to three-story houses and at least four semisubterranean, stone-built, rectangular kivas.

SOURCES: Colton and Baxter 1932; Fewkes 1900; Ellis 1961; Connelly 1979.

Michael B. Stanislawski

MISSISSIPPIAN, a term applied to a widespread prehistoric manifestation in the eastern United States during the period A.D. 800–1500. Usage of the term varies: Some archaeologists say "Mississippian Stage," others say "Mississippian Tradition," "Mississippian Pattern," or "Mississippian Culture." Most, howoever, simply call the archaeological manifestation "the Mississippian."

The emergence of the Mississippian is marked by the appearance of distinctive forms of pottery, commonly tempered with crushed mussel shell, intensive village-based horticulture, the rise of chiefdoms, and the construction on or around a central plaza of large, earthen, platform mounds that served as substructures for temples, elite residences, and council buildings. Other important facets of Mississippian development were the use of the bow and arrow as the major weapon system; a horticultural system based on maize, beans, and squash; religious ceremonialism connected with agricultural production and centered around a fire-sun deity; long-distance trade; increased territoriality and warfare; and the emergence of ranked social systems.

It was during the Mississippian that such huge archaeological sites as Cahokia in Illinois, Moundville in Alabama, Etowah in Georgia, and Spiro in Oklahoma (qq.v.) became dominant regional civic/ceremonial centers. The power of these and other regional Mississippian centers waxed and waned over a 400-year period between A.D. 1100 and 1500; by the time of Spanish exploration in the 16th century, all the major centers had been abandoned. The remaining Mississippian societies, many of which came into face-to-face contact with European explorers, were drastically decreased in population by Old World diseases to which they were highly susceptible.

SOURCES: J. B. Griffin 1985; B. D. Smith 1985.

John A. Walthall

MITCHELL PLANTATION QUARRY, located near the Nottoway River where it crosses the fall line in southern Virginia; a source of chalcedony and of a distinctive, yellow chert favored by Paleoindian and Early Archaic peoples in the immediate area.

SOURCE: McCary and Bittner 1979.

Keith T. Egloff

MITCHELL SITE (1), a large secondary Mississippian (q.v.) mound center on the Mississippi River floodplain in the American Bottom, in southwestern Illinois, dating ca. A.D. 1150–1200. First mapped by Bushnell in 1904, the site probably covered an area of more than 100 acres originally, and evidently comprised eleven mounds, residential areas, and a town plaza with a large, bald cypress post standing in its center. It is believed that Mitchell represents a satellite town associated with the large mound center at the Cahokia Site (q.v.) about 7 miles to the south. Archaeologists from Southern Illinois University, Carbondale conducted major excavations at Mitchell in 1960–1962.

SOURCES: Bushnell 1904; Fowler 1969; Porter 1974.

Charles J. Bareis and Andrew C. Fortier

MITCHELL SITE (2), a fortified community near Mitchell, South Dakota, belonging to the Over Focus (q.v.), which contained long, rectangular, semi-subterranean houses and pottery with angled shoulders and broad, trailed designs reminiscent of Middle Mississippian pottery from sites like Aztalan and Cahokia (qq.v.). Excavated in 1938 by E. E. Meleen, the Mitchell Site is estimated to date ca. A.D. 1000–1300.

SOURCES: Meleen 1938; Wedel 1961.

Patricia J. O'Brien

MITTAMATALIK LOCALITY, a location on Pond Inlet, North Baffin Island, where Therkel Mathiassen and Guy Mary-Rousseliere have investigated several sites dating from earliest Pre-Dorset time through the Thule Phase (qq.v.) to modern Inuit. This was the departure point for a well-documented mid–19th-century migration of a small Inuit band through the High Arctic to northeastern Greenland. The band reintroduced such lost traits as kayaks and bows and arrows to the isolated Polar Eskimo.

SOURCES: Mathiassen 1927; Mary-Rousseliere 1976.

Moreau S. Maxwell

MOANING CAVE, a deep limestone cavern on the western slope of the Sierra Nevada Mountains in Calaveras County, in central California, containing an extensive deposit of human bones; one of the first archaeological sites reported in California. Speleotherm age dating developed by P. C. Orr suggested that the bones might be from 12,000 to 50,000 years old, but a subsequent radiocarbon assays on calcite covering a human femur indicated that the femur had been placed in the cave only about 1400 years ago.

SOURCES: Wallace 1951; P. C. Orr 1952; Broecker et al. 1960.

R. E. Taylor and L. A. Payen

MOAPA GRAY WARE, an olivine-tempered ceramic found all across the Virgin Province (q.v.) of the Western Anasazi Culture in Arizona, Utah, and Nevada. It was used from Basketmaker III times (ca. A.D. 500) to ca. A.D. 1000. Both jars and bowls are present, some of them bearing painted designs that reflect the changes from Lino to Black Mesa (q.v.) to Sosi and Dogoszhi styles.

SOURCES: Colton 1952; Myhrer and Lyneis 1985.

Margaret M. Lyneis

MOAPA PHASE, the analog of Basketmaker II (q.v.) for the Virgin Province (q.v.) of the Western Anasazi Culture, occupying the upper Moapa and lower Virgin valleys of southern Nevada and Zion National Park, Utah, and estimated to date ca. A.D. 1–500. Moapa Phase peoples, like Basketmaker II peoples, are assumed to have cultivated maize to supplement a basic diet of hunted and collected foods. Habitation sites consist of one or a few large house pits grouped on high bluffs overlooking valley floors. Distinctive artifacts include large, crude projectile points suited for use with atlatl rather than on arrows. Pottery is absent. The Moapa Phase was defined by Richard Shutler, Jr.

SOURCES: Schroeder 1955; Shutler 1961.

Margaret M. Lyneis

MOBRIDGE SITE, an earthlodge village near Mobridge, South Dakota, occupied at two distinct periods (A.D. 1600–1650 and 1675–1700), together with two associated cemeteries. The village areas, never dug professionally, were badly damaged by relic hunters and highway construction. The cemeteries, following early sampling by W. H. Over and Matthew Stirling, were excavated extensively by William M. Bass in 1968–1970 and Douglas H. Ubelaker in 1971. Approximately 789 individuals were recovered, the largest population of human skeletal remains from the northern Plains. About 20 percent of the burials from the 1675–1700 cemetery contained European artifacts; the burials from the earlier cemetery contained none.

SOURCES: Merchant 1973; Merchant and Ubelaker 1977.

William M. Bass

MOCCASIN BLUFF SITE, a multicomponent site on the St. Joseph River in southwestern Michigan, excavated by Hale Smith in 1948. Projectile points with bifurcate bases indicate some occupation as early as the Middle

Archaic; other points resembling the Raddatz and Lamoka (q.v.) types are of Late Archaic provenance. Early Woodland pottery (Marion Thick type) and Middle Woodland Havana wares suggest a strong association with Illinois.

Largely on the basis of this site, R. L. Betteral and H. G. Smith defined three Late Woodland phases: Brems (A.D. 700–1050), Moccasin Bluff (A.D. 1050–1300), and Berrien (A.D. 1400–1600). Components of the latter two phases yielded shell-tempered pottery similar to Fisher and Huber wares of northeastern Illinois and Indiana. Grit-tempered pottery also was present.

SOURCES: Yarnell 1964; Cleland 1966; Bettaral and Smith 1973.

Margaret B. Holman

MOCKINGBIRD GAP SITE, a multicomponent open camp in the Jornada del Muerto, an intermontane basin in central New Mexico, particularly noteworthy for its extensive lithic assemblage of the Clovis Complex (q.v.), estimated to date ca. 9150 B.C. Excavations in 1966–1969 by R. H. Weber and G. A. Agogino and, in subsequent years, by Weber yielded numerous Clovis points (q.v.), mostly discarded basal fragments. These display a wide range in style and size, but there is a high frequency of small specimens from 50 down to less than 25 millimeters long.

Associated lithics include end and side scrapers, gravers, thin flake scraper-knives, cores, simple utilized flakes, and abundant debitage. Both nearby and distant lithic sources were exploited, some as far away as extreme northwestern New Mexico and northwestern Texas. The few remaining traces of bone suggest that bison were among the prey of the Clovis hunters.

In later components were, respectively, Cody Complex (q.v.) projectile points, Early to Late Archaic lithics, and a cluster of pithouses associated with 17th-century glazewares, perhaps from a Piro or Tompiro refugee occupation.

SOURCES: Weber and Agogino n.d.a, n.d.b; Weber 1973.

Robert H. Weber

MOCKLEY WARE, a shell-tempered, Middle Woodland pottery found from southern Delaware to the lower James River, in Virginia. Radiocarbon dated to ca. A.D. 200–900, it occurs typically as medium to large jars with direct rims and rounded or semiconical bottoms, and cordmarked, net-impressed, or plain exterior surfaces.

SOURCES: Stephenson et al. 1963:105–109; Artusy 1976:3–4; Egloff and Potter 1982:103–104.

Stephen R. Potter

MODOC HORIZON, the "historically modern" component of the archaeological sequence in the Klamath Basin of northeastern California as originally defined by L. S. Cressman in 1940.

SOURCE: Moratto 1984:444.

Michael J. Moratto

MODOC ROCK SHELTER, a deeply stratified, multicomponent site at the edge of the central Mississippi River Valley in Randolph County, in southwestern Illinois, excavated in the 1950s by the Illinois State Museum and the University of Chicago and in the 1980s by the Illinois State Museum and the University of Wisconsin, Milwaukee. Artifacts and biotic remains were superbly preserved in 8.5 meters of alluvial and colluvial deposits that had been protected by sandstone overhangs. Excavations and research, which focused on Early, Middle, and Late Archaic components, have documented major changes in human settlement and subsistence practices during the period ca. 7000–2100 B.C. These cultural changes were in part related to mid-Holocene climatic effects on resources.
SOURCES: M. L. Fowler 1959; Styles et al. 1983.

Bonnie W. Styles

MOGOLLON CLASSIFICATION SYSTEM. See Southwestern Classification Systems.

MOGOLLON CULTURE, the prehistoric culture that occupied south-central and southwestern New Mexico, east-central and southeastern Arizona, northern Chihuahua, and adjacent Sonora ca. A.D. 200–1450. The culture was defined originally by E. W. Haury on the basis of his excavations at Mogollon Village and the Harris site, both in southwestern New Mexico. Haury traced the then already well-known Mimbres (q.v.) culture back to earlier Mogollon pithouse villages and argued that a Mogollon Culture had developed independently of the Anasazi Culture (q.v.) to the north. After J. O. Brew challenged the validity of this concept, a debate persisted until other Mogollon manifestations had been documented by several researchers in what now are defined as the Cibola (q.v.), San Simon, Forestdale, Black River, and Jornada (q.v.) provinces.

The basic attribute that gave integrity to the Mogollon Culture was brownware pottery, whose distribution lay generally along and south of the Mogollon Rim in Arizona, and along the less well-defined south edge of the Colorado Plateau in New Mexico. In the Anasazi area, pottery was made from gray- and white-firing clays, whereas in the Mogollon area brown- and red-firing clays from volcanic deposits dominated. This division promoted regional comparison of other Mogollon and Anasazi traits until evidence for the Mogollon Culture became so overwhelming that debate ceased.

Unlike the Anasazi Culture, the Mogollon Culture did not survive recognizably up to the historic period, most of its homeland having been abandoned by A.D. 1400. Remnants of some Mogollon groups evidently merged with Anasazi peoples to become what is known as the Western Pueblo or Western Anasazi.

SOURCES: Haury 1936, 1940; Nesbitt 1938; P. S. Martin 1943; Sayles 1945; Brew 1946; Lehmer 1948; Reed 1948.

Stewart Peckham

MONACAN FARM DISTRICT, an area of floodplain on the James River in the central Piedmont of Virginia, where in 1930 D. I. Bushnell found artifacts dating from Early Archaic through the postcontact period, including Early Woodland ceramics. A postcontact feature probably was associated with the 18th-century Huguenot settlement of Manakintown.

SOURCES: Bushnell 1930; Winfree 1972; Mouer 1983.

Keith T. Egloff

MONKS MOUND, the largest prehistoric earthen mound in North America and the focal point of the Cahokia (q.v.) temple-mound complex, located on the Mississippi River floodplain in the American Bottom, in southwestern Illinois. Consisting of four terraces representing multiple building stages, the mound rises to a height of about 30 meters above the floodplain and covers an area of some 15 acres. The period of its construction and/or occupation began with the Lohmann Phase (ca. A.D. 1000), or possibly earlier, and continued through the Sand Prairie Phase (ca. A.D. 1400). The chief residence of Cahokia's political-religious leader probably stood on Monks Mound, which also may have been the center of major ceremonial activities. It is widely believed that many of the other mounds at Cahokia were oriented to, or were functionally associated with, Monks Mound. Major excavations in the mound have been conducted by the University of Illinois at Urbana-Champaign; the University of Wisconsin, Milwaukee; Southern Illinois University, Edwardsville; and Washington University, St. Louis.

SOURCES: Bushnell 1904; Reed et al. 1968; Fowler 1969, 1975; Benchley 1974.

Charles J. Bareis and Andrew C. Fortier

MONOCACY SITE, a site on the Potomac River in the Piedmont section of Maryland with seven stratigraphic zones comprising components of the Late Archaic, Early Woodland, and Late Woodland periods, dating ca. 2000 B.C.–A.D. 1600. It was excavated from 1967 to 1970 by the joint efforts of Catholic University, American University, and the University of Maryland.

SOURCES: Ayers and Little 1967:26–38; Ayers 1972; Kavanagh 1982.

Stephen R. Potter

MONROE FOCUS, a complex defined by D. J. Lehmer on the basis of his work at the Dodd Site on the Missouri River in South Dakota. Probably dating ca. A.D. 1000–1500, it is characterized by long, rectangular pithouses

and pottery with S-shaped or flaring rims that is either plain or cord roughened.
SOURCE: Lehmer 1954.

Patricia J. O'Brien

MONTAGUE HARBOUR SITE, a large, culturally stratified shell midden on Galiano Island, British Columbia, where excavations in 1964–1965 by D. H. Mitchell established a clear temporal separation between Locarno Beach, Marpole, and Gulf of Georgia (qq.v.) assemblages.
SOURCE: Mitchell 1971.

Donald H. Mitchell

MONTEZUMA CASTLE, a remarkably well-preserved five-story dwelling that can be entered only by means of a series of ladders, situated in a cave high up in a limestone cliff in Montezuma Castle National Monument, a few miles north of Camp Verde, Arizona. It was built and occupied by Sinaguas of the Verde Province (q.v.) between A.D. 1125 and 1400. West of the castle are the collapsed remains of a similar but smaller three-story structure of the same date. The castle was thoroughly ransacked for artifacts by early settlers and army personnel stationed at Camp Verde, but the smaller dwelling, when excavated by Earl Jackson and S. P. Van Valkenburgh in 1933, yielded a variety of material.

Despite the vandalism at the castle, its original ceilings, doorways, floors, and walled balcony remain to provide architectural details not normally found in ruins in the open. The walls, like those of pueblos in the river valley, are composed of rock and mud, giving the appearance of a mud wall with rock fill. Stone picks found at the site probably were used to mine salt from a nearby deposit. A macaw skeleton indicates trade with people to the south, probably the Hohokam of the Gila–Salt Valley who obtained occasional articles from Mexico.
SOURCE: Jackson and Van Valkenburgh 1954.

Albert H. Schroeder

MONTGOMERY COMPLEX, a Late Woodland (ca. A.D. 900–1450) manifestation centered in the Piedmont section of the Potomac River Valley, characterized by 1- to 2-acre village sites with an oval pattern of trash pits surrounding an open plaza, Shepard Cord-marked pottery (q.v.), obtuse-angle clay pipes, and single flexed or semiflexed burials.
SOURCES: Schmitt 1952:62; Slattery et al. 1966:49–51; Kavanagh 1982:70–74, 79–82.

Stephen R. Potter

MOOREHEAD PHASE, a unit of the Mississippian (q.v.) tradition that followed the Stirling Phase (q.v.) in the American Bottom of southwestern Illinois ca. 1150–1250 A.D. It is characterized by temple-mound complexes, wall-trench structures, and primarily shell-tempered ceramics. Vessel forms include the Mississippian inventory with plates added. Ramey Incised pottery, common in Stirling Phase sites, became less frequent during the Moorehead Phase. There are major Moorehead components at the Mitchell, Cahokia (qq.v.), and Julien sites in the American Bottom.

SOURCES: Fowler and Hall 1972; Porter 1974; Bareis and Porter 1984; Milner 1984.

Andrew C. Fortier and Charles J. Bareis

MOORE SITE, a palisaded village of the Monongahela Woodland Complex, located on the Potomac River in the Appalachian Mountains of western Maryland and dating to the 15th century A.D. It was tested in 1976 by R. G. Handsman and in 1982 by J. F. Pousson.

SOURCE: Pousson 1983.

Stephen R. Potter

MORESBY TRADITION, the earliest subdivision of Queen Charlotte Islands, British Columbia prehistory, dating ca. 6000–3000 B.C.; characterized by small sites and a flaked-stone industry dominated by microblade manufacture. Flaked bifaces and fire-cracked stones are absent, the latter suggesting that stone boiling was unknown.

Adapted to a littoral-maritime environment, the Morseby tradition is thought to represent a culture with ultimately northern relationships.

SOURCES: Fladmark 1975, 1979a.

Knut R. Fladmark

MORROW MOUNTAIN POINT, a small to large chipped-stone projectile-point type distinguished by a triangular blade and a rudimentary haft element formed by an excurvate or pointed base. The classic Middle Archaic horizon marker for the interior Southeast, the type dates ca. 5200–4500 B.C. and is distributed throughout the Tennessee River drainage, the Piedmont, and surrounding areas from the Carolina coast to northeastern Mississippi.

SOURCES: Lewis and Kneberg 1951; DeJarnette et al. 1962:63; Coe 1964:37,43; J. W. Griffin 1974; Jefferson Chapman 1977; Bense 1983.

Eugene M. Futato

MORTLACH SITE (also known as the BESANT MIDDEN), a multicomponent site in central Saskatchewan with thirteen distinct occupations attributed to eight different cultural units, covering the period from ca. 1400 B.C. to very late prehistoric times. Excavations there by Boyd Wettlaufer in 1954 were the first major excavations in the Canadian Plains. The Plains Side-notched Point System, the Besant Phase, the Pelican Lake Complex

(qq.v.), and the McKean-Duncan-Hanna Complex are represented at the site, along with other less well-known cultural units.
SOURCE: Wettlaufer 1955.

Margaret Hanna

MORTON SITE, a large, multicomponent, habitation and burial-mound complex in the central Illinois River Valley, probably occupied over the period from ca. 600 B.C. to ca. A.D. 1300 and comprising major Red Ocher, Spoon River Mississippian, and Oneota components (qq.v.). University of Chicago field schools held there in the 1930s under the direction of Fay-Cooper Cole and Thorne Deuel developed field and analytical techniques that still are widely employed today. Rosters from the field schools are a veritable Who's Who of individuals who later became eminent in American archaeology.
SOURCE: Cole and Deuel 1937:57–111.

Alan D. Harn

MOSTIN SITE, a deeply stratified site located near Clear Lake in northern California; the location of one of the earliest cemeteries known in North America. It contained nine cultural and natural levels; the deepest one (radiocarbon dated at ca. 9000 B.C.) contained a large number of human burials. An organic fraction obtained from human bones has been radiocarbon dated at ca. 8500 B.C.
SOURCES: Kaufman 1980; Moratto 1984:99–101, 112–113.

Michael J. Moratto

MOUND CITY, a group of at least 25 densely spaced mounds—most of them enclosed by a low embankment—located on the Scioto River just north of Chillicothe, Ohio. Intermittent major excavations beginning early in the 19th century and continuing over the years have discovered, under the mounds, remains of single-room structures where rituals and social gatherings took place, as well as cremated human remains, deposits of both burned and unburned exotic goods, and utilitarian artifacts of the Hopewell Culture (q.v.). The site appears to have been in use between ca. A.D. 100 and 250.
SOURCES: Squier and Davis 1848;54–55, pl. 19, 186–286 passim; Mills 1922; Barnhart 1985; Baby and Langlois n.d.; J. A. Brown n.d.; Brown and Baby n.d.

N'omi B. Greber

MOUNDS PLANTATION SITE, one of the important early Caddoan sites in Caddo Parish, in northwestern Louisiana, comprising a large plaza, nine surviving mounds, and multiple habitation and activity areas. It occupies a secondary terrace fronting a relict channel of Red River some 3 kilometers west of the river's present course. It was investigated by C. B. Moore in 1912 and by R. R. McKinney and C. H. Webb between 1950 and 1962.

The site witnessed the transition from Coles Creek (q.v.) to Caddo I (ca. A.D. 900–1100), and it is coeval with the Gahagan and Crenshaw (qq.v.) ceremonial sites in the heart of Caddo country. The Coles Creek occupation established the plaza and the initial stages of at least four mounds; it also left evidence of heavy occupation along the terrace front. A log-covered Caddo I tomb, radiocarbon dated to the 11th century A.D., contained five groups of sequentially placed burials of 21 individuals, including fetuses, with copper ornaments, ornamented cane matting, exotic lithics, and a bowl with hand-and-eye and cross symbols. Secondary group and individual burials attributed to the Bossier and Belcher (qq.v.) cultures of the 15th to 17th centuries A.D. also were found in two mounds.

SOURCES: C. B. Moore 1912:524–525; Webb and McKinney 1975:39–127.

Clarence H. Webb

MOUNDS STATE PARK, a state-administered recreation area on a high bluff overlooking the White River in Madison County, in Indiana, comprising a number of geometric enclosures and probable burial mounds. The little systematic excavation undertaken there has been primarily in the "Great Mound," a circular enclosure measuring about 100 meters in diameter. Two radiocarbon dates of 60 B.C. and A.D. 230 and an assemblage of artifacts, some from burials, are suggestive of both Adena (q.v.) and Middle Woodland. These have been ascribed by K. D. Vickery to a New Castle Phase (q.v.).

SOURCES: Lilly 1937; Kellar 1969; Vickery 1979; Buehrig and Hicks 1982.

James H. Kellar

MOUNDVILLE SITE, largest and best-known Mississippian (q.v.) site in the Southeast, located on the Black Warrior River in Hale County, in Alabama. Covering over 300 acres and comprising twenty large earthen pyramids, a central plaza, and extensive habitation areas, the site probably was the central community of a chiefdom. Excavations in the mounds and habitation zones by D. L. DeJarnette between 1933 and 1941 have yielded over 2,000 burials—many of them accompanied by elaborate offerings—and tremendous quantities of utilitarian artifacts.

SOURCE: Walthall 1981.

John A. Walthall

MT. EDZIZA (or ICE MOUNTAIN) OBSIDIAN QUARRY, a series of obsidian flows from a now-dormant volcano on the Stikine River in northern British Columbia, comprising at least five chemically distinct obsidians. Associated with them are numerous flaking stations where excavations by K. R. Fladmark in 1981 revealed microblades at some that had been pro-

duced from distinctive types of cores. Few sites have been extensively excavated or well dated, but one microblade component has been radiocarbon
dated to ca. 2900 B.C. A later occupation with lanceolate projectile points
but no microblades dated between 2000 and 800 B.C. Edziza obsidian was
widely distributed in the Cordilleran region from the Skeena River in British
Columbia northward into the southern Yukon, and from the coast into
Alberta and the southwestern District of Mackenzie.
    SOURCES: Fladmark 1984, 1985; Souther 1970.

                                                          Donald W. Clark

MOUNT PLEASANT PHASE, a culture unit dating ca. 300 B.C.–A.D. 800
whose sites occur widely in the Tidewater and Inner Coastal Plain regions
of North Carolina, most frequently along major trunk streams, estuaries,
and the coast. It is characterized by Mount Pleasant Series pottery (q.v.);
small, triangular projectile points; blades; abraders; shell and polished-stone
gorgets; and both primary inhumations and cremations.
    SOURCE: Phelps 1983:32–33.

                                                          Billy L. Oliver

MOUNT PLEASANT POTTERY SERIES, a pebble- or grit-tempered ware
with fabric-impressed, cordmarked, net-impressed, incised, or plain surfaces. Dating ca. 300 B.C.–A.D. 800, it is distributed widely in components
of the Mount Pleasant Phase (q.v.) in the Tidewater and Inner Coastal Plain
regions of North Carolina, where it often occurs in association with Hanover
Ware (q.v.) and an unnamed sand-tempered pottery.
    SOURCE: Phelps 1983:32–33.

                                                          Billy L. Oliver

MOUNT ROYAL SITE, a village and associated large pyramidal mound
of the St. Johns Culture (q.v.) on the St. Johns River in Putnam County, in
Florida, dating from ca. A.D. 1100 to 1513. In the 1890s, C. B. Moore dug
into the mound where he found a number of copper objects, including a
plate of Southern Ceremonial Complex (q.v.) style. A Spanish mission stood
on the site in the 17th century.
    SOURCES: Moore 1894a:16–35, 1894b:130, 137–146; Goggin 1952:55,
87–88.

                                                          Jerald T. Milanich

MOUNT TAYLOR CULTURE, a Middle to Late Archaic unit (ca. 4000–
2000 B.C.) centered on the middle St. Johns River, in Florida, which de-

veloped into the Orange Culture (q.v.). Mount Taylor shell middens often underlie Orange and St. Johns (q.v.) shell middens.

SOURCES: Goggin 1952:40–43, 66–68; Milanich and Fairbanks 1980:147–152.

Jerald T. Milanich

MOYAONE WARE, a ceramic of the Late Woodland and early historic periods (ca. A.D. 1300–1650) in the upper coastal plain of the Potomac River Valley. Tempered with sand, occasionally mixed with crushed quartz, vessels are small to medium sized with globular bodies and rounded or slightly conical bases. The ware is divided into three types: Moyaone Cord-impressed, Moyaone Incised, and Moyaone Plain.

SOURCES: Stephenson et al. 1963:120–125; Egloff and Potter 1982:112.

Stephen R. Potter

MUDDY RIVER PHASE, the analog of Basketmaker III (q.v.) for the Virgin Province (q.v.) of the Western Anasazi Culture occupying an area bounded on the east by Kanab, Arizona, on the west by the lower Moapa Valley of southern Nevada, and including Zion National Park in southwestern Utah. The phase, which was defined by Richard Shutler, Jr., is estimated to date ca. A.D. 700–900.

Sites comprise clusters of from one to five pithouses, smaller than those of the preceding Moapa Phase (q.v.), situated on low gravel benches adjacent to valley floors. Pottery is present, but it is sparse and usually plain. Decorations, when present, resemble the black-on-gray Lino designs of the Anasazi area farther east. Arrow points replaced dart points at the beginning of the phase, and a dependence on maize, beans, and squash, supplemented by collected wild foods and products of the hunt, is assumed.

SOURCES: Schroeder 1955; Shutler 1961.

Margaret M. Lyneis

MUD GLYPH CAVE, a cave in the mountains of west-central Virginia, containing curvilinear and rectilinear glyphs traced with the fingers through a veneer of mud spread over a rock face. Three radiocarbon dates on charcoal found at the base of the wall gave dates from A.D. 995 to 1060.

SOURCE: Faulkner n.d.b.

Keith T. Egloff

MULBERRY (or TAYLORS or MCDOWELL) MOUNDS, a complex comprising a village and three mounds of the Appalachian Mississippian period (ca. A.D. 1250–1670), located on the Wateree River in Kershaw County, in South Carolina. First reported by William Blanding in 1948, it was excavated by A. R. Kelly in 1952 and has been the subject of more recent studies by the University of South Carolina.

SOURCES: L. G. Ferguson 1974; Merry and Pekrul 1983; Sassaman 1983; DePratter 1985c; Depratter and Judge 1986.

Michael Trinkley

MUMMY CAVE, a stratified rockshelter in the Absaroka Mountains of northwestern Wyoming that was occupied ca. 7000 B.C.–A.D. 1200. Excavated by Wilfred Husted and Robert Edgar in 1966, it contained evidence of a long series of radiocarbon dated Altithermal Period cultures. All levels produced large quantities of mountain sheep (*Ovis canadensis*) remains.
SOURCES: McCracken 1978; Wedel et al. 1968.

George Frison

MUND SITE, a stratified, multicomponent site on the Mississippi River floodplain of the American Bottom in southwestern Illinois; excavated by archaeologists from the University of Illinois at Urbana-Champaign in 1979–1980. They identified deeply buried Archaic, Early Woodland, Middle Woodland, and Late Woodland remains and features, including a Mund Phase village comprising more than 160 pits and several structures—the earliest known example of horticulturally based village sedentism in the central Mississippi River Valley (ca. A.D. 500). Data from the Mund site led to the definition of both the Middle Woodland, Cement Hollow Phase (150–1 B.C.) and the Late Woodland, Mund Phase (A.D. 400–600).
SOURCES: Fortier et al. 1983; Bareis and Porter 1984:113–118.

Andrew C. Fortier

MUNKERS CREEK PHASE, a Middle Archaic culture unit in the Flint Hills and western Osage Plains of eastern Kansas, dating ca. 3500–3000 B.C.; characterized by large camps on the floodplains of major drainages and an artifact assemblage including diagnostic, chipped-stone, lanceolate points with parallel stems, knives, axes, gouges, and pottery effigies in the form of human heads. The William Young Site (q.v.) is the type site for the phase.
SOURCE: Witty 1982.

Thomas A. Witty, Jr.

MURPHY SITE, a large, Caborn-Welborn Phase (q.v.), Late Mississippian town in the southern portion of Posey County, in Indiana, partially excavated in 1898 by Clifford Anderson, under the direction of W. K. Moorehead, for the Robert S. Peabody Foundation. The substantial collection obtained, mostly from burials, represents the earliest work in Indiana for which notes and cultural materials survive. They now are curated by Indiana University.

SOURCES: Moorehead 1906; W. K. Adams 1949:25–47; Green and Munson 1978.

James H. Kellar

MUSQUEAM NORTHEAST SITE, a shell midden at the mouth of the Fraser River in southwestern British Columbia, excavated by C. E. Borden between 1972 and 1974, where more than 450 rare artifacts made of wood and bark (basketry, cordage, netting, wrapped stone sinkers, wooden wedges, bent-wood fishhooks, and other items) were collected from water-saturated deposits identified with the Locarno Beach Phase (q.v.). Radiocarbon dated to ca. 1000 B.C., these are among the oldest artifacts of their kind yet found on the Northwest coast. A later occupation containing no perishable items was attributed to the Marpole Phase (q.v.).

SOURCE: Borden 1976.

David J. W. Archer

N

NACO SITE, a location in southern Arizona where, in 1952, E. W. Haury discovered eight Clovis points (q.v.) among the bones of a mammoth. It was apparent that the points had tipped spears with which the mammoth was killed.
  SOURCES: Haury et al. 1953; Wormington 1957:53–55.

Edward B. Jelks

NAKNEK. an archaeological area on the Alaska Peninsula (see Brooks River–Naknek Drainage Sites).

NALAKIHU. See Citadel Pueblo/Nalakihu.

NAMU SITE, a site on the rugged central coast of British Columbia, occupied continuously or nearly continuously from ca. 7700 B.C. to the historic period. Partially excavated by J. J. Hester in 1969–1970 and by R. L. Carlson in 1977–1978, this is the oldest dated site on the British Columbia coast.
  SOURCES: Hester and Nelson 1978; R. L. Carlson 1979.

Roy L. Carlson

NANOOK SITE, a Middle Dorset Phase community, on Cape Tanfield (q.v.), Baffin Island; radiocarbon dated ca. 400 B.C.–A.D. 100, excavated by a Michigan State University team in 1966. Dwellings apparently were partially communal with a single common wall and several kitchen enclosures. The site evidently was abandoned in the first century A.D. when the Dorset population of the central region is thought to have declined. W. H.

Arundale's report on Nanook constitutes the most detailed description to date (1986) of a Middle Dorset site.
SOURCES: Arundale 1976; Maxwell 1973.

Moreau S. Maxwell

NAOMIKONG POINT SITE, a predominantly Middle Woodland site with a radiocarbon date of A.D. 430 ± 400, located on the shore of Whitefish Bay on Lake Superior in Michigan. The 296 ground-stone netsinkers found by George Quimby, James Fitting, and Donald Janzen during a series of excavations there between 1965 and 1967, plus a favorable natural setting and ethnohistoric descriptions of fishing in the region, combine to suggest that the site was a fishing station.
SOURCE: D. E. Janzen 1968.

Margaret B. Holman

NAPOLEON HOLLOW SITE, an open, stratified, multicomponent site at the west edge of the Illinois River Valley in Pike County, in Illinois; excavated by M. D. Wiant in 1979–1980. Buried in interfingered colluvial and alluvial deposits was a lengthy series of components attributed to these culture periods: Early Middle Archaic, ca. 5000 B.C.; Middle Archaic, two occupations at ca. 4300 B.C. and 3600 B.C., respectively; Late Archaic, Titterington Phase (q.v.), ca. 2000 B.C.; Early Woodland, Marion Phase, ca. 500 B.C.; Middle Woodland, Havana-Hopewell, ca. 0–A.D. 200; and Late Woodland, ca. A.D. 850. The site's long, well-dated sequence of Archaic (q.v.) hunter-gatherer occupations, coupled with a comparable sequence at the Koster Site (q.v.) some 50 kilometers downriver, refined regional culture history significantly and improved the understanding of both settlement variation and the evolution of sedentism. The Havana-Hopewell component, thought to have been functionally associated with burial-mound sites on nearby bluff crests, is comparable to Stuart Struever's conception of a Middle Woodland mortuary camp. In addition, the closely dated geologic strata documented important details of local Holocene depositional history.
SOURCES: Struever 1968; Wiant et al. 1983:147–164; Styles 1985; Wiant and McGimsey 1986.

Michael D. Wiant

NASE SITE, a stratified site occupied from Early Archaic through the Woodland periods, located on the Chickahominy River in the interior coastal plain of Virginia. Excavated in 1963 by H. A. MacCord and in 1978 by

S. M. Perlman, the site is well known for its outstanding series of Early and Middle Woodland strata and features.
SOURCES: MacCord 1964a; Mouer 1984.

Keith T. Egloff

NATCHITOCHES ENGRAVED POTTERY, the best known and most widely spread ceramic type of the historic Caddo Indians, occurring as resident ware at a dozen sites around Natchitoches, Louisiana, and as resident or trade ware northwestward along the Red River as far west as Montague County, in Texas, and Jefferson County, in Oklahoma. It occurs also on the Sabine and Ouachita rivers and as trade ware in Norteño Focus (q.v.) sites, at Natchez, at Tunica sites in southern Louisiana, at Mobile Bay, and on the Arkansas River at the Douglas and Greer sites. It is a finely potted, shell-tempered ware, chiefly in the form of bowls although some bottles and effigy vessels were made. It is usually buff to gray-brown in color but often is red-filmed. Exteriors are completely covered with curvilinear meanders and scrolls formed of plain and ticked lines filled with white or red pigment.
SOURCES: C. H. Webb 1945:63–63, pls. 11–14; Suhm et al. 1954:334–35; Harris and Harris 1980.

Clarence H. Webb

NATIVE POINT LOCALITY, a place on southeastern Southampton Island, Northwest Territories, where Dorset Phase (q.v.) sites T–1, T–2 (qq.v.), and T–3 were excavated by H. B. Collins in the 1950s.
SOURCES: Collins 1956a, 1956b.

Moreau S. Maxwell

NAUJAN SITE, a prehistoric village at Repulse Bay, north of Southampton Island at the base of the Melville Peninsula, Northwest Territories; the type site of the 13th-century A.D. Classic Thule Phase. Therkel Mathiassen defined the Thule culture (see Thule Phase) on the basis of twelve houses that he excavated there in 1925.
SOURCE: Mathiassen 1927.

Moreau S. Maxwell

NAYLIER PHASE, a pre-A.D.–750 phase of the Cohonina Province, Patayan Division, Hakataya Culture (qq.v.) in Arizona. Dwellings were round jacales with slab-lined firepits. Artifacts include platform and trough type metates, plus pottery types Deadman's Gray, Fugitive Red, intrusive plainware from

the Sinagua Province (q.v.), and Kana-a-Black-on-white, an Anasazi (q.v.) intrusion.
SOURCES: McGregor 1951, 1967.

Albert H. Schroeder

NAYUK COMPLEX. See Anaktuvuk Pass Sites.

NEAR IPIUTAK, a local, early aspect of the Ipiutak Phase (q.v.) at Point Hope and at a burial site near Kotzebue, Alaska. It is closely related to the Norton Tradition (q.v.) in the strict sense, or it may be considered transitional between Norton and Ipiutak within the context of a Norton Tradition (q.v.).
SOURCES: Larsen and Rainey 1948; D. D. Anderson 1978.

Donald W. Clark

NEBO HILL PHASE, an Archaic (q.v.) culture unit centered in northwestern Missouri and eastern Kansas, radiocarbon dated to ca. 2600–1000 B.C. Diagnostics of the phase include lanceolate and slightly stemmed Nebo Hill type projectile points, bifacial hoes and gouges, an elaborate ground-stone tool inventory (including three-quarter-grooved greenstone axes, rectangular celts, and ovate and rectangular manos), and fiber-tempered Nebo Hill pottery (q.v.). The Nebo Hill Phase is part of a post-hypsithermal, pan-Prairie Peninsula technocomplex that includes the Sedalia and Titterington phases (qq.v.) to the east and that descends from the late hypsithermal Munkers Creek and Helton phases (qq.v.) of eastern Kansas and western Illinois, respectively.
SOURCES: Shippee 1948; Kenneth Reid 1984a.

Kenneth C. Reid

NEBO HILL POTTERY, the earliest date ceramic type from midcontinental North America. Small, plain sherds of this fiber-tempered earthenware have been found in several sites in the lower Missouri River basin. The type was radiocarbon dated to ca. 1605 B.C. at the type site (23CL11); a series of thermoluminescence dates on associated heat-treated chert at another site clusters between 1620 and 1500 B.C. Nebo Hill sherds resemble contemporaneous fiber-tempered wares in the southeastern United States more closely than they do initial Early Woodland wares in the Midwest.
SOURCES: Kenneth Reid 1984a, 1984b.

Kenneth C. Reid

NEBRASKA PHASE, a unit of the Central Plains Tradition (q.v.) occurring along the Missouri River and a short distance up its tributaries in eastern Nebraska, western Iowa, and northeastern Kansas. Dating ca. A.D. 1050–1400, the phase is thought to be ancestral to the Coalescent Tradition (q.v.)

of North and South Dakota and, in turn, to the Arikara and/or Pawnee tribes. Sites contain square lodges with rounded corners that were erected in pits; these occur in lines, in loose clusters, or as isolated houses. Characteristic artifacts are utilitarian ceramics and tools of chipped and ground stone, bone, and shell. A mixed economy is indicated, featuring corn horticulture and hunting of a wide variety of game animals.

SOURCES: Strong 1935; Blakeslee and Caldwell 1979; Hotopp 1982.

Donald J. Blakeslee

NEHAWKA QUARRIES, an extensive series of pits dug to mine the fine gray-blue, speckled flint from the Virgil Series limestones in Cass County, in Nebraska. Flint from these quarries litters the prehistoric sites of many periods in southeastern Nebraska.

SOURCES: Blackman 1903, 1905; Strong 1935.

Patricia J. O'Brien

NEOESKIMO, a collective term designating all of the eastern Arctic cultures following the Paleoeskimo (q.v.): specifically, the Thule/Ruin Island (qq.v.), Historic Contact, and Modern Inuit phases. The living Inuit are known to be lineal descendants of the earliest Neoeskimo.

SOURCE: Maxwell 1976b.

Moreau S. Maxwell

NEOSHO FOCUS, a poorly understood, late prehistoric complex dominated by plain ceramics and other artifacts characteristic of the late Mississippian period (q.v.), occupying the eastern flanks of the Ozark Uplift along the Grand (or Neosho) River and its tributaries in northeastern Oklahoma. The small quantities of decorated pottery bear incised and punctated designs similar to those on Oneota (q.v.) pottery to the northeast but rare or absent in other complexes of eastern Oklahoma. Some suspect that the focus began earlier than late Mississippian times. Knowledge of this complex is based primarily on materials from the upper levels of rockshelters excavated by Works Progress Administration crews who did not leave complete descriptions of the sites.

SOURCE: Rohrbaugh 1984.

Charles L. Rohrbaugh

NESIKEP TRADITION, a culture unit of interior British Columbia thought by David Sanger, who initially defined it in 1969, to represent 7,000 years of cultural continuity. He concluded that the tradition replaced the Lochnore Complex (q.v.) ca. 5000 B.C. and continued with little change in subsistence pattern (mainly the use of anadramous salmon, land mammals, and certain plants), in lithic tools, or in stone-flaking techniques until culminating with the ethnographic Salish in modern times. A. H. Stryd later divided the Nesikep into an early segment (predating ca. 800 B.C. and characterized by a well-developed microblade industry) and a late segment (dating after 800 B.C. and marked by the absence of microblades and the presence of pithouses).

Several local and regional phases have been proposed for Late Nesikep, including the Kamloops Phase (q.v.) occupying the entire mid-Fraser and Thompson river drainages; the Lillooet and Nicola phases in the Fraser Valley near Lillooet; the Thompson and Shuswap phases (qq.v.) of the south Thompson River area; and the Chiliwist and Cassimer Bar phases of the Okanagan Valley.

Several researchers now question the existence of the continuity that is the basis for the Nesikep Tradition. The appearance, ca. 1400 B.C., of the pithouse and more sedentary winter settlements probably reflects an intensification in salmon usage and suggests that the ethnographic subsistence pattern does not have a 7,000-year antiquity.

SOURCES: Sanger 1969; Fladmark 1982b:95–156; Lawhead and Stryd n.d.

Arnoud H. Stryd

NEVILLE SITE, a fishing station on the Merrimack River, in New Hampshire, occupied for more than 8,000 years, beginning at least as early as the Middle Archaic period (i.e., before 5,700 B.C.). Peaks of occupation occurred between ca. 6000 and 4000 B.C. and following 3000 B.C. D. F. Dincauze's work at Neville provided the first dated evidence of Middle Archaic cultures along the New England coast; it stands as a model for chronology in southern New England.

SOURCE: Dincauze 1976.

James A. Tuck

NEVIN SITE, a Late Archaic site near Blue Hill, Maine containing well-preserved human burials of the Moorehead, or Maritime Archaic, tradition (qq.v.); excavated by D. S. Byers prior to World War II. Artifacts associated with the burials included harpoons, daggers, stone plummets, and other materials, some of which compare closely with artifacts from coastal sites farther north. Nevin is one of the few Archaic sites in Maine and Atlantic Canada with good organic preservation.

SOURCE: Byers 1979.

James A. Tuck

NEWARK EARTHWORKS, a group of mounds and embankments—originally extending over more than 500 hectares—located within Newark, Ohio, on tributaries of the Licking River. Embankment shapes included an octagon, a square, two large circles, many smaller circles, parallel connecting walls, and irregular walls. As recorded in 1848, wall height varied from near 5 to less than 1 meter. Artifacts found during the few recorded mound excavations are of the Hopewell Culture (q.v.). Recent studies have suggested that at least part of the complex, including the octagon, was constructed using a common unit of measurement and may have been designed to include lunar siting lines.

SOURCES: Atwater 1820:126–131, pl. 2; Squier and Davis 1848:67–72, 72n, pl. 25; Cyrus Thomas 1889; Dache Reeves 1936; Dragoo and Wray 1964; Hively and Horn 1982.

N'omi B. Greber

NEWBERRY CAVE, a dry cave located in the south-central Mojave Desert of southern California which apparently functioned as a magico-religious site. Split-twig figurines, similar to examples known primarily from the Grand Canyon region, were among the most numerous artifacts recovered during excavations conducted by G. A. Smith in the 1950s. Quartz crystals, wrapped feathers, sinew-wrapped bighorn sheep dung, and pictographs portraying bighorn sheep are suggestive of ritual activities. The predominant projectile-point forms are of the Elko series (q.v.). Eight radiocarbon assays on split-twig figurines and dart-shaft fragments range from ca. 1800 to ca. 1000 B.C.

SOURCES: G. A. Smith 1963; Davis and Smith 1981.

L. A. Payen

NEW CASTLE PHASE, a Middle Woodland culture unit proposed by K. D. Vickery on the basis of limited excavations at two "ceremonial centers": Mounds State Park and the New Castle Site (qq.v.), both in east-central Indiana. Five radiocarbon dates range between 60 B.C. and A.D. 230. The cultural assemblage, primarily derived from burials, is reminiscent of the more developed Hopewell assemblages in Ohio and Illinois, but in much attenuated form. J. B. Griffin has referred to this regional variant as "reluctant Hopewell."

SOURCES: Swartz 1971:135, 1976; Vickery 1979.

James H. Kellar

NEW CASTLE SITE, a Middle Woodland mound group identified with the New Castle Phase (q.v.), located at the juncture of the Big Blue and Little Blue rivers in Henry County, in east-central Indiana. Partially excavated by B. K. Swartz between 1965 and 1972, the site originally comprised ten circular enclosures and two burial mounds.

SOURCES: Lilly 1937; Swartz 1976.

James H. Kellar

NEWINGTON SITE, a stratified midden on the Mattaponi River in the interior coastal plain of Virginia, tested by R. W. Winfree in 1966. It contained a rich assortment of artifacts, particularly ceramics, that span the entire Woodland period.

SOURCE: Winfree 1969.

Keith T. Egloff

NEW MELONES SITES, a series of nearly 700 archeological sites—approximately 100 of which were excavated by various researchers between 1968 and 1985—that were impacted by the New Melones Reservoir on the Stanislaus River in the central Sierra Nevada foothills, in California. Data from the sites document a record of cultural activity spanning some 10,000 years, ranging from Paleoindian hunting camps to 19th-century boom towns of the Gold Rush.
SOURCE: Moratto et al. 1986.

Michael J. Moratto

NEW RIVER PHASE, a term proposed by D. S. Phelps for the archaeological expression of Early Woodland culture in the southern coastal region of North Carolina. No components of this hypothetical phase, which should data ca. 1000–300 B.C., have been excavated as of 1987; its only manifestation is the occurrence of New River Series pottery (q.v.) in the area. However, the term has been adopted as an interpretive and organizational aid by researchers.
SOURCES: Loftfield 1976; Phelps 1983:31.

Billy L. Oliver

NEW RIVER POTTERY SERIES (1), an inclusive term for all shell-tempered pottery in the New and Tennessee river drainages of southwestern Virginia. Dating ca. A.D. 1200–1650, the globular and bowl-shaped vessels occasionally have strap handles and net-impressed, cordmarked, or plain surfaces. The series represents a complex mixture of wares that developed from, and were continually affected by, the Mississippian Tradition (q.v.) of Tennessee and the Fort Ancient Tradition (q.v.) of the Ohio River Valley.
SOURCES: Clifford Evans 1955; Holland 1970; K. T. Egloff n.d.b.

Keith T. Egloff

NEW RIVER POTTERY SERIES (2), a coarse, sand-tempered ceramic with simple-stamped, cordmarked, fabric-impressed, net-impressed, or plain surfaces; a diagnostic type of the Deep Creek Phase (q.v.) that occupied the Tidewater area of southern coastal North Carolina ca. 1000–300 B.C. D. S. Phelps recently subsumed this series under the Deep Creek Pottery Series (q.v.) in a scheme for standardizing pottery typology in coastal North Carolina.
SOURCES: Loftfield 1976:149–154; Phelps 1983.

Billy L. Oliver

NIGHTFIRE ISLAND SITE, a multicomponent site on the edge of lower Klamath Lake just south of the Oregon-California line which was occupied at varying levels of intensity between ca. 4000 B.C. and A.D. 1600. It was excavated by LeRoy Johnson, Jr., in 1966 and later was studied and reported by C. G. Sampson. Changes in the pattern of human occupation over time were correlated with climatic fluctuations; the latter were recorded in a bristlecone pine climatic curve for the White Mountains of California. Changes in the lake-marsh setting, including rising and falling lake levels, were correlated with changes in the role of the site as a base for exploiting local resources. First a waterfowling station, it later became a semipermanent pithouse village, then a small fishing village, and finally was abandoned shortly before the beginning of historical times. Situated in modern Modoc territory, the site records a long in situ evolution of the ethnographically known lake-marsh-adapted Klamath-Modoc lifeway.

SOURCE: Sampson 1985.

C. Melvin Aikens

NIGHT WALKER'S BUTTE VILLAGE, a 19th-century Hidatsa village site in North Dakota that was occupied ca. A.D. 1750–1800. It was excavated in the 1950s by personnel of the Inter-Agency Archeological Salvage Project, who assigned it to the Knife River (q.v.) Phase on the basis of its ceramic and lithic artifact types.

SOURCE: W. R. Wood 1986.

Patricia J. O'Brien

NIOBRARA (or GRAHAM) JASPER, a caramel to dark-brown chert that occurs as lenticular nodules in the Upper Cretaceous Series of the Niobrara Chalk formations in western Kansas and Nebraska. This material was used extensively by Central Plains prehistoric peoples, from Paleoindian (q.v.) to protohistoric times.

SOURCE: Wedel 1985.

Patricia J. O'Brien

NODENA PHASE. See Nodena Site.

NODENA SITE, a mound group associated with a central plaza and a chunky field in northeastern Arkansas; the entire complex form a rectangular arrangement of 6.2 hectares. It is the type site for the Nodena Phase and also for the Nodena type projectile point and Nodena Red and White pottery. The site dates to the first half of the phase, whose total existence spanned the period ca. A.D. 1400–1650. The Upper Nodena site was extensively investigated between 1897 and 1941 by an avocational archaeologist, Dr. James Hampson, who invited the universities of Alabama and Arkansas to work there as well. Excavations by D. F. Morse in 1973 produced large quantities of corn and beans. There are 61 known sites of the

Nodena Phase, which probably was the Province of Pacaha, visited by the De Soto expedition in 1541.
SOURCES: D. F. Morse 1973; Morse and Morse 1983.

Dan F. Morse

NOGALES CLIFF HOUSE, a Gallina Phase (q.v.) site about 3 kilometers west of Llaves in north-central New Mexico, situated in a rincon on the west side of Spring Canyon some 150 meters above the stream. Dendrodated to A.D. 1239–1267, the site contained eleven contiguous, rectangular houses of typical Gallina Phase style built on two levels, together with at least 20 storage cists. F. C. Hibben excavated the site in 1939 and recovered numerous perishable items.
SOURCES: Hibben 1940; Blumenthal 1940:10–13; Pattison 1968.

Herbert W. Dick

NOLANDS FERRY SITE, a multicomponent, Late Woodland (ca. A.D. 900–1600) village surrounding a central plaza, located near the confluence of Tuscarora Creek and the Potomac River, in Maryland. Tests in 1978 by the Archeological Society of Maryland under the supervision of the Maryland Geological Survey, produced cord-marked pottery similar to the Page Cord-marked (q.v.) type from the main occupation.
SOURCES: D. W. Peck 1980:2–18; Kavanagh 1982.

Stephen R. Potter

NOLAN POINT, a dart-point type dating ca. 2650–2150 B.C.; a diagnostic trait of the Clear Fork Phase (q.v.) in central Texas, whence it ranges westward to the lower Pecos River region, occurring there in the later part of the Eagle Nest Phase. It has a slender, leaf-shaped blade; rounded to squarish shoulders; and a mildly expanding, alternately beveled stem with a straight to slightly convex base. Nolan is associated with the early proliferation of burned-rock middens on the Edwards Plateau during the Middle Archaic period.
SOURCES: Suhm and Jelks 1962; Prewitt 1981; Turner and Hester 1985.

Elton R. Prewitt

NORTEÑO FOCUS, an 18th- and 19th-century culture unit in northern Texas and southern Oklahoma, defined in 1961 by L. F. Duffield and E. B. Jelks, which has been identified with the five tribes of the historic Wichita Confederacy: Tawakoni, Yscani, Waco, Kichai, and Wichita proper. A number of Norteño sites investigated by several archaeologists have yielded a large number of distinctive artifacts, both of Wichita and of European (especially French) origin.

SOURCES: Duffield and Jelks 1961:69–75; Bell et al. 1967; E. M. Davis 1970.

James E. Corbin

NORTH BAY CULTURE, a northern tier Middle Woodland expression, dating ca. 500 B.C.–A.D. 500, defined on the basis of several sites on Wisconsin's Door County peninsula and offshore islands. The culture seems to have been only marginally influenced by cultures in southern Wisconsin and Illinois. Primary communication was to the east, through the Upper Great Lakes, and northward into Canada. North Bay shares certain affinities with the Laurel Culture (q.v.) and probably represents a maritime adaptation.

SOURCE: Mason 1967.

David Overstreet

NORTH BAY WARE, a kind of pottery in the form of thick-walled, conoidal vessels with dentate-stamped, linear-stamped, incised, and pseudo-scallop-shell decorations. Associated with the so-called northern tier Middle Woodland developments in Wisconsin, Minnesota, Michigan, and Ontario, the ware has greater affinities with ceramic styles to the north and east than with those to the south.

SOURCE: Mason 1967.

David Overstreet

NORTH CREEK GRAY WARE, a variety of Tusayan (q.v.) Gray Ware pottery comprising plain, black-on-gray, and corrugated types, found in the Virgin Province (q.v.) of the western Anasazi Culture (q.v.) in Arizona, Utah, and Nevada. Thought to date to Pueblo I–II times (ca. A.D. 700–1150), the ware includes all local sand-tempered gray pottery in which the sand is dominated by quartz grains.

SOURCES: Colton 1952; Dalley and McFadden 1985.

Margaret M. Lyneis

NORTHERN ARCHAIC TRADITION, a broad culture unit characterized by notched and oblanceolate projectile points, notched-pebble implements, and a very high frequency of flakes beveled to form simple end scrapers. It was defined initially by D. D. Anderson at Onion Portage (q.v.) in the Denbigh Flint Complex (ca. 2200 B.C.) and postdates the American Paleo-Arctic Tradition. Early and late phases (Palisades and Portage) were recognized; both lack a microblade industry.

Elements of Northern Archaic technology dating between 4000 B.C. and A.D. 100, and in some cases associated with microblades, occur in a region extending westward from the Mackenzie River to the western and northern coasts of Alaska. Some generalists have expanded the tradition to include

the modern archaeological cultures of the Athapaskan Tradition (q.v.). The tradition comprises many different local phases and may be viewed as a loose and varying congeries of horizon and period styles.
SOURCES: D. D. Anderson 1968; Dumond 1977.

Donald W. Clark

NORTHERN PLATEAU (or CANADIAN PLATEAU), a subarea of the Plateau Culture Area (q.v.) defined by culture traits as well as by geography.
SOURCE: V. F. Ray 1939.

Frank C. Leonhardy

NORTHERN SIDE-NOTCHED POINT, a large projectile point with a straight to concave base and deep, comma-shaped side notches. Found mostly around the northern fringe of the Great Basin, they date ca. 5000–2000 B.C. and are a diagnostic trait of the Menlo Phase in Surprise Valley, California.
SOURCES: O'Connell 1975; Heizer and Hester 1978.

Robert G. Elston

NORTHERN SINAGUA PROVINCE, a province of the Sinagua Division, Hakataya Culture (qq.v.) that occupied the plateau south of the Little Colorado River in Arizona, between Wupatki and Flagstaff on the west and the Winslow area on the east and encompassing Anderson Mesa on the south. In the mid–1060s, a large area between Flagstaff and Wupatki was blanketed with a heavy ash fall from the volcanic eruption that created Sunset Crater. This formed an excellent moisture-retaining soil that attracted neighboring farming people of the Anasazi, Mogollon, and Hohokam cultures (qq.v.). Bringing new cultural elements with them, they transformed the local Northern Sinagua pattern into a blend that later entered the Verde Valley to the south and ultimately reached the Gila-Salt region beyond.
SOURCE: Colton 1946.

Albert H. Schroeder

NORTHWEST MICROBLADE TRADITION, the first construct assimilating all the northwestern interior microblade industries into one culture unit, developed in the 1950s by R. S. MacNeish on the basis of the Campus, Pointed Mountain, and Little Arm sites (qq.v.) in Alaska, the District of Mackenzie, and the Yukon Territory, respectively. The tradition encompasses a broad temporal range; most component assemblages date between 4000 and 500 B.C. Among the numerous sites ascribed at least in part to the tradition are Bezya (q.v.) in northwestern Alberta; Canyon and Little Arm (qq.v.) in the southern Yukon Territory; Pointed Mountain and Fisherman Lake (qq.v.) in the southwestern District of Mackenzie; Mt. Edziza (q.v.) in northern British Columbia; and Healy Lake (q.v.) and Tuktu (see Anaktuvuk Pass Sites) in Alaska.

Some have questioned whether the diverse assemblages containing microblades constitute a single cultural tradition, and some have defined other traditions to account for parts of MacNeish's Northwest Microblade Tradition (see Northwest Microblade Tradition).

SOURCES: MacNeish 1954, 1964.

Donald W. Clark

NORTHWEST RIVERINE TRADITION, an integrative concept used by G. R. Willey in his monumental *An Introduction to American Archaeology* in an effort to characterize all of Plateau prehistory between A.D. 500 and 1850 as it was known in the early 1960s. Although taught in many classrooms, this extremely generalized concept has not been used seriously by archaeologists working in the Plateau area.

SOURCE: Willey 1966:404–407.

Frank C. Leonhardy

NORTON MOUNDS, a group of seventeen burial mounds built during the first two centuries A.D., located along the Grand River in Kent County, in Michigan. Excavations by Richard Flanders in 1963–1964 disclosed graves with lavish offerings having similarities to Illinois Hopewell (q.v.) artifacts.

SOURCE: Griffin et al. 1970.

Charles E. Cleland

NORTON TRADITION PHASE, a major Paleo-eskimo (q.v.) archaeological culture, extending from the Mackenzie River delta in the Northwest Territories around the coast of Alaska to the Gulf of Alaska, and dating from 500 B.C. or earlier to ca. A.D. 1100. It was defined initially by J. L. Giddings, Jr., mainly on the basis of his work at the Iyatayet Site (q.v.) on Norton Sound, Alaska. Typical attributes of the tradition include well-made points, tips (end blades), and side blades for arming weapons; relatively thin linear- and check-stamped pottery; highly distinctive, discoidal scraper bits; broad, flat labrets; toggling harpoon heads of somewhat archaic design; and numerous prosaic implements such as notched-pebble weights and crude stone lamps.

Better known Norton sites include Cape Prince of Wales, Cape Nome, Unalakleet, Nunavak Island, Chagvan Bay, and Platinum; local phases include the Smelt Creek–Weir Falls phases of the Brooks River–Naknek area and the Lakes Phase of the Ugashik drainage. The extent to which the Norton Tradition was ancestral to any of the Eskimos is open to interpretation, but current belief holds that the Yup'ik Eskimo south of Norton Sound are descendants of Norton people.

SOURCES: Larsen and Rainey 1948; Giddings 1964, 1967; Bockstoce 1979; Dumond 1981; Shaw and Holmes 1982.

Donald W. Clark

NORWOOD CHERT, a light to dark gray, banded, tabular chert that outcrops at a single locale along Lake Michigan in Antrim County, in Michigan. It is the predominate chert type used for tool production by prehistoric peoples from the Straits of Mackinac along the western side of lower Michigan as far south as the Grand River Valley. Geologically, this chert is associated with the Petoskey limestone of the late-middle Devonian Traverse Group.
SOURCE: Cleland 1973; Leudtke 1976.

Charles E. Cleland

NOWLIN MOUND, a large Adena (q.v.) mound formerly located in Dearborn County, in southeastern Indiana that contained a number of log tombs and a modest quantity of artifacts typical of the period. G. A. Black's excavation of this mound in 1934–1935 was one of the first systematic explorations of an Ohio Valley burial mound, and his report still stands as a model of methodological description.
SOURCE: Black 1936.

James H. Kellar

NUKLEET SITE, a location at Cape Denbigh (q.v.), Alaska on the Bering Sea coast that has produced an important assemblage of artifacts related to the Thule Tradition or Neoeskimos (qq.v.). Excavated in 1948–1949 by J. L. Giddings, Jr., and by Wendell and Helen Oswalt, the site was occupied during the greater part of the second millennium A.D. The term Nukleet sometimes is used to designate a particular form of the Thule culture that occurs on the Alaskan coastal mainland south of the Bering Strait, exclusive of the Gulf of Alaska region.
SOURCE: Giddings 1964.

Donald W. Clark

NUKUSUSUTOK SITE, a late Pre-Dorset Phase (q.v.) site near Nain, Labrador, excavated in the 1920s by the Torngat Project (q.v.). A house with a well-defined mid-passage (q.v.) is seen as a link with Independence II (q.v.) of the High Arctic. The excavators identified the site with the terminal Pre-Dorset Phase (ca. 700 B.C.), but a radiocarbon date places the site about 450 years earlier.
SOURCE: Cox 1978.

Moreau S. Maxwell

NUNGUVIK SITE, a pithouse community dating from the early Dorset Phase (ca. 500 B.C.) to the late Thule Phase (ca. A.D. 1200) (q.v.) situated on Navy Board Inlet, North Baffin Island. Excavations by Guy Mary-Rousseliere between the 1960s and 1980s revealed a sequence of houses that demonstrated stylistic shifts within the Dorset continuum. Although the nonlithic assemblage from House 46 was typically Early Dorset, the lithic inventory contained 9 percent spalled burins, a condition unlike that at other Dorset sites save those on southern Baffin Island. Caribou were the predominant source of food.

SOURCES: Mary-Rousseliere 1976, 1979a, 1979b.

Moreau S. Maxwell

NUULLIT (or NUGDLIT) SITE, a Late Dorset–Early Thule (ca. A.D. 1000–1200) (qq.v.) village comprising 60 Thule Phase houses on northwestern Greenland; excavated in the 1940s by Erik Holtved. Holtved defined a Nugdlit Phase comprising the earlier occupation (unassociated with Norse trade materials), presuming it to precede the Ruin Island Phase (q.v.) and therefore the earliest eastern Thule expression. Questioning that interpretation, K. M. McCullogh combined the entire occupation into a single Ruin Island Phase representing the earliest Neoeskimo manifestation in the eastern High Arctic.

SOURCES: Holtved 1954; McCullogh 1986.

Moreau S. Maxwell

O

OAKALLA PHASE, the terminal (ca. 3050–2650 B.C.) Early Archaic man-ifestation in central Texas, defined by E. R. Prewitt in 1981. Sites are small and contain burned-rock middens and hearths lined with flat rocks. Diag-nostics are triangular projectile-point types Baird and Tortugas (q.v.) (some-times both are simply called Early Triangular) and gouges. There are major components at the Wounded Eye, Greenhaw, and John Ischy sites.
SOURCES: Sorrow 1969:18–19, 23; Weir 1979:29; Luke 1980:43–44; Prewitt 1981:78–79.

Frank A. Weir

OAK GROVE CULTURE, the earliest (ca. 5500–3000 B.C.) of the three prehistoric phases in the Santa Barbara region of coastal southern California. Distinguishing traits are semisubterranean pithouses, extended burials with red ocher, millingstones, and crude projectile points.
SOURCES: D. B. Rogers 1929; Moratto 1984:124–127.

Michael J. Moratto

OAK HILL PHASE, the earliest manifestation of Iroquois culture in New York state, dating to the 13th and 14th centuries and characterized by large, often fortified villages whose occupants were horticulturalists. Their artifacts foreshadow those used by historically known Iroquois people. Social and political organization underwent changes during this period which even-tually led to the formation of the League of the Five Nations known from historic times.
SOURCE: Ritchie 1980.

James A. Tuck

OAK ISLAND PHASE, a late prehistoric (ca. A.D. 800–1700) culture unit south of the Neuse River in southern coastal North Carolina. Distinctive traits include Oak Island Series pottery (q.v.), rectangular houses, refuse

pits, and ossuaries. The phase is considered to be contemporaneous with the Colington Phase (q.v.) to the north.
SOURCES: Loftfield 1976; Phelps 1983:49.

Billy L. Oliver

OAK ISLAND POTTERY SERIES, a shell-tempered ware with cordmarked, net-impressed, fabric-impressed, or plain surfaces, affiliated with the Oak Island Phase (q.v.) of southern coastal North Carolina and dating ca. A.D. 800–1700. This pottery sometimes is referred to as "hole tempered" because the particles of shell originally in the paste have decomposed, leaving empty spaces in their stead. The White Oak and Colington pottery series (qq.v.) are similar and are probably related.
SOURCES: South 1976:20–21; Loftfield 1976; Phelps 1983.

Billy L. Oliver

OBSIDIAN HYDRATION DATING, a method of inferring how long ago a piece of obsidian was fractured by measuring the amount of progressive alteration to the fracture surface caused by the absorption of water from the environment. Factors influencing the hydration rate include time, temperature, and the chemical composition of the obsidian.
SOURCE: Michels and Bebrich 1971.

R. E. Taylor

OCCANEECHI SITE, the apparent location of Achonechy Town, visited by John Lawson in 1701; situated on the Eno River near Hillsborough, North Carolina. J. L.Coe's tests between 1938 and 1941 were inconclusive; however, R. S. Dickens, Jr., later discovered burials at the site aligned in a cemetery-like pattern, along with the remains of structures and palisades, all associated with abundant European trade items.
SOURCE: Dickens et al. 1985.

Billy L. Oliver

OCEAN BAY TRADITION, a culture unit on the south coast of Alaska spanning the period from ca. 4000 B.C. to some time after 1000 B.C. Stone was worked exclusively by chipping at the beginning of Ocean Bay I (the earlier of the two phases within the tradition); tools of ground and polished slate appeared later in the phase and almost completely supplanted chipped-stone tools during Ocean Bay II at some localities. On the Pacific side of the Alaska Peninsula, the later phase, which there is called Takli Birch, extended into a more recent period than did Ocean Bay II and took on characteristics of the Kachemak Tradition (q.v.).

Ocean Bay sites are unobtrusive compared to the large, deep village-midden sites typical of the region, which led to their relatively late discovery. The principal excavated sites are Sitkalidak Roadcut in the Kodiak Islands

and a Takli Island site near the Alaska Peninsula. Other components have been dug on Afognak Island, Uganik Island, and Karluk (q.v.) in the Kodiak group, at Pedro Bay on Lake Iliamna, at the Brooks River Strand Phase in the Naknet drainage (q.v.), and at Kaflia on the Alaska Peninsula.
    SOURCES: G. H. Clark 1977; D. W. Clark 1979, 1982; Dumond 1981.

Donald W. Clark

OCHOA PHASE, the final phase of the Eastern Extension Sub-Province (q.v.) sequence of the Jornada Province, Mogollon Culture (qq.v.), dating ca. A.D. 1350/1400–1450. The phase's geographical distribution is greatly contracted from that of previous phases, being restricted to the southeastern corner of New Mexico south of Hobbs.
    Structures include both pithouses and small pueblos of from one to several rooms with slab-based, presumably jacal-type walls of poles and adobe. Ceramics are dominated by the locally made Ochoa Brown and Ochoa Corrugated types. Most of the intrusive pottery types of the earlier Maljamar Phase (q.v.) are still present, though in smaller numbers. Artifacts of note include basally notched Garza type arrow points, numerous small end scrapers, and an occasional Harahey type knife (a four-edged, diamond-shaped, alternately beveled form typical of the Panhandle Aspect [q.v.] to the northeast). Hunting and gathering formed the economic base as bison clearly became more important. The Ochoa Phase is best represented at the Merchant and Andrews Lake sites.
    SOURCE: Leslie 1979.

R. N. Wiseman

OCMULGEE SITE, a Mississippian (q.v.) mound center dating ca. A.D. 900–1100, located on the Macon Plateau in central Georgia. In the 1930s, A. R. Kelly and others excavated extensively there, investigating several mounds, exploring portions of the associated village area, and uncovering an elaborate earthlodge and an early historic period trading post. An apparent lack of continuity with earlier cultures in the region has led some researchers to suggest that Ocmulgee represents an intrusion by a Mississippian population from the west, but present (1986) evidence for this is inconclusive.
    SOURCES: A. R. Kelly 1938; Fairbanks 1946, 1956.

Paul A. Webb

OCONTO SITE, one of the most thoroughly reported cemeteries of the Old Copper Culture (q.v.), located in northeastern Wisconsin. Early radio-

carbon dates from the site of around 4500 B.C. have stimulated much discussion regarding the age of copper metallurgy in Wisconsin.
SOURCE: Ritzenthaler and Wittry 1957.

David Overstreet

OGDEN-FETTIE SITE, a large Middle Woodland habitation center and
group of more than 30 burial mounds at the confluence of the Illinois and
Spoon river valleys in central Illinois, dating ca. A.D. 1–250. A trench en-
circles the central mounds. The Dickson family excavated several of the
mounds and opened the Ogden Mound and other area mounds for public
viewing in the 1920s. The universities of Illinois and Chicago also dug there
in 1929 and 1931. Ogden-Fettie is the type site for the Ogden Phase of the
Middle Woodland Havana Hopewell culture, as well as for related ceramic
types.
SOURCES: Cole and Deuel 1937:171–181; P. J. Munson 1967.

Alan D. Harn and Duane Esarey

OJO DE AGUA, a name that has been applied to two separate sites in
Sonora: one on a bluff overlooking the floodplain of the upper Rio Sonora
in north-central Sonora; the other, in the northeastern part of the state
immediately south of Fronteras. The former, excavated by R. A. Pailes in
1975, is a typical site of the later Rio Sonora Culture (q.v.), with numerous
foundations of rectangular surface structures and incised-punctated pottery
with red painted zones. One of two sites dominating this part of the river
valley, it is estimated to date ca. A.D. 1000–1500.

The other Ojo de Agua site has above-ground adobe structures, abundant
pottery, and clear affiliations with the Chihuahuan Province—so much so
that it has been described as "peripheral Casas Grandes" (q.v.).
SOURCES: Sauer and Brand 1931; Pailes 1980, 1984; Braniff Cornejo 1985.

Richard A. Pailes

OKAK 3 SITE, a late Dorset Phase (q.v.) settlement on the Labrador coast
midway between Hebron and Nain, excavated in the 1970s by the Torngat
Project (q.v.). Running through the middle of a paved pithouse that was
radiocarbon dated to ca. A.D. 1000 were two parallel rows of upright rock
slabs, demonstrating the persistence of such mid-passage features on the
Labrador at a relatively late date.
SOURCE: Cox 1978.

Moreau S. Maxwell

OKIALIVIALUK (or OKIVILIALUK) SITE, a settlement dating from classic
Thule Phase (q.v.) times to the Historic Contact period, situated near Lake
Harbour; excavated by a Michigan State University team in 1977. Semi-
subterranean houses and qarmat (q.v.) demonstrated a series of changes

between early Thule and modern times. Later houses indicated a longer persistence of bowhead whale hunting than elsewhere in the eastern Arctic. One of the earliest Thule houses contained a small wooden figurine depicting a Norse Viking.

SOURCES: Sabo and Sabo 1978; Sabo III 1981.

Moreau S. Maxwell

OKVIK PHASE, an early Eskimo manifestation on the Asian side of the Bering Sea; noted for its ivory carvings of human torsos and roughly executed, freehand incised art that is similar to Old Bering Sea (q.v.) Style I. It is thought to have preceded other Old Bering Sea phases, but its age and sequential position have not been conclusively established. Okvik, the type site, is located on one of the tiny Punuk islands outlying St. Lawrence Island. Extensively mined by St. Lawrence Islanders for the ivory art trade, it was excavated in 1934 by O. W. Geist and described in 1941 by F. G. Rainey.

SOURCES: Rainey 1941; Arutiunov and Sergeev 1964.

Donald W. Clark

OLD BERING SEA PHASE, an early (ca. A.D. 1–500) Eskimo phase on the Asian side of the Bering Sea (including St. Lawrence and the Diomede Islands); famous for elaborate curvilinear-incised decorations carved on ivory implements. Recognized in 1926 by Diamond Jenness, who called it the "archaic Bering Sea culture," it later was verified through the excavations of H. B. Collins at Gambell (q.v.) on St. Lawrence Island and elsewhere. Implement styles, technology, and pottery of the phase contrast markedly with those of the contemporary late Norton and Ipiutak phases (qq.v.) on the Alaskan mainland. Okvik (q.v.) art often is classified with the earliest Old Bering Sea style.

SOURCES: Jenness 1928; Geist and Rainey 1936; Collins 1937; Collins et al. 1973.

Donald W. Clark

OLD COPPER, a term initially applied to early metallurgy in Wisconsin, which may be as old as 7000 B.C.—the oldest metallurgy in North America and perhaps in the Old World as well. Prehistoric peoples annealed and cold-hammered 99 percent pure copper nuggets from the Lake Superior basin into a wide range of artifacts: projectile points, woodworking tools, needles, awls, and various ornaments. The densest concentration of these artifacts is in eastern Wisconsin; however, copper in raw and finished form was traded throughout the eastern United States.

Recently, the term *Old Copper Culture* (q.v.) has become synonymous with a regional Late Archaic mortuary complex.
SOURCE: Ritzenthaler 1957b.

David Overstreet

OLD COPPER CULTURE, one of a widespread set of Late Archaic burial practices that has been distinguished on the basis of region, "diagnostic" artifacts, and raw materials. Regionally associated with eastern Wisconsin, where it was first defined, and with Michigan's western Upper Peninsula, the culture, which dates ca. 3000–1000 B.C., is distinguished by copper artifacts—projectile points, knives, socketed adzes and axes, needles, awls, fishing gear, bracelets, and beads—placed in burials.
SOURCES: Ritzenthaler and Wittry 1957; Quimby and Spaulding 1957.

Margaret B. Holman

OLD CORDILLERAN CULTURE, an early, widespread, generalized culture that probably was ancestral to most archaeological complexes of western North America; initially defined by B. R. Butler in 1961. First thought to be coeval with the Clovis Culture (q.v.) of the Great Plains at ca. 9500–9000 B.C., it later was determined to be much younger. The concept was important for the controversy it generated.
SOURCES: B. R. Butler 1961, 1965b.

Frank C. Leonhardy

OLD CROW FLATS LOCALITIES, places along the Old Crow River in the northern Yukon Territory where gravel bars have yielded numerous fossilized bones of Pleistocene fauna that eroded from their original locations in the river bluffs, together with both apparent and unequivocal bone artifacts. Included among the latter are bones with cut marks, mammoth bone cores, facetted or polished bones (not necessarily artifacts), and bones which may have been fractured by humans. The attribution of artifact status to these modified bones, which have been dated in the range of 60,000–26,000 B.C. or older, has been questioned by many archaeologists. Occasional definitive stone, bone, and antler implements have been found on the gravel bars, but those that have been dated are of Holocene age.
SOURCES: Jopling et al. 1981; Irving and Harington 1973; Bonnichsen 1979; Morlan 1980.

Donald W. Clark

OLD NUULLIT (or GAMMEL NUGDLIT) SITES, a series of Paleoeskimo (q.v.) components radiocarbon dated to ca. 2500–2000 B.C., lying 9 to 11 meters above sea level on Wolstenhom Fjord, north of Thule in northwestern Greenland. Eigil Knuth, who excavated the sites, considers the artifacts he found there to be older than those of Independence I (q.v.), to which,

however, they are related), making them the oldest cultural materials known for the eastern Arctic. Lithic artifacts are smaller and more expertly made than those of Independence I, and they lack the lateral stem notching characteristic of Independence I lithics. Dwellings lack mid-passages.
SOURCE: Knuth 1977–78.

Moreau S. Maxwell

OLD RIVER PERIOD. See Galveston Bay Focus.

OLD STONE FORT, a stone enclosure in central Tennessee of long antiquarian interest. Excavations in 1966 by Charles Faulkner confirmed a Middle Woodland (ca. A.D. 100–300) affiliation and similarities to other enclosures of the same period.
SOURCES: Squier and Davis 1848; Joseph Jones 1876; Faulkner 1968.

Jefferson Chapman

OLD WHALING PHASE, an early (ca. 1300 B.C.) whaling culture unit known from a single site at Cape Krusenstern (q.v.), Alaska, that was discovered and excavated by J. L. Giddings, Jr., in 1959. Evidence of whaling consists in accumulations of baleen whale bones and large, relatively broad flint blades that may have tipped whaling harpoons. Among other artifacts are large points, end scrapers, and knives, many specimens of each group with hafting notches on the sides. Temporally, the phase falls between the Denbigh Flint and coastal Choris phases (qq.v.), but its implement styles show a close relationship to neither. There are possible ties, however, with a contemporary site on Wrangel Island in the Soviet Arctic. After the phase's decline, whaling seems to have disappeared from the area until whaling with harpoons appeared much later.
SOURCES: Giddings 1962a, 1962b, 1966, 1967; Giddings and Anderson (in press).

Donald W. Clark

OLIVER PHASE, an agriculturally based, Late Woodland/Upper Mississippian (ca. A.D. 1000–1100) cultural expression in the middle White River Valley in central Indiana. Its most prominent element is a ceramic complex that includes minor amounts of Fort Ancient (q.v.) material, especially curvilinear guilloche decoration, and corded/punctated/collared vessels more typical of cultures to the north, e.g. Oneota (q.v.).
SOURCES: J. B. Griffin 1943a; Dorwin 1971.

James H. Kellar

OLSEN-CHUBBOCK SITE, a bison-kill site of the Firstview Complex (q.v.) in east-central Colorado near the Kansas border where, in 1958, J. B. Wheat excavated the remains of about 190 *Bison bison occidentalis*. The type site

for the complex with a radiocarbon date of 8200 ± 500 B.C., it provided important insights into Paleoindian bison utilization and butchering practices.
    SOURCE: Wheat 1972.

                                                              Patricia J. O'Brien

O'MALLEY SHELTER, a site on the upper reaches of a Colorado River tributary in southeastern Nevada, containing Archaic, Sevier/Fremont, Anasazi (qq.v.), and late prehistoric components that span the last 7000 years. Excavated in 1969–1970 by D. B. Madsen and D. D. Fowler, the site helped confirm the early artifact sequence in the eastern Great Basin. It also helped date the spread of Paiute/Shoshoni-like artifacts throughout the Great Basin.
    SOURCE: Fowler et al. 1973.

                                                              David B. Madsen

ONE GUN PHASE, a late (A.D. 1700–1750) archaeological culture in southern Alberta that appears to represent an intrusive population movement from the Middle Missouri area. The main evidence for its existence is the Cluny Site (q.v.), an earthlodge village in the Bow River valley east of Calgary, but there also are a number of possibly affiliated open campsites which typically contain undercut storage pits and distinctive artifacts (pitted manos, grinding slabs, scapula knives, and pottery) that are similar to Middle Missouri forms. There is some evidence to suggest that the One Gun phase represents a splinter Hidatsa group.
    SOURCES: Forbis 1977; Byrne 1978.

                                                              William J. Byrne

ONEOTA TRADITION, a long-standing (ca. A.D. 900–1500) culture unit centered in southern Wisconsin and northwestern Illinois consisting of several phases: the Silvernale Phase (ca. A.D. 1100), restricted to the margins of the Mississippi River in southwestern Wisconsin; the Green Bay Phase, Wisconsin, the northernmost reported Oneota cluster whose adaptive strategy and chronology are poorly known; the Grand River Phase, an intermediate development in east-central Wisconsin dating ca. A.D. 1150–1300; the Lake Winnebago Phase (ca. A.D. 1350–1500), perhaps the climax of Oneota development in Wisconsin; the Koshkonong Phase an early (ca. A.D. 1000) development in southeastern Wisconsin which, in terms of ceramic design, shared some features with Mississippian cultures to the south; and the Orr Phase, a protohistoric/historic expression probably associated with the historic Ioway tribe. The Oneota Tradition encompasses a series of

highly successful horticultural-hunting-gathering groups who controlled major waterways for more than five centuries.
SOURCES: Overstreet 1978; R. L. Hall 1962.

David Overstreet

ONION FIELD SITE, a Late Woodland village on the Roanoke River in the southern Piedmont of Virginia, where H. A. MacCord in 1969 found storage and hearth pits, human burials, postmolds, and a thick midden containing Dan River (q.v.) pottery.
SOURCE: J. A. Williams 1978.

Keith T. Egloff

ONION PORTAGE SITE, a location on the Kobuk River in northeastern Alaska that was occupied for at least 9,000 years (up to the early 18th century A.D.); excavated by J. L. Giddings, Jr., in 1941 and by Giddings and D. D. Anderson in the 1960s. There are cultures represented at the site with both interior and coastal affiliations, including the Akmak Phase of the American Paleo-Arctic Tradition (the earliest phase represented at Onion Portage), several phases of the Northern Archaic Tradition, several Paleoeskimo phases (Denbigh Flint, Choris, Ipiutak), the Itkillik Complex, and the Arctic Woodland Culture facies of the Thule Tradition (qq.v.).
SOURCES: Giddings 1966, 1967; D. D. Anderson 1968, 1970a, 1970b.

Donald W. Clark

OPTIMA FOCUS, a late prehistoric unit in the Oklahoma panhandle, described in 1950 by Virginia Watson, on the basis of cultural materials from the Stamper site, as a northern variant of the Panhandle Aspect (q.v.). Stamper and related sites now are considered affiliates of the Antelope Creek Phase (q.v.), and the term Optima Focus has become obsolete.
SOURCES: Watson 1950; Duffield 1964; Lintz 1978, 1984b.

Christopher Lintz

ORAIBI PUEBLO, perhaps the oldest continuously occupied site in the United States, located on the tip of Hopi Third Mesa in northeastern Arizona where, according to tradition, people of the Shungopavi Pueblo Bear Clan settled ca. A.D. 1150. Visited by Coronado's men in 1540, it was the site of a large Spanish Franciscan mission and church built ca. A.D. 1629 and burned by Indians in 1680, at which time the Spaniards were either killed or expelled.

Oraibi was of traditional western Hopi style, with parallel rows of houses from one to four stories high and thirteen or more kivas in or near the wide areas (streets) between the rows. Archaeologial evidence suggests that there were several episodes of immigrants moving into the village between A.D.

1150 and 1700. It was the largest Hopi pueblo in 1906 with a population of 1200 or more, but it had declined to less than 100 people by the 1930s.
SOURCES: Colton 1932; Hargrave 1932a; Titiev 1944; F. H. Ellis 1961.

Michael B. Stanislawski

ORANGE CULTURE, a Late Archaic culture (ca. 2000–500 B.C.) in eastern and central Florida, which evolved into the St. Johns Culture (q.v.). It is distinguished by fiber-tempered pottery.
SOURCES: Goggin 1952:43–47; Bullen 1955b, 1972; Milanich and Fairbanks 1980:152–157.

Jerald T. Milanich

ORANGE POTTERY SERIES, a fiber-tempered ceramic dating between 2000 and 1000 B.C., found along the St. Johns River in northeastern Florida. The earliest varieties occur as plain, flat-bottomed bowls and pans. Later, incised and punctated decorations were added, most commonly in diamond, chevron, and herringbone patterns.
SOURCE: Jenkins et al. 1986.

John A. Walthall

ORCOQUISAC PERIOD. See Galveston Bay Focus.

ORO GRANDE SITE, a thin but extensive midden on a terrace of the Mojave River northwest of Victorville in San Bernardino County, in southern California. Excavation in 1978 disclosed a Late Period occupation characterized by Cottonwood type projectile points, shell beads of southern California coastal origin, and the absence of pottery. Six radiocarbon determinations on associated hearth features bracket the period A.D. 800–1300. A human and animal trackway dated to ca. 3000 B.C. was discovered in river sediments underlying the midden.
SOURCE: Rector et al. 1983.

L. A. Payen

ORR PHASE. See Oneota Tradition.

OSHARA TRADITION, an Archaic hunting and gathering culture that occupied the Four Corners area of the Southwest from ca. 5500 B.C. to ca. A.D. 400. It has been divided into five phases on the basis of projectile-point form, artifact assemblages, and inferred socioeconomic organization. These phases, which trace the development of sedentary Anasazi (q.v.) agriculturalists from nomadic bands of hunters and gatherers, can be summarized as follows: In the Jay (ca. 5000–4800 B.C.) and Bajada (ca. 4800–3300 B.C.) phases (qq.v.) of Early Archaic affiliation, small nomadic bands subsisted by foraging and hunting a wide range of plants and animals, following a relatively unstructured annual schedule. During the San Jose Phase (q.v.), dating ca. 3300–1800 B.C., a moister climate and improvements in food processing allowed more intense, more efficient utilization of local resources. The population was still organized in small bands, and in some areas there was a population increase. Maize horticulture was introduced and practiced on a limited basis during the Armijo Phase (q.v.) of ca. 1800–800 B.C. In some areas, this produced a small seasonal food surplus and a concomitant aggregation of the population in the fall, or in the fall and winter, which led to greater complexity of socioceremonial interaction. During the En Medio Phase (q.v.) of ca. 800 B.C.–A.D. 400, which encompassed the Basketmaker II Phase of the Anasazi Culture, maize horticulture increased in importance, although hunting and gathering were still the mainstays of the economy. Increased population pressure and the associated need to broaden and better structure the economic base led to a well-developed seasonal round and probably to a well-established socioceremonial cycle.

SOURCES: Irwin-Williams and Tomkins 1968; Irwin-Williams and Haynes 1970; Irwin-Williams 1973, 1979.

Cynthia Irwin-Williams

OSSUARY, a mass human burial in a prepared pit or vault; a form of burial practiced by many prehistoric North American peoples, especially east of the Rocky Mountains.

OTARRE STEMMED POINT, the outmoded name for a kind of projectile point that now is included within the Small Savannah River Stemmed type (q.v.).

SOURCES: Keel 1976:194–196; Oliver 1981.

Billy L. Oliver

OTOWI (or POTSUWI'I) RUIN, a Rio Grande Anasazi pueblo of the Classic Period (q.v.), dating ca. A.D. 1250–1600, located near Los Alamos, New Mexico, an ancestral village of modern San Ildefonso Pueblo. Partially excavated in 1915 by Mrs. L. L. W. Wilson, it comprised five masonry houseblocks of about 450 ground-floor rooms and as many as 250 upper-story rooms; ten kivas, including two within houseblocks; and a reservoir. Associated ceramics were Santa Fe Black-on-white; Wiyo Black-on-white; Biscuitware (q.v.) types A, B, and C; Potsuwi'i Incised; Sankawi Black-on-cream; and intrusive Rio Grande Glaze (q.v.) groups A, B, D, E, and F. Tree-ring dates for Otowi of 1414–1491 cover only part of the time range ascribed to the pottery types.

SOURCES: Mrs. L. L.W. Wilson 1916; Hewett and Dutton 1953.

Stewart Peckham

OVER FOCUS, a unit of the Midwestern Taxonomic System (q.v.) dating ca. A.D. 1000–1300, which includes sites like Brandon, Mitchell, and Twelve

Mile Creek (qq.v.) on the Big Sioux and lower James rivers in southeastern South Dakota. Distinctive traits of the focus are its rectangular houses and the Middle Mississippian influences reflected in its ceramic styles.
SOURCE: Wedel 1961.

Patricia J. O'Brien

OVERHANGING MANO, a hand-held grinding stone that is longer than the width of the flat-slab metate with which it is used. The metate's lateral edges are rounded, and the mano is shaped so that its grinding surface conforms to, and hangs over, the metate's edge. While such manos occasionally may have been shaped by use, most were carefully shaped by design. Overhanging manos and their corresponding metates are found throughout central Mesoamerica, as well as in southern Sonora and in Desert Hohokam sites (qq.v.) in the Papagueria, Arizona.
SOURCES: Ekholm 1942:197; Pailes 1972:287–292, pl. 12.

Richard A. Pailes

OVERPECK POTTERY, a type that appears to have been coeval with Riggins Fabric Impressed (q.v.) at ca. A.D. 900–1600 but differs from that type in having cordmarked surfaces and more complex decorative motifs. Defined at the Overpeck site (q.v.) on the Pennsylvania side of the lower Delaware River, it occurs throughout southeastern Pennsylvania, New Jersey, Delaware, and northeastern Maryland—an area in which it is the latest aboriginal ceramic type.
SOURCE: Forks of the Delaware Chapter 14 1980.

Ronald A. Thomas

OVERPECK SITE, a multicomponent site on the west bank of the Delaware River in southeastern Pennsylvania, comprising several Woodland (q.v.) occupations, and estimated to date ca. A.D. 800–1600. Excavations by the Forks of the Delaware Chapter, SPA, unearthed human burials, settlement features, and numerous artifacts. The Overpeck Pottery (q.v.) ceramic category was defined on the basis of pottery taken from this site.
SOURCE: Forks of the Delaware Chapter 14 1980.

Ronald A. Thomas

OWASCO CULTURE, the immediate precursor of Iroquois culture in New York state, dating ca. A.D. 1000–1300. Characteristic traits are ceramics impressed with cord-wrapped paddles, obtuse-angle smoking pipes with pronounced straight stems, and an economy making use of both locally available natural resources and corn, beans, and squash. Unfortified upland

villages of up to 3 acres consisted of elongated houses that were ancestral to the Iroquois longhouse.
SOURCE: Ritchie 1969:272–300.

James A. Tuck

OWENS VALLEY BROWN WARE, a type of plain brown pottery made by coiling and scraping techniques; characteristic of the later prehistoric/ protohistoric period in east-central California (southeastern Sierra and western Great Basin) after A.D. 1000–1300. It was first recognized and described in 1951 by H. S. Riddell, Jr., at the Cottonwood Creek Site (q.v.) in Owens Valley (q.v.), California.
SOURCES: Riddell 1951; Moratto 1984.

L. A. Payen

OWENS VALLEY LOCALITY, a large, comparatively well-watered valley situated between the highest section of the Sierra Nevada (to its west) and the White-Inyo Mountains (to its east) in eastern California. The valley was occupied historically by the Owens Valley Paiute, who, in comparison to other aboriginal groups in the Great Basin, were notable for their high population densities, sedentary settlement pattern, and complex sociopolitical organization. R. L. Bettinger, who conducted archaeological surveys and excavations in the valley from 1972 to the present, has documented a series of important adaptive changes that occurred there between 2500 B.C. and the present, culminating in an adaptation comparable to that noted ethnographically by J. H. Steward. Bettinger's research suggests that the pine nut, the most important food source of the Owens Valley Paiute, was not exploited extensively by prehistoric peoples until after ca. A.D. 600. This and other major adaptive changes appear to contradict the concept that the Desert Culture (q.v.) maintained a stable long-time subsistence pattern.

Bettinger has defined four phases for the Owens Valley:

Phase	Diagnostic Traits	Dates
Clyde Phase	Little Lake Series projectile points	2500–1200 B.C.
Cowhorn Phase	Elko Series projectile points (q.v.)	1200 B.C.–A.D. 600
Baker Phase	Rose Spring and Eastgate projectile points	A.D. 600–1300
Klondike Phase	Cottonwood Series and Desert Side-Notched projectile points (q.v.)	A.D. 1300–historic

SOURCES: Steward 1933; Bettinger 1975, 1976, 1977.

Robert L. Bettinger

OXBOW COMPLEX, a Prairie Archaic complex in Saskatchewan that is identified by its side-notched projectile points, which are similar to points at Plains sites in the United States: e.g., the Simonsen, Turin, and Logan

Creek sites (qq.v.). The type site, Oxbow-Dam, which dates ca. 3250 B.C., was excavated in 1956 by R. W. Nero and B. A. McCorquodale.

SOURCE: Nero and McCorquodale 1958.

Patricia J. O'Brien

OZARK BLUFF-DWELLER CULTURE, a culture defined by M. R. Harrington in the early 1920s on the basis of investigations at several rockshelters in southwestern Missouri and northwestern Arkansas, and viewed by him as a long-lived adaptation to the region, combining hunting, agriculture, fishing, and gathering of natural foods. He also defined Pre-Bluff-Dweller and Post-Bluff-Dweller cultures from stratigraphic sequences in some of the rockshelters.

One of the culture's more outstanding technical achievements was basketry, well-preserved examples of which were found in dry rockshelter deposits, and which Harrington compared to the works of the Basketmaker III Culture (q.v.) in the American Southwest. Because of correspondences in ceramics, he also speculated that the Bluff-Dweller Culture either was ancestral to the Caddoan cultures of southern Arkansas or became amalgamated with the Caddoan populations. Present-day archaeologists attribute the Bluff-Dweller Culture to Woodland and Mississippian (qq.v.) peoples of the period ca. A.D. 700–1500.

SOURCES: M. R. Harrington 1924a, 1924b; Scholtz 1975; J. A. Brown 1984b.

George Sabo III

OZARK ROCK-ART SITES, a series of pictograph and petroglyph sites in Arkansas and Missouri, attributed to Woodland and Mississippian peoples of ca. A.D. 700–1500 which provide unique, vivid representations of their artistry and symbolism. Ideological symbols include circles, snakes, crosses, masks, and human figures whose posture and accoutrements suggest that most were created for ceremonial use. Hunting-magic symbols are few. Along the western fringes of the Ozarks occurs a different rock-art tradition, perhaps reflecting Plains influence, that displays an anthropomorphically centered iconography.

SOURCE: Fritz and Ray 1982.

Gayle J. Fritz

OZETTE VILLAGE SITE, a settlement at Cape Alava on the Pacific coast in Washington, the westernmost point in the coterminous United States, occupied for some 2000 years into modern times. In the historic period, it was the southernmost of five villages of the Makah, a Nootkan-speaking people closely related to the Nitnat of Vancouver Island.

R. D. Daugherty conducted intensive excavations at Ozette between 1966 and 1981 with field crews made up largely of students from Washington State University and members of the Makah Tribe. One part of the village had been buried by mud flows at several different times over the past 800 years. Excavations there in a level dating to the 16th century A.D. produced more than 50,000 artifacts, the remains of numerous houses, and masses of faunal material. Most of the 179 categories of artifacts were made from normally perishable substances (wood, bark, and grasses), and were in an excellent state of preservation, owing to the protective environment created by the mud slides. Included were over 3000 woven objects, 7 looms and items of weaving equipment, 115 wooden bows, 124 wooden shafts for whaling and sealing harpoons, hundreds of fishhooks, over a thousand wooden trays and bowls, and numerous examples of artistic carving in wood. These objects, in all stages of manufacture, provided important information on manufacturing techniques.

SOURCES: Kirk and Daugherty 1974; J. P. Friedman 1975; Edward Friedman 1976; Mauger 1978; Gleeson 1980; Wessen 1982; DePuydt 1983; Gill 1983; Heulsbeck 1983; Samuels 1983.

Richard D. Daugherty

P

PACE MCDONALD SITE, a multicomponent site on the middle Neches River drainage in eastern Texas, comprising two Caddoan mounds, an associated village area, six possible borrow pits, and an apparent minor Archaic occupation. Tests in both mounds by A. T. Jackson in 1933 revealed that the smaller, circular mound is composed primarily of ash, while the larger, elliptical mound evidently resulted from multiple construction events and may cover the remains of at least one submound structure. Originally, both Early and Late Caddoan occupations were thought to be represented, but more recent studies of the collections from the site suggest a predominantly transitional, Middle Caddoan occupation, dating ca. A.D. 1250–1450.

SOURCES: Jackson n.d.a.; Newell and Krieger 1949:194–196; Gilmore 1973:74–75, 155–158; Kleinschmidt 1982:198–239.

Jan Guy

PADRE PHASE, an expression of the Northern Sinagua Tradition of the Flagstaff Province (qq.v.) in north-central Arizona during the period ca. A.D. 1130–1200. Sites of the phase are very numerous over the entire Flagstaff area, which suggests a population increase as well as geographical expansion. Square or rectangular, masonry-lined pithouses were the dominant dwelling style, although pithouses of other shapes and pueblos of from one to five rooms also occur. Occasionally, a pithouse's masonry walls extended above the ground surface. Roofs were supported either by timbers placed across the tops of the walls or by a system consisting of a center ridge pole resting on two centrally located posts. Entry was via a roof hatch rather than through the ramp, which is typical of earlier Sinaguan pithouses. Ventilators usually were present. Although there was considerable range in size, most pithouses were small (about 15 square meters of floor area). Some kivas have been reported that are like a standard pithouse except for a raised bench at one end. Extremely large community rooms or great kivas also are known from some sites.

Burial forms include extended and flexed inhumations as well as primary and secondary cremations. These occur randomly at small sites, but there are formal cemeteries at larger sites, in which inhumations and cremations occupy separate areas. Pottery was the same as that of the preceding Angell and the succeeding Elden phases, consisting of the paddle-and-anvil-produced Winona Brown, Angell Brown, and Sunset Plain types and their redware, smudged, and polished varieties. Trade pottery was primarily late Pueblo II period types from the Kayenta and Winslow Anasazi areas.

SOURCES: Colton 1939b:39–40, 1946:270–272, 312–314; McGregor 1941b, 1965; Schroeder 1961c; T. A. Lee, Jr. 1962.

Peter J. Pilles, Jr.

PAGE CORDMARKED WARE, a limestone-tempered, Late Woodland pottery, first described by J. B. Griffin in 1944 from sherds found at the Keyser Farm Site (q.v.) in the Shenandoah River Valley of northwestern Virginia; later found in the upper James River drainage and in the New River drainage in West Virginia. A diagnostic attribute is a cord-decorated, thickened rim or collar.

SOURCES: Manson et al. 1944; Geier and Boyer 1982; Maslowski and King 1983.

Keith T. Egloff

PAINT LICK MOUNTAIN PICTOGRAPHS, a series of paintings made with red ocher on a rock face at Paint Lick Mountain in southwestern Virginia; the only known surviving pictographs in Virginia. The stylized figures apparently represent a deer, a turtle, eagles, an arrow, people, and the sun. According to Garrick Mallery, the pictographs were first reported in 1766 and were visited and described by a Dr. W. J. Hoffman in 1886.

SOURCE: Mallery 1893.

Keith T. Egloff

PAISLEY CAVES, a series of small caves on a Pleistocene beach terrace east of Summer Lake in south-central Oregon, excavated by L. S. Cressman in 1937 and 1938. He found sandals and other artifacts buried under Mazama volcanic ash (q.v.) that was deposited ca. 4700 B.C. Well below the volcanic ash in one cave were found several rudely flaked fragments of stone points and scrapers in association with an apparent hearth and a few horse and camel bones. At the time these finds were made, it was commonly held that the Great Basin Desert Culture was quite recent, dating perhaps 1000 to 2000 years ago. The Paisley Caves gave the first strong indication that humans were present in the northern Great Basin at a much earlier period, before the time of the Mazama eruption (then estimated to date between

5000 and 10,000 years ago) when now-extinct Pleistocene horses and camels still roamed the region.

SOURCES: Cressman et al. 1940; Cressman 1942; Cressman 1966.

C. Melvin Aikens

PALEOESKIMO, a term adopted at a conference in 1973 to designate all of the prehistoric phases that preceded the entry of Thule/Ruin Island (qq.v.) people into the eastern Arctic region at the beginning of the second millennium A.D.

SOURCE: Maxwell 1976a.

Moreau S. Maxwell

PALEOINDIAN, a term applied to a late Pleistocene (ca. 11,000–4000 B.C.) cultural tradition whose remains are spread thinly across North America from the western fringes of the Great Plains to the Atlantic, between southern Canada and northern Mexico. The term also has been applied to early archaeological finds in South America. In North America, the name Paleo-American sometimes has been used synonymously.

Paleoindians hunted large, now-extinct mammals, especially the Columbian mammoth, *Bison antiquus*, horses, and camels. Although evidence is scant, they surely also ate nuts, seeds, roots, and other vegetal foods. Their physical type is poorly known owing to scarcity of skeletal remains.

Lanceolate, chipped-stone spear points of several distinctive types are the most diagnostic Paleoindian tools. Other characteristic artifacts include stone knives fashioned from parallel-sided blades, small snub-nosed end scrapers, tiny graver points, and long pointed tools of uncertain use made of elephant ribs or ivory.

Earlier sites are mostly places where animals were killed and butchered; campsites are rare. Typical kill sites are bison jumps (q.v.), where herds were driven over cliffs or into ravines, and small lakes where animals were killed from ambush when they came to drink.

Three major Paleoindian cultures have been defined: Clovis (ca. 11,000–9000 B.C.), Folsom (ca. 9000–7000 B.C.), and Plano (ca. 7000–4000 B.C.) (qq.v.). Each culture has distinctive types of tools, especially projectile points.

SOURCES: F. H. H. Roberts, Jr. 1940, 1945; Suhm et al. 1954:16–18; H. M. Wormington 1957; Krieger 1964:51–59; Frison 1978; Shutler 1983.

Edward B. Jelks

PALISADE RUIN, a briefly occupied (A.D. 1310–1314) Coalition Period (q.v.) pueblo on the northwestern frontier of the Tewa Basin Province (q.v.), on the Rio Chama west of Abiquiu, New Mexico. Investigated in 1958 by Stewart Peckham, the U-shaped, 60-room block of adobe-walled dwelling rooms was fortified with a pole palisade on the east side of its plaza. A

semisubterranean grinding room and a round, underground kiva were its other principal features. Decorated pottery types found at the sites were Santa Fe Black-on-white and two variants of Wiyo Black-on-white.
SOURCE: Peckham 1981.

Stewart Peckham

PALMER CORNER-NOTCHED POINT, a small, Early Archaic (ca. 10,000–8000 B.C.) projectile point with a straight, heavily ground base and deeply serrated blade edges. Widely distributed in the eastern United States, it often is found in association with small, snub-nose end scrapers virtually identical to scrapers found at many late Paleoindian sites.
SOURCES: Coe 1964:67; Oliver 1985.

Billy L. Oliver

PALMETTO BEND SITES, a series of sites on the lower Navidad and Lavaca rivers on the central Texas coast. Investigations by several archaeologists, mostly in the 1970s, revealed prehistoric and historic remains that constitute the primary systematic data base for the archaeology of the Matagorda Bay region.
SOURCE: Texas Archeological Survey Staff 1981.

Lawrence E. Aten

PALUGVIK SITE, the principal archaeological site of Prince William Sound, south-central Alaska, excavated by Frederica de Laguna in 1933 following surveys in 1930. Together with information from other sites, it provided the basis for a prehistory of the Chugach Eskimo. Although the base of this Kachemak Tradition (q.v.) site has been dated to ca. A.D. 200, the upper levels are not dated, and further work in the region will be required to fully document Chugach ethnogenesis.
SOURCE: de Laguna 1956.

Donald W. Clark

PANDALE POINT, a Middle Archaic dart-point type dating ca. 5050–1950 B.C., considered diagnostic of the Eagle Nest Phase of the lower Pecos River region of southwestern Texas. Its slender blade is alternately beveled; the weak shoulders are usually rounded; and the expanding stem with weakly concave to weakly convex base also is alternately beveled, but opposite to that of the blade. The combination of beveling on blade and stem creates a distinctive propellerlike twist of up to 90 degrees to the overall point. Pandale shares attributes with the culturally related Nolan (q.v.) and Travis types of central Texas.

SOURCES: Suhm and Jelks 1962; D. S. Dibble n.d.a.; Turner and Hester 1985.

Elton R. Prewitt

PANHANDLE ASPECT, a unit of the Midwestern Taxonomic System (q.v.) dating ca. A.D. 1000–1500, defined by A. D. Krieger to include a number of complexes in the panhandle areas of Texas and Oklahoma, e.g., the Antelope Creek and Optima foci (qq.v.) whose architecture was Pueblo inspired, but whose other material culture was Plains-like.

SOURCE: Wedel 1961.

Patricia J. O'Brien

PAPAGUERIA PROVINCE, a vast stretch of arid desert south of the lower Gila River in southern Arizona and extreme northwestern Sonora. It was occupied from Paleoindian times to the historic period, when the Papago and their western neighbors, the Sand Papago, lived there. Population densities were always low because of the marginal nature of the environment. The lack of permanent streams dictated reliance on floodwater farming or on irrigation using water from wells and potholes.

Gila Pueblo undertook an extensive survey of the province in 1929 to locate the western and southern boundaries of the "red-on-buff" (Hohokam [q.v.]) culture. In the 1940s the Arizona State Museum conducted research on the Papago Indian Reservation, including excavations at Valshni Village and Jack Rabbit Ruin.

The Hohokam occupation of the province appears to have been closely related to that of the Tucson Basin Province (q.v.). The pottery tradition, lumped under the general rubric of Sonoran Brown Ware, consistently parallels the painting styles of the Tucson Basin. Fortified hill sites (Cerros de Trincheras [q.v.]) are similar to those in the Gila Bend Province (q.v.). Ball courts and platform mounds are infrequent or absent in all parts of the province except at its northeastern fringe along Santa Rosa Wash. Village sites usually are smaller and more scattered than in the Phoenix and Tucson basins.

Current reconstructions indicate that Hohokam settlements in the Papagueria Province began ca. A.D. 600 during the last Pioneer Period (q.v.) and continued through the A.D. 1200s. E. W. Haury contrasted the lower levels of cultural activity of these "Desert Hohokam" people to their "River Hohokam" relatives who occupied the better-watered valleys to the north and east. There is evidence suggesting a Hohokam-Papago continuum in the province.

SOURCES: Gladwin and Gladwin 1930a; Scantling 1939; Haury 1950; Withers 1973; Masse 1980a; McGuire and Schiffer 1982.

David E. Doyel and John S. Cable

PAQUIME PHASE. See Casas Grandes Province.

PARACHUKLA (or PALLACHUCOLA) SITE, a late 17th-century Appalachicola (Lower Creek) village on the Savannah River at Stokes Bluff, South Carolina, where heavy erosion in the early 20th century exposed burials and "house floors." In 1937, Marmaduke Floyd recorded several burials and collected artifacts from the site, including pottery and European trade items.
SOURCES: J. R. Caldwell 1948, 1952.

Michael Trinkley

PARKIN SITE, the type site for the Parkin Phase and for pottery type Parkin Punctate, located in northeastern Arkansas and dating ca. A.D. 1400–1650. It probably is the site of the capital of the Province of Casqui, visited by the De Soto expedition in 1541. Covering 7 hectares, it comprises seven earthen mounds—the largest standing 6.5 meters high—and a large, rectangular, 3-meter-deep midden. It is bordered on three sides by a wide ditch and on the fourth by the St. Francis River. Besides typical protohistoric artifacts, a 16th-century glass bead and a brass hawk bell have been found at the site. It is the best-preserved example of a post-A.D. 1400 Native American town in the Mississippi Valley.
SOURCES: H. A. Davis 1966; Klinger 1977; P. A. Morse 1981; Morse and Morse 1983.

Phyllis A. Morse

PATAYAN DIVISION, a division of the Hakataya Culture (q.v.) comprising three provinces—Cerbat, Prescott, and Cohonina (qq.v.)—located in the plateau country of northwestern Arizona between the Flagstaff area and the Colorado river. Earlier sites appear to have been small, short lived, and seasonally occupied. They contain the remains of oval and rectangular jacales, commonly outlined with rocks.
SOURCE: Colton 1939a.

Albert H. Schroeder

PATRICK PHASE, a terminal Late Woodland unit, dating ca. A.D. 600–800, first defined in the American Bottom of southwestern Illinois at the 1971 Cahokia Ceramic Conference. Earlier, it was included within the Early Bluff culture; however, in the American Bottom, Early Bluff has been subdivided into three Late Woodland phases: Rosewood, Mund (q.v.), and Patrick. The Patrick Phase is characterized by courtyard villages, keyhole structures, small-post basin structures, earth ovens, cordmarked jars with interior lip impressions, and a complex subsistence system based on horticulture. The first known occurrence of maize and of the bow and arrow in southwestern Illinois was in this phase.

SOURCES: Bareis and Porter 1984; Fortier et al. 1984; J. E. Kelly et al. 1984.

Andrew C. Fortier and Charles J. Bareis

PATRICKS POINT SITE, a deep shell midden in Humboldt County on the northwestern coast of California, where extensive excavations by the University of California, Berkeley, in 1948 disclosed four cultural levels spanning the period from ca. A.D. 1400 to historic times. Bone and shell artifacts found there were especially important in defining late period ritual activities and changes in sea-mammal hunting techniques.

SOURCE: Elsasser and Heizer 1966.

Michael J. Moretto

PAUGVIK SITE, a large 19th-century Eskimo settlement on Bristol Bay at the mouth of the Naknek River on the Alaska Peninsula that has attracted the attention of Aleš Hrdlička, Helge Larsen, and D. E. Dumond, who tested it, respectively, in 1931, 1948, and 1961. J. W. VanStone and Dumond carried out substantive excavation there in 1985. Ethnohistorical and archaeological research on this rich site is yielding information on local native responses to technological, religious, cultural, and administrative changes during the Russian and American contact periods.

SOURCE: Dumond 1981.

Donald W. Clark

PAVIK PHASE. See Brooks River-Naknek Drainage Sites.

PAW PAW SITE, a terminal Middle Woodland or early Late Woodland village dating ca. 700–1000, located on the Potomac River in the Appalachian Mountains of western Maryland. Discovered in 1983 by C. D. Curry and tested the same year by M. Kavanagh, this single-component site produced a unique ceramic assemblage showing some similarities to the Buck Garden type of the Ohio River drainage.

SOURCES: Curry 1983; Kavanagh 1984.

Stephen R. Potter

PAYSON PHASE, a phase of the East Verde Province of the Sinagua Division, Hakataya Culture (qq.v.) in Arizona, dating ca. A.D. 1150–1300.

Sites include large and small compound centers, plus rural farmsteads with water-control devices.
SOURCE: Redman and Hohmann 1986.

Albert H. Schroeder

PAYUPKI SITE, a pueblo on Hopi Second Mesa in northeastern Arizona, built ca. A.D. 1690–1696 by Rio Grande Tewa refugees and abandoned ca. 1742 upon their return to the Rio Grande. It was a stone-built, hollow-square, central-plaza site of from one to two stories with about 200 rooms, two or more kivas, and a population of from 300 to 400. It is particularly noteworthy for its rectangular Rio Grande style settlement pattern and its Payupki Polychrome pottery, with densely packed geometric designs on Rio Grande jar and bowl forms, which became the typical pottery of the Hopi Province (q.v.) ca. A.D. 1700–1800. The site has been partially excavated by unknown persons.
SOURCES: Victor Mindeleff 1891:59–60; E. C. Adams 1979:59–73.

Michael B. Stanislawski

PEACHTREE SITE, a multicomponent mound and village site in the Appalachian Summit region of southwestern North Carolina, where excavations by J. D. Jennings in 1933–1934 revealed a more or less continuous occupation from the Mississippian, Pisgah Culture (q.v.), dating ca. A.D. 1000–1450, through the historic Cherokee period.
SOURCES: Setzler and Jennings 1941; Dickens 1976.

Paul A. Webb

PEALE POINT SITE, a Thule Phase (q.v.) settlement comprising eleven houses, occupied at intervals from the beginning of the 13th century A.D. to the 18th century; loated 13 kilometers west of the town of Frobisher Bay, Baffin Island. Douglas Stenton excavated the site in 1981 and found abundant game remains from aglu (q.v.) seal hunting and from whale hunting. One well-stratified house documented the changes from a sealed Classic Thule midden to a later Post-Classic occupation. Stenton hypothesized that full winter occupation of the site was doubtful because it lies more than 100 kilometers north of the food-rich winter floe edge (q.v.).
SOURCE: Stenton 1983.

Moreau S. Maxwell

PEARSON SITE, an important component of the Norteño Focus (q.v.) near the mouth of Hooker Creek, on the floodplain of the Sabine River in Rains County, in Texas, tentatively identified as a village of the Tawakoni or another tribe of the Wichita Confederacy. Investigations there by L. F.

Duffield and E. B. Jelks in 1960 produced a collection of artifacts, both Indian and European, dating ca. A.D. 1780–1800.
SOURCE: Duffield and Jelks 1961.

James E. Corbin

PEASE BRUSHED-INCISED POTTERY, a widespread Caddo (q.v.) ware found in northwestern Louisiana, southwestern Arkansas, and eastern Texas; a major type of the late Alto (q.v.), Haley, and Bossier (q.v.) foci, dating primarily to the Caddo II–III period (ca. A.D. 1200–1500). A culinary ware tempered with clay grit, or sometimes with bone, it features tall jars with barrel-shaped bodies and moderate to high recurved rims. The buff to dark-gray exterior surfaces are totally covered by vertical or horizontal bands of incising or brushing, which are enclosed by applique ridges or lines formed of nodes or punctations. Fire clouds and soot staining are frequent.
SOURCES: C. H. Webb 1948, 1983; Suhm and Jelks 1962:119–20.

Clarence H. Webb

PEBBLE TOOL, a cobble with a crude cutting edge produced by direct, hard-hammer percussion, generally with unifacial flaking that is confined to one end or side of the artifact; the dominant tool type at a number of early sites in the Pacific Northwest which is thought to be late Pleistocene or early post-Pleistocene in age.
SOURCES: Borden 1968b; Grabert 1979.

David J. W. Archer

PECOS CLASSIFICATION. See Southwestern Classification Systems.

PECOS MISSION, the Spanish mission-convento complex of La Nuestra Señora de Los Angeles de Porciuncula, located at Pecos National Monument, New Mexico. It was established between A.D 1617 and 1621, razed during the Pueblo Revolt of 1680, partially rebuilt later, and permanently abandoned ca. 1812. Investigations between 1915 and 1971 by several archaeologists guided the preservation of buildings, resolved the conflicting historical accounts of church architecture, and provided insights into the process of missionizing local Indians.
SOURCES: A. C. Hayes 1974; Kessell 1979.

Larry V. Nordby

PECOS (or CICUYE) PUEBLO, a major pueblo in northern New Mexico; the focus of A. V. Kidder's pioneering effort in Southwestern stratigraphic excavation from 1915 to 1929. He selected it because he believed that it would link early Anasazi (q.v.) and historical populations.

About A.D. 1300, atop an earlier building, a preplanned structure, termed the Quadrangle or North Pueblo, which completely surrounded an enclosed plaza, was built. Patently defensive in design, the four- to five-story Quadrangle proper had approximately 245 ground-floor rooms that were arranged in suites from three to six rooms deep radiating outward from the plaza. Galleries or covered walkways surmounted the terraced interior. Ground-floor rooms had no exterior doorways; access to the complex was controlled at three or four gates, each of which had an adjoining, rectangular "guardhouse" kiva. Twenty-two circular, subterranean kivas, used at various times in the life of the pueblo, are scattered both inside the Quadrangle's plaza and across the surrounding trash middens. In addition to the Quadrangle itself, there are an unknown number of discontiguous roomblocks.

During the more than five centuries of occupation before its abandonment in 1838, Pecos grew to power by participating in trading networks that exchanged Rio Grande glazeware (q.v.) pottery, Plains bison products, maize, cotton garments, and other items. By ca. A.D. 1525, the distinctive Pecos Glaze-polychrome pottery was being manufactured at the site, and Apache traders were camping nearby. These events produced an eclectic material culture reflected in Kidder's excavations in middens and rooms, and in the more than 1500 burials that he exposed.

SOURCES: Parsons 1925; Hooton 1930; Kidder 1931, 1932, 1958; Kidder and Shepard 1936.

Larry V. Nordby

PEDERNALES POINT, a Middle Archaic dart-point type associated strongly with burned-rock middens in central Texas, a diagnostic trait of the Round Rock Phase (q.v.), dating ca. 1550–650 B.C. The blade is long and slender to moderately broad and stubby; the stem is rectangular with straight or convex edges and a deep basal concavity. Stylistically Pedernales grades into the preceding Bulverde (q.v.) and the succeeding Marshall (q.v.) types.

SOURCES: Suhm et al. 1954; Weir 1976; Prewitt 1981.

Elton R. Prewitt

PEE DEE CULTURE (or PHASE), a Mississippian (q.v.) period (ca. A.D. 1200–1500) cultural expression, defined in 1952 by J. L. Coe; best known from its type site, Town Creek (q.v.), in south-central North Carolina. Pee Dee village sites and palisaded ceremonial-civic centers with mounds and burial houses occur on the Pee Dee and Wateree rivers of the Carolina Piedmont and Coastal Plain. Distinctive artifacts include small, triangular, chipped-stone points; ground-stone celts and discs; bone tools; complicated-stamped pottery (including burial urns); stone and clay pipes; and marine-shell beads and gorgets. The settlement pattern is one of ceremonial-civic

centers surrounded by satellite villages and hamlets, possibly indicative of a small chiefdom-level society.
SOURCES: Coe 1952; J. J. Reid 1965; Ward 1983.

Roy S. Dickens, Jr.

PEE DEE PENTAGONAL POINT, a small, usually asymmetrical, pentagonal projectile point with a straight or concave base; made from a thin primary flake by pressure flaking. Dating ca. A.D. 1450–1550, the type's distribution is concentrated in and around Montgomery County, in North Carolina.
SOURCE: Coe 1964:49.

Billy L. Oliver

PEE DEE POTTERY SERIES, the main ware of the Pee Dee Phase of the lower Piedmont in North Carolina and South Carolina, dating ca. A.D. 1450–1550; a well-fired, sand-tempered ceramic with rectilinear and curvilinear complicated-stamped, burnished, textile-impressed, and plain surface treatments. Rosettes, punctations, fillets, applied nodes, and incised motifs constitute the main decorative elements. Interiors are invariably smoothed or burnished. Vessel forms include globular jars, hemispherical bowls, and cazuela bowls. Extremely large pots were used for primary interment of infants.
SOURCES: Coe 1952:309; J. J. Reid 1967.

Billy L. Oliver

PELICAN LAKE COMPLEX, a congeries of corner-notched projectile points (the Pelican Lake type), end scrapers, ovoid bifaces, chipped-stone drills, and bone artifacts found at the Mortlach, Long Creek (qq.v.), and other sites in Saskatchewan, dating ca. 1350 B.C.–A.D. 100. Sites include camps, bison pounds, and cairn-covered graves containing secondary burials. A similar complex in Manitoba is sometimes called the Larter Phase.
SOURCES: D. R. King 1961; Kehoe 1974; Epp and Dyck 1983.

Thomas F. Kehoe

PELICAN STONES, carved stone (usually steatite) sculptures that appear to be generalized pelican representations; found in late period or Canaliño (q.v.) sites along the southern California coast. Also reported from this same area are small steatite model canoes and effigies of whales and other sea mammals.
SOURCE: Hoover 1974.

L. A. Payen

PENINSULAR WOODLAND, a catch-all term for Late Woodland occupations in Michigan's upper and lower peninsulas and in coastal Wisconsin, particularly small camps that have produced protohistoric materials, cord-marked pottery, and projectile points.

SOURCE: Quimby 1960:88.

Charles E. Cleland

PENNSYLVANIA JASPER QUARRIES, a series of high-quality, brown jasper outcrops in southeastern Pennsylvania which were extensively quarried by aboriginal peoples from Paleoindian to Late Woodland times (ca. 10,000 B.C.–A.D. 1600). At nearby workshops, quarried stone was fashioned into blanks which were distributed throughout the Middle Atlantic region for future tool manufacture. Some blanks of this distinctive jasper have been found as far away as New England and the Southeast.
SOURCE: Wyantt n.d.

Ronald A. Thomas

PENOKEE STONE MAN, the figure of a man outlined with small stones, 15 meters long by 9 meters wide, atop a ridge at the edge of the Smoky Hill River valley in northwestern Kansas. The body is rectangular, the head is circular with big ears, the arms are upraised, the legs are straight with feet turned out, and male genitalia are represented. The head is oriented to the west, the feet to the east. Cultural affiliation is attributed to an early historic Plains Indian nomadic group. First reported in 1879, the figure is listed on the National Register of Historic Places.
SOURCES: Williston 1879; Witty 1978a.

Thomas A. Witty, Jr.

PENSACOLA CULTURE, a unit of the Mississippian tradition (q.v.) occupying the Gulf coast between Mobile Bay and Louisiana from ca. A.D. 1200 into the colonial period; defined mainly on the basis of a distinctive shell-tempered ceramic assemblage. Several regional variants have been recognized.
SOURCE: Knight 1984.

Jerald T. Milanich

PERALTA COMPLEX, a presumed Archaic (q.v.) complex in west-central Sonora with lithic artifacts similar to Cochise Culture (q.v.) material found in southern Arizona. It is probably a southern manifestation of the Cochise tradition.
SOURCE: Fay 1955.

Richard A. Pailes

PERDIZ POINT, a type of late (ca. 1300–1750 A.D.) arrow point with a triangular blade (frequently serrated), strong barbs, and a contracting stem, occurring commonly from western Louisiana across eastern and central Texas to the Trans-Pecos region of western Texas, and from southern Oklahoma on the north to the Texas Gulf coast and northern Tamaulipas, Nuevo

Leon, and Chihuahua on the south. Perdiz is a diagnostic trait of the Toyah Phase (q.v.) of central Texas and also occurs in late Caddoan, Trans-Pecos, and coastal phases.

SOURCES: J. C. Kelley 1947a; Suhm et al. 1954; Jelks 1962; Prewitt 1981; Turner and Hester 1985.

Elton R. Prewitt

PERMUDA ISLAND SITE, a vast Middle and Late Woodland shell midden, occupied from ca. 300 B.C. to A.D 1650, which covers virtually the entire length of Permuda Island in Stump Sound, in Onslow County, North Carolina. Cheryl Claassen, B. L. Oliver, and T. C. Loftfield, who investigated the site at different times between 1979 and 1984, reported dense concentrations of shell refuse, trash pits, small ossuaries, and rectangular houses.

SOURCES: Claassen n.d.; Loftfield n.d.b.; Loftfield and Watson n.d.

Billy L. Oliver

PERROS BRAVOS PHASE. See Casas Grandes Province.

PERSHING SITE, the remains of a large pithouse village in Anderson Canyon, just east of Anderson Mesa, approximately 60 kilometers southeast of Flagstaff, Arizona. It was occupied from the later A.D. 700s to ca. 1175, with the heaviest usage after 1000. In 1958 and 1960, J. C. McGregor excavated four burials and seventeen structures, including two possible community lodges.

SOURCES: McGregor 1958a, 1961; J. P. Wilson 1969.

Donald E. Weaver, Jr.

PETAGA POINT SITE, a stratified, multicomponent site at the head of the Rum River on Lake Ogechie in east-central Minnesota; tested by Leland Cooper in 1965 and investigated more extensively by Peter Bleed in 1966. Bleed's work included the first excavation and interpretation of an Old Copper Complex (q.v.) habitation site in Minnesota. Sparse Middle Woodland and dense Late Woodland components are also present at Petaga Point.

SOURCES: L. R. Cooper n.d.; Bleed 1969.

Gordon R. Peters

PETERSON SITE, a large multicomponent (Middle and Late Woodland) village on the Fox River, dating ca. A.D. 1100; representative of the large, palisaded, Late Woodland villages of southeastern Wisconsin that are related to the Effigy Mound Culture (q.v.). Aztalan collared ware, Madison ware,

and corn were found in refuse pits at the site by L. A. Brazeau and David Overstreet during excavations in 1978.
SOURCE: Brazeau et al. 1979.

David Overstreet

PHILLIPS SITE, a village of the Sierra Blanca Sub-Province (q.v.), Jornada Province, Mogollon Culture in southeastern New Mexico, comprising some 40 small Corona Phase (q.v.) roomblocks and limited Lincoln Phase (q.v.) remains. It is estimated to date ca. A.D. 1100–1300. J. H. Kelley's limited excavations there in 1956 focused on the Lincoln Phase component.
SOURCE: J. H. Kelley 1984.

R. N. Wiseman

PHOENIX BASIN PROVINCE, an area in south-central Arizona comprising a number of structural basins, including those of the middle Gila and lower Salt rivers and their tributaries. The term "Hohokam core area" is commonly applied to this province because the traits most widely accepted as diagnostic of the Hohokam Culture (q.v.) occur there: large-scale canal irrigation; cremation burial practices; red-on-buff pottery; shallow pithouse architecture; compounds containing houses made of caliche-adobe; ball courts; platform mounds; and distinctive, ornamental, marine-shell and carved-stone industries.

A long history of archaeological investigations in the province began with F. H. Cushing's excavations in 1886–1887 at the Los Muertos Site and other large village sites in the Salt River Valley. The Hohokam Culture was formally defined in the late 1930s as a result of the efforts of Gila Pueblo. In the early 1930s, H. S. Gladwin and others conducted surveys in the province and excavated at the Snaketown Site (q.v.), which produced a more complete picture of the Hohokam Culture's time depth and unique developmental sequence. E. W. Haury's additional work at Snaketown reinforced the conclusions of the original excavators with some notable revisions.

It is now known that in the river valleys of the province there were scores of large Hohokam villages of more than 100 hectares each, and hundreds of miles of irrigation canals. A typical large village was surrounded by a few or many small satellite villages and contained from one to five ball courts, numerous mounds, plazas, compounds, residential areas, cemetery areas, rock-art stations, agricultural field areas, and roasting ovens.
SOURCES: Gladwin et al. 1937; Haury 1945, 1976; Doyel 1981; Wilcox et al. 1981.

John S. Cable and David E. Doyel

PICKWICK POINT, a large, often crude, shouldered type of Late Archaic projectile point with a straight or contracting stem. Dating ca. 3000–1000 B.C., it occurs primarily in the western Tennessee River Valley of Alabama and Tennessee.

SOURCES: Smith and Smith 1960; Cambron and Hulse 1964:94, 1975:103; Alexander 1982:72.

Eugene M. Futato

PICTOGRAPH CAVE, the largest of a series of caves in Yellowstone County, in Montana, notable for a series of pictographs on its walls and for its stratified cultural deposits. Excavations by H. M. Sayre in 1937 produced Paleoindian materials including Eden/Scottsbluff points (q.v.) from Layer I, corner-notched points of the Middle Prehistoric Period from Layer II, and small, triangular, side-notched points of the Late Prehistoric Period from Layer III.
SOURCE: Mulloy 1958.

Patricia J. O'Brien

PICURIS (or SAN LORENZO) PUEBLO, a multicomponent village on the north side of the Rio Pueblo in south-central Taos County, in New Mexico, occupied from ca. A.D. 1150 to the present (1988). Excavations there by H. W. Dick in 1960–1965 disclosed remains representing nine distinct phases: Taos or Valdez (ca. A.D. 1150–1250), Santa Fe (ca. A.D. 1250–1300), Talpa (ca. A.D. 1300–1375), Vadito (ca. A.D. 1375–1490), San Lazaro (ca. A.D. 1490–1600), Trampas (ca. A.D. 1600–1696), Cuartelejo (A.D. 1696–1706), Apodaca (A.D. 1706–1864), and Penasco (A.D. 1864–present). Archaeological study of these phases at Picuris has documented long-term changes in prehistoric architecture and in the typology of pottery and other artifacts. It also has traced the acculturation that has taken place since the late 16th century following contact with Europeans.
SOURCES: Dick 1965b; D. N. Brown 1973; Schroeder 1974.

Herbert W. Dick

PIEDRA PHASE, a late Pueblo I manifestation of the Pecos Classification (q.v.), dating ca. A.D. 850–950, in the Upper San Juan Province (q.v.). The basic settlement pattern was continued from the preceding Rosa Phase (q.v.) but with many more village-size sites. Foreign-trade items (marine-shell ornaments, pottery, lithic-knapping materials, and other goods) appear in relatively high frequencies in the large village sites, which are interpreted as mercantile points of redistribution to the outlying, smaller sites. Big kivas, classified as Shabikeschchee-type religious structures, constitute unique focal points within each central-place village and are likely sites of redistributive barter.

Studies in the Navajo Reservoir District indicate that river cutting began as early as A.D. 800, thereby lowering the floodplain water table which, in turn, impacted corn horticulture. In response, Piedra Phase peoples relocated their settlements upstream so as to utilize unentrenched alluvial soils for cropping, and by A.D. 900 more and more people had aggregated in larger and larger villages in the middle and upper reaches of the Navajo Reservoir area. These relocations evidently were effected by "leapfrogging" over the heads of upstream blocking settlements that were unaffected by the lowered water table.

For the first time, settlements in the lowland canyon bottoms were stockaded, apparently so that they could serve as places of refuge during attack. A combination of the stockades, a high incidence of burned sites and structures, and evidence of cannibalism, group burials, and occasional incinerated bodies in pithouses all point to the advent of internecine warfare, thought to have been the result of severe competition for the scarce, arable lands of the floodplain.

SOURCES: F. H. H. Roberts, Jr. 1930; Reed 1958; Schroeder 1963; Eddy 1966, 1972, 1974; Flinn et al. 1976.

Frank W. Eddy

PIGEON PHASE, an expression of the early Middle Woodland culture in southern North Carolina dating ca. 200 B.C.–A.D. 300. Its most distinctive traits are Pigeon Series pottery (q.v.); small, weakly notched or eared projectile points; bone and antler awls; hammerstones; celts; expanded-center bar gorgets; and smoking pipes of both stone and clay. Little is known of ceremonial, settlement, or subsistence practices.

SOURCES: Keel 1976:61–62; Dickens 1976.

Billy L. Oliver

PIGEON POTTERY SERIES, a quartz-tempered ware thought to represent part of a northward spread of Deptford-type paddle stamping from the Georgia Piedmont into southern North Carolina in the early part of the Middle Woodland period, ca. 200 B.C.–A.D. 300. It is the chief pottery type of the Pigeon Phase (q.v.). Surfaces are check stamped, simple stamped, brushed, or plain; vessel forms include conical jars, open hemispherical bowls, and small, flat-based jars with tetrapodal supports. The only decoration is an occasional notched or paddle-marked lip.

SOURCES: Keel 1976:256–260; Dickens 1976.

Billy L. Oliver

PIKE BAY SITE, the southernmost Laurel Culture (q.v.) site in Minnesota containing a burial mound; located south of Lake Vermilion. Excavations in the mound by L. A. Wilford in 1940 disclosed that it was constructed of fill containing a substantial amount of Laurel material that had been taken from an associated habitation area. The mound also contained intrusive Blackduck burials. The ceramic assemblage from the site defines the Pike Bay Phase, the earliest phase of the Laurel Culture in Minnesota.

SOURCES: Wilford 1950a; Stoltman 1962, 1973; D. L. Webster 1967; Lukens 1963; Lugenbeal 1976.

Gordon R. Peters

PILCHER CREEK SITE, a large site in the Blue Mountains of northeastern Oregon, excavated by D. R. Brauner in 1982–1983, which contained large assemblages attributed to the Windust and Cascade phases (qq.v.). Pilcher Creek and Lind Coulee (q.v.) are the only major Windust Phase sites known outside major river canyons.
SOURCE: Brauner 1985.

Frank C. Leonhardy

PILON PHASE. See Casas Grandes Province.

PINCKNEY ISLAND SHELL MIDDEN, a stratified, Early to Late Woodland midden in Beaufort County, in South Carolina that contained components of the Deptford, Mount Pleasant, and St. Catherines phases (qq.v.). Michael Trinkley totally excavated large sections of the site between 1978 and 1980 and collected important evidence about Early and Middle Woodland settlement and subsistence patterns. Radiocarbon dates indicate that the site was occupied during the period ca. 480 B.C.–A.D. 1385.
SOURCE: Trinkley 1981a.

Michael Trinkley

PINDI PHASE, an early Coalition phase of the Tano Province (q.v.) in north-central New Mexico, dating ca. A.D. 1220/1250–1300; named for Pindi Pueblo on the Santa Fe River. Numerous small farmsteads and villages, as well as several large pueblos, were typical in both the Santa Fe and Galisteo basins. Villages consisted of clustered houses and house blocks, or extensive one- and two-story apartment complexes with associated kivas. Both surface dwellings and pithouses were present. Agricultural fields were located along the margins of streams and arroyos.

Characteristic stone artifacts are slab metates and side-notched arrow points. The carbon-painted pottery type Santa Fe Black-on-white and a variety of indented-corrugated grayware types dominate the ceramic inventory. Trade pottery from the west includes polychromes. Extensive manufacture of bird bone awls may have begun at this time, and the raising of domestic turkeys became economically important. Cordmarked pottery and tools made of Alibates (q.v.) chert reflect trade connections with peoples of the Great Plains. Rock art, which basically followed the Plateau Anasazi style, emphasized anthropomorphs and quadrupeds, sometimes arranged in hunt scenes. The intrusion of Keresan peoples from the west may have begun late in the Pindi Phase.

SOURCES: Stubbs and Stallings 1953; Hammack n.d.

                                                                    Richard W. Lang

PINE RIVER WARE, a pottery class dating ca. A.D. 700 that represents an in-situ Late Woodland development in Michigan's northern lower peninsula. The ware is stylistically transitional between Middle Woodland Laurel vessels from sites in the Straits of Mackinac region and early Late Woodland Mackinac Ware vessels from the same region.

SOURCES: Holman 1978, 1984.

                                                                  Margaret B. Holman

PINEY BRANCH QUARRY, one of the largest boulder quarries on the Atlantic slope, used primarily during the Late Archaic (ca. 3000–1100 B.C.) period as a source of quartzite and quartz; tested by W. H. Holmes in 1889–1890 and by B. A. Munford in 1981.

SOURCES: W. H. Holmes 1890, 1897:33–62; Munford 1982.

                                                                   Stephen R. Potter

PINSON SITE, a large mound/village complex in southwestern Tennessee. Most of the mounds are associated with a Middle Woodland (q.v.) mortuary complex that dates ca. A.D. 1–300 and shows strong affinities to the Hopewell Culture (q.v.).

SOURCES: Mainfort 1980; Mainfort et al. 1985.

                                                                  Jefferson Chapman

PINTO BASIN SITES, a series of prehistoric encampments along the banks of a dry watercourse at Pinto Basin in eastern Riverside County, in California; thought to have been first inhabited during a wet cycle, beginning ca. 3000 B.C. Artifacts, limited to surface finds, include distinctive shouldered projectile points with concave bases. Similar assemblages have been recognized at many other sites in the desert region of southern California.

SOURCES: Campbell and Campbell 1935; Wallace 1962.

                                                                       L. A. Payen

PINTO/GYPSUM COMPLEX, a culture unit of the southern California deserts defined in 1939 by M. J. Rogers, who dated it between 800 B.C. and A.D. 200. It included Pinto points (q.v.), Gypsum Cave points, plano-convex bifaces, scraper planes, choppers, hammerstones, and flat grinding slabs. Nearly all subsequent schemes recognized separate Pinto and Gypsum complexes; Pinto is the earlier of the two. Most investigators now would date Pinto ca. 5000–2000 B.C. and Gypsum ca. 1500 B.C.–A.D. 600.

SOURCES: M. J. Rogers 1939; Bettinger and Taylor 1974; C. N. Warren 1984.

Robert L. Bettinger

PINTO POINT, a heavy, often crudely made projectile-point type with a triangular blade, a narrow stem, and an indented base, occurring in southeastern California and estimated to date ca. 5000–2000 B.C.

SOURCES: Campbell and Campbell 1935; Harrington 1957.

L. A. Payen

PIONEER PERIOD, the earliest of the Hohokam Culture's (q.v.) four periods whose age has been the focus of a long-standing debate, in which two main schools of thought have emerged: The "long-count" school favors an early beginning date, and the "short-count school" argues for a much later beginning date. Recent excavations in downtown Phoenix have provided support for both camps, confirming the "short-count" dating of the previously defined Pioneer phases but also recognizing a new phase (Red Mountain, q.v.) bridging the Archaic-to-Hohokam transition. J. S. Cable and D. E. Doyel have estimated that the Pioneer Period dates ca. A.D. 1–700.

The Pioneer Period has been divided into five phases:

Red Mountain Phase. Dating A.D. 1–300, this phase is characterized by a crude, plain, brown pottery representing the initial stages of ceramic production; small, square pithouses; flexed inhumations; and shallow basin metates. Subsistence was based on wild resources and floodwater farming; the settlement pattern was probably biseasonal, and social organization was egalitarian.

Vahki Phase. Dating ca. A.D. 300–450, this phase is distinguished by sophisticated redware and thin, polished, plainware pottery; small, rectangular pithouses; clay figurines; one-end, open-trough metates; and large, square, communal houses that probably were used for ritual or other specialized purposes.

Estrella and Sweetwater. Dating ca. A.D. 450–550 and ca. A.D. 550–625, respectively, it was during these phases when decorated pottery first appeared.

Snaketown Phase. Dating ca. A.D. 625–700, this phase is typified by irrigation agriculture; larger houses; cremations; caliche-capped mounds; and larger, more numerous villages. These changes suggest a shift toward a ranked society by the end of the phase.

SOURCES: Gladwin et al. 1937; Gladwin 1948; Haury 1976; Wilcox and Shenk 1977; Plog 1980; Schiffer 1982; Cable and Doyel 1986.

John S. Cable and David E. Doyel

PIPE SITE, a Grand River Phase site of the Oneota Tradition (q.v.), located on the eastern shore of Lake Winnebago in eastern Wisconsin; representative of permanent, horticultural-hunting-gathering villages during the period

A.D. 1150–1250. David Overstreet, who dug there between 1975 and 1978, reported domestic structures, an adjacent cemetery, and large faunal and floral assemblages.

SOURCE: Overstreet 1981.

David Overstreet

PISCATAWAY POINT, a long, slender projectile point with narrow shoulders, contracting stem, and pointed or rounded base, usually made from quartz by fine pressure flaking. Found in northern Virginia and the coastal plain of southern Maryland, the type originally was thought to be of Late Woodland age but now is considered to be a Late Archaic type dating ca. 4000–3000 B.C.

SOURCES: Stephenson et al. 1963:146–147; Steponaitis 1980:14.

Stephen R. Potter

PISGAH CULTURE, (or PHASE), a Mississippian (q.v.) period culture (ca. A.D. 1100–1500) found throughout the south Appalachian highlands, especially in the mountain valleys of western North Carolina; thought to represent at least one of the late prehistoric antecedents of the Cherokee. It was named and first described by Patricia Holder in 1966 on the basis of earlier work by J. L. Coe. The distinctive pottery combines traditional southeastern complicated stamping with collared-and-punctated vessel rims that are characteristic of the Midwest and Northeast. In addition to pottery vessels, there are clay pipes and discs; small, triangular, chipped-stone points; ground-stone celts; bone awls; and marine-shell beads and gorgets. Sites represent small to medium-size villages, with a few larger villages having platform mounds built over earlier earth-covered ceremonial buildings.

SOURCES: Keel 1976; Dickens 1976, 1978, 1979, 1985.

Roy S. Dickens, Jr.

PISGAH POTTERY SERIES, the primary diagnostic artifact type of the Pisgah Phase (q.v.) in the mountains of North Carolina, dating ca. A.D. 1000–1550. The typical vessel shape is a globular jar with an everted rim to which a clay strip has been added to form a collar. Some exterior surfaces are plain; others are check stamped, complicated stamped (rectilinear or curvilinear), or, rarely, impressed with basketry, corncobs, cordage, fabric, or netting. Rim decorations include bands of punctations, incised patterns, and appendages in the form of handles, nodes, vertical lugs, or applied strips. Tempering is fine to coarse river sand, crushed quartz, and, occasionally, shell.

SOURCES: P. P. Holden 1966:64–77; Dickens 1976:172–186.

Billy L. Oliver

PITHOUSE, a common form of dwelling in much of North America made by digging a pit into the ground and covering it with a weatherproof superstructure. The bottom of the pit served as the house's floor and the sides of the pits as the lower part of the house's walls. Pithouses varied greatly in depth, size, and complexity of superstructure. A detailed chronological sequence of pithouse styles has been developed for prehistoric Southwestern cultures.

Frank C. Leonhardy

PITTSBERG VILLAGE, the type site of the Cohonina Province of the Patayan Division, Hakataya Culture (qq.v.), occupied ca. A.D. 700–1200. When L. L. Hargrave excavated the site in 1938, he exposed a number of house structures with various ground plans and a "fort" that were outlined with low walls of rock and mud. The houses exhibited signs of repeated alteration during the Cataract Phase (q.v.), ca. A.D. 900–1100, suggesting seasonal reuse. San Francisco Mountain Gray Ware, commonly with fugitive red exteriors, was the dominant pottery. Contact with Anasazi (q.v.) neighbors to the east is indicated by some of the pottery styles. Hargrave found long, unnotched obsidian arrow points, but ornaments and animal bones were scarce. Cremation of the dead is postulated, and agriculture may have been practiced.

SOURCE: Hargrave 1938.

Albert H. Schroeder

PLAINS SIDE-NOTCHED POINT SYSTEM, a typological classification for the ubiquitous small, triangular, side-notched projectile points of the northern Plains.

SOURCE: Kehoe 1966.

Thomas F. Kehoe

PLAINVIEW SITE, a Paleoindian (q.v.) communal bison kill on the southern high plains in Hale County, in Texas, manifested by a bone bed containing the remains of about 100 *Bison antiquus* that apparently were driven over the valley wall of Running Water Draw onto the valley floor ca. 8000 B.C. Eighteen complete, broken, or reworked projectile points, constituting the type collection for the Plainview type point, and several lithic butchering tools were recovered from the deeply buried bone bed by Glen L. Evans and Grayson Meade between 1945 and 1949. The Plainview bone bed lay

within a well-stratified sequence of sediments and soils that record climatic cycles in the late Pleistocene and Holocene.
SOURCE: Sellards et al. 1947.

Vance T. Holliday and Eileen Johnson

PLANO CULTURE, the most recent of the three major Paleoindian (q.v.) cultures, dating ca. 7000 to 4000 B.C., whose sites have been reported in relative abundance over North America east of the Rocky Mountains. Territorial Plano bands apparently followed a hunting-gathering mode of existence, with particular emphasis on hunting large animals, particularly *Bison antiquus* during the waning of the Pleistocene and their successors, *B. bison* in the early Holocene. Plano peoples possessed a basic tool kit of chipped-stone projectile points, knives, scrapers, and gravers; bone fleshing tools also occur commonly in their sites.

In recent years, a number of regional phases—including Plainview, Horner, Sisters Hill, Frederick, Hell Gap, Portales, and Agate Basin (qq.v.)—have been subsumed within the Plano culture by various researchers. These phases are distinguished from one another by differences in the forms of projectile points and other artifacts, as well as by differences in geographical distribution. Some points that would be identified with the early Archaic (q.v.) if found in the eastern United States would be ascribed to the Plano Culture if found in the Plains.
SOURCES: Quimby 1960; Mason 1962; Jennings 1968.

Edward B. Jelks

PLAQUEMINE CULTURE, a late prehistoric culture that evolved directly out of the preceding Coles Creek Culture (q.v.) in coastal Louisiana and the lower Mississippi River Valley. Temple-mound construction in the area reached its maximum development in Plaquemine times. Groups of large pyramidal mounds arranged around plaza areas served as ceremonial/trade centers, while the general population lived in villages along natural stream levees. Distinctive traits include fully developed agriculture based on maize; decorated pottery decorated with brushing, rectilinear incising, and engraving; and rectangular houses of wall-trench and wattle-and-daub construction.
SOURCES: Quimby 1951; Neuman 1984:258–271.

William G. Haag

PLATEAU CULTURE AREA, a region extending from central Oregon northward into central British Columbia and from the Cascade Mountains eastward to the Great Plains. Aboriginally, the area was occupied by hunting-gathering peoples with technologies designed to exploit riverine resources. Two subareas are recognized: the Northern Plateau and the

Southern Plateau, sometimes called respectively the Canadian and American plateaus.
SOURCE: V. F. Ray 1939.

Frank C. Leonhardy

PLATEAU HORIZON. See Thompson Phase.

PLATEAU MICROBLADE TRADITION, a long-standing tradition well represented on the Canadian Plateau and found occasionally on the Columbia Plateau (q.v.). Defined by David Sanger in 1968, it is distinguished from neighboring microblade traditions by several distinctive attributes of its conical cores. Sanger dated the tradition ca. 5500–1000 B.C., but uncertainty about its age has increased recently. K. R. Fladmark has suggested an age of ca. 4600–2000 B.C. with some possible later manifestations. S. Lawhead and A. H. Stryd recently found substantial numbers of microblades in the Highland Valley of British Columbia that dated to the first millennium A.D.
SOURCES: Sanger 1968b; Fladmark 1982b; Ludowicz 1983.

Arnoud H. Stryd

PLATFORM PIPE, a carved-stone or pottery smoking pipe having a bowl set in the middle of a roughly rectangular platform; the most common pipe style of the Middle Woodland period (ca. 100 B.C.–A.D. 500). They vary widely in size and shape. Bowls may be from nearly spherical to tubular, or may be in the form of animals, birds, reptiles, or, more rarely, human heads. The vast majority of the effigies were found in Ohio at Mound City and the Tremper Mound (qq.v.); others are from sites of the Hopewell Culture (q.v.) over much of eastern North America. Some, usually of plainer styles, occur in Late Woodland or later sites.
SOURCES: Squier and Davis 1848:242–245, 251–271; Mills 1916; J. B. Griffin 1952:figs. 16, 22, 33, 34, 37, 50, 61, 63, 140, 141, 170, 172; Barnhart 1985.

N'omi B. Greber

PLAYA INDUSTRY, a unit in M. J. Rogers' culture sequence of 1939 for the lower Colorado River Basin. Estimated to date between 1200 and 800 B.C., it comprised two phases: Playa I (characterized by scrapers, scraper planes, and plano-convex and lenticular knives) and Playa II (characterized by scrapers of various kinds, scraper planes, choppers, borers, reamers, blades, and chipped-stone amulets). Both phases were later subsumed in C. N. Warren's San Dieguito complex (q.v.), thought to date ca. 8000–7000

B.C., which, in turn, was subsumed in S. F. Bedwell's Western Pluvial Lakes Tradition (q.v.), dating ca. 9000–5000 B.C.
    SOURCE: M. J. Rogers 1939.

Robert L. Bettinger

PLAZA SITE, a late McDonald (q.v.) Phase (ca. A.D. 1150–1250) pueblo located in the Hopi Buttes north of Winslow, Arizona, which served as a cultural center for the entire surrounding locality. Excavations by G. J. Gumerman in 1967 exposed a large enclosed plaza, a block of five residential rooms with a kiva, an exterior great kiva, and an exterior regular kiva.
    SOURCE: Gumerman and Skinner 1968.

George J. Gumerman

PLENGE SITE, one of the largest known Paleoindian (q.v.) sites in eastern North America, located on a terrace of the Muscontetcong River in northwestern New Jersey, where excavations by H. C. Kraft in 1972 produced a wide range of fluted projectile-point forms and other artifacts. No occupational features were found at the site, which had been extensively disturbed by plowing.
    SOURCES: Kraft 1973, 1977:269; D. R. Snow 1980:130–132.

Edward B. Jelks

PLUM BAYOU CULTURE. See Toltec Site.

PLUM NELLY SITE, a multicomponent, stratified site near the mouth of the Potomac River, occupied intermittently from ca. 6800 B.C. to A.D. 1500. The site has contributed substantially to an understanding of the Late Archaic and Middle Woodland cultures of the region, owing to the variety of its features, artifacts, and faunal and floral remains, and to their excellent state of preservation.
    SOURCE: Potter 1982:276–331.

Stephen R. Potter

POINT BARROW SITES, a series of sites in the vicinity of Point Barrow at Alaska's extreme northwestern point, known to explorers and early anthropologists who often purchased collections mined from the sites by local Inupiat Eskimo. Following brief investigations by several people between 1912 and 1928, J. A. Ford conducted the first substantial excavations in 1932 and 1936 at the Utkiavik-Barrow (Utquiagvik), Nuwuk, Nunagiak, and Birnirk (q.v.) sites; he used his findings to define the Birnirk Phase (q.v.) and its role in the development of the Thule Tradition (q.v.). Harvard University's excavations in the 1950s are largely unpublished. D. J. Stanford's work at Walakpa and other sites traced the development of Thule out of Birnirk and documented an earlier occupation related to the Denbigh

Flint Complex and the Norton Tradition (qq.v.). In 1981 A. A. Dekin, Jr., directed extensive salvage excavations at the Utquiagvik Site, and in 1982 native collectors discovered the widely publicized "Frozen Family."
SOURCES: J. A. Ford 1959; Stanford 1976; Dekin 1981; Lobdell and Dekin 1984.

Donald W. Clark

POINTED MOUNTAIN SITE, a site near Fort Liard in the southwestern District of Mackenzie, excavated by R. S. MacNeish in 1952 and by J. F. V. Millar in 1967 and later. MacNeish's original formulation of the Northwest Microblade Tradition (q.v.) was based largely on materials from the site. Millar's work considerably enlarged the collection from the Pointed Mountain Complex of that tradition.
SOURCES: MacNeish 1954; Millar 1981.

Donald W. Clark

POINT HOPE SITES, a group of major sites at Point Hope, Alaska: the Ipiutak (Ipiutak Phase, q.v.), Old Tigara (later Thule Tradition, q.v.), and Jabbertown (early Thule Tradition and Near Ipiutak Phase, q.v.), together with ancient Ipiutak cemeteries and mounds of the Near Ipiutak Phase. Spectacular discoveries at Ipiutak in 1939–1941 by Helge Larsen and F. G. Rainey overshadowed other excavations of the time there. Later work on these sites by the University of Alaska is largely unpublished.
SOURCES: Larsen and Rainey 1948; Rainey 1971.

Donald W. Clark

POINT OF PINES LOCALITY, an area some 95 kilometers east of Globe, Arizona, that encompasses a number of habitation settlements, pithouse villages, masonry pueblos, and agricultural structures, spanning the period ca. A.D. 600–1400, as well as some earlier Archaic remains. The most notable of the sites is the Point of Pines Ruin, a 600-room pueblo with an associated great kiva and a plaza, built in a number of construction episodes between A.D. 1200 and 1400, and spanning the Tularosa, Pinedale, Canyon Creek, and Point of Pines phases of the Mogollon Culture (q.v.). The pueblo was variously rebuilt several times during this period.
From 1946 to 1960, E. W. Haury and others directed annual University of Arizona field schools in the locality, primarily at the Point of Pines Site, which trained some 300 students in archaeological excavation techniques and related scholarly studies. The sites have produced important evidence about the processes of settlement aggregation within the complex community, decentralization to small communities, mortuary practices, artifact technologies, possible long-distance immigration, a catastrophic fire within the pueblo, and architectural and settlement strategies through time. They also have contributed to a better understanding of the complex interactions

that developed between the Mogollon-Western Pueblo peoples, the Anasazi peoples of the Colorado Plateau, and the desert peoples to the south of Point of Pines.

SOURCES: Haury 1958; Woodbury 1961.

Alexander J. Lindsay, Jr.

POINT REVENGE CULTURE, an Indian culture of coastal Labrador dating ca. A.D. 1–1600. Sites are small, usually consisting of cobble hearth features and a simple chipped-stone tool complex, the most distinguishing characteristic of which is the almost exclusive use of Ramah chert as a raw material.

SOURCE: Fitzhugh 1975.

James A. Tuck

POJOAQUE GRANT SITE, an important multicomponent Anasazi community of the Developmental Period (q.v.), located north of Santa Fe, New Mexico. Excavations in 1953 by S. A. Stubbs revealed pithouses, alignments of adobe-walled surface rooms (both dwelling and storage), small kivas, and a great kiva. Possible influence from the Chaco Province (q.v.), or even Chaco outlier status, is indicated by intrusive pottery from northwestern New Mexico (types Red Mesa Black-on-white and Gallup/Chaco Black-on-white) and by locally made copies of those types. There are tree-ring dates of A.D. 677–1133 for the site, but the early end of the range is questionable.

SOURCES: Stubbs 1954; Wendorf and Reed 1955; Robinson et al. 1972.

Stewart Peckham

POLLOCK SITE, a large pueblo of at least 40 rooms located at the mouth of Kinnikinnick Canyon on the east slope of Anderson Mesa in northern Arizona; the only extensively excavated late pueblo in the region. The main occupation was from ca. A.D. 1250 to 1325. Constructed of sandstone slab masonry, the pueblo is arranged in a compact mass, including small courts and a rectangular kiva. Associated with the main pueblo are burials, scattered small pueblos, a possible ball court, and extensive agricultural terraces, check dams, and waffle gardens. These farming remains are among the best preserved and most extensive agricultural systems known for the region.

J. C. McGregor dug or outlined 30 rooms in 1953 and 1955. One large square kiva-like room was 5.2 meters on a side and had a flagstone floor and benches.

SOURCES: McGregor 1955, 1956.

Donald E. Weaver, Jr.

POMONA FOCUS, a Middle Ceramic cultural entity, dating ca. A.D. 1000–1500, defined from excavations at numerous sites in the Dissected Till Plains, Flint Hills, and Osage Cuestas of eastern Kansas. Subsistence was based on hunting, gathering, and limited horticulture. Sites, usually on floodplains, include both nucleated villages and extended communities of simple, mud-daubed dwellings, usually with an oval floor plan. House types, pottery, and the presence of both small, triangular and large, corner-notched projectile points have led some researchers to associate the focus with the earlier Plains Woodland groups.

SOURCES: Witty 1967, 1981; Wilmeth 1970.

Thomas A. Witty, Jr.

POPES CREEK SITE, an extensive shell midden on the left bank of the Potomac River in southern Maryland, discovered by E. R. Reynolds in 1878, investigated by W. H. Holmes in 1890, and tested in 1985 by the Archeological Society of Maryland, under the supervision of the Maryland Geological Survey. It is the type site for Popes Creek Ware (q.v.), a Middle Woodland pottery dating ca. 500 B.C.–A.D. 200.

SOURCES: E. R. Reynolds 1883:23–24; W. H. Holmes 1907:113–128.

Stephen R. Potter

POPES CREEK WARE, a sand-tempered, net- or cord-impressed ceramic of Middle Woodland affiliation (ca. 500 B.C.–A.D. 200), found in the coastal plain between southern Maryland and the James River, in Virginia. Vessels are large, wide-mouthed jars with direct rims and walls that descend in slight, even curves to a conical base. Infrequent exterior decoration consists of incised horizontal lines or chevron patterns, or of finger-smoothed horizontal lines.

SOURCES: W. H. Holmes 1903:153–155; Stephenson et al. 1963:92–96; Egloff and Potter 1982:99.

Stephen R. Potter

PORT AU CHOIX, Newfoundland, the location of major sites of the Paleoeskimo Groswater and Dorset (qq.v.) peoples plus a large cemetery of the Maritime Archaic Tradition (q.v.). Excellent preservation of human skeletons and organic artifacts at the cemetery, which dates ca. 2000–1300 B.C., provided a picture of a people well adapted to life in coastal Newfoundland. Living sites of the Groswater Phase represent the terminal occupation of early Paleoeskimos on the island of Newfoundland, which ended ca. 200 B.C. A series of Dorset housepits on raised beaches spans virtually the entire Dorset occupation of Newfoundland, ca. A.D. 100–500.

SOURCES: Harp 1964; Tuck 1976.

James A. Tuck

PORT AU CHOIX SITE 2, a middle to late Dorset Phase (q.v.) site on the Newfoundland coast at the Strait of Belle Isle, where in the 1960s and 1970s Elmer Harp, Jr., excavated 36 house pits that had been dug into the beach

shingle. He found therein a distinctive and remarkably conservative artifact assemblage spanning the period from the 1st to the 7th century A.D.
SOURCE: Harp 1976.

Moreau S. Maxwell

PORT MOLLER SITE, the principal site at Port Moller on the north side of the Alaska Peninsula near the Historic Aleut-Eskimo territorial boundary; properly called the Village, or Hot Springs Village Site (q.v.). First investigated by E. M. Weyer in 1928, this extensive site with 200 possible dwelling depressions also has been the focal point of several Japanese expeditions in the 1960s and 1970s. The site's location near an ethnic boundary poses questions concerning identification of its occupants during the past 3000–3500 years. The early inhabitants probably were Paleo-Aleuts.
SOURCES: Weyer 1930; W.B. Workman 1966; McCartney 1969; Dumond et al. 1975; Okada 1980.

Donald W. Clark

PORT REFUGE LOCALITY, a place on the northwestern tip of Devon Island, Northwest Territories, where in 1972 Robert McGhee excavated the Gull Cliff, the Upper Beaches, and the Cold sites (qq.v.). The latter two, identified with the Independence I Phase (q.v.), had linearly dispersed tent remains with stone box hearths or mid-passages and nontoggling harpoon heads. They contrasted with Gull Cliff, closer to sea level, and attributed to the Pre-Dorset Phase (q.v.), which had toggling harpoon heads and clustered tent remains.
SOURCE: McGhee 1979.

Moreau S. Maxwell

POSNICK SITE, a site occupied from Paleoindian times through the Woodland period (qq.v.), located on the Chickahominy River in the interior coastal plain of Virginia. Tested by H. A. MacCord in 1964 and by J. Harper in 1971, the site is well known for its ceramic variation illustrative of interaction between related cultures of the Piedmont and the coastal plain.
SOURCES: MacCord and Owens 1965; Mouer 1984.

Keith T. Egloff

POST-CONTACT COALESCENT PERIOD, a time (ca. A.D. 1675–1862) marked by the impact of Euroamerican culture on the coalescing Central Plains and Middle Missouri traditions (qq.v.). The lifeways and material culture of the Mandan, Hidatsa, and Arikara—the major tribes in the middle

Missouri River Valley area—were changed very dramatically by white peoples' fur trade, diseases, warfare, and land encroachment.
SOURCE: Lehmer 1971:136–179.

Patricia J. O'Brien

POST-MCKENZIE PHASE, the last phase of the Middle Pecos Sub-Province (q.v.) of the Jornada Province, Mogollon Culture, in eastern New Mexico, dating ca. A.D. 1300. The only structures noted are tipi rings (q.v.) at one site. Sites have the appearance of camps occupied by nonsedentary, nonagricultural people. Glaze ceramics and greater use of obsidian indicate increased contacts with the Middle Rio Grande Province (q.v.). Arrow points are side notched with a third notch in the base.

A. J. Jelinek, using the trends and contacts traced through the sub-province's phase sequence, postulates that the people of the Post-McKenzie Phase abandoned the middle Pecos River region in favor of a bison-hunting lifeway and eventually became the Plains-dwelling Kiowa of the historic period.
SOURCE: Jelinek 1967.

R. N. Wiseman

POT CREEK PUEBLO, a multicomponent site located on the Fort Burgwin Research Center, in New Mexico, investigated by Fred Wendorf in 1957–1958, R. K. Wetherington in 1959–1967, E. L. Green in 1961, and several others since 1967. Valdez Phase pithouses dating ca. A.D. 1000–1200 underlay a Pot Creek Phase (ca. A.D. 1200–1250) pueblo and kiva that were largely destroyed by the construction of a multistoried, coursed adobe pueblo containing an estimated 300 ground-floor rooms in nine roomblocks, built around a plaza and a great kiva. The largest community in the Northern Rio Grande Province at the time (ca. A.D. 1250–1350), this last component is attributed to the Talpa Phase and is believed to be ancestral to the historic Taos and Picuris (qq.v.) pueblos.
SOURCES: Wetherington 1968; E. L. Green 1976.

Patricia L. Crown

POTOMAC CREEK SITE, a late precontact and possibly early contact Algonkian village known as Patawomeke, located on the Potomac River in northern Virginia. This major palisaded village of the Potomac chiefdom was excavated by W. J. Graham between 1935 and 1937 and by T. D. Stewart in 1939–1940.
SOURCES: T. D. Stewart 1939, n.d.; Schmitt 1965.

Stephen R. Potter

POTOMAC CREEK WARE, a sand- and quartz-tempered pottery of Late Woodland and early historic affiliation, occurring in the area between Baltimore and northwestern Virginia and dating ca. A.D. 1300–1650. Vessels are globular with everted or straight rims and rounded bases; sometimes there are cord impressions on the rim.

SOURCES: W. H. Holmes 1903:155–156; Schmitt 1965:10–11; Egloff and Potter 1982:112.

Stephen R. Potter

POTOMAC POINT, a small, thin projectile point in the approximate shape of an equilateral triangle with a straight or concave base, commonly made of quartz. Of protohistoric-historic age (ca. A.D. 1350–1650), its distribution is mainly in the piedmont and coastal plain sections of the Potomac River Valley and along Maryland's western shore.

SOURCES: Stephenson et al. 1963:145–146; Steponaitis 1980:17; Waselkov 1982:281–289.

Stephen R. Potter

POTTER CREEK CAVE, a limestone cave situated above the McCloud River in Shasta County, in northern California, first excavated in 1902–1903 by J. C. Merriam as part of the University of California's systematic program, begun in 1899, to establish the antiquity of man on the Pacific Coast. A sizable assemblage of Pleistocene fauna was unearthed, including ground sloth, horse, bison, camel, shrub ox, mammoth, and short-faced bear. Several implement-like bone splinters, a flaked pebble, and charcoal were found, apparently in the same deposits as the extinct animal remains. Reexamination of the cave in 1965 by L. A. Payen established that at least some of these materials belonged to a late Holocene occupation that has been radiocarbon dated at ca. 60 B.C. The bone accumulation, including the tool-like bone splinters, were attributed to activities of large Pleistocene carnivores.

SOURCES: W. J. Sinclair 1904; Putnam 1906; Payen and Taylor 1976.

L. A. Payen

POTTERY MOUND, a Classic Period (q.v.), Rio Grande Anasazi pueblo in the Middle Rio Grande Province (q.v.) on the Rio Puerco southwest of Albuquerque, New Mexico. Between 1954 and 1962, F. C. Hibben explored this settlement of coursed-adobe construction, thought to have been built on a prepared platform mound ca. A.D. 1325 and abandoned before 1450. Of the seventeen kivas, sixteen were rectangular; the other was circular. All but two of them had from 3 to 38 layers of polychrome murals depicting ritual paraphernalia, ceremonies, deific figures, stylized representations of elements important in prehistoric Pueblo religion (e.g., maize, rain, lightning, feathers, parrots, serpents), and figures seemingly related to formalized warfare.

SOURCES: Hibben 1966, 1975.

Stewart Peckham

POTTS POINT, a corner-notched projectile-point type, originally defined by B. C. McCary in 1953 at the Potts Site (q.v.), located on the Chickahominy River in the interior coastal plain of Virginia. In 1983 C. R. Geier found Potts points associated with Middle Woodland ceramics at the Skiffes Creek Site in Newport News, Virginia.

SOURCES: McCary 1953; Coe 1964; Geier and Barber 1983.

Keith T. Egloff

POTTS SITE, a stratified Woodland (q.v.) site, on the Chickahominy River in the interior coastal plain of Virginia; the type site for the Potts type projectile point (q.v.). When tested by B. C. McCary in 1953, it produced a wide variety of artifacts illustrating the development of Indian culture through the Woodland period. Clifford Evans in 1955 based his seriation of coastal ceramics on the Potts Site.

SOURCES: McCary 1953; Clifford Evans 1955.

Keith T. Egloff

POVERTY POINT CULTURE, a transitional culture that participated in the change from an Archaic band existence to the village/regional center/ large ceremonial center complex of the Southeastern Formative period. Basically a riverine culture, it is manifested chiefly in the large river valleys of the lower Ohio, lower Arkansas, and lower Mississippi systems, from the Missouri boot heel to the Gulf of Mexico, but spreading to the lateral lesser streams and along the Gulf from mid-Louisiana to the Florida panhandle. It began by 2000 B.C., flourished between 1200 and 800 B.C., and had declined by 600 B.C., to be supplanted by the Tchula and Tchefuncte cultures (q.v.). Chiefdom status is postulated.

A hunting, fishing, and gathering economy prevailed; therefore, an ecological constant was the location of sites in contact zones which permitted exploitation of diverse resources. Horticulture involving squash, chenopodium seeds, and possibly other plants has been postulated but is unproven. Intense cooking in shallow basins and earth ovens produced char-blackened middens; Poverty Point objects (q.v.), stone vessels, and fiber-tempered pottery suggest new food resources or culinary innovations. Bolas and stone-tipped darts hurled with the atlatl were used in hunting.

Of the more than 200 recorded Poverty Point components, most occur in clusters of from 10 to 25 relatively small sites grouped around large regional centers. Stone tools were made mainly of local materials, but the centers and many other sites have yielded exotic lithics, sometimes traded from long distances; steatite, hematite, copper, galena, slate, quartz, and jasper are widespread. At the major centers, art forms were expressed on baked clay objects, steatite vessels, hematite plummets, gorgets, and an extensive lapidary industry.

SOURCES: Ford and Webb 1956; J. A. Ford et al. 1955; C. H. Webb 1968, 1982; Gibson 1974.

Clarence H. Webb

POVERTY POINT OBJECTS, baked balls of clay, usually from 4 to 8 centimeters in diameter, that were molded and smoothed with the hands and fingers into three basic shapes—biconical, spheroidal, and cylindrical—then impressed or grooved with the fingers in several different ways before baking. Found at most sites of the Poverty Point Culture (q.v.), they are especially abundant in earth ovens and in heavily carbonized middens around shallow cooking pits, suggesting culinary use—probably as substitutes for stones, which are very rare locally, in some method of baking or roasting. It also has been proposed that they were used as net weights, slingshot projectiles, or counters. An estimated 24 million of these objects were made at the Poverty Point Site (q.v.).

SOURCES: Ford and Webb 1956; J. A. Ford et al. 1955; C. H. Webb 1977, 1982.

Clarence H. Webb

POVERTY POINT SITE, the ceremonial center and hub of trade and manufacturing for the Poverty Point Culture (q.v.), flourishing between 1500 and 600 B.C. It is in western Carroll Parish, in northeastern Louisiana, on the eastern edge of Macon Ridge, standing some 5 or 6 meters above the Mississippi River floodplain. When occupied, the site lay about halfway between the then-active channels of the Mississippi to the east and the Arkansas to the west (ca. 20 kilometers from each). There were relict channels of the Arkansas nearby, affording easy access to the entire domain of the center's parent culture.

The site comprises a complex of many major components: a huge village laid out in a semioctagonal pattern, six earthen mounds, and numerous occupation and activity areas, all stretching along an 8-kilometer section of Macon Ridge. The village, approximately 1200 meters across, consists of six concentric ridges from 2 to 3 meters high that were built of soil taken from the spaces between the ridges. Concentrated middens, pits, hearths, earth ovens, and occupational debris indicate habitation atop and on the slopes of the ridges.

The great Mound A, one of the largest on the continent, is oval with a crest that trends north-south, is 207 meters long at the base, and stands at present about 23 meters high. A preserved ramp and platform 91 meters long connect Mound A to the westernmost village ridge. The conical Mound

B, over 6 meters high, possibly contains the remains of a crematory. Motley Mound, 2.3 kilometers to the north, and Lower Jackson Mound, 2.5 kilometers to the south, are units of the complex; but two lower mounds on the eastern margin may relate to later occupations by Tchefuncte, Marksville, and Coles Creek (qq.v.) peoples. Surface investigations and subsurface tests at this spectacular site have been carried out by numerous people between 1950 and the present; the most notable work has been done by J. A. Ford, C. H. Webb, R. S. Neitzel, and Jon L. Gibson.

SOURCES: C. B. Moore 1913; Ford and Webb 1956; Gibson 1974; C. H. Webb 1977, 1982.

Clarence H. Webb

PRAIRIE PHASE, an Early Woodland–Middle Woodland unit restricted to the Prairie du Chien locality in southwestern Wisconsin. Defined by J. B. Stoltman in 1981, it dates ca. A.D. 100. Sites are interpreted as stations for freshwater mussel procurement on the lowland floodplain of the Mississippi River. The Prairie Phase is related to, although somewhat later than, the Black Sand Phase (q.v.) as defined in Illinois.

SOURCE: Stoltman 1979.

David Overstreet

PRAIRIE WARE, a ceramic style associated with Early–Middle Woodland in the Upper Mississippi River Valley, typically consisting of sandy-paste vessels with incised-over-cordmarked and fingernail-punctated decorations.

SOURCE: Stoltman 1979.

David Overstreet

PRATT FOCUS, a poorly known culture complex defined in 1959 by W. R. Wedel, basically as a grouping of distinctive pottery types found at the type site, 14PT1 in Pratt County, in Kansas. The pottery has affinities to Great Bend Aspect (q.v.) ceramics, but also to pottery from sites in New Mexico. The focus probably dates ca. A.D. 1400.

SOURCE: Wedel 1959.

Patricia J. O'Brien

PRE-CADDO CERAMICS, early (ca. 200 B.C.–A.D. 700) pottery in eastern Texas, southeastern Oklahoma, southwestern Arkansas, and northwestern Louisiana that predates the Caddoan cultures of the region. It typically occurs as undecorated, grog- and grit-tempered and/or sandy-paste vessels in the shape of simple jars and bowls. Generally considered part of a more widespread Middle to Late Woodland ceramic tradition, these wares exhibit local variations in vessel shape and paste characteristics. In the northern part of their distribution, the grog- and/or sand-tempered wares known as Williams Plain and Bois D'Arc Plain apparently are ancestral to some later

Caddoan forms. In the south, early sandy-paste wares (e.g., Bear Creek Plain) precede grog- and bone-tempered Caddoan wares. These early ceramics often occur in conjunction with Tchefuncte and Marksville-Troyville pottery, particularly in the south. In the Caddoan regions of Arkansas and Louisiana, some wares of the pre-Caddo ceramic tradition fall within the general Early Mississippian tradition as expressed in the Marksville, Troyville, and Coles Creek phases (qq.v.).
    SOURCES: Jelks 1965; E. M. Davis 1970; M. P. Hoffman 1970; Wyckoff 1970:97–103; Story 1981:145–147.

                                                          James E. Corbin

PRE-DORSET PHASE, an early expression of the Paleoeskimo, Arctic Small Tool Tradition (qq.v.), extending across northern Canada from Banks Island on the west to Labrador on the east. Radiocarbon dated to ca. 2000–1000 B.C., it is thought by most archaeologists to be the cultural predecessor of the Dorset Phase (q.v.). Settlements consisted of clusters of tents outlined by rocks. Lithic assemblages—similar to those of Alaska's Denbigh Flint Complex (q.v.)—are dominated by spalled burins, many of them polished in later parts of the phase. Harpoon heads are of toggling, open socket (female) styles. Pre-Dorset is seen by most authorities as distinct from Independence I (q.v.), but discussion continues over the relative ages of the two phases.
    SOURCES: McGhee 1978:37–51; Maxwell 1985:77–111.

                                                          Moreau S. Maxwell

PRESCOTT PHASE, a phase of the Prescott Province, Patayan Division, Hakataya Culture (qq.v.) in Arizona; estimated to date ca. A.D. 900–1000 on the basis of intrusive Black Mesa Black-on-white and Tusayan Black-on-red Anasazi pottery, which occurs in association with the local Verde Gray and black-on-gray types. Dwellings were oval pithouses outlined with rocks and having two roof-support posts but no ramp or vestibule. Clay figurines occur in sites of the phase, as do both basin and trough metates; the latter suggests the practice of agriculture. Notched stones in and on house floors may have supported raised platforms for storing crops above the moisture-laden earth.
    SOURCES: Gladwin and Gladwin 1934; Colton 1939a.

                                                          Albert H. Schroeder

PRESCOTT PROVINCE, a manifestation of the Patayan Division of the Hakataya Culture (qq.v.), located in Arizona between the Big Sandy and upper Verde rivers north of Prescott and south of the Walapai Plateau. Comprising two phases—Prescott and Chino (qq.v.)—the province was defined in 1930 by Winifred and H. S. Gladwin, who based its geographic distribution on the occurrence of Prescott Gray Ware pottery. People of the province had some dependence on agriculture, and they had contacts with peoples of the Agua Fria, Cerbat, and Cohonina provinces (qq.v.).

SOURCES: Gladwin and Gladwin 1930a; Euler and Dobyns 1962.

Albert H. Schroeder

PRINCE GEORGE WARE, a net-, fabric-, or cord-impressed, pebble-tempered pottery with a row of widely spaced finger pinches or reed punctations below the vertical rim. Dating ca. 300 B.C. to A.D. 400, the ware is restricted to the interior coastal plain of central Virginia.

SOURCES: Clifford Evans 1955; Egloff and Potter 1982; K. T. Egloff n.d.a.

Keith T. Egloff

PRINCE RUPERT HARBOUR SEQUENCE, a temporally ordered series of culture units based on excavations at twelve sites in Prince Rupert Harbour, in northern British Columbia. Three periods have been recognized in the continuous and cumulative cultural development in the harbour area, reflecting increasing socioeconomic complexity through time in a broadly based littoral way of life:

Period III. Dating 3000–1500 B.C., Period III is the initial period during which the basic economic pattern became established on a small scale. Occupation levels contain few artifacts, little variety in faunal remains, rare structural features, and shallow midden deposits. Traits include pebble tools; shell adze blades and points; wedges, chisels, awls, points, pendants, beads, and harpoons of bone; simple, geometric, incised decorations on harpoons and other utilitarian objects.

Period II. Dating 1500 B.C.–A.D. 500, this period is a period of greater social interaction and economic growth. Shell middens become more extensive and contain features suggesting more continuous occupation. There are many burials, some with physical injuries apparently inflicted in warfare; the distribution of grave goods suggests some degree of status differentiation. Flaked- and ground-stone tools increase in frequency, art objects are more numerous, geometric decoration motifs become more elaborate, the first zoomorphic art pieces appear, and exotic items (e.g., obsidian tools) are indicative of trade with other areas.

Period I. Dating A.D. 500–1830, this period is marked by the development of the lifeway followed by the historic Coast Tsimshian Indians. Distinctive traits are semipermanent winter villages of substantial size and social complexity, a well-established zoomorphic art tradition, and an elaborate inventory of both stone and organic artifacts. European goods appear late in

Period I; after 1830, Prince Rupert Harbour was abandoned by the Coast
Tsimshian as a major activity center.
SOURCES: MacDonald and Inglis 1976, 1980–1981.

Patricia D. Sutherland

PROMONTORY CULTURE. See Fremont Culture.

PRYOR STEMMED COMPLEX, one of the terminal Paleoindian (q.v.)
complexes that are strongly oriented to the foothills and mountains in Wyoming and Montana; proposed by George Frison and Donald Grey in 1980.
Several radiocarbon dates place its age at ca. 6300–5800 B.C.; its full geographic spread has not yet been determined. The Pryor Stemmed projectile-
point type, defined by Wilfred Husted in 1969, is the complex's chief diagnostic trait.
SOURCES: Husted 1969; Frison and Grey 1980.

George Frison

PUEBLO, a term meaning town or village in Spanish that was applied by
16th-century Spanish explorers to the village-dwelling Indians of New Mexico and to their settlements. In modern usage, the term is usually specific
and is capitalized; e.g., Pueblo Indians, Pueblo Culture, Cochiti Pueblo,
Pueblo Bonito. Sometimes, the term also is used uncapitalized in nonspecific
reference to Puebloan sites: e.g., "a 30-room pueblo."

Stewart Peckham

PUEBLO ALTO, a pueblo of the classic and late periods of the Bonito Phase
(q.v.), positioned high on the mesa that overlooks Chaco Canyon in northwestern New Mexico. Built ca. A.D. 1030 and abandoned by A.D. 1132, it
comprised about 236 single-story rooms and more than seventeen kivas but
had no great kiva. There also was a huge refuse mound.
    Noted for its wealth of material-culture analyses (sparse for other great-
houses in Chaco Canyon), Pueblo Alto was one of a cluster of greathouses
(the others were Pueblo Bonito, Pueblo del Arroyo, Chetro Ketl, and Kin
Kletso [qq.v.]), that formed the heart of the Chaco phenomenon. It served
as an important point in a visual communications and road network extending throughout the San Juan Basin, and it was connected to other
greathouses (New Alto, Chetro Ketl, Pueblo Bonito, and Penasco Blanco)
by masonry walls and roads. W. J. Judge's and T. C. Windes' excavation
of about 10 percent of the site between 1976 and 1979 led to refinement

of the Chacoan chronology and to the development of new theories regarding the Chaco phenomenon.

SOURCE: Windes 1987.

Thomas C. Windes

PUEBLO BONITO, a magnificent ruin of the Bonito and Mesa Verde phases (qq.v.) in Chaco Culture National Historical Park, in New Mexico. Its Spanish name, "Beautiful Town," is apt for the 650-room pueblo up to four stories high, parts of which (including some intact rooms) are still (in 1987) well preserved. The site also has over 60 kivas, three great kivas, and two huge, walled middens containing trash discarded during a 50-year period of the site's four centuries of occupation, starting ca. A.D. 919.

Pueblo Bonito is the type site for the Bonito Phase, the period between A.D. 900 and 1150 which saw the rise of great, multistoried, Chacoan pueblos in northwestern New Mexico. Excavated by Richard Wetherill and G. H. Pepper between 1896 and 1899 and by N. M. Judd between 1921 and 1927, the site is noted not only for its great size and fine masonry architecture, but also for its wealth of unusual cultural materials, unsurpassed in the Southwest: jewelry made of turquoise, shell, jet, and stone; pottery vessels such as incense burners and cylindrical jars; copper bells and macaws from Mesoamerica; and carved wooden canes.

SOURCES: Pepper 1920; Judd 1964.

Thomas C. Windes

PUEBLO COLORADO, one of the Salinas pueblos located about 6.5 kilometers south of the Tabira Site and east of the Gran Quivira Site (qq.v.) in central New Mexico. Pottery collected from the surface indicates that it probably was occupied ca. A.D. 1325–1625.

SOURCE: Hayes et al. 1981.

Frances Levine

PUEBLO DEL ARROYO, a classic Chacoan greathouse of the Bonito and Mesa Verde phases (qq.v.), located in Chaco Culture National Historical Park, in New Mexico. Its name, meaning "Home Beside the Water's Edge," describes its location on the edge of Chaco Wash, across from Pueblo Bonito (q.v.). The ruin consists of approximately 284 rooms—some partly intact and reaching four stories high—and more than fifteen kivas. Neither a great kiva nor a large refuse mound is evident.

Pueblo del Arroyo was built ca. A.D. 1060, was abandoned ca. 1140, and was reoccupied in the 13th century. A complex of rooms and kivas was attached to its back wall in the early 1100s, including an unusual tri-wall structure (q.v.), the only one of its kind in Chaco Canyon. The type site for

Chaco-McElmo Black-on-white pottery (q.v.), Pueblo del Arroyo was excavated between 1923 and 1926 by Karl Ruppert.
SOURCES: Judd 1959; Vivian 1959.

Thomas C. Windes

PUEBLO DEL ENCIERRO, a Rio Grande Anasazi village of the Classic Period (q.v.), comprising about 250 adobe-walled, ground-level rooms, seven small kivas, one "big kiva," and six early Classic pithouses. Though there are small Developmental and Coalition period components, tree-ring dates show the principal occupation to have been between A.D. 1401 and 1520, with a later, possibly Spanish reuse of some rooms in the 18th century. The predominant pottery is Rio Grande glazeware (q.v.) that shows possible ties to Tano-speaking pueblos in the Galisteo Basin and Puye areas.
SOURCES: A. H. Warren 1979.

Stewart Peckham

PUEBLO GRANDE, a large Hohokam (q.v.) ruin encompassing about 35 hectares, situated on the north bank of the Salt River in the city of Phoenix, Arizona. Both a National Landmark and a Municipal Monument, the main ruin is that of a large, rectangular platform mound consisting of caliche-adobe retaining walls filled with earth to produce an elevated platform on which residences or special-purpose rooms of elite families once stood. Such platform mounds first appeared during the Classic Period (ca. A.D. 1100–1450), the final stage of the Hohokam Culture (qq.v.).

Pueblo Grande has had a long history of archaeological investigation, beginning with F. H. Cushing and the Hemenway Southwest Expedition of 1887. The platform mound was partially excavated in the 1930s as an outgrowth of Works Progress Administration and Civilian Conservation Corps programs. Recent research indicates that the site originally contained two or three ball courts, a multistory building, numerous roomblocks and compounds, and an extensive pre-Classic occupation extending back to at least A.D. 400. The archaeological sequences defined at Snaketown (q.v.), covering the period ca. A.D. 1–1100, and at Casa Grande, running from ca. A.D. 1100 to 1450, represent the entire Hohokam culture sequence as understood in 1987.
SOURCES: J. D. Hayden 1957; Wilcox and Sternberg 1983; Wilcox and Doyel 1987.

David E. Doyel and John S. Cable

PUEBLO GRANDE DE NEVADA. See Lost City and Lost City Phase.

PUEBLO PARDO, one of the Salinas pueblos located about 5 kilometers south of the Gran Quivira Site (q.v.) in central New Mexico, excavated by

J. H. Toulouse, Jr., and R. L. Stephenson in 1960. It was occupied ca. A.D. 1560–1600/1650.

SOURCES: Toulouse and Stephenson 1960; Hayes et al. 1981.

Frances Levine

PUNUK PHASE, an ancestral Eskimo culture unit in the Asian–St. Lawrence Island sequence, dating to the second half of the first millennium and the beginning of the second millennium A.D.; noted for the restraint of its incised art, which tends to be geometric in contrast to the curvilinear flourishes of the immediately preceding art of the Old Bering Sea Phase (q.v.). The type site, in the tiny Punuk Islands of the St. Lawrence group, was excavated in 1928 by H. B. Collins, who named the phase. Important Punuk remains on St. Lawrence Island have come from sites near Gambell (q.v.), excavated by Collins, and from the Kukulik (q.v.) Mound, excavated by Otto Geist and F. G. Rainey. Intergradational Thule-Punuk or Western Thule artifacts have been found at the Kurigitavik Site, in Cape Prince of Wales.

SOURCES: Collins 1937, 1940, 1962.

Donald W. Clark

PUYE CLIFF DWELLINGS, a complex of Classic Period (q.v.) Rio Grande Anasazi ruins west of Espanola, New Mexico, excavated between 1909 and 1926 by E. L. Hewett. On a mesa top is a 700-room, multistoried, masonry-walled pueblo enclosing a rectangular plaza; adjacent to it are a water reservoir and three subterranean kivas excavated into bedrock. Against the cliffs below the mesa top are several kivas, together with hundreds of cavate rooms (q.v.) carved into the soft volcanic tuff forming the mesa. Other masonry-walled dwelling rooms up to three stories high were built against cliff faces in front of the cavate rooms.

The earliest construction at Puye was a small pueblo that probably was built in the A.D. 1200s and was razed by 1400 to accommodate the large mesa-top village, which was built by makers of Biscuitware pottery (q.v.). Abandoned by the early 1500s, the village was reoccupied by 1530 by makers of glaze-decorated pottery—possibly Tano-speaking Pueblo Indians moving into the area from the south. Oral traditions hold that Puye was occupied by the ancestors of the modern Santa Clara Pueblo Indians.

SOURCES: Morley 1910; Hewett and Dutton 1953.

Stewart Peckham

Q

QARMAK (pl. QARMAT), a Neoeskimo (q.v.) autumn dwelling consisting of a shallow pit covered with skins. Modern Inuit qarmat often are on prepared wooden floors.

Moreau S. Maxwell

QUAD POINT, a large, lanceolate, sometimes fluted, chipped-stone projectile-point type, probably of late Paleoindian (q.v.) affiliation, believed to date ca. 8000–7000 B.C. The type is found throughout the Ohio and Tennessee river drainages and adjacent areas, and eastward to the Carolina coast. Similar points found in Florida and Georgia are called Suwannee points.

SOURCES: Soday 1954; Cambron and Waters 1959; Cambron and Hulse 1964, 1975:107.

Eugene M. Futato

QUAD SITE, a Paleoindian (q.v.) site, thought to date ca. 10,000–8000 B.C., where F. J. Soday in 1951 collected large numbers of early forms of projectile points and other stone tools from the eroded surfaces of two ridges near Decatur, Alabama. Quad was one of the earliest recognized Paleoindian sites east of the Mississippi River.

SOURCE: Soday 1954.

John A. Walthall

QUALLA CULTURE (or PHASE), a protohistoric to historic (A.D. 1500–1800) culture following the Pisgah Culture (q.v.) in the archaeological sequence of the South Appalachians, occurring mainly in western North Carolina; originally defined by B. J. Egloff in 1967. Many of its later sites have been correlated with historically documented Cherokee towns. Artifacts include bold, complicated-stamped, and plain-incised pottery vessels; pottery discs; small, triangular, chipped-stone points; ground-stone celts and

discs; bone tools; and marine-shell beads and gorgets. Historic period sites also contain European trade goods. Early, small to medium-sized Qualla villages were clustered and palisaded; later villages consisted of strings of houses loosely grouped on river floodplains. Some large sites contain a small platform mound.
SOURCES: B. J. Egloff 1967; L. G. Ferguson 1971; Dickens 1978, 1979, 1985.

Roy S. Dickens, Jr.

QUALLA POTTERY SERIES, a Lamar-like, grit-tempered, pottery style associated with the Qualla Phase (q.v.) and identified with the historic Cherokee of ca. A.D. 1550–1900 in the western mountains of North Carolina. It is characterized by folded, finger-impressed rim fillets, bold incising, and large sloppy, carved, stamped designs. Six surface treatments occur: complicated stamped, plain, burnished, check stamped, cordmarked, and corncob impressed. Vessel shapes include simple and carinated bowls, globular jars with short necks, and large jars with constricted mouths. Qualla pottery is believed to have developed directly from Pisgah Series pottery of the Pisgah Phase (qq.v.).
SOURCES: B. J. Egloff 1967:34–45; Keel 1976; Dickens 1976.

Billy L. Oliver

QUAPAW. See Arkansas Post.

QUARAI SITE, a multicomponent site near Punta de Agua, New Mexico consisting of the 17th-century Franciscan mission complex of La Purisima Concepcion de Curac, the foundations of an earlier, smaller chapel, and about nine unexcavated Pueblo house mounds and associated plazas dating ca. A.D. 1300–1672. Quarai was purchased by the Museum of New Mexico in 1913, was declared a State Monument in 1935, and was transferred to the newly created Salinas National Monument in 1981.

E. L. Hewett excavated the church and convento complex in 1913, and the Archaeological Society of New Mexico conducted excavations in the South Mound in 1916. The Museum of New Mexico and the University of New Mexico, in conjunction with the Civilian Conservation Corps, began stabilizing and landscaping the monument in 1934–1936, work that was completed in 1938–1940 by the Works Progress Administration. Stanley Stubbs explored the early chapel foundations in 1959, and the Museum of New Mexico restabilized the church and convento between 1972 and 1979.

Few of the archaeological field studies at Quarai have been published,

but the information unearthed there documents important episodes of culture change among the protohistoric Puebloans.
SOURCES: J. P. Wilson 1973; Stubbs and Stallings 1959.

Frances Levine

QUERECHO PHASE, the earliest (ca. A.D. 950–1100/1150) phase of the Eastern Extension Sub-Province of the Jornada Province, Mogollon Culture (qq.v.), in the southeastern corner of New Mexico. It is distinguished from the preceding late Archaic, Hueco Phase by the appearance of ceramics and a shift in use from the spear and atlatl to the bow and arrow. Structures which left identifiable archaeological remains evidently did not appear until the end of the phase, although excavations in two sites have uncovered prepared clay "pads" used as living surfaces. Ceramics include Jornada Brown (q.v.) and locally made cognatese; Cebolleta Black-on-white has been noted as an intrusive. Corner-notched arrow points are typical, and grinding equipment includes the basin metate and its characteristic oval, one-hand mano. Subsistence was based upon hunting and gathering.
SOURCE: Leslie 1979.

R. N. Wiseman

QUICKSBURG SITE, a palisaded Woodland (q.v.) village on the North Fork of the Shenandoah River in northwestern Virginia, containing house patterns, burials, and storage pits. Predominant ceramics were Page and Keyser wares (qq.v.). The site was studied by C. G. Holland in 1966 and by H. A. MacCord in 1969.
SOURCES: Holland 1966; MacCord 1973.

Keith T. Egloff

QUILILUKAN SITE, the type site for the Post Classic period (ca. A.D. 1350–1400) of the Thule Phase (q.v.), located near Pond Inlet on North Baffin Island, Northwest Territories. Therkel Mathiassen, who excavated there in the 1920s, found 60 harpoon heads that demonstrated a progression of styles from Naujan to later types. There was a reduced emphasis on whaling at the site, as well as a shift from deep winter pithouses to shallower qarmat (q.v.) and winter snow houses.
SOURCE: Mathiassen 1927.

Moreau S. Maxwell

R

RABBIT MOUNT SITE, a Woodland (q.v.) midden in the Groton Plantation locality (q.v.), Hampton County, South Carolina, where J. B. Stoltman's excavations in 1964 revealed a significant Stallings Phase occupation with the earliest radiocarbon date associated with pottery in the United States: 2505 ± 135 B.C. Stoltman found abundant pottery, lithics, worked bone, faunal and floral remains, and evidence of a Stallings Phase structure in the midden.

SOURCES: Stoltman 1966, 1974a.

Michael Trinkley

RADDATZ ROCKSHELTER, one of several rockshelters in the driftless area of Wisconsin excavated by W. L. Wittry in the 1950s. Source of the type sample for the Raddatz Side-Notched projectile-point type, this site played an important role in the definition of Archaic and Woodland sequences in central Wisconsin.

SOURCE: Wittry 1959a.

David Overstreet

RADFORD POTTERY SERIES, a term originally used comprehensively to include all limestone-tempered pottery in the New River and Tennessee River drainages of southwestern Virginia; now limited to an undecorated, net-, cord-, and corncob-impressed ware dating ca. A.D. 1000–1650.

SOURCES: Clifford Evans 1955; Holland 1970; K. T. Egloff n.d.b.

Keith T. Egloff

RADIOCARBON DATING, the principal physical dating method used in North American archaeology. Radiocarbon (carbon 14) is produced in the atmosphere by the action of cosmic rays. Metabolic processes maintain a constant concentration of carbon 14 in living organisms, both plant and animal. At an organism's death, the residual carbon 14 activity in its surviving tissue decreases at a constant rate through radioactive decay. The method can be used to infer the age of organic materials up to about 50,000 years old by measuring residual carbon 14 activity. The use of accelerator mass spectrometry has allowed the use of much smaller samples (measured in milligrams of carbon) and potentially may extend the time frame to about 100,000 years.

SOURCES: Libby 1955; R. E. Taylor, Jr. 1978.

R. E. Taylor

RAINBOW HOUSE, a Classic Period (q.v.) Rio Grande Anasazi ruin in Cañon de los Frijoles, Bandelier National Monument, in New Mexico; excavated by F. C. V. Worman in 1948–1950. Consisting of 46 masonry rooms in two houseblocks, plus a round subterranean kiva, it has been dated by dendrochronology between A.D. 1421 and 1453. Pottery types, about equally divided between early to middle-range Rio Grande glazewares and Biscuitware (qq.v.), indicate at least some earlier occupation in the 14th century A.D.

SOURCE: Caywood 1966.

Stewart Peckham

RAISCH-SMITH SITE, an extensive Archaic (q.v.) component covering about 2 hectares along Four Mile Creek in Preble county, in Ohio, within Hueton Woods State Park. Excavations in 1933, 1945, and 1948–1950 by avocational archaeologists and the Ohio Historical Society produced numerous chipped- and ground-stone tools, including unfinished tubular bannerstones (q.v.).

SOURCES: Moffett 1949; J. B. Griffin 1955; Mayer-Oakes 1955:232; Long 1962.

N'omi B. Greber

RAISEBECK MOUND GROUP, a site in Grant County, in southwestern Wisconsin, comprising both Middle and Late Woodland mounds. Excavated by W. C. McKern in 1932, it was one of many sites incorporated in C. W. Rowe's analysis of the Effigy Mound Culture (q.v.).

SOURCE: Rowe 1956.

David Overstreet

RAMOS BLACK POTTERY, a polished blackware that occurs as bowls and jars of varying shape, also as effigies and hand drums; a hallmark of the Medio and Tardio periods of the Casas Grandes Culture (q.v.) of northwestern Chihuahua. Over two-thirds of the Ramos Black vessels found at

the Casas Grandes Sites (q.v.) were funeral furniture, a practice that continued into the following period.
SOURCES: Di Peso 1974: vol. 2; Di Peso et al. 1974:vol. 6.

Gloria J. Fenner

RANGE SITE, a large, multicomponent site on the Mississippi River floodplain in the American Bottom, in southwestern Illinois. Excavations there by the University of Illinois at Urbana-Champaign from 1977 through 1981 exposed over 5500 pits and houses attributed to numerous occupations, from the Late Archaic (ca. 3000 B.C.) to the Oneota (ca. A.D. 1400) traditions, and revealed a continuous sequence of community plans from the terminal Late Woodland (ca. A.D. 600) through the Mississippian (ca. A.D. 1150) periods.
SOURCES: Kelly and Fortier 1983; Bareis and Porter 1984.

Charles J. Bareis and Andrew C. Fortier

RAPIDAN MOUND, a burial mound radiocarbon dated to A.D. 1440, located on the Rapidan River in the northern Piedmont of Virginia. In 1894, Gerard Fowke described the mound and dug a large trench in it; in 1979–1980, C. G. Holland, S. D. Speiden, and David van Roijen tested what was left of it. The Rapidan and Jefferson's (q.v.) mounds are the only documented burial mounds in the Piedmont. Each held hundreds of individuals, evidently representing all ranks within the society.
SOURCES: Fowke 1894; Holland et al. 1983.

Keith T. Egloff

RAT INDIAN CREEK, a location adjacent to the Klo-kut Site (q.v.) near Old Crow in the northern Yukon Territory which, along with other sites in the area, has contributed significantly to the definition of a prehistoric Athapaskan (q.v.) sequence of nearly 3000 years' duration. First tested in 1968 by R. E. Morlan, further tested in 1972–1973, and extensively excavated in 1976–1978 as part of the University of Toronto Northern Research Programme, the site has produced a large number of bone and antler implements, an artifact class often missing in sites of the boreal forest because of poor organic preservation. On the basis of changes in lithic technology, including a reduced frequency of bifacially flaked artifacts, R. J. Le Blanc has proposed two phases for the sequence: an earlier Old Chief Phase (ca. 900 B.C.–A.D. 700) and a later Klo-kut Phase (A.D. 700 to mid–19th-century European contact).
SOURCE: Le Blanc 1984.

Donald W. Clark

RATTLERS BIGHT PHASE, the terminal Maritime Archaic (q.v.) manifestation along the cental Labrador coast, preceding occupation of the area by Paleoeskimos. Habitation sites dating between 2000 and 1500 B.C. some-

times contain large multifamily longhouses and elaborate burials equivalent in many respects to those in Newfoundland and the Maritimes. Rattlers Bight economy appears to have been largely marine oriented.
SOURCE: Fitzhugh 1972.

James A. Tuck

RAYMOND FOCUS, a poorly defined Late Woodland expression in the western portions of extreme southern Illinois, essentially representing the entire local Late Woodland sequence (ca. A.D. 400–800) except for its terminal portion (Dillinger Focus, q.v.). The type site is on the Big Muddy River north of Carbondale, in Jackson County. Raymond ceramics, primarily grit tempered and cordmarked, are generally similar to ceramics of other Late Woodland complexes in the southern Midwest. Raymond pottery is comparable to contemporaneous pottery in the American Bottom to the north.
SOURCE: Maxwell 1951.

Brian M. Butler

REAGAN SITE, a site in northwestern Vermont, excavated by W. R. Ritchie in 1952, that produced a number of fluted projectile points of several shapes—mostly triangular, lanceolate, and pentagonal—all dating to late Paleoindian times (ca. 9000–8000 B.C.).
SOURCES: Ritchie 1953; D. R. Snow 1980:142–143.

Edward B. Jelks

RECTANGULAR KIVA, a subterranean or semisubterranean kiva (q.v.), or ceremonial room, typical of the later Sinagua, Hopi Mesa (qq.v.), Tsegi, and Point of Pines (q.v.) prehistoric cultures of northeastern Arizona and of the Zuni and Mimbres cultures of New Mexico after A.D. 1000–1250, and thus diagnostic of Western Pueblo traditions. Constructed with stone walls and often covered with matting and clay, they had a raised bench across the southern or spectators' end with a ventilator shaft underneath, which rose to the surface in back. The northern (sacred) floor area had a central firepit with a deflector in front, a sipapu hole (through which Kachinas emerged and descended, as did the original Hopi people), and sets of from three to five anchor holes for looms. All kivas had stone-paved floors and were entered by ladder through a central hatchway in the roof.
SOURCES: Watson Smith 1972; E. C. Adams 1982, 1983.

Michael B. Stanislawski

REDBANKS/POINT SAUBLE/BEAUMIER FARM, a locality on the eastern shore of Green Bay, Wisconsin; the site of a large Oneota/Winnebago village and of an earlier Late Woodland occupation. The type site for Point

Sauble Collared Ceramics, it also is thought to be the location of explorer Jean Nicolet's landfall in 1650.
SOURCE: Freeman 1956.

David Overstreet

REDBIRD PHASE, a unit of the Plains Village Tradition consisting of earth-lodge villages clustered near the mouth of the Niobrara River and Ponca Creek in northeastern Nebraska; provisionally attributed to the late pre-historic and protohistoric Ponca Indians. Related campsites occur up the Niobrara River to the west and along the Elkhorn River to the south.
SOURCE: W. R. Wood 1965.

W. Raymond Wood

RED CEDAR RIVER FOCUS, a Middle Woodland burial complex of north-western Wisconsin related to Hopewellian cultures (q.v.) to the south; es-timated to date ca. A.D. 200. The burials are notable for the use of clay funeral masks.
SOURCE: L. R.Cooper 1933.

David Overstreet

RED HILL SITE, a Late Woodland village on the Roanoke River in the southern Piedmont of Virginia, tested in 1965 by H. A. MacCord, who found storage pits, hearths, faunal remains, and pottery (Dan River [q.v.] Ware predominating).
SOURCE: Segall 1981.

Keith T. Egloff

REDHOUSE PHASE, a late Pueblo III manifestation on Cedar Mesa in the Cedar Mesa Province (q.v.), southeastern Utah, consisting of small, scattered sites on the mesa tops and cliff dwellings in the canyons. Dating ca. A.D. 1225–1270, it followed the Woodenshoe Phase (q.v.) and was the terminal Anasazi occupation on the mesa. Having Mesa Verde (q.v.) style architecture and ceramics, Redhouse is roughly equivalent to the terminal Pueblo III occupation on Mesa Verde, although on a much smaller scale. In some respects, it resembles the Horsefly Hollow Phase (q.v.) of the Red Rock Plateau.
SOURCE: Matson and Lipe 1978.

R. G. Matson

RED MOUNTAIN PHASE. See Pioneer Period.

RED OCHER CULTURE, term designating a series of related Late Archaic–Early Woodland mortuary complexes associated with the Marion Culture in the Upper Mississippi River Valley. No habitation sites have been reported. It is not clear when the use of copper implements, large ceremonial spears, Turkey-Tail points, and red ocher were first employed in the broader Great Lakes region. As most Red Ocher sites have been exposed accidentally by modern earthmoving activities, few sites have been investigated with carefully controlled excavation techniques.

SOURCES: Ritzenthaler and Quimby 1962; Overstreet 1980.

David Overstreet

RED-ON-BUFF POTTERY, a distinctive ware of the Hohokam Culture (q.v.) in southern Arizona typified by red designs painted on a buff-slipped ground. Unlike the neighboring Mogollon and Anasazi (qq.v.) people who made their pots by the coil-and-scrape technique, the Hohokam used the paddle-and-anvil method to shape vessels by compressing unfired clay fillets or coils between an anvil on the interior surface and a paddle on the exterior surface. Decorative styles and technological details of the ware underwent changes through time which serve as valuable time markers to the archaeologist.

The first comprehensive typology of Hohokam decorated pottery was developed by E. W. Haury on the basis of excavations in 1934–1935 at the Snaketown Site (q.v.) on the Gila River. His types formed a framework for the first Hohokam chronology, in which each pottery type represented a different culture phase. The earliest Hohokam pottery, termed red-on-gray, was unslipped. The tradition of slipping surfaces began in the Snaketown Phase (q.v.) and was common in the Phoenix Basin (q.v.) and provinces to the north. Pottery with unslipped surfaces, however, continued to be the norm in the more southerly provinces (i.e., Tucson Basin, San Pedro, and Papagueria [qq.v.]), where it is known as the red-on-brown tradition.

SOURCES: Gladwin et al. 1937; Haury 1976; Masse 1982.

John S. Cable and David E. Doyel

RED ROCK POINT SITE, a Groswater Dorset Phase component on Hamilton Inlet, Labrador, excavated by W. W. Fitzhugh. A radiocarbon date of ca. 250 B.C. indicates an overlap between Groswater Dorset and the other Paleoeskimo (q.v.) phase, Early Dorset.

SOURCE: Fitzhugh 1972.

Moreau S. Maxwell

REEDY CREEK SITE, a Late Woodland village on the Dan River in the south-central Piedmont of Virginia. When G. N. Coleman dug the site in 1975, he found a midden, several features (including a small semisubter-

ranean structure), and a wide variety of charred floral and faunal remains associated with Clarksville Series pottery (q.v.).
SOURCE: Coleman et al. 1982.

Keith T. Egloff

REFUGE CULTURE, an Early Woodland (ca. 1100–500 B.C.) manifestation defined by A. J. Waring on the basis of his 1947 excavations at the Refuge Site in Jasper County, in South Carolina. Components of the culture also have been investigated at the Second Refuge and Alligator Creek sites (qq.v.). Other sites, including shell middens and small camps, occur on the coastal plain of South Carolina and Georgia. Refuge ceramics are characterized by a coarse, gritty paste, simple stamping, and simple vessel forms.
    SOURCES: Waring 1968; Peterson 1971; Thomas and Larsen 1979; Trinkley 1982; Lepionka et al. n.d.

Michael Trinkley

RENIER SITE, one of two reported late Paleoindian (q.v.) cremations near the city of Green Bay, Wisconsin, investigated by R. J. Mason and Carol Irwin in 1959. Heat-shattered Eden-Scottsbluff projectile points (qq.v.) were found in association with calcined human remains.
SOURCE: Mason and Irwin 1960.

David Overstreet

RENNER SITE, the type site of the Kansas City Hopewell Phase (q.v.) located near Parkville, Missouri; excavated by W. R. Wedel in the 1930s. It is a large habitation site whose pottery exhibits decorative motifs derived from Illinois Hopewell communities near St. Louis, whose projectile points are Hopewell types (Ensor, Gibson, Steuben, and Snyders), and whose end scrapers are the blocky and circular varieties of the central Illinois River Valley.
    SOURCES: Wedel 1943; A. E. Johnson 1976.

Patricia J. O'Brien

RESCH SITE, a midden from 3 to 4 feet thick covering an area of about a hectare, situated on a low terrace of Potter's Creek, a tributary of the Sabine River in Harrison County, in Texas. The site was discovered by three avocational archaeologists of Marshall, Texas, F. E. Murphey, W. G. Ellis, and H. R. Green. Over a period of several years in the 1960s, with the guidance of C. H. Webb and the assistance of numerous relatives, friends, and volunteers, they excavated nearly 300 5-foot squares in the midden, collecting more than 41,000 artifacts, nut shells, and faunal specimens.
    Important aspects of this small site were (1) its similarity to numerous multicomponent, seasonally occupied sites in the uplands of the Trans-Mississippi Southeast; (2) its intermittent uses during a period of four mil-

lennia, from the Middle Archaic to the Caddoan period (ca. 3000 B.C.–A.D. 1200); (3) the uses of local lithic materials throughout this period; (4) a shift from dart to arrow use in Coles Creek (q.v.) and Caddo (q.v.) I times; (5) indigenous ceramic development from ca. 400 B.C. to ca. A.D. 1200 (Caddo I), featuring clay, bone, and sand aplastics; (6) introduction of Lower Mississippi Valley ceramics, including Tchefuncte, Marksville, Troyville (qq.v.), and Coles Creek styles.

SOURCE: Webb et al. 1969.

Clarence H. Webb

RESERVOIR LAKES PHASE, a late Paleoindian (ca. 8000–4000 B.C.) complex whose components have yielded variations of Scottsbluff, Agate Basin, Eden, Hell Gap, and Plainview (qq.v.) type projectile points. It is probably related to the Lakehead Complex of the Thunder Bay area in Ontario. While the phase's geographic limits are poorly defined, the densest concentration of its materials is at a series of reservoir lakes along the Cloquet and Beaver rivers northeast of Duluth, Minnesota.

SOURCES: Steinbring 1974; Fox 1975, 1980; Dawson 1983.

Gordon R. Peters

RESOLUTE LOCALITY, a place on Cornwallis Island, Northwest Territories, where late Dorset Phase and early Thule Phase (qq.v.) sites were excavated in the early 1950s by H. B. Collins. Although the Dorset components are very late and the Thule components very early, there is no indicated contact between the two phases. Artifacts from the Thule components are typologically some of the earliest in the eastern Arctic.

SOURCE: Collins 1955.

Moreau S. Maxwell

RIDGE RUIN, a major Elden Phase (q.v.) pueblo of the Sinagua Tradition (q.v.), located in north-central Arizona and dating ca. A.D. 1100–1200. The main pueblo was two stories tall in places, had over twenty ground-floor rooms, and was built on top of an earlier pithouse settlement. It is the best example of an Elden Phase central place, being located on a hill along what is believed to have been a prehistoric trade route, and having inner and outer plazas, a large community room, ball courts, and a high frequency of trade items. The only site in northern Arizona with two ball courts, it appears to have been the hub of a settlement system comprising a number of sites scattered around the sides of a large lava flow. Some of these sites were small pithouse settlements that may eventually have aggregated into Ridge Ruin.

J. C. McGregor and M. A. Wetherill tested Ridge Ruin and the sites around it in 1939 as part of a project to investigate ball courts and the suspected presence of the Hohokam Culture (q.v.) in northern Arizona. On the basis of one room's masonry style, they hypothesized a migration of Chaco Anasazi (qq.v.) people to the Flagstaff region, but this is now doubted. In another room, they found the so-called Magician's Burial (q.v.), one of the most spectacular burials yet found in the Southwest.

Ridge Ruin and Winona Village (q.v.) have provided much of the data used in defining phase concepts and cultural development in the Flagstaff Province between A.D. 1064 and 1200.

SOURCES: McGregor 1941a, 1943; Fish et al. 1980.

Peter J. Pilles, Jr.

RIGGINS FABRIC IMPRESSED POTTERY, a Late Woodland type dating ca. A.D. 900–1600 that is very widespread on the middle Atlantic coastal plain. Exterior vessel surfaces bear impressions of fabric-wrapped paddles; bodies are tempered with finely crushed quartz or other locally available stone. The type is usually undecorated, but sometimes there are incised linear decorations or cord impressions below a vessel's rim.

SOURCE: McCann 1957.

Ronald A. Thomas

RING HOUSE, a style of shallow residential pithouse, consisting of an oval or circular main room and an attached antechamber, which appeared during the Los Pinos Phase (q.v.), ca. A.D. 1–400, in the Upper San Juan Province (q.v.) of northern New Mexico and southern Colorado. The hemispherical superstructure was made of cribbed logs; the main room was outfitted with a central fire basin and usually with several storage pits. The name comes from a ring of river cobbles laid around the edge of the house floor.

SOURCES: Morris and Burgh 1954; Fenenga and Wendorf 1956; Eddy 1961, 1966, 1972.

Frank W. Eddy

RIO ABAJO PROVINCE, a little-studied area along the Rio Grande (largely between Belen on the north and the northern end of Elephant Butte Lake on the south), and along the Rio Salado, a western tributary, all within New Mexico. A reconnaissance in 1980 by M. P. Marshall and H. J. Walt recorded sites of the Paleoindian and Archaic periods, as well as sites identified with the Mogollon Culture (q.v.) on the basis of their abundant brownware pottery and both locally made and intrusive painted wares. Marshall and Walt proposed a provisional phase sequence for the period A.D. 300–1670 that traces cultural development in the province from the beginning

of permanent agricultural settlements to historically documented, Piro-speaking Pueblo people reported by Spaniards in the 17th century.
SOURCE: Marshall and Walt 1984.

Stewart Peckham

RIO DE FLAG PHASE, the best-known preeruptive phase of the Northern Sinagua Tradition (q.v.) in north-central Arizona, coeval with the early Pueblo II period from ca. A.D. 900 to the eruption of Sunset Crater (q.v.) in A.D. 1064/1066. Sites of the phase, which occur over most of the Northern Sinagua territory, have a greater geographic spread to the east than do sites of the preceding phases. The distribution of sites may reflect a response to a warmer, drier climate that began ca. A.D. 900, for they are concentrated along the east flanks of the San Francisco Peaks where there are more springs and greater precipitation than elsewhere in the region. Large alluvial basins, called parks, at the bases of the peaks contain prime farmlands. By settling on the margins of these parks, the Sinaguans could employ several farming strategies: dry farming on the parks, ak chin (q.v.) floodwater farming where drainages from the parks entered the margins of the parks, and check-dam farming along the washes on the sides of the peaks.

Pithouses continued to be subrectangular, circular, and square, and they continued to have central firepits, four-post roof-support systems, and lateral ramp entries to the east side of the house. Ventilators, bulbous alcoves rather than ramp entries, pithouse walls completely or partially lined with stone masonry, timber-lined pithouse walls, and pithouses constructed on low earthen mounds are known for the phase. In addition to pithouses, small masonry structures—probably field houses used for seasonal farming activities—have been reported. Exceptionally large pithouses, called community rooms, at some of the larger sites are assumed to have served the same community integrative function as Anasazi great kivas (q.v.). These occur only at larger sites close to optimal farmlands, thought to have been major villages in a hierarchical settlement system.

The dominant local pottery for the Rio de Flag Phase, as for the entire preeruptive period, was Rio de Flag Brown ware. Intrusives from the Cohonina Province (q.v.) and the Kayenta Anasazi area form a large part of the ceramic assemblage; pottery from the Hohokam (q.v.) area, although rare, is present. Soil- and water-control devices include irrigation ditches and check dams. Burials are predominantly extended, although a few are flexed.
SOURCES: Colton 1939b:37–39, 1946:269–270, 312–314; DeBoer 1976; J. P. Wilson 1969:49–186.

Peter J. Pilles, Jr.

RIO GRANDE CLASSIC PERIOD, a period of the Tano Province in north-central New Mexico between ca. A.D. 1350 and the founding of the Spanish colonial capital of Santa Fe in 1610. The period has the potential of future division into several phases as archaeological understanding improves.

This was a time when many pueblos with from several hundred to a thousand or more inhabitants dotted the province, all of them apparently located at springs or on perennial streams. The Galisteo Basin became a major population center. Important communities included Agua Fria (School House), Arroyo Hondo, Blanco, Cieneguilla, Colorado, Galisteo, Largo, San Lazaro, San Marcos, She, Ogapoge, and San Cristobal. N. C. Nelson partially excavated many of these between 1912 and 1915, collecting large samples of pottery that later were used by H. P. Mera in his important ceramic studies.

Town plans varied; the preferred plan had one or more roomblock arrangements, each enclosing a plaza. Reservoirs were more common than previously, and there was an intensive mixture of bottomland ditch and floodwater irrigation, pit gardening, and upland dry farming of terraced ridges, slopes, and swales. Galisteo Black-on-white pottery (q.v.) gradually went out of production during the 1400s and was replaced by various red, yellow, gray, and polychrome wares decorated with glaze paints. The unindented-corrugated and smeared-over, indented-corrugated gray and brownwares prominent during the preceding Galisteo Phase (q.v.) were replaced by plain-surfaced culinary wares. Export of pottery made in the province flourished. Rock art focused strongly on kachina motifs, probably reflecting the introduction of the kachina cult. Mining in the Cerrillos was expanded to include lead ore for use in making pottery glaze paints.

Following the droughts of the 1400s and early 1500s, the overall population probably declined as many farmsteads and farm fields were abandoned. Trade with Plains peoples and/or middlemen continued, and there may have been a major incursion of Plains nomads. In 1540, the first of several Spanish exploration parties visited the province, presaging the period's conclusion with the establishment of Santa Fe.

SOURCES: N. C. Nelson 1914; Mera 1940.

                                                    Richard W. Lang

RIO GRANDE CLASSIFICATION SYSTEM. See Southwestern Classification Systems.

RIO GRANDE COMPLEX, an Archaic (q.v.) complex in northern New Mexico and southern Colorado, proposed by K. H. Honea in 1969 in his redefinition of E. B. Renauds's Upper Rio Grande Culture. Honea viewed the complex as potentially deriving from the Agate Basin Complex (q.v.) of the Plains, and as comprising several sequential phases, beginning with the Quemado Phases and continuing through unnamed phases correlative with the San Jose, Lobo, and Atrisco complexes. Cynthia Irwin-Williams has since divided the Quemado Phase into earlier Jay and later Bajada phases (qq.v.) within her broadly defined Oshara Tradition (q.v.), which probably originated ultimately in the San Dieguito Complex (q.v.) of the far West. In both concept and nomenclature, the Oshara Tradition has replaced the Rio Grande Complex in the literature.

SOURCES: Renaud 1942; Honea 1969.

Richard W. Lang

RIO GRANDE GLAZE-PAINT POTTERY, a series of ceramic wares made by the Rio Grande Anasazi during their Classic Period (q.v.) in the Middle Rio Grande, Galisteo Basin, Salinas, Rio Abajo, and (briefly and late) Tewa Basin and Picuris provinces (qq.v.). Introduced ca. A.D. 1315–1325 from the Upper Little Colorado and Zuni provinces of west-central New Mexico and Arizona, this pottery was decorated with a lead-fluxed pigment that fired to a black, brown, or, rarely, apple-green glaze. Bichrome decoration—glaze on a red, orange, yellow, or tan ground—occurred early and also in the 1600s; polychrome decorations with glaze paint used to frame solid red elements occurred throughout. Glaze paint was used exclusively as decoration (not as a waterproofing agent) on slipped surfaces of water jars, food bowls, canteens, and "ceremonial" vessels, but not on pottery used for cooking.

A. V. Kidder and A. O. Shepard studied glazewares from Pecos Pueblo (q.v.) and distinguished six roughly sequential groups (Pecos Glazes I–VI), using rim form, slip color, type of temper, and the degree to which the glaze paint ran during firing as criteria. Shepard's petrographic analyses showed that most early glaze-paint pottery at Pecos had been imported from other pueblos; only the last two groups were made locally.

H. P. Mera, finding that glaze-paint pottery in the Middle Rio Grande Province did not follow the Pecos sequence, distinguished a series of over a dozen named types and placed them into six groups designated alphabetically. Recent petrographic studies by A. H. Warren provide more precise dates for Mera's ceramic groups (all dates are A.D.): Glaze A, 1315–1425; Glaze B, 1400–1450; Glaze C, 1400/1425–1500; Glaze D, 1490–1515; Glaze E, 1515–1600/1650; Glaze F, 1650–1700+.

Late glaze-paint pottery types have been found on 18th-century Navajo sites in the Upper San Juan Province (q.v.) and as intrusions at sites in western Texas and central Kansas.

SOURCES: Mera 1933; Kidder and Shepard 1936; Shepard 1942; A.H. Warren 1979.

Stewart Peckham

RIO SONORA CULTURE, the local manifestation of a widespread cultural tradition, found throughout the eastern ranges of Sonora, from the extreme southern part of the state northward to the Fronteras Basin. It was first defined by Monroe Amsden in 1928 on the basis of a series of sites in the upper Rio Sonora Valley. In the south, it is represented by the Los Camotes–

San Bernardo (qq.v.) phase sequence, beginning ca. A.D. 700 and lasting until the Spanish entrada in the 1530s. In the north, extensive research has been conducted only in the upper Rio Sonora Valley; only a few surveys have been carried out in neighboring valleys.

The culture is characterized throughout by the presence of ceramics decorated with punctating and linear incising. On the north, the decoration includes the use of red paint in addition to, or together with, texturing, producing a ceramic that in varying degrees resembles red-painted, textured types in northeastern Chihuahua. In the south, the use of red pigment on textured pottery is absent.

Dwellings comprise two basic types: pithouses and above-ground structures. Pithouses have been found only in the north, where they preceded surface structures but continued in use probably until historic times. The remains of surface dwellings are of two kinds: those with only a foundation remaining and those with standing walls of crude stone masonry. The latter are found only in the south on certain sites situated on hilltop prominences. Ball courts appear in Rio Sonora Valley sites sometime after A.D. 1150.

Stone bowls and overhanging manos (q.v.) are common in the south; decorated stone spindle whorls, shaft smoothers, and turquoise beads are typical artifacts in the north. Chihuahuan polychromes are the predominant intrusive pottery in northern sites, indicating close ties with the Casas Grandes Site (q.v.).

SOURCES: Amsden 1928; Pailes 1972, 1976, 1980, 1984.

Richard A. Pailes

RIO SONORA INCISED WARE, a general term for a brownware pottery decorated with textured patterns produced by incising and punctating before firing; found throughout the eastern mountain zone of Sonora in sites of the Rio Sonora Culture (q.v.). In form and decoration, many sherds are identical to the Casas Grandes Incised and Convento Incised types in Chihuahua, differing only in clay and temper. Others are reminiscent of Playas Red Incised, also found in Chihuahua. In southern Sonora appear the cognate types Los Camotes Incised, San Bernardo Incised, and San Bernardo Punctate Incised which, except for lacking the red pigment combined with texturing, are identical to the ware farther north.

SOURCES: Pailes 1972, 1980, 1984.

Richard A. Pailes

RIVERSIDE SITE, a large multicomponent cemetery and village site near the mouth of the Menominee River in Menominee County, in Michigan. Excavations by Robert Hruska between 1961 and 1963 disclosed a large number of burials dating to both Late Archaic and Middle Woodland times. Lavish grave goods are predominantly from the later period, although Old

Copper (q.v.) artifacts were found in some graves as well as in the village area.
SOURCE: Hruska 1967.

Charles E. Cleland

RIVERTON CULTURE, an Archaic (q.v.) expression known from several sites along the Wabash River near Vincennes, Indiana, defined by H. D. Winters in 1969. Dating ca. 1500 to 1000 B.C., the hunting-gathering culture is distinguished by a rich variety of stone and bone tools and by a settlement pattern comprising year-round settlements plus seasonally occupied bases, hunting, and transient camps.
SOURCE: Winters 1969.

Edward B. Jelks

ROADCUT SITE, a multicomponent, stratified site on the Columbia River, 180 miles from its mouth, where it cuts through the Cascade Range; spanning some 9000 years of occupation, one of the longest sequences in northwestern America. Excavated from 1953 to 1956 by L. S. Cressman and students, the site's most significant material came from the lower three strata. Although yielding only a few flaked-stone and bone artifacts, Stratum I produced an early radiocarbon date of ca. 7835 B.C. Artifacts from Stratum II, with a radiocarbon date of ca. 5725 B.C., included large chipped-stone projectile points, a variety of other flaked-stone tools, and waterworn pebbles with pecked grooves, an inventory similar to that of the Windust Phase (q.v.). Stratum II was additionally significant because of its rich bone and antler industry. Thousands of salmon vertebrae together with many bird and mammal bones demonstrate excellent adaptation at this early time to the Northwest environment.

The bone and antler industry declined and disappeared in Stratum III. Stratum IV, with radiocarbon dates of 5925 and 4140 B.C., produced a few nondiagnostic artifacts. From Strata V and VI, not dated, came a variety of late projectile points, cobble choppers, peripherally flaked cobbles, small flake tools, and some carved stone and bone artifacts. The period of European contact was marked by the appearance of copper and iron artifacts.
SOURCES: Cressman et al. 1960; D. G. Rice 1972.

Robert E. Greengo

ROANOKE LARGE TRIANGULAR POINT, a triangular, chipped-stone projectile point with slightly concave sides and base; a type of the Vincent and Deep Creek phases (qq.v.) of North Carolina and Virginia. Dating ca.

1000–300 B.C., the type signals the introduction of the triangular point tradition to the area.
SOURCES: Coe 1964:110–111; Oliver 1985.

Billy L. Oliver

ROANOKE WARE, a shell-tempered, simple-stamped ceramic, defined by M. C. Blaker in 1952 from sherds found earlier by J. C. Harrington at the original Fort Raleigh, in North Carolina. The ware, very rarely incised below the rim, occurs mainly in the estuarine coastal plain of northern North Carolina and southern Virginia, most often in 16th- and 17th-century sites.
SOURCES: J. C. Harrington 1948; Blaker 1952; Egloff and Potter 1982.

Keith T. Egloff

ROARING RAPIDS PHASE, the earliest phase of the Cerbat Province of the Patayan Division, Hakataya Culture (qq.v.) in northwestern Arizona. It was defined largely from a component at the Willow Beach Site (q.v.) that contained choppers, shell artifacts, cooking pits, arrow points, and intrusive Anasazi (q.v.) pottery by which the component was cross-dated to pre-A.D. 750. There was a radiocarbon date of ca. A.D. 450 in an underlying preceramic level.
SOURCE: Schroeder 1961b.

Albert H. Schroeder

ROARING SPRINGS CAVE. See Catlow and Roaring Springs Caves.

ROBERTS CLASSIFICATION SYSTEM. See Southwestern Classification Systems.

ROBLES PHASE. See Casas Grandes Province.

ROCHE-A-CRIS, an outcrop of resistant sandstone towering above the surrounding countryside in Adams County, in Wisconsin on which many glyphs have been carved, including geometric forms, canoes, arrows, and so-called "crow's feet." Tentative interpretations indicate that late prehistoric peoples are responsible for the glyphs, which now are protected within Roche-A-Cris State Park.
SOURCES: Ritzenthaler 1950; Hazlett and Hazlett 1965.

David Overstreet

ROCK ISLAND, a small island just off the tip of Door County, Wisconsin, notable for several sites affiliated with the North Bay Culture (q.v.). It also

is known as the Island of the Potawatomies because that tribe lived there in the 17th century.
SOURCE: Mason 1982.

David Overstreet

ROCKPORT FOCUS (or PHASE), the primary post-Archaic culture unit on the central Texas coast, dating between A.D. 1100 and the 18th century and attributed to the prehistoric and early historic Karankawa tribes. Distinctive traits are Rockport Ware (q.v.) pottery, arrow points, and evidence of hunting-gathering subsistence.
SOURCES: Suhm et al. 1954:125–128; Corbin 1974.

Lawrence E. Aten

ROCKPORT WARE, a series of three pottery types (Rockport Plain, Rockport Black on Gray, and Rockport Incised), dating between ca. A.D. 1100 and the late 18th century, found widely at sites in a 40-kilometer-wide zone along the Texas coast between Matagorda and Corpus Christi bays. The ceramic technology and vessel shapes are similar to those of Goose Creek Ware (q.v.) in the bordering area to the east. Decorations were produced on the exterior vessel surfaces both by incising/impressing and by painting with melted asphalt. Designs are of two distinct styles: straight-line geometric patterns, similar to those on Goose Creek Ware, and patterns that often are reminiscent of designs found in northeastern Mexico, made up of dots, meanders, zigzags, and punctations. Rockport Ware evidently was primarily the product of historic and prehistoric tribes of the Karankawa group.
SOURCES: Suhm et al. 1954:382–385; Story 1968.

Lawrence E. Aten

ROGERS SPRING SITE, a multiple burned-rock midden and 19th-century Euroamerican site on the edge of the Balcones Escarpment, near Austin in central Texas. Excavated by A. T. Jackson in 1933 and by E. R. Prewitt in 1974, the site produced important information on rates of disturbance in burned-rock middens.
SOURCES: Lathan n. d.; Prewitt 1976.

Elton R. Prewitt

ROOD CULTURE (or PHASE), a Mississippian culture dating ca. A.D. 900–1400 whose sites are distributed along the lower Chattahoochee River and its tributaries in southwestern Georgia and southeastern Alabama. Some important sites are Rood's Landing, Cool Branch, Singer-Moye, and Cemochechobee, which is a large village with three platform mounds. The material culture is characterized by plain, incised, and punctated pottery vessels, triangular chipped-stone points, ground-stone celts and discs, and pottery-pipes and discs. Among ceremonial-elite items are copper headdresses, effigy pottery, and marine-shell beads. The Rood Culture probably represents a chiefdom level of social organization.

SOURCES: J. R. Caldwell 1955; McMichael and Kellar 1960; G. S. Schnell 1981.

Roy S. Dickens, Jr.

ROOSEVELT PHASE, a phase of the Salado Province of the Sinagua Division, Hakataya Culture (qq.v.) in Arizona, dating ca. A.D. 1200–1300. The phase is distinguished by the association of local pottery types Tonto Brown (a variety of Alameda Brown Ware, q.v.), Pinto Black-on-red, and Pinto Polychrome with intrusive Mogollon (q.v.) types from the east and north: Salado Red, St. Johns Polychrome, Pinedale Black-on-white, and others. Material culture changes from the preceding Miami Phase (q.v.) are said to have been numerous, but the phase remains poorly reported. Houses were similar to those of the Miami Phase.

SOURCES: Doyel 1976a, 1976b.

Albert H. Schroeder

ROOSEVELT-TONTO PROVINCE, a culture area in central Arizona, centered around Roosevelt Lake and encompassing the upper Salt River drainage system between the mountainous regions of the Mogollon Culture (q.v.) to the east and the low desert environments of the Hohokam Culture (q.v.) to the west and south. Investigations in the region by Gila Pueblo in the 1920s and 1930s included the excavation of Roosevelt Site 9:6, one of the type sites of the Colonial Period (q.v.) of the Hohokam Culture. Subsequently, excavations at the Snaketown Site (q.v.) in the Phoenix Basin Province (q.v.) revealed a Hohokam Culture pattern identical to that at Roosevelt 9:6. The red-on-buff pottery styles and technology were the same, as was the pithouse architecture. A mixture of Hohokam and Puebloan traits has been reported at several sites in the Roosevelt-Tonto Province, but only one ball court has been recorded there.

By A.D. 1100, the Hohokam Culture pattern was replaced in the province by the Salado Culture, but whether this replacement represents an actual demographic shift or simply a cultural change or admixture has not yet been determined.

SOURCES: Haury 1932; Gladwin and Gladwin 1935; Doyel 1976b, 1978.

John S. Cable and David E. Doyel

ROSA PHASE, an expression of the early Pueblo I Stage of the Pecos Classification (q.v.) within the Upper San Juan Province (q.v.) dating ca. A.D. 700–850. A typical settlement consisted of a pithouse, a surface structure, scattered trash, and exterior pits and hearths. Pithouses were of both the small, shallow, Sambrito Phase (q.v.) style and the larger Plains style. After A.D. 750, the latter evolved into the larger elaborate type house with some combination of ventilator, fire basin, partition walls, ash pits or warming pits, and a deflector. Surface structures in the form of rectangular jacales (q.v.) reappeared after A.D. 750, some containing a fire basin indicative of year-round used in conjunction with the residential pithouses.

The introduction of the bow to replace the atlatl during Rosa Phase times probably amplified both warfare and big-game hunting. The large number of sites during this period suggests a population peak, which, along with changes in rainfall patterns and the beginnings of headward river entrench-ment, may have affected horticultural production adversely, leading to local warfare and drift migration. Another apparent response to these demo-graphic and environmental changes was the rise of new religious customs: hunting magic, family-directed ritual held within the pithouse and shaman-directed cults having to do with weather and river control.

SOURCES: E. T. Hall, Jr. 1944; R. L. Carlson 1965; Schoenwetter and Eddy 1964; Eddy 1966, 1972, 1974.

Frank W. Eddy

ROSEGATE POINT SERIES, a series of small, corner-notched, chipped-stone projectile points with expanding bases dating ca. A.D. 700–1300, distributed throughout the desert West. Previously, the series comprised two separate types: Rose Spring Corner-notched and Eastgate Expanding Stem.

SOURCES: Lanning 1963; D. H. Thomas 1981.

David Hurst Thomas

ROSENKRANS FERRY SITE, a Delmarva-Adena Phase (q.v.) cemetery in the Upper Delaware River Valley, dating ca. 500 B.C. It was excavated by avocational archaeologists and tested by Edmund Carpenter in 1950. Grave goods and mortuary practices suggest status differentiation within the so-ciety represented, as well as long-distance trade.

SOURCES: Carpenter 1950; Kraft 1976.

Ronald A. Thomas

ROSENSTOCK DISTRICT, an area in Maryland's Monocacy River Valley comprising three sites with collective occupations dating from Middle Ar-chaic through Late Woodland times, including two separate Late Woodland complexes.

SOURCE: Kavanagh 1982.

Stephen R. Potter

ROSENSTOCK SITE, a village of the Montgomery Complex (q.v.) located on the Monocacy River, in Maryland and dating to the 15th century A.D.

It was tested in 1979 by the Archeological Society of Maryland, under the supervision of the Maryland Geological Survey.

SOURCE: Kavanagh 1982.

Stephen R. Potter

ROSE SPRING SITE, a deeply stratified, multicomponent site in Rose Valley just south of Owens Valley (q.v.) in eastern California, excavated by F. A. Riddell in 1956 and reported later by E. P. Lanning. The site yielded a sequence of projectile-point types that were known to be widely distributed within the Great Basin, but whose respective ages had until then been suspected but not demonstrated. Without the benefit of radiocarbon dates, Lanning estimated the temporal ranges for the most important of these types roughly as follows.

Point Type	Date
Little Lake (Pinto) Series (q.v.)	3000–1500 B.C.
Elko Series (q.v.)	1500 B.C.–A.D. 500
Rose Spring Series	A.D. 500–1300
Eastgate Expanding-Stem	A.D. 500–1300
Cottonwood Series (q.v.)	A.D. 1300–historic
Desert Side-Notched (q.v.)	A.D. 1300–historic

Subsequent radiocarbon dates for this and other sites in the western Great Basin where these point types have been found clearly substantiated these inferred dates, usually within a margin of one or two centuries.

SOURCES: Lanning 1963; Clewlow et al. 1970.

Robert L. Bettinger

ROSWELL PHASE, the later of two phases belonging to the incompletely defined southern sector of the Middle Pecos Sub-Province (q.v.) of the Jornada Province, Mogollon Culture, in eastern New Mexico. As no sites have been excavated, the phase's distinguishing criteria are based upon surface ceramics and similarities with the McKenzie Phase (q.v.) of the northern sector. Thus, dates of ca. A.D. 1200–1300 are suggested.

Roswell Brown (a cognate of Jornada Brown, q.v.) continues as a dominant pottery type, and Jornada Brown occurs in almost equal quantities. Chupadero Black-on-white (q.v.) is the dominant painted type; contemporary types from the northern sector are found in small quantities. Sherds of types from the Socorro area (Rio Abajo Province, q.v.) are the main but infrequent intrusives from farther afield.

SOURCE: Jelinek 1967.

R. N. Wiseman

ROUND LAKE PERIOD. See Galveston Bay Focus.

ROUND ROCK PHASE, the second and terminal phase of the Middle Archaic in central Texas, following the Clear Fork Phase (q.v.) and dating ca. 2000–650 B.C. Site features include large stone-lined hearths; small basin-shaped hearths; tremendous, mounded accumulations of densely packed, fire-cracked stones; and, in the Llano uplift area, possibly circular structure foundations. The many large open and rockshelter sites of the phase throughout central Texas seem to reflect a dense population.

The Pedernales type dart point (q.v.), a form with prominent shoulders or barbs and a parallel-sided, bifurcated stem, is the chief diagnostic of the phase. The duration of this type—well over 1,000 years—exceeds that of all other point types in the area. Other tools in the assemblage include a great variety of bifaces, grinding stones, and bone tools, and a few unifaces. Wunderlich, Greenhaw, and Loeve-Fox (q.v.) are some of the major excavated Round Rock sites.

Limited descriptions of a Round Rock culture, phase, or focus were made, respectively, by E. B. Sayles in 1935, by C. N. Ray between 1938 and 1948, and by J. C. Kelley in 1947. F. A. Weir defined the phase more fully in 1976.

SOURCES: J. C. Kelley 1947a:124; Leroy Johnson, Jr. et al. 1962:25–27; Weir 1976:128–133, 1979:53–55; Prewitt 1981:80.

Frank A. Weir

ROUND VALLEY PHASE, a phase of the East Verde Province of the Sinagua Division, Hakataya Culture (qq.v.) in Arizona, dating ca. A.D. 1300–1350. The phase is represented by a few large, central sites; the extent of the rural occupation is unknown.

SOURCE: Redman and Hohmann 1986.

Albert H. Schroeder

ROWE VALLEY SITE, a late Toyah Phase (q.v.) campsite, dating ca. A.D. 1720–1730, on the San Gabriel River in east-central Texas, dug in 1982–1984 by the Texas Archeological Society under the direction of E. R. Prewitt. Broad horizontal excavation revealed a circular camp pattern with a discrete butchering station and numerous chipping stations.

SOURCES: Prewitt 1982b, 1983b, 1984.

Elton R. Prewitt

RUBY SITE, a Besant Phase (q.v.) bison-kill site in eastern Wyoming, dating ca. A.D. 250, which was investigated by George Frison in 1968 and 1969. Remains of a large corral and drive lines for penning the animals, a large religious structure beside the corral, and a large nearby processing area constitute the most sophisticated evidence of pre-horse bison procurement on the High Plains.

SOURCES: Frison 1971, 1978.

George Frison

RUGGLES OUTLET SITE, a late Thule Phase house on the Lake Hazen (qq.v.) outlet, partly excavated in 1881 by A. W. Greeley and completed by M. S. Maxwell in 1958. Since the occupants apparently died in the house,

a complete inventory of household effects was still present when the house was excavated, thus providing a single time frame for 14th- to 15th-century Inugsuk Phase (q.v.) materials.
SOURCE: Maxwell 1960.

Moreau S. Maxwell

RUIN ISLAND PHASE, one of the first, if not the first, culture unit of the eastern Canadian Arctic, radiocarbon dated to ca. A.D. 1200; first described by E. Holtved in 1954 and defined in detail by Karen McCollogh in 1986. Distinctive traits include pithouses without sleeping platforms but with open fire kitchens in alcoves and a number of Alaska-related traits such as specific styles of harpoon heads and needle cases. The spread of Ruin Island peoples has been traced by finds of Sicco type harpoon heads from southern Victoria Island northward to Lancaster Sound, thence westward, then northward to Ellesmere Island and northwestern Greenland. The phase is restricted to the High Arctic region.
SOURCES: Holtved 1954; McCollogh 1986.

Moreau S. Maxwell

RUSSELL CAVE, a large cavern in Jackson County, in Alabama where intensive excavation in 1956–1958 and 1962 revealed deeply buried Early to Middle Archaic strata dating ca. 8000–4000 B.C. In 1961 the National Geographic Society purchased Russell Cave and donated the property to the National Park Service.
SOURCE: J. W. Griffin 1974.

John A. Walthall

S

SAATUT SITE, a Middle Dorset site on Navy Board Inlet, North Baffin Island, radiocarbon dated to ca. 170 B.C. Excavations there by Guy Mary-Rousseliere in the 1970s and 1980s provided data that compared well with data from the nearby Nunguvik Site (q.v.). Like Middle Dorset houses in Labrador (see Koliktalik Site), a house at Saatut had a paved entry passage that was outlined with stone slabs.
SOURCE: Mary-Rousseliere 1979a.

Moreau S. Maxwell

SABLE SITE, a Late Archaic–Early Woodland site on the Saluda River floodplain in Richland County, South Carolina that dates ca. 500 B.C. When T. M. Ryan excavated there in 1972, he discovered Deptford (q.v.) Phase pottery and lithics, as well as several pit features.
SOURCE: Ryan 1972a.

Michael Trinkley

SACATON PHASE, a phase of the Salado Province of the Sinagua Division, Hakataya Culture (qq.v.) in Arizona, dating ca. A.D. 1000–1150. It is based on excavations at a few sites with pit or jacal structures that differ in important respects from houses of the Hohokam (q.v.) core area to the west. Round, slab-lined surface structures, none of which have been excavated, also have been reported. The phase is named for Sacaton Red-on-buff pottery, which occurs at small sites that may have been seasonally occupied. Also reported from these sites is intrusive Snowflake Black-on-white pottery of the Mogollon Culture (q.v.).
SOURCES: Doyel 1976a, 1976b.

Albert H. Schroeder

SADMAT SITE, a series of "pebble mounds," rock cairns, rock alignments, and habitation areas in the Lahontan Basin, in central Nevada. They were discovered and explored in the 1960s by Y. Saddler and E. M. Mateucci,

who collected more than 3000 artifacts from the site, including Great Basin Stemmed projectile points, scrapers, gravers, and drills estimated to date from the Paleoindian period. Although the mounds may prove to be historic, they are at an elevation suggesting prehistoric origins.
SOURCES: Tuohy 1968, 1981.

David Hurst Thomas

SAFETY HARBOR CULTURE, a Mississippian (q.v.) culture dating ca. A.D. 1000–1700, centered around Tampa Bay, Florida, that developed out of Weeden Island (q.v.) cultures and correlates with the historic Tocobaga and Mocoso Indians. Major sites usually consist of a temple mound, a burial mound, and a village midden. Political organization was of the local chiefdom form.
SOURCES: Willey 1949a; Griffin and Bullen 1950; Bullen 1951b, 1952, 1955a, 1978; Sears 1967; Milanich and Fairbanks 1980:204–210; Luer and Almy 1981.

Jerald T. Milanich

SAGLEK BAY LOCALITY, a location on the Labrador coast north of Hebron where several important Paleoeskimo (q.v.) sites were excavated in the 1970s by J. A. Tuck. He considers early lithic material (dating ca. 1860 B.C.) from the sites to be more closely related to Independence I (q.v.) of the High Arctic than to the Pre-Dorset (q.v.) of Baffin Island and the Melville Peninsula.
SOURCE: Tuck 1975.

Moreau S. Maxwell

ST. ALBANS SITE, a stratified, multicomponent site buried deeply in the alluvium of the Kanawha River near St. Albans, West Virginia, excavated in the late 1960s by B. J. Broyles. More than 10 meters of deposits, consisting of a series of cultural strata separated by zones of sterile alluvium, spanned nearly 10,000 years of prehistory, beginning ca. 8000 B.C. The sequence of artifacts—especially projectile points—provided a useful chronological array of Archaic styles that has been used as a reference datum by numerous archaeologists over a broad area of eastern North America.
SOURCE: Broyles 1971.

Edward B. Jelks

ST. CATHERINES CULTURE, a Late Woodland (ca. A.D. 1100) expression found on the Georgia and southern South Carolina coast, defined by J. R. Caldwell in 1971. Sites include mortuary-mound complexes, small villages, and scattered shell middens. St. Cartherine pottery is tempered with small particles of low-fired clay; surface treatments include fine cordmarking, burnishing, and net impressing. A poorly developed shell-bead and bone industry is associated.

SOURCES: J. R. Caldwell 1971; Trinkley 1981a; Larsen and Thomas 1982; Brooks et al. 1982.

Michael Trinkley

ST. CROIX WARE, a Late Middle to Late Woodland, transitional ceramic series occurring across northwestern Wisconsin and central Minnesota, and northward into the Red River Valley of western Minnesota and the Dakotas. One of the pottery types associated with the Arvilla Complex (q.v.), St. Croix dates ca. A.D. 500–800. Vessels are grit tempered and subconoidal to rounded, and have slightly constricted necks with vertical rims. Bodies are textile roughened; rims are decorated with dentate-stamped and fine cord-wrapped-dowel impressions.

SOURCES: Caine 1966, 1974, 1983; Gibbon and Caine 1980.

Christy Hohman-Caine

ST. HELENA PHASE, a unit of the Central Plains Tradition (q.v.) located in northeastern Nebraska and southernmost South Dakota, probably dating ca. A.D. 1200–1450. Sites consist of scattered earthlodges on ridgetops, hill slopes, or broad terraces at the mouths of major creeks. Houses are square with rounded corners and extended entryways. Mortuary features include individual burial pits, ossuaries, and possibly charnel houses. Attributes of artifacts and architecture indicate contact with the Middle Missouri Tradition (q.v.) and to a lesser extent with Oneota (q.v.). St. Helena is closely related to the Loup River Phase (q.v.) and is ancestral to the Coalescent Tradition (q.v.).

SOURCES: P. A. Cooper 1936; Blakeslee 1978; Blakeslee and O'Shea 1981.

Donald J. Blakeslee

ST. JOHNS CULTURE, a major culture distributed throughout eastern and central Florida, especially within the St. Johns River drainage and adjacent lake system, dating from 500 B.C. to the Spanish colonial period. A distinctive chalky-ware pottery is found in both mound and village sites. In historic times, St. Johns correlates with various Timucuan Indian groups.

SOURCES: Goggin 1952:47–58, 68–70; Deagan 1978; Milanich and Fairbanks 1980:145–166.

Jerald T. Milanich

ST. JONES RIVER ADENA SITE, a relatively large mortuary site near Lebanon, Delaware discovered by accident in 1960; it proved to be an important manifestation of the Delmarva-Adena Phase (q.v.), dating ca. 400 B.C. Excavations in 1960 by Leon DeValinger revealed the presence of mass graves exhibiting complex mortuary behavior. Grave furnishings consisted of large numbers of exotic artifacts, including big bifaces maufactured from Flint Ridge (q.v.), Ohio chalcedony, tobacco pipes of Portsmouth, Ohio fire stone, and copper beads, cups, and gorgets.

SOURCES: DeValinger 1970; R. A. Thomas 1976.

Ronald A. Thomas

ST. JOSEPH COMPLEX, a terminal Archaic (q.v.) and Early Woodland cultural manifestation in southwestern lower Michigan, dating ca. 1000–100 B.C. The Berrien, Three Oaks, and Wymer projectile-point types are diagnostics. They and a variety of other tools usually were made from immediately available till cherts, but some were made from exotic stones, especially Burlington and Upper Mercer (q.v.) cherts which suggests that exchange was oriented toward the south and east. Pollen data coupled with plant and animal remains from four sites in Berrien County indicate a favorable environment for diffuse adaptations.

SOURCE: Garland et al., n.d.

Margaret B. Holman

ST. MUNGO CANNERY SITE, a multicomponent shell midden on the Fraser River Delta in British Columbia, dating ca. 2530 B.C.–A.D. 1500, first recorded by H. I. Smith in 1898; excavated by Gay Frederick in 1968–1969 and by Leonard Ham in 1982–1983. From a house floor dated ca. 2530 B.C. came a two-dimensional steatite engraving of a mustelid/fish, the earliest known example of Coast Salish religious art. At that time, the site was occupied seasonally during migrations of eulachon, sturgeon, and salmon, which were taken with dip nets and set lines and by trolling. The fish were preserved by drying on raised frames and by smoking in smoke-houses. The early Coast Salish families who occupied the site were wealthy and had a well-developed religious and ceremonial life.

SOURCES: Calvert 1970; Borden 1975; Ham et al. n.d.a.

Leonard Ham

ST. MUNGO CULTURE, an early hunting, fishing, and gathering culture of the Lower Fraser River, in British Columbia, radiocarbon dated to 2550–1350 B.C. Components at the St. Mungo Cannery and Glenrose Cannery sites (qq.v.) represent semisedentary settlements with large wooden dwellings. The use of watercraft is inferred. Deer, wapiti, beaver, harbor seal, and waterfowl were hunted; sturgeon, salmon, and flatfish were taken; bay mussels and other shellfish were collected.

Typical artifacts include pebble and cortex spall tools; chipped-stone points, knives, and scrapers; pieces esquillies; incised, chipped, and ground slate objects; abraders; edge-ground cobbles and hammerstones; antler and bone wedges; and a variety of bone tools and ornaments. Mussel shell adze blades, barbed bone and antler harpoon heads, and zoomorphic and anthropomorphic stone carvings occur rarely. Red ocher is often associated with burials, which occur typically in middens.

In 1975 C. E. Borden grouped the St. Mungo Phase (originally defined by R. G. Matson), the Eayem Phase of the Fraser River Canyon, and the Mayne Phase of the Gulf of Georgia, within a single *Charles Phase*. The association of the St. Mungo and Eayem phases is generally accepted, but their association with the Mayne Phase is less certain.

The St. Mungo Culture probably developed in situ from the Old Cordilleran Tradition (q.v.). It exhibits major elements of the Northwest Coast Culture Tradition and, in the Fraser Delta, is succeeded by the Locarno Beach Culture (q.v.), although no direct developmental link between the two has been established.

SOURCES: Calvert 1970; R. L. Carlson 1970; Boehm 1973; Borden 1975; Matson 1976; Ham et al. n.d.a.

Gay Frederick

SALADO PROVINCE, a manifestation of the Southern Sinagua Division, Hakataya Culture (qq.v.), in Arizona, dating ca. A.D. 750–1450. The province has not been well defined. Rectangular to circular slab- or rock-outlined structures are typical dwellings. The Tonto Brown variety of Almeda Brown Ware (q.v.) was the dominant plain pottery, but a few sherds of Hohokam (q.v.) types Santa Cruz and Sacaton Red-on-buff have been reported. Some early sites in the area have been identified with the Hohokam Culture because they contain a ball court, Hohokam house types, or red-on-buff pottery.

The post–A.D. 1100 sites have Sinagua redware pottery and rock-walled structures, the latter changing from individual rooms at first to later compact, pueblo-like buildings consisting of contiguous rooms. Stone, shell, and bone crafts are unimpressive and on a par with materials from earlier sites. Extended inhumations are common.

The phases of the Salado Province, revised several times, are extremely tentative as currently (1987) defined, and they pertain primarily to the Globe-Miami area. The phases include Santa Cruz, Sacaton, Miami, Roosevelt, and Gila (qq.v.). The term Salado has been applied to sites in southwestern New Mexico and southeastern Arizona in recent years, even though they differ in many respects from Salado sites in central Arizona. Such usage has obscured the concept of a Salado culture unit, which has never been adequately described.

SOURCES: Doyel 1976a; Schroeder 1960.

Albert H. Schroeder

SALINAS PROVINCE, an archaeological area east of the Rio Grande in New Mexico, encompassed by the eastern foothills of the Manzano Mountains, the southwestern part of the Estancia Basin, and the northern end of the Tularosa Basin. At playas and springs in the Estancia Basin, Paleoindian sites have yielded a wide range of projectile-point types. Archaic and early Puebloan occupations, although present in the area, have been little researched; both Mogollon and Anasazi (qq.v.) attributes have been reported.

The following sequence of foci for the province has been proposed by J. H. Touolouse, Jr., and R. L. Stephenson on the basis of limited reconnaissance and testing at Pueblo Pardo: Claunch Focus (Pueblo III, ca. A.D. 1200–1300), Arroyo Seco Focus (Pueblo III, ca. A.D. 1200–1300), Gran Quivira Focus (early Pueblo IV, ca. A.D. 1300–1425), Pueblo Colorado Focus (mid-Pueblo IV, ca. A.D. 1400–1500), Pueblo Pardo Focus (late Pueblo IV–early Pueblo V, ca. A.D. 1500–1650), and Salinas Focus (Pueblo V, ca. A.D. 1600–1675).

Most field work in the Salinas Province has been at protohistoric pueblos and Spanish colonial Franciscan mission sites, but questions still remain regarding the cultural and linguistic affiliations of the people who occupied them.

SOURCES: A. C. Hayes 1981; Toulouse and Stephenson 1960.

Frances Levine

SALINAS RED POTTERY, an unslipped, sand-tempered, utility ware that probably dates ca. A.D. 1615–1672; found in the Salinas Province (q.v.), New Mexico, at the Abo, Quarai, and Gran Quivira sites (qq.v.). Shapes include ollas, bowls, flanged-rim soup plates, and candlesticks.

SOURCES: Toulouse 1949; Hayes et al. 1981.

Frances Levine

SALMON RUIN, a large Anasazi (q.v.) pueblo on the San Juan River near Farmington, New Mexico, excavated between 1970 and 1978 by Cynthia Irwin-Williams in conjunction with the San Juan County Museum Association. Originally established between A.D. 1088 and 1094 as an outlier colony of the culture centers in Chaco Canyon, it was enlarged in A.D. 1105–1106. By ca. A.D. 1270, its original inhabitants had largely abandoned the pueblo, but local San Juan Anasazi people reoccupied it ca. A.D. 1130 and remained until ca. 1270, when a catastrophic fire made it uninhabitable.

The original Chacoan (q.v.) community formed three sides of a south-facing rectangle, centered around a plaza, and comprised about 150 ground-floor and 100 second-floor rooms, a great kiva in the plaza, and a "tower kiva" in the north roomblock. Most of the rooms were organized into four-room suites leading back from the plaza; ceramics from the suites indicated that they were occupied by both Chaco-derived and Anasazi-derived people.

Skilled specialists dominated local craft activities, including masonry, architecture, and chipped- and ground-stone tool production. Corn grinding, corn parching, and other domestic activities took place at community locations rather than in residential suites. Despite a relatively egalitarian economic structure, Chacoan society at Salmon evidently was dominated by a semistratified elite class who exercised considerable community authority through control of secular and esoteric information.

SOURCE: Irwin-Williams and Shelley n.d.

Cynthia Irwin-Williams

SAMBRITO PHASE, a manifestation in the Upper San Juan Province (q.v.) that is equivalent in time, but not in cultural content, to the Basketmaker III Stage of the Pecos Classification (q.v.). Dating ca. A.D. 400–700, the phase marks the first appearance of the true pithouse in the province, while Sambrito Brown type pottery becomes more common than in the preceding Los Pinos Phase (q.v.). A typical settlement consists of a row of from one to seven small, shallow pithouses facing the San Juan River. With them are undercut pits with burned sides, thought to have been used as earth ovens for roasting corn and cooking wild game.

Between A.D. 500 and 600, long-distance trade routes introduced gray-ware pottery and shell ornaments made from Gulf of California marine shells to the Upper San Juan Province: the pottery from the Mesa Verde Province (q.v.) just to the west, the ornaments via the Hohokam Culture (q.v.) of southern Arizona. Early Sambrito Phase sites dating ca. A.D. 400–500 usually contain a few pieces of locally made Sambrito Brown pottery. Intrusive Mesa Verde gray pottery, both decorated and plain, was added to the pottery inventory ca. A.D. 500–600, as were Rosa Gray and Brown wares ca. A.D. 600–700.

SOURCES: Dittert et al. 1963; Hester and Shiner 1963; Eddy and Dregne 1964; Schoenwetter and Eddy 1964; F. W. Eddy 1966, 1972.

Frank W. Eddy

SAM KAUFMAN SITE, a multicomponent Caddoan (q.v.) site in Red River County, in Texas, occupied from the Caddo II period (ca. A.D. 1200) to Caddo V (ca. A.D. 1700); excavated by James Sciscenti in 1968. There were two mounds, both resulting from intensive midden accumulation and house construction. One contained grog-tempered pottery dating ca. A.D. 1000; the other, dating ca. A.D. 1400, contained shell-tempered pottery and numerous house floors. Burial patterns suggest that ranked status and interregional trade networks existed in both the Late and the Early Caddo periods.

SOURCE: Harris 1953; Harris et al. 1954; Harris and Wilson 1956; Skinner et al. 1969.

James E. Corbin

SAN BERNARDO INCISED POTTERY, a type found in the upper foothills of southern Sonora in sites of the San Bernardo Phase (q.v.), beginning sometime between A.D. 1050 and 1250, and lasting until historic times. The decoration consists of panels of parallel incised lines combined at various

angles to form geometric patterns above a vessel's shoulder. The type appears to be a southern variant of textured pottery characteristic of the Rio Sonora Culture (q.v.).
SOURCE: Pailes 1972:215–217, pl. 3.

Richard A. Pailes

SAN BERNARDO PHASE, the second of the Rio Sonora's (q.v.) two phases in southern Sonora. It replaced the Los Camotes Phase (q.v.) between A.D. 1050 and 1250 and lasted until historic times. Sites consist of small villages and rancherias on the terraces of watercourses within easy reach of arable land. Dwellings were above-ground, rectangular structures with stone foundations. The main pottery types are San Bernardo Incised and San Bernardo Punctate Incised (qq.v.), both southern variants of the textured pottery characteristic of the Rio Sonora Culture (q.v.). Other artifacts include stone bowls, axes, shaft abraders, and overhanging manos (q.v.).
SOURCE: Pailes 1972:371–382.

Richard A. Pailes

SAN BERNARDO PUNCTATE INCISED POTTERY, a type found in the upper foothills of southern Sonora that is characteristic of the San Bernardo Phase (q.v.), beginning ca. A.D. 1050/1250 and lasting until historic times. Decorations consist of panels of parallel incised lines and punctations forming geometric patterns above a vessel's shoulder. The type appears to be a southern variant of textured Rio Sonora Culture (q.v.) pottery.
SOURCE: Pailes 1972:215–217, pl. 5.

Richard A. Pailes

SANDERS SITES, a series of mounds and villages in Waupaca County, in Wisconsin, excavated by W. M. Hurley in 1966–1967. The most recent (1975) synthesis of the Effigy Mound Culture (q.v.) was based in large part on Hurley's work at the Sanders sites.
SOURCE: Hurley 1975.

David Overstreet

SAN ANTONIO DE PADUA PHASE. See Casas Grandes Province.

SANDIA CAVE, a stratified cave in central New Mexico where in 1939 F. C. Hibben found 19 unusual, single-shouldered projectile points and other tools in a deeply buried stratum of late Pleistocene age, which also contained bones of mastodon, horse, camel, mammoth, and bison. Above this stratum was a layer of culturally sterile yellow ocher and, above that, a limestone breccia containing bones of extinct Pleistocene fauna (horse, camel, mammoth, ground sloth, bison, and wolf) and a number of stone and bone artifacts, including several lanceolate projectile points, two of which were of the Folsom type (q.v.).

A few Sandia points, as Hibben named the one-shouldered specimens, have been reported from other sites. The most notable of these is the Lucy Site, to the north of Sandia Cave, where several Sandia points and other early points have been found on the eroded surface of Pleistocene lake deposits.

SOURCES: Hibben 1941; Wormington 1957:85–91.

Edward B. Jelks

SANDIA POINT, an early (ca. 10,000 B.C.?), one-shouldered, chipped-stone projectile point type having some features reminiscent of unshouldered Paleoindian points such as Clovis, Folsom, and the various Plano types (qq.v.). While a number of surface finds have been reported, the only Sandia points found in geological context to date came from the lowest cultural stratum at Sandia Cave (q.v.), New Mexico, where they were stratigraphically older than artifacts of the Folsom Culture (q.v.). Firm dates for the type have not been established and its full geographic range is uncertain.

SOURCES: Hibben 1941, 1946; Wormington 1957:85–91.

Edward B. Jelks

SAN DIEGUITO COMPLEX, an early (ca. 8000–7000 B.C.) culture unit identified on the California coast in the San Diego area in 1929 by M. J. Rogers, who later (1939) associated it with the Malpais and Playa I and II complexes (qq.v.) of the southern California and southern/west-central Nevada deserts. As now perceived, the complex represents an ancient tradition distinct from the Desert Culture (q.v.) in its reliance on hunting rather than gathering. Typical artifacts are leaf-shaped knives, small leaf-shaped projectile points, stemmed and shouldered points, scrapers of various forms, engraving tools, and chipped-stone crescents. Milling equipment of any kind is notably lacking. In 1970 S. F. Bedwell included the desert manifestations of the San Dieguito Complex in his Western Pluvial Lakes Tradition (q.v.).

SOURCES: M. J. Rogers 1929, 1939; C. N. Warren 1967; Bedwell 1970.

Robert L. Bettinger

SAND POINT SITE, a large, primarily Late Woodland site with nineteen burial mounds on Michigan's Keweenaw Peninsula, excavated by Winston Moore in 1970–1971. Habitation areas provided evidence of net fishing, flint knapping, and copper working. Mound structure plus stylistic attributes of Sand Point Ware suggest a close association with the Lakes Phase (q.v.) of north-central Wisconsin. Radiocarbon dates of A.D. 1055±55 and 1220±55, coupled with the presence of Oneota and Middle Mississippian (qq.v.) sherds indicate occupation during the later part of the Late Woodland Period.

SOURCES: Cremin et al. 1980; Wyckoff 1981.

Margaret B. Holman

SAND PRAIRIE PHASE, a unit of the Mississippian Tradition that followed the Moorehead Phase (qq.v.) in the American Bottom of southwestern Illinois ca. A.D. 1250–1400. First defined at the 1971 Cahokia Ceramic Conference, the phase is characterized by nearly square wall-trench structures, ceramics dominated by shell-tempered jars, and effigy vessels associated with human burials. Mortuary patterns comprise both primary and secondary interments, usually located near San Prairie residences. The phase represents the terminal Mississippian occupation of the American Bottom and marks the collapse of all Mississippian mound centers in the area.

SOURCES: Fowler and Hall 1972; Szuter 1979; Milner 1983, 1984; Bareis and Porter 1984.

Andrew C. Fortier and Charles J. Bareis

SANDY LAKE WARE, a shell- or grit-tempered, Late Woodland pottery, intially described by Leland Cooper and Elden Johnson from excavations at the Scott and Osufsen sites in north-central Minnesota, and from the Fickle Site in northwestern Wisconsin. The ware is distributed throughout the northern half of Minnesota, northward to the Thunder Bay area of Ontario and into southeastern Manitoba. The heaviest concentration is in the Mississippi headwaters region of Minnesota. Vessels are globular with cordmarked or smoothed-over cordmarked surface treatment. Decoration includes lip notching and both interior and exterior punctating. Sandy Lake is tentatively assigned to the Wanikan Culture (ca. A.D. 1000–1750), which may be proto-Assiniboine or proto-Eastern Dakota.

SOURCES: Cooper and Johnson 1964; Gibbon 1976; Birk 1977, 1979; Arthurs 1978; Lugenbeal 1978; Elden Johnson n.d.

Gordon R. Peters

SAN GERONIMO PHASE, a manifestation of the middle and later parts of the Early Archaic in central Texas, dating ca. 6000–2500 B.C.; defined by F. A. Weir in 1976. Sites, which tend to be small, typically contain large hearths lined with flat limestone slabs, scatters of fire-cracked stones, chipped-stone gouges, bifaces, unifaces, denticulates, and several types of corner- or basal-notched dart points (e.g., Gower, Hoxie [qq.v.], and Jetta). Major sites are Wilson-Leonard, Jetta Court, Youngsport, Granite Beach, and Tombstone Bluff.

SOURCES: Shafer 1963:64–65; Crawford 1965:76–79; Weir 1976:14–15; We-solowsky et al. 1976:45–47; Prewitt 1982a:77–78.

Frank A. Weir

SANILAC PETROGLYPHS, a group of more than 100 petroglyph figures carved into a large rock in Greenleaf Township, in Sanilac County, Michigan. The site was donated to the state by the Michigan Archaeological Society in 1978 for a historical park.

SOURCES: Hatt et al. 1958; Weston 1975.

Charles E. Cleland

SAN ISIDRO SITE, an early multicomponent campsite near Monterrey, Nuevo León, excavated in 1962 by J. F. Epstein. The earliest component, represented by hearths of fire-cracked limestone, were associated with percussion-flaked choppers, unifaces, and bifaces. With the second component (probably dating ca. 7000 B.C.) were Plainview and Lerma type projectile points of the Paleoindian (q.v.) period together with a number of Clear Fork gouges. The last occupation was by Archaic peoples. San Isidro's major significance lies in the possibility that the earliest component dates to a time (pre–8000 B.C.?) before bifacial projectile points were commonly used in North America. It also documents the presence of Paleoindian peoples in Nuevo León.

SOURCE: Epstein 1968.

Edward B. Jelks

SAN JACINTO WARE, a grog-tempered, plain or incised ceramic comprising several types and varieties; a major constituent of ceramic technology in coastal and interior southwestern Louisiana and southeastern Texas. It first appeared in southwestern Louisiana ca. A.D. 100, and from there it diffused slowly westward until it reached Galveston Bay ca. A.D. 1000. It continued as a major culture element through the 17th century and as a minor element into the early 19th century. Vessel forms are not well known, but the paste and the incised decorations are closely related to pottery of the Coles Creek and, perhaps, the Marksville cultures (qq.v.) of the Lower Mississippi River Valley. Apparently, San Jacinto Ware was primarily a product of the historic and prehistoric Atakapa tribes.

SOURCE: Aten 1983:241–242.

Lawrence E. Aten

SAN JOSE PHASE, the third phase of the Oshara Tradition (q.v.) in the Four Corners area of the Southwest, dating ca. 3300–1800 B.C. During this period, a relatively moist climate served to improve the character, quantity, quality, and reliability of a number of the economically important plant and animal species of the region. Archaeological sites increased both in size and in number in comparison to the preceding Bajada Phase (q.v.), and extensive midden stains indicate that they were occupied less ephemerally and probably repeatedly. The presence of fifteen hearths at a single hunting camp suggests the existence of large special-activity groups, and irregular posthole patterns in campsites indicate some form of temporary structures.

Large ovens filled with fire-cracked cobbles appeared during the phase, and ground-stone tools came into general use. Artifact assemblages tend to be dominated by large chopping tools and scrapers fashioned from thin flakes. Continuity in projectile-point forms was maintained, but there were a few innovations: serrated blade margins, relatively shorter stems, and trends toward decreased overall length, more widely expanding stems, and deeper serrations.

These tool-kit changes are interpreted as denoting more and more orientation toward a mixed foraging subsistence base. On the whole, the evidence suggests an increasingly successful and more localized adaptation. Resource exploitation, which became more systematic, intensive, and inclusive, may have been somewhat seasonally structured. Better climatic conditions and improvements in food-processing techniques appear to have allowed for an increase in population, but not to the point where severe pressure was placed on essential economic resources or on the stability of the social system.

SOURCES: Irwin-Williams and Haynes 1970; Irwin-Williams 1973, 1979.

Cynthia Irwin-Williams and Patricia A. Hicks

SAN JOSE SITE, a major site in the upper Rio Sonora Valley in north-central Sonora, the largest site in the Baviacora segment of the valley, with more than 60 pithouses, an equal number of surface structures, and a large enclosure that has been interpreted as a ball court. Estimated dates for the site range from A.D. 1000 to 1500.

SOURCES: Pailes 1980, 1984.

Richard A. Pailes

SAN JUAN PHASE, a late prehistoric occupation in the San Juan Islands, Washington, representing the antecedants of the historic Straits Salish Indians. The shell-midden components of the phases have yielded numerous bone barbs from composite fishhooks, barbed bone projectile points, small toggling harpoon heads, bone chisels, antler wedges, nephrite adze or chisel blades, and shell knives. There is little or no chipped stone in the components, which may represent seasonal occupations. This content differs little

from that of components in adjacent Salish territory dating A.D. 1200–1800, and all form part of the developed Coast Salish pattern.
SOURCE: R. L. Carlson 1960.

Roy L. Carlson

SAN MARCOS PHASE, the earliest (ca. 1000 B.C.–A.D. 200) Late Archaic phase in central Texas, defined by F. A. Weir in 1976. Sites occur on stream terraces and in rockshelters; bison-kill sites are found at the western edge of the phase's territory. Burned-rock scatters and small, circular, stone-lined hearths are typical features. The chief diagnostics are the broad-bladed dart-point types Castroville (q.v.), Montell, Marshall (q.v.), and Marcos. Other artifacts include millingstones, backed knives, corner-tang knives, bifaces, and unifaces. Major components have been dug at the Oblate, Evoe Terrace, and Crumley sites. The Uvalde Phase (q.v.), as defined by E. R. Prewitt in 1981, is approximately equivalent to Weir's San Marcos Phase.
SOURCES: T. C. Kelly 1961:250–253; Leroy Johnson, Jr. et al. 1962:92; Sorrow et al. 1967:18–20; Weir 1976:133–136.

Frank A. Weir

SAN PATRICE CULTURE, a late Paleoindian (q.v.) or Early Archaic culture thought to date ca. 8000–6000 B.C. More than 100 upland sites are known in Louisiana, eastern Texas, and southern Arkansas where the culture's diagnostic trait, the San Patrice type projectile point (q.v.), has been found on the surface. The best-known excavated sites are Wolfshead in Texas and John Pearce in Louisiana (qq.v.), where San Patrice points were found together with side-notched points, Albany side scrapers, and a variety of small flaked tools similar to those of western Paleoindian small-tool kits. These artifacts are all made of local stones. The San Patrice Culture appears to be related to the makers of projectile-point types Meserve to the west and Dalton to the east and north (qq.v.), both of which share typological similarities with the San Patrice point.
SOURCES: C. H. Webb 1946; Duffield 1963; Webb et al. 1971.

Clarence H. Webb

SAN PATRICE POINT, a wide, stubby, chipped-stone projectile point with a triangular blade, a concave base, and weak shoulders; the diagnostic trait of the transitional Paleoindian-Archaic San Patrice Culture (q.v.), dating between 8000 and 6000 B.C. The base and proximal edges are smoothed, and the blade edges are pressure trimmed, beveled, or, rarely, serrated. Proximal thinning was produced by striking from one to three flakes from the base. Two varieties, Hope and St. Johns, have been recognized. In contrast to many Paleoindian types that often were made of imported stones,

San Patrice points were made, with rare exceptions, only from local cherts and flints.

SOURCES: C. H. Webb 1946; Duffield 1963; Webb et al. 1971; Suhm and Jelks 1962:243–44.

Clarence H. Webb

SAN PEDRO PROVINCE, a culture area comprising the San Pedro River and Aravaipa Creek drainages in southern Arizona, the southern reaches of which contain the densest Paleoindian and Archaic sites recorded in the state. On the southeastern periphery of the Hohokam Culture's (q.v.) domain, the province reflects contacts with the neighboring Mogollon Culture (q.v.) through quantities of Mimbres Black-on-white and polished redware pottery found in sites that are essentially of Hohokam affiliation. It is possible that populations of both cultures intermingled in the San Pedro area to produce what W. S. Fulton and Carr Tuthill have referred to as the Dragoon Culture (q.v.).

The earliest pottery-producing sites in the San Pedro Province are Pioneer Period Hohokam types dating ca. A.D. 400–500. Colonial (ca. A.D. 700–900) and Sedentary (ca. A.D. 900–1100) period sites occur, both in upland locations that would have been optimal for dry farming and along main streams where irrigation may have been practiced. Several larger sites contain ball courts.

After the Colonial Period, the distinctive red-on-brown pottery of the Dragoon Culture emerged; there is no agreement on whether this should be interpreted as a regionalization of Hohokam or of San Simon Branch Mogollon culture. The later (ca. A.D. 1150–1300) ceramic assemblage parallels the sequence in the Tucson Basin; later settlements correspond to settlements of the Tanque Verde Phase in the Tucson Basin. A unique Western Pueblo (q.v.) complex containing stone-masonry pueblos, square kivas, stone-lined fire boxes, corrugated and polychrome pottery, and other Puebloan traits has been reported at the Reeve Ruin and elsewhere by C. C. Di Peso. The latest (ca. A.D. 1250–1400) sites show affinities with the Salado Culture's (q.v.) stone pueblos and its distinctive polychrome and red-on-brown pottery. There also may have been early Apachean sites in the province.

SOURCES: Fulton and Tuthill 1940; Di Peso 1958; Franklin and Masse 1976; Masse 1980a, 1980b, 1980c.

David E. Doyel and John S. Cable

SAN PEDRO STAGE. See Cochise Culture.

SANTA CRUZ PHASE, a phase of the Salado Province of the Sinagua Division, Hakataya Culture (qq.v.) in Arizona, dating ca. A.D. 750. The phase was defined primarily on the basis of an excavated site in which notched stones were found on a house floor which contained Hohokam (q.v.) pottery of the Santa Cruz Red-on-buff and Gila Butte Red-on-buff types. Most sites of the phases have quantities of the Tonto Brown variety of Alameda Brown Ware (q.v.), with or without Gila Plain from the Gila-Salt Province (q.v.). Excavated Santa Cruz Phase houses deviate in plan from houses in the Hohokam area to the west. A small Hohokam colony in the area is suggested by the presence of a ball court east of Globe.

SOURCES: Doyel 1976a, 1976b; Brandes 1957.

Albert H. Schroeder

SANTA ROSA ISLAND, one of the Santa Barbara Channel islands off the southern California coast, where several hundred archaeological sites have been recorded. The island has been the subject of extensive geological, archaeological, and paleontological investigations since the late 19th century. Following World War II, P. C. Orr excavated several sites of Pleistocene age containing "hearths," burned bones of dwarf mammoths, and other presumed evidence of human activity. Nonetheless, the presence of humans on the island earlier than ca. 8000 B.C. has not been confirmed.

SOURCES: P. C. Orr 1958; Moratto 1984:54–59.

Michael J. Moratto

SAQQAQ (or SARQAQ) PHASE, an early (ca. 1500–1100 B.C.) Paleo-eskimo (q.v.) phase on Greenland, represented by clusters of circular pit-houses with central stone-slab hearths at Disko Bay on the coast and at Itinnera in the interior. The lithic tool inventory resembles that of the Pre-Dorset Phase (q.v.) except that virtually all spalled burins are polished on both faces and have tapering stems. Tapering-stem end blades (arrow tips?) also are occasionally polished. Other distinctive traits are round, small to medium-sized soapstone lamps, and rare nontoggling harpoon heads similar to those of Independence I (q.v.).

SOURCES: Meldgaard 1961:15–23; Maxwell 1985:103, 107.

Moreau S. Maxwell

SASKATCHEWAN BASIN COMPLEX, the major indigenous ceramic complex of the upper Saskatchewan River basin, found mainly in central and southern Alberta. There are two chronologically distinct variations: an Early Variant (ca. A.D. 250–1150) and a Late Variant (ca. A.D. 1000–1850), distinguished from one another primarily by differences in pottery decoration and form.

SOURCE: Byrne 1973.

William J. Byrne

SATCHELL COMPLEX, a manifestation characterized by stone tools made of argillite, represented mainly at sites in southeastern Michigan and western Ontario. Although initially there was some controversy as to whether the complex dated to Early Archaic or to Late Archaic, a series of radiocarbon dates clustering around 1800 B.C. has led to current agreement that the term designates a Late Archaic complex. However, projectile points similar to the Eden and Scottsbluff types (qq.v.) made of argillite have been found in the region, indicating earlier use of this material.

SOURCES: Peske 1963; Roosa 1965, 1966; Kenyon 1981.

Margaret B. Holman

SAUGEEN CULTURE, a western variant of the Point Peninsula Culture, found north of Lakes Erie and Huron. It began ca. 700 B.C., but its terminal date is uncertain. Like most other Initial Woodland peoples, the Saugeen people were hunters and gatherers who used ceramics and participated in the elaborate burial practices typical of the first millennium B.C. in many parts of eastern North America.

SOURCE: J. V. Wright 1972a.

James A. Tuck

SAVANNAH RIVER PHASE, a very widespread Archaic (q.v.) expression, dating ca. 3000–1000 B.C., occupying the territory between the Appalachian Mountains and the Atlantic coast between New Jersey and northern Florida. Distinctive traits are Savannah River Stemmed projectile points (q.v.), fiber-tempered ceramics, steatite vessels, grooved axes, polished-stone atlatl weights, antler atlatl hooks, grooved and perforated netsinkers, bone fish-hooks, drills, bone pins (often incised with geometric designs), and both bundle burials and flexed inhumations. Earlier and later subphases have been identified at several stratified sites in North Carolina.

SOURCES: Coe 1964; Oliver 1981:36–38.

Billy L. Oliver

SAVANNAH RIVER STEMMED POINT, the dominant projectile-point type of the Savannah River Phase (q.v.) of the Late Archaic period (ca. 3000–1000 B.C.), found along much of the East Coast of the United States. It is a large point with a broad, triangular blade, a straight or slightly contracting stem, and a straight, incurvate, or excurvate base. The same form also has been called Appalachian Stemmed, Benton Stemmed (q.v.), Kays Stemmed, and Koens-Crispin (q.v.). Several subtypes have been described.

SOURCES: Coe 1964:44–45; Oliver 1981.

Billy L. Oliver

SAVITCH FARM/KOENS-CRISPIN SITES, two adjacent sites at Marlton, New Jersey, that both contained cremation burials associated with furnishings of the Late or Terminal Archaic period of the Middle Atlantic region. Grave goods included well-made bannerstones, shaft smoothers, large

Koens-Crispin type (q.v.) spear points, and other utilitarian items. The sites are estimated to date ca. 2500 B.C.

SOURCES: Hawkes and Linton 1916; Regensburg 1970.

Ronald A. Thomas

SAYLES COMPLEX, an assemblage consisting largely of percussion-flaked scraper planes, scrapers, choppers, and various kinds of millingstones; defined on the basis of finds at the Sayles Site in Cajon Pass, between the Mojave Desert and the Los Angeles Basin in southern California. Dating ca. 1000 B.C.–A.D. 1000, the complex is thought to represent a blending of coastal Millingstone and desert Pinto Basin (qq.v.) traits.

SOURCE: Kowta 1969.

L. A. Payen

SCALLORN POINT, a type of small, corner-notched projectile point associated with Woodland (q.v.) cultures in the central and northern plains and a diagnostic trait of the Austin Phase (q.v.) in central Texas. Scallorn and similar forms are thought to be some of the earliest arrow points, as distinguished from dart points, in much of central North America.

SOURCES: Suhm et al. 1954; Jelks 1962; Prewitt 1981; Turner and Hester 1985.

Elton R. Prewitt

SCHARBAUER (or MIDLAND) SITE, a locality near the town of Midland in western Texas where, in 1953, Keith Glasscock, Fred Wendorf, and others collected from the ground surface most of a female human cranium and several postcranial bones that evidently had eroded from Pleistocene deposits. A number of Folsom and other types of Paleoindian (qq.v.) projectile points were also found nearby on the eroded surface. Included were points of the same size and shape as Folsom points, but having no flutes, which sometimes are called Midland points.

Chemical and geological studies indicated that the bones, which are commonly known as Midland Man (or Woman), probably date ca. 8000 B.C. This is one of the few finds to date of human skeletal material that can be identified confidently with Paleoindians.

SOURCES: Wendorf et al. 1955; Wormington 1957:141–246.

Edward B. Jelks

SCHMIDT SITE, a predominately Late Archaic site of controversial date in the Saginaw Valley, in Michigan that was investigated by a University of Michigan team in 1964 and by a Western Michigan University team led by Jerry Fairchild in 1973. Abundant bifaces and a high frequency of mammal and bird remains support the hypothesis that the site was occupied in fall and winter.

SOURCES: Cleland and Kearney 1966; Taggart 1967; Fairchild 1977.

Margaret B. Holman

SCHULTZ COMPLEX, the expression of Early Woodland culture in the Saginaw Valley, in Michigan, as exemplified by the Schultz Site (q.v.). It has been postulated that the complex represents a systemic adaptation comprising changes in scheduling to incorporate squash cultivation, mussel exploitation, the use of pottery in processing nuts, the use of stemmed projectile points, and the construction of mounds to bury the dead.

SOURCE: Ozker 1982.

Margaret B. Holman

SCHULTZ PHASE, a culture unit in north-central Kansas, originally defined by Charles Eyman as a burial complex but now recognized as a Plains or Late Woodland phase (ca. A.D. 400–700) comprising both habitation and burial-mound sites. The economy focused on gathering and hunting, especially deer; no evidence of cultigens has been found, but pigweed, lambsquarter, and walnut were important vegetal foods. The dead were cremated and their ashes broadcast in the fill of mounds while they were being constructed on bluffs overlooking major stream drainages.

SOURCES: Phenice 1969; Eyman 1966; O'Brien et al. 1973; Parks n.d.

Patricia J. O'Brien

SCHULTZ SITE, a large, stratified, multicomponent site at the confluence of the Tittabasassee and Shiawassee rivers where they join in Michigan to form the Saginaw River; excavated between 1962 and 1965 by J. E. Fitting. As the prehistoric natural setting of the site has been intensively studied and reported, there is information on local zoology and water dynamics, plus analyses of fauna, mollusks, wood, and other botanical remains from the site.

Doreen Ozker has studied the Early Woodland component at the site (cf. Schultz Complex) intensively from the viewpoint of systemic change. In the later of two Middle Woodland levels, there was a circular stockade which has been interpreted as a ceremonial area. Ceramics from village debris are local products but are similar to Havana, Hopewell, and Baehr wares in Illinois. Fish were an important food item during the Middle Woodland occupation.

A Late Woodland component, less intensively occupied than the preceding ones, has yielded Eastern Complex corn and a radiocarbon date of 1180 ± 100.

SOURCES: Yarnell 1964; Cleland 1966; Fitting 1972; Ozker 1982.

Margaret B. Holman

SCHUYLER AREA SOAPSTONE QUARRIES, a series of quarry pits in soapstone outcrops that parallel the east side of the Blue Ridge Escarpment, near the James River in the western Piedmont of Virginia. After initial identification by D. I. Bushnell in 1926, C. G. Holland described the quarries in detail in 1960 and, in 1981, by means of neutron activation analysis, he studied the distribution of bowls and other artifacts made from the soapstone.

SOURCE: Bushnell 1930; Holland 1960b; Holland et al. 1981.

Keith T. Egloff

SCIOTO TRADITION, an interpretive model proposed by O. H. Prufer that views materials of the Hopewell Culture (q.v.) as an overlay upon a separate, evolving, secular culture which began in the Early Woodland period (Adena Phase) and continued into Late Woodland times (Peters Phase).

SOURCES: Prufer et al. 1965:127–136; Prufer 1968:4, 1975:10–15.

N'omi B. Greber

SCOGGIN SITE, a small bison pound or corral site in western Wyoming, dating ca. 2500 B.C., where animals were driven over a low escarpment and down a steep slope into a corral. Investigations in 1970 by George Frison produced McKean type lanceolate projectile points plus large, unnamed, side-notched points, in contextual association with bison remains.

SOURCE: Lobdell 1974.

George Frison

SCOTT COUNTY PUEBLO, a seven-room pueblo ruin in western Kansas where excavations by S. W. Williston and H. T. Martin in 1898 produced mainly Plains Indian pottery and chipped-stone material, but also some southwestern Puebloan artifacts. Utilizing Spanish documents, Williston identified the site as El Cuartelejo, a large Cuartelejo Apache rancheria to which Pueblo Indians fled to escape Spanish rule in the late 17th century. W. R. Wedel investigated the site intensively in 1939 and assigned the Apache component to the Dismal River Aspect (q.v.). In 1970 T. A. Witty, Jr., reexcavated the pueblo and restored the ruins to their 1898 configuration as an interpretive exhibit.

SOURCES: H. T. Martin 1909; Wedel 1959:422–468; Williston 1899; Witty 1983.

Thomas A. Witty, Jr.

SCOTTSBLUFF POINT, a late Paleoindian (q.v.) projectile-point type, dating ca. 7100–6000 B.C., distributed widely on the Great Plains. Specimens of the type are long, parallel-sided points, lenticular in cross section, with a rectangular stem, weak shoulders, and parallel flake scars.
SOURCES: Barbour and Schultz 1932; Wormington 1957.

Patricia J. O'Brien

SCOTTSBLUFF SITE, a bison-kill site near Scottsbluff, Nebraska, where in 1932 C. B. Schultz and E. H. Barbour discovered the type specimens of the Scottsbluff projectile-point type (q.v.) in association with *B. occidentalis*.
SOURCES: Barbour and Schultz 1932; Wormington 1957.

Patricia J. O'Brien

SCOTT'S LAKE BLUFF SITE, a village and mortuary complex of the South Appalachian Mississippian period (ca. A.D. 1250–1350), located approximately a kilometer from the Scott's Lake Mounds (q.v.) on the shore of Lake Marion in Clarendon County, in South Carolina. L. G. Ferguson, who discovered the site eroding into Lake Marion in 1973, salvaged 25 individual flexed, bundled, and cremated burials, some of them in Pee Dee-like urns.
SOURCE: Carter and Chickering 1973; DePratter and Judge 1986.

Michael Trinkley

SCOTT'S LAKE (or FORT WATSON) MOUNDS, a South Appalachian Mississippian mound group that originally comprised two or three mounds, located on the edge of Lake Marion in Clarendon County, in South Carolina. Dating ca. A.D. 1600, it was partially excavated by L. G. Ferguson in 1972–1973.
SOURCES: J. J. Reid 1965, 1967; L. G. Ferguson 1975.

Michael Trinkley

SEAHORSE GULLY SITE, a site on the west coast of Hudson Bay in the Keewatin District, thought to represent a southward penetration of Late Pre-Dorset peoples ca. 900 B.C. When R. J. Nash excavated the site, he discovered houses with paved floors resembling Independence-type mid-passages (see Independence I).
SOURCE: R. J. Nash 1969.

Moreau S. Maxwell

SEA PINES SHELL RING, a Thom's Creek (q.v.) Phase component on the south end of Hilton Head Island in Beaufort County, in South Carolina. Excavations were conducted there in the 1950s by A. J. Waring, in 1966

by A. R. Calmes, and in the 1970s by Larry Lepionka. There are two radiocarbon dates on the site: 1450 ± 110 B.C. and 1160 ± 110 B.C..
SOURCES: Calmes n.d.a.; Trinkley 1980a.

Michael Trinkley

SEATED HUMAN FIGURE BOWL, a distinctive artifact type of the Fraser River stone-sculpture complex in southwestern British Columbia and northwestern Washington, probably dating between 400 B.C. and A.D. 400. In most of the nearly 60 known specimens, the principal figure is a human with an emaciated or skeletal body, but a fully fleshed face, whose arms and legs embrace a bowl. The face is turned slightly upward, the mouth is often open, and the hair is drawn into a prominent top-knot. A subsidiary figure or face—usually a lizard or snake—ornaments the bowl's front.
SOURCES: Duff 1956, 1975.

Donald H. Mitchell

SECOND REFUGE SITE, a multicomponent, Early Woodland shell midden about 2 meters deep on the Little Back River in Jasper County, in South Carolina. Larry Lepionka, who excavated the site in 1979–1980, found Irene, Savannah, and Deptford pottery in its upper levels and Refuge Phase (qq.v.) materials in its lower levels. The latter provided important information about Refuge Phase subsistence practices, settlement pattern, and ceramics typology.
SOURCES: Waring 1968; Lepionka et al., n.d.

Michael Trinkley

SEDENTARY PERIOD, the third period of the Hohokam Culture (q.v.), dating ca. A.D. 900–1100 and including a single phase, Sacaton (q.v.). Sedentary Period cultural patterns reflect those of the earlier Colonial Period (q.v.), with some notable absences and some new traits, and presage those of the Classic Period (q.v.). Sacaton Red-on-buff pottery often exhibits poor-quality design work, with emphasis on broad-line, rectilinear and curvilinear patterns; some complex designs appear to replicate woven textile patterns. Although the flared-rim bowl form of the Colonial Period continues and effigy forms are elaborated, large decorated jars with low-placed "Gila Shouders" are more common. Small quantities of polished redware also occur. The Snaketown Site (q.v.) may have emerged as a major center of pottery manufacture during the late Colonial and Sedentary periods.

Architectural styles continued to emphasize shallow, elliptical pithouses; some especially large ones (65–80 square meters) have been reported. At the Snaketown and Gatlin sites, true platform mounds made their first appearance. There was some experimentation with caliche-adobe as a wall-building material, anticipating a common practice of the following Classic Period. Subsistence based on irrigation farming in the riverine provinces and on floodwater farming in the more arid provinces remained constant or, in some places, even expanded. Ball courts continued in use at major villages.

A Santan Phase has been proposed as a transitional phase between the Sedentary and Classic periods, but it has not been verified through stratigraphic excavations.

SOURCES: Gladwin et al. 1937; Haury 1976; Doyel 1981; Wilcox and Sternberg 1983.

David E. Doyel and John S. Cable

SEIP SITE, a group of at least 30 mounds within and near a large geometric earthwork on Paint Creek, west of Chillicothe, Ohio. W. C. Mills excavated Seip Mound 1 in 1907; H. C. Shetrone excavated the Seip-Pricer Mound in 1925–1929. Both mounds covered large, multisection, Hopewell (q.v.) civic-ceremonial structures that contained evidence of a range of activities. Floor plans and artifact distributions were similar to those at the Edwin Harness Mound (q.v.). When use of the buildings was discontinued, a separate mound was erected over each section. At Seip-Price, these early stages were later covered by one tremendous mound—the second largest of the Ohio Hopewell Culture. Between 1971 and 1977, R. S. Baby exposed simple Hopewell structures dating ca. A.D. 100–500 under other mounds of the Seip group.

SOURCES: Squier and Davis 1848:58–59, pl. 21, no. 2; Mills 1909; Shetrone and Greenman 1931; Baby and Langlois 1979; Greber 1979a, 1981, 1983:86–92; Konigsberg 1985.

N'omi B. Greber

SELBY BAY PHASE, a Middle Woodland (ca. A.D. 200–900) phase occupying the pan-Chesapeake Bay region from the Delmarva Peninsula to Virginia's coastal plain. Distinctive traits are cordmarked and net-impressed Mockley Ware (q.v.) pottery and, in some areas, Selby Bay or Potts projectile points (qq.v.).

SOURCES: Mayr 1972; H. T. Wright 1973:21–22; Steponaitis 1980:15–16; Potter 1982:118–126, 334–347.

Stephen R. Potter

SELBY BAY POINT, a crudely made type of projectile point with an elongated blade, straight to slightly excurvate edges, and either a weakly stemmed or side-notched hafting element. Found in Middle Woodland sites in Delaware, Maryland, and northern Virginia, the type dates ca. A.D. 200–900.

SOURCES: R. A. Thomas et al. n.d.; Steponaitis 1980:15–16; Potter 1982:125–126.

Stephen R. Potter

SELDON ISLAND CORD-MARKED POTTERY, a type of steatite-tempered pottery in the form of conical jars with haphazardly cord-marked exterior surfaces. Dating ca. 800 B.C., it occurs in Early Woodland sites in Delaware, Maryland, and northern Virginia.
SOURCES: Slattery 1946:263–265; Artusy 1976:2.

Stephen R. Potter

SELDON ISLAND SITE, an Early Woodland (ca. 1000–800 B.C.) base camp on Seldon Island in the Piedmont section of the Potomac River, Maryland. Excavated by R. G. Slattery and H. V. Stabler in 1945, it is the type site for Seldon Island Cord-marked pottery (q.v.).
SOURCE: Slattery 1946:262–266.

Stephen R. Potter

SERMERMIUT SITE, a multicomponent site on Disko Bay, Greenland, excavated by Therkel Mathiassen, H. E. Larsen, and Jørden Meldgaard in the 1950s. It provided the first data on the Saqqaq Phase (q.v.), which was separated stratigraphically from early Middle Dorset and Neoeskimo materials.
SOURCES: Larsen and Meldgaard 1958; Mathiassen 1958.

Moreau S. Maxwell

SERPENT MOUND, an earthen effigy of a serpent about 210 meters long on a high terrace above Brush Creek in Adams County, in Ohio. F. W. Putnam partly excavated the mound and reconstructed it in 1888 but found no artifacts in it. At the same time, he also dug a conical mound south of the serpent and a habitation area at the base of the terrace. In the conical mound, he found artifacts of the Adena Culture (q.v.); in the habitation area, he discovered Fort Ancient (q.v.) artifacts superposed over Adena materials.
SOURCES: Squier and Davis 1848:96–98, pl. 35; Putnam 1890; Willoughby 1919; J. B. Griffin 1943a:56–64.

N'omi B. Greber

SEVIER CULTURE. See Fremont Culture.

SEVIER/FREMONT CULTURE. See Fremont Culture.

SEWEE SHELL RING, a Thom's Creek Phase site in Charleston County, in South Carolina with a radiocarbon date of 1345 ± 110 B.C. It was excavated by W. E. Edwards in 1965.

SOURCES: Trinkley 1980a; Edwards n.d.

                                                              Michael Trinkley

SHABIK'ESHCHEE VILLAGE, an Eastern Anasazi pithouse village on the lower bench of Chacra Mesa in Chaco Culture National Historical Park, New Mexico. The type site for the Basketmaker (q.v.) III period (not only for Chaco Canyon, but for the entire Anasazi region), it had at least twenty dwellings, a great kiva, 45 storage cists, and two refuse mounds. Tree-ring dates indicate an initial occupation in the 6th century A.D.; the date of abandonment is uncertain.

The Basketmaker III dwellings, dug from 50 to 100 centimeters into the ground, were round to rectangular and from 3 to 4 meters across. Some were lined with vertical slabs. Four interior posts supported the roofs, which were made of poles, brush, and mud. Floor features included mud- or slab-lined firepits, an upright deflector stone, bins made of stone slabs, and a sipapu (a small, round hole in the floor between the firepit and the north wall). Entrance was through an antechamber, generally located to the south of the main room.

Shabik'eshchee's great kiva was 12 meters in diameter and about a meter deep. It had a low bench faced with sandstone slabs around its interior perimeter, a firepit, a deflector, and four roof-support posts. There was no sipapu.

F. H. H. Roberts, Jr., excavated Shabik'eshchee in 1927, exposing eighteen houses, a kiva, and 45 cists. In 1973, A. C. Hayes and John Thrift dug portions of two more pithouses and obtained additional tree-ring samples.

SOURCES: F. H. H. Roberts, Jr. 1929b; McKenna and Truell 1986.

                                                         Frances Joan Mathien

SHALLOW LAKE SITE, a multicomponent site consisting of discontinuous middens and six mounds covering some 24 hectares, located in the Quachita Valley of south-central Arkansas. Its ten components span almost 10,000 years—from the Dalton Culture (q.v.) to the historic period—and document the entire archaeological sequence of the Felsenthal region of the lower Mississippi River Valley. Excavated by the Arkansas Archeological Survey in 1975, Shallow Lake is the type site for two Mississippian (q.v.) phases: Gran Marais and Caney Bayou.

SOURCE: Rolingson and Schambach 1981.

                                                         Frank F. Schambach

SHANNON SITE, a large, palisaded village on the North Fork of the Roanoke River in southwestern Virginia with a possible occupation date of A.D. 1550–1600. J. L. Benthall tested the site in 1966, uncovering storage

pits, hearths, human burials, and circular house patterns. Ceramics were an unusual mixture of Radford, Dan River, and New River (qq.v.) wares.
SOURCES: Benthall 1969a; Mecklenburg 1969.

Keith T. Egloff

SHASTA COMPLEX, a late period assemblage dating from ca. A.D. 500 to the historic contact period, found in the north coastal ranges and the northern Sacramento Valley, in California. Small barbed arrow points of the Gunther Barbed type, pine-nut and spire-lopped *Olivella* shell beads, large chert bifaces, and basket-hopper mortars are distinctive traits.
SOURCE: Meighan 1955.

L. A. Payen

SHAYMARK SITE, an early (ca. 2000 B.C.) Pre-Dorset (q.v.) site on the outskirts of the town of Frobisher Bay, Baffin Island, Northwest Territories; excavated in 1962 by a Michigan State University team. Some lithic artifacts suggest a possible earlier occupation by Independence I (q.v.) peoples.
SOURCE: Maxwell 1973.

Moreau S. Maxwell

SHEFFIELD SITE, a multicomponent campsite on the floodplain of the St. Croix River in east-central Minnesota, initially excavated by L. A. Wilford in 1951, 1955, and 1956 and later, in 1959–1960, by P. Jenson. The largest component, dating ca. A.D. 1300–1800, is an Oneota (q.v.) summer hunting and fishing camp, possibly related to the Blue Earth Phase of south-central Minnesota. Middle Woodland, Late Woodland (Kathio Phase), and Early Historic components also are present.
SOURCES: Wilford n.d.d.; Gibbon 1973.

Gordon R. Peters

SHEPARD CORD-MARKED POTTERY, a quartz- or granite-tempered, Late Woodland (ca. A.D. 900–1450) type, found in the northern Shenandoah Valley of Virginia, the Hagerstown Valley of Maryland, and the Piedmont section of the Potomac Valley. Vessels have globular bodies, semiconical or rounded bases, and slightly constricted necks. Decorations consist of oblique lines, either incised or made with a cord-wrapped paddle edge, and, sometimes, applique strips.
SOURCES: Schmitt 1952:62; Slattery et al. 1966:50; R. M. Stewart 1982:76–77; Kavanagh 1982:70–74.

Stephen R. Potter

SHEPARD SITE, a Late Woodland village, dating ca. A.D. 900–1450, on the left bank of the Potomac River in the Maryland Piedmont. Excavated in 1936–1939 by R. G. Slattery and H. V. Stabler, in 1952–1955 by N.

Yinger and R. Fout, and in 1955 by H. A. MacCord, it is the type site for the Montgomery Complex and for Shepard Cord-marked pottery (qq.v.).
SOURCES: Schmitt 1952; MacCord et al. 1957.

Stephen R. Potter

SHERMER SITE, a large, fortified village of the terminal Middle Missouri Tradition (q.v.) on Alkali Creek, a tributary of the Missouri River in North Dakota. Excavated by J. E. Sperry in 1965–1966, it has been dated by dendrochronology to between A.D. 1485 and 1543. Like the related Huff Site (q.v.), it probably was a prehistoric Mandan-Hidatsa settlement.
SOURCE: Sperry 1968.

Patricia J. O'Brien

SHOCKOE SLIP SITE, a stratified site below the falls of the James River in Richmond, Virginia, tested by Mark Druss and J. R. Saunders in 1977. It yielded a wide range of floral and faunal remains, associated with Middle and Late Woodland ceramics showing strong Piedmont relationships.
SOURCE: Mouer 1984.

Keith T. Egloff

SHOOP SITE, a hillside near Enterline in eastern Pennsylvania, from whose surface several different people in the 1930s and 1940s collected 48 complete and fragmentary Paleoindian projectile points, plus a variety of chipped-stone scrapers and knives, gravers, and lamellar blades and cores. After analyzing the material, John Witthoft described a distinctive way of striking blades from cores and flutes from projectile points which he named the Enterline Chert Industry.
SOURCE: Witthoft 1952.

Edward B. Jelks

SHORTY SITE, a two-component site on Cape Tanfield (q.v.) on the southeastern coast of Baffin Island, Northwest Territories, excavated by a Michigan State University team in 1974. A small Thule Phase (q.v.) pithouse that had been dug through an earlier Dorset Phase (q.v.) midden still had its complete whale-rib roof structure in place, providing unique data on a single-family Thule residence. Materials from the midden suggested that the site was first used by early Late Dorset people, but strictly as a base for spring hunting of immature seals.
SOURCES: Maxwell 1980, 1985.

Moreau S. Maxwell

SHULDHAM ISLAND 9 SITE, a 14th-century, late Dorset Phase (q.v.) site on Saglek Bay, northern Labrador. When he excavated there in 1980, Callum Thomson found many lithic artifacts, the most significant being a series of soapstone artistic pieces that included a figurine of a clothed Dorset man with an upstanding collar. The carvings bear general resemblances to Dorset styles, but to date they are a unique find.

SOURCES: Thomson 1981, 1982.

Moreau S. Maxwell

SHUNGOPAVI SITES, a series of four sites representing the mother villages of Hopi Second Mesa in northeastern Arizona; one of the oldest, largest, and most important Hopi settlements which, according to tradition, was founded by Bear clans from the Kayenta area, together with Squash and Cloud clans from the Upper Colorado or Sinagua areas. Archaeological evidence dates the beginnings of the earliest site (Shungopavi I) to ca. A.D. 1200.

This first village of some 300 to 400 persons was shifted to a new location (Shungopavi II) a few hundred meters to the south ca. A.D. 1400. A third village (Shungopavi III) was established later, just south of a Spanish Franciscan mission and compound built in 1629. Then, Shungopavi II and III were both abandoned in 1680 following the destruction of the church and mission in the Pueblo Revolt, after which Shungopavi IV, which still survives, was founded. This Western Hopi style, parallel-row pueblo consists of stone-built houses from one to three stories high and contains five semi-subterranean, stone-built rectangular kivas. A complete ceremonial cycle is still observed.

A suburb, Shipaulovi, was established in 1680 across a wash from Shungopavi proper. It was of the Upper Little Colorado/Rio Grande, hollow-square, central-plaza style, with one- to three-story, stone-built houses and three outside, semisubterranean, stone-built, rectangular kivas.

J. W. Fewkes surveyed and tested the Shungopavi sites in the 1890s; L. L. Hargrave and the Museum of Northern Arizona worked there in the 1920s and 1930s.

SOURCES: Fewkes 1900; Hargrave 1930; Colton 1932b; Ellis 1961; Connelly 1979.

Michael B. Stanislawski

SHUSWAP HORIZON. See Shuswap Phase.

SHUSWAP PHASE, the earliest (ca. 2000–400 B.C.) of three prehistoric phases in the South Thompson River Valley, the western Shuswap Lake area, and the adjacent highlands of British Columbia; defined by Thomas Richards and Michael Rousseau in 1982. It is characterized by unbarbed projectile points with concave bases and basal-lateral ears; the use of poor-quality local stones for tools; a well-developed bone and antler industry; poorly developed trade; large, oval housepits, probably with flat roofs and side entrances; and flexed, single interments inside houses. Origins of the phase presumably lie in either the Lehman Phase or the Old Cordilleran Culture (qq.v.). Richards and Rousseau assign the Shuswap Phase to a more widespread Shuswap Horizon of the mid-Fraser and Thompson river drainages.

SOURCE: Rousseau and Richards 1986.

Arnoud H. Stryd

SICHOMOVI SITE, a pueblo located between Walpi and Hano in northeastern Arizona, considered a suburb of Walpi. Established ca. A.D. 1760–1782, probably by Rio Grande Tewa or Zuni Asa clans, it was built in the Rio Grande/Upper Little Colorado Style, originally with approximately 50 stone-built rooms (population about 100) of one or two stories around a central plaza in which were two rectangular, stone-built, semisubterranean kivas. The site was surveyed by Victor Mindeleff in the 1880s and was tested by B. E. Holmes and T. G. Birkedal between 1980 and 1985.

SOURCES: Victor Mindeleff 1891; Hargrave 1931; Ellis 1961; Holmes and Stanislawski 1986.

Michael B. Stanislawski

SIERRA BLANCA SUB-PROVINCE, a division of the Jornada Province (q.v.) of the Mogollon Culture, occupying an area in central New Mexico ca. A.D. 500?–1450. J. H. Kelley has devised two contemporaneous phase sequences for the sub-province: the Corona and Lincoln phases (qq.v.) in the northern sector, and the early and late Glencoe Phase (q.v.) in the south. The earliest ceramic-period occupations in both sectors remain undefined. Cultural similarities are strongest with the El Paso Sub-Province (q.v.) of the Jornada Province to the southwest, the Mimbres Province to the west, and the Salinas Province (q.v.) of the Anasazi Culture to the northwest.

SOURCE: J. H. Kelley 1984.

R. N. Wiseman

SIGNAL BUTTE SITE, a three-component, stratified site on a large mesa southeast of Scottsbluff, Nebraska, excavated by W. D. Strong in 1932. Like Ash Hollow Cave (q.v.), it played an important role in initial chronological ordering of Central Plains (q.v.) archaeological culture units. Signal Butte I, the lowest level, which contained lanceolate projectile points with some resemblance to the Folsom type (q.v.), probably was of Paleoindian (qq.v.) affiliation. Signal Butte II produced early late Archaic materials dating ca. 2000 B.C. Signal Butte III comprised two layers: a component of the Dismal River Aspect (q.v.), containing some glass beads and trade copper along with aboriginal artifacts, and, below that, an Upper Republican Aspect (q.v.) component.

SOURCES: Strong 1935:224–239; Champe 1946:58–60.

Patricia J. O'Brien

SIKYATKI SITE, a large prehistoric village at the east base of Hopi First Mesa in northeastern Arizona, inhabited from ca. A.D. 1350 to ca. 1400. Known to the Hopi as Yellow House or Yellow Water, it was a stone-built, hollow-square, central-plaza pueblo of one- and two-story buildings and several possible plaza kivas, with a population of at least 300 to 500 people. There are cemeteries with both seated (flexed) and extended burials to the west, southwest, and southeast. J. W. Fewkes briefly excavated the site in 1895.

Sikyatki is notable for (1) its Rio Grande style village plan; (2) its elaborate, polished but unslipped yellowware (Sikyatki Polychrome) painted in black, brown, and red with curvilinear, free-form designs that emphasize birds and bird wings, reptiles (including the plumed serpent), man-eagles, rainclouds, sun figures, tadpoles, moths, butterflies, human figures, and panels of geometric patterns—all on new vessel forms with squat outlines and very sharp shoulders; and (3) evidence that coal was used for firing pottery, which may have contributed to its light yellow color.

According to tradition, Sikyatki was founded by the Kokop (Firewood) Clan, later was occupied by the Coyote and Wolf clans of Kokopynyama village, and eventually was destroyed by inhabitants of Second Mesa villages led by the people of Old Walpi. Survivors are said to have fled to Oraibi or Awatovi (qq.v.).

SOURCES: Fewkes 1896, 1898a, 1910, 1919; Hargrave 1931, 1937.

Michael B. Stanislawski

SILUMIUT SITE, a group of Thule Phase (q.v.) houses, radiocarbon dated to ca. A.D. 1100–1250, located on Roes Welcome Sound, Northwest Territories, about 200 kilometers south of the Naujan Site (q.v.). A. P. McCartney's excavations there in the 1970s disclosed a site rich in details about the development of eastern Thule from Classic to Post-Classic times. Earlier houses were winter deep pithouses, typologically contemporaneous with houses at the Naujan Site; toward the end of the occupation such houses were being deserted for snow houses on the fast ice (q.v.).

SOURCE: McCartney 1977.

Moreau S. Maxwell

SILVER BLUFF SITE, a major multicomponent site on the Savannah River in Aiken County, in South Carolina, occupied by both prehistoric and protohistoric Indians. Thought by some scholars to be the location of Cofitachique, visited by De Soto in 1540, it was the site of a Yuchi village between

1746 and 1750. J. D. Scurry and J. W. Joseph conducted archaeological studies at Silver Bluff in 1979–1980.
SOURCE: Scurry et al. 1980.

Michael Trinkley

SILVERNALE PHASE. See Oneota Tradition.

SIMONSEN SITE, a stratified site on the Little Sioux River near Quimby, Iowa, where in 1958 side-notched projectile points and other stone tools were found among bones of the extinct *Bison occidentalis* in a stratum that was radiocarbon dated to 6480±520 B.C.
SOURCES: Frankforter and Agogino 1959; Agogino and Frankforter 1960; Beals 1965.

George A. Agogino and Duane C. Anderson

SINAGUA DIVISION, an expression of the Hakataya Culture (q.v.) in Arizona south of the Little Colorado River, between the San Francisco Peaks on the west almost to Winslow on the east, and extending southwestward into the Tonto Basin and the valleys of the Verde, East Verde, and Agua Fria rivers. The division's domain corresponds to the distribution of Alameda Brown Ware (q.v.) pottery and its series; its phases were occupied for varying periods between ca. A.D. 500 and 1400/1450. According to Hopi tradition, some Sinagua peoples are thought to have moved to the middle Colorado River and then to Hopi country, arriving there by A.D. 1450. Other Sinaguans are believed to have moved into the Gila-Salt area in the 1100s.

There are several provinces within the division that were influenced through time in one way or another by the Anasazi Culture to the north, the Mogollon Culture to the east, and the Hohokam Culture to the south (qq.v.). Pre–1100 Sinaguan burial practices have not been established; but, after 1100, they buried their dead (many, but not all, of whom had occipitally flattened crania) in an extended position oriented in various directions. This contrasts with the Anasazi's flexed burials and lambdoidal cranial deformation.

Redware and smudged-interior pottery appeared in the 1100s among the Sinagua. These traits are not found among the more western Hakataya except for redware along the lower Colorado River. The Sinagua also adopted pueblo-style architecture in the 1100s.
SOURCES: Colton 1946; Schroeder 1960.

Albert H. Schroeder

SISTERS HILL SITE, a location near Buffalo, Wyoming, where a deeply buried occupation zone, excavated in 1961 by George Agogino, produced three Hell Gap (q.v.) type projectile points along with chipped-stone scrapers, gravers, and knives. Bones of mule deer, antelope, squirrel, rabbit, and porcupine were associated. A radiocarbon date of 7689 B.C. indicates that Sisters Hill is slightly more recent than other dated sites with Hell Gap points.

SOURCES: Agogino 1961; Agogino and Galloway 1965.

George A. Agogino

SITE 38LX5, a large site containing Middle Archaic through Late Woodland components, located in the Congaree Creek drainage in Lexington County, in South Carolina. Excavations in 1978 by D. G. Anderson revealed several relatively short-term Archaic and Woodland occupations. Michael Trinkley investigated the site further in 1980 and discovered a Deptford (q.v.) Phase component with features. Six radiocarbon dates indicate that the site was occupied from ca. 2750 B.C. to ca. A.D. 80.

SOURCES: D. G. Anderson n.d.a; Trinkley 1980c.

Michael Trinkley

SITE 38SU83, a Yadkin Phase seasonal campsite in Sumter County, in South Carolina, excavated in 1985 by D. B. Blanton and P. E. Brockington. They carried out a detailed analysis of its ceramic and lithic assemblages and obtained an average radiocarbon date (on three specimens) of ca. 380 B.C.

SOURCES: Blanton et al. n.d.; Trinkley et al. 1985.

Michael Trinkley

SITES BC 50 AND 51, two small, related, Bonito Phase (q.v.) sites in Chaco Culture National Historical Park, New Mexico. Bc 50 is a pueblo of approximately 30 rooms and four kivas dating from the late 11th to the mid–12th century. Bc 51, with over 50 rooms and seven kivas, dates to the same period. A shared trash midden lies between them, and there are earlier pit structures and surface rooms at both sites.

D. D. Brand excavated Bc 50 in 1936; Clyde Kluckhohn excavated Bc 51 in 1937. While stabilizing the sites in 1949–1950, Gordon Vivian dug a few additional rooms in Bc 51. Their work demonstrated the contemporaneity of such small sites with the large pueblos such as Pueblo Bonito and Pueblo del Arroyo (qq.v.) in Chaco Canyon, which brought into question some of the phase descriptions originally outlined for the Pecos Classification (q.v.).

SOURCES: Brand et al. 1937; Kluckhohn and Reiter 1939.

Frances Joan Mathien

SKAMEL PHASE. See Fraser Canyon Sequence.

SKOGLUND'S LANDING SITE, a two-component site on Graham Island, Queen Charlotte Islands, British Columbia, excavated by K. R. Fladmark in 1969. A few waterworn pebble tools and flakes were found in the lower

component, an ancient marine beach, now ca. 15 meters above sea level and thought to date ca. 8000–6000 B.C. The upper component contained a large assemblage of flaked-stone unifaces and cores, dating ca. 2500–500 B.C., the local manifestation of the Transitional Complex (q.v.).
SOURCE: Fladmark 1970.

Knut R. Fladmark

SKRAELING ISLAND SITE, a settlement comprising a large number of Ruin Island Phase (q.v.) houses on Skraeling Island, off the coast of Ellesmere Island in the eastern Canadian Arctic; excavated by Karen McCollogh. Data from this site, which has been radiocarbon dated to the 13th century A.D., and from related sites on the nearby Bache Peninsula (q.v.) provided the basis for defining this distinctive phase of the Neoeskimo Tradition (q.v.). To date (1988), known houses and artifacts of the Ruin Phase are restricted to the Canadian and Greenland shores of Davis Strait in the High Arctic. Strong Alaskan attributes suggest that the phase is either an initial aspect of the Thule Phase (q.v.) migration or a separate migration that followed earlier Thule people coming from Birnirk Phase (q.v.) sites in northern Alaska.
SOURCE: McCollogh 1986.

Moreau S. Maxwell

SLAUGHTER CREEK PHASE, a Late Woodland manifestation in Sussex County, in Delaware, dating ca. A.D. 1000–1600 and distinguished by a horticultural/shellfishing economy and by Townsend Ware (q.v.) ceramics, triangular projectile points manufactured from local pebble jasper, a wide range of bone tools, shell middens, storage pits, semi-subterranean houses, and both single and ossuary burials. The phase was initially defined as a focus under the Midwestern Taxonomic System (q.v.).
SOURCES: Weslager 1968; R. A. Thomas 1976.

Ronald A. Thomas

SLOAN SITE, a Dalton-period (q.v.) cemetery in northeastern Arkansas, dating ca. 8000 B.C. Excavations there by D. F. Morse in 1974 exposed a series of artifact clusters that were interpreted as sets of offerings originally placed in individual graves. The grave outlines were not discernible, and the skeletons had almost completely decomposed because of high soil acidity; however, in an area of 130 square meters, more than twenty grave locations could be identified on the basis of artifact distribution. The 448

artifacts found, most of them complete and in pristine condition, included projectile points, preforms, adzes, end scrapers, flakes, cores, and cobbles.
SOURCES: Morse 1975; Morse and Morse 1983.

Dan F. Morse

SMALL SAVANNAH RIVER STEMMED POINT, a lineal descendant of the earlier Savannah River Stemmed type (q.v.), this small to medium-sized projectile point has a broad triangular blade, a rectangular stem, and a straight, incurvate, or excurvate base. Dating to the latter part of the Late Archaic period (ca. 2000–1000 B.C.), specimens of the type have been found at stratified sites in coastal South Carolina and in the Piedmont and mountains of North Carolina.
SOURCES: South 1959; Oliver 1981:151–154.

Billy L. Oliver

SMELT CREEK PHASE. See Brooks River-Naknek Drainage Sites.

SMILING DAN SITE, an open, stratified, multicomponent site in Scott County, in Illinois, comprising Middle Archaic (ca. 4000 B.C.), Middle Woodland (ca. 70 B.C.-A.D. 370), and Late Woodland (ca. A.D. 850) components buried in colluvium at the edge of a creek valley tributary to the Illinois River. M. B. Sant and B. D. Stafford focused their excavations there in 1979–1980 on the Middle Woodland (Havana-Hopewell) component, a thick, extensive midden in which they discovered three structures and 182 pit features. They recovered well-preserved floral and faunal remains and a large quantity of ceramic and lithic artifacts; many of the latter were made of imported stone. This was the first Middle Woodland base settlement in the lower Illinois River Valley to be analyzed comprehensively.
SOURCE: Stafford and Sant 1985.

Michael D. Wiant

SMITH CREEK CAVE, a site overlooking the southwestern arm of Pleistocene Lake Bonneville in Snake Valley, in eastern Nevada, which contained a complete sequence of projectile-point types from the Rosegate Series through the Great Basin Stemmed Series, as well as a variety of lithic tool types, bone tools, and perishables. The artifacts and hearths suggest two sporadic habitational uses for the site: one ca. 9000 B.C. and another about 2000 years ago. Willis and George Evans dug at the cave in 1925; M. R. Harrington conducted further excavations in 1932; and Alan Bryan did extensive work there in 1936, 1955, 1968, 1971, and 1974.
SOURCES: M. R. Harrington 1934; A. R. Bryan 1979.

David Hurst Thomas

SMITH SITE (formerly known as the LAUREL SITE), the type site for the Initial Woodland, Laurel Culture (q.v.) in Minnesota, situated along the south bank of the Rainy River on the border between Minnesota and Ontario. Both Laurel and Blackduck (Late Woodland) components are represented in the habitation area and in the burial mound complex. The "Grand Mound," the largest burial mound in Minnesota, stands on the Smith Site along with four other Laurel burial mounds. The Blackduck burials in these mounds are considered intrusive. Excavations have been conducted intermittently at the Smith Site by several different researchers from 1884 through 1985.

SOURCES: Bryce 1904; Jenks 1935; Wilford 1950a; D. L. Webster 1967; Stoltman 1973; Lugenbeal 1976.

Gordon R. Peters

SMOKY HILL PHASE, a culture unit in Kansas, originally defined in 1959 by W. R. Wedel as the Smoky Hill Aspect, consisting of two foci: Manhattan and Saline. The Nebraska, Upper Republican (qq.v.), and Smoky Hill phases constitute the Central Plains Tradition (q.v.), which dates ca. A.D. 1000–1500 and, on the basis of evidence from the Witt Site (q.v.) in Kansas, is attributed to ancestral Pawnee and Arikara. Diagnostic features of the phase are square earthlodges with a central fireplace and four main interior posts, small triangular projectile points, and globular pottery that is often collared.

SOURCES: O'Brien 1984b; Wedel 1959.

Patricia J. O'Brien

SMYTH POTTERY SERIES, a steatite-tempered pottery with net-impressed, scraped, or plain surfaces, found occasionally in southwestern Virginia and dating ca. A.D. 1200–1400.

SOURCE: Holland 1970.

Keith T. Egloff

SNAKETOWN PHASE. See Pioneer Period.

SNAKETOWN SITE, a large Hohokam (q.v.) settlement on the Gila River approximately 40 kilometers south of Phoenix, Arizona, containing two ball courts, over 60 mounds, hundreds of houses, and extensive canal-irrigation systems. Gila Pueblo conducted initial excavations there in 1934–1935 for the express purposes of investigating the origins of and defining the chronology of the Hohokam Culture. A basic outline of Hohokam prehistory was achieved for the Pioneer through the Sedentary Period (ca. A.D. 1–1100), but serious disagreements about the chronology gradually emerged. E. W. Haury's excavations at the site 30 years later did much to expand Hohokam Culture history but failed to resolve the issues of chronology and Hohokam origins.

For many years, Snaketown was the only extensively excavated Hohokam site, and as a result it has been the central focus of discussions concerning the culture. Recently, data from the site have been used to produce new models of Hohokam social and economic organization.

SOURCES: Gladwin et al. 1937; Haury 1976; Wilcox et al. 1981; Cable and Doyel 1986.

David E. Doyel and John S. Cable

SNIPES SITE, a primarily Early Ceramic Period (ca. A.D. 700) site in Cass County, in Texas, with a later, light Caddo occupation. Excavations there by E. B. Jelks in 1952 demonstrated an association between Williams Plain pottery (Jelks' Baytown-like) and Coles Creek pottery, Alba arrow points, and Gary dart points (qq.v.).

SOURCE: Jelks 1965:41–55.

James E. Corbin

SNOWDRIFT VILLAGE SITE, a late (ca. 1000 A.D.) Dorset Phase (q.v.) village on Dundas Island off the northwestern tip of Devon Island, Northwest Territories; excavated by Robert McGhee. It is the only Late Dorset site completely reported to date (1988). The village comprised five houses with paved and rock-lined mid-passages, and it contained harpoon heads of Late Dorset type.

SOURCE: McGhee 1981b.

Moreau S. Maxwell

SNYDER SITE, a Late Archaic site in south-central Kansas, now inundated by El Dorado Lake; excavated between 1968 and 1971 by R. D. Grosser and Tyler Bastian. Three phases (Chelsea, El Dorado [qq.v.], and Walnut), dating ca. 2800–50 B.C., constitute the earliest and longest temporally defined Archaic sequence in the Central Plains. Semisedentary occupations and diverse exploitation of the biotic resources were documented for the earliest phases, Chelsea and El Dorado. The Walnut Phase people were more transient, made more limited use of the biotic resources, and had acquired the bow and arrow. A Late Woodland phase, Butler, was also recognized at the site.

SOURCES: Grosser 1973, 1977.

Roger D. Grosser

SOHO PHASE. See Classic Period, Hohokam Culture.

SOLEBAAKEN SITE, an Independence II component, dating ca. 1000 B.C., on Polaris Promontory, northwestern coastal Greenland; excavated in 1958

by Eigil Knuth. Because of its intermediate location, it provided linkage between Independence sites of Peary Land and Ellesmere Island.
SOURCE: Knuth 1967.

Moreau S. Maxwell

SOLOMON RIVER PHASE, a relatively early (850–1250 A.D.) unit of the Upper Republican Aspect (q.v.) in north-central Kansas. Excavations by Preston Holder in the area to be inundated by Glen Elder Reservoir disclosed fourteen habitation sites and an ossuary assigned to the phase. Most were on the first river terrace; some had multiple or single houses and others were houseless, temporary, seasonal campsites.

Culture traits include subterranean pits, cord-marked and incised pottery, and stone artifacts typical of Central Plains Tradition (q.v.) forms. Remains of corn, squash, and sunflowers were found, along with bones of prairie game animals (bison and pronghorn) and, less commonly, bottomland forest species (deer, cottontail, squirrel, and raccoon). The river provided large numbers of mussels and a few species of fish and turtles.

Through analyses of materials and locational data, house floors were ordered temporally, the average number of inhabitants per household was calculated, and, by ethnographic analogy, family structure and post-marital residence patterns were inferred.
SOURCES: Lippincott 1976, 1978; Krause 1982.

Kerry Lippincott

SONOTA COMPLEX, a regional manifestation in Alberta, Saskatchewan, Montana, and the Dakotas of a widespread tradition, dating to the first six centuries A.D., which selectively exploited the plains-riverine environments of north-central North America. Sites of the complex typically contain bison bones, stone projectile points, butchering and hide-preparation tools, bone implements, and small amounts of pottery.

Along streams in the eastern Dakotas, Sonota artifacts occur in low, domed, earthen, burial mounds and campsites, in which pottery is relatively common and there is a variety of elaborate and, at times, exotic stone, bone, shell, copper, vegetal, and pigment specimens, usually associated with mound interments. The mounds, with their subfloor chambers and necrolia, along with certain ceramics found in both the mounds and the campsites, reflect influences from Hopewell (q.v.) societies east and southeast of the Plains, which probably were connected with the acquisition by Hopewell peoples of such highly prized western resources as obsidian and Knife River flint (q.v.).
SOURCE: Neuman 1975.

Robert W. Neuman

SOUTH APPALACHIAN MISSISSIPPIAN CULTURE, a general term for a fusion of traditional Middle Mississippian Culture with indigenous population of Georgia, South Carolina, and contiguous parts of Alabama, Florida, North Carolina, and Tennessee. Dating ca. A.D. 1000–1650, the culture was characterized by large villages (frequently palisaded), temple mounds, a large population, agriculture, a distinctive cermonialism, and a chiefdom level of sociopolitical organization.

SOURCES: L. G. Ferguson 1971; J. B. Griffin 1967.

Michael Trinkley

SOUTHERN CEREMONIAL COMPLEX (or SOUTHERN CULT), a complex of ceremonial objects that occurs with burials of high-status individuals in mounds at Mississippian (q.v.) sites across the southeastern United States. Among the more spectacular items are elaborately carved marine-shell gorgets and dippers, monolithic axes, and repousse copper plates. Design elements include costumed dancing human figures, raptorial birds, sun circles, swastikas, plumed rattlesnakes, "weeping eyes," human hands, and "bilobed arrows." Some of these elements are similar to motifs in Mesoamerica; others are reminiscent of Hopewell motifs. The complex occurs most often at major ceremonial centers, including the Spiro, Moundville, and Etowah sites (qq.v.).

SOURCES: Waring and Holder 1945; Krieger 1945; J. H. Howard 1968.

Edward B. Jelks

SOUTHERN PLATEAU, a subarea of the Plateau Culture Area (q.v.) defined by culture traits as well as by geography. It sometimes is called the American Plateau or the Columbia Plateau (q.v.).

SOURCES: V. F. Ray 1939.

Frank C. Leonhardy

SOUTHERN PLATEAU TRADITION, an integrative concept proposed by W. W. Caldwell and O. L. Mallory in 1967 to account for apparent similarities in archaeological complexes found throughout the southern Plateau region between 1000 B.C. and the historic period. Less generalized than Willey's Northwest Riverine Tradition (q.v.), it implied a distinction between the respective archaeological cultures of the northern and southern Plateau areas. Neither the concept nor the term has found acceptance among Plateau researchers.

SOURCES: Caldwell and Mallory 1967; Leonhardy 1968.

Frank C. Leonhardy

SOUTHWESTERN CLASSIFICATION SYSTEMS. Since 1927, individuals and organizations have developed six important systems for describing and classifying prehistoric cultures in the Southwest. Three of them (the Pecos, Gladwin, and Rio Grande systems) continue to see use today (1988), although only as classificatory devices for helping develop explanatory models of cultural processes.

Pecos Classification. Developed in 1927 at the first Southwestern Archeological Conference (which, in 1988, is still held annually as the Pecos Conference) held at the ruins of Pecos Pueblo, New Mexico, this system proposed eight "chronologically sequent periods":

Basketmaker I, or Early Basketmaker (5500 B.C.–A.D. 1): a postulated nonagricultural, nonpottery-making, atlatl-using, hunting-gathering stage.

Basketmaker II, or Basketmaker (A.D. 1–450): an agricultural, nonpottery-making, atlatl-using stage.

Basketmaker III, or Late Basketmaker, or Post-Basketmaker (A.D. 450–700/750): a pithouse- and slabhouse-building stage whose people did not practice skull deformation.

Pueblo I, or Proto-Pueblo (A.D. 700/750–900): the first stage when cranial deformation was practiced; neck-corrugated pottery was introduced; and villages composed of rectangular, true-masonry houses were established.

Pueblo II (A.D. 900–1050): a stage of widespread proliferation of small villages; cooking vessels' entire surfaces were covered with elaborate corrugations.

Pueblo III, or Great Period (A.D. 1050–1300): a stage characterized by large communities, great development of the arts, and growth of intensive local specialization.

Pueblo IV, or Proto-Historic (A.D. 1300–1600): a stage when the populated area contracted, corrugated pottery gradually disappeared, and there was a general decline from the preceding cultural peak.

Pueblo V, or Historic (A.D. 1600–present): the period from A.D. 1600 to the present.

Roberts Classification. Proposed by F. H. H. Roberts, Jr., in 1935, the system was designed to remove the restrictive chronological connotations and other limitations of the Pecos Classification. Roberts proposed more general terms:

Basketmaker for Basketmaker II;

Modified Basketmaker for Basketmaker III;

Developmental Pueblo for Pueblo I and II;

Great Pueblo for Pueblo III;

Regressive Pueblo for Pueblo IV;

Historic Pueblo for Pueblo V.

Gladwin Classification. Proposed by Winifred and H. S. Gladwin in 1934 to correlate " . . . stages through which all people in the Southwest are believed to have passed, but which do not coincide either in time or in geographical relations," this system set up a heirarchical system of *roots* (major cultures such as Basketmaker, Hohokam, and Hakataya [qq.v.]), each of which was divided into several *stems* (e.g., San Juan, Little Colorado, and Playas). Each stem was subdivided into *branches* (e.g., Mesa Verde, Chaco,

Kayenta, and Cibola), which, in turn, were broken down into *phases*—units whose sites shared uniformly common characteristics. The Gladwins' phases are not to be confused with the phases of the Midwestern Classification System (q.v.), which are approximately equivalent to stems in the Gladwin system. Only branches and phases are used occasionally in the Southwest today (1987).

Colton Classification. Devised by H. S. Colton, this system substituted the term *focus* of the Midwestern System for the Gladwin system's *phase* and changed the root names to make them more equivalent to those commonly used for the basic Southwestern cultures: Anasazi, Mogollon, Hohokom, and (in this volume) Hakataya (qq.v.). Colton inferred that branches of the Gladwin system, which he retained, probably were equivalent to Indian tribes.

Rio Grande Classification. Proposed by Fred Wendorf and E. K. Reed in 1955 to circumvent their difficulties in trying to apply the Pecos Classification to the Rio Grande Anasazi region, where in some areas sites were infrequent and data sparse, this system lumped Basketmaker III through Pueblo II together as a *Developmental Period,* which was followed by a *Coalition Period* when Western Anasazi migrants became assimilated into the Rio Grande villages. Wendorf and Reed's *Classic Period* is the same as Pueblo IV of the Pecos Classification. Their classification system is still in general use for the cultures of the Rio Grande provinces.

Mogollon Classification. Developed by J. B. Wheat, this system created a descriptive-developmental sequence of five numbered periods (using Arabic numerals) for the Mogollon Culture (q.v.). The periods were based specifically on house types, ceremonial architecture, village plans, practices for disposing of the dead, pottery types, and minor handicrafts.

SOURCES: Kidder 1927; Gladwin and Gladwin 1934; F. H. H. Roberts, Jr. 1935b; Colton 1939a; Wendorf and Reed 1955; Wheat 1955.

Stewart Peckham

SOUTH YALE SITE, a river-terrace location in the lower Fraser Canyon of British Columbia where, in 1963 and in 1970, C. E. Borden found artifacts that he thought predated 7000 B.C. They consist mainly of crude, unifacial pebble tools (q.v.), plus several hammerstones, waste from the manufacture of the pebble tools, and a few retouched and utilized flakes. There were none of the points and knives typical of the Milliken and Mazama (qq.v.) phases that occupied the region between 7000 and 4000 B.C. Borden has suggested that the site represents a series of late Pleistocene encampments of hunters and gatherers possessing a stone industry related to the Asian pebble-tool tradition. Others have argued that the South Yale pebble-tool assemblage is a product of specialized seasonal activities by peoples of the Milliken Phase.

SOURCES: D. H. Mitchell 1965; Browman and Munsell 1969; Borden 1975.

David J. W. Archer

SPAIN SITE, a small settlement of earthlodges on Bull Creek in Lyman County, South Dakota, now covered by Lake Francis Case, formerly Fort Randall Reservoir. Excavated in 1953 by Carlyle Smith, it has been identified as a winter village of the Shannon Phase of the Extended Coalescent Variant and is thought to date from the early years of the 17th century.

Two round earthlodges and an extremely rich midden were the principal features investigated. The pottery is characterized by horizontally incised rims, called "Category B" by P. L. Cooper. A large quantity of potsherds and artifacts of stone, bone, and antler vary little from those found in closely contemporary sites of both the Middle Missouri and Coalescent traditions. In addition to the Shannon Phase material, a few Plains Woodland artifacts and a Paleoindian projectile point were found during the excavation.

SOURCES: P. L. Cooper 1949; Smith and Grange 1958.

Carlyle S. Smith

SPANISH DIGGINGS, a prehistoric quartzite quarry in southeastern Wyoming which was attributed to Spaniards by early Euroamerican settlers because they thought that the Indians of the region would not have expended the enormous labor that clearly was required to dig the extensive quarry holes. Today we know that the Indians quarried stone there for thousands of years.

SOURCE: Frison 1978.

Patricia J. O'Brien

SPANISH MOUNT SITE, a Thom's Creek Phase (q.v.) shell midden on Edisto Island, in Charleston County, South Carolina which was excavated in 1973–1974 by Donald Sutherland. There are two radiocarbon dates on the site: 1870±185 B.C. and 2220±350 B.C.

SOURCES: Donald Sutherland 1973, 1974; Trinkley 1980a.

Michael Trinkley

SPENCER LAKE MOUNDS AND CAMPS, a site in northwestern Wisconsin, excavated by W. C. McKern and Ralph Linton in 1936, where boards with steel-axe cut marks and a horse skull found in a mound burial showed that mound construction persisted into historic times in the region.

Data from these and related sites led McKern to identify the Clam River Focus (q.v.) with the Santee Sioux.

SOURCES: McKern 1963; J. B. Griffin 1964a; Ritzenthaler 1964.

David Overstreet

SPIRO PHASE, a late prehistoric (ca. A.D. 1250–1450) manifestation of the Caddo Tradition (q.v.), consisting of small habitation sites dispersed in the Arkansas River Valley, together with a series of civic-ceremonial centers, each of which served a cluster of habitation sites. With an economy based on corn agriculture supplemented with wild-plant foraging and hunting, including the hunting of bison, the Spiro Phase achieved the greatest degree of social complexity and cultural elaboration of the tradition.

The rectangular dwellings had gabled roofs and clay-daubed walls. The principal features at a typical civic-ceremonial center were a platform mound, one or more mounds covering buried structures, and specialized public buildings. The elite usually were buried in the flanks of the platform mounds, sometimes accompanied with conch-shell artifacts, copper plates, copper-headed axes, pearl beads, elaborate cloaks and skirts, and other items of wealth and luxury. An exception was at the Spiro Site (q.v.) in eastern Oklahoma, where elite burials were placed on a large submound mortuary floor along with a large quantity of rich necrolia. Ordinary individuals, inhumed in cemeteries, usually were accompanied with modest offerings.

SOURCES: Brown et al. 1978; J. A. Brown 1984a; Rohrbaugh 1984.

James A. Brown

SPIRO SITE, the principal civic-ceremonial center of the Arkansas River Valley Caddo (q.v.) culture, dating ca. A.D. 850–1450; located in eastern Oklahoma. Its plundering between 1933 and 1935 was dramatically publicized by the host of spectacular artifacts taken from the main (Craig) mound. Scientific excavations by Forrest Clements between 1936 and 1941, and further work by several researchers since 1979, have documented eleven mounds and an adjoining 32-hectare habitation area.

The Craig mound consisted of four cones conjoined along a single line about 120 meters long. At the north end stood the largest cone, consisting of a multistage platform mound topped by a cone, beneath which was a dismantled mortuary structure that is world famous for the trove it yielded of copper, marine-shell, wooden, and fabric articles of unparalleled richness for the Mississippian (q.v.) period. The other earthworks consist of two platform mounds, two burial mounds, and six mounds covering dismantled mortuary structures. During the Spiro Phase (q.v.), ca. A.D. 1250–1450, there was no longer a resident population at the site; the support population occupied a number of separate sites within a 3-kilometer radius.

SOURCES: Clements 1945; K. G. Orr 1946; H. W. Hamilton 1952; J. D. Rogers 1982; J. A. Brown 1984a.

James A. Brown

SPLIT ROCK CREEK MOUNDS, a group of dome-shaped burial mounds at the juncture of the Big Sioux River and Split Rock Creek in southeastern South Dakota. They date ca. A.D. 500 and are the type site for the Split Rock Creek Focus. Excavated in 1939 by W. H. Over, they have affinities with Woodland mounds of the Red River Aspect in Minnesota and Iowa.
SOURCE: Over and Meleen 1941.

Patricia J. O'Brien

SPOONER LAKE SITE, the type site for the Early Archaic Spooner Phase (q.v.), located at an elevation of 7000 feet above sea level, overlooking a meadow at the head of a major pass between Lake Tahoe and Carson Valley, Nevada. In the center of the site is a group of bedrock metates and mortars which were used for processing plant food. Although the site contained many flaked-stone and ground-stone tools, it lacked structural or storage features and apparently was used for thousands of years as a field camp for hunting, gathering, and possibly fishing. The site produced several Pinto (q.v.) and Humboldt Concave Base type projectile points. Two radiocarbon dates obtained on charcoal samples are 5140 and 2970 B.C.
SOURCE: Elston 1971.

Robert G. Elston

SPOONER PHASE, a poorly understood Early Archaic expression on the eastern slope of the northern Sierra Nevada and adjacent western Great Basin in Nevada (see Spooner Lake Site).
SOURCES: Heizer and Elsasser 1953; Elston 1971; Elston et al. 1977.

Robert G. Elston

SPOON RIVER TRADITION, a unit of the Middle Mississippian culture pattern that occupied the central Illinois River Valley between the Sangamon River and Peoria Lake ca. A.D. 1050–1450. The tradition reflects the result of a small population intrusion from the large Cahokia Site (q.v.) to the south and the acculturation, through their influence, of the receptive indigenous population. Although this movement was both sociopolitically and economically motivated and was oriented to the primary Mississippian center at Cahokia, Spoon River communities still maintained close secular contacts with one another, as well as with their regional neighbors. Thus, despite adoption of such salient Mississippian characteristics as a structured nonegalitarian society, population consolidation, sedentism, sophisticated engineering, profuse ceremonial equipment, shell-tempered pottery, triangular arrow points, rectangular wall-trench houses, and corn horticulture,

indications are that Spoon River society was neither as highly structured nor as dependent on horticulture as were the larger centers to the south.
SOURCES: Cole and Deuel 1937:220–221; Harn 1975, 1980.

Alan D. Harn

SPORADIC SPANISH CONTACT PHASE. See Casas Grandes Province.

SPRING CREEK TRADITION, an early Late Woodland ceramic tradition in the northwestern region of southern lower Michigan, dating ca. A.D. 600–1100. Spring Creek vessels are similar to wares of the Wayne and Allegan traditions (qq.v.).
SOURCES: Fitting 1968; Brashler 1981.

Margaret B. Holman

SQUIRREL DAM SITE, one of several stratified sites in the North Lakes District of north-central Wisconsin that R. J. Salzer used in establishing a regional cultural sequence extending from late Paleoindian through late Historic times.
SOURCE: Salzer 1969.

David Overstreet

STAHL (or LITTLE LAKE) SITE, a Desert Culture (q.v.) component near Little Lake, between Owens Valley and China Lake, California. Excavated in 1956 by M. R. Harrington, who believed it to represent a single occupation of the Pinto Culture dating between 2000 and 1000 B.C., it was the first open residential site reported in the Great Basin. The site contained a wide variety of artifacts, including manos, metates, scrapers, scraper planes, choppers, drills, and projectile points. Although Pinto and Gypsum type points (q.v.) were abundant, both earlier (Silver Lake and Lake Mojave, q.v.) and later (Elko, q.v., Rose Spring, and Desert Side-notched, q.v.) point types also were common.
SOURCE: M. R. Harrington 1957.

Robert G. Elston

STALLING'S ISLAND CULTURE (or PHASE), a Late Archaic (ca. 3000–1000 B.C.) archaeological expression found throughout the lower Piedmont and coastal plain of South Carolina and Georgia. Sites variously represent small camps, base camps, and occasionally seasonal macro-band camps or small seasonal villages. Shell middens, including ring middens, occur on the coast. Many sites, especially those along the coast, contain fiber-tempered pottery that may be the oldest pottery in North America. Sites in the interior often contain soapstone vessels instead of pottery. There also are large, stemmed, Savannah River type (q.v.) projectile points, perforated soapstone slabs, bone tools, ground-stone grooved axes, and burials with shell beads.

SOURCES: Claflin 1931; Fairbanks 1942; Miller 1949; Bullen and Greene 1970; DePratter 1975.

Roy S. Dickens, Jr.

STALLING'S ISLAND POTTERY SERIES, the earliest known pottery in North America, dating between 2500 B.C. and 1000 A.D.; distributed along the Georgia-South Carolina coast. Tempered with plant fibers, it occurs mostly as plain vessels, although punctated and incised decorations are known.
SOURCES: Jenkins et al. 1986.

John A. Walthall

STALLING'S ISLAND SITE, a stratified, Late Archaic (ca. 2750–1750 B.C.) shell midden located on an island in the Savannah River near Augusta, Georgia, that shows clearly the continuity between preceramic Late Archaic assemblages and subsequent assemblages with first plain, then decorated, fiber-tempered ceramics. Originally about 155 meters long by 90 meters wide and nearly 2 meters thick, the midden has been investigated by several excavators since 1870, most notably by the Cosgroves of the Peabody Museum in 1929.
SOURCES: C. C. Jones 1873; Claflin 1931; Fairbanks 1942; Bullen and Greene 1970.

Paul A. Webb

STANFIELD-WORLEY SITE, a large rockshelter in Colbert County, in Alabama containing deeply buried Early to Middle Archaic (ca. 9000–4000 B.C.) cultural components; excavated by D. L. DeJarnette in 1961–1962.
SOURCE: DeJarnette et al. 1962.

John A. Walthall

STANLY STEMMED POINT, an Early Archaic (ca. 6000–5000 B.C.) projectile-point form intermediate between the Kirk Stemmed and Savannah River Stemmed types (qq.v.), found along the Atlantic Coast between New Jersey and northern Florida. It has a broad, triangular blade and a small, square stem with an incurvate base.
SOURCE: Coe 1964:34–35.

Billy L. Oliver

STARR POINT, a triangular arrow point with mildly concave blade edges and a deeply concave base, dating ca. A.D. 1300–1750; considered diag-

nostic of the Brownsville (q.v.) and Mier phases in southern Texas and northern Tamaulipas and Nuevo León.
SOURCES: J. C. Kelley 1947b; Suhm and Jelks 1962; Turner and Hester 1985.

Elton R. Prewitt

STAR VALLEY PHASE, a phase of the East Verde Province of the Sinagua Division, Hakataya Culture (qq.v.) in Arizona, described as a rural adaptation of the earlier Union Park Phase (q.v.). Dating ca. A.D. 1000–1150, the phase is best known from farmsteads with rock-lined pithouses.
SOURCE: Redman and Hohmann 1986.

Albert H. Schroeder

STARVED ROCK SITE, a rocky eminence overlooking the Illinois River in northern Illinois that was occupied by Indians from early Archaic (q.v.) to historic times (ca. 8000 B.C. to the early 17th century), and long thought to be the site of La Salle's late 17th-century Fort St. Louis. Between the 1940s and the 1980s, several different archaeologists have excavated in Starved Rock's stratified deposits, where they discovered numerous features and many artifacts representing the different cultures that inhabited the site.
SOURCES: Mayer-Oakes 1951; Westover 1984; Jelks and Hawks n.d.

Edward B. Jelks

STEAMBOAT HOT SPRING LOCALITY, an area a few miles south of Reno, Nevada, comprising a complex of archaeological sites, many of which have been destroyed in recent years by highway construction and urban development. Excavations were conducted at some of the sites in 1971 and 1972 by R. G. Elston and J. O. Davis. A Washoe Indian winter village in the area reportedly was an important center for manufacturing lithic tools from locally quarried basalt and chalcedonic sinter. Debitage densities in some sites were extremely high. One site contained a human burial; another, a pithouse associated with a single type (Steamboat) of lanceolate projectile point, dating ca. 1500 B.C.
SOURCE: Elston and Davis 1972.

Robert G. Elston

STEED-KISKER PHASE, a culture unit in the vicinity of Kansas City, Missouri, dating ca. A.D. 1000–1250, consisting of a series of family farmsteads and attendant cemeteries and ancillary sites (e.g., shrines and storage camps). No villages of the phase have been discovered. The population, which appears to have migrated from the Cahokia (q.v.) area near St. Louis about A.D. 1000, was made up of farmers who practiced the busk or green corn ceremonies but did not have a stratified society like Cahokia's. The type site is the Steed-Kisker Site, overlooking the juncture of the Platte River with the Missouri.

SOURCES: Wedel 1943; Shippee 1972; O'Brien 1978, n.d.; McHugh et al. n.d.

Patricia J. O'Brien

STEENS MOUNTAIN LOCALITY, a major fault-block mountain range in central Oregon, flanked by desert basins—Carlow Valley on the west and the Alvord Desert on the east—where D. K. Grayson, P. J. Mehringer, Jr., and C. M. Aikens conducted extensive archaeological and environmental studies between 1978 and 1981. Pollen cores from lake sediments, plant macrofossils from pack-rat middens, and sand-dune stratigraphy provided a regional record of paleoenvironments over the last 9000 years; the archaeological site survey showed that human settlement size and number fluctuated in concert with climatic changes. Sites were more numerous but smaller during cool/moist periods, and were less numerous but larger during warm/dry periods. Shifting patterns of population size and nucleation are indicated. Excavations at several cave and open sites, and study of collections obtained earlier from Catlow and Roaring Springs caves (q.v.), provided radiocarbon dates, detailed cultural inventories, and evidence of dietary remains for parts of the cultural sequence.

SOURCES: Jones et al. 1983; Beck 1984; Wigand 1985; Wilde 1985; Mehringer 1985.

C. Melvin Aikens

STERNS CREEK FOCUS, a complex of Plains Woodland affiliation occurring along the Missouri River in eastern Nebraska, probably dating ca. A.D. 500–900; defined by W. D. Strong in 1935. The small, inconspicuous sites typically contain arrow points resembling the Scallorn type (q.v.), grit-tempered pottery with scalloped rims, and, occasionally, squash seeds. C. R. Keyes reported similar sites across the Missouri in southwestern Iowa.

SOURCES: Strong 1935:175–196, 267–288; Keyes 1949:96–97.

Patricia J. O'Brien

STEUBEN SITE, a group of burial mounds and an associated shallow, stratified habitation area located in the central Illinois River Valley, southern Marshall County, in Illinois; occupied principally during Middle Woodland times (ca. 100 B.C.-A.D. 250). It is the type site for the Steuben Phase of the Middle Woodland Tradition, as well as for a variety of late Middle Woodland ceramic and projectile-point styles. The site was partially excavated by

the Schoenbeck and Morse families in the early 1950s and was tested by the University of Michigan Museum of Anthropology in 1956.
SOURCES: Schoenbeck 1947, 1948, 1949; Morse 1963.

Alan D. Harn

STIRLING PHASE, a unit of the Mississippian Tradition that followed the Lohmann Phase (q.v.) in the American Bottom, in southwestern Illinois. Dating ca. A.D. 1050–1150, Stirling is characterized by wall-trench structures and shell-tempered pottery, including the Ramey Incised type which first appeared during the phase. Elaborately carved bauxite figurines with snake and plant motifs demonstrate a complex religious symbolism associated with agricultural practices. The settlement system is typified by major administrative-ceremonial centers, secondary satellite towns and villages, and numerous isolated farmsteads. There was broad interregional exchange, and Stirling influences are apparent over a wide area of the Midwest.
SOURCES: Fowler and Hall 1972; Prentice and Mehrer 1981; Bareis and Porter 1984; Emerson and Jackson 1984; Finney and Fortier 1985.

Andrew C. Fortier and Charles J. Bareis

STONE-VAULTED MOUNDS, earthen mounds containing stone-walled burial vaults, located on bluffs overlooking large habitation sites along both sides of the Missouri River in the vicinity of Kansas City. Many such mounds have been excavated by several archaeologists between the early and the late 20th century. The vaults are approximately square, usually with an extended entryway facing south or east. Their walls are made of dry-laid limestone slabs. Dating ca. A.D. 1–500, they reflect the mortuary practices of the Kansas City Hopewell (q.v.) peoples.
SOURCES: Fowke 1922; Wedel 1943; Larsen and O'Brien 1973; Tjadon 1974.

Patricia J. O'Brien

STONY CREEK WARE, originally a catchall category for all sand-tempered pottery in various parts of Virginia; now restricted to a fabric-, net-, and cord-impressed ware, dating ca. 500 B.C. to A.D. 800, found near the town of Stony Creek, Virginia.
SOURCES: Clifford Evans 1955; Binford 1964; Egloff and Potter 1982.

Keith T. Egloff

STRAND PHASE. See Brooks River-Naknek Drainage Sites.

STRATTON PLACE SHELL RING, a Thom's Creek Phase (q.v.) site in Charleston County, in South Carolina that was extensively investigated by Michael Trinkley in 1979, primarily to examine the ring's interior.

SOURCES: Trinkley 1980b, 1985.

Michael Trinkley

SUDDEN SHELTER, a site on the eastern margin of the Wasatch Plateau in central Utah with deposits spanning the period from 5000 to 1300 B.C. Excavated by J. D. Jennings in 1974, the site reflects shifting patterns of resource exploitation by Archaic hunter-gatherers.
SOURCE: Jennings et al. 1980.

David B. Madsen

SUGAR CAMP HILL SITE, the type site for the Crab Orchard Focus and ultimately for the Crab Orchard Tradition (q.v.), situated on Crab Orchard Creek in Williamson County, in Illinois; now submerged by Crab Orchard Lake. Excavated by M. S. Maxwell in 1939–1940, this predominantly Middle Woodland village site often has been incorrectly referred to as the Crab Orchard Site.
SOURCE: Maxwell 1951:78–174.

Brian M. Butler

SUGARLOAF QUARRY, the major quarry of Coso obsidian, located at Sugarloaf Mountain, California; a complex pile of rhyolite domes and flows where high-quality obsidian is available in surface rubble and talus. Interconnected pits and benches extending over an area more than 2 miles long were dug into the margin of the largest flows by stone knappers seeking obsidian for tool manufacture. Colluvium in and below the mining zone is mostly obsidian debitage and quarry debris. Coso obsidian was transported westward to the southern California coast and also occurs in western Nevada sites in the Great Basin.
SOURCES: Ericson et al. 1976; Elston and Zeier 1984.

Robert G. Elston

SUGAR QUARTZ, a term that has been applied to Hixton silicified sandstone (see Hixton Site) by collectors since the late 1800s and that often has appeared in the archaeological literature. The appellation derives from the granular but shiny texture of this sandstone.

David Overstreet

SULLY SITE, the largest known earthlodge village on the Missouri River, comprising over 400 lodges and three different burial areas, occupied by the Arikara ca. 1650–1760. R. L. Stephenson excavated the village area from 1956 through 1958. A. L. Bowers dug 49 burials in one cemetery area in 1930–1931; W. M. Bass dug 636 burials in another cemetery in 1956–

1958. Burials were predominantly wood covered and flexed, with heads oriented west to north. There were cultural items in 63 percent of the graves.
SOURCES: Bass n.d.; Jantz and Ubelaker 1981.

William M. Bass

SULPHUR SPRING STAGE. See Cochise Culture.

SUMMER ISLAND SITE, a stratified site off the Garden Peninsula in Delta County, in Michigan; investigated by David Brose in 1967. Although Brose identified Late Woodland, Upper Mississippian, and Historic Period components, the greatest occupation (with radiocarbon dates of A.D. 70 ± 280, A.D. 250 ± 100, and A.D. 160 ± 130) took place in Middle Woodland times. Fishing gear (togglehead harpoons, net shuttles, gorges, and net sinkers) and an abundance of bones from spring-spawning fish indicate that fishing was the primary subsistence activity. Ceramics reflect Northern Tier/Lake Forest, Middle Woodland affinities. It is hypothesized that from 25 to 40 people, probably members of a patrilocal band, occupied Summer Island.
SOURCES: Binford and Quimby 1963; Brose 1970.

Margaret B. Holman

SUNNYVALE SKELETON, a human skeleton of controversial age unearthed in 1972 at the Sunnyvale East Drainage Channel in the southern portion of San Francisco Bay, California. Initially, an amino acid racemization date measurement of 70,000 years drew attention to the skeleton; later radiocarbon determinations indicated that it actually is no older than ca. 4000 B.C.
SOURCES: Bada and Helfman 1975; Taylor et al. 1983.

R. E. Taylor and L. A. Payen

SUNSET CRATER, a cinder cone northeast of Flagstaff, Arizona, whose prehistoric volcanic eruptions left substantial lava flows and ash deposits. Much archaeological research in the Flagstaff Province (q.v.) has been devoted to dating the eruptions and to determining their impacts on the peoples who were living in the area at the time. Different dates have been advanced by different researchers, but there currently (1988) is a strong consensus, based partly on paleomagnetic dating of lava flows, that the crater erupted episodically between A.D. 1064 and 1250.

From the 1930s to the 1970s, it was widely believed that the thousands of acres of fertile farmland created by the ash fall from the 1064–1066 eruptions attracted many people from surrounding culture areas. This supposed population increase, together with interactions between the immigrants and local populations, was thought to have accelerated and greatly influenced Sinaguan cultural development. However, in the 1970s and 1980s, this interpretation was reevaluated, and now most authorities hold that the supposed population increase has been vastly exaggerated, and that the evidence for multicultural migration is not convincing. Some effects thought to have resulted from the cinder fall were more likely due to a climatic change from relatively dry to extremely moist conditions.

SOURCES: Robinson 1913; McGregor 1936b, 1941; Colton 1936, 1939b, 1945a, 1946, 1947, 1962; D. S. King 1949; Smiley 1958; Schroeder 1961c; Stanislawski 1963a, 1963b; Breternitz et al. 1967; Shoemaker and Kieffer 1974; Shoemaker 1977; Pilles 1978, 1979; Fish et. al. 1980.

Peter J. Pilles, Jr.

SUNSET PHASE, the second of the Northern Sinagua (q.v.) phases in north-central Arizona, contemporaneous with the Pueblo I period at ca. A.D. 700–900. Sites of the phase have been found over most of the northern Sinagua territory south and east of the San Francisco Peaks. The circular to subsquare houses are similar to those of the preceding Cinder Park Phase (q.v.) in shape and in major features: four main roof supports, a central firepit, and a ramp entry on the east side. A few have posts set around the edges of the floor, presumably to hold wooden planks in place along the walls.

Rio de Flag Brown pottery continued as the dominant type. Trade pottery came primarily from the Kayenta Anasazi area, although Deadmans Gray and Deadmans Fugitive Red sherds from the Cohonina Province (q.v.) also have been found in some quantity. Irrigation ditches were probably used in the latter part of the phase. Burials probably were extended. The phase is named after Sunset Crater (q.v.), in whose general vicinity many of the excavated Sunset Phase sites were located.

SOURCES: Colton 1939b:37, 1946:269, 312–314.

Peter J. Pilles, Jr.

SURPRISE VALLEY, a large, deep valley in northeastern California where J. F. O'Connell, after extensive surveys and excavations, identified five archaeological phases:

Phase	Time Markers	Dates
Menlo Bah Phase	Northern Side-Notched projectile points (q.v.)	4500–2500 B.C.
Bare Creek Phase	Bare Creek (Little Lake) projectile points	2500–1000 B.C.
Emerson Phase	Elko Series projectile points (q.v.)	1000 B.C.–A.D. 500
Alkali Phase	Rose Spring/Eastgate projectile point	A.D. 500–1400
Bidwell Phase	Desert Side-Notched and Cottonwood Series projectile points	A.D. 1400–Historic

Surprise Valley is perhaps most noted for its large, semisubterranean pithouses of the Menlo Bah Phase that suggest multifamily living units and a sedentary or semisedentary settlement pattern. Brush wikiups found in all succeeding phases suggest smaller family-sized living units and greater residential mobility. Coincident changes in fauna support the interpretation that this shift in social/settlement pattern was a response to environmental deterioration after 2500 B.C. In very recent times, the Surprise Valley Paiute immigrated into the valley from Burns, Oregon.

SOURCES: O'Connell and Hayward 1972; O'Connell 1975.

Robert L. Bettinger

SU SITE, the type site for the Pine Lawn Phase of the Mogollon Culture (q.v.), located near Reserve, New Mexico. Excavated by P. S. Martin and J. B. Rinaldo between 1939 and 1946, it consisted of 23 shallow, oval to circular pithouses with ramp entrances and interior storage pits, but no interior hearths. One larger semisubterranean structure probably was an early form of Mogollon great kiva (q.v.). Pottery types found at SU were the earliest Mogollon types: Alma Plain, Alma Rough, and San Francisco Red (Saliz Variety). Several tree-ring dates suggest occupation before A.D. 500. As no remains of domesticated plants were found, it appears that the SU Site Indians subsisted by hunting and gathering.

SOURCES: P. S. Martin 1940, 1943; Martin and Rinaldo 1947.

Stewart Peckham

SWANNANOA PHASE, the earliest (ca. 800–200 B.C.) ceramic-bearing manifestation in the mountains of North Carolina, distinguished by the Swannanoa pottery series (q.v.).

SOURCE: Keel 1976:50, 230–231.

Billy L. Oliver

SWANNANOA POTTERY SERIES, the earliest (ca. 800–200 B.C.) ceramic in North Carolina's Appalachian Summit area: a quartzite- or coarse sand-tempered ware, typically cord marked or fabric impressed, but occasionally check stamped, simple stamped, or plain. Conical jars and shallow bowls are common vessel shapes; bases may be conical, conical with a nipple-like protrusion, or slightly flattened. Swannanoa pottery is comparable in age, form, and style to pottery of the Watts Bar and Kellogg phases of Tennessee and Georgia.

SOURCE: Keel 1976:230–231.

Billy L. Oliver

SWANNANOA STEMMED POINT, a small, thick, triangular-bladed projectile point with a relatively long stem and a straight, excurvate, or incurvate base. All known specimens are made of black or gray chert. Dating ca. 800–200 B.C., this type represents the terminal expression of the stemmed-point tradition in the Appalachian Summit area of North Carolina, where it co-occurs with large, triangular points characteristic of the Early Woodland period. Swannanoa Stemmed evolved from the Gypsy Stemmed type, as overall size decreased and chert became a preferred raw material.

SOURCES: Keel 1976:196–198; Oliver 1981.

Billy L. Oliver

SWANSON SITE, a palisaded, late prehistoric village of rectangular houses, located near Chamberlain, South Dakota. The large standard deviation of the single radiocarbon date, A.D. 1100 ± 250, makes the time of occupation uncertain.

Swanson was assigned by W. R. Hurt in 1950 to the Over Focus (q.v.), a unit now identified with the Initial Variant of the Middle Missouri Tradition (q.v.). It is closely related to the Cambria Site in southern Minnesota and to the Mill Creek sites of northwestern Iowa. Pottery from the site exhibits Woodland-type cord marking on vessels of Mississippian shapes as well as distinctly local attributes. Swanson may be an ancestral village of the Mandan culture.

SOURCES: Hurt 1951; Lehmer 1971.

Wesley R. Hurt

SWEETWATER PHASE. See Pioneer Period.

SWIFT CREEK CULTURE (or PHASE), a late Middle Woodland (ca. A.D. 200–600) culture whose remains extend from the Gulf of Florida into the coastal plain and Piedmont regions of Alabama, Georgia, and South Carolina. It was named and described by G. R. Willey in 1949. Diagnostic artifacts include pottery vessels with intricate, well-executed, curvilinear-complicated stamping; chipped-stone spear and arrow points; and ground-stone gorgets, tubular pipes, boat stones, plummets, and celts. Burials at some sites contain late Hopewell ritual necrolia. Sites represent semipermanent villages and transient camps; some large sites contain burial mounds and, occasionally, small platform-like mounds. A tribal level of social organization is indicated.

SOURCES: A. R. Kelly 1938; Willey 1949a; J. R. Caldwell 1958; Kellar et al. 1962.

Roy S. Dickens, Jr.

SWIFT CREEK POTTERY SERIES, a Middle Woodland (ca. A.D. 300), sand-tempered ceramic found in the coastal plain region of Georgia, Florida, and Alabama. It often took the form of conoidal jars with flat bases, some-times with tetrapodal supports. Curvilinear and rectilinear designs were applied to vessel surfaces with carved wooden paddles.

SOURCE: Jennings and Fairbanks 1939.

John A. Walthall

SWIFT CREEK SITE, a Middle Woodland mound and village site, occupied ca. A.D. 500–750, situated on the Ocmulgee River a short distance south of the Macon Plateau in central Georgia. Excavations by A. R. Kelly in the 1930s demonstrated that the mound was an accretional structure and pro-duced quantities of distinctive, finely executed pottery of the Swift Creek Complicated-Stamped type.

SOURCES: A. R. Kelly 1938; Kelly and Smith n.d.

Paul A. Webb

T

T-1 SITE, the first Early Dorset site reported in detail, located at Native Point on Southampton Island, Northwest Territories; excavated in the 1950s by H. B. Collins.

SOURCE: Collins 1956a.

Moreau S. Maxwell

T-2 SITE, a Late Dorset site at Native Point, Southampton Island, Northwest Territories, which, together with the Early Dorset T-1 (q.v.) and Middle Dorset T-3 sites, provided the first detailed descriptions of Dorset (q.v.) assemblages at ca. 400 B.C., ca. A.D. 1, and ca. A.D. 600. The three sites were excavated by H. B. Collins in the 1950s.

SOURCE: Collins 1956b.

Moreau S. Maxwell

TABIRA SITE (or PUEBLO BLANCO), one of the Salinas pueblos dating ca. A.D. 1200–1670s, located at the east end of Mesa Jumanes in central New Mexico. Stanley Stubbs excavated a small chapel there in 1959.

SOURCES: Stubbs and Stallings 1959; Hayes et al. 1981.

Frances Levine

TABIRA WARE, a relatively uncommon Puebloan ceramic dating between ca. 1545 and 1672 that evidently was made only at the Gran Quivira, Tabira, and Pueblo Pardo sites (qq.v.), New Mexico. It may be either plain or decorated with black-on-white or polychrome (yellow, red, and black) designs; the most common motifs are feathers, kachinas, and animals laid out in panels on ollas and pitchers.

SOURCE: Hayes et al. 1981.

Frances Levine

TACUICHAMONA CULTURE, a culture defined by Carl Sauer and Donald Brand in 1931 from sites in the foothills of northern Sinaloa; now subsumed into the Rio Sonora Culture (q.v.).

SOURCES: Sauer and Brand 1931; Pailes 1972, 1976.

David A. Phillips, Jr.

TAHOE REACH PHASE, the earliest known phase (ca. 7000–5000 B.C.) on the eastern slope of the northern Sierra Nevada and adjacent western Great Basin in California and Nevada; thought to represent a very low-density human population with a Pre-Archaic strategy of foraging and big-game hunting. Diagnostic artifacts are edge-ground Great Basin Stemmed points. A site at the mouth of Squaw Valley has produced a radiocarbon date of 6180 B.C. but no diagnostic artifacts.

SOURCES: Elston et. al. 1977; Elston 1982.

Robert G. Elston

TAKLI ISLAND SITES, two sites on Takli Island on the south side of the Alaska Peninsula, excavated in 1964–1965 by D. E. Dumond, which, together with other sites of the area, have yielded evidence of an archaeological sequence extending from 4000 B.C. into the historic period. At certain times, the sequence shows links between the Pacific and Bering Sea regions; at other times, relationships are restricted to the Gulf of Alaska region. The earliest phase, Takli Alder, is nearly identical to Ocean Bay I (q.v.) on Kodiak Island; the next earliest phase, Takli Birch, which is characterized by dual ground-slate and flaked-stone industries, exhibits elements of both Ocean Bay II (q.v.) and the Kachemak Tradition (q.v.).

SOURCES: G. H. Clark 1977; Dumond 1971.

Donald W. Clark

TALAQUAK (or TALARAQ) LOCALITY, a small peninsula on McKellar Bay near Lake Harbour (q.v.), on Baffin Island's southern coast, where several Dorset and Thule phase (qq.v.) sites were excavated by a Michigan State University team between 1963 and 1979. At many places, early and late Thule pithouses cut through late Dorset middens. The house sequence, which continued through the Historic Contact period, provided data on ecological changes and on the role of social organization in cultural adaptation to such changes.

SOURCE: Sabo 1981.

Moreau S. Maxwell

TALKING CROW SITE, a multicomponent village site on the Missouri River, just below the Big Bend Dam, in South Dakota; investigated by Carlyle Smith in 1950–1952. It has special regional significance because of its four components identifiable as: (1) a Plains Woodland occupation of ca. A.D. 600; (2) a fortified village of the Initial Coalescent Variant, intrusive from the Central Plains (ca. A.D. 1425–1500); (3) a village of the post-contact Coalescent Variant (ca. A.D. 1725), attributed to the Arikara; and

(4) a component documented as modern Dakota (Sioux), 1865–1950. A large collection of potsherds from the site provided data for the establishment of ceramic types of temporal and geographic importance throughout the Middle Missouri area.

SOURCES: C. S. Smith 1960, 1963, 1977; Wedel 1961.

Carlyle S. Smith

TAMAULIPAS SEQUENCE, a culture classification for parts of Tamaulipas developed by R. S. MacNeish, based on his field research there in the late 1940s and early 1950s. For the Sierra de Tamaulipas and its environs, he proposed nine phases and complexes: Diablo (older than 10,000 B.C.), Lerma (ca. 8000–7000 B.C.), Nogales (ca. 5000–3000 B.C.), La Perra (ca. 3000–2000 B.C.), Almagre (ca. 2000–1700 B.C.), Laguna (ca. 600–1 B.C.), Eslabones (ca. A.D. 1–500), La Salta (ca. A.D. 500–900), and Los Angeles (ca. A.D. 1200–1780).

MacNeish defined these phases for the coastal plain of Tamaulipas: Nogales (ca. 5000–3000 B.C.), Repelo (ca. 3000–1900 B.C.), Abasolo (ca. 1900 B.C.–A.D. 100), Las Flores (ca. A.D. 100–1300), Catan (ca. A.D. 100–1800), and Panuco (ca. A.D. 1300–1500). He defined eight phases for southwestern Tamaulipas: Inficrno (ca. 7000–5400 B.C.), Ocampo (ca. 4000–2200 B.C.), Flacco (ca. 2200–1900 B.C.), Guerra (ca. 1900–1200 B.C.), Mesa de Guaje (ca. 1200–500 B.C.), Palmillas (ca. A.D. 200–800), San Lorenzo (ca. A.D. 1000–1450), and San Antonio (ca. A.D. 1450–1800).

MacNeish reported evidence of incipient agriculture at some sites in Tamualipas, but most of his phases can be assigned to hunting-gathering peoples of Archaic (q.v.) affiliation. Many artifacts, especially projectile points, resemble Archaic types of central and southern Texas. There has been no substantive field research in these areas of Tamaulipas since MacNeish's of the 1950s.

SOURCES: MacNeish 1947, 1958b, 1961.

Edward B. Jelks

TANFIELD/MORRISSON SITE, an extensive Early Dorset Phase (q.v.) community on Cape Tanfield on the southern coast of Baffin Island, Northwest Territories, that had sod houses as well as a shallow pithouse roofed with small pieces of driftwood. Excavated in 1966 by a Michigan State team, the site produced much information on the development of Early Dorset culture ca. 500–300 B.C.

SOURCE: Maxwell 1973.

Moreau S. Maxwell

TANGLE LAKES SITES, an archaeological district on the south flanks of the Alaska Range that was investigated by Frederick Hadleigh West, mainly during the 1970s. Microblade components at several Tangle Lakes sites figure prominently in Hadleigh West's delineation of the Denali Complex (q.v.), which he described as part of a Beringian Tradition. Other components, including ones with side-notched projectile points ascribed to the Northern Archaic Tradition (q.v.), are present.

SOURCES: Hadleigh West 1975, 1980, 1981.

Donald W. Clark

TANO (or GALISTEO-SANTA FE) PROVINCE, a culture area located entirely within the Santa Fe River and Galisteo Creek basins of the Rio Grande drainage in north-central New Mexico. In late prehistoric and early historic times, the province was occupied primarily by the Tano, or Southern Tewa Indians (a Puebloan people), but its southwestern corner was dominated by the Keres. The province had become a significant center of Rio Grande Anasazi (q.v.) culture by the A.D. 900s, and it was major population center between 1300 and 1680. The hill country known as the Cerrillos was important in turquoise and lead mining. Both a black-on-white pottery in the Mesa Verde whiteware tradition and later glaze-painted wares were extensively exported from the Tano Province to surrounding areas.

Six major periods have been recognized within the Tano area: Paleoindian, Early Archaic (qq.v.), Developmental, Coalition, Classic, and Early Historic.

Paleoindian Period (ca. 9500–6000 B.C.). A few Paleoindian artifacts have been found in the area, mainly projectile points of the Llano and Plano cultures (qq.v.), made of exotic chert or obsidian. Sites include rockshelters and mesa-top game overview stations.

Early Archaic Period (ca. 4800–1800 B.C.). The early Archaic Period is represented in the Tano Province by the Bajada and San Jose phases of the Oshara Tradition (qq.v.), cultures formerly included in the Rio Grande Complex (q.v.).

Developmental Period (ca. 1800 B.C.–A.D. 900/1250). During this period there was a transition from the hunting-gathering life style of late Archaic peoples into the early stages of the Anasazi Culture's (q.v.) agriculturally based economy. The period is represented by three late Archaic culture units (Armijo Phase [ca. 1800–1500 B.C.], Cochise Culture ca. [1500–800 B.C.]), and En Medio Phase [ca. 800 B.C.–A.D. 400], qq.v.), and by three Anasazi units (Basketmaker [q.v.] III–Pueblo I [ca. A.D. 400–870/900], Red Mesa Phase [ca. A.D. 870/900–1050], and Tesuque Phase [ca. A.D. 1050–1220/1250], qq.v.). All of these cultural expressions occur beyond, as well as within the Tano Province.

Coalition Period (ca. A.D. 1220/1250–1350). This was a period marked by a coalescence of Anasazi peoples in the Tano Province to form a relatively homogeneous regional cultural pattern. Two phases have been defined for the period: Pindi (ca. A.D. 1220/1250–1300) and Galisteo (ca. A.D. 1300–1350) (qq.v.).

Classic Period (ca. A.D. 1350–1610). The Anasazi Culture in the Tano Province reached its climax during this period. For a detailed description, see Rio Grande Classic Period.

Early Historic Period (A.D. 1610–1821). This period began with the founding of a permanent Spanish settlement at Santa Fe and ended with Mexican independence. By 1620 an extensive Spanish mission system had been established and European influences were becoming strongly integrated into Puebloan culture. Indian potters had adopted European forms; sheep, goats, cattle, horses, wheat, several vegetables, orchard culture, metal tools, and other European traits were introduced.

Spanish control of labor, demands for goods and services, the Christianization process: all these tore at the economic, social, political, and religious fabric of Puebloan culture. There was a major decline in the native population owing to epidemics of new diseases, warfare, and other factors. A successful revolt by the Indians in 1680 was followed by intertribal warfare and, in 1692, by Spanish reconquest. By 1693, the only major pueblo still occupied appears to have been Santo Domingo of the Keres, although Pueblo Galisteo was re-established in 1706 as a buffer against the Apaches. After a period of warfare with the Comanches, those Tanos remaining at Galisteo abandoned that pueblo and joined the Keres at Santo Domingo. The last glaze-painted pottery seems to have been made between 1650 and 1700.

SOURCES: Schroeder 1972; Lang 1977, 1980a; Phillips and Seymour 1982.

Richard W. Lang

TAOS BLACK-ON-WHITE POTTERY, a ceramic having a crushed-rock-tempered body with a white-slipped surface on which designs resembling Chaco Province (q.v.) styles were painted with black mineral pigment. A common type of the Eastern Anasazi in the Northern Rio Grande Province of the southwestern United States, it occurs primarily as globular jars (rarely as bowls and ladles) and dates ca. A.D. 1000–1400.

SOURCES: Mera 1935; Peckham 1963; Wetherington 1968:51–54.

Patricia L. Crown

TAOS INCISED POTTERY, a sand-tempered, gray to gray-brown ceramic, dating ca. A.D. 950–1200 and associated with the Eastern Anasazi in the Northern Rio Grande Province of the southwestern United States. Jars and miniature bowls exhibit distinctive linear and herringbone designs made by incising with tools or fingernails.

SOURCES: Mera 1935:4, 6; Wetherington 1968:60; E. L. Green 1976:36–37.

Patricia L. Crown

TAOS PROVINCE, a culture area conveniently conforming to the boundaries of Taos County in northern New Mexico, with the Rio Grande running north to south through its center. Archaic remains in the province, dating between ca.

5000 B.C. and A.D. 500, include stone rings marking the former locations of brush and/or skin shelters, a variety of dart points, and numerous choppers, flake knives, and scrapers made from fine-grained, volcanic stones.

Developmental Period (ca. A.D. 500–1200) sites of the Anasazi Culture (q.v.) consist of dispersed pithouses, occurring either singly or in pairs, on stream terraces, with occasional rude jacal and coursed-adobe surface dwellings, mostly for storage. Maize horticulture was practiced, and Taos Black-on-white pottery (q.v.) was the major ceramic type.

The Coalition Period (ca. A.D. 1200–1325) saw the end of pithouse habitation and the growth of communities made up of adobe surface houses, kivas, and plazas. Carbon-painted wares appeared in the form of Santa Fe Black-on-white pottery.

During the Classic Period (ca. A.D. 1325–1598), two mega-pueblos, Taos and Picuris (qq.v.), reached their apogee with from 2000 to 3000 inhabitants each. A series of glaze-painted pottery types was traded to Taos and Picuris from sites to the south, while indigenous, carbon-painted, black-on-white wares continued to be made locally.

In the Historic Period (A.D. 1598–present), Europeans introduced many new items, customs, and constraints, including grains, fruits, animals, metals, weapons, Christianity, suppression of Indian religious ceremonies, Spanish as a second language, and a new political system. Indigenous matte-painted, polychrome pottery came into use, along with burnished redware pots in Spanish shapes. The Indian population became drastically reduced through catastrophic epidemics of European diseases.

Components of the following phases and complexes occur in the Taos Province (all dates are A.D.): Valdez Phase (ca. 900–1250), Taos Phase (ca. 900–1300), Santa Fe Phase (ca. 1250–1300), Talpa Phase (ca. 1250–1375), Vadito Phase (ca. 1375–1490), San Lazaro Phase (ca. 1490–1600), Trampas Phase (ca. 1600–1696), Cuartelejo Phase (1696–1706), Apodaca Phase (1706–1846), Penasco Phase (1846–present), Complex I (900–1300), and Complex II (1300–1600).

SOURCES: Ellis and Brody 1964:316–327; Wetherington 1968; Dick 1965b; 1968:77–94; Woolsey 1980.

Herbert W. Dick

TAOS PUEBLO, an extant, five-story, adobe pueblo consisting of two room-blocks, located at the foot of the Sangre de Cristo Mountains in northern New Mexico, Northern Rio Grande Province; northernmost of the Eastern Pueblos. A single trench dug in 1961 by F. H. Ellis and J. J. Brody indicates occupation since ca. A.D. 1450.

SOURCES: Ellis and Brody 1964; Bodine 1979.

Patricia L. Crown

TARDIO PERIOD. See Casas Grandes Province.

TAYE LAKE PHASE, a phase of the Northern Archaic Tradition (q.v.) in the southwest Yukon, defined by R. S. MacNeish in 1964 on the basis of his excavations at the Taye Lake Site. Dating ca. 2500 B.C.-A.D. 400, the phase is characterized by large side-notched projectile points.

SOURCES: MacNeish 1964; W. B. Workman 1978.

Donald W. Clark

TAYLOR MOUND, a multi-component burial mound overlooking the Missouri River in extreme northeastern Kansas. Originally it contained both Valley Focus and Nebraska Phase (qq.v.) burials, but the latter became badly disturbed by vandals. Excavations in the main undisturbed part of the mound by P. J. O'Brien in 1968 revealed a Valley Focus limestone-lined cist containing 7 skulls and 3 clusters (bundles?) of human long bones, an arrangement suggesting some social ranking of the population. A foot above the cist was a cremation layer which held the burnt remains of at least three individuals and which produced three radiocarbon dates averaging A.D. 1–100 ± 100 years. Also in the cist were diagnostic Valley Cord Roughened pottery as well as Hopewellian (q.v.) sherds.

SOURCE: O'Brien 1971.

Patricia J. O'Brien

TAYLOR SITE, an Early Archaic (ca. 8000 B.C.) site on the Congaree River floodplain in Lexington County, in South Carolina; the type site for the Taylor projectile point. James Michie excavated the site in 1970 and found Paleoindian projectile points and hearths attributed to the Palmer and Dalton (q.v.) cultures.

SOURCE: Michie 1971.

Michael Trinkley

TCHEFUNCTE CULTURE, a coastally oriented culture that spanned the centuries from ca. 500 B.C. to A.D. 200 in an area extending from northwestern Florida to northwestern Louisiana. Tchefuncte peoples, who primarily exploited the coastal environment and the lowlands of the lower Mississippi Valley, were the first in the area to use pottery extensively. Their habitation sites consist of scattered, small middens located on natural levees or on higher marginal lands. Burials were placed in the middens or covered with small earthen mounds. Many Archaic traits continued in this Early Woodland culture.

SOURCE: Ford and Quimby 1945.

William G. Haag

TCHEFUNCTE SITE, the type site for the Tchefuncte Culture (q.v.), located on the north shore of Lake Pontchartrain in St. Tammany Parish, in Louisiana. Almost completely excavated with Works Progress Administration

labor in 1941, the site consisted of two contiguous shell middens containing many flexed burials in pits.
SOURCE: Ford and Quimby 1945.

                                                                    William G. Haag

TERTIARY HILLS LITHIC SOURCE, a deposit of a distinctive kind of fused tuff which, in its luster and its off-white, gray, buff, and red-brown colors, resembles puddings prepared from commercial mixes. Exposed along a small tributary of Tate Lake in the Tertiary Hills southwest of Fort Norman, District of Mackenzie, it was traded throughout the western District of Mackenzie and occasionally in more distant places, including northern Alberta.
SOURCE: Cinq-Mars 1973.

                                                                    Donald W. Clark

TESUQUE BY-PASS SITE, a habitation site on Rio Tesuque north of Santa Fe, New Mexico, in the Tewa Basin Province (q.v.), containing components of the Developmental and Coalition periods of the Rio Grande Anasazi Culture (qq.v.). C. H. McNutt excavated there in 1955 and exposed a shallow pithouse without associated pottery; several middle to late Developmental Period jacales; and parts of two kivas, one of which was associated with a twelve-room Coalition Period pueblo.
SOURCE: McNutt 1969.

                                                                    Stewart Peckham

TESUQUE PHASE, a late Developmental phase of the Tano Province (q.v.) of north-central New Mexico, named for related manifestations in the southern Tewa Basin. The phase appears to date ca. A.D. 1050–1220/1250, a time of continued population growth in the Santa Fe Valley, with expansion into previously uninhabited locales adjacent to springs and perennial streams. Small farmsteads were numerous; there were at least a few villages and one large community of some 100 surface rooms and associated pithouses and/or kivas. Buildings were of jacal, coursed adobe, or stone masonry construction.

Diagnostic pottery types are Kwahe'e Black-on-white (q.v.) and indented-corrugated grayware. Side-notched arrow points became common. Trade connections with peoples to the south and west are indicated by quantities of imported obsidian, chert, and pottery, including black-on-white types Socorro, Gallup, and Puerco, and black-on-red types Wingate, Puerco, and St. Johns. Carbon paint began to supplant mineral paint in whiteware technology late in the phase. Turquoise mining and processing continued in the Cerrillos.

SOURCES: Lang 1977, 1980b.

Richard W. Lang

TEWA BASIN PROVINCE, the domain of the Rio Grande Anasazi (q.v.) (the ancestors of the modern Tewa-speaking Pueblo Indians), encompassing the western drainage of the Sangre de Cristo Mountains north of Santa Fe, New Mexico; the eastern and northern flanks of the Jemez Mountains (Pajarito Plateau) north of Frijoles Canyon; the lower Rio Chama Valley drainage; and the Rio Grande north of Espanola to Velarde, New Mexico.

A. F. A. Bandelier's pathfinding survey of the area in the 1880s revealed a wealth of ruins which attracted the attention of E. L. Hewett, who, in the 1890s, made a more intensive survey of the Pajarito Plateau. In 1907, Hewett organized the first formal archaeological project in the entire Rio Grande region: a unique series of multidisciplinary studies at Puye, Tyuonyi (qq.v.), Tsirege, and Tsankawi, all of which yielded Biscuitware (q.v.) pottery characteristic of the Rio Grande Classic Period (q.v.) in the Tewa Basin Province.

H. P. Mera, during his surveys of the area in the 1920s, recognized Developmental and Coalition period (q.v.) sites, but only one was excavated before World War II. In the 1950s and 1960s, archaeological salvage excavations near the Los Alamos National Laboratory, along highways, and even in occupied pueblos gave greater definition to the province, setting it apart from the Northern and Middle Rio Grande provinces (q.v.), especially in terms of the San Juan Anasazi origins for much of the Tewa Basin's population after A.D. 1200.

SOURCES: Bandelier 1890–1892; Hewett 1906; Mera 1935; Hewett and Dutton 1953; Wendorf and Reed 1955; Wendorf and Miller 1959; Ortiz 1969.

Stewart Peckham

TEXARKANA FOCUS, a now-outmoded term coined by A. D. Krieger in 1946 for a division of his Fulton Aspect (q.v.). Centered in Bowie County, Texas, and probably postdating A.D. 1500, this unit currently is ascribed to the Late Caddo or Caddo V classifications (see Caddo Tradition).

SOURCES: Krieger 1946:205–214; Suhm et al. 1954:203–208; E. M. Davis 1970; Wyckoff 1974:143–149.

James E. Corbin

TEXAS STREET SITE, a locality of disputed significance in the Mission Valley area of San Diego, California, where finds of deeply buried stone cores, flakes, and hearth-like features have been reported by George Carter at various times since the 1940s. Carter has argued that these materials constitute evidence for human occupation dating to the Sangamon Inter-

glacial period, more than 80,000 years ago. Both the human origin of the finds and the dating of their geological context have been disputed.
SOURCES: Carter 1957; Minshall 1976; Moratto 1984:60–62.

L. A. Payen

THALIA POINT SITE, an early (ca. 1710 B.C.) Paleoeskimo (q.v.) site on northern Labrador north of Nain, excavated by the Torngat Project (q.v.). Although most of the artifacts are typologically close to more northern Pre-Dorset (q.v.) artifacts, the excavators consider Thalia Point partially related to Independence I (q.v.).
SOURCES: Cox 1978; Fitzhugh 1980.

Moreau S. Maxwell

THERIAULT SITE, a chert quarry on Briar Creek in Burke County, in Georgia, utilized from Paleoindian through Woodland times; one of the largest quarries in the South Carolina-Georgia area and the source of much of the chert found in coastal plain sites of the region. Excavated by William Edwards in 1966, it subsequently was largely destroyed by vandals.
SOURCE: Brockington 1971b.

Michael Trinkley

THOMAS RIGGS SITE, a fortified site with rectangular houses in South Dakota which shares many similarities with the Huff and Shermer sites (qq.v.) of the Terminal Middle Missouri Tradition, and which, like them, probably was a prehistoric Mandan-Hidatsa village. Excavated by E. E. Meleen in 1940, it has been dated by dendrochronology to A.D. 1477–1516.
SOURCE: Meleen 1949.

Patricia J. O'Brien

THOMPSON PHASE, a late prehistoric (ca. 400 B.C.-A.D. 800) phase that precedes the Kamloops Phase (q.v.) in the South Thompson River valley, the western Shuswap Lake area, and the adjacent uplands of British Columbia. Distinctive traits include well-made corner- and base-notched, barbed projectile points; small, circular, or oval housepits; villages located on old river terraces at some distance from present watercourses. Microblades are absent, and ground-stone artifacts are rare. Thomas Richards and Michael Rousseau assign the Thompson Phase, along with the similar Lillooet Phase of the mid-Fraser drainage, to a Plateau Horizon (q.v.).
SOURCES: Wilson and Carlson 1980; Rousseau and Richards 1986.

Arnoud H. Stryd

THOM'S CREEK CULTURE, a Late Archaic-Early Woodland (ca. 1800–900 B.C.) expression defined by J. B. Griffin in 1945, whose sites—small camps, base camps, and large year-round villages—occur throughout the coastal plain in South Carolina. Thom's Creek shell middens are common on the coast, including shell rings that probably were occupied year-round. Interior sites usually are small, indicating temporary, perhaps seasonal use. Common artifacts on the coast include Thom's Creek pottery, finely worked bone tools, Savannah River and Small Savannah River stemmed projectile points, shell beads, worked whelk shells, and, occasionally, steatite.

SOURCES: J. B. Griffin 1945; Phelps 1968; Trinkley 1980a, 1980b.

Michael Trinkley

THULE PHASE, the earliest expression (with Ruin Island, q.v.) of the eastern Neoeskimo (q.v.) Tradition, ultimately distributed over all the eastern Arctic; defined by Therkel Mathiassen in 1927. Dwellings were large, deep pithouses walled with sod, rocks, and whalebone, and roofed with skins supported by whale jaws and ribs. Entered through tunnels, these had raised sleeping platforms above paved floors and were heated with soapstone oil lamps. Other distinctive traits were gear for both aglu (q.v.) and open-water hunting; the umiak (q.v.); paraphernalia for hunting baleen (predominantly bowhead) whales; and sleds pulled by dogs.

Although not yet determined with certainty, the time of the Thule Phase's appearance probably was between A.D. 1000 and 1200. Distinctive periods within the phase have not been well defined, but a generally recognized Classic Period (as at Naujan, q.v.) is marked by the use of winter pithouses and emphasis on whale hunting. In the following Postclassic Period, the pithouse was abandoned for the autumn qarmat (q.v.) and, on the fast ice, for the snow house; harpoon-head styles changed; and bowhead whale hunting decreased. This period was followed by a time of more regionally oriented ecological adaptations and by decreased homogeneity in material culture.

The ill-defined Historic Contact Period began in 1576 with Martin Frobisher's exploration of Frobisher Bay and Henry Hudson's explorations, in 1610, of Hudson Strait and Hudson Bay. It ended in the mid–19th century with various voyages in search of John Franklin's crew.

SOURCES: Mathiassen 1927; McGhee 1978:83–102; Maxwell 1985:247–294.

Moreau S. Maxwell

TIBURON PLAIN POTTERY, a prehistoric type of the Seri, found along the Sonoran coast and on Tiburon Island; also known as Tiburon Island Thinware and as Eggshell pottery because of its remarkable thinness relative to vessel size. Some vessels as much as 66 centimeters high have walls only 3 millimeters thick. The type appeared sometime between A.D. 700 and 1400 and lasted until ca. 1800.

SOURCE: Bowen 1976a.

Richard A. Pailes

TIKORALAK SITE, an early (ca. 740 B.C.) Groswater Dorset Phase (q.v.) component on Hamilton Inlet, Labrador, excavated by W. W. Fitzhugh. A

major source of data for defining the phase, it is one of the earliest Groswater
Dorset sites, overlapping in time the latest Pre-Dorset sites.
SOURCE: Fitzhugh 1972.

Moreau S. Maxwell

TIM ADRIAN SITE, a shallow, single-component, Hell Gap (q.v.) site near
Norton, Kansas, situated beside an outcrop of Niobrara Jasper (actually
chert) on the first terrace of Walnut Creek, a secondary tributary of the
Republican River. A large quantity of lithic material recovered from the
1.6-hectare site by P. J. O'Brien, A. E. Johnson, and A. M. White in 1980
consists of primary debitage, retouched flakes, Paleoindian-type end scrapers, and a variety of side scrapers, choppers, gravers, spokeshaves, and
bifaces. One Hell Gap projectile point was found. Microscopic analysis
indicated that the tools were used on dense materials such as wood or bone.
The site is interpreted as a specialized, limited-activity location—dating ca.
8100–7700 B.C.—to which the Paleoindian occupants returned intermittently, probably in the summer, to quarry chert and manufacture bone and/
or wooden artifacts.
SOURCE: O'Brien 1984a.

Patricia J. O'Brien

TIP FLUTING, a distinctive flaking technique used on Dorset Phase (q.v.)
chert end blades. Flakes are pressed from the distal tip of a triangular end
blade toward the proximal base, providing an especially sharp tip.

Moreau S. Maxwell

TIPI RING, a ring of stones marking the former location of a tipi. The
stones, which weighted down the edge of the tipi's cover, were left behind
when the tipi was packed up and hauled away. Sometimes there is a hearth
inside a ring and/or a gap in the stone arrangement where the tipi entry
was located. Tipi rings are widely distributed in the Northern Plains.
SOURCES: T. F. Kehoe 1958, 1960.

Thomas F. Kehoe

TITTERINGTON PHASE (formerly TITTERINGTON FOCUS), a nonceramic, Late Archaic (ca. 2500–1900 B.C.) cultural/technological horizon
of the southern Prairie Peninsula border in west-central Illinois and central
Missouri, represented by small hunting and/or processing camps, base settlements, and mortuary sites. Diagnostic artifacts include Etley, Sedalia, and
Wadlow type bifaces. Titterington Phase stone tools are distinctive because
they generally were not heat treated.

SOURCES: T. G. Cook 1976:65–68; Emerson 1984; Fortier and Emerson 1984; Wiant et al. 1983.

Michael D. Wiant

TITUS PHASE (or FOCUS), a protohistoric-historic (ca. A.D. 1600–1700) culture unit in northeastern Texas, initially defined by A. D. Krieger as part of his Fulton Aspect (q.v.) but now included within the Late Caddo or Caddo V categories (see Caddo Tradition).

SOURCES: Krieger 1946:230–241; Suhm et al. 1954:189–195; E. M. Davis 1970:48–50; Thurmond 1981.

James E. Corbin

TIZON BROWN WARE, a type of plain brown pottery made by the paddle-and-anvil technique; a characteristic trait of the late prehistoric/protohistoric period in interior southern California. The ware evidently was introduced from western Arizona and the lower Colorado River Valley not later than A.D. 800, then it diffused westward across the California deserts.

SOURCE: Moratto 1984:369, 421, 425.

L. A. Payen

TOBIAS SITE, a Little River Focus site of the Great Bend Aspect (q.v.) in south-central Kansas, dating ca. A.D. 1300–1600. W. R. Wedel's intensive investigations at this protohistoric Wichita Indian village in Rice County, in Kansas added greatly to knowledge of council circles (q.v.), one of which was present at the site. Geneseo series pottery was the most distinctive artifact category.

SOURCE: Wedel 1959.

Patricia J. O'Brien

TOLTEC SITE, a group of eighteen earthen mounds enclosed within an embankment 1.6 kilometers long, located in central Arkansas and dating ca. A.D. 700–900; the type site of the Plum Bayou Culture. Now an Arkansas state park, the complex covers some 40 hectares. Mound A is conical and 15 meters high; Mound B is pyramidal and 11.5 meters high. Ceramics at the site are unique but have some similarities to the pottery of the Coles Creek Phase (q.v.) of the lower Mississippi River region. Considerable lithic debris is present, which is unusual for the area.

SOURCES: Cyrus Thomas 1894:243–245; Rolingson 1982.

Martha A. Rolingson

TOM'S CREEK SITE, a multicomponent site on Tom's (or Thom's) Creek in Lexington County, in South Carolina occupied from the Early Archaic through the Woodland period (ca. 8000 B.C.-A.D. 1200). It was explored by J. L. Michie in 1969 and by Donald Sutherland in 1970. The type site for Thom's Creek pottery, it produced a long sequence of Archaic projectile-point types.

SOURCES: J. B. Griffin 1945; Michie 1969; Trinkley 1976a.

Michael Trinkley

TONTO NATIONAL MONUMENT, the location near Miami, Arizona, of two Gila Phase, Salado Province (qq.v.) cliff dwellings, dating ca. A.D. 1300–1450. These multistoried pueblos are constructed in large caves, and their original ceilings are still preserved, resting on the pueblos' walls of cobbles and mud. The ruins are similar to the pueblo known as Montezuma Castle (q.v.) in the Verde Valley. The lower ruin of 19 rooms is better preserved than the large 40-room upper ruin. Gila Polychrome, the dominant decorated pottery type, is associated at both ruins with the local Tonto Brown variety of Alameda Plain Ware (q.v.). The museum at the monument's visitor center exhibits a sample of ceramics, a fine collection of fabrics, vegetal materials, and other artifacts from the sites.

SOURCE: Steen et al. 1962.

Albert H. Schroeder

TOPANGA CANYON, a locality in Los Angeles County, in California containing a number of stratified habitation sites that were investigated by several different archaeologists between 1946 and 1957. The lowest components of these sites (Phase I) were characterized by scraper planes, milling stones, and manos. The Phase II middle components were distinguished by small projectile points, incised stones, and cogged stones. Typical traits of Phase II upper components were rock-lined ovens, flexed burials, mortars, pestles, and numerous millingstones. Radiocarbon data suggest that Phase I began earlier than 3000 B.C. and that Phase III lasted until about the beginning of the Christian era.

SOURCES: Treganza and Malamud 1950; Treganza and Bierman 1958; Moratto 1984:126–127.

Michael J. Moratto

TORNGAT PROJECT, a multiacademic and museum archaeological project led by W. W. Fitzhugh of the Smithsonian Institution that explored prehistoric cultural and environmental factors on the coast of Labrador in the late 1970s and 1980s.

SOURCE: Fitzhugh 1980.

Moreau S. Maxwell

TORTUGAS POINT, a thick dart-point type of simple triangular shape occurring commonly in Middle and Late Archaic sites (dating ca. 2600 B.C. to A.D. 1000) in southern Texas and northeastern Mexico.

SOURCES: Suhm et al. 1954; MacNeish 1958b; Sorrow 1969; Turner and Hester 1985.

Elton R. Prewitt

TOWN CREEK (or FRUTCHEY) SITE, a ceremonial complex of the Pee Dee Culture (q.v.) dating ca. A.D. 1350–1450, located on the Little River near Mount Gilead, North Carolina. Archaeological explorations began there in 1937 under the sponsorship of the Works Project Administration and continued steadily until the present (1987) under the direction of J. L. Coe. In the 1950s, the temple mound, associated structures, and a palisade enclosure were reconstructed on the basis of the archaeological data. Town Creek is the type site for Pee Dee Pottery Series (q.v.).
SOURCE: Coe 1983.

Billy L. Oliver

TOWNSEND SITE, a manifestation of the Late Woodland, Slaughter Creek Phase (q.v.) on the Atlantic coast of Delaware, dating ca. A.D. 1000–1600. Discovered and excavated by avocational archaeologists, but analyzed and interpreted in part by Smithsonian Institution archaeologists, the site contained hundreds of storage/trash pits, each of which yielded potsherds; finished artifacts of stone, bone, and shell; and food remains, especially animal bones and marine shells. Townsend Ware (q.v.), a widely distributed ceramic series, was named for the site.
SOURCE: Omwake and Stewart 1963.

Ronald A. Thomas

TOWNSEND WARE, a shell-tempered, fabric-impressed pottery, occurring as large to small wide-mouthed jars with direct rims, conoidal bodies, and rounded or semiconical bases. Found between Delaware and Virginia in Late Woodland and early historic sites, it dates ca. A.D. 900–1650 and is divided into four types: Rappahannock Fabric-impressed, Rappahannock Incised, Townsend Corded, and Townsend Herringbone.
SOURCES: Blaker 1963:14–22; Daniel Griffith 1977; Egloff and Potter 1982:107–109.

Stephen R. Potter

TOXAWAY VILLAGE, an 18th-century Cherokee settlement, now inundated by the Keowee Reservoir in Oconee County, in South Carolina. In 1968, William Edwards unearthed house patterns and other features there, as well as large quantities of Cherokee artifacts.
SOURCE: Beuschel n.d.

Michael Trinkley

TOYAH PHASE, the terminal prehistoric culture unit in central Texas (ca. A.D. 1200–1750) with a subsistence based primarily on plant gathering and hunting of deer and bison. Characteristic artifacts are contracting-stem arrow points (especially the Perdiz type), end scrapers, four- and two-edged beveled knives, blade tools, drills, bone awls, deer-ulna flakers, milling-stones, ornaments of shell and bone, and bone-tempered pottery. Rock-shelters and stream terraces were favored camping places; common features include large, flat hearths, basin-shaped pits, and burials that sometimes show evidence of violent death. Typical sites are Kyle Rockshelter (q.v.), Hoxie Bridge, Oblate, and Smith Rockshelter. The Toyah Focus, named and briefly described by J. C. Kelley in 1947, was described in more detail by E. B. Jelks in 1962. E. R. Prewitt designated this unit a phase in 1981.

SOURCES: J. C. Kelley 1947a; Suhm 1957; Jelks 1962:24–26; Bond 1978:53–238; Prewitt 1981:83–84.

Frank A. Weir

TRAIL CREEK CAVES, a series of small shelters on the Seward Peninsula, in western Alaska, which were utilized by hunters from about 7000 B.C. into modern times. Components at Trail Creek, excavated by Helge Larsen in 1949–1950, produced a few microblades and antler points grooved for microblades to which a radiocarbon date of 7120 B.C. is thought to apply. Also found were artifacts of the Denbigh Flint Complex (q.v.), numerous lanceolate projectile points attributed to the inland Choris Phase (q.v.) at approximately 1000 B.C., and materials from later Norton, Ipiutak, Thule (qq.v.), and modern Eskimo occupations.

SOURCE: Larsen 1968.

Donald W. Clark

TRANQUILLITY SITE, a locality in Fresno County, in California, inves-tigated by several researchers between 1939 and 1944, where a series of human skeletons initially was thought by some to be coeval with bones of extinct bison, camel, and horse, largely because chemical analysis showed similar fluorine levels in the human and animal bones. However, later ra-diocarbon determinations on two Tranquillity burials yielded dates of only about 600 B.C.

SOURCES: Hewes 1946; Angel 1966; Berger et al. 1971.

Michael J. Moratto

TRANSITIONAL COMPLEX, a unit of the provisional Queen Charlotte Island, British Columbia culture sequence, distinguished by unifacial flaked-stone assemblages in non-shell midden contexts, dating between ca. 2500 B.C. and A.D. 500+. Technological continuity with the earlier Moresby Tradition (q.v.) appears in scrapers, flake cores, and flake tools; however, by this time, the older microblade complex had been replaced by the possibly functionally equivalent bipolar core system. Most Transitional Complex sites—e.g., Skoglund's Landing Point and Lawn Point (qq.v.)—show evi-

dence of the beginning of ground and polished stone, suggesting relationships with the contemporary Graham Tradition (q.v.).
SOURCES: Fladmark 1970, 1975.

Knut R. Fladmark

TRANS-MISSISSIPPI SOUTH, a biogeographically based archaeological
subarea of eastern North America defined in 1970 by F. F. Schambach, who
considers it comparable in size and cultural significance to traditional archaeological subareas such as the lower Mississippi Valley, the Ohio Valley,
and the Southeast. Occupying a zone of typically southeastern Woodland
environment west of the lower Mississippi River Valley and east of the
Plains in parts of Missouri, Arkansas, Oklahoma, Louisiana, and Texas,
this subarea possesses its own distinct cultures (e.g., Fourche Maline and
Caddo, q.v.) and its own distinct interpretive problems.
SOURCES: Schambach 1970; Schambach et al. 1982.

Frank F. Schambach

TREMPEALEAU BAY SITES, a Middle Woodland complex of Havana-
related mounds and villages adjacent to Trempealeau Bay on the Mississippi
River in southwestern Wisconsin, reported by W. C. McKern in 1931.
Included are the Nicholls, Shrake, and Schwert mound groups. The sites
now are assigned to the Trempealeau Phase (q.v.).
SOURCES: McKern 1931; Stoltman 1979.

David Overstreet

TREMPEALEAU PHASE, Middle Woodland analog in southwestern Wisconsin to Havana Hopewell developments in Illinois and Ohio; estimated
to date ca. 200 B.C.-A.D. 100. The phase was defined by J. B. Stoltman in
1979, largely on the basis of mortuary contexts and ceramic affinities.
SOURCES: Stoltman 1979.

David Overstreet

TREMPEALEAU SITE, a group of three truncated pyramidal mounds at
Trempealeau, Wisconsin, investigated in 1903 by G. H. Squier, who reported finding red-slipped ceramics of Middle Mississippian affiliation in
the mounds. This is the northernmost known occurrence of such pottery in
the Upper Mississippi Valley.
SOURCE: G. H. Squier 1905.

David Overstreet

TREMPER MOUND, a large, sprawling, Ohio Hopewell (q.v.) mound
closely surrounded by a low embankment, located near the confluence of
Pond Creek and the Scioto River just north of Portsmouth, Ohio. W. C.
Mills' excavations in 1915 exposed a submound structure consisting of a

large central area with several appended sections, within which were concentrations of lithic debris and unworked bone, as well as prepared deposits of artifacts and mass interments of cremated human remains. A large and a small cache of platform pipes (q.v.) were found, many of them carved from Ohio pipestone which probably came from sources in the nearby hills. On typological grounds, the site has been ascribed to early Hopewell peoples, possibly at ca. 100 B.C.–A.D. 150.

SOURCES: Squier and Davis 1848:83–84, pl. 29, no. 4; Mills 1916; J. B. Griffin 1943a:210–215; Webb and Snow 1945:200–217; Prufer 1968:45–50, 148–153.

N'omi B. Greber

TRIGG SITE, a palisaded village on the New River in the mountains of southwestern Virginia, occupied from Late Woodland to protohistoric times. First described by C. G. Holland in 1970, it was completely excavated in 1974–1975 by H. A. MacCord and W. T. Buchanan, who recorded 762 features including numerous storage pits and human burials. The burials contained both European trade items and traditional Native American artifacts.

SOURCES: Holland 1970; Buchanan n.d.

Keith T. Egloff

TRIHEDRAL ADZE, a large, keel-backed, ground-stone tool, often fashioned of rhyolite and obviously designed for woodworking. Numerous examples have been found with Eden and Scottsbluff projectile points (qq.v.) in eastern Wisconsin and Ontario. Associated with the Cody Complex (qq.v.), they are thought to be the earliest ground-stone tools in North America.

SOURCE: Overstreet n.d.b.

David Overstreet

TRINCHERAS CULTURE, a major culture in north-central Sonora, primarily between the Rio San Miguel on the east and the Rio Seco on the west, and extending into extreme southern Arizona. A few Trincheras sites are known from the Rio Moctezuma and Rio Sonora valleys, but the greatest concentration is in the Rio Magdalena and Rio Altar basins. On the basis of ceramic cross-dating, the culture is thought to date between A.D. 800 and Spanish contact in the 16th century.

Sites consist of terraced hillsides and ridges, with crude masonry walls stabilizing the terraces, and, frequently, circular or rectangular rock-walled enclosures on the hilltops, where they may have served a defensive function. The characteristic decorated pottery is Trincheras Purple-on-Red (q.v.), a brownware that was slipped red, then painted with geometric designs in specular hematite paint. Less common are Trincheras Polychrome and Trincheras Redware. The decorated pottery is reminiscent of several Hohokam types in Arizona, leading some to classify the Trincheras Culture as a southern variant of the Hohokam Culture (q.v.). Large quantities of marine shells found in Trincheras sites, commonly in the form of manufacturing debris, suggest that the Trincheras Culture was the source of the abundant shell found in Hohokam sites.

SOURCES: Sauer and Brand 1931; A. E. Johnson 1963, 1966.

Richard A. Pailes

TRINCHERAS PURPLE-ON-RED POTTERY, a brownware of the Trincheras Culture in north-central Sonora that was slipped red and decorated in geometric patterns with a paint made of specular hematite which, when fired, produced a distinctive purplish color. It is thought to date ca. A.D. 800–1100.

SOURCE: A. E. Johnson 1966.

Richard A. Pailes

TRINITY ASPECT, a Late Archaic (q.v.) expression in north-central Texas comprising two foci, Carrollton and Elam. Defined in the early 1950s by W. W. Crook, Jr., and R. K. Harris, the aspect is known from a number of small campsites along the upper Trinity River and its tributaries. Artifacts include a variety of chipped-stone projectile points, scrapers, knives, and axes.

SOURCES: Crook and Harris 1952, 1954; Suhm et al. 1954:76–80.

Edward B. Jelks

TRINITY DELTA SITES. See Wallisville Sites.

TRI-WALL STRUCTURE, a type of circular, triple-walled building from 13 to 22 meters in diameter and about 2 meters high that occurs in sites of the late Bonito and Intermediate phases (qq.v.) in the Chaco and Upper San Juan provinces (qq.v.) in New Mexico. Partition walls divide the outer wall rings into roughly equal-sized compartments which are arrayed around a central core. There are tri-wall structures at Pueblo del Arroyo, at Aztec Ruin (qq.v.), and at the Holmes Group, but too few of these structures have been investigated to determine feature patterns or to permit sound inferences regarding their function.

Bi-wall structures, a possibly related architectural form with one less circumferential wall, are distributed similarly to tri-walled structures. Both types are widely considered to be important components of Anasazi (q.v.) esoteric public architecture, possibly used for holding ceremonies.

SOURCES: Vivian 1959; Lekson 1984.

Peter J. McKenna

TROYVILLE CULTURE, a Woodland (q.v.) expression dating ca. A.D. 300–600 that followed the Marksville Culture and preceded the Coles Creek Culture (qq.v.) in the lower Mississippi River Valley. Platform mounds—

not necessarily pyramidal—first appeared in the area during Troyville times, in association with large, bathtub-shaped fire pits. Ceramics include red-zoned and red-slipped wares, commonly cordmarked; the Edwards variety of the Mulberry Creek Cord Marked type is the most distinctive and wide-spread style. Dog burials are a distinctive Troyville trait.

SOURCES: Belmont 1967, 1982; Gibson 1982; Williams and Brain 1983:404–405.

William G. Haag

TROYVILLE SITE, a large mound complex at the confluence of the Black and Little rivers in Catahoula Parish, in Louisiana, now almost totally destroyed by highway construction and town development. Originally, there were thirteen mounds, twelve of which were truncated pyramids; the other (the so-called Great Mound) was a stepped pyramid capped by a 35-foot conical mound. The mounds were enclosed on two sides by a low wall of earth, remnants of which are still discernible. There was a definite Marksville (q.v.) component at the site that predated the mound construction; most of the sherds collected from the surface are "classic" Coles Creek (q.v.) types.

SOURCES: W. M. Walker 1936; Neuman 1984.

William G. Haag

T-SHAPED DOORWAY, a doorway to a dwelling whose upper part is wide and its lower part narrow, creating a roughly T-shaped entry. Ventilation holes can also take this form. T-shaped doorways occur in many Southwestern sites of the Anasazi, Mogollon, and Casas Grandes cultures (qq.v.).

SOURCE: Love 1975.

David A. Phillips, Jr.

TUCK CARPENTER SITE, a large Caddo (q.v.) IV Period cemetery in Camp County, in Texas, radiocarbon dated to the 16th century A.D. Excavations there between 1963 and 1967 by R. L. Turner and R. W. Walsh unearthed unusual stemmed (goblet-shaped) vessels suggesting possible contact with the De Soto expedition (A.D. 1542).

SOURCE: R. L. Turner, Jr. 1978.

James E. Corbin

TUCSON BASIN PROVINCE, an area encompassing the middle Santa Cruz River drainage in southern Arizona that was occupied in late prehistoric times by the Hohokam Culture (q.v.). Owing to the drainage system's relatively high elevation of from 700 to 1100 meters above sea level, farming practices differed in important ways from the canal-irrigation farming of the Hohokam in the Phoenix Basin (q.v.) to the northwest. While irrigation was practiced along the Santa Cruz River floodplain, there is evidence that floodwater farming techniques also were used throughout the province. Typical Hohokam shell and stone artifacts are abundant, but ceramic styles and other material-culture traits of the Tucson Basin (q.v.) Hohokam diverged through time from those of the Phoenix Basin Hohokam. The Tucson Basin's brownware vessels, either unslipped or wash slipped, contrast with the buff-colored, slip-decorated vessels of the Phoenix Basin. Also, polychrome ceramic styles in the Tucson Basin were more heavily influenced by northern Mexican traditions than were those in the Phoenix Basin.

Ball courts and, later, platform mounds are quite numerous in the Tucson Basin. The late prehistoric culture shows affinities with both Puebloan (q.v.) and north-Mexican cultures. Current interpretations ascribe equal antiquity to culture sequences in the Tucson and Phoenix basins, and they recognize an Archaic-to-Hohokam transition in both provinces. There also may have been a continuum from Hohokam to protohistoric or historic Indian cultures.

SOURCES: Di Peso 1956; J. D. Hayden 1957; Greenleaf 1975b; Doyel 1977, 1984; I. T. Kelly 1978; Jacobs and Hartman 1984.

David E. Doyel and John S. Cable

TUKTU COMPLEX. See Anaktuvuk Pass Sites.

TUKTU SITE. See Anaktuvuk Pass Sites.

TULARE LAKE (or WITT) SITE, a zone along an old shoreline of Tulare Lake in the southern San Joaquin Valley, California, where Clovis-like fluted projectile points, Lake Mojave points (q.v.), chipped-stone crescents, and a wide variety of scraping/cutting implements have been collected by D. Witt and other amateur investigators over a period of more than three decades. The locality also has produced heavily mineralized fragments of human, bison, ground sloth, and horse bones.

SOURCE: Riddell and Olsen 1969.

L. A. Payen

TULAROSA AND CORDOVA CAVES, two dry caves near Reserve, New Mexico, containing materials attributed to the Mogollon Culture (q.v.) of ca. A.D. 300–1100. P. S. Martin and J. B. Rinaldo excavated them in 1950–1951 to validate the local culture sequence established at open sites and to obtain perishable foodstuffs and artifacts of wood and fiber not ordinarily preserved in open sites.

SOURCE: Martin et al. 1952.

Stewart Peckham

TUNACUNNHEE SITE, a Middle Woodland mound and village site in northwestern Georgia's Lookout Valley, dating ca. A.D. 150 and consisting of four stone-and-earth burial mounds and an associated habitation area.

In 1973, J. R. Caldwell and R. W. Jefferies discovered burials within and beneath the mounds which contained a variety of exotic offerings indicating strong contact with the Ohio Hopewell Culture (q.v.). Such items occurred only in mortuary contexts, however, and Hopewellian influence did not seem to have extended to other aspects of the society.

SOURCES: Jefferies 1976, 1979.

Paul A. Webb

TUNNEL ENTRY, a below-ground entryway typical of Thule Phase (q.v.) houses, designed to retain heat in the living quarters. Initially thought to be characteristic only of Neoeskimo houses, tunnel entries recently have been discovered in houses of the middle Dorset Phase (q.v.).

Moreau S. Maxwell

TURIN SITE, a location near Turin, Iowa, where four deeply buried skeletons ascribed to the Middle Archaic were found. One had been sprinkled with red ocher and had shell beads at the ankles. A sample of bones gave a radiocarbon date of 2770 B.C. ±250.

SOURCES: Frankforter 1955; Ruppe 1955, 1956; Fisher et al. 1984; Frankforter and Agogino 1959.

Duane C. Anderson

TURKEY FOOT RIDGE SITE, a pithouse village of the Mogollon Culture (q.v.) in the Pine Lawn Valley, Cibola Province (q.v.), near Reserve, New Mexico; excavated in 1947–1948 by P. S. Martin and J. B. Rinaldo. Fifteen pithouses built during the Georgetown, San Francisco, and Three Circle phases showed a change from round to rectangular forms. An intermediate version of a Mogollon great kiva (q.v.) also was present.

Brownware utility pottery from the site has textured (scored, incised, punched, banded, and plain-corrugated) exterior surfaces. Painted pottery (Mogollon Red-on-brown) appeared first in the San Francisco Phase and was followed by Three Circle Red-on-white and Mangas (or Mimbres Bold Face) Black-on-white—the same sequence seen in the Mimbres Province. There is some doubt, however, that these types were made in the Cibola Province. Anasazi pottery—Red Mesa Black-on-white, perhaps from the southern part of the Zuni Province—appeared during the Three Circle Phase. A series of 45 tree-ring dates suggests that some of the pithouses were built ca. A.D. 780.

SOURCES: Martin et al. 1949; Martin and Rinaldo 1950a.

Stewart Peckham

TURKEY HILL PHASE, a late phase of the Northern Sinagua Tradition of the Flagstaff Province (qq.v.) in north-central Arizona. It marks a dramatic regrouping of the Sinagua population into a few sites near Flagstaff and into a few others on Anderson Mesa in the Chevelon-Chavez Province (q.v.). This aggregation has been interpreted as indicative of an abandonment of the immediate Flagstaff area, with removal to Anderson Mesa and Verde Valley. However, surveys in the latter areas indicate pre–1200 A.D. populations large enough to account for the larger, later pueblos there without augmentation from outside.

The only sites known for this period in the vicinity of Flagstaff are Elden (q.v.), Turkey Hill, Old Caves, and Two Kivas pueblos, with Wupatki Pueblo (q.v.) farther to the south. The pueblos generally are large (over twenty rooms in size) and often are multistoried. Their layout in block or linear form follows that of the preceding Elden Phase (q.v.). Rectangular kivas with benches continue, but no community rooms or ball courts of this period are known in the Flagstaff area.

The earlier variations in burial practices seem to have ended with the Turkey Hill Phase, since only extended inhumations are known from the few excavated sites of the phase. Burial in cists, sometimes lined with stone slabs and covered by slabs or branches is more common than in previous times.

With the separation of the main population into two areas, Flagstaff and Anderson Mesa, there was a concomitant separation of local pottery types, which reflects the differences in available clays and tempering materials in the respective areas. In the Flagstaff area, Sunset Plain, Angell Brown, and their redware, smudged, and polished varieties continued to dominate; on Anderson Mesa, the most common pottery types were Grapevine Brown, Kinnikinnick Brown, Chavez Brown, and their redware, smudged, and polished varieties. However, every known Turkey Hill Phase site contains all these pottery types, indicating that contact between the two major population centers was maintained.

SOURCES: Cummings 1930; Colton 1939b:42–43, 1946:72–74, 312–314; J. P. Wilson 1969:25–27.

Peter J. Pilles, Jr.

TURKEY-TAIL POINT, a medium to large, often thin and delicately chipped, bipointed, leaf-shaped projectile point with shallow side notches, typically manufactured from Wyandotte chert (q.v.). Caches of more than 100 specimens have been reported. The type is associated with a transitional Late Archaic-Woodland period—and especially with the Red Ocher Complex—in a region extending from the Great Lakes southward into Tennessee.

SOURCES: Binford 1963; Didier 1967; Justice 1984.

James H. Kellar

TURNER FARM SITE, a large site in coastal Maine containing evidence of Archaic (q.v.) occupations as early as 3200 B.C. and of the Susquehanna Tradition, as well as burials from the mid-second millennium B.C. and

materials attributed to more recent ceramic-using peoples of Woodland affinity. Maritime adaptation is indicated in all periods, but the site may have functioned as a large base camp from which both marine and terrestrial species were exploited.
SOURCE: Bourque 1975.

James A. Tuck

TURNER-LOOK SITE, an open Fremont Culture (q.v.) community on the Colorado Plateau near the Utah-Colorado border, probably dating ca. A.D. 1000–1300 and containing characteristically eastern Fremont masonry structures. H. M. Wormington, who excavated there in the 1930s and 1940s, used data from the site as the basis for her definition of the Fremont Culture.
SOURCE: Wormington 1955.

David B. Madsen

TURNER SITE, a group of approximately fifteen mounds attributed on typological grounds to Middle and Late Hopewell (q.v.) peoples, located within and near a geometric earthwork on the Little Miami River east of Cincinnati, Ohio. F. W. Putnam's and C. L. Metz's work there between 1882 and 1908 constitutes the most systematic excavation of a large Hopewell site in Ohio. The earthen embankment included a large oval, three circles, a long narrow enclosure, and a graded way. Within the oval were found the main cemetery and, under seven conjoined mounds, a major civic-ceremonial area. There were other typical Hopewell ritual activity areas under parts of the embankments and under other scattered mounds; habitation areas also were identified. Some features are as yet uninterpreted, e.g., series of pits with attached flues found in one of the structures.
SOURCES: Whittlesey 1851; Willoughby 1917; Willoughby and Hooton 1922; Prufer 1964, 1968; Greber 1979a.

N'omi B. Greber

TURNGAASITI SITE, one of the Belcher Islands sites (q.v.); an early Dorset Phase (or possibly a transitional Pre-Dorset/Dorset) component that demonstrated a very early penetration of Dorset people into southern Hudson Bay. Excavations by Elmer Harp, Jr., in 1975 produced artifacts resembling those of both the Groswater Dorset Phase and the Avinga Site (qq.v.).
SOURCE: Harp 1976.

Moreau S. Maxwell

TURTLE BAY PERIOD. See Galveston Bay Focus.

TUSAYAN RUIN, a typical U-shaped Western Anasazi pueblo on the Grand Canyon's south rim in Arizona, consisting of about sixteen habitation and storage rooms, two kivas, and a central plaza. It was excavated by E. W.

Haury and H. S. Gladwin in 1929. Dating to the late Pueblo II-early Pueblo III period (ca. A.D. 1185–1225), it probably was one of the last sites occupied by the Anasazi (q.v.) before they abandoned the area.
SOURCE: Haury 1931.

Janet R. Balsom

TUVAALUK PROJECT, a multidisciplinary study of the prehistory of Ungava Bay, Quebec, and particularly of Diana Bay at its northwestern corner. The field research, conducted in the 1970s, was led by Patrick Plumet of the University of Quebec at Montreal.

Moreau S. Maxwell

TUWIUCA FOCUS, a division of the Winslow Branch of the Anasazi Culture (qq.v.) in northeastern Arizona, dating ca. A.D. 1200–1300 and characterized by masonry pueblo villages with associated kivas and Winslow Orange Ware (q.v.) ceramics. The focus was named for the type site, Homolovi IV or Tuwiuca, in Hopi country.
SOURCES: Fewkes 1904; Colton and Hargrave 1937:135–140; Colton 1939a:68–69, 1956.

Donald E. Weaver, Jr.

TUZIGOOT PHASE, a phase of the Verde Province of the Sinagua Division, Hakataya Culture (qq.v.), dating ca. A.D. 1300–1450, defined on the basis of excavations at Tuzigoot Pueblo and Montezuma Castle (qq.v.). Pueblo architecture continued as in the preceding Honanki Phase (q.v.), but buildings were large, and some apparently were multistoried with associated plazas. Other continuing traits were extended burials, irrigation, field houses, and garden plots.

Tuzigoot Brown, Red, and Smudged pottery like that of the Honanki Phase continued in use; intrusive wares from the Hopi country included Jeddito Black-on-white and Winslow Polychrome. The Tuzigoot Phase marked the end of pueblo-type architecture in the Verde Valley, which was occupied by Yavapai Indians when first visited by Spaniards in 1583.
SOURCES: Caywood and Spicer 1935; Jackson and Van Valkenburgh 1954.

Albert H. Schroeder

TUZIGOOT PUEBLO, a hilltop pueblo with walls of rock and mud, located at the national monument of the same name near Clarkdale, Arizona. Occupied between A.D. 1125 and 1400/1450 by Sinuaga of the Verde Province (qq.v.), the pueblo was mostly one story high but appears to have had two stories in a few spots. Excavations there by L. R. Caywood and E. H. Spicer in 1933–1934 produced the most complete collection of Sinagua crafts from any one site. These constitute the basic data for the late phases of the province.

Living on hilltops had several advantages: Rock for building is exposed there; drainage is a natural feature, breezes help cool the hot summer temperatures while unobstructed sunlight provides warmth in winter; exposure to the first and last light of day lessens the need for firewood for light; and hilltops are above the insects that infest the stream valleys below.
SOURCE: Caywood and Spicer 1935.

Albert H. Schroeder

TWELVE MILE CREEK SITE, a bison kill in Logan County, in Kansas excavated in 1895 by H. T. Martin; the first site in the Western Hemisphere dug by a scientifically trained person that demonstrated the contemporaneity of humans and Ice Age animals. A fluted projectile point, probably a resharpened Clovis point (q.v.), was associated with the bones of extinct bison. The point was stolen not long after the discovery, and only a photograph and a drawing of it remain.
SOURCES: Williston 1902; Rogers and Martin 1984.

Richard A. Rogers

TWENHAFEL SITE [spelling varies], a large mound and village complex in the Mississippi River floodplain in Jackson County, in Illinois; known principally as a Middle Woodland complex, although it also contains Mississippian and Late Woodland components. Thought originally to have consisted of some 25 mounds and extensive village areas, the site is the only large Middle Woodland mound complex along the Mississippi River in southern Illinois, and it has been interpreted as one of the regional centers of the Hopewell Interaction Sphere. Excavations by M. L. Fowler in 1957 and by J. R. Caldwell in 1958 have never been fully published.
SOURCES: Hofman 1979; Struever and Houart 1972.

Brian M. Butler

TWIN SISTERS PHASE, a Late Archaic culture unit in central Texas, dating ca. 50 B.C.-A.D. 1200; defined by F. A. Weir in 1976. Sites are mostly on stream terraces and in rockshelters, where characteristic features include stone-lined hearths, mussel-shell caches, and circular arrangements of stones that may be related to shelters of some kind. A few living surfaces have been reported, suggesting organization of living space according to social units. Burials are always flexed.

The Ensor type dart point (q.v.) is the chief diagnostic. Other common artifacts include chipped-stone axes, perforators, gravers, hammerstones, grinding stones, chert cores, side unifaces, and several forms of bifaces. Such exotic articles as boat stones, gorgets, and ornaments made of marine and freshwater shells are found occasionally. Components of the phase have been excavated at a number of sites, including Oblate, Site 41-BT-6, and several sites at the Belton Reservoir.

SOURCES: Miller and Jelks 1952; Johnson et al. 1962:87–90; Weir 1976:136–137; Young 1985:23–53.

Frank A. Weir

TWO DOG SITE, one of the two type sites of the Greenwood Phase (q.v.), Plains Woodland, located in the Neosho River valley of the Kansas Flint Hills, radiocarbon dated to A.D. 1050±145. Excavations by T. A. Witty, Jr., in 1962 disclosed a large, oval house floor.
SOURCE: Witty 1982.

Thomas A. Witty, Jr.

TYARA SITE, one of the first early (ca. 500 B.C.) Dorset Phase (q.v.) sites described in detail, located on Sugluk Island at the northeastern corner of Hudson Bay. It was excavated between 1957 and 1959 by W. E. Taylor, Jr., who, after comparing it to the Arnapik Site (q.v.) on Mansell Island, concluded that there was cultural continuity between Pre-Dorset and Dorset.
SOURCE: W. E. Taylor, Jr. 1968.

Moreau S. Maxwell

TYUONYI SITE, a Classic Period (q.v.), Rio Grande Anasazi pueblo in Frijoles Canyon, Bandelier National Monument, New Mexico; excavated by E. L. Hewett between 1909 and 1912. The oval, masonry-walled structure surrounds a plaza, within which are three small kivas. Nearby are a Rio Grande big kiva (q.v.), several hundred cavate rooms (q.v.), and masonry rooms built into and against the cliffs on the canyon's north side.

The full sequence of Rio Grande Glazewares (q.v.) dominated the pottery sequence from Hewett's excavations, but there were lesser amounts of Biscuitwares (q.v.) from the Tewa Basin Province (q.v.), along with wares of both the late Developmental and Coalition periods (qq.v.). The pottery revealed that the pueblo was occupied over a much longer time than the period of A.D. 1386–1521 indicated by tree-ring dates.

Located near the northernmost extent of the Middle Rio Grande Province (q.v.), Frijoles Canyon is close to a dividing line between the distribution areas of Biscuitware and Rio Grande Glazeware pottery.
SOURCES: Hendron 1940; Hewett and Dutton 1953.

Stewart Peckham

U

UGASHIK NARROWS PHASE, an early (ca. 7000–6000 B.C.) phase in the Ugashik River drainage of the Alaska Peninsula, intensively investigated by the University of Oregon during the 1970s. In most respects, the Ugashik sequence is similar to the Bering Sea-related sequence in the Brooks River-Naknek Drainage area (q.v.): American Paleo-Arctic Tradition (Ugashik Narrows Phase), Northern Archaic Tradition (Ugashik Knoll Phase), Arctic Small Tool Tradition, Norton Tradition, and Neoeskimo or Thule Tradition (qq.v.). Strong representation of the Northern Archaic, once thought to be a boreal forest adaptation, is noteworthy. Ugashik Narrows, the earliest known phase in southwestern Alaska (radiocarbon dated to between 6000 and 7000 B.C.) in some respects is quite variant from the American Paleo-Arctic Tradition as initially defined by D. D. Anderson, but that may help bridge the typological gap between the Anangula (q.v.) Blade Complex and other early blade industries.

SOURCES: Dumond et al. 1976; Henn 1978.

Donald W. Clark

ULU, the distinctive, round-bladed "woman's knife" of the modern Inuit. The form extends well back into prehistoric times, first appearing ca. A.D. 1000 in the early Thule Phase (q.v.) of the eastern Arctic.

Moreau S. Maxwell

UMIAK, a kind of large, skin-covered boat used in the eastern Arctic from the Thule Phase (ca. A.D. 1000) to the Historic Contact period for whale hunting and for transporting families to new settlement locations. It has been called the "woman's boat" because it traditionally was rowed by women in traveling to new locations; however, men also used umiaks for whale hunting.

Moreau S. Maxwell

UMINGMAK SITE, a Pre-Dorset (q.v.) component on Banks Island, Northwest Territories, dating ca. 1400 B.C., whose occupants relied more on muskox hunting than on seacoast resources for a livelihood. Excavated by W. E. Taylor, Jr., Umingmak, along with the related Shoran Site, provided data on the farthest west penetration of eastern Pre-Dorset people.
SOURCE: W. E. Taylor, Jr. 1967.

Moreau S. Maxwell

UNIFLITE SITE, a multicomponent site in Onslow County, in North Carolina, occupied chiefly by Late Woodland people ca. A.D. 1400. T. C. Loftfield dug there in 1978 and found shell-tempered pottery, rectangular houses, refuse pits, hearths, dog burials, and a wealth of floral and faunal remains.
SOURCE: Loftfield n.d.a.

Billy L. Oliver

UNION PARK PHASE, a phase of the East Verde Province of the Sinagua Division, Hakataya Culture (qq.v.) in Arizona, dating ca. A.D. 900–1000 and based on the occurrence of Hohokam (Santa Cruz Phase [q.v.]) elements on the surface of unexcavated sites. Sherds of earlier Gila Butte and Snaketown Red-on-buff pottery, also of Hohokam affiliation, have been reported at other sites, but their significance is not clear.
SOURCE: Redman and Hohmann 1986.

Albert H. Schroeder

UNIVERSITY VILLAGE SITE, a site on the southwestern edge of San Francisco Bay, California, investigated in the 1950s by B. A. Gerow. Analysis of data associated with burials led him to conclude that two culturally and morphologically distinct traditions coexisted in central California between 1500 and 1000 B.C.—one in the San Francisco Bay region, the other (the "Early Horizon") in central California.
SOURCES: Gerow 1969; Moratto 1984.

Michael J. Moratto

UNKAR CHRONOLOGY, a sequence of four Anasazi (q.v.) phases developed to interpret the settlement history of the Unkar Delta locality (q.v.) in the Grand Canyon of the Colorado River. Based strictly on ceramics typology, the phases are Medicine Valley, ca. A.D. 900; Vishnu, ca. A.D. 1050–1070; Zoraster, ca. A.D. 1075–1100; and Dox, ca. A.D. 1100–1150. Each phase is defined by identifying the narrowest interval of time at which all of its diagnostic pottery types overlap. This chronology has not been widely used; most researchers prefer the Pecos Classification (q.v.) with slight modifications to reflect site-specific data for the Grand Canyon Province (q.v.).

SOURCES: Euler et al. 1979; Schwartz et al. 1980.

Janet R. Balsom

UNKAR DELTA LOCALITY, an area located along the Colorado River of the Grand Canyon, Arizona; one of the largest settlement areas within the Grand Canyon Province (q.v.), comprising more than 50 Western Anasazi (q.v.) sites that span the period ca. A.D. 900–1150. Excavations there by members of the School of American Research between 1967 and 1969 disclosed dwellings, storage bins, kivas, agricultural features, fire pits, and various activity areas. Data from this work constitute much of the baseline for interpreting the Anasazi settlement in the Grand Canyon. The Unkar Chronology (q.v.)—consisting of the Medicine Valley, Vishnu, Zoraster, and Dox phases—was developed to interpret the settlement history of the locality.

SOURCE: Schwartz et al. 1980.

Janet R. Balsom

UPPER BEACHES SITE. See PORT REFUGE LOCALITY.

UPPER COLUMBIA RIVER REGION, an archaeological region in the Plateau, extending along the Columbia River from its confluence with the Okanagan River in Washington to its headwaters in British Columbia.

Frank C. Leonhardy

UPPER HAT CREEK SITES, a group of more than 200 prehistoric sites near the town of Hat Creek in southern British Columbia, located by David Pokotylo and his students between 1976 and 1982. Their study—the first major archaeological investigation of an upland area in the Canadian Plateau away from the major river valleys—showed that root-roasting ovens appeared ca. 300 B.C. and that root processing, while present in historic times, was more intense before the Kamloops Phase (q.v.), which began ca. A.D. 800.

SOURCES: Pokotylo 1978; Pokotylo and Froese 1983.

Arnoud H. Stryd

UPPER MERCER FLINT, a material used for making chipped-stone tools, quarried from a limestone member of the Pennsylvanian System that outcrops in much of the eastern third of Ohio. The names of specific quarry areas—e.g., Warsaw, Coshocton, and Nellie (a chert)—have been used in archaeological reports to identify sources.

SOURCES: Holmes 1919; Stout and Schoenlaub 1946:39–60.

N'omi B. Greber

UPPER REPUBLICAN ASPECT. See Upper Republican Phase.

UPPER REPUBLICAN PHASE, one of the phases—along with the Nebraska and Smoky Hill phases (qq.v.)—constituting the Central Plains Tradition (q.v.). Dating ca. A.D. 1000–1500, it focuses on the Republican River in southern Nebraska and northern Kansas. Small, unfortified village sites are typical, containing square earthlodges having four interior posts around the fireplace. Ceramics are sand- or gravel-tempered, globular jars with collared rims.

SOURCE: Wedel 1959.

Patricia J. O'Brien

UPPER SAN JUAN PROVINCE, an area of some 8450 square kilometers in the San Juan River drainage of northern New Mexico and southern Colorado, in which a distinctive development of the Anasazi Culture (q.v.) took place during the period ca. A.D. 1–1125. Field work has been carried out in the province since 1921 by several investigators, most notably J. A. Jeançon, F. H. H. Roberts, Jr., F. C. Hibben, E. T. Hall, Jr., R. L. Carlson, and F. W. Eddy. Their research has produced a complete chronology of Anasazi developments in the province comprising seven genetically related phases, spanning the Basketmaker and early Pueblo stages of the Pecos Classification (qq.v.). The phases are (from early to late) Los Pinos, Sambrito, Rosa, Piedra, Arboles, Largo-Gallina, and Chimney Rock (qq.v.).

At ca. A.D. 850, during the Rosa Phase, the tradition bifurcated into two diverging lines of development: (1) the Rosa-Gallina branch, reflecting settlement and population shifts away from the San Juan River toward the uplands on the south flank of the basin, and (2) the Piedra-Chimney Rock arm of the Pueblo Tradition, representing a cultural divergence by communities that drifted northward to the base of the San Juan Mountains. As a result of these movements, much of the axial center of the basin had been abandoned by ca. A.D. 1000. These settlement shifts were effected by drift migration as individual site groups relocated by "leapfrogging" other communities, both along river bottomland and in the upland. Climatic change coupled with headward entrenchment of the San Juan have been posited to account for these settlement relocations.

Evidently, the San Juan Province was completely depopulated between A.D. 1125 and 1700, then was reoccupied in the 18th century by Navajo of the Gobernador Phase (q.v.). The Athapaskan-speaking Navajo were, in turn, forced out of the province by the Southern Ute in the last quarter of the century.

SOURCES: Jeancon 1922; F. H. H. Roberts, Jr. 1925, 1929a, 1930; Hibben 1938; E. T. Hall, Jr. 1944; Bolton 1950; U.S. Geological Survey 1958; Dittert et al. 1961; R. L. Carlson 1965; Eddy 1966, 1972, 1974, 1977; E. C. Adams 1975; Truell 1975; Mackey and Holbrook 1978; Tucker 1981; Eddy and O'Sullivan 1986.

Frank W. Eddy

UPPER SAURATOWN SITE, a multicomponent complex on the Dan River in Stokes County, in North Carolina, believed to be the location of Upper Sauratown, a historically documented village of the Siouan-speaking Saura Indians. Investigations by J. L. Coe between 1972 and 1981 revealed circular houses, numerous palisade lines, features, and human burials. There are two major components: The earlier dates ca. A.D. 1550; the later, identified with the historic Saura, ca. A.D. 1680.

SOURCE: Ward 1983.

Billy L. Oliver

UUMMANNAQ (or UMANAQ) LOCALITY, a place of late Thule Phase (q.v.) development on northwestern Greenland.

SOURCE: Jordan 1984.

Moreau S. Maxwell

UVALDE PHASE, a Late Archaic manifestation in central Texas, first described briefly as the Uvalde Focus by J. C. Kelley in the 1940s; defined more fully in 1981 by E. R. Prewitt. F. A. Weir's San Marcos Phase (q.v.) comprises essentially the same congeries of traits as Prewitt's Uvalde Phase.

SOURCES: J. C. Kelley 1947a:124, 1947b; Weir 1976:134–136; Prewitt 1981:81.

Frank A. Weir

UWHARRIE POTTERY SERIES, a quartz-tempered ceramic with net-impressed, cord-marked, or scraped surface treatment, dating ca. A.D. 400–1000; a common type throughout the Piedmont region. It preceded and was transitional to the Dan River Pottery Series (q.v.).

SOURCE: Coe 1964.

Billy L. Oliver

UWHARRIE TRIANGULAR POINT, a medium-sized, narrow, isosceles-triangular projectile-point type associated with Middle and early Late

Woodland occupations, dating ca. A.D. 400–1000, in the North Carolina Piedmont.
SOURCE: Coe 1964:49.

Billy L. Oliver

UYAK SITE, a site on Uyak Bay, Kodiak Island where Alĕs Hrdlička in 1931–1936 undertook, with mining cars, the most extensive, though not the most scientific, excavation ever done at a single site in Alaska. His collections, held by the Smithsonian Institution, constitute the largest extant assemblage of Kachemak Tradition and Koniag Phase (qq.v.) artifacts. Called "Our Point" by Hrdlička and the Jones Point Site by the Smithsonian, it was named the Uyak Site by R. F. Heizer, who later analyzed Hrdlička's collections. The large human skeletal series recovered by Hrdlička continues to be utilized by physical anthropologists.
SOURCES: Hrdlička 1944; Heizer 1956.

Donald W. Clark

V

VAHKI PHASE, see Pioneer Period.

VAIL SITE, a Paleoindian (q.v.) site on the bank of Aziscohos Lake in northwestern Maine, where more than 4,000 stone tools have been collected, most of which were exposed by lake erosion. Included in the artifact inventory are fluted projectile points, scrapers, gravers, and knives. Two radiocarbon dates average around 9000 B.C.
    SOURCES: Gramley and Rutledge 1981; MacDonald 1983:99–100.

Edward B. Jelks

VALLEY FOCUS, a culture unit dating ca. A.D. 100–300 that is distributed from south-central and southeastern Nebraska to the Kansas River drainage in north-central Kansas. Identified with Valley Cord-Roughened pottery, the focus has some Hopewellian characteristics including burial in mounds, sometimes in stone-lined cists.
    SOURCES: Hill and Kivett 1940; Kivett 1949; O'Brien 1971.

Patricia J. O'Brien

VALLEY SITE, the type site for the Valley Focus (q.v.), located in Valley County, in Nebraska; excavated in 1939 by A. T. Hill.
    SOURCES: Hill and Kivett 1940; Kivett 1949; O'Brien 1971.

Patricia J. O'Brien

VANTAGE PHASE, a culture unit dating ca. 6000–2500 B.C. that followed the Windust Phase (q.v.) in the Middle Columbia River sequence. It is characterized by microblades, Cascade type projectile points (q.v.), leaf-shaped knives, and, in a late subphase (ca. 4700–2500 B.C.), Cold Springs

Side-Notched points (q.v.) as well. The Vantage and Cascade (q.v.) phases are coeval and closely comparable.
SOURCE: Galm et al. 1981.

Frank C. Leonhardy

VAUGHN SITE, a Neoeskimo (q.v.) site on Cape Parry, Northwest Territories, similar to the Jackson Site (q.v.); excavated by William E. Taylor, Jr. Wooden elements in houses suggested an eastern extension of the Alaskan Nunagliak Phase.
SOURCE: W. E. Taylor, Jr. 1972.

Moreau S. Maxwell

VENADITO BROWN WARE, a fine brown pottery from Cueva de Colmena in southern Sonora, where it appears stratigraphically earlier than Batacosa Brown and Huatabampo Brown (qq.v.). It possesses characteristics of both those types, suggesting that it may be ancestral to them. Although Venadito Brown dates prior to A.D. 200 and is the earliest known pottery type in Sonora (indeed, one of the earliest types in the entire Southwest), it is a curious fact that it is technically superior to succeeding types.
SOURCE: Pailes 1972:232–236.

Richard A. Pailes

VENTANA CAVE, a large, deeply stratified rockshelter in the Papagueria Province (q.v.), in extreme south-central Arizona, that contained evidence of human occupation spanning some 12,000 to 14,000 years. E. W. Haury's excavations in 1941–1942 disclosed a sequence beginning with a Paleoindian (q.v.) occupation ca. 12,000–10,000 B.C.; continuing with numerous Archaic (q.v.) levels dating ca. 10,000 B.C.–A.D. 1, in which materials of the Cochise and Amargosa cultures (qq.v.) were mixed; following with a Hohokam (q.v.) occupation from ca. A.D. 1 to 1450; and concluding with protohistoric and historic Papago camp deposits. Ventana Cave provided valuable information about the adaptive diversity and cultural affiliations of the Paleoindian and Archaic populations of southern Arizona and also established a continuity between the Hohokam peoples of the Papagueria and the modern Papago Indians.
SOURCES: Haury 1950; Bayham 1982.

John S. Cable and David E. Doyel

VERDE PROVINCE, an expression of the Southern Sinagua Province, Sinagua Division, Hakataya Culture (qq.v.), primarily in the middle Verde Valley, Arizona; formerly referred to as the Los Reyes Branch. Five phases (Hackberry, Cloverleaf, Camp Verde, Honanki, and Tuzigoot [qq.v.]) span the period ca. A.D. 700–1450. The Verde Province differs from the Flagstaff Province (q.v.) in early house architecture, in local plainware ceramics, and in the appearance of intrusive Hohokam (q.v.) traits and colonies between A.D. 800 and 1100. What little is known of the upper Verde Valley suggests that comparable phases there may differ in time and content from those of the middle valley.

SOURCES: Colton 1946; Schroeder 1960; Fish and Fish 1977.

Albert H. Schroeder

VERDE RIVER PROVINCE, a culture area on the extreme northern periphery of the Hohokam Culture's (q.v.) territory, comprising the drainage system of the Verde River and surrounding mountain ranges. Cosmos Mindeleff surveyed the Verde Valley in the 1880s and recorded numerous archaeological sites there. In the 1920s, Gila Pueblo extended its survey into the area, and, in the late 1950s, the Museum of Northern Arizona conducted excavations in the upper Verde Valley to refine the local culture sequence.

The pottery, pithouse styles, shellwork, stonework, and other elements of material culture from these investigations indicate a Hohokam affiliation. Ball courts are numerous in the province, especially toward the southern end, and platform mounds have been recorded. Three phases corresponding respectively to the Pioneer (ca. A.D. 1–700), Colonial (ca. A.D. 700–900), and Sedentary (ca. A.D. 900–1100) periods (qq.v.) of the Hohokam sequence have been defined.

The Verde Valley was one of the major north-south trade routes in the region, which may account for the mixture of traits found in sites there. During the Sedentary Period, cultural relations in the province became complex. By A.D. 1100, the Sinagua Culture emerged in the upper Verde Valley, while Hohokam patterns were maintained near the lower Verde-Salt river confluence.

SOURCES: Cosmos Mindeleff 1896; Gladwin and Gladwin 1930b; Colton 1939b; Breternitz 1960; Fish et al. 1980.

John S. Cable and David E. Doyel

VICTORIA BLUFF SHELL MIDDEN, a St. Catherines Culture (q.v.) site in Beaufort County, in South Carolina with a radiocarbon date of A.D. 1380 ± 75, excavated by Michael Trinkley in 1980.

SOURCE: Trinkley 1981a.

Michael Trinkley

VIEJO PERIOD. See Casas Grandes Province.

VILLAGE OF THE GREAT KIVAS, a site of the classic and late periods of the Bonito Phase (q.v.), located about 120 kilometers southwest of Chaco Canyon on the Pueblo of Zuni Indian Reservation near Gallup, New Mexico. It consists of a Chacoan great kiva (q.v.) and a two-story building of about 120 rooms, both built in the A.D. 1000s, together with other houseblocks and a second great kiva that presumably are of later date. The ruins have deteriorated badly owing to lack of stabilization efforts.

This is the best-documented southern Chacoan outlier, although F. H. H. Roberts, Jr.'s report on his work there in 1930 is mainly descriptive, with little artifact analysis. The site's potential for investigating Chaco-Zuni interaction makes it especially important.
SOURCE: F. H. H. Roberts, Jr. 1932.

Thomas C. Windes

VINCENT POTTERY SERIES, a sand-tempered ware comprising cord-marked and fabric-impressed varieties, found in Early Woodland sites in the northern Piedmont of North Carolina. Conical bowls and large straight-sided jars are the most common vessel forms.
SOURCES: Coe 1964:101–102; Ward 1983; Phelps 1983.

Billy L. Oliver

VINCENT TRIANGULAR POINT, a large, triangular projectile point with concave sides and base; affiliated with the Vincent Phase (ca. A.D. 300–400) of the Early Woodland period in the northern North Carolina Piedmont. Specimens of the type sometimes have been identified as Roanoke Large Triangular points (q.v.).
SOURCE: Coe 1964:110–111.

Billy L. Oliver

VIRGIN PROVINCE, the westernmost territory of the Western Anasazi Culture in the high, forested Colorado Plateau region of northwestern Arizona and southwestern Utah, and in the hot desert of far southwestern Utah and southern Nevada. Prior to ca. A.D. 900, architecture and pottery resembled those of the western Anasazi peoples to the east; both areas had small, scattered, pithouse communities and pottery decorated with Lino/Kina-a style designs. Two pottery wares are distinctive of the province at that period: Logandale Gray and Moapa Gray (qq.v.).

After ca. A.D. 900, communities were laid out as curves of storage rooms with attached or detached habitation rooms. Corrugated pottery was manufactured, and designs on locally made black-on-gray wares resemble Black Mesa (q.v.) and Sosi/Dogoszhi designs. Kivas are rare and late in the Colorado Plateau portion of the province and apparently are missing altogether in southern Nevada.

The phase sequence for the Virgin Province is Moapa, ca. A.D. 1–500; Muddy River, ca. A.D. 500–700; Lost City, ca. A.D. 700–1100; and Mesa

House, ca. A.D. 1100–1150 (qq.v.). Anasazi occupation of the province is thought to have ended by ca. A.D. 1150.

SOURCES: Shutler 1961; Aikens 1966.

Margaret M. Lyneis

VISHNU PHASE. See Unkar Chronology.

W

WACHESAW LANDING SITE, a site on the east bank of the Waccamaw River north of Georgetown, South Carolina, containing Mississippian (q.v.) and protohistoric components; excavated by Michael Trinkley in 1982–1983 and by J. L. Michie in 1984. It produced Pee Dee (q.v.) and Wachesaw Series pottery (the latter probably made by Waccamaw Indians in the late 17th and early 18th centuries), many features, postmolds, burials, European trade goods, and both faunal and floral remains.

SOURCES: Trinkley et al. 1983; Michie 1984.

Michael Trinkley

WADE POINT, a thin, straight-stemmed, medium-sized, chipped-stone projectile point with pronounced barbs, dated ca. 1500–400 B.C. It is associated with terminal preceramic and early ceramic cultures in the middle and lower Tennessee River Valley and in adjacent regions of Alabama, Mississippi, and Tennessee.

SOURCES: Cambron and Hulse 1964:110, 1975:122; Faulkner and McCollough 1974:149; McCollough and Faulkner 1978; P. M. Thomas Jr. 1980.

Eugene M. Futato

WAKEMAP MOUND, a deeply stratified site in the Columbia River gorge, visited by Lewis and Clark in 1805, where three controlled excavations between 1924 and 1957 revealed occupational and cultural debris in three main strata, ranging in age from ca. 500 A.D. to the early 19th century. A 30-centimeter-thick basal stratum, deposited on bedrock, contained a few nondiagnostic artifacts. Stratum 2, 4 meters thick, comprised a complex series of organic and inorganic substrata, some of which were interpreted as successive floors of rectangular wood-framed houses with mat siding built on the same location over a period of many years. Stratum 3, a layer of sand up to 1.5 meters thick, contained few artifacts but was associated with nineteen housepits.

Many artifacts, largely from Stratum 2, included chipped- and ground-stone items, objects of abraded and polished bone and antler, and implements embellished by incising, pecking, abrading, and painting in an art style related to that of the Northwest coast, but distinctive to the region and comparable in complexity and symbolism to Hopewell (q.v.) art.

SOURCES: Strong et al. 1930; W. W. Caldwell 1956; B. R. Butler 1965a.

Robert E. Greengo

WALAM OLUM, a purported Native American tribal document composed of painted symbols on bark that is alleged to have chronicled a period from creation to the coming of Europeans into the New World. C. F. Rafinesque, an early 19th-century naturalist, is said to have made copies of the original and to have translated it from the Delaware language; however, both the original (if it ever existed) and his copies have been lost. In 1931 the Indiana Historical Society initiated research to determine whether the allegorical history expressed in the Walam Olum might be confirmed by comparison with the historical insights gained from anthropological studies of the American Indian. While there remain serious questions concerning the authenticity of the Walam Olum, the research that went on for two decades in the 1930s and 1940s involved many scholars in eastern North America and had a profound impact on archaeology by reason of the financial support provided.

SOURCE: Indiana Historical Society 1954.

James H. Kellar

WALHALLA GLADES RUIN, a Western Anasazi (q.v.) site on the north rim of the Grand Canyon near Cape Royal, Arizona, comprising four large habitation rooms, five or more smaller storage rooms, and at least eight enclosures. This is the largest site of its kind thus far recorded on Walhalla Glades, an area that was used for farming between ca. A.D. 1050 and 1150. Excavation by members of the School of American Research in 1969–1970 has added greatly to knowledge of Anasazi agricultural practices at the Grand Canyon.

SOURCE: Schwartz et al. 1981.

Janet R. Balsom

WALLISVILLE (or TRINITY DELTA) SITES, a heavy concentration of shell middens on the upper reaches of Galveston Bay, Texas, where excavations by several archaeologists between 1966 and 1986 produced a highly detailed record of the technology, subsistence practices, and settlement patterns of local peoples between the late Middle Archaic period (ca. 1000 B.C.) and the mid–19th century. Results of this work, which are still emerging, constitute the foundation of contemporary archaeological research in upper coastal Texas.

SOURCES: Aten 1983:171–189, 1984; Stokes 1985.

Lawrence E. Aten

WALNUT CANYON NATIONAL MONUMENT, a locality in the Northern Sinagua Province (q.v.) near Flagstaff, Arizona, containing a series of masonry cliff dwellings built into overhangs in the canyon walls and other sites along the canyon's rims. Check dams across shallow arroyos held water and soil for crops. Several of the sites, attributed to the Elden and Turkey Hill phases (qq.v.), have been tree-ring dated to the A.D. 1100s and early 1200s. Early Flagstaff settlers removed the contents from most of the cliff dwellings, but later scientific excavations produced artifacts that now (1987) are exhibited in a museum portraying the lifeways of the canyon's prehistoric inhabitants.

SOURCE: Colton 1932b.

Albert H. Schroeder

WALNUT GROVE SHELL MIDDEN, a two-component site on Awendaw Creek in Charleston County, in South Carolina; excavated by Michael Trinkley in 1981. The McClellanville pottery series was based on a sample from the major component, which dated to the Middle Woodland period. Below that was an Early Woodland component with no shell.

SOURCE: Trinkley 1981c.

Michael Trinkley

WALPI SITES, four prehistoric and historic Hopi villages at First Mesa, in northeastern Arizona. The first site (Walpi I), atop the mesa at its south tip, dates ca. A.D. 1250–1350. Walpi II was established on the lower terrace to the west by Bear Clan people ca. A.D. 1400 and was occupied first by them, and later by people of the Snake Clan, until ca. 1680. Spaniards built a chapel or visita on the lower terrace near the south tip of the mesa ca. 1620, around which a new community, Walpi III, grew. Following destruction of local churches and visitas and the murder of Spanish priests during the Pueblo Revolt, the inhabitants of Walpi II and III abandoned their homes ca. 1680 and jointly founded Walpi IV at the original site of Walpi I. This survives as the modern pueblo.

Historic Walpi IV, the "Mother Village" of First Mesa, was built in three parallel rows of about 500 stone houses rising from two to four stories high, with six rectangular, semisubterranean, stone-built kivas located in two plaza areas near the east cliff edge. Population in the 1700s and 1800s may have been from 800 to 1000, but, by the mid–20th century, there had been a decline to 150 houses and only from 60 to 80 people.

Victor Mindeleff mapped Walpi in 1891; L. L. Hargrave surveyed it in 1930–1931; and E. C. Adams conducted excavations there between 1975 and 1977.
SOURCES: Victor Mindeleff 1891; Hargrave 1931; Ellis 1961; E. C. Adams 1979, 1982.

Michael B. Stanislawski

WAREKECK WARE, a shell-tempered, plain ceramic defined by L. R. Binford in 1965 and attributed to the Weanock Indians who lived along the Nottoway River in southeastern Virginia in the mid–17th century.
SOURCES: Binford 1965; Egloff and Potter 1982.

Keith T. Egloff

WARE PLAIN, an Early Woodland pottery of the lower Delaware River Valley, dating ca. 500 B.C., which shows influence from and/or continuity with the steatite-tempered wares that preceded it in the area. Like vessels of the earlier Marcey Creek Ware (q.v.), Ware Plain vessels have flat bottoms and smoothed exterior and interior surfaces. They are, however, tempered with large fragments of crushed stone and have slab bottoms and coiled sides. Ware Plain was defined by Catherine McCann on the basis of her excavations at the Ware Site in New Jersey.
SOURCE: McCann 1950.

Ronald A. Thomas

WARNER VALLEY LOCALITY, a place in south-central Oregon a few miles north of the California-Oregon boundary where, in the middle 1960s, M. L. Weide conducted a wide-ranging archaeological survey in the valley and adjacent uplands. She defined a lacustrine-oriented subsistence network in this unusually well-watered Great Basin setting, which contained a series of lakes fed by springs and runoff from adjacent higher elevations. This prehistoric hunter-gatherer band territory—as it was conceived—centered on several large midden sites, apparently villages, in waterside locations on the valley floor. Outlying exploitative camps also were recognized in an area of dunes and sloughs at the north end of the valley and around small, shallow, ephemeral lakes on the nearby Hart Mountain upland. The system as defined existed between ca. 2500 B.C. and A.D. 1500. Although historically the area was northern Paiute territory, it has been suggested that in earlier times it may have been occupied by the Klamath, who during the ethnographic period maintained their characteristic lake-marsh adaptation in the Sycan Marsh/Klamath Lakes region west of Warner Valley.
SOURCES: Weide 1968, 1974.

C. Melvin Aikens

WARREN WILSON SITE, a multicomponent, stratified site on the Swannanoa River in Buncombe County, in North Carolina; occupied from the Middle Archaic period (ca. 5000 B.C.) through the Mississippian period (to ca. A.D. 1550). A Pisgah Phase (q.v.) village of ca. A.D. 1450 has been the major research focus. Excavations at the site from 1966 to 1982 by J. L. Coe and from 1983 to 1986 by R. S. Dickens, Jr., have produced abundant information about the Pisgah, Savannah River (q.v.), and other represented phases.

SOURCES: Dickens 1976; Keel 1976.

Billy L. Oliver

WASHINGTON PASS CHERT, a pink to orangish, opaline stone that outcrops in the Chuska Mountains' Washington Pass in northwestern New Mexico. This high-quality material was imported into Chaco Canyon, some 110 kilometers to the east, during the Bonito Phase (q.v.), where it evidently was the favored material for flaked-tool production, especially at great-houses. Patterns of lithic use and distribution suggest that Washington Pass chert was disseminated in Chaco Canyon through periodic population aggregation.

SOURCE: Cameron 1984.

Peter J. McKenna

WASHINGTON SQUARE MOUND SITE, a Caddo II (ca. A.D. 1250–1350) mound complex in the city of Nacogdoches, Texas, which, before extensive damage by modern construction activities, appears to have consisted of a mortuary mound and two structural mounds surrounding a plaza. Excavations in the mortuary mound (the only one intact enough for thorough study) by J. E. Corbin in 1979–1980 revealed the presence of numerous deep-shaft pits for both single and multiple human burials. There was an average of about fifteen ceramic vessels per individual in the two burials that were dug. Ceramic styles indicate an intermediate position between the George C. Davis Site (q.v.) and later Caddoan (q.v.) complexes of the area; ties to northeastern Texas and adjacent sections of Arkansas and Louisiana also are apparent. Artifact concentrations suggest localized special-activity areas within the plaza.

SOURCE: Corbin n.d.

James E. Corbin

WASHITA RIVER FOCUS, a complex in the Washita River drainage of central Oklahoma, dating ca. A.D. 1100–1400, that was ancestral to and/ or contemporaneous with the cultural traditions that gave rise to the historic Wichita Indians.

SOURCE: Bell 1973.

Patricia J. O'Brien

WAUBESA CONTRACTING-STEMMED POINT, the Wisconsin analog of the Adena (q.v.) type projectile point. The type spans Early and Middle Woodland times (ca. 300 B.C.-A.D. 100).

SOURCE: Ritzenthaler 1967.

David Overstreet

WAUKESHA FOCUS, a unit encompassing the Hopewell (q.v.) manifestations in southeastern Wisconsin, dating ca. A.D. 200. The Cutler mound group in Waukesha County is the type site. Waukesha differs from other Havana-related Middle Woodland complexes in Wisconsin in that exotic items are often found in the village debris rather than in mortuary contexts. This has been interpreted as a deemphasis of the high status accorded a few privileged individuals in other Middle Woodland groups.
SOURCE: Salzer n.d.a.

David Overstreet

WAYNE MORTUARY COMPLEX, a burial pattern in Michigan's lower peninsula dating ca. A.D. 700–1000. Wayne Tradition (q.v.) pottery, projectile points, chert blanks, cache blades, antler harpoons and handles, copper awls, celts, drills, disc-shaped slate or chert scrapers, pipes, and beads of both shell and copper appear regularly as grave goods, but there is a high degree of variability in the kinds and quantities of goods with particular burials. Flexed or bundled skeletons, sometimes in mounds, occur both as group and as isolated interments.
SOURCES: Halsey 1976, 1981.

Margaret B. Holman

WAYNE TRADITION, an early Late Woodland ceramic tradition of southeastern lower Michigan and the Saginaw Valley, with strong similarities to coeval wares in southern lower Michigan, thus indicating fluid stylistic boundaries. Dates of the tradition are controversial, but a reasonable estimate places its beginning at ca. A.D. 600, its termination in southeastern Michigan at ca. A.D. 900, and its termination in the Saginaw region at ca. A.D. 1200.
SOURCES: Fitting 1965; Brashler 1973, 1981; Halsey 1976.

Margaret B. Holman

WEAVER SITE, a multicomponent village and mortuary site near the mouth of Duck Creek in the central Illinois River Valley, occupied throughout much of prehistory. Best known for its terminal Middle Woodland occupation, it is the type site for the Weaver Tradition (or Focus) and for Weaver Ware ceramics. It was partially excavated by the Wray family between 1933 and 1958, and it was tested by R. S. MacNeish in 1944 and 1945. Domestic features pertaining to Weaver and early Mississippian (q.v.) occupations

have been excavated, along with burial mounds associated with Mississippian and Middle Woodland residents.
SOURCE: Wray and MacNeish 1961.

Alan D. Harn

WEBB PHASE, a Middle Woodland expression dating ca. A.D. 600–1000, defined from grave furnishings (which were primarily utilitarian) at the Island Field Site (q.v.) on the west shore of Delaware Bay.
SOURCES: Thomas and Warren 1970:1–32; Custer 1984:136–143.

Ronald A. Thomas

WEBER I SITE, a stratified site on the Cass River in Saginaw County, in Michigan, dug by William Lovis in 1982. The first occupation, probably an autumn hunting and collecting camp dating ca. 4200–2300 B.C., is the only Middle Archaic component excavated to date in Michigan. In a later, disturbed component of the early Late Woodland, Wayne Tradition (q.v.)—likewise an autumn camp—nuts were found. Geological assessment of the Weber I site agrees with artifact and radiocarbon indications of age. Thus, shortly after the Middle Archaic occupation, the site was inundated by Lake Nipissing's maximum high-water stage; it was reoccupied after the water had receded.
SOURCE: Lovis n.d.

Margaret B. Holman

WEEDEN ISLAND CULTURE, a post-Middle Woodland, pre-Mississippian (qq.v.) culture that occupied much of northern Florida, southwestern Georgia, and southeastern Alabama ca. A.D. 200–1000. Their pottery, which includes animal and human effigies from mounds, is among the finest prehistoric pottery of the eastern United States.
SOURCES: Willey 1945, 1949a:396–452, 510–512; Sears 1956; Milanich 1980; Milanich and Fairbanks 1980:89–143; A. S. Cordell 1984; Milanich et al. 1984.

Jerald T. Milanich

WEIR PHASE. See Brooks River-Naknek Drainage Sites.

WEIS ROCKSHELTER, a site in a small canyon tributary to the lower Salmon River in Nez Perce National Historical Park, in Idaho. Excavations there in 1961–1962 by B. R. Butler provided much of the data critical to his concept of the Old Cordilleran Culture (q.v.).
SOURCE: B. R. Butler 1962.

Frank C. Leonhardy

WELLINGTON BAY SITE, one of the Pre-Dorset (q.v.) sites along the Ekalluk River on Victoria Island, Northwest Territories; excavated by W. E. Taylor, Jr., in the 1960s. This middle to late Pre-Dorset (ca. 1200 B.C.)

expression had a more inland orientation (e.g., caribou hunting) than is found at coastal sites of the region.
SOURCE: W. E. Taylor, Jr. 1967.

                                                                             Moreau S. Maxwell

WEST ATHENS HILL SITE, a quarry-workshop-habitation station, the largest known Paleoindian (q.v.) site in New York, located in Greene County. R. E. Funk excavated there in 1966 and found more than 1400 artifacts attributed to the Clovis Culture (q.v.), including fluted projectile points, knives, and scrapers.
SOURCES: Funk 1973; Ritchie 1980:xv-xvi.

                                                                             Edward B. Jelks

WEST BERKELEY SITE, a very large shell midden on the eastern edge of San Francisco Bay, California; first excavated in 1902 by archaeologists from the University of California, Berkeley. Later excavators argued that the materials recovered from the site provided the first clear evidence of an Early Horizon (q.v.) occupation in the San Francisco Bay region, dating as early as 2000–1500 B.C.
SOURCE: Moratto 1984:258–261.

                                                                             Michael J. Moratto

WESTERN BASIN TRADITION, a proposed sequence of cultural development for the Maumee Valley of northwestern Ohio spanning the period from ca. 1000 B.C. to A.D. 1400.
SOURCES: Stothers 1975; Stothers et al. 1979.

                                                                             N'omi B. Greber

WESTERN PLUVIAL LAKES TRADITION, a culture unit defined by S. F. Bedwell, who perceived it as an early postglacial culture that left distinctive artifacts along the shorelines of extinct Pleistocene lakes throughout the western Great Basin, from central Oregon to southern California. The principal diagnostic markers of this tradition are large, stemmed, lanceolate projectile points, variously termed Windust (q.v.), Parman, Haskett (q.v.), Great Basin Stemmed, Lake Mohave (q.v.), and Silver Lake, according to the localities in which they are found. Large, leaf-shaped bipoints also are characteristic. It was originally presumed that the tradition reflected an early adaptation to lakeshore environments as they existed in the Great Basin in final Pleistocene/initial Holocene times, but, in fact, the representative point types occur over a much broader area than the western Great Basin, including California, the Columbia Plateau, the Snake River Plain, and British Columbia, where pluvial lakes were not characteristic of the natural setting. It now appears that these projectile-point types immediately followed in time and were perhaps derivative from the large, lanceolate points of the

Paleoindian Clovis Culture (q.v.) of ca. 10,000–9,000 B.C. They clearly are associated with a way of life much broader or more varied than the lacustrine pattern originally envisaged, but the nature of this lifeway remains to be fully defined.

SOURCE: Bedwell 1973.

C. Melvin Aikens

WESTERN PUEBLO, a concept developed by E. K. Reed to describe late prehistoric trends in the western Mogollon (q.v.) area of eastern Arizona and western New Mexico. It recognizes a synthetic culture that incorporated both Mogollon and Anasazi (q.v.) traits and traditions and that cannot be explained solely as an outgrowth of earlier Mogollon patterns.

SOURCES: Reed 1948; A. E. Johnson 1965.

David A. Phillips, Jr.

WEST JEFFERSON CULTURE, an Emergent Mississippian (ca. A.D. 850–1000) expression in the upper Black Warrior River drainage of north-central Alabama; defined by N. J. Jenkins in 1974. It was the first culture of the region to develop an effective horticultural system based on maize. The Bessemer Site 2 (q.v.) was their major ceremonial center.

SOURCE: Jenkins and Nielson 1974.

John A. Walthall

WEST RIVER SITE, an Adena (q.v.) cremation and burial site on Maryland's western shore of Chesapeake Bay. Excavations there by T. L. Ford, Jr., in 1954–1955 produced diagnostic Adena artifacts, including blocked-end tubular pipes, hematite pyramids, copper beads, gorgets of Ohio shales, and large stemmed blades and points of flint from Harrison County, Indiana, and Flint Ridge, Ohio.

SOURCES: Dragoo 1963:283; T. L. Ford, Jr. 1976:63–76.

Stephen R. Potter

WET LEGGETT PUEBLO, a six-room Mogollon Culture (q.v.) surface dwelling in the Cibola Province (q.v.) near Reserve, New Mexico; excavated by P. S. Martin and J. B. Rinaldo in 1949. Constructed of boulder masonry, it documents the adoption of surface architecture in the province ca. A.D. 1000 after centuries of pithouse construction. Related sites showing much experimentation with the new building method contain Mogollon brownware culinary pottery and Reserve Black-on-white ware, both characteristic of the Reserve Phase (A.D. 1000–1075/1100). The masonry construction and black-on-white pottery are seen as evidence of strong ties to the Anasazi Culture (q.v.) to the north. This is supported by a clear cultural differentiation at this time between the Cibola Province and the Mimbres Province to the south.

SOURCES: Martin and Rinaldo 1950b; Bluhm 1957; Peckham 1958.

Stewart Peckham

WHEELER CULTURE, the first culture in the middle South to make pottery; resident in the western Tennessee River Valley ca. 1200–600 B.C. The relatively crude, fiber-tempered earthenware was shaped by working a slab of clay into shallow bowl and jar forms. Wheeler components occur frequently in upper levels of the great shell middens along the Tennessee River.

SOURCE: Jenkins 1975.

John A. Walthall

WHELAN PHASE (or COMPLEX), a Late Caddo (A.D. 1500–1600) culture unit, possibly ancestral to the Titus Phase (q.v.), centered on the middle reaches of Big Cypress Creek in northeastern Texas. The phase was defined on the basis of E. M. Davis' excavation, in 1958, of four small mound sites, each of which had been heaped over the burned remains of two or more circular, nondomestic structures.

SOURCES: E. M. Davis 1970:47–48, n.d.; Wyckoff 1971; Thurmond 1981.

James E. Corbin

WHITE DOG PHASE, an expression of the Basketmaker (q.v.) II tradition at Marsh Pass in the Cedar Mesa Province (q.v.) of southeastern Utah. The phase's material culture resembles that of the Grand Gulch Phase of the western part of the same province, but it contrasts strongly with the Basketmaker II material found near Durango, Colorado, and with the Los Pinos Phase (q.v.) material found in northeastern New Mexico.

SOURCES: Colton 1939a; Morris and Burgh 1954; Eddy 1961; Lipe 1970; Matson and Lipe 1978.

R. G. Matson

WHITEFORD SITE (also known as the PRICE SITE), a late prehistoric (ca. A.D. 1300) cemetery complex in the Smoky Hill River Valley of east-central Kansas, excavated in 1937 by G. L. Whiteford, an amateur archaeologist, who exposed the skeletons of 146 individuals and left them in place as a commercial educational exhibit called the Indian Burial Pit. The burials are interpreted as belonging to the Smoky Hill Phase (q.v.) of the Central Plains Tradition (q.v.). The site has been designated a National Historic Landmark.

SOURCES: Whiteford 1941; Wedel 1959.

Thomas A. Witty, Jr.

WHITE HOUSE RUIN (LOWER), the westernmost Chacoan outlier, located 130 kilometers west of Chaco Canyon near Chinle in Canyon de Chelly, Arizona. It was investigated by E. H. Morris in 1926. Ascribed to the Bonito and Mesa Verde phases (qq.v.), the ruin is composed of about 60 multistory rooms and a Chaco-style kiva which were built ca. A.D. 1070 on the banks of a wash which has washed away part of the site. Mesa Verdeans and Navajo occupied the site in later times. White House is unusual in the Chinle-de Chelly Province for its large rooms, Chacoan-style masonry, and use of ponderosa pine for roofing timbers. The site's importance lies in its potential for explicating interactions between the Chacoan, Kayentan, and Mesa Verdean cultures.

SOURCE: Cosmos Mindeleff 1897.

Thomas C. Windes

WHITE MOUND PHASE, an expression of the Eastern Anasazi, early Pueblo Period I (ca. A.D. 700–800) in the Chaco Province (q.v.) of northwestern New Mexico. Sites of this period share many similarities throughout the Anasazi region and are characterized by a gradual shift from subsurface to surface dwellings. Subsistence was based on horticulture, hunting, and gathering, probably with seasonal occupation of some sites.

A typical site has a large, deep pithouse in front of a group of contiguous residential suites arranged in an arc, each suite comprising a large living room backed by two storage rooms. The pithouses, each of which apparently housed from one to three families, were still four-primary-post models with a central firepit, numerous storage pits, a large ventilator, and wing walls separating the floor into two primary use areas. There often was a work area sheltered with a ramada between the residential units and the pithouse. Trash was deposited to the east or southeast of the pithouse.

The surface rooms, made of mud supported by posts and upright stone slabs at the wall bases, often were not fully enclosed, which suggests that they were for seasonal, warm-weather use. Storage rooms ranged from small, bathtub-shaped units to large, rectangular ones. No great kivas have been reported at White Mound Phase sites in the Chaco Province.

Ceramics of the phase are mainly carryovers from the Basketmaker (q.v.) period: predominantly Lino Gray and La Plata Black-on-white, with White Mound Black-on-white becoming important. Kana'a Gray pottery is not present in Chaco Canyon sites, or it occurs in sparse amounts, despite its prevalence as a type marker for the Pueblo I Period elsewhere in the Anasazi region. Early San Juan Redwares occur rarely on Chacoan sites.

SOURCES: Gladwin 1945; McKenna and Truell 1986.

Thomas C. Windes

WHITE MOUND VILLAGE, the type site for the White Mound Phase of the Anasazi Culture (qq.v.) located in northwestern New Mexico and dating ca. A.D. 700–800. Excavations there in 1936 by H. S. Gladwin established the phase as a distinct period of Anasazi development in the Chaco Province (q.v.), dating between the earlier Basketmaker pithouse villages of the La

Plata Phase (q.v.) and the later Anasazi pueblos with their greater development of surface architecture, formalization of kivas, and sophistication in material culture.

White Mound Village consisted of three crescentic houseblocks of eight, seven, and ten rooms, respectively, plus six pithouses and several intramural hearths and storage pits. The pithouses, now more consistently oriented toward the south than previously, continued to have a divided floor plan with a storage area south of the central firepit. Also, a true ventilator system had replaced the large antechamber entry of the preceding La Plata Phase.

The houses were constructed of upright-slab and horizontal masonry. Their rooms frequently were semisubterranean, of "bath-tub" shape, and generally devoid of floor features. Domestic hearths and storage pits were located under ramadas between the houseblocks and pithouses. Ceramics, featuring nested chevron lines, were still in the black-on-white Lino tradition, but their decorations were more complex than those of earlier types.
SOURCE: Gladwin 1945.

Peter J. McKenna

WHITE OAK POINT SITE, a deeply stratified shell midden on the lower Potomac River, Virginia, where extensive excavations by G. A. Waselkov in 1978 revealed 26 separate components dating from Late Archaic (ca. 2000 B.C.) to ca. A.D. 1700. The site provided detailed information on shell midden formation, subsistence practices, and culture chronology.
SOURCES: Waselkov 1982, 1985.

Stephen R. Potter

WHITE OAK POTTERY SERIES, a shell-tempered ware with cordmarked, fabric-impressed, smoothed, simple-stamped, or net-impressed surfaces, distributed over the central and southern Tidewater region of North Carolina. Some archaeologists subsume the type, which dates ca. A.D. 800–1650, within the Oak Island Series (q.v.); others view the White Oak, Oak Island, and Colington (q.v.) series as distinctive regional variations of the shell-tempering tradition.
SOURCES: Loftfield 1976:157–163; Phelps 1983.

Billy L. Oliver

WHITE ROCK ASPECT, a complex in north-central Kansas, thought to date ca. A.D. 1500–1600, that comprises two foci: Glen Elder (q.v.) and Blue Stone. Its diagnostic pottery is the Walnut Decorated Lip type, which has affinities with Oneota Tradition (q.v.) pottery.
SOURCE: Rusco 1960.

Patricia J. O'Brien

WHITTLESEY TRADITION, a culture unit in northeastern Ohio, dating ca. A.D. 1000–1650 and characterized by large village sites (e.g., South Park and Tuttle Hill)—typically located upon isolated, high bluffs and cut off by embankment walls—containing much habitation debris and some burials. Small, probably special-purpose sites also are known. Subsistence included maize-squash-bean agriculture, fishing, hunting, and the use of wild trees and plants. Diagnostic ceramics include Tuttle Hill Notched, Reeve Opposed, Fairport Harbor Filleted, and Parker Festooned.

SOURCES: Whittlesey 1851, 1871; Greenman 1937b; Morgan and Ellis 1943; Morgan 1952:96–97, fig 36; Fitting 1964; Brose 1976.

N'omi B. Greber

WILDCAT CANYON SITE, a very complex, multicomponent site on the Middle Columbia River 34 miles east of The Dalles, Oregon, excavated by D. L. Cole between 1959 and 1968. Later, Rick Minor and D. E. Dumond defined four phases based on Cole's field work: Phillipi, a homolog of the Windust Phase (q.v.), older than 6000 B.C.; Canyon, ca. 4500–3000 B.C.; Wildcat, ca. 500 B.C.–A.D. 1100; and Quinton, ca. A.D. 1100–1800, probably the archaeological expression of the prehistoric Tenino.

SOURCE: Dumond and Minor 1983.

Frank C. Leonhardy

WILD CHERRY SITE, a probable Connestee Phase (q.v.) village site dating ca. A.D. 800, now under Kcowee Reservoir in Pickens County, in South Carolina. Excavations there by Bernard Golden in 1967 revealed a number of features, including one containing over 56 kilograms of charred acorns and other organic material.

SOURCE: Beuschel n.d.

Michael Trinkley

WILLIAMSON SITE (1), the largest known Paleoindian site in Virginia, located near the fall line in the southern part of the state. Extending for about a mile along both sides of Cattail Creek, this was a heavily utilized quarry and base camp. B. C. McCary, who first reported it in 1951, tested it in 1965 and in 1972, finding an intact Paleoindian horizon 0.8 to 1.0 feet thick. From the site's surface came thousands of Paleoindian artifacts, all made from the local Cattail Creek chert: numerous fluted points, end and side scrapers, preforms, cores, wedges, drills, reamers, bifacial knives, spokeshaves, gravers, perforators, denticulates, and beaked tools.

SOURCES: McCary 1951, 1978, 1983; Benthall and McCary 1973; McCary and Bittner 1978.

Keith T. Egloff

WILLIAMSON SITE (2), a stratified, multicomponent site on Eagle Creek, a tributary of the Neosho River, in the western Osage Plains of east-central Kansas; excavated by T. A. Witty, Jr., in 1963. The two upper components contained lithic artifacts, respectively, of the Middle and Early Ceramic

periods. The lower and major component was a campsite of the Late Archaic, El Dorado Phase (q.v.), radiocarbon dated to ca. 3600 B.C., where
two adult, female, human burials were found along with the partial skeleton
of a small dog. The Table Rock and Lamokan projectile-point types pre-
dominated in the El Dorado component.
SOURCE: Schmits 1980a.

Thomas A. Witty, Jr.

WILLIAM YOUNG SITE, a large, stratified, multicomponent site on the
upper Neosho River drainage in the Flint Hills of eastern Kansas; excavated
in 1962 and 1964 by T. A. Witty, Jr. Zone I, the upper component, contained
Euroamerican, Plains Woodland, and possibly Late Archaic materials. Zone
II yielded projectile points of the Late Archaic, El Dorado Phase (q.v.). The
deepest component, Zone III, with a radiocarbon date of 3390 B.C. ±160
years, consisted of a series of Middle Archaic habitation levels associated
with abundant residue of lithic procurement and reduction. Zone III is the
type component of the Munkers Creek Phase (q.v.).
SOURCE: Witty 1982.

Thomas A. Witty, Jr.

WILLOW BEACH PHASE, the phase of the Amacava Province of the Laquish Division, Hakataya Culture (qq.v.) that followed the Roaring Rapids
Phase (q.v.) in northwestern Arizona. It is represented by the upper level of
the stratified Willow Beach Site (q.v.) about 24 kilometers below Hoover
Dam on the Arizona bank of the Colorado River. Pyramid Gray, a common
type in the Mohave Desert of southern California, dominated the pottery
inventory at Willow Beach, indicating relationships to the west. Asphaltum
and steatite from southern California also were present, as was pottery type
Cerbat Brown of the Cerbat Province (q.v.).
SOURCE: Schroeder 1961b.

Albert H. Schroeder

WILLOW BEACH SITE, a stratified campsite of the Hakataya Culture (q.v.)
on the Arizona bank of the Colorado River about 24 kilometers below
Hoover Dam. Excavated by A. H. Schroeder in 1950, it contained preceramic and ceramic levels spanning the period ca. 250 B.C.–A.D. 1150. The
Basketmaker II and Amargosa II periods (qq.v.) of southern California were
represented in the earliest preceramic levels; California elements became
more common in the uppermost preceramic level.
    There were two ceramic levels, both of which contained some Anasazi
(q.v.) intrusives. The lower level was dominated by Cerbat Brown pottery
of the Cerbat Province (q.v.); the upper was dominated by Pyramid Gray
of the Amacava Province. Also in the upper level were Paiute ceramics and

arrow points, an association similar to that at Pine Park Shelter, an Anasazi site in southwestern Utah where Hakataya ceramics occurred as intrusives.

Willow Beach provided the primary stratigraphic evidence of prehistoric cultural developments in the region. It also demonstrated links between cultures of northern Arizona and California which probably developed through abalone-shell trade from the West Coast to Anasazi peoples prior to A.D. 500, and that continued later (ca. A.D. 700?) while the Anasazi were mining turquoise in southern Arizona.

SOURCE: Schroeder 1961b.

Albert H. Schroeder

WILLOW CREEK SITE, a stratified coastal midden in southern Monterey County on the central California coast; occupied from ca. A.D. 100 until historic contact. Investigated by R. F. Heizer in 1951 and by R. K. Beardsley in 1952, the midden was found to consist of two vertically and horizontally stratified components whose respective cultural materials contrasted both in style and in relative frequency. It has been suggested that the site was situated astride a prehistoric political boundary and was occupied alternately by two adjacent tribal groups.

SOURCE: Pohorecky 1976.

Michael J. Moratto

WILMINGTON (or HANOVER) WARE, a Middle Woodland ceramic estimated to date ca. A.D. 500–1000, found on the coastal plain of Georgia, South Carolina, and southern North Carolina. Possibly developed from ware of the preceding Deptford Culture (q.v.), it may eventually have given rise to the pottery of the St. Catherines Culture (q.v.). Wilmington is tempered with large quantities of crushed sherds; surfaces are heavily cordmarked, plain, brushed, or (on the northern coast) fabric impressed. A related ware, Walthour, was defined by Works Progress Administration investigators on the Georgia coast.

SOURCES: Caldwell and Waring 1939; South 1960; DePratter 1979.

Michael Trinkley

WILSON MOUNDS, a group of at least eleven Middle Woodland burial mounds on Dogtown Hills, an erosional remnant adjacent to the Wabash River in White County, in Illinois. In 1950, several mounds were investigated by a field party jointly sponsored by the Illinois State Museum, the University of Chicago, and Southern Illinois University. They found mortuary remains that were quite varied, ranging from central log-tomb complexes to less formally organized cemeteries. These mounds, along with the nearby Hue-

bele Village Site, formed the basis for what came to be known as Wabash Valley Hopewellian.
SOURCE: Neumann and Fowler 1952.

Brian M. Butler

WINDGATE PHASE, a phase of the late Pueblo II period (ca. A.D. 1070–1110) on Cedar Mesa in the center of the Cedar Mesa Province (q.v.) of southeastern Utah; the local equivalent of the Mancos Phase of the Mesa Verde Province (q.v.). Characterized by small sites scattered in highland, deep-soil locations, the Mesa Verde Tradition, Windgate Phase was the first occupation on the mesa after a hiatus that began ca. A.D. 750.
SOURCE: Matson and Lipe 1978.

R. G. Matson

WINDMILLER PATTERN, previously termed the "Early Horizon" (q.v.) (ca. 2500–500 B.C., a socioeconomic adaptation in the Delta locality of central California that is marked by intensive use of riverine and marsh resources, well-developed flaked- and ground-stone industries, extensive trade, and a mortuary complex with ventrally extended burials and distinctive shell and stone artifacts. The Windmiller Site, in Sacramento County, is the type site.
SOURCES: Ragir 1972; Fredrickson 1973.

Michael J. Moratto

WINDUST CAVES, a group of nine caves on the Snake River near Pasco, Washington. Excavations at Cave C by H. S. Rice between 1957 and 1961 established that, in the Southern Plateau, assemblages dominated by stemmed projectile points were stratigraphically earlier than assemblages dominated by Cascade points (q.v.). The stemmed-point assemblages date ca. 8800–6000 B.C.
SOURCE: H. S. Rice 1965.

Frank C. Leonhardy

WINDUST PHASE, a phase dating ca. 8800–6000 B.C. that is represented throughout the southeastern Plateau region and is coeval with the Phillipi Phase of the southwestern Plateau. Windust components are characterized by a variety of stemmed projectile points, atlatl spurs, atlatl weights, burins, and many other kinds of implements. Cascade points (q.v.) occur in small numbers. Early human skeletal material from Marmes Rockshelter (q.v.) is referable to the Windust Phase.
SOURCES: D. G. Rice 1972; Galm et al. 1981.

Frank C. Leonhardy

WINDUST POINT, a type of stemmed projectile point dating between ca. 8800 and ca. 7000 or 6000 B.C., found throughout the Southern Plateau and Northern Great Basin; characteristic of the Windust (q.v.) and Phillipi phases. It has a convex blade, shoulders of varying prominence, and a slightly expanding to contracting stem with a straight or concave base. Basal grinding is a hallmark. The type was first recognized in an early stratigraphic context at Windust Caves (q.v.). The informally named Lind Coulee Point (q.v.) is a variety of the type.

SOURCES: H. S. Rice 1965; D. G. Rice 1972.

Frank C. Leonhardy

WINDY RIDGE SITE, a multicomponent Archaic and Woodland (qq.v.) extractive site delineated by a surface lithic scatter on a piedmont ridge near Winnsboro, South Carolina. In 1977, J. H. House and R. W. Wogaman excavated the site using a spatially dispersed sampling design. This is perhaps the only site of this type to have been so thoroughly excavated.

SOURCES: House and Wogaman 1978; Ward 1980.

Michael Trinkley

WINGINA SITE, a multicomponent site on the James River in the western Piedmont of central Virginia, occupied intermittently during the Late Archaic and more intensively during the Middle and Late Woodland periods. Gerard Fowke first identified the site in the late 19th century; in 1950, C. G. Holland reported on a surface collection made there; in 1955, Clifford Evans analyzed the surficial sherds in his study of Virginia ceramics; in 1971, H. A. MacCord tested the site and reported hearths, refuse-filled pits, house patterns, and a foot-thick midden.

SOURCES: Holland 1950; Clifford Evans 1955; MacCord 1974a.

Keith T. Egloff

WINONA FOCUS, a culture unit centered in the Winona, Arizona, area east of Flagstaff, dating ca. A.D. 1070–1100. Hallmark traits are Hohokam (q.v.) style pithouses, ball courts, trash mounds, primary and secondary cremation burials, human clay figurines, shell ornaments, projectile points, and locally made Hohokam-style pottery, including some with red-on-buff painted designs. The focus originally was viewed as representing a migration of approximately 1000 Hohokam people from the Verde Valley to the Flagstaff area to take advantage of farmlands created by the initial eruptions of Sunset Crater (q.v.) in A.D. 1064–1066. Interaction between these Hohokam (and other) immigrants and Sinaguan peoples was thought to have created a new cultural pattern that characterized the Flagstaff, Verde Valley, and Phoenix areas after A.D. 1120.

Reanalysis, however, has noted that the Hohokam-like items are rare, generally isolated occurrences that do not constitute a complete Hohokam assemblage. Many of the items have local antecedents and lasted well past A.D. 1100. Thus, according to this interpretation, the presence of Hohokam-like traits in this Sinaguan culture area can best be explained as a local development resulting from increased Sinaguan participation in regional exchange systems, with possibly some Hohokam trading outposts in the area.

SOURCES: McGregor 1937a, 1937b, 1937c, 1941a; Colton 1939b:48, 1946:270, 312–314; Schroeder 1949, 1961c, 1975, 1977; Rouse 1958; Pilles 1979; Fish et al. 1980.

Peter J. Pilles, Jr.

WINONA VILLAGE, a cluster of eight sites spread over a 65-hectare area east of Flagstaff, Arizona, where J. C. McGregor and M. A. Wetherill, between 1935 and 1939, excavated 30 structures, six trash mounds, a ball court, 45 cremated burials, and 22 inhumed burials. R. E. Kelly excavated further there in 1964. Their work was a major source of the data used in defining the phase system of the Northern Sinagua Tradition (q.v.). Two of the sites in the group are type sites: NA2133A for the Winona Focus (q.v.) and NA2135C for the Angell Phase (q.v.). Stratigraphic analysis of pottery from the trash mounds established a plainware sequence for the Sinagua and aided in determining the temporal relationships of several intrusive black-on-white pottery types.

Each site consists of four or more pithouses along the edges of "trash" mounds which, since they contained burials, may actually have been intentionally constructed as burial mounds. A major integrating feature for the sites is a Casa Grande (q.v.) style ball court, one of only fourteen in the entire Flagstaff Province (q.v.).

Winona Village is considered one of the earliest examples of the highly stylized and patterned central places that are better known from the later Elden Phase (q.v.). Such villages are thought to have been key components of regional exchange and interaction systems. Winona Village is listed in the National Register of Historic Places and has been designated a National Historic Landmark.

SOURCES: McGregor 1937a, 1937b, 1937c, 1941a; Bartlett 1941; R. E. Kelly 1969; Fish et al. 1980.

Peter J. Pilles, Jr.

WINSLOW BRANCH, a regional division of the Anasazi Culture (q.v.) in Arizona, located along the central Little Colorado River from the vicinity of Holbrook on the east to Leupp on the west. As originally defined by H. S. Colton, it was characterized by Little Colorado White Ware, Little Colorado Gray Ware, Winslow Orange Ware, and Homolovi Orange Ware pottery (qq.v.); extended burials; and early pithouse architecture followed by masonry pueblos with enclosed plazas and kivas. Other material culture showed a blend of Anasazi and Mogollon (q.v.) traits.

The Winslow Branch included four foci: Holbrook, ca. A.D. 900–1100; McDonald, ca. A.D. 1100–1200; Tuwiuca, ca. A.D. 1200–1300; and Homolovi, ca. A.D. 1300–1400 (qq.v.). Subsequent modification by Colton and G. J. Gumerman added the Hopi Buttes area to the Winslow Branch and modified the sequence and duration of foci, and Gumerman changed the overall designation to the Central Little Colorado Province (q.v.).

SOURCES: Colton 1939a:66–69; Gumerman 1969; Gumerman and Skinner 1968.

Donald E. Weaver, Jr.

WINSLOW ORANGE WARE, the major decorated ware from sites along the Little Colorado River and its tributaries in northeastern Arizona between A.D. 1300 and 1400. As first defined by H. S. Colton and L. L. Hargrave, this ware included six types: Tuwiuca Orange, Tuwiuca Black-on-orange, Tuwiuca Polychrome, Winslow Polychrome, Jeddito Black-on-orange, and Jeddito Polychrome. Colton subsequently revised the ware's description to include six additional types: Chavez Pass Black-on-red, Chavez Pass Polychrome, Homolovi Black-on-red, Homolovi Polychrome, Black Ax Plain, and Black Ax Polychrome. The polychrome types all have black and white painted designs.

SOURCES: Colton and Hargrave 1937:134–143; Colton 1956.

Donald E. Weaver, Jr.

WINSLOW PROVINCE, a minor western Anasazi (q.v.) manifestation centered in the high desert of the Little Colorado River Valley in northern Arizona, where it occupies a major zone of cultural interaction between various traditions from all directions. This is evidenced by artifacts and architectural forms, which exhibit a melding of cultural traditions resulting from the natural east-west route afforded by the river and the desert, an environmental corridor sandwiched between major highlands to the north and south.

The first substantial, distinctive tradition in the province appeared ca. A.D. 1000 and survived until ca. A.D. 1300, when large pueblos such as the Homolovi group were established along the Little Colorado as many drier places were abandoned. Sites, which tend to be small except directly along the river, display a variety of architectural forms: small pithouses mixed with surface structures, mud walls with masonry, Mogollon (q.v.) house forms with Anasazi features, and great kivas (q.v.) associated with smaller round or rectangular kivas. Little Colorado White Ware (q.v.) ceramics predominate at the sites, some of which seem to have been ceremonial/economic centers.

SOURCES: Colton 1939a; Gumerman and Skinner 1968.

George J. Gumerman

WITT SITE. See Tulare Lake Site.

WOLFE NECK POTTERY, a recently defined major type in the middle Delmarva Peninsula that also has been recognized throughout the Middle Atlantic region. An Early Woodland ceramic characterized by crushed grit temper and lack of decoration, it has thick walls and either net-impressed or cord-marked exterior surfaces. The type has been radiocarbon dated to the first millennium B.C.

SOURCE: Griffith and Artusy 1977.

Ronald A. Thomas

WOLFSHEAD SITE, an Archaic (ca. 4000–1 B.C.) campsite in San Augustine County, in eastern Texas; excavated by L. F. Duffield in 1960. The earliest occupation is typified by San Patrice (q.v.) and other Early Archaic dart-point forms; the middle occupation, by expanding stem and side-notched points; and the last occupation, by sandy paste, Pre-Caddoan pottery and contracting stem points.

SOURCE: Duffield 1963.

James E. Corbin

WOMACK SITE, a Norteño Focus (q.v.) village on the Red River in Lamar County, in Texas, tentatively identified as a historic Kichai Indian village visited by members of the Bernard de la Harpe expedition in 1719. Excavations there by University of Texas archaeologists in 1931 revealed middens, burials, probable house remains, and artifacts of both indigenous and European manufacture. The Womack Site was identified as a component of the Caddoan Glendora Focus by A. D. Krieger in 1946 before the Norteño Focus had been defined.

SOURCES: Krieger 1946:164; Suhm et al. 1954:221–225; Duffield and Jelks 1961:70; Harris et al. 1965.

James E. Corbin

WOODENSHOE PHASE, an expression of the early Pueblo III period (ca. A.D. 1150–1225) on Cedar Mesa in the Cedar Mesa Province (q.v.) of southeastern Utah; the westernmost extension of the Mesa Verde tradition at the time. The phase, which followed the Clay Hills Phase (q.v.) on Cedar Mesa, is characterized by small, scattered, highland sites that equate roughly with sites of the McElmo Phase in the Mesa Verde Province (q.v.).

SOURCE: Matson and Lipe 1978.

R. G. Matson

WOODLAND, a major cultural tradition—distinguished by cord-marked or fabric-impressed pottery, burial mounds, and agriculture—that followed the Archaic tradition over much of eastern North America, including the Midwest, the Southeast, the Northeast, and the eastern Great Plains. Its age varies somewhat from one region to another, but Woodland traits had appeared by 1000 B.C. or somewhat earlier and the tradition continued until replaced by other cultures (for example, the Mississippian in the Southeast and the Plains Village Tradition in the Plains), generally between A.D. 700

and 1200. Early, Middle, and Late Woodland periods are recognized in most areas. Adena and Hopewell (qq.v.) are classic Woodland cultures.

SOURCES: Willey 1966:267–292; Griffin 1967, 1978:235–258; Tuck 1978; Caldwell and Henning 1978:123–125.

Edward B. Jelks

WOODRUFF OSSUARY, a Keith Focus (q.v.) burial in Phillips County, in Kansas; excavated by M. F. Kivett in 1946. It comprised the remains of 61 individuals representing the population's total age range of both sexes, all evidently in generally good health except for a high incidence of tooth caries after the age of twenty. Associated with the articulated, partly articulated, and disarticulated skeletons were Harlan Cord-Roughened pottery, Scallorn arrow points (q.v.), hundreds of disk shell beads, and many shell pendants.

SOURCE: Kivett 1953.

Patricia J. O'Brien

WOOLLEY MAMMOTH SITE, a locality in the Wreck Canyon region of Santa Rosa Island (q.v.), California, where in 1975 John Woolley discovered a large, circular feature of red-burned sediments containing abundant charcoal, burned mammoth bones, and chipped-stone materials. C. R. Berger, who dug the feature in 1976, concluded that it was a hearth and that the chipped-stone items were artifacts. Radiocarbon analysis of four charcoal samples from the feature indicated an age of greater than 40,000 years.

SOURCE: Berger 1982.

R. E. Taylor

WRIGHT SITE, a Copena Complex (q.v.) village covering about 1.5 acres and two associated burial mounds in the Tennessee Valley of northwestern Alabama. Excavations by W. G. Haag in 1939 disclosed the remains of round timber structures in the village and, in the nearby mounds, over 50 burials associated with typical Copena necrolia of copper, galena, stone, and marine shell.

SOURCE: Webb and DeJarnette 1942.

John A. Walthall

WUPATKI PUEBLO, a Pueblo II–III (ca. A.D. 1120–1225) site of Kayenta Anasazi/Sinagua (qq.v.) affiliation; located in Wupatki National Monument about 35 miles northeast of Flagstaff, Arizona. One of the largest sites in the Flagstaff region and one of the few that has been extensively excavated, the pueblo originally consisted of a three-story masonry structure estimated to have had about 100 rooms, an amphitheater, a ball court, and a midden area. L. L. Hargrave and H. S. Colton directed the bulk of the excavations there in 1933–1934; E. K. Reed and D. J. Jones dug three rooms in 1940–1941; and A. J. Lindsay, Jr., and G. J. Gumerman excavated the ball court in 1965. M. B. Stanislawski studied the numerous artifacts from the site, which included many perishable remains (textiles and basketry) as well as shell objects, copper bells, parrot burials, and other exotic items.

SOURCES: Colton 1946:55–63; Stanislawski 1963b.

Bruce Anderson

WYANDOTTE CAVE, a large cave complex in Crawford County, in Indiana; the type station for which Wyandotte chert (q.v.) was named. It also was the source of raw material for all known Middle Woodland artifacts made of aragonite—predominantly platform pipes and reel-shaped gorgets—that occur in major Hopewell (q.v.) centers from Iowa through the Ohio Valley into south-central Tennessee. There is clear evidence of prehistoric mining of aragonite at the "Pillar of the Constitution," a formation about 1000 meters from the cave's entrance. Epsomsite also may have been collected from the cave in prehistoric times.

SOURCES: Gray et al. 1983; Tankersley et al. (in press).

James H. Kellar

WYANDOTTE CHERT, a typically blue-gray, microcrystalline, nonfossiliferous, lustrous, high-quality chert that occurs in both nodular and tabular forms in the Ste. Genevieve limestone in western Harrison and eastern Crawford counties, in Indiana. It probably also is present in adjacent portions of Kentucky, but it has not been firmly documented there. The name derives from exposures and workshop debris in Wyandotte Cave (q.v.), Indiana. This chert was intensively and extensively utilized in the middle Ohio Valley from Paleoindian through Middle Woodland times, and artifacts apparently manufactured from it have been reported in the Great Lakes and Southeast areas. In the literature, it also has been called Wyandotte flint, Indiana hornstone, and Harrison County flint.

SOURCES: Fowke 1928; Seeman 1975; Myers 1981; Basset and Powell 1984.

James H. Kellar

WYLIE FOCUS, a late prehistoric (ca. A.D. 1300–1600) cultural expression concentrated along the East Fork of the Trinity River in Collin and Rockwall counties, Texas; defined by R. L. Stephenson in 1950 largely on the basis of the type site, Hogge Bridge. Sites are small villages containing evidence of maize agriculture, hunting, fishing, and gathering. Their most unique feature is the presence in each site of a large, round pit 20 to 40 meters in diameter, with an earthen ridge around its perimeter. Flexed burials sometimes were placed in the ridge, in the pit floor, or elsewhere in the site. The artifact inventory includes a mixture of both Plains and late Caddoan pottery types.

SOURCES: Stephenson 1952; Suhm et. al 1954:87–92.

Edward B. Jelks

WYTHE POTTERY SERIES, a sand-tempered ceramic of southwestern Virginia west of the Blue Ridge escarpment, dating ca. A.D. 1300–1650; considered a western variant of the Dan River Series (q.v.). Vessels occasionally have folded rims, notched lips, and finger-pinches or incised lines below the lip; surfaces are plain or textured with net, cord, or corncob impressions.

SOURCES: Holland 1970; P. S. Gardner 1980.

Keith T. Egloff

Y

YADKIN POTTERY SERIES, a quartz-tempered ceramic with fabric-impressed, linear check-stamped, and burnished-over cordmarked surface finishes. Dating ca. 300 B.C.-A.D. 400, Yadkin pottery occurs in the Piedmont areas of North and South Carolina.
SOURCE: Coe 1964:30–32.

Billy L. Oliver

YADKIN TRIANGULAR POINT, a large, well-made, triangular projectile point with a concave base and straight sides, pressure flaked from fine-grained, nonporphyritic materials. Widespread in the Piedmont of North Carolina and dating ca. 300 B.C.-A.D. 400, the type appears to represent a refinement of the earlier Badin Triangular point (q.v.).
SOURCE: Coe 1964:45–46.

Billy L. Oliver

YANKEETOWN PHASE, a Late Woodland (ca. A.D. 900) archaeological manifestation predominantly in southwestern Indiana and the adjacent areas of Kentucky and Illinois. The culture content is significant because it includes both Woodland and some Mississippian elements and because it represents a transition toward settled village life typical of the Late Prehistoric interval in the area. The Yankeetown Site (q.v.) is the type site for the phase.
SOURCES: Blasingham 1953, n.d.; Winters 1963:83; Dorwin and Kellar n.d.

James H. Kellar

YANKEETOWN SITE, a large, buried, multicomponent site in the Ohio River floodplain in Warrick County, in Indiana; the type site for the transitional Late Woodland-Early Mississippian Yankeetown Phase (q.v.). Diagnostic elements are a distinctive grog-tempered, incised or notched, appliqued pottery and a few bowl-shaped vessels.

SOURCES: Blasingham 1953, n.d.; Winters 1963; Dorwin and Kellar n.d.

James H. Kellar

YARBROUGH SITE, a stratified, primarily Archaic (ca. 6000–200 B.C.) site in Van Zandt County, in eastern Texas, excavated by a Work Projects Administration team in 1941. Stratigraphic data from the site were used by LeRoy Johnson, Jr., in 1962 as a basis for his definition of the La Harpe Aspect (q.v.). These data demonstrated the evolution of dart-point styles (generally from expanding to contracting stem forms) within the Archaic and the adoption of sandy-paste pottery by Terminal Archaic peoples of eastern Texas.

SOURCE: LeRoy Johnson, Jr. 1962.

James E. Corbin

YEOCOMICO WARE, a protohistoric-historic (A.D. 1500–1700) pottery tempered with oyster shell; found in the coastal plain of northeastern Virginia and southeastern Maryland. Vessels have thin walls and either mildly constricted necks or direct rims; forms include small cups, medium-sized bowls, and globular jars with rounded bases. The ware comprises three types: Yeocomico Plain, Yeocomico Scraped, and Yeocomico Cord-marked.

SOURCES: Waselkov 1982:288–289; Potter 1982:222–227, 376–379; Egloff and Potter 1982:112–114.

Stephen R. Potter

YEO SITE, a specialized, limited-activity Middle Woodland site (ca. A.D. 600) on Camp Branch of the Little Platte River in northwestern Missouri; excavated by P. J. O'Brien in 1976. Part of the ancillary site system associated with large, permanent, Kansas City Hopewell (q.v.) villages near the mouths of major drainages, Yeo was a seasonal camp used for collecting hickory and domestic *Iva* in early October. It produced important information about the nature of specialized limited-activity areas and about starchy seed domestication in the Woodland period.

SOURCE: P. J. O'Brien 1982.

Patricia J. O'Brien

YOUNGE TRADITION, a culture unit in southeastern Michigan defined by the presence of Late Woodland ceramics. It is divided into three phases: Younge, A.D. 900–1100; Springwells, A.D. 1100–1250; and Wolf, A.D. 1250–1450. Typical Younge Tradition artifacts are elbow pipes, triangular arrow points, and ceramics similar to Glen Meyer ceramics in western

Ontario. Burials, often in ossuaries, sometimes have perforated long bones or crania.

SOURCES: Greenman 1937a; Fitting 1965, 1966.

Margaret B. Holman

YUHA SKELETON, a nearly complete human skeleton of controversial age, excavated by W. M. Childers and E. Burton in 1972 in the Yuha Desert region of the Salton Sea Basin, in Imperial County, California. An age of from 19,000 to 22,000 years was initially assigned to this burial, but a later series of radiocarbon measurements directly made on samples of Yuha bone gave a date of ca. 2000 B.C.

SOURCES: Bischoff et al. 1976; Stafford et al. 1984.

R. E. Taylor and L. A. Payen

YUMAN CULTURE, a name formerly used for the Hakataya Culture (q.v.).

YUQUOT SEQUENCE, the evolution of a culture based on four radio-carbon-dated strata at the Yuquot Site (q.v.) on the west coast of Vancouver Island, British Columbia, showing cultural continuity and gradual change from before 2300 B.C. to the present.

Zone I. Dating pre–2300 to ca. 1000 B.C., Zone I contained artifact types that became more refined in later periods; however, they document the presence of all basic manufacturing, fishing, and hunting technologies for exploiting the maritime environment effectively.

Zone II. Dating from ca. 1000 B.C. to A.D. 800, Zone II contained a wide range of artifact types (including those of Zone I): pecked- and ground-stone celts; flaked-stone wedges; whalebone wedges; sandstone abraders and saws; a whalebone cedar-bark shredder; a wide range of bone needles and awls; abundant fishing paraphernalia (gorges, elements of composite fishhooks, toggling harpoon heads for salmon); nontoggling harpoon heads for sea mammals; perforated animal teeth and bones; tubular birdbone beads; carved whalebone clubs; and bird-bone whistles. Superimposed rock-rimmed fire pits suggest permanent house frames.

Zone III. Dating from A.D. 800 to 1790, Zone III appears to represent Nootkan culture as it is known from early historical and ethnographical accounts. Most artifact types in Zones I and II continue in more refined forms and with greater size variations, but there are two important new technological developments: (1) composite, toggling harpoon heads for hunting whales and other large sea mammals and (2) stone-shanked, composite, trolling fishhooks for salmon.

Faunal remains from Zones II and III show that a wide range of animal resources was exploited consistently, including 22 species of marine mollusks, salmon, rockfish, ling cod, the coast deer (the most common mammal species), whales, northern fur seals, and a great variety of birds, especially the now nearly extinct short-tailed albatross, the common murre, and the glaucous-winged gull.

Zone IV. Dating from A.D. 1790 to the present, Zone IV represents the period when Nootkan culture was exposed directly to European influences. Although Yuquot became an important base for the maritime fur trade and for European exploration in the late 18th century, relatively few traces of European presence at that time were found. Native material culture continued essentially unchanged, and resource exploitation followed the prehistoric pattern with only a few exceptions. Quantities of ceramic, glass, and metal artifacts dating from the late 19th century onward indicate a period of acculturation and native involvement in a monetary economy.

SOURCES: Dewhirst 1978, 1980; Clarke and Clarke 1980; McAllister 1980; Olive Jones 1981; Lueger 1981.

John Dewhirst

YUQUOT SITE, a large village midden on the southeastern tip of Nootka Island, British Columbia, which currently provides the longest unbroken archaeological record for the west coast of Vancouver Island. More than 5 meters of deposits comprise four stratigraphic zones that record the Yuquot sequence (q.v.), spanning a period from ca. 2300 B.C. to the present. Yuquot reflects a highly maritime-oriented culture that gradually became more specialized over time, developing in relative cultural isolation until contact with Europeans in the late 18th century. Yuquot then became a major base for the maritime fur trade and European exploration. Since the mid–19th century, the site has been the summer village of the Mowachaht confederacy, a union of tribal groups of Nootka Sound.

SOURCES: Dewhirst 1978, 1980.

John Dewhirst

Z

ZEBREE SITE, an Early Mississippian (ca. A.D. 800–1000) site in northeastern Arkansas; the type site for the Big Lake Phase and the best expression to date of the Varney Horizon. It is rectangular in plan, 1.15 hectares in size, and originally was fenced. Excavations by D. F. Morse between 1968 and 1976 revealed a pit where a large central post once stood and a series of midden concentrations forming a semicircle around the pit. Features included small rectangular houses and large bell-shaped pits for corn storage. Characteristic ceramics are Varney Red Filmed handleless jars, bowls, salt pans, hooded bottles, and toy pots; Mississippi Plain handless jars and bowls; and Wickliffe Thick funnels. Other material culture included a microlithic industry, bone harpoons, notched arrow points, stone discoidals, chert hoe fragments, and other typical Mississippian artifacts. Zebree has produced a wealth of significant information concerning the emergence of the Mississippian (q.v.) culture.

SOURCES: Morse and Morse 1983, n.d.

Dan F. Morse

ZIMMERMAN SITE, a large late prehistoric and early historic village site on the north bank of the Illinois River in northern Illinois, identified as the Grand Village of the Kaskaskia Indians, a subgroup of the Illinois tribe, who French explorers reported were living in the vicinity between 1673 and 1691. Excavated by the Illinois State Museum and the University of Chicago in 1947, and by the LaSalle County Historical Society between 1970 and 1972, Zimmerman has produced a large amount of information on village plan, diet, artifacts, and burial practices of the Kaskaskia and their prehistoric antecedants.

SOURCES: J. A. Brown 1961; M. K. Brown 1975.

Edward B. Jelks

ZORASTER PHASE. See Unkar Chronology.

ZUMA CREEK SITE, a coastal site in the Santa Barbara region of California; dug by S. L. Peck in 1947–1948. Dating ca. 3000–1000 B.C., it is characterized by core tools, cogged stones, and secondary interments under milling stones.
    SOURCE: S. L. Peck 1955.

L. A. Payen

Appendix: Sites Listed Geographically

Each site listed here has a separate entry in the dictionary. Sites mentioned in the dictionary, but not having separate entries, are listed in the index.

ALASKA: Anaktuvuk Pass, Anangula Blade, Batza Tena, Birnirk, Brooks River-Naknek Drainage, Cape Alitak Petroglyph, Cape Krusenstern Area, Chaluka, Daxatkanada, Dry Creek, Gallagher Flint, Gambell, Ground Hog Bay 2, Hidden Falls, Hot Springs Village, Ipiutak, Iyatayet, Kachemak, Kukulik, Mesa, Nukleet Site, Onion Portage, Palugvik, Paugvik, Point Barrow, Point Hope, Port Moller, Takli Island, Talaquak Locality, Tangle Lakes, Trail Creek Caves, Uyak.

ALABAMA: Bessemer, Moundville, Quad, Russell Cave, Stanfield-Worley.

ALBERTA: Bezya, Cluny, Lake Athabaska.

ARIZONA: Awatovi, Casa Grande, Chavez Pass Ruins, Chevelon Ruin, Chodistaas, Citadel Pueblo/Nalakihu, Cottonwood Creek Ruin, Crack-in-Rock Pueblo, Elden Pueblo, Foote Canyon Pueblo, Grapevine Pueblo, Grasshopper, Hano, Homolovi, Jeddito 264, King's Ruin, Kinnikinnick Ruin, Kwaika'a, Lehner, Magician's Burial, Mishongnavi, Montezuma Castle, Naco, Oraibi Pueblo, Payupki, Pershing, Pittsberg Village, Plaza, Point of Pines Locality, Pollock, Pueblo Grande, Ridge Ruin, Shungopavi, Sichomovi, Sikyatki, Snaketown, Tonto National Monument, Tusayan Ruin, Tuzigoot Pueblo, Unkar Delta Locality, Ventana Cave, Walhalla Glades Ruin, Walnut Canyon National Monument, Walpi, White House Ruin, Willow Beach, Winona Village, Wupatki Pueblo.

ARKANSAS: Arkansas Post, Battle Mound, Baytown, Brand, Breckenridge, Cherry Valley, Cooper, Crenshaw, Helena Mounds, Holman Shelter, Huntsville, Nodena, Ozark Rock Art, Parkin, Shallow Lake, Sloan, Toltec, Zebree.

BRITISH COLUMBIA: Charlie Lake Cave, Chase Burial, Dodge Island, Glenrose Cannery, Lawn Point, Locarno Beach, Lochnore-Nesikep Locality, Marpole, Milliken, Montague Harbour, Mt. Edziza Obsidian Quarry, Musqueam Northeast, Namu, St. Mungo Cannery, Skoglund's Landing, South Yale, Upper Hat Creek Sites, Yuquot.

CALIFORNIA: Alder Hill Quarry, Arlington Springs, Augustine, Borax Lake, Bordertown, Buena Vista Lake, Calico, Casa Diablo Quarry, Coso Petroglyphs, Cottonwood Creek, Crane Flat, C. W. Harris, Del Mar Skeleton, Diablo Canyon, Ellis Landing, Emeryville, Gunther Island, Karlo, La Brea Skeleton, Laguna Beach Skeleton, Little Harbor, Los Angeles Skeleton, Malaga Cove, Martis, Moaning Cave, Mostin, Newberry Cave, New Melones, Oro Grande, Patricks Point, Pinto Basin, Potter Creek Cave, Rose Spring, Santa Rosa Island, Stahl, Sugarloaf Quarry, Sunnyvale Skeleton, Texas Street, Topanga Canyon, Tranquillity, Tulare Lake, University Village, West Berkeley, Willow Creek, Woolley Mammoth, Yuha Skeleton, Zuma Creek.

CHIHUAHUA: Casas Grandes, Convento.

COLORADO: Chimney Rock Pueblo, Dent, Frazier, Gordon Creek Burial, Jones-Miller, Jurgens, Lindenmeier, Turner-Look.

DELAWARE: Island Field, Rosenkrans Ferry, St. Jones River Adena, Townsend.

DISTRICT OF COLUMBIA: Piney Branch Quarry.

FLORIDA: Crystal River, Fort Center, Fort Walton, Key Marco, Lake Jackson, Little Salt Spring, McKeithen, Mount Royal.

GEORGIA: Etowah, Hollywood, Irene, King, Kolomoki, Mandeville, Ocmulgee, Stalling's Island, Swift Creek, Theriault, Tunacunnhee.

GREENLAND: Ammassalik, Cape Tyson, Comer's Midden, Dodemansbukgt, Hellebaek, Independence Fjord, Itinnera, Julianehab, Kangek, Kolnaes, Nuullit, Old Nuullit, Sermermiut, Solebaaken, Uummannaq Locality.

IDAHO: Hatwai, Weis Rockshelter.

ILLINOIS: Baumer, Cahokia, Crable, Dickson Mounds, Go-Kart North, Great Salt Springs, Havana, Kincaid, Klunk-Gibson Mounds, Knight Mound, Koster, Larson, Liverpool, Lunsford-Pulcher, Maples Mills, Mitchell (1), Modoc Rockshelter, Monks Mound, Morton, Mund, Napoleon

Hollow, Ogden-Fettie, Range, Smiling Dan, Starved Rock, Steuben, Sugar Camp Hill, Twenhafel, Weaver, Wilson Mounds, Zimmerman.

INDIANA: Alton, Angel, Bone Bank, Crib Mound, Fort Ouiatenon, Griesmer, Mann, Mounds State Park, Murphy, New Castle, Nowlin Mound, Wyandotte Cave, Yankeetown.

IOWA: Cherokee Sewer, Lewis Central School, Simonsen, Turin.

KANSAS: Blue River Kansa Village, Coal-Oil Canyon, Coffey, Curry, Fanning, Infinity, James Younkin Mound, Kansas Monument, Lansing Man, Malone, Milbourn, Olsen-Chubbock, Penokee Stone Man, Scott County Pueblo, Snyder, Stone-Vaulted Mounds, Tim Adrian, Tobias, Twelve Mile Creek, Two Dog, Whiteford, Williamson (2), William Young, Woodruff Ossuary.

KENTUCKY: Indian Knoll, Jewell.

LABRADOR: Avayalik, Buxhall, Dog Bight, Hamilton Inlet, Koliktalik, Nukususutok, Okak 3, Saglek Bay Locality, Shuldham Island 9, Thalia Point, Tikoralak.

LOUISIANA: Belcher Mound, Coral Snake Mound, Gahagan Mound, Gold Mine, John Pearce, Marksville, Mounds Plantation, Poverty Point, Tchefuncte, Troyville.

MAINE: Nevin, Turner Farm, Vail.

MARYLAND: Accokeek Creek, Biggs Ford, Conowingo, Devil Bliss Bridge, Harlan Mill Steatite Quarry, Juhle, Martins Pond, Monocacy, Moore, Nolands Ferry, Paw Paw, Plum Nelly, Popes Creek, Rosenstock, Seldon Island, Shepard, West River.

MASSACHUSETTS: Bull Brook.

MICHIGAN: Andrews, Barnes, Dumaw Creek, Feeheley, Fletcher, Holcombe, Juntunen, Lasanen, Marquette Mission, Moccasin Bluff, Naomikong Point, Norton Mounds, Riverside, Sand Point, Sanilac Petroglyphs, Schmidt, Schultz, Summer Island, Weber I.

MINNESOTA: Browns Valley, Bryan Site, Itasca, McKinstry, Minnesota Woman, Petaga Point, Pike Bay, Sheffield, Smith.

MISSISSIPPI: Gordon.

MISSOURI: Ozark Rock Art, Renner, Yeo.

MONTANA: Anzick, Bootlegger Trail, Hagen, MacHaffie, Pictograph Cave.

NEBRASKA: Ash Hollow Cave, Hudson-Meng, Lime Creek, Logan Creek, Meserve, Nehawka Quarries, Scottsbluff, Signal Butte, Valley.

NEVADA: Alta Toquima, Bordertown, Falcon Hill Caves, Gatecliff Shelter, Hidden Cave, Humboldt Lakebed, Kings Beach, Leonard Rockshelter, Lost City Locality, Lovelock Cave, Mesa House, O'Malley Shelter, Sadmat, Smith Creek Cave, Spooner Lake, Steamboat Hot Spring Locality.

NEW BRUNSWICK: Augustine Mound.

NEWFOUNDLAND: Gargamelle Cove, L'anse aux Meadows, Port au Choix, Port au Choix 2.

NEW HAMPSHIRE: Neville.

NEW JERSEY: Abbott Farm, Plenge, Savitch Farm/Koens-Crispin.

NEW MEXICO: Abo, Apache Creek Pueblo, Arrowhead Ruin, Aztec Ruin, Bis Sa'ani, Block Lookout Ruin, Blackwater Draw, Bloom Mound, Bonnell, Casa Rinconada, Cerrito, Chetro Ketl, Cornfield Taos, Evans, Folsom, Forked Lightning Pueblo, Gran Quivira, Guadalupe Ruin, Higgins Flat Pueblo, Huerfano Mesa Village, Kin Kletso, Kuaua Pueblo, Llano, Marcia's Rincon Community, Mayhill, Mockingbird Gap, Nogales Cliff House, Otowi Ruin, Palisade Ruin, Pecos Mission, Pecos Pueblo, Phillips, Picuris Pueblo, Pojoaque Grant, Pot Creek Pueblo, Pottery Mound, Pueblo Alto, Pueblo Bonito, Pueblo Colorado, Pueblo del Arroyo, Pueblo del Encierro, Pueblo Pardo, Puye Cliff Dwellings, Quarai, Rainbow House, Ring House, Salmon Ruin, Sandia Cave, Shabik'eshchee Village, BC 50, BC 51, SU, Tabira, Tesuque By-pass, Tularosa and Cordova Caves, Turkey Foot Ridge, Tyuonyi, Village of the Great Kivas, Wet Leggett Pueblo, White Mound Village.

NEW YORK: Frontenac Island, Lake Lamoka, West Athens Hill.

NORTH CAROLINA: Baum, Coweeta Creek, Doerschuk, Donnaha, Garden Creek, Hardaway, Haw River, Jordan's Landing, Keyauwee, Lowder's Ferry, Occaneechi, Peachtree, Permuda Island, Town Creek, Uniflite, Upper Sauratown, Warren Wilson.

NORTH DAKOTA: Biesterfeldt, Huff, Inkster, Like-a-Fishhook Village, Night Walker's Butte Village, Shermer.

NORTHWEST TERRITORIES: Aberdeen, Abverdjar, Acasta, Alarnerk, Annawak, Arnapik, Avinga, Baker Lake, Ballantine, Bell, Bernhard Harbour, Bloody Falls, Brooman Point, Buchanan, Buchanan Lake, Burton Bay, Button Point, Cape Sparbo, Cape Tanfield, Clachan, Closure, Crystal II, Cumberland Sound, Dismal II, Dubawnt, Eureka Sound, Ferguson Lake, Fisherman Lake, Franklin Tanks, Gull Cliff, Igloolik Locality, Inuarfissuaq, Jackson, Joss, K'aersut, Kaleruserk, Kapuivik, Karluk Island, Kemp, Killiktee, Killilugak, Kingaaluk, Kittigazuit, Lagoon, Lake Harbour Locality, Lake Hazen Locality, Lonesome Creek, Longhouse, Loon, Malerualik, Mary's Hill, Mill Island, Migod, Mittamatalik Locality, Nanook, Native Point Locality, Naujan, Nunguvik, Okialivialuk, Peale Point, Pointed Mountain, Port Refuge Locality, Quililukan, Resolute Locality, Ruggles Outlet, Saatut, Seahorse Gully, Shaymark, Shorty, Silumiut, Skraeling Island, Snowdrift Village, T–1, T–2, Tanfield/Morrisson, Tertiary Hills Lithic Source, Turngaasiti, Tyara, Umingmak, Vaughn, Wellington Bay.

NOVA SCOTIA: Debert.

NUEVO LEON: Cueva de la Zona, San Isidro.

OHIO: Adena Mound, Baum Village, Edwin Harness, Flint Ridge, Fort Ancient, Hopewell, Incinerator, Leimach, McGraw, Madisonville, Marietta Earthworks, Meadowcroft Rockshelter, Mound City, Newark Earthworks, Raisch-Smith, Seip, Serpent Mound, Tremper, Turner.

OKLAHOMA: Domebo, Spiro.

ONTARIO: Belcher Island.

OREGON: Catlow and Roaring Springs Caves, Dirty Shame Rockshelter, Five Mile Rapids, Fort Rock Cave, Kawumkan Springs Midden, Nightfire Island, Paisley Caves, Pilcher Creek, Steens Mountain Locality, Warner Valley Locality, Wildcat Canyon.

PENNSYLVANIA: Overpeck, Pennsylvania Jasper Quarries, Shoop.

QUEBEC: Belanger, Diana Bay, Gulf Hazard, Hochelaga, Ivugivik.

SASKATCHEWAN: Long Creek, Mortlach.

SONORA: Botonapa, Cerro de los Gentiles, La Mora, La Playa, Las Delicias del Sur, Las Trincheras, Ojo de Agua, San Jose.

SOUTH CAROLINA: Adamson Mound, Alligator Creek, Arant's Field, Awendaw Shell Midden, Bass Pond Dam, Callawassie Island Burial Mound, Cal Smoak, Charles Towne, Chauga, Chester Field Shell Ring, Clear Mount, Daws Island, Dunlap, Edenwood, Fig Island Shell Rings, Fish Haul, Ford's Skull Creek Shell Ring, Greenhill Mound, Green's Shell Enclosure, Guernsey, Holiday, Horse Island Shell Ring, I. C. Few, Jeremy Island Midden, Keowee Town, Lighthouse Point Shell Ring, Love, McCollum Mound, Mattassee Lake, Minim Island Shell Midden, Mulberry Mounds, Parachukla, Pinckney Island Shell Midden, Rabbit Mount, Sable, Scott's Lake Bluff, Scott's Lake Mounds, Sea Pines Shell Ring, Second Refuge, Silver Bluffs 38LX5, 38SU83, Spanish Mount, Stratton Place Shell Ring, Taylor, Tom's Creek, Toxaway Village, Victoria Bluff Shell Midden, Wachesaw Landing, Walnut Grove Shell Midden, Wild Cherry, Windy Ridge.

SOUTH DAKOTA: Arzberger, Brandon, Crow Creek, Four Bear, La Roche, Leavenworth, Mitchell (2), Mobridge, Spain, Split Rock Creek Mounds, Sully, Swanson, Talking Crow, Thomas Riggs.

TENNESSEE: Chota-Tanasee, Chucalissa, Eva, Hiwassee Island, Icehouse Bottom, Old Stone Fort, Pinson, Wright.

TEXAS: Addicks, Alibates Flint Quarries, Andrews Lake, Arenosa Shelter, Baker Cave, Bee Cave Canyon Shelter, Bentsen-Clark, Bob Williams, Bonfire Shelter, Cervenka, Choke Canyon, Culpepper, De Shazo, Devils Mouth, Devils Rockshelter, Equipaje Spring, Fate Bell Shelter, George C. Davis, Gilbert, Hale Mound, Harroun, Hatchel-Mitchell, Hinds Cave, Infierno Camp, Jake Martin, Jonas Short, Knight's Bluff, Kyle, Lewisville, Livermore Cache, Loeve, Loeve-Fox, Lubbock Lake, Mackin, Mayhew, Miami, Midland Man, Miller, Millington, Pace McDonald, Palmetto Bend, Pearson, Plainview, Resch, Rogers Springs, Rowe Valley, Sam Kaufman, Scharbauer, Snipes, Tuck Carpenter, Wallisville, Washington Square Mound, Wolfshead, Womack, Yarbrough.

UTAH: Backhoe Village, Caldwell Village, Cowboy Cave, Danger Cave, Fish Springs Caves, Great Salt Lake Marsh, Hogup Cave, Median Village, Sudden Shelter.

VERMONT: Reagan.

VIRGINIA: Bessemer, Bowman, Brown Johnson, Buzzard Rock, Camden District, Chula Soapstone Quarry, Cornett, Crab Orchard, Croaker Landing, Daugherty's Cave, Deep Bottom, Deshazo, Elk Island, Elm Hill, Ely Mound, Flanary, Flint Run District, Flowerdew Hundred, Hand, Hansonville, Hatch, Hayes' Creek Mound, Hirsh Mound, Hoge, Hopewell Airport,

Ingles Bottom, Irwin, Jefferson's Mound, John East Mound, John Green, Keyser Farm, Koehler, Leggett, Lewis Creek Mound, Marcey Creek, Maury Street, Maycock Point, Miley, Mitchell Plantation Quarry, Monacan Farm District, Mud Glyph Cave, Nase, Newington, Onion Field, Paint Lick Mountain Pictographs, Posnick, Potomac Creek, Potts, Quicksburg, Rapidan Mound, Red Hill, Reedy Creek, Schuyler Area Soapstone Quarries, Shannon, Shockoe Slip, Trigg, White Oak Point, Williamson (1), Wingina.

WASHINGTON: Alpowa, Cattle Point, Five Mile Rapids, Kettle Falls, Lind Coulee, Marmes Rockshelter, Ozette Village, Roadcut, Wakemap Mound, Windust Caves.

WEST VIRGINIA: St. Albans.

WISCONSIN: Aztalan, Bass Quarry, Big Bend Mound Group, Boas Mastodon, Carcajou Point, Convent Knoll, Crabapple Point, Cutler Mound and Village, Diamond Bluff, Durst Rockshelter, Gottschall Rockshelter, Heins Creek, Hixton, Horicon, Interstate Park, Lasley's Point, Midway Village, Millville, Oconto, Peterson, Pipe, Raddatz Rockshelter, Raisebeck Mound Group, Redbanks/Point Sauble/Beaumier Farm, Renier, Roche-a-Cris, Rock Island, Sanders, Spencer Lake Mounds and Camps, Squirrel Dam, Trempealeau, Trempealeau Bay.

WYOMING: Agate Basin, Big Horn Medicine Wheel, Brewster, Carter/Kerr-McGee, Casper, Colby, Hanson, Hell Gap, Horner, Medicine Lodge Creek, Mummy Cave, Ruby, Scoggin, Sisters Hill, Spanish Diggings.

YUKON TERRITORY: Bluefish Caves, Canyon, Engigstciak, Gladstone, Klo-Kut, Old Crow Flats Localities, Rat Indian Creek.

References

ABBREVIATIONS

A	*Awanyu*
AA	*American Anthropologist*
AAAM	*American Anthropological Association Memoirs*
AAn	*American Antiquity*
AAr	*The Arizona Archaeologist* (Phoenix)
AASOP	*Arizona Archaeological Society, Occasional Papers*
AASRS	*Arkansas Archeological Survey Research Series*
ABC	*Anthropology in British Columbia* (British Columbia Provincial Museum, Victoria)
ABS	*American Behavioral Scientist*
AcA	*Acta Arctica* (Copenhagen)
ACM	*Annals of the Carnegie Museum* (Pittsburgh)
AENA	*Archaeology of Eastern North America*
AFP	*Amerind Foundation, Publication* (Dragoon, Arizona)
AFS	*Anthropological Field Studies* (Department of Anthropology, Arizona State University, Tempe)
AG	*The American Geologist*
AINATP	*Arctic Institute of North America, Technical Paper*
AJPA	*American Journal of Physical Anthropology*
AJS	*American Journal of Science*
ALCUOP	*Archeology Laboratory, Department of Anthropology, Catholic University, Occasional Publications* (Washington, D.C.)
ALRTAM	*Anthropological Laboratory Report, Texas A&M University* (College Station)
ALSS	*Anthropological Laboratory Special Series* (Texas A&M University, College Station)
AM	*Archaeology in Montana*
AMNHM	*American Museum of Natural History Memoirs* (New York)
AmP	*American Pioneer*
AmS	*American Scientist*
An	*Anthropologica*

AnP	*Anthropological Papers* (Museum of Anthropology, University of Michigan, Ann Arbor)
ANYAS	*Annals of the New York Academy of Sciences*
AP	*Anthropological Papers* (Bureau of American Ethnology, Smithsonian Institution, Washington, D.C.)
APAMNH	*Anthropological Papers, American Museum of Natural History* (New York)
APAOBC	*Activities of the Provincial Archaeologist's Office of British Columbia* (Victoria)
APNMC	*Anthropological Papers, National Museums of Canada* (Ottawa)
APNPS	*Anthropological Papers, National Park Service* (Washington, D.C.)
APSFA	*Anthropological Papers, Stephen F. Austin State University* (Nacogdoches, Texas)
APUA	*Anthropological Papers of the University of Alaska* (Fairbanks)
APUAr	*Anthropological Papers of the University of Arizona* (Tucson)
APUG	*Anthropological Papers of the University of Georgia* (Athens)
APUO	*Anthropological Papers of the University of Oregon* (Eugene)
APUPM	*Anthropological Publications of the University Museum* (University of Pennsylvania, Philadelphia)
APUT	*Anthropological Papers, The University of Texas* (Austin)
AR	*Archeological Report* (U.S. Department of Agriculture, Southwestern Region, Albuquerque)
Ar	*Archaeology*
ArA	*Arkansas Archeology* (Fayetteville)
ARBSU	*Archaeological Reports, Boise State University* (Boise, Idaho)
Arc	*Arctic*
ArcA	*Arctic Anthropology*
Arch	*Archaeometry*
Arcl	*The Archeolog*
ARPM	*Archaeological Reports. Peabody Museum of Archaeology and Ethnology* (Harvard University, Cambridge, Massachusetts)
ARPRR	*Archaeological Research Program, Research Report* (Southern Methodist University, Dallas)
ARRO	*Archaeological Research Report* (Ontario Ministry of Culture, Recreation, Historical and Research Branch, Toronto)
ARS	*Archeological Research Series* (National Park Service, Washington, D.C.)
ArS	*Archeological Studies* (Maryland Geological Survey)
ARSI	*Annual Report of the Smithsonian Institution* (Washington, D.C.)
Art	*The Artifact* (El Paso Archaeological Society, El Paso)
AS	*The American Scholar*
ASAJ	*ASA Journal*
ASAMS	*Archaeological Survey of Alberta Manuscript Series* (Edmonton)
ASAOP	*Archaeological Survey of Alberta Occasional Papers* (Edmonton)
ASASC	*Archaeological Survey Association of Southern California, Papers*
ASC	*Archaeological Studies, Circular* (State Archaeological Commission, Pierre, South Dakota)

ASCP   *Archaeological Survey of Canada Papers* (Ottawa)
ASCSA   *Adams State College Series in Anthropology* (Alamosa, Colorado)
ASKSHS   *Anthropological Series, Kansas State Historical Society* (Topeka)
ASMAS   *Arizona State Museum Archaeological Series* (Tucson)
ASMB   *Archeological Society of Maryland Bulletin*
ASMHS   *Arizona State Museum Contribution to Highway Salvage Archae-ology in Arizona* (Tucson)
ASMSU   *Anthropological Series, Michigan State University, Publications of the Museum* (East Lansing)
ASNJB   *Archaeological Society of New Jersey Bulletin*
ASNJN   *Archaeological Society of New Jersey Newsletter*
ASSDNR   *Anthropological Series, Saskatchewan Department of Natural Re-sources* (Regina)
ASSP   *Antiquities Section Selected Papers*
ASt   *Anthropological Studies* (Institute of Archeology and Anthropology, University of South Carolina, Columbia)
ASUAP   *Arizona State University Anthropological Research Papers* (Tempe)
ASUD   *Archaeological Series, Department of Anthropology, University of Denver* (Denver)
ASUT   *Archaeology Series, Department of Anthropology, The University of Texas* (Austin)
ASVQB   *Archaeological Society of Virginia Quarterly Bulletin*
ASVSP   *Archaeologcial Society of Virginia Special Publication*
AW   *Arizona and the West*
BAEB   *Bureau of American Ethnology Bulletin* (Smithsonian Institution, Washington, D.C.)
BASD   *Bulletin of the Archaeological Society of Delaware*
BASNC   *Bulletin of the Archaeological Society of North Carolina*
BCGS   *B.C. Geographic Series* (University of British Columbia, Vancouver)
BCS   *B.C. Studies* (University of British Columbia, Vancouver)
BJ   *The Bluejay* (Saskatchewan Museum of Natural History, Regina)
BLMCRS   *Bureau of Land Management Cultural Resources Series*
BLMNC   *Bureau of Land Management, Nevada, Contributions to the Study of Cultural Resources, Technical Papers*
BLMUCR   *Bureau of Land Management, Utah, Cultural Resources Series*
BMAS   *Bulletin of the Massachusetts Archaeological Society*
BPA   *Bulletin, Phillips Academy, Department of Archaeology* (Andover, Massachusetts)
BPAP   *Ballena Press Anthropological Papers* (Ballena Press)
BPMCM   *Bulletin of the Public Museum of the City of Milwaukee*
BRSSS   *Bureau of Research in the Social Sciences, Study* (The University of Texas, Austin)
BTAPS   *Bulletin of the Texas Archeological and Paleontological Society*
BTAS   *Bulletin of the Texas Archeological Society*
BTMM   *Bulletin of the Texas Memorial Museum* (The University of Texas, Austin)
CA   *Contributions to Archaeology* (Gila Press, Scottsdale, Arizona)

CAAB	*Canadian Archaeological Association Bulletin*
CAAH	*Contributions to American Archaeology and History* (Carnegic Institute of Washington, Washington, D.C.
CAH	*Contributions to Anthropological History* (Ball State University, Muncie, Indiana)
CAIRP	*Center for Archaeological Investigations, Research Paper* (Southern Illinois University, Carbondale)
CAn	*Current Anthropology*
CASAP	*Complete Archaeological Services Associates Papers* (Cortez, Arizona)
CASC	*Center for Archaeological Studies, Contributions to Anthropological Studies* (Albuquerque)
CC	*Coleccion Científica* (Instituto Nacional de Antropoligia e Historia, Mexico City)
CCAF	*Contributions du Centre d'Etudes Arctiques et Finno-Scandinaves* (Paris)
CCPA	*Colorado College Publications in Archeology* (Colorado Springs)
CFSMAH	*Contributions of the Florida State Museum, Anthropology and History* (Gainesville)
CGJ	*Canadian Geographical Journal*
CISB	*Cranbrook Institute of Science Bulletin*
CIWB	*Carnegie Institute of Washington, Bulletin* (Washington, D.C.)
CJA	*Canadian Journal of Archaeology*
CM	*Century Magazine*
CMAI	*Contributions from the Museum of the American Indian* (Heye Foundation, New York)
CMGP	*Contributions to the Museum of the Great Plains* (Lawton, Oklahoma)
CN	*COSCAPA Newsletter*
CoM	*Colorado Magazine*
CPRM	*COAS Publishing and Research Monograph* (Las Cruces, New Mexico)
CRD	*Cultural Resource Document* (Santa Fe National Forest, New Mexico)
CRRSFU	*Current Research Reports, Simon Fraser University* (Burnaby, British Columbia)
CSAJ	*Central States Archaeological Journal*
CSASM	*Central States Archaeological Societies Memoir*
CUCARF	*Contributions of the University of California Archaeological Research Facility* (Berkeley)
DASFUP	*Department of Archaeology, Simon Fraser University, Publications* (Burnaby, British Columbia)
DAUCO	*Department of Archaeology, University of Calgary, Occasional Papers* (Calgary, Alberta)
DMP	*Denver Museum of Natural History Proceedings* (Denver)
DMPS	*Denver Museum of Natural History, Popular Series* (Denver)
DRIPSS	*Desert Research Institute Publications in the Social Sciences* (Reno, Nevada)

DRITS	*Desert Research Institute Technical Report Series* (Reno, Nevada)
DSMSB	*Delaware State Museum Series Bulletin* (Dover)
EG	*Early Georgia*
EIS	*Etudies/Invit/Studies*
EM	*Early Man* (Center for American Archeology, Kampsville, Illinois)
EMUP	*Ethnology Monographs, Department of Anthropology, University of Pittsburgh* (Pittsburgh)
ENMUCA	*Eastern New Mexico University Contributions in Anthropology* (Portales)
EP	*El Palacio*
ESAFB	*Eastern States Archaeological Federation Bulletin*
EWURAH	*Eastern Washington University, Reports in Archaeology and History* (Cheney)
F	*Fieldiana* (Field Museum of Natural History, Chicago)
F:A	*Fieldiana: Anthropology* (Field Museum of Natural History, Chicago)
FA	*Florida Anthropologist*
FASP	*Florida Anthropological Society Publications*
FBRC	*Fort Burgwin Research Center* (Dallas)
FGSRI	*Florida Geological Survey, Report of Investigations*
FHQ	*Florida Historical Quarterly*
FMNHAS	*Field Museum of Natural History, Anthropological Series* (Chicago)
FO	*Folk* (Copenhagen)
Ga	*The Gamut* (Cleveland State University, Cleveland)
GCAS	*Grand Canyon Archaeological Series* (School of American Research Press, Sante Fe)
GCM	*Grand Canyon Natural History Association Monograph*
GLIMH	*Great Lakes Informant, Michigan History Division*
GM	*Geoscience and Man*
GR	*Geographical Review*
GSAA	*Geological Society of America Abstracts with Programs*
GSAB	*Geological Society of America Bulletin*
GSAMP	*Geological Survey of Alabama, Museum Papers*
GSOB	*Geological Survey of Ohio Bulletin*
GT	*Geografisk Tidsskrift* (Copenhagen)
HA	*History and Archaeology* (Parks Canada, Environment Canada, Ottawa)
HE	*Human Ecology*
HSA	*Highway Salvage Archaeology*
I	*Inksherds*
IAB	*Indiana Archaeological Bulletin*
IASB	*Illinois Archaeological Survey Bulletin* (Urbana)
IASM	*Illinois Archaeological Survey Monograph* (Urbana)
IHB	*Indiana History Bulletin*
INM	*Indian Notes and Monographs* (Museum of the American Indian, Heye Foundation, New York)
IR	*Investigation Reports* (Inter-Agency Archeological Service, National Park Service, Washington, D.C.)

ISMRI	*Illinois State Museum, Reports of Investigations* (Springfield)
ISMRPA	*Illinois State Museum, Papers in Anthropology* (Springfield)
ISMSP	*Illinois State Museum, Scientific Papers* (Springfield)
IVAPRS	*Illinois Valley Archaeological Program Research Papers* (Springfield)
IVCOP	*Imperial Valley College Occasional Paper* (El Centro, California)
JAA	*Journal of Alabama Archaeology*
JANSP	*Journal of the Academy of Natural Sciences of Philadelphia*
JAS	*Journal of Archaeological Science*
JCA	*Journal of California Anthropology*
JCGBA	*Journal of California and Great Basin Anthropology*
JFA	*Journal of Field Archaeology*
JHAA	*Journal for the History of Astronomy, Archeoastronomy*
JIAS	*Journal of the Iowa Archaeological Society*
JISAS	*Journal of the Illinois State Archaeological Society* (Fairbury)
JKAA	*Journal of the Kansas Anthropological Association*
JMH	*Journal of Mississippi History*
JNDA	*Journal of the North Dakota Archaeological Association*
JNWA	*Journal of New World Archaeology*
JWAS	*Journal of the Washington Academy of Sciences* (Washington, D.C)
K	*The Kiva*
KAAB	*Kansas Anthropological Association Bulletin*
KAAN	*Kansas Anthropological Association Newsletter*
KACRS	*Kampsville Archaeological Center Research Series* (Kampsville, Illinois)
KCRSI	*Kansas City Review of Science and Industry*
KSA	*Kampsville Seminars in Archaeology* (Center for American Archaeology, Kampsville, Illinois)
KUQ	*Kansas University Quarterly* (Lawrence)
LA	*Louisiana Archaeology*
LAHPR	*Laboratory of Archaeology and History, Project Reports* (Washington State University, Pullman)
LAN	*Laboratory of Anthropology Notes* (Museum of New Mexico, Santa Fe)
LASB	*Louisiana Archaeological Society Bulletin*
LATSB	*Laboratory of Anthropology, Technical Series, Bulletin* (Museum of New Mexico, Santa Fe)
LGSAS	*Louisiana Geological Survey, Department of Conservation, Anthropological Study* (New Orleans)
LM	*Living Museum* (Illinois State Museum, Springfield)
LMB	*Logan Museum Bulletin* (Beloit, Wisconsin)
LMPAB	*Logan Museum Publications in Anthropology* (Beloit, Wisconsin)
LT	*La Tierra* (Southern Archaeological Association)
M	*The Masterkey*
MA	*The Missouri Archaeologist*
MaA	*Maryland Archeology*
MAAA	*Memoirs, American Anthropological Association*
MAQ	*Manitoba Archaeological Quarterly* (Winnipeg)
MASM	*Missouri Archaeological Society Memoir*

MASN	*Missouri Archaeological Society Newsletter*
MASRS	*Missouri Archaeological Society Research Series*
MASSP	*Missouri Archaeological Society Special Publications*
MCAS	*Memoirs of the Colorado Archaeological Society*
MDAHAR	*Mississippi Department of Archives and History, Archaeological Report*
MG	*Meddelelsen om Grønland* (Copenhagen)
MGSFR	*Maryland Geological Survey, Division of Archeology, File Report*
MGSM	*Miami Geological Survey Memoir*
MH	*Minnesota History*
MHM	*Maryland Historical Magazine*
MHMCA	*Memoirs of the Harvard Museum of Comparative Anatomy*
MHTMS	*Maryland Historical Trust Monograph Series*
MiA	*The Michigan Archaeologist*
MiH	*Michigan History*
MinA	*The Minnesota Archaeologist*
MJA	*Midcontinental Journal of Archaeology*
MJASP	*Midcontinental Journal of Archaeology, Special Paper*
MMAUM	*Memoirs of the Museum of Anthropology, University of Michigan* (Ann Arbor)
MN	*Museum Notes* (Museum of Northern Arizona, Flagstaff)
MNAB	*Museum of Northern Arizona Bulletin* (Flagstaff)
MNACS	*Museum of Northern Arizona Ceramic Series* (Flagstaff)
MNARP	*Museum of Northern Arizona Research Paper* (Flagstaff)
MNMHS	*Museum of New Mexico Highway Salvage* (Santa Fe)
MNMPA	*Museum of New Mexico Papers in Anthropology* (Santa Fe)
MNMRR	*Museum of New Mexico, Research Records* (Santa Fe)
MP	*Medallion Papers* (Gila Pueblo, Globe, Arizona)
MPM	*Monographs. Peabody Museum* (Harvard University, Cambridge, Massachusetts)
MPMPA	*Milwaukee Public Museum, Publications in Anthropology*
MPMPAH	*Milwaukee Public Museum, Publications in Anthropology and History*
MPS	*Minnesota Prehistoric Series* (Minnesota Historical Society, St. Paul)
MPTMM	*Miscellaneous Papers, Texas Memorial Museum* (The University of Texas, Austin)
MS	*Monograph Series* (University of New Mexico and the School of American Research)
MSAA	*Memoirs of the Society for American Archaeology*
MSAR	*Monographs of the School of American Research* (Santa Fe)
MUNSES	*Memorial University of Newfoundland, Institute of Social and Economic Research, Newfoundland Social and Economic Studies* (St. John's)
N	*Nature*
NAA	*North American Archaeologist*
NaH	*Natural History* (American Museum of Natural History, New York)
NARN	*Northwest Anthropological Research Notes*
NASR	*Nevada Archaeological Survey Reports* (Reno)

NASRP   *Nevada Archaeological Survey Research Paper* (Reno)
NB   *Note Book* (Laboratory of Anthropology, University of Nebraska, Lincoln)
NCACP   *North Carolina Archaeological Council Publication* (Raleigh)
NCIASN   *Northwest Chapter of the Iowa Archeologcial Society Newsletter*
NDH   *North Dakota History*
NG   *National Geographic* (National Geographic Society, Washington, D.C.)
NH   *Nebraska History* (Lincoln)
NHSQ   *Nevada Historical Society Quarterly*
NMA   *New Mexico Anthropologist* (University of New Mexico, Albuquerque)
NMCAP   *National Museums of Canada Anthropological Papers* (Ottawa)
NMCB   *National Museums of Canada Bulletin* (Ohawa)
NMCBAS   *National Museums of Canada Bulletin, Anthropological Series* (Ottawa)
NMESES   *National Museum of Ethnology, Senri Ethnological Series* (Osaka)
NMMMS   *National Museum of Man, Mercury Series* (Ottawa)
NMPA   *Navajo Nation Cultural Resource Management Program, Papers in Anthropology* (Window Rock, Arizona)
NPSPA   *National Park Service Publications in Archaeology* (Washington, D.C.)
NPSTP   *National Park Service Transactions and Proceedings Series* (Washington, D.C.)
NSHSPA   *Nebraska State Historical Society Publications in Anthropology* (Lincoln)
NSMAP   *Nevada State Museum Anthropological Papers* (Carson City)
NSMB   *Nebraska State Museum Bulletin* (Lincoln)
NVA   *Nevada Archaeologist*
NUAPSP   *Northwestern University Archaeological Program, Scientific Papers* (Evanston, Illinois)
NWRRI   *New World Research, Report of Investigations* (Pollock, South Dakota)
NYASA   *New York Academy of Sciences, Annals*
NYSMSB   *New York State Museum and Science Service Bulletin*
OA   *Ontario Archaeology*
OAHSQ   *Ohio State Archaeological and Historical Society Quarterly*
OASB   *Oklahoma Anthropological Society Bulletin*
OASM   *Oklahoma Anthropological Society Memoir*
OASOP   *Oklahoma Archaeological Survey Studies in Oklahoma's Past*
OASP   *Oklahoma Anthropological Society Special Publication*
OCARRI   *Office of Cultural and Archaeological Research, Report of Investigations* (University of West Florida, Pensacola)
OCMAUM   *Occasional Contributions from the Museum of Anthropology, University of Michigan* (Ann Arbor)
OhA   *Ohio Archaeologist*
OI   *Outdoor Indiana*
OJS   *Ohio Journal of Science*

OMASC	*W. H. Over Museum, Archaeological Studies, Circular*
OPAJMU	*Occasional Papers in Anthropology. James Madison University* (Harrisonburg, Virginia)
OPAUM	*Occasional Papers, Department of Anthropology, University of Manitoba* (Winnipeg)
OPCAI	*Occasional Papers, Center for Archaeological Investigations* (Southern Illinois University, Carbondale)
OPISC	*Occasional Papers, Idaho State College* (Pocatello)
OPISCM	*Occasional Papers of the Idaho State College Museum* (Pocatello)
OPISUM	*Occasional Papers of the Idaho State University Museum* (Pocatello)
OPLAM	*Occasional Papers of the Los Angeles Museum of History, Science, and Art* (Los Angeles)
OPMA	*Occasional Publications in Minnesota Anthropology* (Minnesota Archaeological Society, Fort Snelling)
OPMSU	*Occasional Papers, Anthropological Research Center* (Memphis State University)
OPSC	*Occasional Papers, Archaeological Society of South Carolina*
OPUA	*Occasional Papers, Anthropology and Historical Preservation Cooperative Park Studies Unit* (University of Alaska, Fairbanks)
OSAIR	*Office of the State Archaeologist of Iowa Report* (Iowa City)
P	*Plateau* (Museum of Northern Arizona, Flagstaff)
PA	*The Plains Anthropologist*
PAAE	*Publications in American Archaeology and Ethnology* (University of California, Berkeley)
PACN	*Plains Archeological Conference Newsletter*
PAIAA	*Papers of the Archaeological Institute of America* (Harvard University, Cambridge, Massachusetts)
PAM	*The Plains Anthropologist, Memoir*
PAPS	*Proceedings of the American Philosophical Society* (Philadelphia)
PAr	*Publications in Archaeology* (Ohio Historical Society, Columbus)
PArc	*Publications in Archeology* (National Park Service, Washington, D.C.)
PASNM	*Papers of the Archaeological Society of New Mexico*
PATVA	*Publications in Anthropology, The Tennessee Valley Authority*
PAVU	*Publications in Anthropology, Vanderbilt University* (Nashville)
PCA	*Plains Conference Abstracts*
PDAA	*Publications of the Department of Anthropology and Archaeology* (University of Kentucky, Lexington)
PFBRC	*Publications of the Fort Burgwin Research Center* (Southern Methodist University, Dallas, Texas)
PFWH	*Publications of the Frederick Webb Hodge Annual Publication Fund* (Los Angeles)
PGMAP	*Pueblo Grande Museum, Anthropological Papers* (Phoenix)
PIAS	*Proceedings, Indiana Academy of Science* (Indianapolis)
PJNPE	*Memoirs of the American Museum of Natural History, Publications of the Jesup North Pacific Expedition* (New York)
PMAMP	*Papers in Manitoba Archaeology, Miscellaneous Papers* (Winnipeg)
PMAS	*Papers of the Michigan Academy of Science, Arts, and Letters*

PMR	*Peabody Museum Reports* (Cambridge, Massachusetts)
PN	*Polar Notes*
PnA	*Pennsylvania Archaeologist*
PNAS	*Proceedings of the National Academy of Sciences*
PNHSM	*Proceedings of the Natural History Society of Maryland* (Baltimore)
PPANS	*Proceedings of the Philadelphia Academy of Natural Sciences* (Philadelphia)
PPASE	*Papers of the Phillips Academy Southwestern Expedition* (Yale University Press, New Haven, Connecticut)
PPFA	*Papers of the Robert S. Peabody Foundation for Archaeology*
PPM	*Papers of the Peabody Museum of American Archaeology and Ethnology* (Cambridge, Massachusetts)
PR	*Prehistoric Records* (Northwestern Archeology Program, Northwestern University, Evanston, Illinois)
PrIAS	*Proceedings of the Iowa Academy of Science*
PRMAS	*Proceedings, Minnesota Academy of Science*
PRS	*Prehistory Research Series* (Indiana Historical Society, Indianapolis)
PS	*Popular Series* (Saskatchewan Museum of Natural History, Regina)
PSAA	*Papers of the School of American Archaeology* (Santa Fe, New Mexico)
PSM	*Popular Science Monthly*
PTASP	*Papers of the Texas Archeological Salvage Project* (The University of Texas, Austin)
PUSNM	*Proceedings of the U.S. National Museum* (Washington, D.C.)
QCPA	*Queens College Publications in Anthropology* (Flushing, New York)
QR	*Quaternary Research*
RAA	*Reports in Archaeology and Anthropology* (University of Kentucky, Lexington)
RBMAH	*Ripley P. Bullen Monographs in Anthropology and History* (Florida State Museum, Gainesville)
RBSP	*River Basin Surveys Papers* (Bureau of American Ethnology, Smithsonian Institution, Washington, D.C.)
RBSPSA	*River Basin Surveys, Publications in Salvage Archeology* (Smithsonian Institution, Washington, D.C.)
RCC	*Reports of the Chaco Center* (National Park Service)
RI	*Reports of Investigations* (Great Lakes Archaeological Research Center, Inc., Waukesha, Wisconsin)
RIBSU	*Reports of Investigations* (Archaeological Resources Management Services, Ball State University, Muncie, Indiana)
RIDAUT	*Report of Investigations, Department of Anthropology, University of Tennessee* (Knoxville)
RIISM	*Reports of Investigations* (Illinois State Museum, Springfield)
RIWSU	*Reports of Investigations, Laboratory of Anthropology* (Washington State University, Pullman)
RMEA	*Revista Mexicana de Estudios Antropologicos* (Mexico City)
RMHA	*Reports in Mackinac History and Archaeology* (Michigan State Park Commission)

RMS	*Research Manuscript Series* (Institute of Archeology and Anthropology, University of South Carolina, Columbia)
RRGABL	*Research Reports, Glenn A. Black Laboratory of Archaeology* (Indiana University, Bloomington)
RRNGS	*Research Reports, National Geographic Society* (Washington, D.C.)
RRRM	*Research Records of the Rochester Museum of Arts and Sciences* (Rochester, New York)
RRS	*Research Report Series* (Virginia Research Center for Archaeology, Yorktown)
RRTAS	*Research Report, Texas Archeological Survey* (The University of Texas, Austin)
RSCF	*Research Series, Chicora Foundation, Inc.* (Columbia, South Carolina)
RSTDC	*Research Series, Division of Archaeology, Tennessee Department of Conservation* (Nashville)
RT	*Researches and Transactions of the New York State Archaeological Association* (Rochester)
S	*Science*
SA	*Scientific American*
SAAAA	*Society for American Archaeology, Archives of Archaeology*
SAAP	*Society for American Archaeology, Papers*
SACB	*Southeastern Archaeological Conference Bulletin*
SACN	*Southeastern Archaeological Conference Newsletter*
SAn	*Series in Anthropology* (University of Colorado Press, Boulder)
SBMB	*Santa Barbara Museum of Natural History, Department of Anthropology Bulletin*
SBOAS	*Special Bulletin, Oklahoma Anthropological Society*
SCA	*Smithsonian Contributions to Anthropology* (Smithsonian Institution, Washington, D.C.)
SCAn	*South Carolina Antiquities*
SCIAN	*South Carolina Institute of Archeology and Anthropology Notebook* (University of South Carolina, Columbia)
SCK	*Smithsonian Contributions to Knowledge* (Smithsonian Institution, Washington, D.C.)
SCRA	*South Carolina Research in Anthropology* (Department of Anthropology, University of South Carolina, Columbia)
SDMP	*San Diego Museum of Man Papers* (San Diego)
SEA	*Southeastern Archaeology*
SH	*Sound Heritage* (Aural History Division, Provincial Archives of British Columbia, Victoria)
SICA	*Smithsonian Institution Contributions to Anthropology* (Smithsonian Institution, Washington, D.C.)
SIS	*Southern Indian Studies*
SJA	*Southwestern Journal of Anthropology*
SJCB	*Sacramento Jr. College, Department of Anthropology, Bulletin*
SL	*Southwestern Lore*
SLOOP	*San Luis Obispo County Archaeological Society Occasional Paper*

SMATS	*Southwestern Monuments Association, Technical Series* (Globe, Arizona)
SMC	*Smithsonian Miscellaneous Collections* (Smithsonian Institution, Washington, D.C.)
SMP	*Southwest Museum Papers*
SMSR	*Southwestern Monuments Special Report*
SMUCA	*Southern Methodist University Contributions in Anthropology* (Dallas)
SN	*SCIAA Notebook* (South Carolina Institute of Archeology and Anthropology, University of South Carolina, Columbia)
SOP	*Studies in Oklahoma's Past* (Oklahoma Archaeological Survey, University of Oklahoma, Norman)
SP	*Scientific Papers* (Illinois State Museum, Springfield)
SPu	*Scientific Publications* (Cleveland Museum of Natural History, Cleveland)
SSB	*Social Science Bulletin* (University of Arizona, Tucson)
SSPA	*Soil Systems Publications in Archaeology* (Soil Systems, Inc., Phoenix)
SUISM	*State University of Iowa Staff Magazine* (Ames)
Sy	*Syesis*
T	*Timeline*
TA	*Tennessee Archaeologist*
TAMP	*Tennessee Archaeological Society, Miscellaneous Papers*
TAPS	*Transactions of the American Philosophical Society* (Philadelphia)
TAPSR	*Texas Antiquities Permit Series* (Texas Antiquities Committee, Austin)
TAr	*Texas Archeology*
TARB	*Toledo Area Aboriginal Research Bulletin*
TASPM	*Texas Archeological Salvage Project, Miscellaneous Papers* (The University of Texas, Austin)
TASPS	*Survey Reports, Texas Archeological Salvage Project* (The University of Texas, Austin)
TASSP	*Texas Archeological Society Special Publication*
TBAP	*Texas State Building Commission Archeology Program Report* (Austin)
TC	*The Chesopiean*
TDAS	*Transactions of the Delaware Academy of Science*
TDHPA	*Texas State Department of Highways and Public Transportation, Publications in Archaeology* (Austin)
Teb	*Tebiwa*
TG	*Tidskritet Grønland*
THCASR	*Texas Historical Commission Archeological Survey Report* (Austin)
TIAS	*Transactions of the Illinois State Academy of Sciences*
TJS	*The Texas Journal of Science*
TM	*The Midden*
TMa	*Technical Manual* (Pan American Union, Washington, D.C.)
TMMB	*Texas Memorial Museum Bulletin* (The University of Texas, Austin)

TMP	*Tebiwa Miscellaneous Papers of the Idaho State University Museum of Natural History* (Moscow)
Tr	*Tracts* (Western Reserve Historical Society)
Tra	*Transactions* (The Historical and Scientific Society of Manitoba, Winnipeg)
TRB	*Tree-Ring Bulletin*
TRec	*The Record*
TTUGS	*Texas Tech University Graduate Studies* (Lubbock)
TTUMJ	*Texas Tech University Museum Journal* (Lubbock)
UAAP	*University of Arizona, Anthropological Papers* (Tucson)
UAMP	*University of Alaska Miscellaneous Publication* (Government Printing Office for the University of Alaska, Washington, D.C.)
UAOARRI	*University of Alabama, Office of Archaeological Research, Report of Investigations* (University)
UAOARRS	*University of Alabama, Office of Archaeological Research, Research Series* (University)
UASSB	*University of Arizona Social Science Bulletin* (Tucson)
UCAR	*University of California Anthropological Records*
UCARFC	*University of California Archaeological Research Facility Contributions*
UCASR	*University of California Archaeological Survey Reports* (Berkeley)
UCLAAR	*University of California, Los Angeles, Archaeological Survey, Annual Report*
UCPA	*University of California Publications in Anthropology*
UCPAE	*University of California Publications in American Archaeology and Ethnology* (Berkeley)
UCPAOP	*University of Chicago, Publications in Anthropology, Occasional Papers* (Chicago)
UCPG	*University of California Publications in Geography* (Berkeley)
UDB	*University of Denver Bulletin*
UGLAS	*University of Georgia, Laboratory of Archaeology Series* (Athens)
UGSA	*University of Georgia Series in Anthropology* (Athens)
UIAMP	*Department of Anthropology, University of Illinois at Urbana-Champaign, FAI–270 Archaeological Mitigation Project Report* (Urbana)
UIARMS	*University of Idaho Anthropological Research Manuscript Series* (Moscow)
UIB	*University of Illinois Bulletin* (Urbana)
UKMPE	*University of Kansas, Museum of Natural History, Popular Education Series* (Lawrence)
UKPA	*University of Kansas Publications in Anthropology* (Lawrence)
UMB	*University Museum Bulletin* (The University Museum, University of Pennsylvania, Philadelphia)
UMM	*University Museum Monograph* (University of Pennsylvania, Philadelphia)
UMMAAP	*University of Michigan, Museum of Anthropology, Anthropological Papers* (Ann Arbor)

UMMAOC	*University of Michigan, Museum of Anthropology, Occasional Contribution* (Ann Arbor)
UMPSS	*University of Montana Publications in the Social Sciences* (Missoula)
UNMAS	*University of New Mexico Bulletin, Anthropology Series* (Albuquerque)
UNMPA	*University of New Mexico Publications in Anthropology* (Albuquerque)
UNMSP	*University of Nebraska State Museum, Special Publication* (Lincoln)
UNS	*University of Nebraska Studies* (n.s.) (Lincoln)
UOAP	*University of Oregon Anthropological Papers* (Eugene)
UOSA	*University of Oregon Studies in Anthropology* (Eugene)
UPMJ	*University of Pennsylvania Museum Journal* (Philadelphia)
USB	*University Science Bulletin* (University of Kansas, Lawrence)
USCIN	*University of South Carolina, Institute of Archeology and Anthropology Notebook* (Columbia)
USDMAC	*University of South Dakota Museum, Archaeological Studies Circular* (Vermillion)
USGSPP	*U.S. Geological Survey Professional Paper*
USNMB	*U.S. National Museum Bulletin* (Smithsonian Institution, Washington, D.C.)
UTB	*University of Texas Bulletin* (Austin)
UTP	*University of Texas Publication* (Austin)
UUAP	*University of Utah Anthropological Papers* (Salt Lake City)
UWPS	*University of Wyoming Publications in Science*
VFPA	*Viking Fund Publications in Anthropology* (Wenner-Gren Fund for Anthropological Research, New York)
VHA	*Volumes in Historical Archeology* (Institute of Archeology and Anthropology, University of South Carolina, Columbia)
VHLNV	*Virginia Historic Landmarks Commission, Notes Virginia*
WA	*World Archaeology*
WACCP	*Western Archeological and Conservation Center Publications in Anthropology* (Western Archeological and Conservation Center, National Park Service, Tucson, Arizona)
WAR	*Western Anasazi Reports* (Cedar City, Utah)
WARCPR	*Washington Archaeological Research Center, Project Report* (Washington State University, Pullman)
WHQ	*The Western Historical Quarterly*
WiA	*The Wisconsin Archaeologist*
WMH	*Wisconsin Magazine of History* (Madison)
WSP	*Water-Supply Paper* (United States Geological Survey, Washington, D.C.)
WTHSSP	*West Texas Historical and Scientific Society Publication* (Sul Ross State Teachers College, Alpine)
WVA	*West Virginia Archaeologist*
WVRI	*West Virginia Geological and Economic Survey, Report of Investigations* (Morgantown)

YPMM   *Yearbook of the Public Museum of Milwaukee* (Milwaukee)
YUPA   *Yale University Publications in Anthropology* (New Haven, Connecticut)

Sources

Ackerman, R. E.
  1968. The Archeology of the Glacier Bay Region, Southeastern Alaska. RIWSU No. 44.
  1974. Post Pleistocene Cultural Adaptations on the Northern Northwest Coast. In *Proceedings, International Conference on the Prehistory and Paleoecology of the Western Arctic and Sub-Arctic*, edited by S. Raymond and P. Schledermann, pp. 1–20. Archaeological Association, Department of Archaeology, University of Calgary.
  1980. Microblades and Prehistory: Technological and Cultural Considerations for the North Pacific Coast. In *Early Native Americans: Prehistoric Demography, Economy, and Technology*, edited by D. L. Browman, pp. 189–197. Mouton.
Ackerman, R. E., T. D. Hamilton, and Robert Stuckenrath
  1979. Early Culture Complexes on the Northern Northwest Coast. CJA 3:195–209.
Adams, E. C.
  1975. *Causes of Prehistoric Settlement Systems in the Lower Piedra District, Colorado*. PhD dissertation, University of Colorado, Boulder.
  1979. *Native Ceramics from Walpi; Walpi Archaeological Project, Phase II*. Inter-Agency Archeological Services, Heritage Conservation and Recreation Service. Santa Fe.
  1982. *Walpi Archaeology Project: Synthesis and Interpretation*. Museum of Northern Arizona. Flagstaff.
  1983. The Architectural Analogue to Hopi Social Organization and Room Use, and Implications for Prehistoric Northern Southwestern Culture. AAn 48:44–61.
Adams, W. K.
  1949. *Archaeological Notes on Posey County, Indiana*. Indiana Historical Bureau. Indianapolis.
  n.d. An Archaeological Assessment of Homolovi I Ruin, near Winslow, Arizona (Site No. AZ–0200781). Report on file at Bureau of Land Management, Phoenix.
Adovasio, J. M.
  1974. Prehistoric North American Basketry. NSMAP 16.
Adovasio, J. M., J. D. Gunn, J. Donahue, and Robert Stuckenrath
  1977. Progress Report on the Meadowcroft Rockshelter: A 16,000 Year Chronicle. In *Amerinds and Their Paleoenvironments in Northeastern North America*, edited by W. S. Newman and Bert Salwen. ANYAS 228:37–159.
Adovasio, J. M., J. Donahue, K. Cushman, R. C. Carlisle, Robert Stuckenrath, J. D. Gunn, and W. C. Johnson
  1983. Evidence from Meadowdcraft Rockshelter. In *Early Man in the New World*, edited by Richard Shutler, Jr., pp. 163–189.

Agenbroad, L. D.
  1978a. Cody Knives and the Cody Complex in Plains Prehistory: A Reassessment. PA 23:159–161.
  1978b. *The Hudson-Meng Site: An Alberta Bison Kill in the Nebraska High Plains*. University Press of America. Washington, D.C.
Agogino, G. A.
  1961. A New Point Type from Hell Gap Valley, Eastern Wyoming. AAn 26(4):558–560.
Agogino, G. A., and W. D. Frankforter
  1960. A Paleo-Indian Bison Kill in Northwestern Iowa. AAn 25(3):414–415.
  1972. The Brewster Site. M34(3):102–107.
Agogino, G. A., and Eugene Galloway
  1965. The Sisters Hill Site: A Hell Gap Site in North-Central Wyoming. PA 10(29):190–195.
Agogino, G. A., and J. J. Hester
  1953. The Santa Ana Pre-ceramic Sites. EP 60(4):131–140.
Agogino, G. A., Irwin Rovner, and Cynthia Irwin-Williams
  1964. Early Man in the New World. S 143(3612):1350–1352.
Ahler, S. A., and R. C. Christensen
  n.d. A Pilot Study of Knife River Flint Procurement and Reduction at Site 32DU508, a Quarry and Workshop Location in Dunn County, North Dakota. Report on file at the State Historical Society of North Dakota, Bismarck.
Aigner, J. S.
  1970. The Unifacial, Core and Blade Site on Anangula Island, Aleutians. ArcA 7(2):59–88.
  1974. Studies in the Early Prehistory of Nikolski Bay: 1937–1971. APUA 16(1):9–25.
Aikens, C. M.
  1965. Excavations in Southwest Utah. UUAP, No. 76.
  1966. Virgin-Kayenta Cultural Relationships. UUAP, No. 79.
  1970. Hogup Cave. UUAP, No. 93.
  in press. Early Man: West. In *Handbook of North American Indians*, Vol. 1. Smithsonian Institution. Washington, D.C.
Aikens, C. M., and Rick Minor
  1978. Obsidian Hydration Dates for Klamath Prehistory. TMP 11.
Aikens, C. M., D. L. Cole, and Robert Stuckenrath
  1977. Excavations at Dirty Shame Rockshelter, Southeastern Oregon. TMP 4.
Aikens, C. M., D. K. Grayson, and P. J. Mehringer, Jr.
  n.d. Final Project Report to the National Science Foundation on the Steens Mountain Prehistory Project. Report on file at the Department of Anthropology, University of Washington, Seattle.
Alexander, L. S.
  1982. Phase II Archaeological Investigations Within the Shelby Bend Archaeological District, Hickman and Maury Counties, Tennessee. UAOARRI No. 21. University.
Allaire, Louis
  1978. L'archaeologie des Kitselas d'apres le Site Stratifie de Gitaus (GdTc:2) sur la Riviere Skeena en Colombie Britannique. NMMMS no. 72. Ottawa.

Allen, J. W., and C. H. McNutt
1955.   A Pit House near Santa Ana Pueblo, New Mexico. AAn 20(3):241–255.
Ambler, J. R.
1961.   *Archaeological Survey and Excavations at Casa Grande National Monument, Arizona.* MA thesis, University of Arizona, Tucson.
1966.   Caldwell Village. UUAP, No. 84.
Ames, K. M., J. P. Greene, and Margaret Pfortner
1981.   Hatwai (10NP143): Interim Report. ARBSU No. 9.
Amsden, Monroe
1928.   Archaeological Reconnaissance in Sonora. SMP, No. 1.
Anderson, D. C.
1966.   The Gordon Creek Burial. SL 32:1–9.
1981.   Mill Creek Ceramics. OSAIR No. 14.
Anderson, D. C., and H. A. Semken
1980.   *The Cherokee Excavations: Mid-Holocene Paleoecology and Human Adaptation in Northwest Iowa.* Academic Press. New York.
Anderson, D. C., Michael Finnegan, J. A. Hotopp, and A. K. Fisher
1978.   The Lewis Central School Site (13PW5): A Resolution of Ideological Conflicts at an Archaic Ossuary in Western Iowa. PA 23(81):183–219.
Anderson, D. D.
1968.   A Stone Age Campsite at the Gateway to America. SA 218(6):24–33.
1970a.   Akmak: An Early Archeological Assemblage from Onion Portage, Northwest Alaska. AcA 16.
1970b.   Microblade Traditions in Northwest Alaska. ArcA 7(2):12–16.
1978.   Tulaaqiac: A Transitional Near Ipiutak–Ipiutak Archaeological Site from Kotzebue Sound, Alaska. APUA 19(1):45–57.
Anderson, D. G.
n.d.a.   Excavations at Four Fall Line Sites: The Southeastern Columbia Beltway Project. Report on file at South Carolina Department of Highways and Public Transportation, Columbia.
n.d.b.   (editor) The Mattassee Lake Sites: Archaeological Investigations Along the Lower Santee River in the Coastal Plain of South Carolina. Report on file at Inter-Agency Archeological Services, National Park Service, Atlanta.
Anderson, D. G., D. J. Hally, and J. L. Rudolph
1986.   The Mississippian Occupation of the Savannah River Valley. SEA 5:32–51.
Anderson, D. G., S. T. Lee, and A. R. Parler, Jr.
1979.   Cal Smoak: A Report of Archaeological Investigations Along the Edisto River in the Coastal Plain of South Carolina. OPSC, No. 1.
Andrews, M. J.
n.d.   An Archaeological Assessment of Homolovi III and Chevelon Ruin, Northern Arizona. Report on file at Department of Anthropology, Northern Arizona University, Flagstaff.
Andrews, R. L., J. M. Adovasio, and R. C. Carlisle
1986.   Perishable Industries from Dirty Shame Rockshelter. UOAP, No. 34, and EMUP, No. 9.
Angel, J. L.
1966.   Early Skeletons from Tranquillity, California. SCA 2(1).

Anonymous
  1924.   George Hubbard Pepper. AA 26:566–567.
  1971.   Mark Raymond Harrington 1882–1971. M 45:84–88.
  n.d.   Notes on file for Site 38RD4, Institute of Archeology and Anthropology,
          University of South Carolina, Columbia.
Apland, B.
  1979.   Reconnaissance Survey in the Rainbow Mountains Region of West-Cen-
          tral British Columbia. APAOBC (Annual Report for the Year 1976):14–36.
Arnold, C. D.
  1981.   The Lagoon Site (OjR1–3): Implications for Paleoeskimo Interactions.
          NMMMS, No. 107.
Arthurs, David
  1978.   Sandy Lake Ware in Northwestern Ontario: A Distributional Study. MAQ
          2(1–2):57–64.
Artusy, Richard
  1976.   An Overview of the Proposed Ceramic Sequence in Southern Delaware.
          MaA 12(2):1–15.
Arundale, W. H.
  1976.   The Archaeology of the Nanook Site: An Exploratory Approach. PhD
          dissertation, Michigan State University, East Lansing.
Arutiunov, S. A., and D. A. Sergeev
  1964.   New Finds in the Old Bering Sea Cemetery at Uelen. In *The Archaeology
          and Geomorphology of Northern Asia: Selected Works*, edited by H. N.
          Michael, pp. 327–332; *Anthropology of the North. Translations from Rus-
          sian Sources* No. 5. University of Toronto Press for the Arctic Institute of
          North America.
Asch, D. L., K. B. Farnsworth, and N. B. Asch
  1979.   Woodland Subsistence and Settlement in West Central Illinois. In *Hope-
          wellian Archaeology: The Chillicothe Conference*, edited by D. B. Brose and
          N'omi Greber, pp. 80–85. Kent State University Press. Kent, Ohio.
Aten, L. E.
  1983.   *Indians of the Upper Texas Coast.* Academic Press. New York.
  1984.   Woodland Cultures of the Texas Coast. In *Perspectives on Gulf Coast
          Prehistory*, edited by D. D. Davis. RBMAH, No. 5:72–93.
Atwater, Caleb
  1820.   Description of the Antiquities Discovered in the State of Ohio and Other
          Western States. In *Archaeologia Americana* 1:105–267. Reprinted in 1973
          with an introduction by Jeremy A. Sabloff in *Antiquities of the New World:
          Early Explorations in Archaeology*, Vol. 1. AMS Press. New York.
Ayers, H. G.
  1972.   *The Archeology of the Susquehanna Tradition in the Potomac Valley.*
          PhD dissertation, Catholic University of America, Washington, D.C.
Ayers, H. G., and J. G. Little
  1967.   18FR100, a Woodland Site in Piedmont, Maryland. ASVQB 22(1):26–
          38.
Baby, R. S.
  1954.   Hopewell Cremation Practices. PAr, No. 1.
  1971.   Prehistoric Architecture: A Study of House Types in the Ohio Valley. OJS
          71 (4):193–198.

Baby, R. S., and S. M. Langlois
1979. Seip Mound State Memorial: Nonmortuary Aspects of Hopewell. In *Hopewell Archaeology: The Chillicothe Conference*, edited by D. B. Brose and N. B. Greber, pp. 16–18. Kent State University Press. Kent, Ohio.
n.d. Excavations of Section 01 and 02, Mounds 8 and 9, Mound City Group National Monument. Report on file at the Ohio Historical Society, Columbus.
Baby, R. S., and Martha Potter
1965. The Cole Complex: A Preliminary Analysis of the Late Woodland Ceramics in Ohio and Their Relationship to the Ohio Hopewell Phase. PAr, No. 2.
Bada, J. L., and P. M. Helfman
1975. Amino Acid Racemization Dating of Fossil Bones. WA 7:160–173.
Bada, J. L., R. A. Schroeder, and G. F. Carter
1974. New Evidence for the Antiquity of Man in North America Deduced from Aspartic Acid Racemization. S 184:791–793.
Bada, J. L., R. Gillespie, J. A. J. Gowlett, and R. E. M. Hedges
1984. Accelerator Mass Spectrometry Radiocarbon Ages of Amino Acid Extracts from California Paleoindian Skeletons. N 312:442–444.
Baerreis, D. A.
1951. The Prehistoric Horizons of Northeastern Oklahoma. UMMAAP No. 6.
1958. Aztalan Revisited. WiA 39(1):2–5.
Baerreis, D. A., and R. A. Bryson
1965. Climatic Episodes and the Dating of the Mississippian Cultures. WiA (n.s.) 46(4):203–220.
Baerreis, D. A., and J. E. Freeman
1958. Late Woodland Pottery in Wisconsin as Seen from Aztalan. WiA 39(1):35–61.
Baker, F. C., J. B. Griffin, R. G. Morgan, G. K. Neumann, and J. L. B. Taylor
1941. Contributions to the Archaeology of the Illinois River Valley, edited by J. B. Griffin and R. G. Morgan. TAPS 32(1).
Bandelier, A. F. A.
1890–1892. Final Report of Investigations among the Indians of the Southwestern United States, Carried on Mainly in the Years from 1880 to 1885 (2 Vols.). PAIAA 3, 4.
Bandi, H-G., and Jørgen Meldgaard
1952. Archaeological Investigations on Clavering O, Northeast Greenland. MG 126:4.
Banks, L. D., and Joe Winters
1975. The Bentsen-Clark Site, Red River County, Texas: A Preliminary Report. TASSP, No. 2.
Barbour, E. H., and C. B. Schultz
1932. The Scottsbluff Bison Quarry and Its Artifacts. NSMB, 1(34).
Bareis, C. J., and J. W. Porter (editors)
1984. *American Bottom Archaeology, a Summary of the FAI–270 Project Contribution to the Culture History of the Mississippi River Valley.* University of Illinois Press. Urbana and Chicago.
Barka, N. F., and B. C. McCary
1976. Early Shell Tempered Pottery in the James River Valley, Virginia. ESAFB No. 36.

Barnhart, T. A.
  1985.   An American Menagerie: The Cabinet of Squier and Davis. T 2(6):2–17.
Barrett, S. A.
  1927.   Reconnaissance of the Citadel Group of Pueblo Ruins in Arizona. YPMM
          6:7–58.
  1933.   Ancient Aztalan. BPMCM 8.
Barrett, S. A., and Alanson Skinner
  1932.   Certain Mounds and Village Sites of Shawano and Oconto Counties,
          Wisconsin. BPMCM 10(5).
Bartlett, Katherine
  1933.   Pueblo Milling Stones of the Flagstaff Region and Their Relation to Others
          in the Southwest. MNAB 3.
  1934.   The Material Culture of Pueblo II in the San Francisco Mountains, Ari-
          zona. MNAB 7.
  1941.   Skeletal Material from Winona and the Ridge Ruin. In *Winona and Ridge
          Ruin, Part I: Architecture and Material Culture*, by J. C. McGregor, pp. 300–
          305. MNAB 18.
  1943.   Onate's Route Across West Central Arizona. P 15(3):33–39.
Bass, W. M.
  1973.   Lansing Man: A Half Century Later. AJPA 38:99–104.
  n.d.   The Physical Anthropology of the Sully Site, 39SL4. Report on file at the
          National Park Service, Washington, D.C.
Bass, W. M., D. R. Evans, and R. L. Jantz
  1971.   The Leavenworth Site Cemetery: Archaeology and Physical Anthropol-
          ogy. UKPA No. 2.
Bassett, John, and R. L. Powell
  1984.   Stratigraphic Distribution of Cherts in Limestones of the Blue River Group
          in Southern Indiana. In *Prehistoric Chert Exploitation: Studies from the
          Midcontinent*, edited by B. M. Butler and E. E. May, pp. 239–251. OPCAI,
          No. 2.
Baumhoff, M. A., and J. S. Byrne
  1959.   Desert Side-notched Points as a Time Marker in California. UCASR, No.
          48:32–65.
Bayham, F. E.
  1982.   *A Diachronic Analysis of Prehistoric Animal Exploitation at Ventana
          Cave.* PhD dissertation, Arizona State University, Tempe.
Beals, J.
  1965.   Simonsen Site Revisited. NCIASN 13(5):35.
Beals, R. L., G. W. Brainerd, and W. Smith
  1945.   Archaeological Studies in Northeast Arizona. PAAE 44(1).
Beck, Charlotte
  1984.   *Steens Mountain Surface Archaeology: The Sites.* PhD dissertation, Uni-
          versity of Washington, Seattle.
Bedwell, S. F.
  1970.   *Prehistory and Environment of the Pluvial Fort Rock Lake Area of South-
          Central Oregon.* PhD dissertation, University of Oregon, Eugene.
  1973.   *Fort Rock Basin Prehistory and Environment.* University of Oregon
          Books. Eugene.

Bell, R. E.
1958. Guide to the Identification of Certain American Indian Projectile Points. OASOP, No. 1.
1960. Guide to the Identification of Certain American Indian Projectile Points. OASOP No. 2.
1972. The Harlan Site, Ck–6, a Prehistoric Mound Center in Cherokee County, Eastern Oklahoma. OASM No. 2.
1973. The Washita River Focus of the Southern Plains. In *Variations in Anthropology: Essays in Honor of John C. McGregor*, edited by D. W. Lathrap and Jody Douglas, pp. 171–187. Illinois Archaeological Survey. Urbana, Ill.
1980. Fourche Maline: An Archaeological Manifestation in Eastern Oklahoma. LASB No. 6.
1984. Arkansas Valley Caddoan: The Harlan Phase. In *Prehistory of Oklahoma*, edited by R. E. Bell, pp. 221–240. Academic Press. New York.
Bell, R. E., and D. A. Baerreis
1951. A Survey of Oklahoma Archaeology. BTAS 22:7–100.
Bell, R. E., E. B. Jelks, and W. W. Newcomb (assemblers)
1967. *A Pilot Study of Wichita Indian Archeology and Ethnohistory.* Final Report for National Science Foundation Grant GS–964. Southern Methodist University. Dallas.
Belmont, J. S.
1967. The Culture Sequence at the Greenhouse Site, Louisiana. SACB, No. 6:27–34.
1982. The Troyville Concept and the Gold Mine Site. LA, No. 9:63–98.
Benchley, E. D.
1974. *Mississippian Secondary Mound Loci: A Comparative Functional Analysis in a Timespace Perspective.* PhD dissertation, University of Wisconsin-Milwaukee.
Bennyhoff, J. A.
1956. An Appraisal of the Archaeological Resources of Yosemite National Park. UCASR 34.
Bense, J. A.
1972. *The Cascade Phase: A Study in the Effect of the Altithermal on a Cultural System.* PhD dissertation, Washington State University, Pullman.
1983. (editor) Archaeological Investigations in the Upper Tombigbee Valley: Phase I. OCARRI No. 3.
Benthall, J. L.
1969a. *Archeological Investigation of the Shannon Site, Montgomery County, Virginia.* Virginia State Library. Richmond.
1969b. *A Preliminary Archeological Survey of the T. M. Gathright Reservoir—Season I.* Virginia Polytechnic Institute and State University. Blacksburg.
n.d. Daugherty's Cave: A Stratified Site in Southwest Virginia. Report on file at the Virginia Research Center for Archaeology, Yorktown.
Benthall, J. L., and B. C. McCary
1973. The Williamson Site: A New Approach. AENA (1)1:127–132.
Berger, Rainer
1974. Advances and Results in Radiocarbon Dating: Early Man in America. WA 7(2):174–184.

1982. The Woolley Mammoth Site, Santa Rosa Island, California. In *Peopling of the New World*, edited by J. E. Ericson, R. E. Taylor, and Rainer Berger, pp. 163–170. Ballena Press. Los Altos, California.

Berger, Rainer, R. Protsch, R. Reynolds, C. Rozaire, and J. R. Sackett
1971. New Radiocarbon Dates Based on Bone Collagen on California Palaeoindians. CUCARF 12:43–49.

Bettarel, R. L., and H. G. Smith
1973. The Moccasin Bluff Site and the Woodland Cultures of Southwestern Michigan. UMMAAP, No. 49.

Bettinger, R. L.
1975. *The Surface Archaeology of Owens Valley, Eastern California.* PhD dissertation, University of California, Riverside.
1976. The Development of Pinyon Exploitation in Central Eastern California. JCA 3(1):81–95.
1977. Aboriginal Human Ecology in Owens Valley: Prehistoric Change in the Great Basin. AAn 42(1):3–17.

Bettinger, R. L., and T. F. King
1971. Interaction and Political Organization: A Theoretical Framework for Archaeology in Owens Valley. UCLAAR 13:137–152.

Bettinger, R. L., and R. E. Taylor
1974. Suggested Revisions in Archaeological Sequences of the Great Basin and Interior Southern California. NASRP 5:1–26.

Beuschel, Leslie
n.d. The Keowee-Toxaway Project: A Partial Report of the Archeology. Report on file at Institute of Archeology and Anthropology, University of South Carolina, Columbia.

Bice, R. A., and W. M. Sundt
1972. *Prieta Vista: A Small Pueblo III Ruin in North-central New Mexico.* Albuquerque Archaeological Society.

Binford, L. R.
1963. Red Ocher Caches from the Michigan Area: A Possible Case of Cultural Drift. SJA 19(1):89–108.
1964. *Archaeological and Ethnohistorical Investigation of Cultural Diversity and Progressive Development among Aboriginal Cultures of Coastal Virginia and North Carolina.* PhD dissertation, University of Michigan, Ann Arbor.
1965. Colonial Period Ceramics of the Nottoway and Weanock Indians of Southeastern Virginia. ASVQB, 19(4):78–87.
1978. *Nunamiut Ethnoarchaeology.* Academic Press. New York.

Binford, L. R., and G. I. Quimby
1963. Indian Sites and Chipped Stone Materials in the Northern Lake Michigan Area. F:A 26(12):277–307.

Binford, L. R., S. R. Binford, Robert Whallon, and M. A. Hardin
1970. Archaeology at Hatchery West. MSAA, No. 24.

Birk, D. A.
1977. Two Sandy Lake Ware Vessels from Onigum Point, Cass County, Minnesota. MinA 36(1):9–15.

1979. Sandy Lake Ware. In *A Handbook of Minnesota Prehistoric Ceramics*, edited by S. F. Anfinson, pp. 175–182. OPMA, No. 5.

Bischoff, J. L., R. Merriam, W. M. Childers, and R. Protsch
1976. Antiquity of Man in America Indicated by Radiometric Dates on the Yuha Burial Site. N 261:128–129.

Black, G. A.
1936. Excavation of the Nowlin Mound. IHB 13(7):201–305.
1967. *Angel Site: An Archaeological, Historical and Ethnological Study.* 2 vols. Indiana Historical Society. Indianapolis.

Blackman, E. E.
1903. Report of Department of Archeology. In *Annual Report of the Nebraska State Board of Agriculture for 1902*, pp. 294–326. Lincoln.
1905. Report of Department of Archeology for 1903 and 1904. In *Annual Report of the Nebraska State Board of Agriculture for 1904*, pp. 207–229. Lincoln.

Blakely, R. L.
1973. *Biological Variation Among and Between Two Prehistoric Indian Populations at Dickson Mounds.* PhD dissertation, Indiana University, Bloomington.

Blaker, M. C.
1952. Further Comments on Simple-Stamped Shell-Tempered Pottery. AAn (17)3:257–258.

Blakeslee, D. J.
1963. Aboriginal Ceramics: The Townsend Site near Lewes, Delaware. Arcl 15(1):14–39.
1978. *The Central Plains Tradition in Eastern Nebraska: Content and Outcome.* OSAIR No. 11:134–143.

Blakeslee, D. J., and W. W. Caldwell
1979. *The Nebraska Phase: An Appraisal.* J & L Reprint. Lincoln.

Blakeslee, D. J., and John O'Shea
1981. *Missouri National Recreational River: Native American Cultural Resources.* (Nebraska State Historical Society, Lincoln)

Blanton, D. B., C. T. Espenshade, and P. E. Brockington, Jr.
n.d. An Archaeological Study of 38SU83: A Yadkin Phase Site in the Upper Coastal Plain of South Carolina. Report on file at the South Carolina Department of Highways and Public Transportation, Columbia.

Blasingham, E. J.
1953. *Temporal and Spatial Distribution of the Yankeetown Cultural Manifestation.* MA thesis, Indiana University, Bloomington.
n.d. Excavation of Yankeetown (12 W 1). Report to the National Park Service.

Bleed, Peter
1969. The Archaeology of Petaga Point: The Preceramic Component. MPS, No. 2.

Bluhm, E. A.
1957. The Sawmill Site: A Reserve Phase Village, Pine Lawn Valley, Western New Mexico. F:A 47(1).

Blumenthal, E. H., Jr.
  1940.   An Introduction to Gallina Archaeology. NMA 4(1):10–13.
Boas, Franz and Berthold Laufer
  1909.   (editors) Putnam Anniversary Volume: Anthropological Essays Presented
          to Frederic Ward Putnam in Honor of His Seventieth Birthday. G. E. Stechert
          & Co. New York.
Bockstoce, John
  1979.   The Archaeology of Cape Nome, Alaska. UMM No. 38.
Bodine, J. J.
  1979.   Taos Pueblo. In *Handbook of North American Indians*, Vol. 9: Southwest,
          edited by W. C. Sturtevant and B. C. Trigger, pp. 255–267. Smithsonian
          Institution. Washington, D.C.
Boehm, S. G.
  1973.   *Cultural and Non-cultural Variation in the Artifact and Faunal Samples
          from the St. Mungo Cannery Site, B. C., DgRr 2.* MA thesis, University of
          Victoria, Victoria.
Bolton, H. E.
  1949.   *Coronado on the Turquoise Trail: Knight of the Pueblos and Plains.*
          University of New Mexico Press. Albuquerque.
  1950.   *Pageant in the Wilderness: The Story of the Escalante Expedition to the
          Interior Basin, 1776.* Utah State Historical Society. Salt Lake City.
Bond, C. L.
  1978.   Three Archaeological Sites at Hoxie Bridge, Williamson County, Texas.
          ALRTAM No. 43:1–296.
Bonnichsen, Robson
  1979.   Pleistocene Bone Technology in the Beringian Refugium. NMMMS,
          ASCP, No. 89. Ottawa.
Borden, C. E.
  1951.   Facts and Problems of Northwest Coast Prehistory. ABC 2:35–57.
  1952.   A Uniform Site Designation Scheme for Canada. ABC 3:44–48.
  1960.   DjRi 3, an Early Site in the Fraser Canyon, British Columbia. Contri-
          butions to Anthropology 1957, NMCB No. 162.
  1961.   Fraser River Archaeological Project. APNMC No. 1.
  1962.   West Coast Crossties with Alaska. AINATP 11:9–19.
  1968a. Prehistory of the Lower Mainland. In *Lower Fraser Valley: Evolution
          of a Cultural Landscape*, edited by A. H. Siemens. BCGS No. 9.
  1968b. A Late Pleistocene Pebble Tool Industry of Southwest British Columbia.
          ENMUCA 1(4):55–69.
  1970.   Culture History of the Fraser-Delta Region: An Outline. In *Archaeology
          in British Columbia, New Discoveries*, edited by R. L. Carlson. BCS Special
          Issue 6–7:95–112.
  1975.   Origins and Development of the Early Northwest Coast Culture to about
          3000 B.C. ASCP No. 45.
  1976.   A Water-Saturated Site on the Southern Mainland Coast of British Co-
          lumbia. In *The Excavation of Water-Saturated Archaeological Sites (Wet
          Sites) on the Northwest Coast of North America*, edited by D. R. Croes.
          ASCP No. 50.

1979.   Peopling and Early Cultures of the Pacific Northwest. S 203(4384):963–971.

Bossu, Jean-Bernard
1982.   *New Travels in North America 1770–1771.* Translated by S. D. Dickinson. Northwest State University Press. Natchitoches, Louisiana.

Bott, K. E.
1981.   44RU7: Archaeological Test Excavations at a Late Woodland Village in the Lower Uplands of Southwest Virginia. RRS No. 2.

Bourque, B. J.
1975.   Comments on the Late Archaic Populations of Central Maine: The View from Turner Farm. ArcA 12(2):35–45.

Bowen, T. G.
1976a.   Seri Prehistory: The Archaeology of the Central Coast of Sonora, Mexico. APUAr, No. 27.
1976b.   Esquema de la Historia de la Cultura Trincheras. In *Sonora: Antropologia del Desierto,* edited by Beatriz Braniff Cornejo and R. S. Felger. CC 27:267–280.

Bowman, P. W.
1960.   Coal-Oil Canyon (14LO1): Report on Preliminary Investigation. KAAB, No. 1.

Boyer, W. P., Jr.
n.d.   Searching for Jefferson's Mound: A Preliminary Report on the 1982 Season at the Carrsbrook Site, 44AB14. Report on file at James Madison University, Harrisonburg, Virginia.

Brand, D. D., Florence M. Hawley, and F. C. Hibben
1937.   Tseh So, a Small House Ruin, Chaco Canyon, New Mexico. UNMAS 2(2).

Brandes, R. S.
1957.   An Archaeological Survey within Gila County, Arizona. Report on file at Arizona State Museum, University of Arizona, Tucson.

Braniff Cornejo, Beatriz
1985.   *La Frontera Protohistorical Pima-Opata en Sonora, Mexico; Proposiciones Arqueologicas Preliminares.* Universidad Nacional de Mexico. Mexico City.

Branstner, S. M.
n.d.   1984 Archaeological Investigations at the Marquette Mission Site. Report on file at The Museum, Michigan State University, East Lansing.

Brashler, J. G.
1973.   *A Formal Analysis of Prehistoric Ceramics from the Fletcher Site.* MA thesis, Michigan State University, East Lansing.
1981.   Early Late Woodland Boundaries and Interaction. ASMSU, No. 3.

Braun, D. P.
1977.   *Middle Woodland–(Early) Late Woodland Social Change in the Prehistoric Central Midwestern U.S.* PhD dissertation, University of Michigan, Ann Arbor.
1979.   Illinois Hopewell Burial Practices and Social Organization: A Reexamination of the Klunk-Gibson Mound Group. In *Hopewell Archaeology: The Chillicothe Conference,* edited by D. S. Brose and N'omi Greber. Kent State University Press. Kent, Ohio.

Brauner, D. R.
   1976.   *Alpowai: The Culture History of the Alpowa Locality*. PhD dissertation, Washington State University, Pullman.
   1985.   *Early Human Occupation in the Uplands of the Southern Plateau*. Department of Anthropology, Oregon State University. Corvallis.
Brazeau, L. A., P. A. Bruhy, and D. F. Overstreet
   1979.   Archaeological Survey and Test Excavations in the Fox River Drainage— Waukesha, Racine, and Walworth Counties. RI, No. 90.
Breternitz, C. D., D. E. Doyle, and M. P. Marshall
   1982.   (editors) Bis s'ana: A Late Bonito Phase Community on Escavada Wash, Northwest New Mexico. NMPA, No. 14.
Breternitz, D. A.
   1957a.   1956 Excavations Near Flagstaff: Part I. P 30(1):22–30.
   1957b.   1956 Excavations Near Flagstaff: Part II. P 30(2):43–54.
   1959.   Excavations at Two Cinder Park Phase Sites. P 31(3):66–72.
   1960.   Excavations at Three Sites in the Verde Valley, Arizona. MNAB 34.
Breternitz, D. A., A. C. Swedlund, and D. C. Anderson
   1960.   Orme Ranch Cave, NA6656. P 33(2):25–39.
   1967.   The Eruption(s) of Sunset Crater: Dating and Effects. P 40(2):72–76.
   1971.   An Early Burial from Gordon Creek, Colorado. AAn 36(2):160–182.
Brew, J. O.
   1946.   Archaeology of Alkali Ridge, Southeastern Utah. PPM 21.
   1979.   Hopi Prehistory and History to 1850. In *Handbook of North American Indians: Southwest*, Vol. 9, edited by W. C. Strutevant and A. A. Ortiz, pp. 514–523. Smithsonian Institution. Washington, D.C.
Brewer, W. H.
   1866.   Alleged Discovery of an Ancient Human Skull in California. AJS 42:424.
Brockington, Paul
   1971a.   South Carolina's Oldest Lady: A Skeleton from 38BU9, Daw's Island, Beaufort County. SN 3(6):128–131.
   1971b.   A Preliminary Investigation of an Early Knapping Site in Southeastern Georgia. SN 3:23–46.
Broecker, W. S., E. A. Olson, P. C. Orr
   1960.   Radiocarbon Measurements and Annual Rings in Cave Formations. N 185:93–94.
Brogan, W. T.
   1981.   The Cuesta Phase: A Settlement Pattern Study. ASKSHS No. 9.
Brookes, S. O.
   1979.   The Hester Site, an Early Archaic Occupation in Monroe County, Mississippi: I. A Preliminary Report. MDAHAR No. 5.
Brooks, M. J., Larry Lepionka, T. A. Rathbun, and John Goldsborough, Jr.
   1982.   Preliminary Archeological Investigations at the Callawassie Island Burial Mound (38BU19), Beaufort County, South Carolina. RMS, No. 185.
Brose, D. S.
   1970.   The Archaeology of Summer Island: Changing Settlement Systems in Northern Lake Michigan. UMMAAP, No. 41.
   1976.   Locational Analysis in the Prehistory of Northeast Ohio. In *Cultural Change and Continuity: Essays in Honor of James Bennett Griffin*, edited by C. E. Cleland, pp. 3–18. Academic Press. New York.

1984. Mississippian Period Cultures in Northwestern Florida. In *Perspectives on Gulf Coast Prehistory*, edited by D. D. Davis, pp. 165–197. University Presses of Florida. Gainesville.

Brose, D. S., and N'omi Greber
1979. (editors) *Hopewell Archaeology: The Chillicothe Conference*. Kent State University Press. Kent, Ohio.

Brose, D. S., and G. W. Percy
1980. Fort Walton Settlement Patterns. In *Mississippian Settlement Patterns*, edited by B. D. Smith, pp. 81–114. Academic Press. New York.

Brose, D. S., J. A. Brown, and D. W. Penney
1985. *Ancient Art of the American Woodland Indians*. H. N. Abrams. New York.

Browman, D. L., and D. A. Munsell
1969. Columbia Plateau Prehistory: Cultural Development and Impinging Influences. AAn 34(3):249–264.

Brown, C. E.
n.d. Notes on Silver Mound. Report on file at the State Historical Society of Wisconsin, Museum Division, Madison.

Brown, D. N.
1973. *Structural Changes at Picuris Pueblo*. PhD dissertation, University of Arizona, Tucson.

Brown, J. A.
1961. (editor) *The Zimmerman Site: A Report on Excavations at the Grand Village of Kaskaskia, La Salle County, Illinois*. ISMRI, No. 9.
1964. The Northeastern Extension of the Havana Tradition. ISMSP 12:107–122.
1966–1985. *Spiro Studies*, vols. 1–5. University of Oklahoma Research Institute. Norman.
1971. (editor) Approaches to the Social Dimensions of Mortuary Practices. MSAA 25.
1979. Charnel Houses and Mortuary Crypts: Disposal of the Dead in the Middle Woodland Period. In *Hopewell Archaeology: The Chillicothe Conference*, edited by D. S. Brose and N'omi Greber, pp. 211–219. Kent State University Press. Kent, Ohio.
1984a. Spiro Focus. In *The Prehistory of Oklahoma*, edited by R. E. Bell, pp. 241–263. Academic Press. New York.
1984b. Prehistoric Southern Ozarks Marginality: A Myth Exposed. MASSP No. 6.
n.d. Inventory and Integrative Analysis: Excavations of Mound City, Ross County, Ohio. Report on file at the Department of Anthropology, Northwestern University, Evanston, Illinois.

Brown, J. A., and R. S. Baby
n.d. Mound City Revisited. Report on file, Department of Archaeology, Ohio Historical Center, Columbus.

Brown, J. A., and R. K. Vierra
1983. What Happened in the Middle Archaic? Introduction to an Ecological Approach to Koster Site Archaeology. In *Archaic Hunters and Gatherers in the American Midwest*, edited by J. L. Phillips and J. A. Brown, pp. 166–195. Academic Press. New York.

582   REFERENCES

Brown, J. A., R. E. Bell, and D. G. Wyckoff
  1978.   Caddoan Settlement Patterns in the Arkansas River Valley. In *Mississippian Settlement Patterns*, edited by B. D. Smith, pp. 169–200. Academic Press. New York.
Brown, L. A.
  1966.   Temporal and Spatial Order in the Central Plains. PA 11(34):294–301.
Brown, M. K.
  1975.   *The Zimmerman Site: Further Excavations at the Grand Village of the Kaskaskia.* ISMRI, No. 32.
Broyles, B. J.
  1966.   Preliminary Report: The St. Albans Site (46KA27), Kanawha County, West Virginia. WVA 19:1–43.
  1971.   Second Preliminary Report: The St. Albans Site, Kanawha County, West Virginia. WVRI 3.
Bruder, J. S.
  1983.   Archaeological Investigations at the Adobe Dam Alternative Site No. 4, Phoenix, Arizona. MNARP, No. 29.
Bryan, A. L.
  1980.   The Stemmed Point Tradition: An Early Technological Tradition in Western North America. In *Anthropological Papers in Memory of Earl H. Swanson*, edited by L. Harten, C. N. Warren, and D. R. Tuohy, pp. 77–107. Idaho State University, Museum of Natural History. Pocatello.
Bryan, A. R.
  1979.   Smith Creek Cave. NSMAP 17:162–253.
Bryan, Kirk
  1935.   Minnesota Man: A Discussion of the Site. S 82(2121):170–171.
  1940.   Geologic Antiquity of the Lindenmeier Site in Colorado. SMC 99(2).
  1954.   The Geology of Chaco Canyon, New Mexico, in Relation to the Life and Remains of the Prehistoric Peoples of Pueblo Bonito. SMC 122(7).
Bryan, Kirk, and C. C. Albritton, Jr.
  1943.   Soil Phenomena as Evidence of Climatic Changes. AJS 214:461–490.
  1984.   The Bryan Site. Min A 43(2).
Bryce, George
  1904.   Among the Mound Builders' Remains. Tra 66:1–33.
Buchanan, W. T., Jr.
  1969.   Deep Bottom Site, Henrico County, Virginia. ASVQB (23)3:103–114.
  n.d.   The Trigg Site, City of Radford, Virginia. Report on file at the Archeological Society of Virginia, Richmond.
Buehrig, J. E., and Ronald Hicks
  1982.   A Comprehensive Survey of the Archaeological Resources of Mounds State Park, Anderson, Indiana with a Proposed Resources Management Plan. RIBSU, No. 6.
Buikstra, J. E.
  1976.   Hopewell in the Lower Illinois Valley: A Regional Approach to the Study of Human Biological Variability and Prehistoric Behavior. NUAPSP, No. 2.
Bullen, R. P.
  1951a.   The Enigmatic Crystal River Site. AAn 17:142–143.
  1951b.   The Terra Ceia Site, Manatee County, Florida. FASP, No. 3.

1952. Eleven Archaeological Sites in Hillsborough County, Florida. FGSRI, No. 8.

1953. The Famous Crystal River Site. FA 6:9–37.

1955a. Archaeology of the Tampa Bay Area. FHQ 34:51–63.

1955b. Stratigraphic Tests at Bluffton, Volusia County, Florida. FA 8:1–16.

1966. Stelae at the Crystal River Site, Florida. AAn 31:861–865.

1972. The Orange Period of Peninsular Florida. In *Fiber-Tempered Pottery in Southeastern United States and Northern Colombia: Its Origins, Context, and Significance*, edited by R. P. Bullen and James Stoltman. FASP 6:9–33.

1978. Tocobaga Indians and the Safety Harbor Culture. in *Tacachale: Essays on the Indians of Florida and Southeastern Georgia During the Historic Period*, edited by J. T. Milanich and Samuel Proctor, pp. 50–58. University Presses of Florida. Gainesville.

Bullen, R. P., and H. B. Greene

1970. Stratigraphic Tests at Stalling's Island, Georgia. FA 23:8–28.

Bunyan, Donald

1979. Harlan I. Smith: Pioneer Contributor to Western Archaeology. TM 11(3):5–8.

Burley, D. V.

1979. The Marpole Site Reassessed. TM 11(4):3–7.

1980. Marpole: *Anthropological Reconstructions of a Prehistoric Northwest Coast Culture Type*. Simon Fraser University Press, Publication No. 8. Burnaby, British Columbia.

Bushnell, D. I.

1905. Cahokia and Surrounding Mound Groups. PPM 3(1):3–20.

1930. Five Monacan Towns in Virginia, 1607. SMC (82)12:1–41.

1937. Indian Sites Below the Falls of the Rappahannock, Virginia. SMC 96(4):1–65.

Bussey, S. D.

1968. Excavations at LA 6462: The North Bank Site. In *The Cochiti Dam Archaeological Salvage Project, Part 1, Report of the 1963 Season*, assembled by C. H. Lange. MNMRR, No. 6.

Butler, B. M.

1971. Hoover-Beeson Rockshelter, 40Cm4, Cannon County, Tennessee. TAMP, No. 9.

1977. *Mississippian Settlement in the Black Bottom, Pope and Massac Counties, Illinois*. PhD dissertation, Southern Illinois University, Carbondale.

Butler, B. M., and R. W. Jefferies

1986. Crab Orchard and Early Woodland Cultures in the Middle South. In *Early Woodland Archeology*, edited by K. B. Farnsworth and T. E. Emerson, pp. 523–534. KSA, No. 2.

Butler, B. R.

1957. Art of the Lower Columbia Valley. Ar 10(3):158–165.

1959. Lower Columbia Valley Archaeology: A Survey and Appraisal of Some Major Archaeological Resources. Teb 2(2):6–24.

1960. *The Physical Stratigraphy of Wakemap Mound, a New Interpretation*. MA thesis, University of Washington, Seattle.

1961. The Old Cordilleran Culture in the Pacific Northwest. OPISUM, No. 5.

1962. Contributions to the Prehistory of the Columbia Plateau. OPISCM, No. 9.

1965a. Perspectives on the Prehistory of the Lower Columbia Valley. Teb 8(1):1–16.

1965b. The Structure and Function of the Old Cordilleran Culture Concept. AA 67(5) Part 1:1120–1131.

1965c. A Report on Investigations of an Early Man Site Near Lake Channel, Southern Idaho. Teb 8(1):1–21.

Byers, D. S.

1954. Bull Brook: A Fluted Point Site in Ipswich Massachusetts. AAn 19(4):343–351.

1956. Additional Information on the Bull Brook Site, Massachusetts. AAn 29(3):274–276.

1959. The Eastern Archaic: Some Problems and Hypotheses. AAn 24(3):233–256.

1979. The Nevin Shellheap: Burials and Observations. PPFA, No. 9.

Byrne, W. J.

1977. The Archaeology and Prehistory of Southern Alberta as Reflected by Ceramics. NMMMS, ASCP, No. 14.

1978. An Archaeological Demonstration of Migration on the Northern Great Plains. In *Archaeological Essays in Honor of Irving B. Rouse*, edited by R. C. Dunnell and E. S. Hall, Jr. Mouton. New York.

Cable, J. S., and D. E. Doyel

1986. Pioneer Period Settlement Pattern and Village Structure in the Phoenix Basin. In *The Hohokam Village: Site Structure and Organization*, edited by D. E. Doyel. Southwestern and Rocky Mountain Division, American Association for the Advancement of Science. Glenwood Springs, Colorado.

Caine, C. A. H.

1966. The Neubauer Lake Woodland Site in Pine County, Minnesota. MinA 28(2):74–107.

1974. The Archaeology of the Snake River Region in Minnesota. In *Aspects of Upper Great Lakes Anthropology: Papers in Honor of Lloyd A. Wilford*, edited by Elden Johnson, pp. 55–63. MPS, No. 11.

1983. *Normative Typological and Systemic Stylistic Approaches to the Analysis of North Central Minnesota Ceramics*. PhD dissertation, University of Minnesota, Minneapolis.

Calabrese, F. A.

1967. The Archeology of the Upper Verdigris Watershed. ASKSHS, No. 3.

Caldwell, J. R.

1943. *Cultural Relations of Four Indian Sites of the Georgia Coast*. PhD dissertation, University of Chicago, Chicago.

1948. Palachacolas Town, Hampton County, South Carolina. JWAS 38:321–324.

1952. Archaeology of Eastern Georgia and South Carolina. In *Archaeology of Eastern United States*, edited by J. B. Griffin, pp. 312–321. University of Chicago Press. Chicago.

1955. Investigations at Rood's Landing, Stewart County, Georgia. EG 2:1–28.
1958. Trend and Tradition in the Prehistory of the Eastern United States. AAAM, No. 88.

Caldwell, J. R., and Robert Hall
1964. (editors) Hopewellian Studies. SP, No. 12.

Caldwell, J. R., and Catherine McCann
1941. *Irene Mound Site, Chatham County, Georgia.* University of Georgia Press. Athens.

Caldwell, J. R., and A. J. Waring, Jr.
1939. Some Chatham County Pottery Types and Their Sequence. SACN 1(5–6).

Caldwell, W. W.
1956. *The Archaeology of Wakemap, A Stratified Site Near The Dalles of the Columbia.* PhD dissertation, University of Washington, Seattle.

Caldwell, W. W., and O. L. Mallory
1967. Hells Canyon Archeology. RBSPSA, No. 6.

Caldwell, W. W., and D. R. Henning
1978. North American Plains. In *Chronologies in New World Archaeology,* edited by R. E. Taylor and C. W. Meighan, pp. 113–145.

Calmes, A. R.
n.d.a. Test Excavations at Two Late Archaic Sites on Hilton Head Island, Beaufort County, S.C. Manuscript on file at Institute of Archeology and Anthropology, University of South Carolina, Columbia.
n.d.b. Excavations at Jenkins Island and Green's Shell Enclosure. Manuscript on file at Institute of Archeology and Anthropology, University of South Carolina, Columbia.

Calvert, S. G.
1970. The St. Mungo Site. In *Archaeology in British Columbia, New Discoveries,* edited by R. L. Carlson. BCS Nos. 6–7.
1980. *A Cultural Analysis of Faunal Remains from Three Archaeological Sites in Hesquiat Harbour, B.C.* PhD dissertation, University of British Columbia, Vancouver.

Cambron, J. W., and D. C. Hulse
1961. A Comparative Study of Some Unfinished Fluted Points and Channel Flakes from the Tennessee Valley. JAA 7(2):88–105.
1964. *Handbook of Alabama Archaeology: Part I, Point Types.* Archaeological Research Association of Alabama. Birmingham.
1975. *Handbook of Alabama Archaeology: Part I, Point Types.* (revised) Archaeological Research Association of Alabama. Birmingham.

Cambron, J. W., and S. A. Waters
1959. Flint Creek Rock Shelter (Part I). TA 15(2):73–87.

Cameron, Cathy
1984. A Regional View of Chipped Stone Raw Material Use in Chaco Canyon. In *Recent Research on Chaco Prehistory.* RCC, No. 8.

Campbell, E. W. C., and W. H. Campbell
1935. The Pinto Basin Site: An Ancient Aboriginal Camping Ground in the California Desert. SMP 9:1–51.

Campbell, E. W. C., W. H. Campbell, Ernst Antevs, C. E. Amsden, J. A. Barbieri, and F. D. Bode
 1937. The Archaeology of Pleistocene Lake Mohave: A Symposium. SMP, No. 11.
Campbell, J. M.
 1959. The Kayuk Complex of Arctic Alaska. AAn 25(1):94–105.
 1961. The Tuktu Complex of Anaktuvuk Pass. APUA 9(2):61–80.
 1962. Cultural Succession at Anaktuvuk Pass, Arctic Alaska. In *Prehistoric Cultural Relations between the Arctic and Temperate Zones of North America*, edited by J. M. Campbell, pp. 39–54. AINATP, No. 11.
 1968. The Kavik Site of Anaktuvuk Pass, Central Brooks Range. APUA 14(1):33–42.
Campbell, J. M., and F. H. Ellis
 1952. The Atrisco Sites: Cochise Manifestations in the Middle Rio Grande Valley. AAn 17(3):211–221.
Campbell, Robert
 1969. *Prehistoric Panhandle Culture on the Chaquaqua Plateau, Southeastern Colorado*. PhD dissertation, University of Colorado, Boulder.
 1976. The Panhandle Aspect of the Chaquaqua Plateau. TTUGS, No. 11.
Campbell, S. N.
 1985. (editor) *Summary of Results, Chief Joseph Dam Cultural Resources Project, Washington*. Office of Public Archaeology, Institute for Environmental Studies, University of Washington. Seattle.
Campbell, T. N.
 1947. The Johnson Site: Type Site of the Aransas Focus of the Texas Coast. BTAPS 18:40–75.
Capes, K. H.
 1963. The W. B. Nickerson Survey and Excavations, 1912–1915, of the Southern Manitoba Mounds Region. NMCAP, No. 4.
Carlson, Catherine
 1979. The Early Component at Bear Cove. CJA No 3:177–194.
Carlson, R. L.
 1960. Chronology of Culture Change in the San Juan Islands, Washington. AAn 25:562–587.
 1965. Eighteenth Century Navajo Fortresses of the Gobernador District. SAn, No. 10.
 1970. Excavations on Mayne Island. In *Archaeology in British Columbia, New Discoveries*, edited by R. L. Carlson. BCS Nos. 6,7.
 1979. The Early Period on the Central Coast of British Columbia. CJA, No. 13.
 1983a. Prehistory of the Northwest Coast. In *Indian Art Traditions of the Northwest Coast*. Archaeology Press, Simon Fraser University. Burnaby, British Columbia.
 1983b. The Far West. In *Early Man in the New World*, edited by Richard Shutler, Jr. Sage Publications. Beverly Hills, California.
Carmichael, P. H.
 1977. A Descriptive Summary of Blackduck Ceramics from the Wanipigow Lake Site Area (EgKx–1), 1975 and 1976. PMAMP, No. 5.

Carpenter, E. S.
   1950.   Five Sites of the Intermediate Period. AAn 15(4):298–321.
Carr, Lucien
   1877.   Report on the Exploration of a Mound in Lee County, Virginia. ARPM, No. 10.
Carter, G. F.
   1957.   *Pleistocene Man at San Diego*. Johns Hopkins Press. Baltimore, Maryland.
Carter, Jacki, and Lee Chickering
   1973.   An Osteological Analysis of the Scott's Lake Bluff Population. SN 5:105–144.
Cassells, E. S.
   1983.   *The Archaeology of Colorado*. Johnson Books. Boulder, Colorado.
Cattanach, G. S., Jr.
   1980.   Long House, Mesa Verde National Park, Colorado. NPSPA, No. 7H.
Caywood, L. R.
   1966.   *Excavations at Rainbow House, Bandelier National Monument, New Mexico*. National Park Service, Southwest Archeological Center. Globe, Arizona.
Caywood, L. R., and E. H. Spicer
   1935.   *Tuzigoot: The Excavations and Repair of a Ruin in the Verde Valley near Clarkdale, Arizona*. Southwestern Monuments, National Park Service. Coolidge, Arizona.
Celnar, P.
   1978.   *Flint Ridge* (reprinted). Ohio Department of Natural Resources, Division of Geological Survey. Columbus.
Chadderdon, M. F.
   1981.   *Baker Cave, Val Verde County, Texas: The 1976 Excavations*. MA thesis, University of Texas at San Antonio.
Champe, J. L.
   1946.   Ash Hollow Cave. UNS (n.s.), No. 1.
Chance, D. H., Jennifer Chance, and J. L. Fagan.
   1977.   Kettle Falls: 1972. UIARMS No. 31.
Chapman, C. H.
   1948.   A Preliminary Survey of Missouri Archaeology Part IV: Ancient Cultures and Sequences. MA 10(4):133–164.
   1975.   *The Archaeology of Missouri, I*. University of Missouri Press. Columbia.
   1980.   *The Archaeology of Missouri, II*. University of Missouri Press. Columbia.
Chapman, Jefferson
   1973.   The Icehouse Bottom Site, 40MR23. RIDAUT, No. 13.
   1975.   The Rose Island Site and the Bifurcate Point Tradition. RIDAUT, No. 14; PATVA, No. 8.
   1977.   Archaic Period Research in the Lower Little Tennessee River Valley—1975: Icehouse Bottom, Harrison Branch, Thirty Acre Island, Calloway Island. RIDAUT, No. 18; PATVA, No. 13.
   1985.   Tellico Archaeology: 12,000 Years of Native American History. PATVA, No. 41.

Chapman, Jefferson, and B. C. Keel
  1978.   Candy Creek/Connestee Components in Eastern Tennessee and Western
        North Carolina and Their Relationship with Adena-Hopewell. In *Hopewell
        Archaeology, The Chillicothe Conference,* edited by David S. Brose and
        Na'omi Greber, pp. 157–161. Kent State University Press. Kent, Ohio.
Chapman, Kenneth
  1951.   Harry P. Mera, 1875–1951. AAn 17:47–48.
Chomko, S. A., and W. R. Wood
  1973.   Linear Mounds in the Northeastern Plains. AM 14(2):1–19.
Christenson, A. L., and W. J. Parry
  1985.   Excavations on Black Mesa 1983: A Descriptive Report. CAIRP, No. 46.
Cinq-Mars, Jacques
  1973.   An Archaeologically Important Raw Material from the Tertiary Hills,
        Western District of Mackenzie, Northwest Territories: A Preliminary State-
        ment. In *Preliminary Archaeology Study, Mackenzie Corridor,* edited by
        Jacques Cinq-Mars. Environmental-Social Committee Northern Pipelines,
        Task Force on Northern Oil Development, Report No. 73–10. Ottawa.
  1979.   Bluefish Cave I: A Pleistocene Eastern Beringian Cave Deposit in the
        Northern Yukon. CJA 3:1–32.
Claasen, Cheryl
  n.d.   Onslow County Archeological Assessment. Report on file at Archaeology
        Branch, North Carolina Division of Archives and History, Department of
        Cultural Resources, Raleigh.
Claflin, W. H., Jr.
  1931.   The Stalling's Island Mound, Columbia County, Georgia. PPM 14(1).
Claggett, S. R., and J. S. Cable
  n.d.   The Haw River Sites: Archaeological Investigations at Two Stratified Sites
        in the North Carolina Piedmont. Report on file at Commonwealth Associates,
        Inc., Jackson, Michigan.
Clark, D. W.
  1970a.   Petroglyphs on Afognak Island, Kodiak Group, Alaska. APUA 15(1):13–
        17.
  1970b.   The Late Kachemak Tradition at Three Saints and Crag Point, Kodiak
        Island, Alaska. ArcA 6(2):73–111.
  1974a.   Koniag Prehistory. (Verlag W. Kohlhammer *Tu Binger Monographien
        zur Urgeschichte,* Vol. 1).
  1974b.   Contributions to the Later Prehistory of Kodiak Island, Alaska.
        NMMMS, No. 20.
  1974c.   Filaments of Prehistory on the Koyukuk River, Northwestern Interior
        Alaska. In *International Conference on the Prehistory and Paleoecology of
        Western North American Arctic and Subarctic,* edited by Scott Raymond and
        Peter Schledermann, pp. 33–46. University of Calgary Archaeological As-
        sociation. Calgary, Alberta.
  1975.   *Technological Continuity and Change within a Persistent Maritime Ad-
        aptation of the Circumpolar Zone.* Mouton. The Hague.
  1977.   Hahanudan Lake: An Ipiutak-Related Occupation of Western Interior
        Alaska. NMMMS, No. 71.
  1979.   Ocean Bay: An Early North Pacific Maritime Culture. NMMMS, No. 86.

1982. An Example of Technological Change in Prehistory: The Origin of a Regional Ground Slate Industry in South-Central Coastal Alaska. ArcA 19(1):103–125.

Clark, D. W., and A. M. Clark
1975. Fluted Points from the Batza Tena Obsidian Source of the Koyukuk River Region, Alaska. APUA 17(2):31–38.

Clark, G. H.
1977. Archaeology on the Alaska Peninsula: The Coast of Shelikof Strait 1963–1965. UOAP, No. 13.

Clark, J. D.
1980. Memorial to Robert Fleming Heizer (1915–1979). JCGBA 1(2):240–245.

Clark, W. E., M. E. Norrisey, and Celia Reed
n.d. A Preliminary Report on the 1977 Excavations of the Buzzard Rock Site, 44RN2. Report on file at Virginia Research Center for Archaeology, Yorktown.

Clarke, L. R., and A. H. Clarke
1980. Zooarchaeological Analysis of Mollusc Remains from Yuquot, British Columbia. The Yuquot Project, Vol. 2, HA, No. 43.

Clausen, C. J., A. D. Cohen, Cesare Emiliani, J. A. Holman, and J. J. Stipp
1979. Little Salt Spring, Florida: A Unique Underwater Site. S 203:609–614.

Clayton, Lee, W. B. Bickley, Jr., and W. J. Stone
1970. Knife River Flint. PA 15(50), pt. 1:282–290.

Cleland, C. E.
1965. Barren Ground Caribou *Rangifer arcticus* from an Early Man Site in Southeastern Michigan. AAn 30(3):350–351.
1966. The Prehistoric Animal Ecology and Ethnozoology of the Upper Great Lakes Region. UMMAAP, No. 29.
1971. The Lasanen Site: An Historic Burial Locality in Mackinac County, Michigan. ASMSU 1(1).
1973. The Pi-Wan-Gop-Ning Prehistoric District at Norwood, Michigan. In *Geology and Environment*. Michigan Basin Geological Society. Lansing.
1982. The Inland Shore Fishery of the Northern Great Lakes: Its Development and Importance in Prehistory. AAn 47(4):761–784.

Cleland, C. E., and Joan Kearney
1966. An Analysis of Animal Remains from the Schmidt Site. MiA 12(2):81–83.

Clements, Forrest
1945. Historical Sketches of Spiro Mound. CMAI 14:48–68.

Clewlow, C. W., Jr.
1967. Time and Space Relations of Some Great Basin Projectile Point Types. UCASR 70:141–149.

Clewlow, C. W., Jr., R. F. Heizer, and R. C. Berger
1970. An Assessment of Radiocarbon Dates for the Rose Spring Site (CA-Iny-372), Inyo County, California. UCARFC 7:19–25.

Cochrane, J.
1878. Antiquities of Mason County, Illinois. ARSI for 1877.

Coe, J. L.
1934. Planning Archaeological Survey of North Carolina. BASNC 1(2).

1952. The Cultural Sequence of the Carolina Piedmont. In *Archaeology of Eastern United States*, edited by J. B. Griffin, pp. 301–311. University of Chicago Press. Chicago.

1964. The Formative Cultures of the Carolina Piedmont. APST 54(5).

1983. Through a Glass Darkly: An Archaeological View of North Carolina's More Distant Past. In *The Prehistory of North Carolina: An Archaeological Symposium*, edited by M. A. Mathis and Jeffrey Crow, pp. 161–177. North Carolina Division of Archives and History, Department of Cultural Resources. Raleigh.

Coe, J. L., and E. Lewis
1952. Dan River Series Statement. In *Prehistoric Pottery of the Eastern United States*, edited by J. B. Griffin. Museum of Anthropology, University of Michigan. Ann Arbor.

Coffin, E. F.
1932. Archaeological Exploration of a Rock Shelter in Brewster County, Texas. INM, No. 48.

Cole, Faye-Cooper, and Thorne Deuel
1937. *Rediscovering Illinois*. University of Chicago Press. Chicago.

Cole, Faye-Cooper, R. E. Bell, J. W. Bennett, J. R. Caldwell, Norman Emerson, R. S. MacNeish, K. G. Orr, and R. K. Willis
1951. *Kincaid, A Prehistoric Illinois Metropolis*. University of Chicago Press. Chicago.

Cole, G. G.
1981. The Murphy Hill Site (1Ms300): The Structural Study of a Copena Mound and Comparative Review of the Copena Mortuary Complex. UAOARRI, No. 3.

Cole, Nancy
1975. *Early Historic Caddoan Mortuary Practices in the Upper Neches Drainage, East Texas*. MA thesis, The University of Texas, Austin.

Coleman, G. N.
n.d. The Koehler Site. Report on file at Virginia Research Center for Archaeology, Yorktown.

Coleman, G. N., Douglas Ubelaker, Michael Trinkley, and Wayne Clark
1982. The Reedy Creek Site, 44 Ha 22, South Boston, Virginia. ASVQB (37)4:150–209.

Collins, H. B.
1937. Archeology of St. Lawrence Island, Alaska. SMC 96(1).

1940. Outline of Eskimo Prehistory. SMC 100:533–592.

1950. Excavations at Frobisher Bay, Baffin Island, N.W.T. NMCB 123:49–63.

1955. Excavations of Thule and Dorset Culture Sites at Resolute, Cornwallis Island, N.W.T. NMCB 136:22–35.

1956a. Archaeological Investigations on Southampton and Coats Islands, N.W.T. NMCB 142:82–113.

1956b. The T–1 Site at Native Point, Southampton Island, N.W.T. APUA 4:63–89.

Collins, H. B., Frederica de Laguna, Edmund Carpenter, and Peter Stone
1962. Eskimo Cultures. *Encyclopedia of World Art*, Vol. 5, columns 1–28. McGraw Hill. New York.

1973. *The Far North: 2000 Years of American Eskimo and Indian Art.* National Gallery of Art. Washington, D.C.

Collins, M. B.

1966. Andrews Lake Sites: Evidence of Semi-sedentary Prehistoric Occupation in Andrews County, Texas. In *Transactions of the Second Regional Archeological Symposium for Southeastern New Mexico and Western Texas.* Midland Archeological Society, Special Bulletin No. 1. Midland, Texas.

Colton, H. S.

1926. The Geographical Distribution of Potsherds in the San Francisco Mountains of Arizona. In *Proceedings: 20th International Congress of Americanists.* Vol. 2:119–121.

1932a. Sunset Crater: The Effect of a Volcanic Eruption on an Ancient Pueblo People. GR 22(4).

1932b. A Survey of the Prehistoric Sites in the Region of Flagstaff, Arizona. BAEB, No. 104.

1936. The Rise and Fall of the Prehistoric Populations of Northern Arizona. S 84(2181):337–343.

1939a. Prehistoric Cultural Units and Their Relationships in Northern Arizona. MNAB, No. 17.

1939b. An Archaeological Survey of Northwestern Arizona, Including the Description of Fifteen New Pottery Types. MNAB, No. 16.

1941. Winona and Ridge Ruin, Part II: Notes on the Technology and Taxonomy of the Pottery. MNAB, No. 19.

1943. Reconstruction of Anasazi History. PAPS 86(2):264–269.

1945a. A Revision of the Date of the Eruption of Sunset Crater. SJA 1(3):345–355.

1945b. The Patayan Problem in the Colorado River Valley. SJA 1(1).

1946. The Sinagua: A Summary of the Archeology of the Region of Flagstaff, Arizona. MNAB, No. 22.

1947. A Revised Date for Sunset Crater. GR 37(1):144.

1952. Pottery Types of the Arizona Strip and Adjacent Areas in Utah and Nevada. MNACS 1:19.

1955. Pottery Types of the Southwest: Ware 8A, 8B, 9A, 9B, Tusayan Gray and White Ware, Little Colorado Gray and White Ware. MNACS, No. 3.

1956. Pottery Types of the Southwest: San Juan Red, Tsegi Orange, Homolovi Orange, Winslow Orange, Awatovi Yellow, Jeddito Yellow and Sichomovi Red Ware 5A, 5B, 6A, 6B, 7A, 7B, 7C. MNACS, No. 3C.

1958. Pottery Types of the Southwest: Wares 14, 15, 16, 17, 18: Revised Descriptions of Alameda Brown Ware, Prescott Gray Ware, and San Francisco Mt. Gray Ware. MNACS, No. 3D.

1960. *Black Sand: Prehistory in Northern Arizona.* University of New Mexico Press, Albuquerque.

1962. Archaeology of the Flagstaff Area. In *New Mexico Geological Society, 13th Field Conference*, pp. 171–172.

1965. Check List of Southwestern Pottery Types. MNACS, No. 2.

Colton, H. S., and F. E. Baxter

1932. *Days in the Painted Desert and the San Francisco Mountains: A Guide.* Northern Arizona Society of Science and Art. Flagstaff.

Colton, H. S., and L. L. Hargrave
  1937. Handbook of Northern Arizona Pottery Wares. MNAB, No. 11.
Connelly, J. C.
  1979. Hopi Social Organization. In *Handbook of North American Indians: Southwest*, Vol. 9, edited by C. W. Sturdevant and A. A. Ortiz, pp. 539–553. Smithsonian Institution. Washington, D.C.
Connor, Sydney
  1943. Excavations at Kinnikinnick, Arizona. AAn 8(4):376–379.
Cook, J. P.
  1952. Pottery Types of the Arizona Strip and Adjacent Areas in Utah and Nevada. MNACS 1:85.
  1969. *The Early Prehistory of Healy Lake, Alaska*. PhD dissertation, University of Wisconsin, Madison.
Cook, T. G.
  1976. Koster: An Artifact Analysis of Two Archaic Phases in Westcentral Illinois. PR, No. 1.
Cooper, L. R.
  1933. The Red Cedar River Variant of the Wisconsin Hopewell Culture. BPMCM 16(2).
  n.d. Preliminary Report on the Archaeological Survey and Excavations, Mille Lacs Kathio State Park, Summer 1965. Report on file at the Minnesota Outdoor Recreation and Resource Commission, St. Paul.
Cooper, Leland, and Elden Johnson
  1964. Sandy Lake Ware and Its Distribution. AAn 29(4):474–479.
Cooper, P. L.
  1936. Archaeology of Certain Sites in Cedar County, Nebraska. In *Nebraska Archeology*, edited by E. H. Bell. University of Nebraska. Lincoln.
  1949. Recent Investigations in Fort Randall and Oahe Reservoirs, South Dakota. AAn 14(4), pt. 1:300–310.
Corbin, J. E.
  1974. A Model for Cultural Succession for the Coastal Bend Area of Texas. BTAS 45:29–54.
  in press. The Washington Square Mound Site. APSFA.
Cordell, A. S.
  1984. Ceramic Technology at a Weeden Island Period Site in North Florida. In *Ceramic Notes 2. Occasional Publications of the Ceramic Technology Laboratory, Florida State Museum*. Gainesville.
Cordell, L. S.
  1979. Prehistory: Eastern Anasazi. In *Handbook of North American Indians*, Vol. 9:131–151.
  1980. *Tijeras Canyon: Analyses of the Past*. Maxwell Museum of Anthropology and University of New Mexico Press. Albuquerque.
  1984. *Prehistory of the Southwest*. Academic Press. Orlando, Florida.
Corley, J. A.
  1970. Proposed Eastern Extension of the Jornada Branch of the Mogollon. In *Transactions of the First Regional Archaeological Symposium for Southeastern New Mexico and Western Texas*. Lea County Archaeological Society. New Mexico.

Cotter, J. L.
1937. The Occurrence of Flints and Extinct Animals in Pluvial Deposits near Clovis, New Mexico. In *Report on the Excavations at the Gravel Pit in 1936*, Part 4. PPANS 89:2–16.
1938. The Occurrence of Flints and Extinct Animals in Pluvial Deposits near Clovis, New Mexico. In *Report on the Field Season of 1937*, Part 4. PPANS 90:113–117.
1952. The Gordon Site in Southern Mississippi. AAn 18(2):110–126.
Cotter, J. L., and J. M. Corbett
1951. Archaeology of Bynum Mounds, Mississippi. ARS, No. 1.
Coupland, Gary
1985. *Prehistoric Cultural Change at Kitselas Canyon*. PhD Dissertatioin, University of British Columbia, Vancouver.
Cox, S. L.
1978. Paleo-Eskimo Occupations of the North Labrador Coast ArcA 15:96–118.
Crabtree, D. E.
1972. An Introduction to Flintworking. OPISUM, No. 28.
Crawford, D. D.
1965. The Granite Beach Site, Llano County, Texas. BTAS 36:71–97.
Cremin, W. M., T. J. Martin, D. K. Rhead, R. D. Hoxie, and L. G. Dorothy
1980. The Sand Point Site (20-BG14). MiA 26(3–4):7–86.
Cressman, L. S.
1942. Archaeological Researches in the Northern Great Basin. CIWP, No. 538.
1956. Klamath Prehistory: The Prehistory of the Culture of the Klamath Lake Area, Oregon. TAPS 46:375–515.
1960. Cultural Sequences at The Dalles, Oregon: A Contribution to Pacific Northwest Prehistory. TAPS 50(10).
1966. Man in Association with Extinct Fauna in the Great Basin. AAn 31(6):866–867.
1977. *Homes of Vanished Peoples*. University of Utah Press. Salt Lake City.
Cressman, L. S., Howel Williams, and A. D. Krieger
1940. Early Man in Oregon: Archaeological Research in the Northern Great Basin. UOSA, No. 3.
1942. Archaeological Studies in the Northern Great Basin. CIWP, No. 538.
Cressman, L. S., D. L. Cole, W. A. Davis, T. M. Newman, and D. J. Scheans
1960. Cultural Sequences at The Dalles, Oregon: A Contribution to Northwest Prehistory. TAPS (n.s.) 50(10).
Cridlebaugh, P. A.
1981. The Icehouse Bottom Site: 1977 Excavations. RIDAUT, No. 35; PATVA, No. 34.
Crook, W. W., Jr., R. K. Harris
1952. Trinity Aspect of the Archaic Horizon: The Carrollton and Elam Foci. BTAPS 23:7–38.
1954. Traits of the Trinity Aspect Archaic: Carrollton and Elam Foci. TR 12(1):2–16.
1957. Hearths and Artifacts of Early Man Near Lewisville, Texas, and Associated Faunal Material. BTAS 28:7–97.

1958. A Pleistocene Campsite Near Lewisville, Texas. AAn 23(3):233–246.

Cross, Dorothy
1941. *Archaeology of New Jersey*, Vol. I. Archaeological Society of New Jersey. Trenton.
1956. *Archaeology of New Jersey*, Vol. II: The Abbott Farm Site. Archaeological Society of New Jersey. Trenton.

Crown, P. A.
1981. *Variability in Ceramic Manufacture at the Chodistaas Site, East-Central Arizona*. PhD dissertation, University of Arizona, Tucson.

Cummings, Byron
1930. Turkey Hill Ruin. MN 2(11).

Curry, D. C.
1983. Archeological Reconnaissance of the Proposed Maryland Route 51 Potomac River Bridge Approaches at Paw Paw, Allegany County, Maryland and Morgan County, West Virginia. MGSFR, No. 180.

Cushing, F. H.
1897. Exploration of Ancient Key-Dweller Remains on the Gulf Coast of Florida. PAPS 25(153):329–448.

Custer, J. F.
1984. *Delaware Prehistoric Archaeology: An Ecological Approach*. University of Delaware Press. Newark.

Cutler, D. C.
1977. Prelude to a Pageant in the Wilderness. WHQ 8(1):5–14.

Daifuku, Hiroshi
1961. Jeddito 264. PPM 33(1).

Dalley, G. F., and D. A. McFadden
1985. The Archaeology of the Red Cliffs Site. BLMUCR, No. 17.

Daugherty, R. D.
1956. Archaeology of the Lind Coulee Site, Washington. PAPS 100(3).
1962. The Intermontane Western Tradition. AAn 28:144–150.

Davis, C. A., and G. A. Smith
1981. *Newberry Cave*. San Bernardino County Museum Association. Redlands, California.

Davis, E. M.
1962. Archeology of the Lime Creek Site in Southwestern Nebraska. UNMSP, No. 3.
1970. Archaeological and Historical Resources of the Red River Basin in Texas, Part II. AASRS 1:27–59.
n.d. The Whelan Site, A Late Caddoan Component in the Ferrell's Bridge Reservoir, Northeastern Texas. Report on file at the Department of Anthropology, The University of Texas, Austin.

Davis, H. A.
1966. An Introduction to Parkin Prehistory. ArA 7:1–40.

Davis, S. D.
1984. (editor) *The Hidden Falls Site, Baranof Island, Alaska*. USDA-Forest Service. Sitka.

Davis, W. A., and E. M. Davis
1960. The Jake Martin Site. ASUT, No. 3.

Dawson, K. C. A.
  1983. Cummins Site: A Late Paleo-Indian (Plano) Site at Thunder Bay, Ontario.
    OA 39:3–31.
Deagan, K. A.
  1978. Cultures in Transition: Fusion and Assimilation among the Eastern Ti-
    mucua. In *Tacachale: Essays on the Indians in Florida and Southeastern
    Georgia during the Historic Period*, edited by J. T. Milanich and Samuel
    Proctor, pp. 89–119. University Presses of Florida. Gainesville.
de Baillou, Clemens
  1965. A Test Excavation of the Hollywood Mound (9Ri1), Georgia. SIS 17:3–
    11.
DeBoer, W. R.
  1976. Archaeological Explorations in Northern Arizona. NA10,754: A Sinagua
    Settlement of the Rio de Flag Phase. QCPA, No. 1.
DeJarnette, D. L.
  1952. Alabama Archaeology: A Summary. In *Archaeology of Eastern United
    States*, edited by J. B. Griffin, pp. 272–284. University of Chicago Press.
    Chicago.
DeJarnette, D. L., and W. S. Webb
  1942. An Archeological Survey of Pickwick Basin in the Adjacent Portions of
    the States of Alabama, Mississippi and Tennessee. BAEB, No. 129.
DeJarnette, D. L., and S. B. Wimberly
  1941. The Bessemer Site: Excavation of Three Mounds and Surrounding Village
    Areas near Bessemer, Alabama. GSAMP, No. 17.
DeJarnette, D. L., E. B. Kurjack, and J. W. Cambron
  1962. Stanfield-Worley Bluff Shelter Excavations. JAA, No. 8.
Dekin, A. A., Jr.
  1975. *Models of Pre-Dorset Culture: Towards an Explicit Methodology*. PhD
    dissertation, Michigan State University, East Lansing.
  1981. *The 1981 Excavations at the Utqiaqvik Archaeological Site, Barrow,
    Alaska*. Public Archaeology Facility, Department of Anthropology, State Uni-
    versity of New York, Binghamton.
de Laguna, Frederica
  1934. *The Archaeology of Cook Inlet, Alaska*. University Museum, University
    of Pennsylvania. Philadelphia.
  1942. The Bryn Mawr Dig at Cinder Park, Arizona. P 14:53–56.
  1956. *Chugach Prehistory*. University of Washington Press. Seattle.
  1960. The Story of a Tlingit Community: A Problem in the Relationship between
    Archeological, Ethnological, and Historical Methods. BAEB, No. 172.
  1975. *The Archaeology of Cook Inlet, Alaska*, 2nd edition. Alaska Historical
    Society. Anchorage.
de Laguna, Frederica, F. A. Riddell, D. F. McGeein, K. S. Lane, and J. A. Freed
  1964. Archeology of the Yakutat Bay Area, Alaska. BAEB, No. 192.
Denton, Joe T.
  1976. No-Name Creek Site: A Terrace Site of the Middle and Late Archaic
    Period in Gillespie County, Texas. TDHPA, No. 7.
DePratter, Chester
  1975. The Archaic in Georgia. EG 3:1–16.

1979. Ceramics. In *Anthropology of St. Catherines Island 2. The Refuge-Deptford Mortuary Complex*, edited by D. H. Thomas and C. S. Larsen, pp. 109–132. APAMNH 56(1).

1985a. Current Research—University of South Carolina. CN 6(1):7–8.

1985b. Adamson Site (38KE11). SN 17:37.

1985c. Mulberry Site (38KE12). SN 17:31–36.

DePratter, Chester, and Christopher Judge
1986. Preliminary Pee Dee Ceramic Sequence for the Wateree Valley, South Carolina. Manuscript on file at Institute of Archeology and Anthropology, University of South Carolina, Columbia.

DePratter, Chester, Charles Hudson, and Marvin Smith
n.d. The Route of Juan Pardo's Explorations in the Interior Southeast, 1566–1568. Manuscript on file at Research Laboratories of Anthropology, University of North Carolina, Chapel Hill.

DePuydt, R. T.
1983. *Cultural Implications of Avifaunal Remains Recovered from the Ozette Site*. MA thesis, Washington State University, Pullman.

Dering, J. P.
1979. *Pollen and Plant Macrofossil Vegetation Record Recovered from Hinds Cave, Val Verde County, Texas*. MS thesis, Texas A&M University, College Station.

Deuel, Thorne
1952. (editor) Hopewellian Communities in Illinois. SP, No. 5.

DeValinger, L.
1970. Report on the Excavation of the St. Jones River Site near Legbanon, Delaware. DSMSB, No. 3.

Dewhirst, John
1978. Nootka Sound: A 4,000 Year Perspective. SH 7(2):1–29.

1980. The Indigenous Archaeology of Yuquot, a Nootkan Outside Village. The Yuquot Project, Vol. 1. HA, No. 39.

Dibble, D. S.
1965. Bonfire Shelter; A Stratified Bison Kill Site in the Amistad Reservoir Area, Val Verde County, Texas. TASPM, No. 5.

1970. On the Significance of Additional Radiocarbon Dates from Bonfire Shelter, Texas. PA 15(50), Pt. 1:251–254.

n.d. Excavations at Arenosa Shelter, 1965–66. Report on file at the Texas Archeological Survey, The University of Texas, Austin.

Dibble, D. S., and Dessamae Lorrain
1968. Bonfire Shelter: A Stratified Bison Kill Site, Val Verde County, Texas. MPTMM, No. 1.

Dibble, David S., and Elton R. Prewitt
1967. Survey and Test Excavations at Amistad Reservoir, 1964–65. TASPS, No. 3.

Dick, H. W.
1965a. Bat Cave. MSAR, No. 27.

1965b. *Picuris Pueblo Salvage Excavations*. No. PB–177047, Clearing House for Federal, Scientific and Technological Information, U.S. Department of Commerce, National Bureau of Standards, Institute for Applied Technology. Springfield, Virginia.

1968. Six Historic Pottery Types from Spanish Sites in New Mexico. In *Collected Papers in Honor of Lyndon Lane Hargrave*, pp. 77–94. PASNM, No. 1.

1976. Archaeological Excavations in the Llaves Area, Santa Fe National Forest, New Mexico, 1972–1974 (Part I—Architecture). AR, No. 13.

1985. Comparisons of Feature Measurements of Pit Houses and Surface Houses of the Gallina Phase of the Anasazi Culture in North Central New Mexico and the Population Estimates of a Village. In *Southwestern Culture History: Collected Papers in Honor of Albert H. Schroeder*, pp. 31–42. PASNM 10:31–42.

Dickens, R. S., Jr.

1970. *The Pisgah Culture and its Place in the Prehistory of the Southern Appalachians*. PhD dissertation, University of North Carolina, Chapel Hill.

1975. A Processual Approach to Mississippian Origins on the Georgia Piedmont. SACB 18:31–42.

1976. *Cherokee Prehistory: The Pisgah Phase in the Appalachian Summit Region*. University of Tennessee Press. Knoxville.

1978. Mississippian Settlement Patterns in the Appalachian Summit Area: The Pisgah and Qualla Phases. In *Mississippian Settlement Patterns*, edited by B. D. Smith, pp. 115–139. Academic Press. New York.

1979. The Origins and Development of Cherokee Culture. In *The Cherokee Indian Nation: A Troubled History*, edited by Duane King, pp. 3–32. The University of Tennessee Press, Knoxville.

1985. The Form, Function and Formation of Garbage-filled Pits on Southeastern Aboriginal Sites: An Archaeobotanical Analysis. In *Structure and Process in Southeastern Archaeology*, edited by R. S. Dickens, Jr. and H. F. Ward. University of Alabama Press, University.

Dickens, R. S., Jr., H. T. Ward, and R. P. S. Davis, Jr.

1985. *The Historic Occaneechi: An Archaeological Investigation of Culture Change*. Research Laboratories of Anthropology, University of North Carolina. Chapel Hill.

Didier, M. E.

1967. A Distributional Study of the Turkey-Tail Point. WiA 48(1):3–73.

Dillehay, Tom D.

1974. Late Quaternary Bison Population Changes on the Southern Plains. AP 19(65):180–196.

Dincauze, D. F.

1974. An Introduction to Archaeology in the Greater Boston Area. AENA 2:39–66.

1976. The Neville Site: 8000 Years at Amoskeag, Manchester, New Hampshire. MPM, No. 4.

1984. An Archaeo-Logical Evaluation of the Case for Pre-Clovis Occupations. In *Advances in World Archaeology*, edited by Fred Wendorf and Angela Close, Vol. 3, pp. 275–323. Academic Press. San Diego.

Dincauze, D. F., and M. T. Mulholland

1977. Early and Middle Archaic Site Distributions and Habitats in Southern New England. NYASA 288:439–456.

Di Peso, C. C.

1951. The Babocomari Village Site on the Babocomari River, Southeastern Arizona. AFP, No. 5.

1953.   The Sobaipuri Indians of the Upper San Pedro River Valley, Southeastern Arizona. AFP, No. 6.

1956.   The Upper Pima of San Cayetano del Tumacacori. AFP, No. 7.

1958.   The Reeve Ruin of Southeastern Arizona. AFP, No. 8.

1968.   Casas Grandes and the Gran Chichimeca. EP 75(4):45–61.

1974.   Casas Grandes: A Fallen Trading Center of the Gran Chichimeca. AFP, No. 9, Vols. 1–3.

1979.   Prehistory: Southern Periphery. In *Handbook of North American Indians*, edited by W. C. Sturtevant and A. A. Ortiz, Vol. 9, pp. 152–161. Smithsonian Institution. Washington, D.C.

Di Peso, C. C., J. B. Rinaldo, and G. J. Fenner

1974.   Casas Grandes: A Fallen Trading Center of the Gran Chichimeca. AFP, No. 9, Vols. 4–8.

Dittert, A. E., Jr., F. W. Eddy, and B. L. Dickey

1963.   Evidence of Early Ceramic Phases in the Navajo Reservoir District. EP 70(1–2):5–12.

Dittert, A. E., Jr., J. J. Hester, and F. W. Eddy

1961.   An Archaeological Survey of the Navajo Reservoir District, Northwestern New Mexico. MSAR, No. 23.

Dixon, E. J.

1975.   The Gallagher Flint Station, An Early Man Site on the North Slope, Arctic Alaska, and Its Role in Relation to the Bering Land Bridge. ArcA 12(1):68–75.

1985.   Cultural Chronology of Central Interior Alaska. ArcA 22(1):47–66.

Donahue, P. F.

1976.   Research in Northern Alberta 1975. ASAOP, No. 2.

Dorwin, J. T.

1971.   The Bowen Site: An Archaeological Study of Culture Process in the Late Prehistory of Central Indiana. PRS 4(4):95–411.

Dorwin, J. T., and J. H. Kellar

n.d.   The 1967 Excavation at the Yankeetown Site. Report to the National Park Service.

Doyel, D. E.

1974.   Excavations in the Escalante Ruin Group, Southern Arizona. ASMAS, No. 37.

1976a.   Revised Phase System for the Globe-Miami and Tonto Basin Areas, Central Arizona. K 41(3–4):241–266.

1976b.   Salado Cultural Development in the Tonto Basin and Gila-Miami Areas, Central Arizona. K 42(1):5–16.

1977.   Rillito and Rincon Period Settlement Systems in the Middle Santa Cruz River Valley: Alternative Models. K 43(2):93–110.

1978.   The Miami Wash Project: Hohokam and Salado in the Globe-Miami Area, Central Arizona. ASMHS, No. 52.

1979.   The Prehistoric Hohokam of the Arizona Desert. AmS 67:544–554.

1981.   Late Hohokam Prehistory in Southern Arizona. CA, No. 2.

1984.   From Foraging to Farming: An Overview of the Preclassic in the Tucson Basin. K 49(3–4):147–165.

Doyel, D. E., and M. D. Elson
 1985. (editors) Hohokam Settlement and Economic Systems in the Central New River Drainage, Arizona. SSPA, No. 4.
Doyel, D. E., and Fred Plog
 1980. (editors) Current Issues in Hohokam Prehistory. ASUAP, No. 23.
Dozier, E. P.
 1954. The Hopi Tewa of Arizona. UCPAE 44(3):259–376.
 1966. Hano, A Tewa Indian Community in Arizona. In *Case Studies in Cultural Anthropology*, edited by George and Louise Spindler. Holt, Rinehart and Winston. New York.
Dragoo, D. W.
 1963. Mounds for the Dead: An Analysis of the Adena Culture. ACM, No. 37.
Dragoo, D. W., and C. F. Wray
 1964. Hopewell Figurine Rediscovered. AAn 30(2):195–199.
Drucker, Lesley, and Susan Jackson
 n.d. Shell in Motion: An Archaeological Study of the Minim Island National Register Site, Georgetown County, South Carolina. Report on file at U.S. Army Corps of Engineers, Charleston District, Charleston.
Duff, Wilson
 1956. Prehistoric Stone Sculpture of the Fraser River and Gulf of Georgia. ABC, No. 5.
 1975. *Images Stone B.C., Thirty Centuries of Northwest Coast Indian Sculpture*. Hancock House. Saanichton, British Columbia.
Duffield, L. F.
 1963. The Wolfshead Site: An Archaic-Neo-American Site in San Augustine County, Texas. BTAS 34:83–141.
 1964. Three Panhandle Aspect Sites at Sanford Reservoir, Hutchinson County, Texas. BTAS 35:19–81.
Duffield, L. F., and E. B. Jelks
 1961. The Pearson Site: A Historic Indian Site in Iron Bridge Reservoir, Rains County, Texas. ASUT, No. 4.
Dumond, D. E.
 1971. A Summary of Archaeology in the Katmai Region, Southwestern Alaska. UOAP, No. 2.
 1977. *The Eskimos and Aleuts*. Thames and Hudson. London.
 1981. Archaeology of the Alaska Peninsula: The Naknek Region, 1960–1975. APUO, No. 21.
Dumond, D. E., and Rick Minor
 1983. Archaeology in the John Day Reservoir: The Wildcat Canyon Site, 35-GM–9. APUO, No. 30.
Dumond, D. E., Leslie Conton, and H. M. Shields
 1975. Eskimos and Aleuts on the Alaska Peninsula: A Reappraisal of Port Moller Affinities. ArcA 12(1).
Dumond, D. E., Winfield Henn, and Robert Stuckenrath
 1976. Archaeology and Prehistory on the Alaska Peninsula. APUA 18(1):17–29.

Dunlevy, M. L.
  1936. A Comparison of the Cultural Manifestations of the Burkett (Nance County) and the Gray-Wolfe (Colfax County) Sites. In *Chapters in Nebraska Archaeology*, edited by E. H. Bell, Vol. 1, Nos. I–IV, No. 2:147–247. University of Nebraska. Lincoln.
Dutton, B. P.
  1963. *Sun Father's Way: The Kiva Murals of Kuaua*. University of New Mexico Press. Albuquerque.
  1981. Excavations at the Pueblo Ruins of Abo. In *Collected Essays in Honor of Erik Kellerman Reed*, edited by A. H. Schroeder, pp. 177–193. PASNM, No. 6.
Eberhart, H.
  1961. The Cogged Stones of Southern California. AAn 26(3):361–370.
Eddy, F. W.
  1961. Excavations at Los Pinos Phase Sites in the Navajo Reservoir District. MNMPA, No. 4.
  1966. Prehistory of the Navajo Reservoir District, Northwestern New Mexico. MNMPA, No. 15(1–2).
  1972. Culture Ecology and the Prehistory of the Navajo Reservoir District. SL 38(1–2):1–75.
  1974. Population Dislocation in the Navajo Reservoir District, New Mexico and Colorado. AAn 39(1):75–84.
  1975. A Settlement Model for Reconstructing Prehistoric Social Organization at Chimney Rock Mesa, Southern Colorado. In *Collected Papers in Honor of Florence Hawley Ellis*, edited by T. R. Frisbie, pp. 60–79. PASNM, No. 2.
  1977. Archaeological Investigations at Chimney Rock Mesa: 1970–1972. MCAS, No. 1.
  1983. Upland Anasazi Settlement Adaptations at Chimney Rock Mesa, Southern Colorado. In *Proceedings of the Anasazi Symposium, 1981*, compiled and edited by J. E. Smith, pp. 141–152. Mesa Verde Museum Association. Mesa Verde National Park.
  n.d. Salvage Archeology in the Laneport Reservoir District, Central Texas. Report on file at the Texas Archeological Survey, The University of Texas, Austin.
Eddy, F. W., and H. E. Dregne
  1964. Soil Tests on Alluvial and Archaeological Deposits, Navajo Reservoir District. EP 71(4):5–21.
Eddy, F. W., and Carol O'Sullivan
  1986. The Federal Management of Archeological Resources in the American West. Ar 39(6):48–52.
Eddy, F. W., A. E. Kane, and P. R. Nickens
  1983. *The Southwestern Colorado Prehistoric Context: Archaeological Background and Research Directions*. Nickens and Associates. Montrose, Colorado.
Eddy, J. A.
  1975. Medicine Wheels and Plains Indian Astronomy. In *Native American Astronomy*, edited by A. F. Aveni, pp. 147–169. University of Texas Press. Austin.

Edwards, W. E.
    n.d.   Preliminary Report on Excavations at Sewee Indian Mound. Manuscript
            on file at Institute of Archeology and Anthropology, University of South
            Carolina, Columbia.
Effland, R. W., A. T. Jones, and R. C. Euler
    1981.   The Archaeology of Powell Plateau: Regional Interaction at Grand Can-
            yon. GCM, No. 3.
Egloff, B. J.
    1967.   An Analysis of Ceramics from Cherokee Towns. MA thesis, University
            of North Carolina, Chapel Hill.
Egloff, K. T.
    n.d.a.   White Park Site (44CF67) in a Fall Zone Study Area. Report on file at
            the Virginia Research Center for Archaeology, Yorktown.
    n.d.b.   Woodland Occupation Along the Clinch and Powell Rivers in South-West
            Virginia: Emphasis on Ceramics. Report on file at the Virginia Research
            Center for Archaeology, Yorktown.
Egloff, K. T., and S. R. Potter
    1982.   Indian Ceramics from Coastal Plain Virginia. AENA 10:95–117.
Egloff, K. T., and Celia Reed
    1980.   Crab Orchard Site: A Late Woodland Palisaded Village. ASVQB
            (34)3:130–148.
Egloff, K. T., and E. R. Turner
    1984.   The Chesapeake Indians and Their Predecessors: Recent Excavations at
            Great Neck. VHLNV, No. 24.
Egloff, K. T., M. B. Barber, and Celia Reed
    n.d.   Leggett Site: A Dan River Agricultural/Riverine Hamlet. Report on file at
            the Virginia Research Center for Archaeology, Yorktown.
Egloff, K. T., M. E. Norrisey Hodges, and Leslie McFaden
    n.d.   Croaker Landing Site. Report on file at the Virginia Research Center for
            Archaeology, Yorktown.
Eighmy, Jeffery
    1984.   Colorado Plains Prehistoric Context. Office of Archeology and Historic
            Preservation, Colorado Historical Society. Denver.
Ekholm, Gordon
    1939.   Results of an Archaeological Survey of Sonora and Northern Sinaloa.
            RMEA 3(1):7–11.
    1940.   The Archaeology of Northern and Western Mexico. In The Maya and
            Their Neighbors, edited by E. L. Hay, pp. 320–330. Appleton-Century. New
            York.
    1942.   Excavations at Guasave, Sinaloa, Mexico. APAMNH, No. 38, part 2.
Elliott, M. L.
    1982.   Large Pueblo Sites near Jemez Springs, New Mexico. CRD, No. 3.
Ellis, F. H.
    1950.   Big Kivas, Little Kivas, and Moiety Houses in Historical Reconstruction.
            SJA 6:286–302.
    1961.   The Hopi, Their History and Use of Lands, Defendant's Exhibit No.
            E500, Docket No. 229, Indian Claims Commission.

1964. A Reconstruction of the Basic Jemez Pattern of Social Organization, with Comparison to Other Tanoan Social Structures. UNMPA, No. 11.

Ellis, F. H., and J. J. Brody
1964. Ceramic Stratigraphy and Tribal History at Taos Pueblo. AAn 29:316–327.

Elsasser, A. L.
1960. The Archaeology of the Sierra Nevada in California and Nevada. UCASR 51

Elsasser, A. L., and R. F. Heizer
1966. Excavation of two Northwestern California Coastal Cities. UCASR 67:1–149.

Elston, R. G.
1971. A Contribution to Washo Archaeology. NASRP, No. 2.
1979. The Archaeology of U.S. 395 Right-of-way Between Stead, Nevada, and Hallelujah Junction, California. Report on file at the Nevada Archaeological Survey, University of Nevada, Reno.
1982. Good Times, Hard Times: Prehistoric Culture Change in the Great Basin. In Man and Environment in the Great Basin, edited by D. B. Madsen and J. F. O'Connell, pp. 186–206. SAAP, No. 2.

Elston, R. G., and J. D. Davis
1972. An Archaeological Investigation of the Steamboat Hot Springs Locality, Washoe County, Nevada. NASR 6(1):9–14.

Elston, R. G., and Charles Zeier
1984. The Sugarloaf Obsidian Quarry. NWC Administrative Publication 313. Naval Weapons Center, China Lake, California.

Elston, R. G., J. D. Davis, A. M. Leventhal, and Cameron Covington
1977. The Archaeology of the Tahoe Reach of the Truckee River. Report on file at the Nevada Archaeological Survey, University of Nevada, Reno.

Elston, R. G., D. F. Hardesty, and Charles Zeier
1982. Archaeological Investigations of the Hopkins Land Exchange, Vol. II. Report on file at the Tahoe National Forest, Nevada City, California.

Emerson, T. E.
1984. The Dyroff and Levin Sites. In American Bottom Archaeology, FAI–270 Site Reports, edited by C. J. Bareis and J. W. Porter, Vol. 9. University of Illinois Press. Urbana and Chicago.

Emerson, T. E., and D. K. Jackson
1984. The BBB Motor Site. In American Bottom Archaeology FAI–270 Site Reports, edited by C. J. Bareis and J. W. Porter, Vol. 6.

Epp, H. T., and Ian Dyck
1983. Tracking Ancient Hunters: Prehistoric Archaeology in Saskatchewan. Saskatchewan Archaeological Society. Regina.

Epstein, J. F.
1968. The San Isidro Site: An Early Man Campsite in Nuevo Leon, Mexico. ASUT, No. 7.

Ericson, J. E.
1977. Egalitarian Exchange Systems in California: A Preliminary View. In Exchange Systems in Prehistory, edited by T. K. Earle and J. E. Ericson, pp. 109–126. Academic Press. New York.

Ericson, J. E., T. A. Hagan, and C. W. Chesterman
    1976. Prehistoric Obsidian Sources in California I: Geological and Geographical Aspects. In *Advances in Obsidian Glass Studies: Archaeological and Geochemical Perspectives.* Noyes Press. Park Ridge, New Jersey.

Essenpreis, P. S.
    1978. Fort Ancient Settlement: Differential Response at a Mississippian–Late Woodland Interface. In *Mississippian Settlement Patterns*, edited by B. D. Smith. Academic Press. New York.

Euler, R. C., and H. F. Dobyns
    1962. Excavation West of Prescott, Arizona. P 34(3).

Euler, R. C., G. J. Gumerman, T. N. V. Karlstrom, J. S. Dean, and R. H. Hevly
    1979. The Colorado Plateaus: Cultural Dynamics and Paleoenvironments. S 205:1089–1101.

Evans, Clifford
    1955. A Ceramic Study of Virginia Archaeology. BAEB, No. 160.

Evans, G. E.
    1961a. *A Reappraisal of the Blackduck Focus or Headwaters Lakes Aspect.* MA thesis, University of Minnesota, Minneapolis.
    1961b. Ceramic Analysis of the Blackduck Ware and Its General Cultural Relationships. PRMAS 29:33–54.

Eyman, C. E.
    1966. *The Schultz Focus: A Plains Middle Woodland Burial Complex in Eastern Kansas.* MA thesis, University of Calgary, Calgary, Alberta.

Ezell, P. H.
    1961. Malcolm Jennings Rogers (1890–1960). AAn 26:532–533.

Fairbanks, C. H.
    1942. The Taxonomic Position of Stalling's Island, Georgia. AAn 7:223–231.
    1946. The Macon Earthlodge. AAn 12:94–108.
    1956. Archeology of the Funeral Mound, Ocmulgee National Monument, Georgia. ARS, No. 3.
    1965. Excavations at the Fort Walton Temple Mound, 1960. FA 18:239–264.

Fairchild, Jerry
    1977. The Schmidt Site: A Pre-Nipissing Village in the Saginaw Valley, Michigan. MA thesis, Western Michigan University, Kalamazoo.

Farmer, M. F.
    1942. Navajo Archaeology of Upper Blanco and Largo Canyons, Northern New Mexico. AAn 8:65–79.

Faulkner, C. H.
    1968. *The Old Stone Fort: Exploring an Archaeological Mystery.* The University of Tennessee Press. Knoxville.
    1972. The Late Prehistoric Occupation of Northwestern Indiana: A Study of the Upper Mississippi Cultures of the Kankakee Valley. PRS 5(1):1–222.
    n.d.a. (editor) Archaeological Investigations in the Tims Ford Reservoir, Tennessee, 1966. Report on file at Department of Anthropology, University of Tennessee, Knoxville.
    n.d.b. Statements on file at Virginia Research Center for Archaeology, Yorktown, Virginia.

Faulkner, C. H., and M. C. R. McCollough
   1974.   Introductory Report of the Normandy Reservoir Salvage Project: Envi-
      ronmental Setting, Typology, and Survey. Normandy Archaeological Project,
      Vol. 1. RIDAUT, No. 11.
Fay, George
   1955.   Pre-pottery, Lithic Complex from Sonora, Mexico. S 121(3152):777–778.
Fenenga, Franklin, and D. F. Wendorf
   1956.   Excavations at the Ignacio, Colorado, Field Camp Site LA 2605. In *Pipe-
      line Archaeology*, edited by Fred Wendorf, Nancy Fox, and Orian L. Lewis,
      pp. 207–214. Laboratory of Anthropology. Santa Fe, New Mexico.
Ferdon, E. N., Jr.
   1967.   The Hohokam "Ball Court": An Alternative View of Its Function. K
      33(1):1–14.
Ferg, Alan
   1983.   LA 25860: The Sheep Chute Site. In *Excavations at Three Developmental
      Period Sites near Zia and Santa Ana Pueblos, New Mexico*. CASAP, No. 2.
Ferguson, A. L. L.
   1941.   The Susquehannock Fort on Piscataway Creek. MHM 36(1):1–9.
Ferguson, L. G.
   1971.   *South Appalachian Mississippian*. PhD dissertation, University of North
      Carolina, Chapel Hill.
   1974. (editor)   Archeological Investigations at the Mulberry Site. SN 6:57–112.
   1975.   Archeology at Scott's Lake—Exploratory Research 1972, 1973. RMS,
      No. 68.
Ferguson, R. B.
   1972. (editor)   The Middle Cumberland Culture. PAVU, No. 3.
Fewkes, J. W.
   1896.   The Prehistoric Culture of Tusayan. AA 9(5):151–174.
   1898a.   Sikyatki and Its Pottery. In *Seventeenth Annual Report of the Bureau of
      American Ethnology: 1895–1896*, pp. 631–728. Smithsonian Institution.
      Washington, D.C.
   1898b.   Preliminary Account of an Expedition to the Pueblo Ruins near Winslow,
      Arizona, in 1896. In *Seventeenth Annual Report of the Bureau of American
      Ethnology: 1895–1896*, pp. 517–539. Smithsonian Institution. Washington,
      D.C.
   1900.   Tusayan Migration Traditions. In *Nineteenth Annual Report of the Bu-
      reau of American Ethnology*, pp. 375–633. Smithsonian Institution. Wash-
      ington, D.C.
   1904.   Two Summers Work in Pueblo Ruins. In *Twenty-Second Annual Report
      of the Bureau of American Ethnology*, Part 1. Smithsonian Institution. Wash-
      ington, D.C.
   1906.   The Sun's Influence on the Form of Hopi Pueblos. AA 8(1):88–100.
   1910.   The Butterfly in Hopi Myth and Ritual. AA 12(4):576–594.
   1912.   Casa Grande, Arizona. In *Twenty-Eighth Annual Report of the Bureau
      of American Ethnology, 1906–07*, pp. 25–179. Smithsonian Institution.
      Washington, D.C.
   1919.   Designs on Prehistoric Hopi Pottery. In *Thirty-Third Annual Report of
      the Bureau of American Ethnology*, pp. 207–284. Smithsonian Institution.
      Washington, D.C.

1927. Archaeological Field Work in Arizona: Field Session of 1926. SMC 78(7):207–232.

Finney, F. A., and A. C. Fortier
1985. The Carbon Dioxide Site. In *American Bottom Archaeology FAI–270 Site Reports*, edited by C. J. Bareis and J. W. Porter, Vol. 13. University of Illinois Press. Urbana and Chicago.

Fish, P. R., and S. K. Fish
1977. Verde Valley Archaeology: Review and Prospective. MNARP, No. 8.

Fish, P. R., P. J. Pilles, Jr., and S. K. Fish
1980. Colonies, Traders and Traits: The Hohokam in the North. In *Current Issues in Hohokam Prehistory*, edited by D. E. Doyel and Fred Plog. ASUAP 23:151–175.

Fisher, A. K., W. D. Frankforter, J. A. Tiffany, S. J. Schermer, and D. C. Anderson
1984. Turin: A Middle Archaic Burial Site in Western Iowa. PA 30(109):195–218.

Fitting, J. E.
1964. Ceramic Relationships of Four Late Woodland Sites in Northern Ohio. WiA 45(4):160–175.
1965. Late Woodland Cultures of Southeastern Michigan. UMMAAP, No. 24.
1966. Radiocarbon Dating the Younge Tradition. AA 31(5):738.
1968. The Spring Creek Site 20MU3, Muskegon County, Michigan. UMMAAP, No. 32.
1970. *The Archaeology of Michigan*. The Natural History Press. New York.
1972. (editor) The Schultz Site at Green Point: A Stratified Occupation Area in the Saginaw Valley of Michigan. MMAUM, No. 4.
1975. *The Archaeology of Michigan*, second edition. Cranbrook Institute of Science. Bloomfield Hills, Michigan.
1976. Archaeological Excavations at the Marquette Mission Site, St. Ignace, Michigan in 1972. MiA 22(2–3):103–250.

Fitting, J. E., J. DeVisscher, and E. Wahla
1966. The Paleo-Indian Occupation of the Holcombe Beach. UMMAAP, No. 27.

Fitzhugh, W. W.
1972. Environmental Archaeology and Cultural Systems in Hamilton Inlet, Labrador: A Survey of the Central Labrador Coast from 3000 B.C. to the Present. SCA, No. 16.
1975. A Comparative Approach to Northern Maritime Adaptations. In *Prehistoric Maritime Adaptations of the Circumpolar Zone*, edited by William Fitzhugh, pp. 339–386. Aldine. Chicago.
1980. Preliminary Report on the Torngat Archaeological Project. Arc 33:585–606.

Fitzwater, R. J.
1962. Final Report on Two Season's Excavations at El Portal, Mariposa County, California. UCLAAR, 1961–1962.

Fladmark, K. R.
1970. Preliminary Report on the Archaeology of the Queen Charlotte Islands. BCS, Nos. 6, 7.
1975. A Paleoecological Model for Northwest Coast Prehistory. ASCP, No. 43.

1978.   A Guide to Basic Archaeological Field Procedures. DASFUP, No. 4.

1979a.   The Early Prehistory of the Queen Charlotte Islands. Ar 32(2):38–45.

1979b.   Routes: Alternate Migration Corridors for Early Man in North America. AAn 44:55–69.

1982a.   Microdebitage Analysis: Initial Considerations. JAS 9:205–220.

1982b.   An Introduction to the Prehistory of British Columbia. CJA 6:95–156.

1984.   Mountain of Glass, Archaeology of the Mount Edziza Obsidian Source, British Columbia, Canada. WA 16(2):139–156.

1985.   *Glass and Ice: A Report on the Archaeology of the Mount Edziza and Spectrum Ranges, Northwestern British Columbia.* Simon Fraser University. Burnaby, British Columbia.

Fladmark, K. R., Diana Alexander, and John Driver

n.d.   Excavations at Charlie Lake Cave (HbRf 39). Report on file at Department of Anthropology, Simon Fraser University, Burnaby, British Columbia.

Flanders, R. E.

1965.   *A Comparison of Some Middle Woodland Materials from Illinois and Michigan.* PhD dissertation, The University of Michigan, Ann Arbor.

Flannery, Regina

1943.   Some Notes on a Few Sites in Beaufort County, S.C. BAEB 133:147–153.

Flaskerd, G. A.

1943.   The A. H. Andersen Site. MinA 9(1):4–21.

Flinn, Lynn, C. G. Turner II, and Alan Brew

1976.   Additional Evidence for Cannibalism in the Southwest: The Case of LA 4528. AAn 41(3):308–318.

Forbis, R. G.

1955.   *The MacHaffie Site.* PhD dissertation, Columbia University, New York.

1960.   The Old Women's Buffalo Jump, Alberta. NMCB 180, Pt. 1.

1961.   Early Point Types from Acasta Lake, Northwest Territories, Canada. AAn 27(1):112–113.

1968.   Fletcher: A Paleo-Indian Site in Alberta. AAn 33(1):1–10.

1977.   Cluny, An Ancient Fortified Village in Alberta. DAUCO, No. 4.

Forbis, R. G., and J. D. Sperry

1952.   An Early Man Site in Montana. AAn 18(2):127–133.

Ford, J. A.

1951.   Greenhouse: A Troyville–Coles Creek Site in Avoyelles Parish, Louisiana. APAMNH 44(1).

1952.   Measurements of Some Prehistoric Design Developments in the Southeastern States. APAMNH 44, Pt. 3:313–384.

1959.   Eskimo Prehistory in the Vicinity of Point Barrow, Alaska. APAMNH 47(1).

1961.   Menard Site: The Quapaw Village of Osotouy on the Arkansas River. APAMNH, No. 48.

1962.   A Quantitative Method for Deriving Cultural Chronology. TM, No. 1.

1963.   Hopewell Culture Burial Mounds Near Helena, Arkansas. APAMNH, No. 50.

1969.   A Comparison of Formative Cultures in the Americas: Diffusion or Psychic Unity of Man? SICA, No. 11.

Ford, J. A., and G. I. Quimby
1945. The Tchefuncte Culture, An Early Occupation of the Lower Mississippi Valley. MSAA, No. 2.
Ford, J. A., and C. H. Webb
1956. Poverty Point, A Late Archaic Site in Louisiana. APAMNH 46(1).
Ford, J. A., and G. R. Willey
1940. Crooks Site, A Marksville Period Burial Mound in La Salle Parish, Louisiana. LGSAS, No. 3.
1941. An Interpretation of the Prehistory of the Eastern United States. AA 43:325–363.
Ford, J. A., Philip Phillips, and W. G. Haag
1955. The Jaketown Site in West-Central Mississippi. APAMNH 45(1).
Ford, R. I.
1975. Re-excavation of Jemez Cave. A 3(3):13–27.
1979. Gathering and Gardening: Trends and Consequences of Hopewell Subsistence Strategies. In *Hopewell Archaeology: The Chillicothe Conference*, edited by D. S. Brose and N'omi Greber, pp. 234–238. Kent State University Press. Kent, Ohio.
Ford, R. I., A. H. Schroeder, and S. L. Peckham
1972. Three Perspectives on Puebloan Prehistory. In *New Perspectives on the Pueblos*, edited by Alfonso Ortiz, pp. 19–39. University of New Mexico Press. Albuquerque.
Ford, T. L., Jr.
1976. Adena Sites on Chesapeake Bay. AENA 4:63–89.
Forks of the Delaware Chapter 14
1980. The Overpeck Site (36BU5). PnA 50(3):1–46.
Fortier, A. C.
1985. The Robert Schneider Site. In *American Bottom Archaeology FAI–270 Reports*, edited by C. J. Bareis and J. W. Porter, Vol. 13. University of Illinois Press. Urbana and Chicago.
Fortier, A. C., and T. E. Emerson
1984. The Go-Kart North Site. In *American Bottom Archaeology FAI–270 Site Reports*, edited by C. J. Bareis and J. W. Porter, Vol. 9. University of Illinois Press. Urbana and Chicago.
Fortier, A. C., F. A. Finney, and R. B. Lacampagne
1983. The Mund Site. In *American Bottom Archaeology FAI–270 Reports*, edited by C. J. Bareis and J. W. Porter, Vol. 13. University of Illinois Press. Urbana and Chicago.
Fortier, A. C., R. B. Lacampagne, and F. A. Finney
1984. The Fish Lake Site. In *American Bottom Archaeology FAI–270 Site Reports*, edited by C. J. Bareis and J. W. Porter, Vol. 8. University of Illinois Press. Urbana and Chicago.
Foster, M. S.
1978. *Loma San Gabriel: A Prehistoric Culture of Northwest Mexico*. Ph.D. dissertation, University of Colorado, Boulder.
Fowke, Gerard
1894. Archaeological Investigation in James and Potomac Valleys. BAEB 23:9–80.

1922.   Archeological Investigations. BAEB, No. 76.

1928.   Archeological Investigations, Part II. In *Forty-Fourth Annual Report of the Bureau of American Ethnology, for 1926–7*, pp. 399–540. Smithsonian Institution. Washington, D.C.

Fowler, D. D., D. B. Madsen, and E. M. Hattori

1973.   Prehistory of Southeastern Nevada. DRIPSS, No. 6.

Fowler, M. L.

1952.   The Clear Lake Site: Hopewellian Occupation. In *Hopewellian Communities in Illinois*, edited by Thorne Deuel. ISMSP, No. 5.

1959.   Summary Report of Modoc Rock Shelter: 1952, 1953, 1955, 1956. ISMRI, No. 8.

1969. (editor)   Explorations into Cahokia Archaeology. IASB, No. 7.

1975. (editor)   Cahokia Archaeology: Field Reports. ISMRPA, No. 3.

Fowler, M. L., and R. L. Hall

1972.   Archaeological Phases at Cahokia. ISMRPA, No. 1.

Fox, W. A.

1975.   The Paleo-Indian Lakehead Complex. ARRO 6:28–49.

1980.   The Lakehead Complex: New Insights. ARRO, No. 13.

Frankforter, W. D.

1955.   Early Indian Skeletons at Turin, Iowa. NCIASN 3(5):4–6.

Frankforter, W. D., and G. A. Agogino

1959.   Archaic and Paleo-Indian Archaeological Discoveries in Western Iowa. TJS 11(4):482–491.

1960.   The Simonsen Site: Report for the Summer of 1959. PA 5(10):65–70.

Franklin, H. H., and W. B. Masse

1976.   The San Pedro Salado: A Case of Prehistoric Migration. K 42(1):47–56.

Frazier, Kendrick

1986.   *People of Chaco: A Canyon and Its Culture*. W. W. Norton & Co. New York.

Fredrickson, D. A.

1973.   *Early Cultures of the North Coast Ranges, California*. PhD dissertation, University of California, Davis.

Fredrickson, D. A., and J. M. Grossman

1977.   A San Dieguito Component at Buena Vista Lake, California. JCA 4(2):173–190.

Freeman, J. E.

1956.   *An Analysis of the Point Sauble and Beaumier Farm Sites*. MA thesis, University of Wisconsin-Madison.

1969.   The Millville Site, A Middle Woodland Village in Grant County, Wisconsin. WiA 50(2):37–88.

Friedman, Edward

1976.   *An Archaeological Survey of Makah Territory: A Study in Resource Utilization*. PhD dissertation, Washington State University, Pullman.

Friedman, J. P.

1975.   *The Prehistoric Uses of Wood at the Ozette Archaeological Site*. PhD dissertation, Washington State University, Pullman.

Frisbie, T. R.
  1967. *The Excavation and Interpretation of the Artificial Leg Basketmaker III–Pueblo I Sites Near Corrales, New Mexico.* MA thesis, University of New Mexico, Albuquerque.
  1973. The Influence of J. Walter Fewkes on Nampeyo: Fact or Fancy? In *Changing Ways of Southwestern Indians, A Historic Perspective*, edited by A. H. Schroeder, pp. 231–244. Rio Grande Press. Glorieta, New Mexico.

Frison, G. C.
  1971. The Bison Pound in Northwestern Plains Prehistory. AAn 36(1):77–91.
  1974. *The Casper Site.* Academic Press. New York.
  1976a. Cultural Activity Associated with Prehistoric Mammoth Butchering and Processing. S 194:728–730.
  1976b. The Chronology of Paleoindian and Altithermal Cultures in the Bighorn Basin, Wyoming. In *Cultural Change and Continuity: Essays in Honor of James Bennett Griffin*, edited by C. E. Cleland. Academic Press. New York.
  1978. *Prehistoric Hunters of the High Plains.* Academic Press. New York.
  1984. The Carter/Kerr-McGee Paleoindian Site: Cultural Resource Management and Archaeological Research. AAn 49(2):288–314.
  in press. *The Horner Site.* Academic Press. New York.

Frison, George, and Bruce Bradley
  1980. *Folsom Tools and Technology at the Hanson Site.* University of New Mexico Press. Albuquerque.

Frison, George, and Donald Grey
  1980. Pryor Stemmed: A Specialized Late Paleoindian Ecological Adaptation. PA 25(87):27–45.

Frison, George, and Dennis Stanford
  1982. *The Agate Basin Site.* Academic Press. New York.

Frison, George, and Lawrence Todd
  1986. *The Colby Mammoth Site.* University of New Mexico Press. Albuquerque.
  1987. *The Horner Site.* Academic Press. New York.

Frison, George, Danny Walker, S. D. Webb, and George Zeimens
  1978. Paleoindian Procurement of *Camelops* on the Northwestern Plains. QR 10:385–400.

Fritz, G. J.
  1984. Identification of Cultigen Amaranth and Chenopod from Rockshelter Sites in Northwest Arkansas. AAn 49(3):558–572.

Fritz, G. J., and Robert Ray
  1982. Rock Art Sites in the Southern Arkansas Ozarks and the Arkansas River Valley. In *Arkansas Archeology in Review*, edited by N. L. Trubowitz and M. D. Jeter, pp. 240–276. AASRS, No. 15.

Fryxell, Roald, T. Bielicki, R. D. Daugherty, C. E. Gustafson, H. T. Irwin, and B. C. Keel
  1968. A Human Skeleton from Sediments of Mid-Pinedale Age in Southeastern Washington. AAn 33(4):511–514.

Fugle, E.
  1962. Mill Creek Culture and Technology. JIAS 11(4).

Fulton, W. S., and Carr Tuthill
   1940.   *An Archaeological Site near Gleeson, Arizona.* The Amerind Foundation,
          Inc. Dragoon, Arizona.
Funk, R. E.
   1978.   Post-Pleistocene Adaptations. In *Handbook of North American Indians,*
          Vol. 15: Northeast, edited by W. V. Sturtevant and B. G. Trigger, p. 16–27.
          Smithsonian Institution. Washington, D.C.
   1983.   The Northeastern United States. In *Ancient North Americans,* edited by
          J. D. Jennings, pp. 303–372. W. H. Freeman & Co. New York.
Futato, E. M.
   1977.   The Bellefonte Site: 1 Ja 300. UAOARRS, No. 2.
   1983.   Archaeological Investigations in the Cedar Creek and Upper Bear Creek
          Reservoirs. UAOARRI, No. 29.
Galm, J. R.
   1984.   Arkansas Valley Caddoan Formative: The Wister and Fourche Maline
          Phases. In *Prehistory of Oklahoma,* edited by R. E. Bell. Academic Press.
          New York.
Galm, J. R., G. D. Hartman, Ruth Masten, and G. O. Stephenson
   1981.   A Cultural Resources Overview of Bonneville Power Administration's
          Mid-Columbia Project, Central Washington. EWURAH 100(16).
Gardner, P. S.
   1980.   *An Analysis of Dan River Ceramics from Virginia and North Carolina.*
          MA thesis, University of North Carolina, Chapel Hill.
Gardner, W. M.
   1974.   (editor)   The Flint Run Paleo-Indian Complex: A Preliminary Report
          1971–73 Seasons. ALCUOP, No. 1.
   1983.   Stop Me If You've Heard This One Before: The Flint Run Paleo-Indian
          Complex Revisited. AENA 11:49–64.
Garland, E. B.
   n.d. (editor)   *Archaeological Investigations in the St. Joseph River Valley, Berrien
          County, Michigan.* Report on file at the State of Michigan Department of
          Transportation, Lansing.
Garrow, P. H.
   1975.   The Woodland Period North of the Fall Line. EG 3:17–26.
Geier, C. R., and Michael Barber
   1983.   The Skiffes Creek Site (44NN7): A Multicomponent Middle Woodland
          Base Camp in Newport News, Virginia. OPAJMU, No. 17.
Geier, C. R., and W. P. Boyer
   1982.   The Gathright Dam–Lake Moomaw Cultural Resource Investigation: A
          Synthesis of the Prehistoric Data. OPAJMU, No. 15.
Geier, C. R., and J. T. Moldenhauer
   1977.   *The Bessemer Site (44B026): A Late Woodland Dan River Cultural Com-
          ponent in Central Western Virginia.* Department of Anthropology, James
          Madison University, Harrisonburg.
Geist, O. W., and F. G. Rainey
   1936.   Archaeological Excavation at Kukulik, St. Lawrence Island, Alaska: Pre-
          liminary Report. UAMP, 2.

Gerber, Art
  1965. An Extraordinary Crib Mound Burial. CSAJ 12(3):91–95.
  1970. Latest Finds at Crib Mound. CSAJ 17(2):87–91.
Gerow, B. A. (with R. Force)
  1969. *An Analysis of the University Village Complex with a Reappraisal of Central California Archaeology.* Stanford University Press. Stanford, California.
Gibbon, G. E.
  1970. The Midway Village Site: An Orr Phase Oneota Site in the Upper Mississippi River Valley. WiA 51(3):79–162.
  1973. The Sheffield Site: An Oneota Site on the St. Croix River. MPS, No. 11.
  1974. A Model of Mississippian Development and Its Implications for the Red Wing Area. MPS 11:129–137.
  1975. The Brower Site. MinA 34(1–2):1–43.
  1976. The Old Shakopee Bridge Site: A Late Woodland Ricing Site on Shakopee Lake, Mille Lacs County, Minnesota. MinA 35(2):2–26.
  1978. A Simplified Algorithm Model for the Classification of Silvernale and Blue Earth Phase Ceramic Vessels. OPMA, No. 2:3–11.
Gibbon, G. E., and C. A. H. Caine
  1980. The Middle to Late Woodland Transition in Eastern Minnesota. MJA 5(1):57–72.
Gibson, J. L.
  1974. Poverty Point, the First North American Chiefdom. Ar 27(2):96–105.
  1982. Old Creek, A Troyville Period Ossuary in La Salle Parish Louisiana: Reflections After a Quarter Century. LA 9:127–204.
Giddings, J. L.
  1940. The Application of Tree-Ring Dates to Arctic Sites. TRB 7(2):10–14.
  1951. The Denbigh Flint Complex. AAn 16(3):193–203.
  1952. The Arctic Woodland Culture of the Kobuk River. UMM.
  1956. Forest Eskimos. UMB 20(2).
  1957. Round Houses in the Western Arctic. AAn 23(2):121–135.
  1960. The Archeology of Bering Strait. CAn 1(2):121–138.
  1962a. Eskimos and Old Shorelines. AS 31(4):585–594.
  1962b. Side-Notched Points near Bering Strait. AINATP 11:35–38.
  1964. *The Archeology of Cape Denbigh.* Brown University Press. Providence, Rhode Island.
  1966. Cross-Dating the Archeology of Northwestern Alaska. S 153(3732):127–135.
  1967. *Ancient Men of the Arctic.* Alfred A. Knopf. New York.
Giddings, J. L., and D. D. Anderson
  1985. *Beach Ridge Archeology of Cape Krusenstern National Monument.* National Park Service. Washington, D.C.
Gill, S. J.
  1983. *Ethnobotany of the Makah and Ozette People, Olympic Peninsula, Washington.* PhD dissertation, Washington State University, Pullman.
Gilliland, M. S.
  1975. *The Material Culture of Key Marco, Florida.* University of Florida Press. Gainesville.

Gillio, D. A.
  1970.   A Reexamination of the Gordon Creek Burial Lithic Material. SL 36:12–
          14.
Gilmore, Kathleen
  1973.   *Caddoan Interaction in the Neches Valley, Texas*. PhD dissertation,
          Southern Methodist University, Dallas.
Gladwin, H. S.
  1928.   Excavations at Casa Grande, Arizona. SMP, No. 2.
  1943.   A Review and Analysis of the Flagstaff Culture. MP, No. 31.
  1945.   The Chaco Branch: Excavations at White Mound and in the Red Mesa
          Valley. MP, No. 33.
  1947.   *Men Out of Asia*. Whittlesey House. New York.
  1948.   Excavations at Snaketown IV: Review and Conclusions. MP, No. 38.
  1957.   *A History of the Ancient Southwest*. Bond Wheelwright. Portland, Maine.
Gladwin, H. S., E. W. Haury, E. B. Sayles, and Nora Gladwin
  1937.   Excavations at Snaketown: Material Culture. MP, No. 25.
Gladwin, Winifred, and H. S. Gladwin
  1930a. The Western Range of the Red-on-buff Culture. MP, No. 5.
  1930b. An Archaeological Survey of the Verde Valley. MP, No. 6.
  1934.   A Method for the Designation of Cultures and Their Variations. MP, No.
          15.
  1935.   The Eastern Range of the Red-on-buff Culture. MP, No. 16.
Gleeson, P. F.
  1980.   Ozette Woodworking Technology. LAHPR, No. 3.
Glennan, W. S.
  1976.   The Manix Lake Industry: Early Lithic Tradition or Workshop Refuse?
          JNWA 1(7):43–61.
Goggin, J. M.
  1949.   Cultural Traditions in Florida Prehistory. In *The Florida Indian and His
          Neighbors*, edited by J. W. Griffin, pp. 13–44. Rollins College Inter-American
          Center. Winter Park, Florida.
  1952.   Space and Time Perspective in Northern St. Johns Archeology, Florida.
          YUPA, No. 47.
Goodman, A. H., and G. J. Armelagos
  1985.   Disease and Death at Dr. Dickson's Mounds. NaH 19(9):12–18.
Goodyear, A. C.
  1974.   The Brand Site: A Techno-Functional Study of a Dalton Site in Northeast
          Arkansas. AASRS, No. 7.
Gordon, B. H. C.
  1975.   Of Men and Herds in Barrenland Prehistory. NMMMS, No. 28.
  1976.   Migod—8000 Years of Barrenland Prehistory. NMMMS 56:310.
Grabert, G. F.
  1979.   Pebble Tools and Time Factoring. CJA 3:165–175.
Gradwohl, David
  1969.   Prehistoric Villages in Eastern Nebraska. NSHSPA, No. 4.
Gramley, R. M., and Kerry Rutledge
  1981.   *A New Paleo-Indian Site in the State of Maine*. AAn 46:354–360.

Grange, R. T., Jr.
    1968.   Pawnee and Lower Loup Pottery. NSHSPA, No. 3.
    1979.   An Archaeological View of Pawnee Origins. NH 60(2):134–160.
    1984.   Dating Pawnee Sites by the Ceramic Formula Method. WA 15(3):274–293.
    n.d.   The I. C. Few Site (38PN2). Report on file at Institute of Archeology and Anthropology, University of South Carolina, Columbia.
Granger, B. H.
    1960.   *Will C. Barnes' Arizona Place Names*. University of Arizona Press. Tucson.
Grant, Campbell
    1981.   The Desert Bighorn and Aboriginal Man. In *The Desert Bighorn*, edited by Gale Monson and Lowell Sumner, pp. 7–39. University of Arizona Press. Tucson.
Grant, C., J. W. Baird, and J. K. Pringle
    1968.   *Rock Drawings of the Coso Range*. Maturango Museum, Publication No. 4. China Lake, California.
Gray, H. H., J. L. Bassett, C. A. Munson, P. J. Munson, and G. S. Fraser
    1983.   Archaeological Geology of the Wyandotte Region, South-Central Indiana (Field Trip 14). In *Field Trips in Midwestern Archaeology*, edited by R. H. Shaver and J. A. Sunderman. The 1983 Annual Meeting of the Geological Society of Avocational and Affiliated Societies at Indianapolis. 2:173–213.
Graybill, J. R.
    1980.   Marietta Works, Ohio, and the Eastern Periphery of Fort Ancient. PnA 50(1–2):51–60.
    1984.   The Eastern Periphery of Fort Ancient. PnA 54(1–2):40–50.
Grayson, D. K.
    1979.   Mount Mazama, Climatic Change, and Fort Rock Basin Archaeo-faunas. In *Volcanic Activity and Human Ecology*, edited by P. D. Sheets and D. K. Grayson, pp. 247–257. Academic Press. New York.
Greber, N'omi
    1979a.   Variations in Social Structure of Ohio Hopewell Peoples. MJA 4:35–78.
    1979b.   A Comparative Study of Site Morphology and Burial Patterns at Edwin Harness Mound and Seip Mounds, 1 and 2. In *Hopewell Archaeology: The Chillicothe Conference*, edited by D. S. Brose and N'omi Greber, pp. 27–38. Kent State University Press. Kent, Ohio.
    1981.   Salvaging Clues to a Prehistoric Culture. Ga, No. 3.
    1983. (editor)   Recent Excavations at the Edwin Harness Mound, Liberty Works, Ross County, Ohio. MJASP, No. 5.
Green, E. L.
    1976.   *Valdez Phase Occupation near Taos, New Mexico*. Fort Burgwin Research Center. Dallas.
Green, F. E.
    n.d.   Archaeological Salvage in the Sanford Reservoir Area. Report on file at the National Park Service, Regional Office, Santa Fe, New Mexico.
Green, R. C.
    1956.   Excavations Near Mayhill, New Mexico. MNMHS, No. 2.

Green, T. J., and C. A. Munson
    1978.   Mississippian Settlement Pattern in Southwestern Indiana. In *Mississippian Settlement Patterns*, edited by B. D. Smith, pp. 293–330. Academic Press. New York.
Greenleaf, J. C.
    1975a.   The Fortified Hill Site near Gila Bend, Arizona. K 40:213–282.
    1975b.   Excavations at Punta de Agua in the Santa Cruz River Basin, Southeastern Arizona. UAAP, No. 26.
Greenman, E. F.
    1932.   Excavations of the Coon Mound and an Analysis of the Adena Culture. OAHSQ 41(3).
    1937a.   The Younge Site. OCMAUM, No. 6.
    1937b.   Two Prehistoric Village Sites Near Cleveland, Ohio. OAHSQ 46:305–366.
    1939.   The Wolf and Furton Sites, Macomb County, Michigan. OCMAUM, No. 8.
    1943.   An Early Industry on a Raised Beach, Near Killarney, Ontario. AAn 8(3):260–265.
Greenman, E. F., and H. C. Shetrone
    1931.   Explorations of the Seip Group of Prehistoric Earthworks. OAHSQ 40(3).
Greenwood, R. S.
    1972.   9000 Years of Prehistory at Diablo Canyon, San Luis Obispo County, California. SLOOP, No. 7.
Greer, J. W., and R. A. Benfer
    1975.   Austin Phase Burials at the Pat Parker Site, Travis County, Texas. BTAS 46:189–216.
Gregory, D. A., and Fred Nials
    1985.   Observations Concerning the Distribution of Classic Period Hohokam Platform Mounds. In *Proceedings of the 1983 Hohokam Symposium: Part I*, edited by A. E. Dittert, Jr., and D. E. Dove, pp. 373–388. AASOP, No. 2.
Gregory, L. B.
    1980.   The Hatch Site: A Preliminary Report. ASVQB 34(4):239–248.
Griffin, J. B.
    1943a.   *The Fort Ancient Aspect.* University of Michigan Press. Ann Arbor.
    1943b.   An Analysis and Interpretation of the Ceramic Remains from Two Sites near Beaufort, S.C. BAEB 133:159–167.
    1945.   Ceramic Collections from Two South Carolina Sites. PMAS 30:465–476.
    1952. (editor)   *Archaeology of Eastern United States.* University of Chicago Press. Chicago.
    1954.   The Chronological Position of the Hopewellian Culture in the Eastern United States. AnP, No. 12.
    1955.   Observations on the Grooved Axe in North America. PnA 25(1):32–44.
    1964a.   Review of the Clam River Focus. WiA 45(2):104–111.
    1964b.   The Northeast Woodland Area. In *Prehistoric Man in the New World*, edited by J. D. Jennings and Edward Norbeck, pp. 223–258. University of Chicago Press. Chicago.
    1967.   Eastern North American Archaeology: A Summary. S 156:175–191.

1977. The University of Michigan Excavations at the Pulcher Site in 1950. AAn 42:462–488.

1978. Late Prehistory of the Ohio Valley. In *Handbook of North American Indians*, Vol. 15:547–559. Smithsonian Institution. Washington, D.C.

1983. The Midlands. In *Ancient North Americans*, edited by J. D. Jennings. W. H. Freeman & Co. New York.

1985. Changing Concepts of the Prehistoric Mississippian Cultures in the Eastern United States. In *Alabama and the Borderlands*, edited by R. R. Badger and L. A. Clayton. University of Alabama Press, University.

Griffin, J. B., and W. H. Sears
1950. Certain Sand-tempered Pottery Types of the Southeast. In *Prehistoric Pottery of the Eastern United States*. Museum of Anthropology, University of Michigan, Ann Arbor.

Griffin, J. B., and A. C. Spaulding
1951. The Central Mississippi Valley Archaeological Survey, Season 1950: A Preliminary Report. JISAS (n.s.) 1:74–81.

Griffin, J. B., R. E. Flanders, and P. F. Titterington
1970. The Burial Complexes of the Knight and Norton Mounds in Illinois and Michigan. MMAUM, No. 2.

Griffin, J. W.
1974. Investigations in Russell Cave, Russell Cave National Monument, Alabama. NPSPA, No. 13.

Griffin, J. W., and R. P. Bullen
1950. The Safety Harbor Site, Pinellas County, Florida. FASP, No. 2.

Griffith, Daniel
1977. Townsend Ceramics and the Late Woodland of Southern Delaware. MA thesis, American University, Washington, D.C.

Griffith, D. R., and R. E. Artusy
1977. Middle Woodland Ceramics from Wolfe Neck, Sussex County, Delaware. Arcl 28(1):1–29.

Grosscup, G. L.
1960. The Culture History of Lovelock Cave, Nevada. UCASR, No. 52.

Grosser, R. D.
1973. A Tentative Cultural Sequence for the Snyder Site, Kansas. PA 18(61):228–238.

1977. *Late Archaic Subsistence Patterns from the Central Great Plains: A Systemic Model*. PhD dissertation, University of Kansas, Lawrence.

Gruhn, Ruth
1961. The Archaeology of Wilson Butte Cave, South-Central Idaho. OPISC, No. 6.

Gubser, N. J.
1965. *The Nunamiut Eskimos: Hunters of Caribou*. Yale University Press. New Haven, Connecticut.

Gulløv, H. C.
1982. Migration et Diffusion: Le Peuplement Inuit de l'Ouest du Groenland a l'Epoque Post Medievale. EIS 6(2):3–20.

Gumerman, G. J.
1969. *The Archaeology of the Hopi Buttes District, Arizona*. PhD dissertation, University of Arizona, Tucson.

1975.   Alternative Models for Demographic Change: Southwestern Examples.
AAn 40(2):104–115.

1984.   *A View from Black Mesa: The Changing Face of Archaeology.* University
of Arizona Press. Tucson.

Gumerman, G. J., and S. A. Skinner

1968.   A Synthesis of the Prehistory of the Central Little Colorado Valley, Arizona. AAn 33(2):185–199.

Gumerman, G. J., and C. S. Weed

1976.   The Question of Salado in the Agua Fria and New River Drainages of
Central Arizona. In *The 1976 Salado Conference,* edited by D. E. Doyel and
E. W. Haury. K 42(1):105–112.

Gundersen, J. N.

1983.   Pipestones of Southeastern South Dakota. PCA:33–34.

1984.   Provenance Analysis of Plains Pipestone Argillites. GSAA 16(6):#39974.

Gunnerson, J. H.

1960.   An Introduction to Plains Apache Archeology: The Dismal River Aspect.
BAEB, No. 173.

Hack, J. T.

1942.   The Changing Physical Environment of the Hopi Indians of Arizona. PPM
8(2).

Hadleigh West, Frederick

1967.   The Donnelly Ridge Site and the Definition of an Early Core and Blade
Complex in Central Alaska. AAn 32(3):360–382.

1975.   Dating the Denali Complex. ArcA 12(1):76–81.

1980.   Late Paleolithic Cultures in Alaska. In *Early Native Americans.* Mouton.
The Hague.

1981.   *The Archaeology of Beringia.* Columbia University Press. New York.

Haggarty, J. C.

1982.   *The Archaeology of Hesquiat Harbour: The Archaeological Utility of an
Ethnographically Defined Social Unit.* PhD dissertation, Washington State
University, Pullman.

Hall, E. S., Jr.

1976.   Contributions to Anthropology: The Interior Peoples of Northern Alaska.
NMMMS, ASCP No. 49.

Hall, E. T., Jr.

1942.   Archaeological Survey of the Walhalla Glades. MNAB, No. 20.

1944.   Early Stockaded Settlements in the Gobernador, New Mexico. In *Studies
in Archaeology and Ethnology,* Vol. 2, part 1. Columbia University Press.
New York.

Hall, G. D., T. R. Hester, and S. L. Black

1986.   *The Prehistoric Sites at Choke Canyon Reservoir, Southern Texas: Results
of Phase II Archaeological Investigations.* Choke Canyon Series, Vol. 10.
Center for Archaeological Research, University of Texas at San Antonio. San
Antonio.

Hall, R. L.

1962.   *The Archaeology of Carcajou Point.* University of Wisconsin Press.
Madison.

Hally, D. J.
    1975. Introduction to the Symposium: The King Site and Its Investigation. SACB
    18:48–54.
Halsey, J. R.
    1976. *The Bussinger Site: A Multicomponent Site in the Saginaw Valley of
    Michigan, with a Review of Early Late Woodland Mortuary Complexes in
    the Northeastern Woodlands.* PhD dissertation, University of North Carolina,
    Chapel Hill.
    1981. The Wayne Mortuary Complex: A New Chapter in Michigan's Prehistoric
    Past. MiH 65(5):17–23.
Ham, L. C.
    1982. *Seasonality, Shell Midden Layers, and Coast Salish Subsistence Activities
    at the Crescent Beach Site, DgRr 1.* PhD dissertation, University of British
    Columbia, Vancouver.
Ham, L. C., Arlene Yip, and Leila Kullar
    n.d.a. A Mitigation Report on the 1982/83 Archaeological Excavations at the
    St. Mungo Cannery Site (DgRr 2), North Delta, B.C. Report on file at Heritage
    Conservation Branch, Ministry of the Provincial Secretary and Government
    Services, Victoria, British Columbia.
    n.d.b. A Charles Culture Fishing Village. Report on file at Heritage Conservation
    Branch, Ministry of the Provincial Secretary and Government Services, Vic-
    toria, British Columbia.
Hamilton, H. W.
    1952. The Spiro Mound. MA, No. 14.
Hammack, L. C.
    n.d. LA 9147: The Waldo Site. In *Salvage Archaeology in the Galisteo Dam
    and Reservoir Area, New Mexico.* Report on file at Laboratory of Anthro-
    pology, Museum of New Mexico, Santa Fe.
Hanes, R. C.
    1980. *Lithic Technology of Dirty Shame Rockshelter, in the Owyhee Uplands
    on the Northeastern Edge of the Great Basin.* PhD dissertation, University
    of Oregon, Eugene.
Hanson, L. H., Jr.
    1970. *The Jewell Site, Bn 21, Barren County, Kentucky.* TAMP, No. 8.
Hargrave, L. L.
    1930. Shungopovi. MN 2(10).
    1931. First Mesa. MN 3(8).
    1932a. Oraibi: A Brief History of the Oldest Inhabited Town in the United
    States. MN 4(7).
    1932b. Guide to Forty Pottery Types from the Hopi Country and the San Fran-
    cisco Mountains, Arizona. MNAB, No. 1.
    1935. The Jeddito Valley and the First Pueblo Towns in Arizona to be Visited
    by Europeans. MN 8(4).
    1937. Sikyatki. MN 9(12).
    1938. Results of a Study of the Cohonina Branch of the Patayan Culture in
    1938. MN 11(6).
    1970. Mexican Macaws. APUAr, No. 20.

Harlow, F. H.
  1973. *Matte-paint Pottery of the Tewa, Keres, and Zuni Pueblos*. Museum of New Mexico Press. Santa Fe.
Harmon, Michael
  1986. Eighteenth Century Lower Creek Adaptation and Use of European Material Culture. VHA, No. 2.
Harn, A. D.
  1975. Cahokia and the Mississippian Emergence in the Spoon River Area of Illinois. TIAS 68:414–434.
  1978. Mississippian Settlement Patterns in the Central Illinois River Valley. In *Mississippian Settlement Patterns*, edited by B. D. Smith, pp. 233–268. Academic Press. New York.
  1980. The Prehistory of Dickson Mounds: The Dickson Excavation. ISMRI, No. 35.
Harp, Elmer, Jr.
  1958. Prehistory in the Dismal Lake Area. Arc 11:218–249.
  1964. The Cultural Affinities of the Newfoundland Dorset Eskimos. NMCB, No. 200.
  1976. Dorset Settlement Patterns in Newfoundland and Southeastern Hudson Bay. In *Eastern Arctic Prehistory: Paleoeskimo Problems*, edited by M. S. Maxwell, pp. 119–138. MSAA, No. 31.
  n.d. Report on Archaeological Investigations in the Belcher Islands During the Summer of 1975. Report on file at Archaeological Survey of Canada, National Museum of Man, Ottawa, Ontario.
Harp, Elmer, Jr., and D. R. Hughes
  1968. Five Prehistoric Burials from Port au Choix, Newfoundland. PN 8:1–47.
Harrington, J. C.
  1948. Plain Stamped, Shell Tempered Pottery from North Carolina. AAn (13)3:251–252.
Harrington, M. R.
  1924a. Explorations in the Ozark Region. INM 1:3–7.
  1924b. The Ozark Bluff-Dwellers. AA 26(1):1–21.
  1927. Some Lake Bed Camp Sites in Nevada. INM 4(1):40–47.
  1933. Gypsum Cave, Nevada. SMP, No. 8.
  1934. American Horses and Ancient Men in Nevada. M 8(6):165–169.
  1937. Excavations of Pueblo Grande de Nevada. BTAPS 9:130–145.
  1948. An Ancient Site at Borax Lake, California. SMP, No. 16.
  1957. A Pinto Site at Little Lake, California. SMP, No. 17.
  1960. The Ozark Bluff-Dwellers. INM, No. 12.
Harrington, M. R., and R. D. Simpson
  1961. Tule Springs, Nevada, with Other Evidences of Pleistocene Man in North America. SMP, No. 18.
Harris, R. K.
  1953. The Sam Kaufman Site, Red River County, Texas. BTAS 24:43–68.
Harris, R. K., and I. M. Harris
  1980. Distribution of Natchitoches Engraved Ceramics. In *Caddoan and Poverty Point Archaeology: Essays in Honor of Clarence Hungerford Webb*, edited by J. L. Gibson. LA, No. 6.

Harris, R. K., and Mr. and Mrs. J. Perkins
  1954. Burials 12, 13, 14 and 15, the Sam Kaufman Site, 19 B3–2. TRec 13(1):2–
         8.
Harris, R. K., and Lester Wilson
  1956. Burial 17, the Sam Kaufman Site, 19 B3–2. TRec 14(4):17–22.
Harris, R. K., I. M. Harris, J. C. Blaine, and J. L. Blaine
  1965. A Preliminary Archeological and Documentary Study of the Womack Site,
         Lamar County, Texas. BTAS 30:287–363.
Hatt, R. T., D. J. Richards, and M. L. Papworth
  1958. The Sanilac Petroglyphs. CISB, No. 36.
Hattori, E. M.
  1982. The Archaeology of Falcon Hill, Winnemucca Lake, Washoe County,
         Nevada. NSMAP, No. 18.
Haury, E. W.
  1931. Kivas of the Tusayan Ruin, Grand Canyon, Arizona. MP, No. 9.
  1932. Roosevelt 9:6, A Hohokam Site of the Colonial Period. MP, No. 11.
  1934. The Canyon Creek Ruin and the Cliff Dwellings of the Sierra Ancha. MP,
         No. 14.
  1936. The Mogollon Culture of Southwestern New Mexico. MP, No. 20.
  1940. Excavations in the Forestdale Valley, East-central Arizona. UASSB, No.
         12.
  1945. The Excavation of Los Muertos and Neighboring Ruins in the Salt River
         Valley, Southern Arizona. PPM 24(1).
  1950. *The Stratigraphy and Archaeology of Ventana Cave, Arizona.* University
         of Arizona Press. Tucson.
  1957. An Alluvial Site on the San Carlos Indian Reservation, Arizona. AAn
         23(1):2–27.
  1958. Evidence at Point of Pines for a Prehistoric Migration from Northern
         Arizona. In *Migrations in New World Culture History*, edited by R. H.
         Thompson, pp. 1–6. UASSB, No. 27.
  1976. *The Hohokam, Desert Farmers and Craftsmen: Excavations at Snake-
         town, 1964–1965.* University of Arizona Press. Tucson.
  1985. *Mogollon Culture in the Forestdale Valley of East-Central Arizona.* Uni-
         versity of Arizona Press. Tucson.
Haury, E. W., Ernst Antevs, and J. F. Lance
  1953. Artifacts with Mammoth Remains, Naco; Arizona. AAn 19(1):1–24.
Haury, E. W., E. B. Sayles, and W. W. Wasley
  1959. The Lehner Mammoth Site, Southeastern Arizona. AAn 24(1):2–30.
Hawkes, E. W., and Ralph Linton
  1916. A Pre-Lenape Site in New Jersey. APUPM 6(2):45–77.
Hawley, Florence
  1936. Field Manual of Prehistoric Southwestern Pottery Types. UNMAS 1(4).
  1941. Tree-ring Analysis and Dating in the Mississippi Drainage. UCPAOP, No.
         2.
  1950. Big Kivas, Little Kivas, and Moiety Houses in Historical Reconstruction.
         SJA 6(3):286–302.
Hawley, Florence, D. D. Brand, and F. C. Hibben
  1937. Tseh So, a Small House Ruin, Chaco Canyon, New Mexico. UNMAS
         2(2).

Hayden, Irwin
   1930.   Mesa House. SMP 4:26–92.
Hayden, J. D.
   1957.   Excavations, 1940, at University Indian Ruin. SMATS, No. 5.
   1976.   Pre-Altithermal Archaeology in the Sierra Pinacate, Mexico. AAn
            41(3):274–289.
Hayes, A. C.
   1964.   The Archeological Survey of Wetherill Mesa, Mesa Verde National Park.
            ARS, No. 7A.
   1974.   The Four Churches of Pecos. University of New Mexico Press.
            Albuquerque.
   1981.   Contributions to Gran Quivira Archeology. PArc, No. 17.
Hayes, A. C., and J. A. Lancaster
   1975.   Badger House Community, Mesa Verde National Park, Colorado.
            NPSPA, No. 7E.
Hayes, A. C., and T. C. Windes
   1975.   An Anasazi Shrine in Chaco Canyon. In Collected Papers in Honor of
            Florence Hawley Ellis. PASNM, No. 2.
Hayes, A. C., J. N. Young, and A. H. Warren
   1981.   Excavation of Mound 7, Gran Quivira National Monument, New Mex-
            ico. PArc, No. 16.
Haynes, C. V., Jr.
   1973.   The Calico Site: Artifacts or Geofacts? S 181(4097):305–310.
   1980.   The Clovis Culture. CJA 1(1):115–121.
Hays, K. A., and E. C. Adams
   n.d.   Excavation and Surface Collection of Homolovi II Ruin. Report on file at
           Arizona State Museum, Tucson.
Hays, T. R.
   1982. (editor)   Archeological Investigations at the San Gabriel Reservoir District,
           Central Texas. Institute of Applied Sciences, North Texas State University.
           Denton.
Hazlett, W. J., and D. J. Hazlett
   1965.   Additional Petroglyphs at Roche-A-Cris. WiA 46(3):191–195.
Heilman, J. M., and R. R. Hoefer
   1981.   Possible Astronomical Alignments in a Fort Ancient Settlement at the
           Incinerator Site in Dayton, Ohio. In Archaeoastronomy in the Americas,
           edited by R. A. Williamson, pp. 157–171. Bellena Press. Los Altos, California.
Heizer, R. F.
   1949.   The Archaeology of Central California I: The Early Horizon. UCAR 12:1–
           84.
   1951.   Preliminary Report on the Leonard Rockshelter Site, Pershing County,
           Nevada. AAn 17:89–98.
   1952.   Petroglyphs from Southwestern Kodiak, Alaska. PAPS 93(1):48–56.
   1956.   Archaeology of the Uyak Site, Kodiak Island, Alaska. UCAR 17(1).
Heizer, R. F., and R. A. Brooks
   1965.   Lewisville—Ancient Campsite or Wood Rat Houses? SJA 21(2):155–165.
Heizer, R. F., and C. W. Clewlow, Jr.
   1968.   Projectile Points from Site NV-Ch–15, Churchill County, Nevada. UCASR
           71:59–88.

Heizer, R. F., and A. B. Elsasser
    1953. Some Archaeological Sites and Cultures of the Central Sierra Nevada.
        UCASR, No. 21.
    1959. *The Archaeologist at Work*. Harper and Row. New York.
    1970. An Ethnographic Sketch of the Paviotso in 1882. CUCARF 7:55–63.
Heizer, R. F., and T. R. Hester
    1978. Great Basin. In *Chronologies in New World Archaeology*, edited by R. E.
        Taylor and C. W. Meighan, pp. 147–199. Academic Press. New York.
Heizer, R. F., and L. K. Napton
    1970. Archaeology and the Prehistoric Great Basin Lacustrine Subsistence Re-
        gime as Seen from Lovelock Cave, Nevada. CUCARF, No. 10.
Heldman, D. P., and R. T. Grange
    1981. *Excavations at Fort Michilimackinac: 1978–1979. The Rue de la Babil-
        lards*. Mackinac Island State Park Commission. Lansing, Michigan.
Helmer, J. W.
    1980. Early Dorset in the High Arctic: A Report from Karluk Island, N.W.T.
        Arc 33:427–442.
Hemmings, E. T.
    1969. An Early Ceramic Site near Beaufort, South Carolina. SN 1(6–9).
    1970a. Preliminary Report of Excavations at Fig Island, South Carolina. SN
        2(2–3).
    1970b. Emergence of Formative Life on the Atlantic Coast of the Southeast.
        RMS, No. 7.
    1978. Cades Pond Subsistence, Settlement, and Ceremonialism. FA 31:141–150.
Henderson, T. K.
    n.d. Archaeological Survey at Chavez Pass Ruin, Coconino National Forest,
        Arizona: The 1978 Field Season. Report on file at Department of Anthro-
        pology, Arizona State University, Tempe.
Hendron, J. W.
    1940. Prehistory of El Rito de los Frijoles, Bandelier National Monument.
        SMATS, No. 1.
Henn, Winfield
    1978. Archaeology on the Alaska Peninsula: The Ugashik Drainage, 1973–1975.
        UOAP, No. 14.
Henning, D. R.
    1961. Oneota Ceramics in Iowa. JIAS 11(2).
    1968. (editor) Climatic Change and the Mill Creek Culture of Iowa. (2 parts)
        JIAS, No. 15.
    1970. Development and Interrelationships of Oneota Culture in the Lower Mis-
        souri River Valley. MA, No. 32.
    1971. Great Oasis Culture Distribution. OSAIR, No. 3.
Henning, D. R., and E. Henning
    1978. Great Oasis Ceramics. OPMA, No. 2.
Hester, J. J.
    1962. Early Navajo Migrations and Acculturation in the Southwest. MNMPA,
        No. 6.
    1972. Blackwater, Locality No. 1. PFBRC, No. 8.

Hester, J. J., and S. M. Nelson
  1978.   Studies in Bella Bella Prehistory. DASFUP, No. 5.
Hester, J. J., and J. L. Shiner
  1963.   Studies at Navajo Period Sites in the Navajo Reservoir District. MNMPA,
          No. 9.
Hester, T. R.
  1971.   Archaeological Investigations at the La Jita Site, Uvalde County, Texas.
          BTAS 42:51–148.
  1982.   Late Paleo-Indian Occupations at Baker Cave, Southwestern Texas. BTAS
          53:101–120.
Hester, T. R., and C. I. Busby
  1977.   A Note on a Pestle Preform from NV-Ch–15, Churchill County, Nevada.
          NASR 10(3):1.
Heulsbeck, D. R.
  1983.   *Mammals and Fish in the Subsistence Economy of Ozette*. PhD disser-
          tation, Washington State University, Pullman.
Hewes, G. W.
  1946.   Early Man in California and the Tranquillity Site. AAn 11(4):209–215.
Hewett, E. L.
  1906.   Antiquities of the Jemez Plateau. BAEB, No. 32.
  1909.   The Excavations at El Rito de los Frijoles. AA 11(4):651–673.
Hewett, E. L., and B. P. Dutton
  1953. (editors)   *Pajarito Plateau and Its Ancient People*. University of New Mex-
          ico Press and School of American Research. Albuquerque.
Hibben, F. C.
  1937.   Excavation of the Riana Ruin and Chama Valley Survey. UNMAS 2(1).
  1938.   The Gallina Phase. AAn 4(2):131–136.
  1940.   *The Gallina Culture of North Central New Mexico*. PhD dissertation,
          Harvard University, Cambridge, Massachusetts.
  1941.   Evidences of Early Occupation in Sandia Cave, New Mexico, and Other
          Sites in the Sandia-Manzano Region. SMC 99(23):1–64.
  1946.   The First Thirty-eight Sandia Points. AAn 11(4):257–258.
  1966.   A Possible Pyramidal Structure and Other Mexican Influences at Pottery
          Mound, New Mexico. AAn 31(4):522–529.
  1975.   *Kiva Art of the Anasazi at Pottery Mound*. KC Publications. Las Vegas,
          Nevada.
Highley, Lynn, Carol Graves, Carol Land, and George Judson
  1978.   Archeological Investigations at Scorpion Cave (41ME7), Medina County,
          Texas. BTAS 49:139–194.
Hildreth, S. P.
  1843.   Pyramids at Marietta. AmP 2:242–248.
Hill, A. T.
  1932.   The Ruins of a Prehistoric House in Howard County, Nebraska. NH,
          No. 13.
Hill, A. T., and M. F. Kivett
  1940.   Woodland-Like Manifestations in Nebraska. NH 21(3):143–243.
Hill, A. T., and George Metcalf
  1942.   The Dismal River Aspect in Chase County, Nebraska. NH 22(2).

Hill, A. T., and W. R. Wedel
　1936. Excavations at the Leary Indian Village and Burial Site, Richardson County, Nebraska. NH, No. 17.
History of Fulton County, Illinois
　1879. Charles C. Chapman and Co. Peoria.
Hively, Ray, and Robert Horn
　1982. Geometry and Astronomy in Prehistoric Ohio. JHAA 4:1–20.
Hobler, P. M.
　1982. Papers on Central Coast Archaeology. DASFUP, No. 10.
Hodge, F. W.
　1916. (editor) Holmes Anniversary Volume of Anthropological Essays. Presented to William Henry Holmes in Honor of his Seventieth Birthday. Washington, D.C.
Hodges, C. T.
　n.d. Letter on file at Virginia Research Center for Archaeology, Yorktown.
Hoffman, J. J.
　1968. The La Roche Sites. RBSPSA, No. 11.
Hoffman, M. P.
　1970. Archeological and Historical Assessment of the Red River Basin in Arkansas. In Archeological and Historical Resources of the Red River Basin, edited by H. A. Davis. AASRS 1:135–194.
Hofman, J. L.
　1979. Twenhafel: A Prehistoric Community on the Mississippi, 500 B.C.–A.D. 1500. LM 41:34–38.
　1984. The Plains Villagers: The Custer Phase. In Prehistory of Oklahoma, edited by R. E. Bell, pp. 287–305. Academic Press. New York.
Hohmann, J. W.
　1982. Sinagua Social Differentiation: Inferences Based on Prehistoric Mortuary Practices. AAr, No. 17.
Holden, Jane
　1955. A Preliminary Report on Arrowhead Ruin. EP 62(4):102–119.
Holden, P. P.
　1966. An Archaeological Survey of Transylvania County, North Carolina. MA thesis, University of North Carolina, Chapel Hill.
Holder, Preston
　1970. The Hoe and the Horse on the Plains. University of Nebraska Press. Lincoln.
Holder, Preston, and Joyce Wike
　1949. The Frontier Culture Complex, a Preliminary Report on a Prehistoric Hunters' Camp in Southwestern Nebraska. AAn 14:260–265.
Hole, Frank, and R. F. Heizer
　1973. An Introduction to Prehistoric Archeology, 3rd edition. Holt, Rinehart and Winston, Inc. New York.
Holland, C. G.
　1948. An Editorial: Touching the History and Archeology of Southwest Virginia. ASVQB (3)1.
　1950. Four James River Sites in Its Middle Course. ASVQB 4(4).

1960a.   Preceramic and Ceramic Cultural Patterns in Northwest Virginia. BAEB (157):1–129.

1960b.   Something About Soapstone. ASVQB 14(4):29–35.

1963.   Two Strata Cuts in the Large Hirsh Mound. ASVQB 18(1):12–19.

1966.   The John Harter Collection from a Site in Southern Shenandoah County. ASVQB 21(2):40–41.

1970.   An Archeological Survey of Southwest Virginia. SCA, No. 12.

Holland, C. G., Clifford Evans, and B. J. Meggers

1953.   The East Mound. ASVQB 7(3).

Holland, C. G., S. E. Pennell, and R. O. Allen

1981.   Geographical Distribution of Soapstone Artifacts from Twenty-One Aboriginal Quarries in the Eastern United States. ASVQB 35(4):200–208.

Holland, C. G., S. D. Speiden, and David van Roijen

1983.   The Rapidan Mound Revisited: A Test Excavation of a Prehistoric Burial Mound. ASVQB 38(1):1–42.

Holliday, V. T.

1982.   *Morphological and Chemical Trends in Holocene Soils at the Lubbock Lake Archaeological Site, Texas.* PhD dissertation, University of Colorado, Boulder.

1983.   Stratigraphy and Soils of the Lubbock Lake Landmark Area. In *Guidebook to the Central Llano Estacado*, edited by V. T. Holliday, pp. 25–80. ICASALS and The Museum, Texas Tech University. Lubbock.

1985.   New Data on the Stratigraphy and Pedology of the Clovis and Plainview Sites, Southern High Plains. QR 23:388-402.

Holliday, V. T., and Eileen Johnson

1986.   A Re-evaluation of the First Radiocarbon Age for the Folsom Culture. AAn 51(2):332–338.

Holliday, V. T., Eileen Johnson, H. Haas, and Robert Stuckenrath

1983.   Radiocarbon Ages from the Lubbock Lake Site, 1950–1980: Framework for Cultural and Ecological Change on the Southern High Plains. PA 28(101):165–182.

Holliday, V. T., Eileen Johnson, M. J. Kazor, and Robert Stuckenrath

1977.   The Garza Occupation at the Lubbock Lake Site. BTAS 48:83–109.

Holman, M. B.

1978.   *The Settlement System of the Mackinac Phase.* PhD dissertation, Michigan State University, East Lansing.

1984.   Pine River Ware: Evidence for In Situ Development of the Late Woodland in the Straits of Mackinac Region. WiA 65(1):32–48.

Holmes, Barbara, and M. B. Stanislawski

1986.   *First Mesa Improvement Project: Historical and Archaeological Data Recovery.* The Hopi Tribe. Oraibi, Arizona.

Holmes, C. E.

1982.   Norton Influence in the Alaskan Hinterland. ArcA 19(2):133–142.

Holmes, W. H.

1890.   A Quarry Workshop of the Flaked-Stone Implement Makers in the District of Columbia. AA 3(1):1–25.

1897.   Stone Implements of the Potomac-Chesapeake Tidewater Province. In *Fifteenth Annual Report of the Bureau of American Ethnology*, pp. 13–150. Smithsonian Institution. Washington, D.C.

1903. Aboriginal Pottery of the Eastern United States. In *Twentieth Annual Report of the Bureau of American Ethnology*. Smithsonian Institution. Washington, D.C.

1905. Notes on the Antiquities of the Jemez Valley, New Mexico. AA 7:198–212.

1907. Aboriginal Shell-Heaps of the Middle Atlantic Tidewater Region. AA 8(1):113–128.

1919. Handbook of Aboriginal Antiquities. Part I: Introduction. The Lithics. BAEB, No. 60.

Holtved, Erik

1944. Archaeological Investigations in the Thule District. MG, No. 141.

1954. Archaeological Investigations in the Thule District Part 3: Nugdlit and Comer's Midden. MG, No. 146.

Honea, K. H.

1969. The Rio Grande Complex and the Northern Plains. PA 14:(43):57–70.

Honerkamp, M. W.

1975. *The Angel Phase: Analysis of a Middle Mississippian Occupation in Southwestern Indiana*. PhD dissertation, Indiana University, Bloomington.

Hooton, E. A.

1930. The Indians of Pecos Pueblo, A Study of their Skeletal Remains. PPASE, No. 4.

Hooton, E. A., and C. C. Willoughby

1920. Indian Village Site and Cemetery near Madisonville, Ohio. PPM 8(1).

Hoover, R. L.

1974. Some Observations on Chumash Prehistoric Stone Effigies. JCA 1:33–40.

Horr, David, and A. E. Johnson

n.d. Petroglyphs of Central Kansas. Report on file at the University of Kansas, Lawrence.

Hotopp, J. A.

1982. Some Observations on the Central Plains Tradition in Iowa. SCA 30:173–192.

Houart, G. H.

1971. Koster: A Stratified Archaic Site in the Illinois Valley. ISMRI, No. 22; IVAPRS, No. 4.

Hough, Walter

1903. *Archaeological Field Work in Northeastern Arizona. The Museum-Gates Expedition of 1901*. U.S. National Museum. Washington, D.C.

1907. Antiquities of the Upper Gila and Salt River Valleys in Arizona and New Mexico. BAEB, No. 35.

1920. Exploration of a Pit House Village at Luna, New Mexico. PUSNM 55(2280):235–296.

1932. Decorative Designs on Elden Pueblo Pottery, Flagstaff, Arizona. PUSNM 81(2930):1–11.

House, J. H., and R. W. Wogaman

1978. Windy Ridge: A Prehistoric Site in the Inter-riverine Piedmont in South Carolina. ASt, No. 3.

Howard, E. B.

1935. Evidence of Early Man in North America, Based on Geological and Archaeological Work in New Mexico. UPMJ 24(2–3):55–171.

Howard, J. H.
  1964. Archeological Investigations in the Toronto Reservoir Area, Kansas. BAEB, No. 189; RBSPSA, No. 38.
  1968. The Southeastern Ceremonial Complex and Its Interpretation. MASM, No. 6.
Hrdlička, Aleš
  1944. The Anthropology of Kodiak Island. Wistar Institute of Anatomy and Biology. Philadelphia.
  1945. The Aleutian and Commander Islands. Wistar Institute of Anatomy and Biology. Philadelphia.
Hruska, Robert
  1967. The Riverside Site: A Late Archaic Manifestation in Michigan. WiA 48(3).
Huckell, B. B.
  1978. Hudson-Meng Chipped Stone. In The Hudson-Meng Site: An Alberta Bison Kill in the Nebraska High Plains, pp. 153–191. University Press of America. Washington, D.C.
Hudson, Charles, Marvin Smith, David Hally, Richard Polhemus, and Chester DePratter
  1985. Coosa: A Chiefdom in the Sixteenth Century Southeastern United States. AAn 50(4):723–737.
Hughes, J. T.
  1949. Investigations in Western South Dakota and Northeastern Wyoming. AAn 14(4):266–267.
Hurley, W. M.
  1975. An Analysis of Effigy Mound Complexes in Wisconsin. UMMAAP, No. 59.
Hurt, W. R.
  1951. Report of the Investigation of the Swanson Site, 39Br16, Brule County, South Dakota, 1950. ASC, No. 3.
Hurt, W. R., W. R. Hurt, Jr., W. G. Buckles, Eugene Fugle, and G. A. Agogino
  1962. Report of the Investigations of the Four Bear Site, 39DW2, Dewey County, South Dakota. OMASC, No. 10.
Husted, Wilfred
  1969. Bighorn Canyon Archeology. RBSPSA, No. 12.
Indiana Historical Society
  1954. Walam Olum: The Migration Legend of the Lenni Lenape or Delaware Indians. Indianapolis.
Inglis, Richard, and G. F. MacDonald
  1979. Skeena River Prehistory. NMMMS, No. 87.
Ingstad, A. S.
  1977. The Discovery of a Norse Settlement in America. Columbia University Press. New York.
Ingstad, Helge
  1954. Nunamiut. W. W. Norton. New York.
Iroquois Research Institute
  1978. Intensive Survey of Cultural Resources, Gathright Lake, Virginia. Fairfax.
Irving, W. N.
  1957. An Archaeological Survey of the Susitna Valley. APUA 6:37–52.

Irving, W. N. and C. R. Harington
  1973.   Upper Pleistocene Radiocarbon-dated Artefacts from the Northern Yu-
    kon. S 179(4071):335–340.
Irwin, A. M., and Ula Moody
  1978.   The Lind Coulee Site (45GR97). WARCPR, No. 53.
Irwin-Williams, Cynthia
  1973.   The Oshara Tradition: Origins of Anasazi Culture. ENMUCA 5(1).
  1979.   Post-Pleistocene Archaeology, 7000–2000 B.C. In *Handbook of North
    American Indians*, Vol. 5: Southwest, edited by W. G. Sturtevant and A. A.
    Ortiz, pp. 31–42. Smithsonian Institution. Washington, D.C.
  n.d.a.   Archaeological Investigations in the Area of the Middle Puerco River,
    New Mexico, May–December 1977. Progress report on file at the Bureau of
    Land Management, Albuquerque.
  n.d.b.   Archaeological Investigations in the Area of the Middle Puerco River
    Valley, New Mexico, May–December 1978. Progress report on file at the
    Bureau of Land Management, Albuquerque.
Irwin-Williams, Cynthia, and C. V. Haynes
  1970.   Climatic Change and Early Population Dynamics in the Southwestern
    United States. QR 1:59–71.
Irwin-Williams, Cynthia, and Sally Tomkins
  1968.   Excavations at En Medio Shelter, New Mexico. ENMUCA 1(2).
Irwin-Williams, Cynthia, Henry Irwin, George Agogino, and C. V. Haynes
  1973.   Hell Gap: Paleo-Indian Occupation on the High Plains. PA 18:40–53.
Irwin-Williams, Cynthia, and P. H. Shelley
  n.d. (editors)   Investigations at the Salmon Site: The Structure of Chacoan Society
    in the Northern Southwest (5 vols.). Report on file at Eastern New Mexico
    University, Portales.
Ives, J. W.
  1985.   A Spational Analysis of Artifact Distribution on a Boreal Forest Archae-
    ological Site. ASAMS, No. 5.
Jack, R. N.
  1971.   The Source of Obsidian Artifacts in Northern Arizona. P 43(3):103–114.
  1976.   Prehistoric Obsidian in California I: Geochemical Aspects. In *Advances
    in Obsidian Glass Studies* edited by R. E. Taylor. Noyes Press. Park Ridge,
    New Jersey.
Jackson, A. T.
  n.d.a.   The Royall or Pace McDonald Place. Report on file at the Texas Arche-
    ological Research Laboratory, The University of Texas, Austin.
  n.d.b.   Trenching of an Earth Mound, L. A. Hale Farm, Titus County, Texas.
    Report on file at the Texas Archeological Research Laboratory, The Univer-
    sity of Texas, Austin.
Jackson, Earl, and S. P. Van Valkenburgh
  1954.   Montezuma Castle Archaeology. SMATS, No. 3.
Jacobs, J. D.
  n.d.   Environment and Prehistory, Baffin Island. Report on file at Department of
    Geography, University of Windsor, Windsor, Ontario.
Jacobs, Mike, and G. H. Hartmann
  1984. (editors)   From Prehistory to History: The Archaeology of the Tucson
    Basin. K 49(3–4).

James, H.C.
   1974.   *Pages from Hopi History*. University of Arizona Press. Tucson.
Janes, S. M.
   1930.   Seven Trips to Mount Livermore. WTHSSP 3:8–9.
Jantz, R. L., and D. H. Ubelaker
   1981.   Progress in Skeletal Biology of the Plains Population. PAM 17.
Janzen, L. M.
   1965.   Early Ellsworth County Pictorial Art. KAAN 11(3).
Janzen, D. E.
   1968.   The Naomikong Point Site and the Dimensions of Laurel in the Lake
           Superior Region. UMMAAP, No. 36.
Jeançon, J. A.
   1922.   *Archaeological Research in the Northeastern San Juan Basin of Colorado
           During the Summer of 1921*. The State Historical and Natural History Society
           of Colorado and the University of Denver. Denver.
   1923.   Excavations in the Chama Valley. BAEB, No. 81.
   1929.   Archeological Investigations in the Taos Valley, New Mexico during 1920.
           SMC, No. 81.
Jefferies, R. W.
   1976.   The Tunacunnhee Site: Evidence of Hopewell Interaction in Northwest
           Georgia. APUG, No. 1.
   1979.   The Tunacunnhee Site: Hopewell in Northwest Georgia. In *Hopewell
           Archaeology: The Chillicothe Conference*, edited by D. S. Brose and N'omi
           Greber, pp. 162–170. Kent State University Press. Kent, Ohio.
Jefferson, Thomas
   1954.   *Notes on the State of Virginia*, edited by William Peden. W. W. Norton
           and Co. New York.
Jelinek, A. J.
   1967.   A Prehistoric Sequence in the Middle Pecos Valley, New Mexico.
           UMMAAP, No. 31.
Jelks, E. B.
   1961.   Excavations at Texarkana Reservoir, Sulphur River, Texas. RBSP, No.
           21; BAEB 179:1–78.
   1962.   The Kyle Site: A Stratified Central Texas Aspect Site in Hill County, Texas.
           ASUT, No. 5.
   1965.   *The Archeology of McGee Bend Reservoir, Texas*. PhD dissertation, Uni-
           versity of Texas, Austin.
   1967. (editor)   The Gilbert Site: A Norteño Focus Site in Northeastern Texas.
           BTAS 37.
Jelks, E. B., and C. D. Tunnell
   1959.   The Harroun Site: A Fulton Aspect Component of the Caddoan Area,
           Upshur County, Texas. ASUT, No. 2.
Jelks, E. B., and P. A. Hawks
   n.d.   *Archeological Explorations at Starved Rock, Illinois (11-Ls-12)*. Report on
           file at Illinois Department of Transportation, Springfield.
Jenkins, N. J.
   1975.   The Wheeler Series and Southeastern Prehistory. FA 28:17–26.
   1979.   Miller Hopewell of the Tomybibee Drainage. In *Hopewell Archaeology:
           The Chillicothe Conference*, edited by D. S. Brose and N'omi Greber,
           pp. 171–180. Kent State University Press. Kent, Ohio.

Jenkins, N. J., and J. J. Nielson
 1974. *Archaeological Salvage Investigations at the West Jefferson Steam Plant Site, Jefferson County, Alabama.* Department of Anthropology, University of Alabama. University.
Jenkins, N. J., D. H. Dye, and J. A. Walthall
 1986. Early Ceramic Development in the Gulf Coastal Plain. In *Early Woodland Archeology*, edited by K. B. Farnsworth and T. E. Emerson, pp. 546–563. Center for American Archeology Press, Kampsville, Illinois.
Jenks, A. E.
 1932. The Problem of the Culture from the Arvilla Gravel Pit. AA 34:455–466.
 1935. Recent Discoveries in Minnesota Prehistory. MH 16:1–21.
 1936. *Pleistocene Man in Minnesota.* University of Minnesota Press. Minneapolis.
 1937a. A Minnesota Kitchen Midden with Fossil Bison. S 86(2228):243–244.
 1937b. Minnesota's Browns Valley Man and Associated Burial Artifacts. MAAA, No. 49.
Jenness, Diamond
 1915. A New Eskimo Culture in Hudson Bay. GR 15:428–437.
 1928. Archaeological Investigations in Bering Strait, 1926. NMCB 50:71–80.
 1941. Prehistoric Cultural Waves from Asia to America. *Smithsonian Institution Annual Report for 1940*, pp. 383–396.
Jennings, J. D.
 1940. A Variation of Southwestern Culture. LATSB, No. 10.
 1941. Chickasaw and Earlier Indian Cultures of Northeast Mississippi. JMH 3(3):155–226.
 1957. Danger Cave. UUAP, No. 27; MSAA, No. 14.
 1964. The Desert West. In *Prehistoric Man in the New World*, edited by J. D. Jennings and Edward Norbeck. University of Chicago Press. Chicago.
 1968. *Prehistory of North America.* McGraw-Hill. New 1978. (editor) *Ancient Native Americans.* W. H. Freeman and Co. San Francisco.
 1980. Cowboy Cave. UUAP, No. 104.
Jennings, J. D., and C. H. Fairbanks
 1939. Pottery Type Descriptions. SACN 1(2).
Jennings, J. D., and Edward Norbeck
 1955. Great Basin Prehistory: A Review. AAn 21(1):1–11.
Jennings, J. D., A. R. Schroedl, and R. N. Holmer
 1980. Sudden Shelter. UUAP, No. 103.
Jensen, H. P., Jr.
 1968. Coral Snake Mound, X16SA48. BTAS 39:9–44.
Jepsen, G. L.
 1951. Ancient Buffalo Hunters in Wyoming. ASNJN 4:22–24.
 1953. Ancient Buffalo Hunters in Northwestern Wyoming. SL 19:19–25.
Johnson, A. E.
 1963. The Trincheras Culture of Northern Sonora. AAn 29:174–186.
 1965. *The Development of the Western Pueblo Culture.* PhD dissertation, University of Arizona, Tucson.
 1966. Archaeology of Sonora, Mexico. In *Handbook of Middle American Indians*, edited by G. F. Ekholm and G. R. Willey, Vol. 4, pp. 26–37. University of Texas Press. Austin.

1976. (editor)   Hopewellian Archaeology in the Lower Missouri Valley. UKPA, No. 8.

1979.   Kansas City Hopewell. In *Hopewell Archaeology: The Chillicothe Conference*, edited by D. S. Brose and N'omi Greber, pp. 86–93. Kent State University Press. Kent, Ohio.

1980.   Archaic Prehistory on the Prairie Plains Border. UKPA, No. 12.

Johnson, A. S., and A. E. Johnson

1975.   K-Means and Temporal Variability in Kansas City Hopewell Ceramics. AAn 40(3):283–295.

Johnson, C. R., Jr.

1963.   Tohalina Bikitsiel: A Pueblo Ruin at Toadlena, New Mexico. EP 70(4):21–32.

Johnson, Eileen

1976.   *Investigations into the Zooarchaeology of the Lubbock Lake Site*. PhD dissertation, Texas Tech University, Lubbock.

1983.   The Lubbock Lake Paleoindian Record. In *Guidebook to the Central Llano Estacado*, edited by V. T. Holliday, pp. 81–106. ICASALS and The Museum, Texas Tech University. Lubbock.

Johnson, Eileen, V. T. Holliday, M. J. Kazor, and Robert Stuckenrath

1977.   The Garza Occupation at the Lubbock Lake Site. BTAS 48:83–109.

Johnson, Elden

1964.   Twenty New Radiocarbon Dates from Minnesota Archaeological Sites. MinA 26(2):34–49.

1969.   *Prehistoric Peoples of Minnesota*. Minnesota Historical Society. St. Paul.

1971.   The Northern Margin of the Prairie Peninsula. JIAS 18:13–21.

1973.   The Arvilla Complex. MPS, No. 9.

n.d.   Sandy Lake Attribute List. Report on file at the Department of Anthropology, University of Minnesota, Minneapolis.

Johnson, Leroy, Jr.

1962.   The Yarbrough and Miller Sites in Northeastern Texas, with a Preliminary Definition of the La Harpe Aspect. BTAS 32:141–284.

1964.   The Devils Mouth Site: A Stratified Campsite at Amistad Reservoir, Val Verde County, Texas. ASUT, No. 6.

Johnson, Leroy, Jr., Dee Ann Suhm, and Curtis D. Tunnell

1962.   Salvage Archeology of Canyon Reservoir: The Wunderlich, Footbridge, and Oblate Sites. BTMM, No. 5.

Johnston, R. B.

1964.   Proton Magnetometry and Its Application to Archaeology: An Evaluation at Angel Site. PRS 4(2):45–140.

1967.   The Hitchell Site. RBSPSA, No. 3.

Jones, A. T.

1968.   A Cross-Section of Grand Canyon Archeology: Excavations at Five Sites Along the Colorado River. WACCP, No. 28.

Jones, B. C.

1982.   Southern Cult Manifestations at the Lake Jackson Site, Leon County, Florida: Salvage Excavation of Mound 3. MJA 7:3–44.

Jones, C. C.

1873.   *Antiquities of the Southern Indians, Particularly of the Georgia Tribes*. Appleton. New York.

Jones, E. E.
    n.d.   A Preliminary Report: The Hoge Site (44TZ6), Burkes Garden, Virginia. Report on file at Virginia Research Center for Archaeology, Yorktown.
Jones, G. T.
    1984.   *Prehistoric Land Use in the Steens Mountain Area, Southeastern Oregon.* PhD dissertation, University of Washington, Seattle.
Jones, G. T., D. K. Grayson, and Charlotte Beck
    1983.   Artifact Class Richness and Sample Size in Archaeological Surface Assemblages. In *Lulu Linear Punctated: Essays in Honor of George Irving Quimby,* edited by R. D. Dunnell and D. K. Grayson, pp. 55–73. UMMAAP, No. 72.
Jones, Joseph
    1876.   Explorations of the Aboriginal Remains of Tennessee. SCK, No. 259.
Jones, Olive
    1981.   Glassware Excavated at Yuquot, British Columbia. The Yuquot Project, Vol. 3. HA, No. 44.
Jopling, A. V., W. N. Irving, and B. F. Beebe
    1981.   Stratigraphic, Sedimentological and Faunal Evidence for the Occurrence of Pre-Sangamonian Artefacts in Northern Yukon. ArcA 34(1):3–33.
Jordan, R. H.
    1979.   Inugsuk Revisited: An Alternative View of Neo-Eskimo Chronology and Culture Change in Greenland. In *Thule Eskimo Culture: An Anthropological Retrospective,* edited by A. P. McCartney. ASCP 88:149–170.
    1980.   Preliminary Results from Archaeological Investigations on Avayalik Island, Extreme Northern Labrador. Arc 33:607–627.
    1984.   Neo-Eskimo Prehistory of Greenland. In *Handbook of North American Indians: Arctic,* edited by W. C. Sturtevant and David Damas, Vol. 5:540–548. Smithsonian Institution. Washington, D.C.
Judd, N. M.
    1926.   Archeological Observations North of the Rio Colorado. BAEB No. 82.
    1954.   The Material Culture of Pueblo Bonito. SMC, No. 124.
    1959.   Pueblo del Arroyo, Chaco Canyon, New Mexico. SMC, No. 138.
    1964.   The Architecture of Pueblo Bonito. SMC 147(1).
    1967.   *The Bureau of American Ethnology: A Partial History.* University of Oklahoma Press. Norman.
    1973.   *The Paleo-Indian Occupation of the Central Rio Grande Valley, New Mexico.* University of New Mexico Press. Albuquerque.
Judge, W. J.
    1973.   *Paleoindian Occupation of the Central Rio Grande Valley in New Mexico.* University of New Mexico Press. Albuquerque.
    1976.   The Development of a Complex Cultural Ecosystem in the Chaco Basin, New Mexico. In *Proceedings of the First Conference on Scientific Research in the National Parks.* NPSTP 5(2):901–906.
    1979.   The Paleo-Indian and Basketmaker Periods: An Overview and Some Research Questions. In *The San Juan Tomorrow,* edited by Fred Plog and Walter Wait, pp. 5–57. National Park Service, Southwestern Regional Office, and the School of American Research. Santa Fe, New Mexico.

1981. Transect Sampling in Chaco Canyon: Evaluation of a Survey Technique. In *Archeological Surveys of Chaco Canyon, New Mexico*, by A. C. Hayers, D. M. Brugge, and W. J. Judge, pp. 107–137. PArc, No. 18A.

Judge, W. J., and J. D. Schelberg
1984. Recent Research on Chaco Prehistory. RCC, No. 8.

Judge, W. J., H. W. Toll, W. B. Gillespie, and S. H. Lekson
1981. Tenth Century Developments in Chaco Canyon. In *Collected Papers in Honor of Erik Kellerman Reed*, edited by A. H. Schroeder, pp. 65–98. PASNM, No. 6.

Justice, Noel
1967. *The Bureau of American Ethnology: A Partial History*. University of Oklahoma Press. Norman.
1984. Diagnostic Projectile Points of Eastern United States Archaeology. MA thesis, Indiana University, Bloomington.

Kaufman, T. S.
1980. *Early Prehistory of the Clear Lake Area, Lake County, California*. PhD dissertation, University of California, Los Angeles.

Kavanagh, Maureen
1982. Archeological Resources of the Monocacy River Region, Frederick and Carroll Counties, Maryland. MGSFR, No. 164.
1984. Phase II Archeological Investigations at the Paw Paw Site (18AG144), Allegany County, Maryland. MGSFR, No. 183.

Keel, B. C.
1976. Cherokee Archaeology: A Study of the Appalachian Summit. University of Tennessee Press. Knoxville.

Kehoe, T. F.
1958. Tipi Rings: The "Direct Ethnological" Approach Applied to an Archaeological Problem. AAn 60(5):861–873.
1960. Stone Tipi Rings in North-Central Montana and the Adjacent Portion of Alberta, Canada: Their Historical, Ethnological, and Archaeological Aspects. BAEB, No. 173; AP, No. 62.
1965. Indian Boulder Effigies. PS, No. 12.
1966. The Small Side-Notched Point System of the Northern Plains. AAn 31(6):827–841.
1973. The Gull Lake Site: A Prehistoric Bison Drive Site in Southwestern Saskatchewan. MPMPAH, No. 1.
1974. The Large Corner-Notched Point System of the Northern Plains and Adjacent Woodlands. In *Aspects of Upper Great Lakes Anthropology: Papers in Honor of Lloyd A. Wilford*, edited by Elden Johnson. MPS 11:129–137.

Kehoe, T. F., and Bruce McCorquodale
1961. The Avonlea Point: Horizon Marker for the Northwestern Plains. PA 6(13):179–188.

Kellar, J. H.
1956. *An Archaeological Survey of Spencer County*. Indiana Historical Bureau. Indianapolis.
1969. New Excavations at Mounds State Park. OI 37(7):4–9.
1970. The Search for Ouiatenon. IHB 47(10):123–133.

1979. The Mann Site and "Hopewell" in the Lower Wabash-Ohio Valley. In *Hopewell Archaeology: The Chillicothe Conference*, edited by D. S. Brose and N'omi Greber, pp. 100–107. The Kent State University Press. Kent, Ohio.

Kellar, J. H., A. R. Kelly, and E. V. McMichael
1962. The Mandeville Site in Southwestern Georgia. AAn 27:336–355.

Kellberg, J. M.
1963. Chert and "Flint" of the Tennessee Area. TA 19:1–7.

Kelley, J. C.
1939. Archaeological Notes on the Excavation of a Pithouse near Presidio, Texas. EP 46(10):221–234.

1947a. The Lehmann Rock Shelter: A Stratified Site of the Toyah, Uvalde, and Round Rock Foci. BTAPS 18:115–128.

1947b. The Cultural Affiliations and Chronological Position of the Clear Fork Focus. AAn 13:97–108.

1949. Archaeological Notes on Two Excavated House Structures in Western Texas. BTAPS 20:89–114.

1956. Settlement Patterns in North-central Mexico. In *Prehistoric Settlement Patterns in the New World*, edited by G. R. Willey, pp. 128–139. VFPA, No. 23.

1957. The Livermore Focus: A Clarification. EP 64(1–2):44–52.

1971. Archaeology of the Northern Frontier: Zacatecas and Durango. In *Handbook of Middle American Indians* 11(2):768–804. University of Texas Press. Austin.

1985. A Review of the Architectural Sequence at La Junta de los Rios. In *Proceedings of the Third Jornada-Mogollon Conference*, edited by M. S. Foster and T. C. O'Laughlin, 23(1–2):149–159.

Kelley, J. C., and Ellen Abbott
1966. The Cultural Sequence on the North Central Frontier of Mesoamerica. In *Arqueología de Mesoamerica*, edited by A. G. Stresser-Pean, pp. 325–344. *Proceedings of the 36th International Congress of Americanists*, Vol. 1. Seville, Spain.

Kelley, J. C., and E. A. Kelley
1975. An Alternative Hypothesis for the Explanation of Anasazi Culture History. In *Collected Papers in Honor of Florence Hawley Ellis*, edited by T. R. Frisbie, pp. 178–223. PASNM, No. 2.

Kelley, J. C., and H. D. Winters
1960. A Revision of the Archaeological Sequence in Sinaloa, Mexico. AAn 25(4):547–561.

Kelley, J. C., T. N. Campbell, and D. J. Lehmer
1940. The Association of Archaeological Materials with Geological Deposits in the Big Bend Region of Texas. WTHSSP, No. 10.

Kelley, J. H.
1984. The Archaeology of the Sierra Blanca Region of Southeastern New Mexico. UMMAAP, No. 74.

Kelly, A. R.
1938. A Preliminary Report on Archeological Explorations at Macon, Georgia. BAEB 119:1–68.

Kelly, A. R., and R. S. Neitzel
   1961.   The Chauga Site in Oconee County, South Carolina. UGLAS, Report 3.
Kelly, A. R., and B. A. Smith
   n.d.   The Swift Creek Site (9Bi3), Macon, Georgia. Report on file at the National
          Park Service, Tallahassee, Florida.
Kelly, I. T.
   1978.   The Hodges Ruin: A Hohokam Community in the Tucson Basin. UAAP,
          No. 30.
Kelly, J. E., and A. C. Fortier
   1983.   The Range Site (11-S-47): The Archaic, Early Woodland, and Middle
          Woodland Components. UIAMP, No. 60.
Kelly, J. E., S. J. Ozuk, and J. A. Williams
   1984.   The Range Site: The Woodland Component. UIAMP, No. 63.
Kelly, R. E.
   1969.   Salvage Excavation at Six Sinagua Sites. P 41(3):112–132.
   1970.   Elden Pueblo: An Archaeological Account. P 42(3):79–91.
Kelly, T. C.
   1961.   The Crumley Site: A Stratified Burnt Rock Midden, Travis County, Texas.
          BTAS 31:239–272.
Kenyon, I. T.
   1981.   The Satchell Complex of Ontario: A Perspective from the Au Sable Valley.
          OA 34:17–44.
Keslin, R. O.
   1958.   A Preliminary Report of the Hahn and Horicon Sites, Dodge County,
          Wisconsin. WiA 39(4):191–273.
Kessell, J. L.
   1979.   *Kiva, Cross, and Crown*. National Park Service. Washington, D.C.
Keur, D. L.
   1941.   Big Bead Mesa: An Archaeological Study of Navajo Acculturation. MSAA,
          No. 1.
   1944.   A Chapter in Navajo-Pueblo Relations. AAn 10:75–86.
Keyes, C. R.
   1949.   Four Iowa Archeologies with Plains Affiliations. In *Proceedings of the 5th
          Plains Conference for Archeology*. Laboratory of Anthropology, University
          of Nebraska. Lincoln.
Keyser, J. D.
   1986.   The Evidence for McKean Complex Plant Utilization. PA 31(113):225–
          235.
Kidder, A. V.
   1915.   Pottery of the Pajarito Plateau and Some Adjacent Regions in New Mex-
          ico. AAAM 2(4).
   1924.   *An Introduction to the Study of Southwestern Archaeology, with a Pre-
          liminary Account of the Excavations at Pecos*. Yale University Press. New
          Haven, Connecticut.
   1927.   Southwestern Archeological Conference. S 66(1716):489–491.
   1931.   The Pottery of Pecos, Vol. I: The Dull-Point Wares. PPASE, No. 5.
   1932.   *The Artifacts of Pecos*. Yale University Press. New Haven, Connecticut.

1936. Speculations on New World Prehistory. In *Essays in Anthropology Presented to Alfred L. Kroeber*, edited by R. H. Lowie, pp. 143–152. University of California Press. Berkeley.

1958. Pecos, New Mexico: Archeological Notes. PPFA, No. 5.

Kidder, A. V., and A. O. Shepard
1936. The Pottery of Pecos, Vol. 2. PPASE, No. 7.

Kincaid, Chris
1983. *Chaco Roads Project Phase I*. Bureau of Land Management. Albuquerque, New Mexico.

King, A. R.
1932. The Artifacts of Pecos. PPASE, No. 6.

1950. Cattle Point, A Stratified Site in the Southern Northwest Coast Region. MSAA, No. 6.

1958. Pecos, New Mexico: Archaeological Notes. PPFA, No. 5.

King, D. R.
1961. The Bracken Cairn: A Prehistoric Burial. BJ 19:45–53.

King, D. S.
1949. Nalakihu: Excavations at a Pueblo III Site on Wupatki National Monument, Arizona. MNAB, No. 23.

King, T. F.
1976. *Political Differentiation among Hunter-Gatherers: An Archaeological Test*. PhD dissertation, University of California, Riverside.

Kingsley, R. G.
1977. *A Statistical Analysis of the Prehistoric Ceramics from the Hacklander Site, Allegan County, Michigan*. MA thesis, Western Michigan University, Kalamazoo.

Kirk, Ruth (with R. D. Daugherty)
1974. *Hunters of the Whale*. Wm. Morrow Co. New York.

Kirkland, Forrest, and W. W. Newcomb, Jr.
1967. *The Rock Art of Texas Indians*. The University of Texas Press, Austin.

Kittleman, L. R.
1973. Mineralogy, Correlation, and Grain-size Distributions of Mazama Tephra and other Postglacial Pyroclastic Layers, Pacific Northwest. GSAB 84:2957–2980.

Kivett, M. F.
1949. A Woodland Pottery Type from Nebraska. In *Proceedings of the Fifth Plains Conference for Archeology, University of Nebraska, Laboratory of Anthropology Note Book*, No. 1, pp. 67–69. Lincoln.

1952. Woodland Sites in Nebraska. NSHSPA, No. 1.

1953. The Woodruff Ossuary, A Prehistoric Burial Site in Phillips County, Kansas. BAEB 154:103–142.

Kivett, M. F., and R. Jensen
1976. Archeological Investigations at the Crow Creek Site (39BF11). NSHSPA, No. 7.

Kleinschmidt, U. K.
1982. *Review and Analysis of the A. C. Saunders Site, 41AN19, Anderson County, Texas*. MA thesis, The University of Texas, Austin.

Klinger, T. C.
    1977. Parkin Archeology: A Report on the 1966 Field School Text Excavations at the Parkin Site. ArA 16(18):45–80.
Kluckhohn, Clyde, and Paul Reiter
    1939. Preliminary Report on the 1937 Excavations, Bc 50–51, Chaco Canyon, New Mexico. UNMAS 3(2):151–162.
Kneberg, Madeline
    1956. Some Important Projectile Point Types Found in the Tennessee Area. TA 12(1):17–28.
    1959. Engraved Shell Gorgets and Their Associations. TA 15(1):1–39.
Knight, V. J., Jr.
    1984. Late Prehistoric Adaptation in the Mobile Bay Region. In *Perspective on Gulf Coast Prehistory*, edited by D. D. Davis, pp. 198–215. University Presses of Florida. Gainesville.
Knudson, R. A.
    1967. Cambria Village Ceramics. PA 12:247–299.
Knuth, Eigil
    1952. An Outline of the Archaeology of Pearyland. Arc 5:17–33.
    1954. The Paleo-Eskimo Culture of Northeast Greenland Elucidated by Three New Sites. AAn 19:367–381.
    1967. Archaeology of the Musk Ox Way. CCAF, No. 5.
    1977–78. The "Old Nugdlit Culture" Site at Nugdlit Peninsula, Thule District, and the "Mesoeskimo" Site Below It. FO 19–20:15–47.
Konigsberg, L. W.
    1985. Demography and Mortuary Practice at Seip Mound One. MJA 10(1):123–148.
Kowta, Makoto
    1969. A Late Milling Stone Assemblage from Cajon Pass and the Ecological Implications of Its Scraper Planes. UCPA, No. 6.
Kraft, H. C.
    1973. The Plenge Site: A Paleo-Indian Occupation Site in New Jersey. AENA 1:56–117.
    1976. The Rosenkrans Site, an Adena-Related Mortuary Complex in the Upper Delaware Valley, New Jersey. AENA 4:9–50.
    1977. Paleo-Indians in New Jersey. In *Amerinds in Northeastern North America*, edited by W. S. Newman and Bert Salwen. ANYAS 288:264–281.
Krantz, Grover
    1979. Oldest Human Remains from the Marmes Site. NARN 13(2):159–174.
Krause, R. A.
    1969. Correlation of Phases in Central Plains Prehistory. PA 14(44):82–96.
    1972. The Leavenworth Site: Archaeology of an Historic Arikara Community. UKPA, No. 3.
    1982. The Central Plains Tradition Revisited: A Critical Review of Recent Interpretations. PA 27:75–82.
Krauskopf, Frances
    1955. *Ouiatenon Documents*. Indiana Historical Society. Indianapolis.

Krieger, A. D.
1944. Archaeological Horizons in the Caddo Area. In *El Norte de Mexico y el Sur de Estados Unidos*, p. 154. Tercera Reunion de Mesa Redonda sobre Problemas Antropologicos de Mexico y Centro America, Sociedad Mexicana de Antropologia. Mexico City.
1945. An Inquiry into Supposed Mexican Influence on a Prehistoric Cult in the Southern United States. AA 47(4):483–515.
1946. Culture Complexes and Chronology in Northern Texas. UTP, No. 4640.
1964. Early Man in the New World. In *Prehistoric Man in the New World*, edited by J. J. Jennings and Edward Norbeck, pp. 23–81. University of Chicago Press. Chicago.

Kroeber, A. L.
1962. The Rancho La Brea Skull. AAn 27(3):416–417.

Kroeber, A. L., and M. J. Harner
1955. Mohave Pottery. UCAR 16(1).

Kunz, M. L.
1982. The Mesa Site: An Early Holocene Hunting Stand in the Iteriak Valley, Northern Alaska. APUA 20:113–122.

Lahren, Larry, and Robson Bonnichsen
1974. Bone Foreshaft from a Clovis Burial in Southwestern Montana. S 186:147–149.

Lallo, J. G., J. C. Rose, and G. J. Armelagos
1980. An Ecological Interpretation of Variation in Mortality Within Three Prehistoric American Indian Populations from Dickson Mounds. In *Early Native Americans: Prehistoric Demography, Economy and Technology*, edited by David Browman, pp. 203–238. Mouton. The Hague.

Lambert, M. F.
1954. Paa-ko: Archaeological Chronicle of an Indian Village in North Central New Mexico. MSAR 19(1–4).

Lang, R. W.
1977. *Archaeological Survey of the Upper San Cristobal Arroyo Drainage, Galisteo Basin, Santa Fe County, New Mexico*. School of American Research, Contract Archaeology Program. Santa Fe, New Mexico.
1980a. *An Archaeological Survey near Agua Fria, Santa Fe County, New Mexico*. School of American Research, Contract Archaeology Program. Santa Fe, New Mexico.
1980b. *An Archaeological Survey of the Prince Estate, Santa Fe County, New Mexico*. School of American Research, Contract Archaeology Program. Santa Fe, New Mexico.
1982. Transformation in White Ware Pottery of the Northern Rio Grande. In *Southwestern Ceramics: A Comparative Overview*, edited by A. H. Schroeder. AAr 15.

Lang, R. W., and A. H. Harris
1984. *The Faunal Remains from Arroyo Hondo Pueblo, New Mexico: A Study in Short-term Subsistence Change*. School of American Research Press. Santa Fe, New Mexico.

Lange, C. H., Jr.
  1941. *The Evans Site: A Contribution to the Archaeology of the Gallina Region, Northern New Mexico.* MA thesis, University of New Mexico, Albuquerque.
  1956. The Evans Site and the Archaeology of the Gallina Region of New Mexico. EP 63(3):72–92.
  1968. The Cochiti Dam Archaeological Salvage Project, Part 1, Report of the 1963 Season. MNMRR, No. 6.
Lanning, E. P.
  1963. The Archaeology of the Rose Spring Site (INY:372). UCPAE 49:237–336.
Lapham, I. A.
  1854. The Antiquities of Wisconsin as Surveyed and Described. SCK, 7, article 4.
Larsen, C. S., and P. J. O'Brien
  1973. The Cochran Mound, 23PL86, Platte County, Missouri. MASN, No. 269.
Larsen, C. S., and D. H. Thomas
  1982. The Anthropology of St. Catherines Island 4. The St. Catherines Period Mortuary Complex. APAMNH 57(4).
Larsen, H. E.
  1951. De Dansk-Amerikanske Alaska-Ekspeditioner 1949–50. GT 51:63–93. Copenhagen.
  1968. Trail Creek: Final Report on the Excavation of Two Caves on Seward Peninsula, Alaska. AcA, No. 15.
Larsen, H. E., and Jørdan Meldgaard
  1958. Paleo-Eskimo Cultures in Disko Bugt, West Greenland. MG 161:1–75.
Larsen, H. E., and F. G. Rainey
  1948. Ipiutak and the Arctic Whale Hunting Culture. APAMNH, No. 42.
Larson, L. H., Jr.
  1959. Middle Woodland Manifestations in North Georgia. SACN 6:54–58.
  1971. Archaeological Implications of Social Stratification at the Etowah Site, Georgia. In *Approaches to the Social Dimensions of Mortuary Practices,* edited by J. A. Brown, pp. 58–67. MSAA, No. 25.
  1972. Functional Consideration of Warfare in the Southeast During the Mississippi Period. AAn 37:383–392.
Lathan, J. M.
  n.d. The Rogers Spring Site, Travis County, Texas. Report on file at the Texas Archeological Research Laboratory, The University of Texas, Austin.
Laughlin, W. S.
  1951. Notes on an Aleutian Core and Blade Industry. AAn 17(1):52–55.
  1963. Eskimos and Aleuts: Their Origins and Evolution. S 142(3593):633–645.
  1975. Aleuts: Ecosystem, Holocene History and Siberian Origin. S 189(4202):507–515.
Laughlin, W. S., and J. S. Aigner
  1966. Preliminary Analysis of the Anangula Unifacial Core and Blade Industry. ArcA 3(2):41–46.
Laughlin, W. S., and W. G. Reeder
  1966. Studies in Aleutian-Kodiak Prehistory, Ecology and Anthropology. ArcA 3(2).

Lawhead, S., and A. H. Stryd
  n.d. Excavations at the Rattlesnake Hill Site (EeRh 61), Ashcroft, B.C. Report on file at the Heritage Conservation Branch, Victoria, British Columbia.

Lazarus, Y. W.
  1970. Salvage Archaeology at Fort Walton Beach, Florida. FA 23:29–42.

Lazarus, Y. W., and R. J. Fornaro
  1975. Fort Walton Temple Mound, Further Test Excavations, DePaux 1973. FA 28:159–177.

Le Blanc, R. J.
  1984. The Rat Indian Creek Site and the Late Prehistoric Period in the Interior Northern Yukon. NMMMS, ASCP, No. 120.
  n.d. The Bezya Site: A Wedge-Shaped Core Assemblage from Northwestern Alberta. Report on file at Archaeological Survey of Alberta. Edmonton, Alberta.

LeBlanc, S. A., and M. E. Whalen
  1980. *An Archaeological Synthesis of South-Central and Southwestern New Mexico.* University of New Mexico, Office of Contract Archaeology. Albuquerque.

Lee, S. T.
  1971. Allendale Site Proves Fruitful. SCAn 3(3):3–9.

Lee, S. T., and A. R. Parler, Jr.
  1972. A Preliminary Report on the Excavations of the Cal Smoak Site. SCAn 4(2):14–18.

Lee, T. A., Jr.
  1962. The Beale's Saddle Site: A Nonconformity? P 34(4):113–128.

Lehmer, D. J.
  1948. The Jornada Branch of the Mogollon. UASSB, No. 17.
  1954. Archeological Investigations in the Oahe Dam Area, South Dakota, 1950–51. RBSPSA, No. 7; BAEB, No. 158.
  1971. Introduction to Middle Missouri Archeology. APNPS, No. 1.

Lehmer, D. J., and W. W. Caldwell
  1966. Horizon and Tradition in the Northern Plains. AAn 31(4):511–516.

Lekson, S. H.
  1983. The Architecture and Dendrochronology of Chetro Ketl. RCC, No. 6.
  1984. Dating the Hubbard Tri-wall and Other Tri-wall Structures. SL 49(4).
  1986. *Great Pueblo Architecture in Chaco Canyon, New Mexico.* University of New Mexico Press. Albuquerque.

Leonhardy, F. C.
  1966. Domebo: A Paleo-Indian Mammoth Kill in the Prairie-Plains. CMGP, No. 1.
  1968. Review of Hells Canyon Archaeology. AAn 33(4):525–526.
  1970. *Artifact Assemblages and Archaeological Units at Granite Point Locality 1, 45WT41, Southeastern Washington.* PhD dissertation, Washington State University, Pullman.

Leonhardy, F. C., and D. G. Rice
  1970. A Proposed Culture Typology for the Lower Snake River Region, Southwestern Washington. NARN 4(1):1–29.

Lepionka, Larry, Donald Colquhoun, Rochelle Marrinan, David McCollum, Mark
    Brooks, John Foss, William Abbott, and Ramona Grunden
    n.d.   The Second Refuge Site, Location 22 (38JA61), Savannah National Wildlife
            Refuge, Jasper County, South Carolina. Report on file at U.S. Fish and Wild-
            life Service, Atlanta, Georgia.
Lepper, B. T.
    1976.   Fluted Point Distributional Patterns in the Eastern United States. MJA
            8:269–285.
    1985.   The Effects of Cultivation and Collecting on Ohio Fluted Point Finds: A
            Reply to Seeman and Prufer. MJA 10(2):241–250.
Leslie, R. H.
    1979.   The Eastern Jornada Mogollon, Extreme Southeastern New Mexico: A
            Summary. In *Jornada Mogollon Archaeology: Proceedings of the First Jor-
            nada Conference*, edited by P. H. Beckert and R. N. Wiseman. New Mexico
            State University. Las Cruces.
Leudtke, Barbara
    1976.   *Lithic Material Distributions and Interaction Patterns During the Late
            Woodland Period in Michigan.* PhD dissertation, University of Michigan,
            Ann Arbor.
Lewis, T. M. N., and Madeline Kneberg
    1946.   *Hiwassee Island: An Archaeological Account of Four Tennessee Indian
            Peoples.* The University of Tennessee Press. Knoxville.
    1951.   Early Projectile Point Forms, and Examples from Tennessee. TA 7:6–19.
    1955.   The A. L. LeCroy Collection. TA 11(2):75–82.
    1958.   *Tribes That Slumber: Indian Times in the Tennessee Region.* The Uni-
            versity of Tennessee Press. Knoxville.
    1959.   The Archaic Culture in the Middle South. AAn 25:161–183.
Lewis, T. M. N., and M. K. Lewis
    1961.   *Eva: An Archaic Site.* The University of Tennessee Press. Knoxville.
Libby, W. F.
    1955.   *Radiocarbon Dating.* University of Chicago Press. Chicago.
Lillard, J. B., R. F. Heizer, and Franklin Fenenga
    1939.   An Introduction to the Archaeology of Central California. SJCB No. 2.
Lilly, Eli
    1937.   *Prehistoric Antiquities of Indiana.* Indiana Historical Society.
            Indianapolis.
    1961.   *Schliemann in Indianapolis.* Indiana Historical Society. Indianapolis.
Linford, L. D.
    1982.   (editor)   Kayenta Anasazi Archaeology on Central Black Mesa, North-
            eastern Arizona: The Pinon Project. NMPA, No. 10.
Lintz, Christopher
    1978.   Panhandle Aspect and Its Relationship with Upper Republican. In *The
            Central Plains Tradition: Internal Development and External Relationships*,
            edited by D. J. Blakeslee. OSAIR, No. 11.
    1984.   The Plains Villagers: Antelope Creek. In *The Prehistory of Oklahoma*,
            edited by R. E. Bell, pp. 325–346. Academic Press. Orlando, Florida.
    1986.   Architecture and Community Variability of the Antelope Creek Phase of
            the Texas Panhandle. OASOP, no. 14.

Lipe, W. D.
1970. Anasazi Communities in the Red Rock Plateau, Southeastern Utah. In *Reconstructing Prehistoric Pueblo Societies*, edited by W. A. Longacre, pp. 84–139. University of New Mexico Press. Albuquerque.

Lippincott, Kerry
1976. *Settlement Ecology of Solomon River Upper Republican Sites in North Central Kansas*. PhD dissertation, University of Missouri, Columbia.
1978. Solomon River Upper Republican Settlement Ecology. In *The Central Plains Tradition: Internal Development and External Relationships*, edited by D. J. Blakeslee, pp. 81–93. OSAIR, No. 11.

Livingston, Henry, Jr.
1791. A View of the Celebrated Indian Fortifications Near the Juncture of the Ohio & Muskingum. *New York Magazine*, frontpiece.

Lobdell, J. E., and A. A. Dekin, Jr.
1984. Introduction to the Frozen Family from the Utqiaqvik Site, Barrow, Alaska, Papers from a Symposium. ArcA 21(1).
1974. The Scoggin Site: A Study in McKean Typology. PA 19(64):123–128.

Loendorf, L. L., S. A. Ahler, and D. A. Davison
1984. The Proposed National Register District in the Knife River Flint Quarries, Dunn County, North Dakota. NDH 51(4):4–20.

Loftfield, T. C.
1976. *A Briefe and True Report . . . : An Archaeological Interpretation of the Southern North Carolina Coast*. PhD dissertation, University of North Carolina, Chapel Hill.
n.d.a. Excavations at 31On33, a Late Woodland Seasonal Village. Report on file at the University of North Carolina, Wilmington.
n.d.b. Preliminary Field Report, Phase I Including Ceramic and Feature Analysis: 31On196 Permuda Island. Report on file at the University of North Carolina, Wilmington.

Loftfield, T. C., and C. B. Watson
n.d. Archaeological Testing and Excavations at 31On96, Permuda Island. Report on file at the University of North Carolina, Wilmington.

Logan, W. D.
1952. Graham Cave: An Archaic Site in Montgomery County, Missouri. MASM 2:1–86.

Long, R. J.
1962. The Raisch-Smith Site Near Oxford, Ohio. OhA 12(3–4):58–68.

Longacre, W. A., S. J. Holbrook, and M. W. Graves
1982. (editors) Multidisciplinary Research at Grasshopper Pueblo, Arizona. APUAr, No. 40.

Lorrain, Dessamae
1967. The Glass Site. In *A Pilot Study of Wichita Indian Archeology and Ethnohistory*, assembled by R. E. Bell, E. B. Jelks, and W. W. Newcomb. Southern Methodist University, Dallas, Texas.

Loud, L. L., and M. R. Harrington
1929. Lovelock Cave. UCPAE, 25(1):1–184.

Love, M. F.
1975. A Survey of the Distribution of T-shaped Doorways in the Greater Southwest. PASNM 2:296–311.

Lovis, W. A.
n.d. (editor) Archaeological Investigations at the Weber I (20SA581) and Weber II (20SA582) Sites, Frankenmuth Township, Saginaw Co., Michigan. Report on file at the Michigan Department of Transportation, Lansing.

Lowther, G. R.
1962. An Account of an Archaeological Site on Cape Sparbo, Devon Island. NMCB 180:1–19.

Ludowicz, Deanna
1983. Assemblage Variation Associated with Southwestern Interior Plateau Microblade Technology. MA thesis, University of British Columbia, Vancouver.

Ludwickson, John
1978. Central Plains Tradition Settlements in the Loup River Basin: The Loup River Phase. In *The Central Plains Tradition: Internal Development and External Relationships*, edited by D. J. Blakeslee, pp. 94–108. OSAIR, No. 11.

Ludwickson, John, and S. R. Holen
(in press) The Loup River Phase. In *Introduction to Nebraska Archeology: 1935–1985*, edited by W. W. Caldwell. Institute for Tertiary and Quaternary Studies. Lincoln.

Ludwickson, John, D. J. Blakeslee, and John O'Shea
n.d. Missouri National Recreational River: Native American Cultural Resources. Report to Inter-Agency Archeological Services, National Park Service, Denver, Colorado.

Lueger, Richard
1981. Ceramics from Yuquot, British Columbia. The Yuquot Project, Vol. 3. HA, No. 44.
n.d. Metal and Miscellaneous Artifacts and Materials from Yuquot, B.C. Report (No. 258) on file at the National Historic Parks and Sites Branch, Parks Canada, Ottawa, Ontario.

Luer, G. M., and M. M. Almy
1981. Temple Mounds of the Tampa Bay Area. FA 34:127–155.

Lugenbeal, E. N.
1976. *The Archaeology of the Smith Site: A Study of the Ceramics and Culture History of Minnesota Laurel and Blackduck*. PhD dissertation, University of Wisconsin, Madison.
1978. The Blackduck Ceramics of the Smith Site (21 KC 3) and Their Implications for the History of Blackduck Ceramics and Culture in Northern Minnesota. MJA 3(1):45–68.

Luke, C. J.
1980. Continuing Archaeology on State Highway 16 in Kerr County, Texas: The Excavations of the Shep Site (41KR109) and the Wounded Eye Site (41KR107). TDHPA, No. 16.

Lukens, Paul
1963. *Some Ethnozoological Implications of Mammalian Fauna from Minnesota Archaeological Sites*. PhD dissertation, University of Minnesota, Minneapolis.

Lyneis, M. M.
1986. Residual Archaeology of the Main Ridge Locality, Pueblo Grande de Nevada. WAR 3:183–259.

McAllister, N. M.
1980. Avian Fauna from the Yuquot Excavation. The Yuquot Project, Vol. 2. HA, No. 43.

McCann, C.
1950. The Ware Site, Salem County, New Jersey. AAn 15:315–331.
1957. Six Late Sites in Southern and Central New Jersey. ASNJB 13:1–10.

McCartney, A. P.
1969. Prehistoric Aleut Influences at Port Moller, Alaska. APUA 14(2):1–16.
1977. Thule Eskimo Prehistory along Northeastern Hudson Bay. NMMMS, No. 70.
1984. Prehistory of the Aleutian Region. In *Handbook of North American Indians: Arctic*, edited by C. W. Sturtevant and David Damas, Vol. 5:119–135. Smithsonian Institution. Washington, D.C.

McCartney, A. P., and C. G. Turner, II
1966. Stratigraphy of the Anangula Unifacial Core and Blade Site. ArcA 3(2):28–40.

McCary, B. C.
1951. A Workshop Site of Early Man in Dinwiddie County, Virginia. AAn 17(1):9–17.
1953. The Potts Site, Chickahominy River, New Kent County. ASVQB 8(1).
1983. Paleo-Indian in Virginia. ASVQB 38(1):43–69.

McCary, B. C., and G. R. Bittner
1978. Excavation of the Williamson Site, Dinwiddie County, Virginia. ASVQB 33(2):45–60.
1979. The Paleo-Indian Component of the Mitchell Plantation Site, Sussex County, Virginia. ASVQB 34(1):33–42.

McClurkan, B. B.
1966. *The Archaeology of Cueva de la Zona de Derrumbes, a Rockshelter in Nuevo Leon, Mexico.* MA thesis, University of Texas, Austin.

McClurkan, B. B., H. P. Jensen, and E. B. Jelks
1980. Jonas Short and Coral Snake Mounds: A Comparison. In *Caddoan and Poverty Point Archaeology*, edited by J. L. Gibson, pp. 173–206. LA, No. 6.

McCollogh, K. M.
1986. *The Ruin Island Phase of Thule Culture in the Eastern High Arctic.* PhD dissertation, University of Toronto.

McCollough, M. C. R., and C. H. Faulkner
1978. (editors) Sixth Report of the Normandy Archaeological Project. Normandy Archaeological Project, Vol. 6. RIDAUT, No. 21.

MacCord, H. A.
1964a. The Philip Nase Site, Henrico County, Virginia. ASVQB 18(4):78–85.
1964b. The Bowman Site, Shenandoah County, Virginia. ASVQB 19(2):43–49.
1964c. The Irwin Site, Prince George County, Virginia. ASVQB 19(2):37–42.
1965. The De Shazo Site, King George County, Virginia. ASVQB 19(4):98–104.
1967. The Hopewell Airport Site, Prince George County, Virginia. ASVQB 22(2):73–80.
1968. Elm Hill Site, Mecklenburg County, Virginia. ASVQB 23(2):63–83.
1969. Camden: A Postcontact Indian Site in Caroline County. ASVQB 24(1):1–55.

1970. The John Green Site, Greensville County, Virginia. ASVQB 25(2):98–138.

1971a. The Lipes Site. ASVQB 26(2):53–106.

1971b. The Brown Johnson Site. ASVQB 25(4):230–272.

1973. The Quicksburg Site, Shenandoah County, Virginia. ASVQB 27(3):121–140.

1974a. The Wingina Site, Nelson County, Virginia. ASVQB 28(4):169–180.

1974b. The Fox Farm Site, Smyth County, Virginia. ASVQB 29(1):1–5.

1979. The Flanary Site, Scott County, Virginia. ASVQB 34(1):1–32.

n.d. Lewis Creek Mound Culture in Virginia. Unpublished manuscript.

MacCord, H. A., and W. T. Buchanan

1980. The Crab Orchard Site, Tazewell County, Virginia. SP, No. 8.

MacCord, H. A., and R. M. Owens

1965. The Posnick Site, Henrico County, Virginia. ASVQB 19(4):88–96.

MacCord, H. A., and C. L. Rodgers

1966. The Miley Site, Shenandoah County, Virginia. ASVQB 21(1):9–20.

MacCord, H. A., and O. D. Valliere

1965. The Lewis Creek Mound, Augusta County, Virginia. ASVQB 20(2):37–47.

MacCord, H. A., Karl Schmitt, and R. G. Slattery

1957. The Shepard Site Study. ASMB, No. 1.

McCormick, O. F., III

1973. Archaeological Resources in the Lake Monticello Area of Titus County, Texas. SMUCA, No. 8.

McCracken, Harold

1978. (editor) *The Mummy Cave Project in North Western Wyoming*. Buffalo Bill Historical Center. Cody, Wyoming.

MacDonald, G. F.

1968. Debert: A Paleo-Indian Site in Central Nova Scotia. APNMC, No. 16.

1983. *Eastern North America*. In *Early Man in the New World*, edited by Richard Shutler, Jr., pp. 97–108. Sage Publications. Beverly Hills, California.

MacDonald, G. F., and R. I. Inglis

1976. *The Dig, An Archaeological Reconstruction of a West Coast Village*. National Museum of Man. Ottawa, Ontario.

1980–1981. An Overview of North Coast Prehistory. In *Fragments of the Past: British Columbia Archaeology in the 1970s*. BCS, No. 48.

McGhee, R. J.

1970. Excavations at Bloody Falls, N.W.T., Canada. ArcA 6:53–73.

1971. An Archaeological Survey of Western Victoria Island, N.W.T. NMCBAS 87:157–191.

1974. Beluga Hunters: An Archaeological Reconstruction of the History and Culture of the Mackenzie Delta Kittegaryumiut. MUNSES, No. 13.

1978. *Canadian Arctic Prehistory*. National Museum of Man. Ottawa, Ontario.

1979. The Paleoeskimo Occupations at Port Refuge, High Arctic Canada. NMMMS, No. 92.

1981a. A Tale of Two Cultures: A Prehistoric Village in the Canadian Arctic. Ar July/August.

1981b.   The Dorset Occupations in the Vicinity of Port Refuge, High Arctic Canada. NMMMS, No. 105.

1984.   Thule Prehistory of Canada. In *Handbook of North American Indians: Arctic*, edited by C. W. Sturtevant and David Damas, Vol. 5:369–376. Smithsonian Institution, Washington, D.C.

McGimsey, C. R., III, and H. A. Davis

1977.   *The Management of Archeological Resources.* Special publication of the Society for American Archaeology. Washington, D.C.

McGovern, T. H.

1980.   Cows, Harp Seals and Church Bells: Adaptation and Extinction in Norse Greenland. HE 8:245–275.

McGregor, J. C.

1936.   Dating the Eruption of Sunset Crater, Arizona. AAn 2(1):15–26.

1937a.   Winona Village. MN 9(7):39–42.

1937b.   Winona Village: A XIIth Century Settlement with a Ball Court Near Flagstaff, Arizona. MNAB, No. 12.

1937c.   A Small Island of Culture Near Flagstaff, Arizona. SL 3(2):28–32.

1941a.   Winona and Ridge Ruin, Part I: Architecture and Material Culture. MNAB, No. 18.

1941b.   *Southwestern Archaeology.* John Wiley & Sons. New York.

1943.   Burial of an Early American Magician. PAPS 86(2):270–298.

1951.   *The Cohonina Culture of Northwestern Arizona.* University of Illinois Press. Urbana.

1952.   The Havana Site. In *Hopewellian Communities in Illinois*, edited by Thorne Deuel. ISMSP, No. 5.

1955.   A Sinagua Kiva. P 7(3):11–17.

1956.   The 1955 Pollock Site Excavations. P 28(3):49–54.

1958a.   The Pershing Site. P 31(2):33–36.

1958b.   *The Pool and Irving Villages.* University of Illinois Press. Urbana.

1961.   The Pershing Site in Northern Arizona. P 34(1):23–27.

1965.   *Southwestern Archaeology* (2nd edition). University of Illinois Press, Urbana.

1967.   *The Cohonina Culture of Mount Floyd, Arizona.* University of Kentucky Press. Lexington.

McGuire, R. H.

1977.   The Copper Canyon–McGuireville Project: Archaeological Investigations in the Verde Valley, Arizona. ASMHS, No. 45.

McGuire, R. H., and M. B. Schiffer

1982. (editors)   *Hohokam and Patayan: Prehistory in Southwestern Arizona.* Academic Press. New York.

McHugh, W. P., G. D. Gardner, and J. Donahue

n.d.   Before Smith's Mill; Archaeological and Geological Investigations. Report on file at U.S. Army Corps of Engineers, Kansas City District, Missouri.

MacKay, J. R., W. H. Mathews, and R. S. MacNeish

1961.   Geology of the Engigstciak Archaeological Site, Yukon Territory. Arc 14(1):25–52.

McKee, Bates

1972.   *Cascadia: The Geological Evolution of the Pacific Northwest.* McGraw-Hill. New York.

McKenna, P. J.
  1984.   The Architecture and Material Culture of 29SJ1360. RCC, No. 7.
McKenna, P. J., and M. L. Truell
  1986.   Small Site Architecture of Chaco Canyon, New Mexico. PArc, No. 18D.
McKennan, Robert, and J. P. Cook
  1970.   Prehistory at Healy Lake, Alaska. *Proceedings of the 8th International
          Congress of Anthropological and Ethnological Sciences* 3:182–184.
McKern, W. C.
  1928.   The Neale and McClaughry Mound Groups. BPMCM 3(3):215–416.
  1930.   The Kletzien and Nitschke Mound Groups. BPMCM 3(4):417–572.
  1931.   A Wisconsin Variant of the Hopewell Culture. BPMCM 10(2):185–328.
  1939.   The Midwestern Taxonomic Method as an Aid to Archaeological Culture
          Study. AAn 4(4):301–313.
  1942.   The First Settlers of Wisconsin. WMH 26(2):153–169.
  1945.   Preliminary Report on the Upper Mississippi Phase in Wisconsin. BPMCM
          16(3):109–285.
  1963.   The Clam River Focus. MPMPA, No. 9.
McKern, W. C., P. F. Titterington, and J. B. Griffin
  1945.   Painted Pottery Figurines from Illinois. AAn 10(3):295–302.
Mackey, J. C., and S. J. Holbrook
  1978.   Environmental Reconstruction and the Abandonment of the Largo-Gal-
          lina Area, New Mexico. JFA 5:29–49.
McMichael, E. V., and J. E. Kellar
  1960.   Archaeological Survey in the Oliver Basin. UGLAS, No. 2.
McNamara, J. M.
  1982.   Summary of the 1981 Excavations at the Conowingo Site, 18CE14.
          MGSFR, No. 172.
  1983.   Summary of the 1982 Excavations at the Conowingo Site, 18CE14.
          MGSFR, No. 176.
MacNeish, R. S.
  1947.   A Preliminary Report on Coastal Tamaulipas, Mexico. AAn 13(1):1–15.
  1952.   Iroquois Pottery Types: A Technique for the Study of Iroquois Prehistory.
          NMCB, No. 124.
  1954.   The Pointed Mountain Site near Fort Liard, Northwest Territories, Can-
          ada. AAn 19(3):234–253.
  1955.   Two Archaeological Sites on Great Bear Lake, N.W.T. NMCB 136:54–
          84.
  1958a. An Introduction to the Archaeology of Southeast Manitoba. NMCB,
          No. 157.
  1958b. Preliminary Archaeological Investigations in the Sierra de Tamaulipas,
          Mexico. TAPS 48(6).
  1959a. Men Out of Asia: As Seen from the Northwest Yukon. APUA 7(2):41–
          70.
  1959b. A Speculative Framework of Northern North American Prehistory as of
          April 1959. An 1(1):1–17 and chart.
  1961.   Recent Finds Concerned with the Incipient Agriculture Stage in Prehistoric
          Mesoamerica. In *Homenaje a Pablo Martinez del Rio*, edited by Ignacio
          Bernal, Jorge Gurria, Santiago Genoves, and Luis Aveleyra, pp. 91–101. In-
          stituto Nacional de Antrolopogia e Historia. Mexico City.

1964. Investigations in Southwest Yukon: Excavations, Comparisons, and Spec-
       ulations. PPFA, No. 6.
McNitt, Frank
  1957. *Richard Wetherill: Anasazi.* University of New Mexico Press.
       Albuquerque.
McNutt, C. H.
  1969. Early Puebloan Occupations at Tesuque By-Pass in the Upper Rio Grande
       Valley. AnP, No. 40.
McPherron, Alan
  1967. The Juntunen Site and the Late Woodland Prehistory of the Upper Great
       Lakes Area. UMMAAP, No. 30.
Madsen, D. B.
  1979. The Fremont and the Sevier: Defining Prehistoric Agriculturalists North
       of the Anasazi. AAn 44(4):711–723.
  1982a. Eastern Great Basin Prehistory. In *Man and Environment in the Great
       Basin*, edited by D. B. Madsen and J. F. O'Connell. SAAP, No. 2.
  1982b. Prehistoric Occupation Patterns, Subsistence Adaptations, and Chro-
       nology in the Fish Springs Area, Utah. BLMCRS, No. 12.
Madsen, D. B., and L. W. Lindsay
  1977. Backhoe Village. ASSP 4(12).
Mainfort, R. C., Jr.
  1979. Indian Social Dynamics in the Period of European Contact: Fletcher Site
       Cemetery, Bay County, Michigan. ASMSU 50(3).
  1980. (editor) Archaeological Investigations at Pinson Mounds State Archaeo-
       logical Area: 1974, 1975, and 1978 Field Seasons. RSTDC, No. 1.
  1985. Wealth, Space, and Status in a Historic Indian Cemetery. AAn 50(3):555–
       579.
  1986. Pinson Mounds: A Middle Woodland Ceremonial Center. RSTDC, No.
       7.
Mainfort, R. C., Jr., G. W. Shannon, Jr., and J. E. Tyler
  1985. 1983 Excavations at Pinson Mounds: The Twin Mounds. MJA 10:49–
       75.
Mallam, R. C.
  1976. The Iowa Effigy Mound Manifestation: An Interpretive Model. OSAIR,
       No. 9.
Mallery, Garrick
  1893. Picture-Writing of the American Indian. *Tenth Annual Report of the
       Bureau of American Ethnology*, pp. 121–122. Smithsonian Institution. Wash-
       ington, D.C.
Mallouf, R. J.
  1976. Archeological Investigations at Proposed Big Pine Lake, 1974–5, Lamar
       and Red River Counties, Texas. THCASR, No. 18.
  1985. *A Synthesis of Eastern Trans-Pecos Prehistory.* MA thesis, The University
       of Texas, Austin.
Manley, P. C.
  1963. Excavation of the Lewis Creek Mound, Augusta County, Virginia. ASVQB
       (18)2:37–42.

Manson, C. P.
  1948.   Marcey Creek Site: An Early Manifestation in the Potomac Valley. AAn
          13(3):223–226.
Manson, C. P., H. A. MacCord, and J. B. Griffin
  1944.   The Culture of the Keyser Farm Site (Page County, Virginia). PMAS
          29:375–435.
Marshall, J. O.
  1969.   *The Glen Elder Focus: The Cultural Affiliations of Archeological Material
          from the Glen Elder Site, 14ML1.* Inter-Agency Archeological Salvage Pro-
          gram, National Park Service. Washington, D.C.
  1972.   The Archeology of the Elk City Reservoir. ASKSHS, No. 6.
Marshall, M. P.
  1982.   *Excavations at Nuestra Senora de Dolores Pueblo (LA 677): A Prehistoric
          Settlement in the Tiquex Province.* Office of Contract Archeology, University
          of New Mexico. Albuquerque.
Marshall, M. P., and H. J. Walt
  1984.   *Rio Abajo: Prehistory and History of a Rio Grande Province.* New Mexico
          Historic Preservation Division. Santa Fe.
Martin, H. T.
  1909.   Further Notes on the Pueblo Ruins in Scott County, Kansas. USB 5(2).
Martin, P. S.
  1940.   The SU Site: Excavations at a Mogollon Village, Western New Mexico,
          1939. FMNHAS 32(1).
  1943.   The SU Site: Excavations at a Mogollon Village, Western New Mexico,
          Second Season, 1941. FMNHAS 32(2).
Martin, P. S., and J. B. Rinaldo
  1939.   Modified Basket Maker Sites, Ackmen-Lowery Area, Southwestern Col-
          orado, 1938. FMNHAS 23(3).
  1947.   The SU Site: Excavations at a Mogollon Village, Western New Mexico,
          Third Season, 1946. FMNHAS 32(3).
  1950a. The Turkey Foot Ridge Site: A Mogollon Village, Pine Lawn Valley,
          Western New Mexico. F:A 38(2).
  1950b. Sites of the Reserve Phase, Pine Lawn Valley, Western New Mexico.
          F:A 38(3).
Martin, P. S., G. I. Quimby, and Donald Collier
  1947.   *Indians Before Columbus.* University of Chicago Press. Chicago.
Martin, P. S., J. B. Rinaldo, and E. R. Barter
  1957.   Late Mogollon Communities: Four Sites of the Tularosa Phase, Western
          New Mexico. F:A 49(1).
Martin, P. S., J. B. Rinaldo, and E. A. Bluhm
  1949.   Cochise and Mogollon Sites, Pine Lawn Valley, Western New Mexico.
          F:A, No. 42.
Martin, P. S., J. B. Rinaldo, E. A. Bluhm, and H. C. Cutler
  1956.   Higgins Flat Pueblo, Western New Mexico. F:A, No. 45.
Martin, P. S., J. B. Rinaldo, H. C. Cutler, and R. T. Grange, Jr.
  1952.   Mogollon Cultural Continuity and Change. F:A, No. 40.
Martin, P. S., Lawrence Roys, and Gerhardt Von Bonin
  1936.   Lowry Ruin in Southwestern Colorado. FMNHAS 23(1).

Marwitt, J. P.
  1970. Median Village and Fremont Regional Variation. UUAP, No. 95.
Mary-Rousseliere, Guy
  1964. The Paleo-Eskimo Remains in the Pelly Bay Region, N.W.T. NMCB
     193:62–183.
  1976. The Paleoeskimo in Northern Baffinland. In *Eastern Arctic Prehistory*,
     edited by M. S. Maxwell. MSAA 31:40–57.
  1979a. A Few Problems Elucidated and New Questions Raised by Recent Dorset
     Finds in the North Baffin Island Region. Arc 32:22–32.
  1979b. The Thule Culture on North Baffin Island: Early Thule Characteristics
     and the Survival of the Thule Tradition. In *Thule Eskimo Culture: An An-
     thropological Retrospective*, edited by A. P. McCartney. NMMMS 88:545–
     75.
Maslowski, R. F., and R. M. King
  1983. *Indian Pottery Types from the Bluestone Reservation*. U.S. Army Corps
     of Engineers. Huntington, West Virginia.
Mason, R. J.
  1962. The Paleo-Indian Tradition in Eastern North America. CA 3(3):227–246.
  1966. Two Stratified Sites on the Door County Peninsula of Wisconsin.
     UMMAAP, No. 26.
  1967. The North Bay Component at the Porte des Morts Site, Door County,
     Wisconsin. WiA 48(4):267–344.
  1969. Laurel and North Bay: Diffusional Networks in the Upper Great Lakes.
     AAn 34:295–302.
  1981. *Great Lakes Archaeology*. Academic Press. New York.
Mason, R. J., and Carol Irwin
  1960. An Eden-Scottsbluff Burial in Northeastern Wisconsin. AAn 26(1):43–
     57.
Masse, W. B.
  1980a. Excavations at Gu Achi. WACCP, No. 12.
  1980b. A Reappraisal of the Protohistoric Sobaipuri Indians of Southeastern
     Arizona. In *The Protohistoric Period in the North American Southwest*, A.D.
     1450–1700, edited by D. R. Wilcox and W. B. Masse, pp. 28–56. ASUAP,
     No. 24.
  1980c. The Hohokam of the Lower San Pedro and the Northern Papagueria:
     Continuity and Variability in Two Regional Populations. In *Current Issues
     in Hohokam Prehistory*, edited by D. E. Doyel and Fred Plog, pp. 205–223.
     ASUAP, No. 23.
  1982. Hohokam Ceramic Art: Regionalism and the Imprint of Societal Change.
     In *Southwestern Ceramics: A Comparative Review*, edited by A. H. Schroe-
     der, pp. 71–105. AAr 15.
Mathiassen, Therkel
  1927. Archaeology of the Central Eskimos, The Thule Culture and its Position
     within the Eskimo Culture. In *Report of the Fifth Thule Expedition, 1921–
     1924*, Vol. 4. Glydendalski Boghandel, Nordisk Forlang. Copenhagen.
  1929. Eskimo Relics from Washington Land and Hall Land. MG 71(3).
     Copenhagen.

1933.   Prehistory of the Angmagssalik Eskimos. MG 92(4).

1958.   The Sermermiut Excavations. MG 161:3.

Mathiassen, Therkel, and Erik Holtved

1936.   The Eskimo Archaeology of the Julianebaab District, with a Brief Summary of the Prehistory of the Greenlanders. MG 118(1).

Mathien, F. J.

1982.   Social and Economic Implications of Jewelry Items of the Chaco Anasazi. In *Recent Research on Chaco Prehistory*. RCC, No. 8.

Matson, R. G.

1976. (editor)   The Glenrose Cannery Site. ASCP, No. 52.

Matson, R. G., and W. D. Lipe

1978.   Settlement Patterns on Cedar Mesa: Boom and Bust on the Northern Periphery. In *Investigations by the Southwestern Anthropological Research Group: An Exercise in Archaeological Cooperation*, edited by R. C. Euler and G. J. Gumerman, pp. 1–12. MNAB, No. 50.

Mauger, J. E.

1978.   Shed Roof Houses at the Ozette Archaeological Site: A Protohistoric Architectural System. WARCPR, No. 73.

Maxwell, M. S.

1950.   A Change in the Interpretation of Wisconsin's Prehistory. WMH 33(4):427–433.

1951.   The Woodland Cultures in Southern Illinois. LMB, No. 7.

1960.   An Archaeological Analysis of Eastern Grant Land, Ellesmere Island, N.W.T. In *Contributions to Anthropology in 1960*. NMCB 180:20–55.

1973.   Archaeology of the Lake Harbour District, Baffin Island. NMMMS, No. 6.

1976a.   Introduction. In *Eastern Arctic Prehistory: Paleoeskimo Problems*, edited by M. S. Maxwell. MSSA, No. 31.

1976b.   Pre-Dorset and Dorset Artifacts: The View from Lake Harbour. In *Eastern Arctic Prehistory: Paleoeskimo Problems*, edited by M. S. Maxwell. MSAA 31:58–78.

1980.   Dorset Site Variation on the Southeastern Coast of Baffin Island. Arc 33:505–516.

1985.   *Prehistory of the Eastern Arctic*. Academic Press. Orlando, Florida.

May, R. V.

1978.   A Southern California Indigenous Ceramic Typology: A Contribution to Malcolm J. Rogers Research. ASAJ 2(1).

Mayer-Oakes, W. J.

1951.   *Starved Rock Archaic*. AAn 16:313–324.

1955.   Prehistory of the Upper Ohio Valley. ACM, No. 34.

Mayr, Thomas

1972.   Selby Bay in Retrospect. MaA 8(1):2–5.

Mead, J. I.

1980.   Is It Really that Old? A comment about the Meadowcroft Rockshelter "Overview." AAn 45:579–582.

Mecklenburg, C. W.

1969.   *Human Skeletal Remains from the Shannon Site, Montgomery County, Virginia*. MA thesis, University of Washington, Seattle.

Meek, Maurice
 1969. Another Crib Mound Banner Stone. CSAJ 16(4):160–163.
Mehringer, P. J., Jr.
 1985. Late-Quaternary Pollen Records from the Interior Pacific Northwest and Northern Great Basin of the United States. In *Pollen Records of Late-Quaternary North American Sediments*, edited by V. M. Bryant and R. G. Holloway, pp. 167–189. American Association of Stratigraphic Palynologists. Dallas.
Meighan, C. W.
 1955. Archaeology of the North Coast Ranges. UCASR 30:1–39.
 1959. The Little Harbor Site, Catalina Island: An Example of Ecological Interpretation in Archaeology. AAn 24(4):383–405.
Meighan, C. W., and C. V. Haynes
 1970. The Borax Lake Site Revisited. S 167(3922):1213–1221.
Meldgaard, Jørdan
 1960. Origin and Evolution of Eskimo Culture in the Eastern Arctic. CGJ 60:64–75.
 1961. Sarqaq-folket ved Itivnera: National Museets Undersogelser i Sommern 1960. TG, January:15–23.
 1962. On the Formative Period of the Dorset Culture. In *Prehistoric Relations between the Arctic and Temperate Zones of North America*, edited by J. M. Campbell. AINATP, No. 11.
 1965. *Nordboerne i Grønland: En Vikingsbygds Historie*. Munksgaard Forlag. Copenhagen.
 1977. The Prehistoric Cultures in Greenland: Discontinuities in a Marginal Area. In *Continuity and Discontinuity in the Inuit Culture of Greenland*, edited by H. P. Kylstra. University of Groningen Arctic Center. Groningen, Netherlands.
Meleen, E. E.
 1938. A Preliminary Report of the Mitchell Indian Village Site and Burial Mounds. ASC, No. 11.
 1948. A Report on an Investigation of the LaRoche Site, Stanley County, South Dakota. USDMAC, No. 5.
 1949. A Preliminary Report on the Thomas Riggs Village Site. AAn 14(3):310–322.
Mera, H. P.
 1931. Chupadero Black-on-White. LATSB, No. 1.
 1932. Wares Ancestral to Tewa Polychrome. LATSB, No. 4.
 1933. A Proposed Revision of the Rio Grande Glaze-paint Sequence. LATSB, No. 5.
 1935. Ceramic Clues to the Prehistory of North Central New Mexico. LATSB, No. 8.
 1938. Some Aspects of the Largo Cultural Phase, Northern New Mexico. AAn 3:236–244.
 1940. Population Changes in the Rio Grande Glaze Plain Area. LATSB 15(1).
 1943. An Outline of the Ceramic Developments in Southern and Southeastern New Mexico. LATSB, No. 11.

Merchant, V. L.
　1973.　*A Cross-Sectional Growth Study of the Protohistoric Arikara from Skeletal Material Associated with the Mobridge Site (39WW1), South Dakota.* MA thesis, American University, Washington, D.C.
Merchant, V. L., and D. H. Ubelaker
　1977.　Skeletal Growth of the Protohistoric Arikara. AJPA 46:61–72.
Merriam, J. C.
　1914.　Preliminary Report on the Discovery of Human Remains in an Asphalt Deposit at Rancho La Brea. S 40(1023):198–203.
Merry, Carl, and Sharon Pekrul
　1983.　A Summary of the 1981 Ditch Excavations at the Mulberry Site. SCAn 15:61–62.
Metcalf, George
　1956.　Additional Data from the Dodd and Phillips Ranch Sites. AAn 21(3):305–309.
　1963.　Small Sites on and about Fort Berthold Indian Reservation, Garrison Reservoir, North Dakota. RBSP, No. 26.
Michels, J. W., and C. A. Bebrich
　1971.　Obsidian Hydration Dating. In *Dating Techniques for the Archaeologist,* edited by H. N. Michael and E. K. Ralph, pp. 164–221. MIT Press. Cambridge, Massachusetts.
Michie, James
　1969.　Excavations at Tom's Creek. SN 1(11):2–16.
　1971.　Excavations at the Taylor Site. SACB 13:47–48.
　1972.　The Edgefield Scraper: A Tool of Inferred Antiquity and Use. SCAn 4(1):1–10.
　1973.　Archaeological Indications for Sea Level 3,500 Years Ago. SCAn 5(1):1–11.
　1974.　A Second Burial from the Daw's Island Shell Midden (38BU9), Beaufort County, South Carolina. SCAn 6(1):37–47.
　1978.　An Intensive Archaeological Test of Edenwood Site 38LX135, Lexington County, South Carolina. SCAn 10(2):454–495.
　1979.　The Bass Pond Dam Site: Intensive Archeological Testing at a Formative Period Base Camp on Kiawah Island, South Carolina. RMS, No. 154.
　1984.　An Initial Archaeological Survey of the Wachesaw/Richmond Plantation Property, Georgetown County, South Carolina. RMS, No. 191.
Milanich, J. T.
　1971a.　The Alachua Tradition of North-Central Florida. CFSMAH, No. 17.
　1971b.　*The Deptford Phase: An Archaeological Reconstruction.* PhD dissertation, University of Florida, Gainesville.
　1978a.　Two Cades Pond Sites in North-Central Florida: The Occupational Nexus as a Model of Settlement. FA 31:151–173.
　1978b.　The Western Timucuans: Patterns of Acculturation and Change. In *Tacachale: Essays on the Indians of Florida and Southeastern Georgia during the Historic Period,* edited by J. T. Milanich and Samuel Proctor, pp. 59–88. University Presses of Florida. Gainesville.
　1980.　Weeden Island Studies—Past, Present, and Future. SACB 22:11–18.

Milanich, J. T., and C. H. Fairbanks
  1980. *Florida Archaeology*. Academic Press. New York.
Milanich, J. T., A. S. Cordell, T. A. Kohler, V. J. Knight, Jr., and B. J. Sigler-Lavelle
  1984. *McKeithen Weeden Island—The Culture of North Florida*, A.D. *200–900*. Academic Press. Orlando.
Millar, J. F. V.
  1981. Interaction between the Mackenzie and Yukon Basins during the Early Holocene. In *Networks of the Past: Regional Interaction in Archaeology*, edited by F. J. Kense and P. G. Duke, pp. 259–294. Archaeological Association of the University of Calgary. Calgary, Alberta.
Miller, Carl
  1949. The Lake Springs Site, Columbia County, Georgia. AAn 15(1):38–51.
Miller, E. O., and E. B. Jelks
  1952. Archaeological Excavations at the Belton Reservoir, Coryell County, Texas. BTAPS 23:168–217.
Miller, J. J., and L. M. Stone
  1970. *Eighteenth-Century Ceramics from Fort Michilimackinac*. The Smithsonian Institution Press. Washington, D.C.
Mills, W. C.
  1902. Excavations of the Adena Mound. OAHSQ 10:451–479.
  1904. Explorations of the Gartner Mound and Village Site. OAHSQ 13:129–189.
  1906. Baum Prehistoric Village. OAHSQ 15:45–136.
  1907. Explorations of the Edwin Harness Mound. OAHSQ 16:113–193.
  1909. Explorations of the Seip Mound. OAHSQ 18:269–321.
  1914. *Archaeological Atlas of Ohio*. Ohio State Archaeological and Historical Society. Columbus.
  1916. Explorations of the Tremper Mound. OAHSQ 25:262–398.
  1917. The Feurt Mounds and Village Site. OAHSQ 26:305–449.
  1922. Explorations of the Mound City Group. OHASQ 31:423–584.
Milner, G. R.
  1983. The East St. Louis Stone Quarry Site Cemetery. In *American Bottom Archaeology FAI-270 Site Reports*, edited by C. J. Bareis and J. W. Porter, Vol. 7. University of Illinois Press. Urbana and Chicago.
  1984. The Julien Site. In *American Bottom Archaeology FAI-270 Site Reports*, edited by C. J. Bareis and J. W. Porter, Vol. 7. University of Illinois Press. Urbana and Chicago.
Mindeleff, Cosmos
  1896. Aboriginal Remains in Verde Valley, Arizona. In *Thirteenth Annual Report of the Bureau of American Ethnology*, pp. 185–261. Washington, D.C.
  1897. Cliff Ruins of Canyon de Chelly, Arizona. In *The Sixteenth Annual Report of the Bureau of American Ethnology:1894–1895*. Smithsonian Institution. Washington, D.C.
  1900. Localization of Tusayan Clans. In *Nineteenth Annual Report of the Bureau of American Ethnology*, pp. 639–653. Smithsonian Institution. Washington, D.C.

Mindeleff, Victor
  1891.   A Study of Pueblo Architecture in Tusayan and Cibola. *8th Annual Report of the Bureau of American Ethnology: 1886–87*, pp. 3–228. Smithsonian Institution. Washington, D.C.
Minshall, H. L.
  1976.   *The Broken Stones: The Case for Early Man in California.* Copley Books. La Jolla, California.
Mitchell, D. H.
  1965.   Preliminary Excavations at a Cobble Tool Site (DjRi 7) in the Fraser Canyon, British Columbia. NMCAP, No. 10.
  1971.   Archaeology of the Gulf of Georgia: A Natural Region and Its Culture Types. Sy 4:Supplement 1.
  1980–1981.   Test Excavations at Randomly Selected Sites in Eastern Queen Charlotte Strait. BCS, No. 48.
Moffatt, C. R.
  1979.   Some Observations on the Distribution and Significance of the Garden Beds of Wisconsin. WiA 60(3):222–248.
Moffett, Ross
  1949.   The Raisch-Smith Site, an Early Indian Occupation in Preble County, Ohio. OAHSQ 58(4):428–441.
Montgomery, Arthur
  1963.   The Source of the Fibrolite Axes. EP 70(1–2):34–48.
Montgomery, H.
  1908.   Prehistoric Man in Manitoba and Saskatchewan. AA 10:33–40.
Montgomery, R. G., Watson Smith, and J. O. Brew
  1949.   Franciscan Awatovi. PPM, No. 36.
Moore, C. B.
  1894a.   Certain Sand Mounds of the St. John's River, Florida, Part 1. JANSP 10:5–128.
  1894b.   Certain Sand Mounds of the St. John's River, Florida, Part 2. JANSP 10:129–246.
  1898.   Certain Aboriginal Mounds of the Coast of South Carolina. JANSP 11:147–16.
  1901.   Certain Aboriginal Mounds of the Northwest Florida Coast, Part 1. JANSP, No. 11.
  1903.   Certain Aboriginal Mounds of the Florida Central West Coast. JANSP, No. 12.
  1907.   Crystal River Revisited. JANSP 13:406–425.
  1912.   Some Aboriginal Sites on Red River. JANSP 14:482–644.
  1913.   Some Aboriginal Sites in Louisiana and Arkansas. JANSP 16:7–99.
  1916.   Some Aboriginal Sites on Green River, Kentucky. JANSP 16(3).
  1918.   The Northwest Florida Coast Revisited. JANSP 16:515–581.
Moore, R. A.
  1983.   Patterns in Synchronic and Diachronic Variation in Prehistoric Lithic Assemblages. In *Cultural Resource Investigations in Blocks VIII and IX, and Testing Operations in Blocks X and XI, Navajo Indian Irrigation Project, San Juan County, New Mexico*, edited by L. E. Vogler, Dennis Gilpin, and J. K. Anderson, pp. 549–692. NMPA, No. 24.

Moorehead, W. K.
1890.   *Fort Ancient, the Great Prehistoric Earthwork of Warren County, Ohio.* Robert Clarke & Co. Cincinnati, Ohio.
1891.   A Description of Fort Ancient. OAHSQ 3:313–315.
1892.   *Primitive Man in Ohio.* Putnams. New York.
1896.   A Description of Fort Ancient. OAHSQ 4:362–377.
1897.   Report of Field Work Carried Out in the Muskingum, Scioto, and Ohio Valley During the Season of 1896. OAHSQ 5:165–274.
1899.   *The Bird-stone Ceremonial: Being an Account of Some Singular Artifacts Found in the United States and Canada.* Allen I. Vosburgh. Saranac Lake, New York.
1906.   Explorations at the Mouth of the Wabash. BPA, No. 3:54–86.
1908.   Fort Ancient, the Great Prehistoric Earthwork of Warren County, Ohio. BPA, No. 4.
1910.   *The Stone Age in North America.* Houghton Mifflin Co. Boston.
1922a. The Hopewell Mound Group of Ohio. FMNHAS 6:73–184, pls. 51–83.
1922b. A Report on the Archaeology of Maine. BPA, No. 5.
1928.   Reports on Archaeological Field Work: Illinois. AA 30:506.
1929.   The Cahokia Mounds. UIB 26(4):7–106.
1932.   Exploration of the Etowah Site in Georgia. *Etowah Papers.* Yale University Press. New Haven.
Moratto, M. J.
1972.   *A Study of Prehistory in the Southern Sierra Nevada Foothills, California.* PhD dissertation, University of Oregon, Eugene.
1984.   *California Archaeology.* Academic Press. New York.
Moratto, M. J., L. H. Shoup, and J. D. Tordoff
1986.   Culture Change in the Central Sierra Nevada, 8000 B.C.–A.D. 1950. *Final Report of the New Melones Archeological Project,* Vol. 9. National Technical Information Service. Washington, D.C.
Morgan, R. G.
1946.   *Fort Ancient.* Ohio State Archaeological and Historical Society. Columbus.
1952.   Outline of Cultures in the Ohio Region. In *Archaeology of Eastern United States,* edited by J. B. Griffin, pp. 83–98. University of Chicago Press. Chicago.
Morgan, R. G., and H. H. Ellis
1943.   The Fairport Village Site. OAHSQ 52:3–64.
Morgan, R. G., and J. H. Rodabaugh
1947.   *Bibliography of Ohio Archaeology.* Ohio State Archaeological and Historical Society. Columbus.
Morgan, R. G., F. C. Baker, J. B. Griffin, G. K. Neumann, and J. L. B. Taylor
1941.   Contributions to the Archaeology of the Illinois River Valley. TAPS (n.s.) 32(1):1–208.
Morlan, R. E.
1973.   The Later Prehistory of the Middle Porcupine Drainage, Northern Yukon Territory. NMMMS, ASCP, No. 11.

1980. Taphonomy and Archaeology in the Upper Pleistocene of the Northern Yukon Territory: A Glimpse of the Peopling of the New World. NMMMS, ASC, No. 94.

Morlan, R. E., and Jacques Cinq-Mars
1982. Ancient Beringians: Human Occupation in the Late Pleistocene of Alaska and the Yukon Territory. In *Paleoecology of Beringia*, edited by D. M. Hopkins, J. V. Matthews, Jr., C. E. Schweger, and S. B. Young, pp. 353–381. Academic Press. New York.

Morley, S. G.
1910. The South House at Puye. PSAA (o.s.), No. 7. Reprinted in 1953 in *Pajarito Plateau and Its Ancient People*, edited by E. L. Hewett and B. P. Dutton. University of New Mexico Press and School of American Research. Albuquerque.

Morris, E. A.
1959. A Pueblo I Site Near Bennett's Peak, Northwestern New Mexico. EP 6(5):169–175.

Morris, E. H.
1919–1928. The Aztec Ruin. APAMNH 26, parts 1–5.
1921. Chronology of the San Juan Area. PNAS 7:18–22.
1939. Archaeological Studies in the La Plata District, Southwestern Colorado and Northwestern New Mexico. CIWB, No. 519.

Morris, E. H., and R. F. Burgh
1954. Basket Maker II Sites near Durango, Colorado. CIWB, No. 604.

Morrison, D. A.
1983. Thule Culture in Western Coronation Gulf, N.W.T. NMMMS, No. 116.

Morrison, R. B.
1964. Lake Lahontan: Geology of Southern Carson Desert. USGSPP, No. 401.

Morse, D. F.
1963. The Steuben Village and Mounds: A Multicomponent Late Hopewell Site in Illinois. UMMAAP, No. 21.
1969. Ancient Disease in the Midwest. ISMRI, No. 15.
1973. (editor) Nodena: An Account of 75 Years of Archeological Investigation in Southeast Mississippi County, Arkansas. AASRS, No. 4.
1974. Paleo-Indian in the Land of Opportunity: Preliminary Report on the Excavations at the Sloan Site (3GE94). In *The Cache River Archeological Project*, edited by M. B. Schiffer and J. H. House, pp. 135–143. AASRS, No. 8.

Morse, D. F., and P. A. Morse
1983. *Archaeology of the Central Mississippi Valley*. Academic Press. New York.
n.d. Zebree Archeological Project. Report on file at the Arkansas Archeological Survey, Fayetteville.

Morse, P. A.
1981. Parkin: The 1978–1979 Archeological Investigations of a Cross County, Arkansas, Site. AASRS, No. 13.

Morss, Noel
1931. The Ancient Culture of the Fremont River in Utah. PPM 12(3).

Motet-White, Anta
1963. Analytic Description of the Chipped Stone Industry from the Snyders Site, Calhoun County, Illinois. In *Miscellaneous Studies in Technology*. UMMAAP 19:1–70.

1968.   The Lithic Industries of the Illinois Valley in the Early and Middle Woodland Period. UMMAAP, No. 35.

Mouer, L. D.
1982.   *Beyond Exchange: Ceramics Composition and the Study of Social and
Political Systems.* Virginia Commonwealth University, Richmond.
1983.   A Review of the Ethnohistory and Archaeology of the Monacans. In
Piedmont Archaeology, edited by J. M. Wittkofski and L. E. Browning.
ASVSP 10:21–39.
1984.   A Review of Virginia Commonwealth University Archeology. ASVQB
(39)2:98–103.

Mouer, L. D., R. L. Ryder, and E. G. Johnson
1981.   The Elk Island Tradition: An Early Woodland Regional Society in the
Virginia Piedmont. ASVQB (36)1, 2:49–76.

Muller, Jon
1978.   The Kincaid System: Mississippian Settlement in the Environs of a Large
Site. In *Mississippian Settlement Patterns,* edited by B. D. Smith, pp. 269–
292. Academic Press. New York.
1983.   The Southeast. In *Ancient North Americans,* edited by J. D. Jennings,
pp. 373–420. W. H. Freeman & Co. New York.
1984.   Mississippian Specialization and Salt. AAn 49(3):489–507.
1986.   *Archaeology of the Lower Ohio River Valley.* Academic Press. New York.

Mulloy, W. T.
1942.   The Hagen Site. UMPSS, No. 1.
1954.   Archaeological Investigations in the Shoshoni Basin. UWPS 8(1).
1958.   A Preliminary Historical Outline for the Northwestern Plains. UWPS
22(1,2).
1965.   Archaeological Investigations along the North Platte River in Eastern
Wyoming. UWPS 31(1–3).

Munford, B. A.
1982.   *The Piney Branch Quarry Site: An Analysis of a Lithic Workshop in
Washington, D.C.* MA thesis, George Washington University, Washington,
D.C.

Munson, C. A.
1980. (editor)   Archaeological Salvage Excavations at Patoka Lake, Indiana.
RRGABL, No. 6.

Munson, P. J.
1967.   A Hopewellian Enclosure Earthwork in the Illinois River Valley. AAn
32:391–393.
1982.   Marion, Black Sand, Morton, and Havana Relationships: An Illinois Valley Perspective. WiA 63:1–17.

Munson, P. J., and R. L. Hall
1966.   An Early Woodland Radiocarbon Date from Illinois. MiA 12:85–87.

Muto, G. R.
1976.   *The Cascade Technique: An Examination of a Levallois-Like Reduction
System in Early Snake River Prehistory.* PhD dissertation, Washington State
University, Pullman.

Myers, J. A.
1981. (editor)   *Archaeological Data Recovery at the Mary Ann Cole Site (12 Cr
1) Crawford County, Indiana.* U.S. Army Corps of Engineers. Louisville,
Kentucky.

Myhrer, Keith, and M. M. Lyneis
  1985. The Bovine Bluff Site: An Early Puebloan Site in the Upper Moapa Valley. BLMNC, No. 15.
Nabhan, Gary
  1982. *The Desert Smells Like Rain: A Naturalist in the Papago Country*. North Point Press. San Francisco.
  1983. *Papago Fields: Arid Lands Ethnobotany and Agricultural Economy*. PhD dissertation, University of Arizona, Tuscon.
Nagle, Christopher
  1978. Indian Occupations of the Intermediate Period on the Central Labrador Coast: A Preliminary Synthesis. ArcA 15(2):119–145.
Nails, Fred, John Stein, and John Roney
  1983. *Chacoan Roads in the Southern Periphery: Results of the Phase II BLM Chaco Roads Project*. Bureau of Land Management. Albuquerque, New Mexico.
Nash, C. H.
  1972. Chucalissa: Excavations and Burials through 1963. OPMSU, No. 6.
Nash, R. J.
  1969. The Arctic Small Tool Tradition in Manitoba. OPAUM, No. 2.
Nelson, C. M.
  1969. The Sunset Creek Site (45KT28) and Its Place in Plateau Prehistory. RIWSU, No. 47.
Nelson, D. E., and G. Will
  1976. Obsidian Sources in the Anahim Peak Area. CRRSFU 3:151–154.
Nelson, N. C.
  1910. The Ellis Landing Shellmound. UCPAE 7(5):357–426.
  1914. Pueblo Ruins of the Galisteo Basin, New Mexico. APAMNH 15(1):41–67.
  1916. Chronology of the Tano Ruins, New Mexico. AA 18(2):159–180.
  1935. Early Migrations of Man to North America. NaH 35:356.
  1937. Notes on Cultural Relations between Asia and America. AAn 2(4):267–272.
Nero, R. W., and B. A. McCorquodale
  1958. Report of an Excavation at the Oxbow-Dam Site. BJ 16(2).
Nesbitt, P. H.
  1938. Starkweather Ruin: A Mogollon-Pueblo Site in the Upper Gila Area of New Mexico, and Affiliative Aspects of the Mogollon Culture. LMPAB, No. 6.
Neuman, R. W.
  1975. The Sonota Complex and Associated Sites on the Northern Plains. NSHSPA, No. 6.
  1984. *An Introduction to Louisiana Archaeology*. Louisiana State University Press. Baton Rouge.
Neumann, G. K., and M. L. Fowler
  1952. Hopewellian Sites in the Lower Wabash Valley. In *Hopewellian Communities in Illinois*, edited by Thorne Deuel, pp. 175–248. SP, No. 5.
Newell, H. Perry, and Alex D. Krieger.
  1949. The George C. Davis Site, Cherokee County, Texas. MSAA, No. 5.

Noble, V. E.
 1983.   *Functional Classes and Inter-Site Analysis in Historical Archaeology: A Case Study from Ouiatenon.* PhD dissertation, Michigan State University, East Lansing.

Noble, W. C.
 1971.   Archaeological Surveys and Sequences in Central District of Mackenzie. ArcA 8(1):102–135.
 1981.   Prehistory of the Great Slave Lake and Great Bear Lake Region. In *Handbook of North American Indians: Subarctic,* edited by W. W. Sturtevant and June Helm, Vol. 6:97–106. Smithsonian Institution. Washington, D.C.

Noël Hume, Ivor
 1962.   An Indian Ware of the Colonial Period. ASVQB (17)1:1–14.

Northrup, S. A.
 1975.   *Turquoise and Spanish Mines in New Mexico.* University of New Mexico Press. Albuquerque.

Nowack, Michael, and Lisa Headington
 1983.   Archeological Investigations in Southeastern Colorado. CCPA, No. 6.

O'Brien, P. J.
 1971.   Valley Focus Mortuary Practices. PA 16(53).
 1972a. A Formal Analysis of Cahokia Ceramics from the Powell Tract. IASM, No. 3.
 1972b. Urbanism, Cahokia and Middle Mississippian. Ar 25(3):188–197.
 1972c. The Sweet Potato: Its Origin and Dispersal. AA 74(3):342–365.
 1978.   Steed-Kisker: A Western Mississippian Settlement System. In *Mississippian Settlement Patterns,* edited by B. D. Smith. Academic Press. New York.
 1982.   The Yeo Site (23L199): A Kansas City Hopewell Limited Activity Site in Northwestern Missouri and Some Theories. PA 27(95).
 1984a. The Tim Adrian Site (14NT604): A Hell Gap Quarry Site in Norton County, Kansas. PA 29(103).
 1984b. Archaeology in Kansas. UKMPE, No. 9.
 n.d.   Cultural Resources Survey of Smithville Lake, Missouri, Vol. 1: Archaeology. Report on File at U.S. Army Corps of Engineers, Kansas City District Office, Missouri.

O'Brien, P. J., Clark Larson, John O'Grady, Brian O'Neill, and Ann S. Stirland.
 1973.   The Elliott Site (14GE303): A Preliminary Report. PA 18(59).

O'Bryan, Deric
 1953.   Excavation of a Cape Dorset Culture Site, Mill Island, West Hudson Strait. In *Annual Report of the National Museum of Canada, 1951–52.* National Museum of Canada. Ottawa, Ontario.

O'Connell, J. F.
 1967.   Elko Eared/Elko Corner-Notched Projectile Points as Time Markers in the Great Basin. UCASR, 70:129–140.
 1975.   The Prehistory of Surprise Valley. BPAP, No. 4.

O'Connell, J. F., and P. S. Hayward
 1972.   Altithermal and Medithermal Human Adaptations in Surprise Valley, Northeast California. In *Great Basin Cultural Ecology: A Symposium,* edited by D. D. Fowler, pp. 25–42. DRIPPS, No. 8.

Oerichbauer, E. S.
  1982.   Archaeological Excavations at the Site of a North West and XY Company
          Wintering Post (47 Bt 26): A Progress Report. WiA 63(3):153–236.
Okada, Hiroaki
  1980.   Prehistory of the Alaska Peninsula as Seen from the Hot Springs Site, Port
          Moller. In *Alaska Native Culture and History*, edited by Y. Kotani and W. B.
          Workman, pp. 103–112. NMESES, No. 4.
Oliver, B. L.
  1981.   *The Piedmont Tradition: Refinement of the Savannah River Stemmed
          Point Type*. MA thesis, University of North Carolina, Chapel Hill.
  1985.   Tradition and Typology: Basic Elements of the Carolina Projectile Point
          Sequence. In *Structure and Process in Southeastern Archaeology*, edited by
          R. S. Dickens, Jr., and H. T. Ward, pp. 195–211. University of Alabama
          Press. University.
  n.d.   Archaeological Investigations at Permuda Island, 31 On 196. Report on file
          at Archaeology Branch, North Carolina Division of Archives and History,
          Department of Cultural Resources, Raleigh.
Omwake, G., and T. D. Stewart
  1963.   (editors). The Townsend Site near Lewes, Delaware. Arcl 15(1):1–72.
O'Neill, Brian
  1980.   The Kansas Petroglyph Survey. Report on file at the Historic Preservation
          Department, Kansas State Historical Society, Topeka.
Opperman, F. A.
  1980.   *A Study of the Prehistoric Ceramics from Maycocks Point, Prince George
          County, Virginia*. Senior thesis, College of William and Mary, Williamsburg,
          Virginia.
  1985.   *Middle Woodland Subsistence Practices at Maycocks' Point (44PG40):
          A Qualitative and Quantitative Analysis*. MA thesis, University of Tennessee,
          Knoxville.
Orr, K. G.
  1946.   The Archaeological Situation at Spiro, Oklahoma: A Preliminary Report.
          AAn 11(4):228–25.
Orr, P. C.
  1952.   Excavations in Moaning Cave. SBMB, No. 1.
  1958.   *Prehistory of Santa Rose Island*. Santa Barbara Museum of Natural His-
          tory. Santa Barbara, California.
  1962.   The Arlington Spring Site, Santa Rosa Island, California. AAn 27:417–
          419.
Ortiz, Alfonso
  1969.   *The Tewa World: Space, Time, Being, and Becoming in a Pueblo Society*.
          University of Chicago Press. Chicago.
Ossenberg, M. S.
  1974.   Origins and Relationships of Woodland Peoples: The Evidence of Cranial
          Morphology. In *Aspects of Upper and Great Lakes Anthropology: Papers
          in Honor of Lloyd A. Wilford*, edited by Elden Johnson, pp. 15–39. MPS,
          No. 11.

Otto, M. P.
  1979.   Hopewell Antecedents in the Adena Heartland. In *Hopewell Archaeology: The Chillicothe Conference*, edited by D. B. Brose and N'omi Greber, pp. 9–14. Kent State University Press. Kent, Ohio.

Over, W. H., and E. E. Meleen
  1941.   A Report on the Investigation of the Brandon Village Site and the Split Rock Creek Mounds. USDMAC, No. 3.

Overstreet, D. F.
  1978.   Oneota Settlement Patterns in Eastern Wisconsin—Some Considerations of Time and Space. In *Mississippian Settlement Patterns*, edited by B. D. Smith. Academic Press. New York.
  1980.   The Convent Knoll Site (47 Wk 327): A Red Ocher Cemetery in Waukesha County, Wisconsin. WiA 61 (1):34–90.
  1981.   Investigations at the Pipe Site (47 Fd 10) and Some Perspectives on Eastern Wisconsin Oneota Prehistory. WiA 62(4):365–525.
  n.d.a. Fieldnotes, Hixton Rockshelter Excavation and Survey. On file at Great Lakes Archaeological Research Center, Inc., Milwaukee, Wisconsin.
  n.d.b. Late PaleoIndian Tool Kits in the Upper Great Lakes. Manuscript on file at Great Lakes Archaeological Research Center, Inc. Milwaukee, Wisconsin.
  n.d.c. Preliminary Reconnaissance—Archaeological and Historic Resources of the Horicon National Wildlife Refuge. Report on file at the U.S. Fish and Wildlife Service, St. Paul, Minnesota.

Ozker, Doreen
  1982.   An Early Woodland Community at the Schultz Site 20SA2 in the Saginaw Valley and the Nature of the Early Woodland Adaptation in the Great Lakes Region. UMMAAP, No. 70.

Pace, R. E., and G. A. Apfelstadt
  1980.   *Allison-Lamotte Culture of the Daugherty-Monroe Site, Sullivan County, Indiana.* Indiana State University. Terre Haute.

Pailes, R. A.
  1972.   An Archaeological Reconnaisance of Southern Sonora and Reconsideration of the Rio Sonora Culture. Phd dissertation, Southern Illinois University, Carbondale.
  1976.   Recientes Investigaciones Arqueologicas in el Sur de Sonora. In *Sonora: Antropologia del Desierto; Primera Reunion de Antropologia e Historia del Noroeste*, edited by Beatriz Braniff C. and R. S. Felger. CC, No. 27.
  1978.   The Rio Sonora Culture in Prehistoric Trade Systems. In *Across the Chichimec Sea: Papers in Honor of J. Charles Kelley*, edited by C. L. Riley and B. C. Hedrick, pp. 134–143. Southern Illinois University Press. Carbondale.
  1980.   The Upper Rio Sonora Valley in Prehistoric Trade. TIAS 72(4).
  1984.   Agricultural Development and Trade in the Rio Sonora. In *Prehistoric Agricultural Strategies in the Southwest*, edited by S. K. Fish and P. R. Fish. ASUAP, No. 33.

Painter, Floyd
  1967.   Geometrically Incised Decorations on Great Neck Ceramics: The Long Creek Midden. Part 3. TC (5)4:94–110.

1979.   The Ancient Indian Town of Chesopeake on the Peninsula of Great Neck. TC (17)4, 5:65–75.

Palmer, H. A.
1954.   A Review of the Interstate Park, Wisconsin Bison Find. PrIAS 61:313–319.

Palmer, H. A., and J. B. Stoltman
1976.   The Boas Mastodon: A Possible Association of Man and Mastodon in Wisconsin. MJA 1:163–177.

Papworth, M. L.
1967.   *Cultural Tradition in the Lake Forest Region During the Late High-Water Stages of the Post Glacial Great Lakes.* PhD dissertation, University of Michigan, Ann Arbor.

Parks, S. G.
n.d.   Test Excavations at 14GE41: A Schultz Focus Habitation. Report on file at the U.S. Army Corps of Engineers, Military Planning Branch, Kansas City, Missouri.

Parson, E. C.
1925.   The Pueblo of Jemez. PPASE, No. 5.

Pattison, N. B.
1968.   *Nogales Cliff House: A Largo-Gallina Site.* MA thesis, University of New Mexico, Albuquerque.

Patton, W. W., Jr., and T. P. Miller
1970.   A Possible Bedrock Source for Obsidian Found in Archaeological Sites in Northwestern Alaska. S 169:760–761.

Payen, L. A., and R. E. Taylor
1976.   Man and Pleistocene Fauna at Potter Creek Cave, California. JCA 3(1):51–58.

Peacock, C. K.
1954.   *Duck River Cache: Tennessee's Greatest Archaeological Find.* J. B. Graham. Chattanooga, Tennessee.

Peacock, W. R. B.
n.d.   The Telep Site: A Late Autumn Fish Camp of the Locarno Beach Culture Type. Report on file at Heritage Conservation Branch, Province of British Columbia, Victoria, British Columbia.

Pearce, J. E., and A. T. Jackson
1933.   A Prehistoric Rock Shelter in Val Verde County, Texas. APUT 1(3); BRSSS, No. 6; UTB, No. 3327.

Peck, D. W.
1980.   Test Excavations at the Nolands Ferry Site, Frederick County, Maryland. MaA 16(1):2–18.

Peck, D. W., and Tyler Bastian
1977.   Text Excavations at the Devilbliss Site, Frederick County, Maryland. MaA 13(2):1–10.

Peck, F. R.
1956.   *An Archaeological Reconnaisance of the East Verde River in Central Arizona.* MA thesis, University of Arizona, Tucson.

Peck, S. L.
1955.   An Archaeological Report on the Excavation of a Prehistoric Site at Zuma Creek, Los Angeles County, California. ASASC, No. 2.

Peckham, Stewart
  1954. A Pueblo I Site near San Felipe Pueblo, New Mexico. HSA 1:41–51.
  1958. Hillside Pueblo: Early Masonry Architecture in the Reserve Area, New
          Mexico. EP 65(3):81–94.
  1963. Two Rosa Phase Sites near Dulce, New Mexico. HSA 4:92–115.
  1979. When Is a Rio Grande Kiva? PASNM 4:55–86.
  1981. The Palisade Ruin: A Coalition Period Pueblo near Abiquiu Dam. PASNM
          6:113–147.
Peckham, Stewart, and E. K. Reed
  1957. Three Pithouse Sites near Albuquerque, New Mexico. HSA 3:39–70.
  1963. Three Sites near Ranchos de Taos, New Mexico. HSA 4:1–28.
Peckham, Stewart, and J. P. Wilson
  n.d.   An Archaeological Survey of Chuska Valley and the Chaco Plateau. Report
          on file at the Museum of New Mexico, Santa Fe.
Peckham, Stewart, Fred Wendorf, and E. N. Ferdon, Jr.
  1956. Excavations near Apache Creek, New Mexico. HSA 2(8):17–86.
Pendergast, J. F., and B. G. Trigger
  1972. Hochelaga and the Dawson Site. In *Cartier's Hochelaga: History and
          Ethnohistory*, edited by J. F. Pendergast and B. G. Trigger, pp. 1–197.
          McGill-Queen's University Press. Montreal, Quebec.
Pepper, G. H.
  1905. Ceremonial Objects and Ornaments from Pueblo Bonito, New Mexico.
          AA 7:183–197.
  1906. Human Effigy Vases from Chaco Canyon, New Mexico. In *Boas Anni-
          versary Volume*, edited by Berthold Laufer, pp. 320–334. Steichert and Com-
          pany. New York.
  1909. The Exploration of a Burial Room in Pueblo Bonito, New Mexico. In
          Anthropoligical Essays: Putnam Anniversary Volume, pp. 196–252. G. E.
          Heckert and Co. New York.
  1920. Pueblo Bonito. APAMNH, No. 27.
Perino, G. H.
  1967. The Cherry Valley Mounds and Banks Mound 3. CSASM, No. 1.
  1968. The Pete Klunk Mound Group, Calhoun County, Illinois: The Archaic
          and Hopewell Occupations (with an appendix on the Gibson Mound Group).
          In *Hopewell and Woodland Site Archaeology*, edited by J. A. Brown, pp. 9–
          124. IASB, No. 6.
  1973a. The Late Woodland Component at the Pete Klunk Site, Calhoun County,
          Illinois. In *Late Woodland Site Archaeology in Illinois I: Investigations in
          South-Central Illinois*, edited by J. A. Brown, pp. 58–89. IASB, No. 9.
  1973b. Gibson Mound 7. In *Late Woodland Site Archaeology in Illinois I:
          Investigations in South-Central Illinois*, edited by J. A. Brown, pp. 211–213.
          IASB, No. 9.
  1983. *Archaeological Research at the Bob Williams Site, Red River County,
          Texas*. Potsherd Press, Museum of the Red River. Idabel, Oklahoma.
Perlman, S. M.
  1983. An Archaeological Excavation at the Falls of the James River: The Maury
          Street Site. ASVQB (38)2:108–123.

Peske, G. R.
    1963.   Argillite of Michigan: A Preliminary Projectile Point Classification and Temporal Placement from Surface Materials. PMAS 48:557–566.
Peters, G. R.
    1978.   Archaeological Survey of Three Proposed Construction Areas and Evaluation of the Horicon Site (47 Do 131) in the Horicon National Wildlife Refuge. RI, No. 44.
Peters, G. R., H. O. Hunn, K. A. Motivans, and D. W. A. Okstad
    n.d.   River Point Site. In *Cultural Resource Management in the Superior National Forest: 1982 Annual Report.* Report on file at Minnesota Historic Society, Fort Snelling.
Peterson, Drexel
    1971.   *Time and Settlement in the Archaeology of Groton Plantation, South Carolina.* PhD dissertation, Harvard University, Cambridge, Massachusetts.
Peterson, L. D., and W. J. Yourd
    n.d.   The Minnesota Trunk Highway Archaeological Reconnaissance Survey: Annual Report 1983. Report on file at the Minnesota Historical Society, Fort Snelling.
Pettigrew, R. M.
    1981.   A Prehistoric Culture Sequence in the Portland Basin of the Lower Columbia Valley. UOAP, No. 22.
Phelps, D. S.
    1968.   Thom's Creek Ceramics in the Central Savannah River Locality. FA 21(1).
    1983.   Archaeology of the North Carolina Coast and Coastal Plain: Problems and Hypotheses. In *The Prehistory of North Carolina: An Archaeological Symposium,* edited by M. A. Mathis and J. J. Crow, pp. 1–51. North Carolina Division of Archives and History, Department of Cultural Resources. Raleigh.
Phenice, T. H.
    1969.   An Analysis of the Human Skeletal Material from Burial Mounds in North Central Kansas. UKPA, No. 1.
Phillips, D. A., Jr., and D. J. Seymour
    1982.   An Archaeological Survey of the Galisteo Dam and Reservoir Area, Santa Fe County, New Mexico. New World Research, Inc. Santa Fe.
Phillips, Philip
    1970.   Archaeological Survey in the Lower Yazoo Basin, Mississippi, 1949–1953. PPM, No. 60.
    1973.   *The Archaeological Reports of Frederic Ward Putnam: Selected from the Annual Reports of the Peabody Museum of Archaeology and Ethnology, Harvard University 1875–1903.* AMS Press, Inc. New York.
Phillips, Philip, and J. A. Brown
    1975–1982.   *Pre-Columbian Shell Engravings from Craig Mound at Spiro, Oklahoma,* 6 vols. Peabody Museum, Harvard University. Cambridge, Massachusetts.
    1983.   (editors). *Archaic Hunters and Gatherers in the American Midwest.* Academic Press. New York.
Phillips, Philip, J. A. Ford, and J. B. Griffin
    1951.   Archaeological Survey in the Lower Mississippi Alluvial Valley, 1940–1947. PPM, No. 25.

Pilles, P. J., Jr.
  1976. Sinagua and Salado Similarities as Seen from the Verde Valley. K 42(1):113–124.
  1978. The Field House and Sinagua Demography. In *Limited Activity and Occupation Sites: A Collection of Conference Papers*, edited by A. E. Ward. CASC 1:119–133.
  1979. Sunset Crater and the Sinagua: A New Interpretation. In *Volcanic Activity and Human Ecology*, edited by P. D. Sheets and D. K. Grayson, pp. 459–485. Academic Press. New York.

Pippin, L. C.
  1979. *The Prehistory and Paleoecology of Guadalupe Ruin, Sandoval County, New Mexico*. Phd dissertation, Washington State University, Pullman.

Plog, F. T.
  1979a. Prehistory: Western Anasazi. In *Handbook of North American Indians: Southwest*, edited by W. C. Sturtevant and A. A. Ortiz, Vol. 9:108–120. Smithsonian Institution. Washington, D.C.
  1979b. Alternative Models of Prehistoric Change. In *Transformations, Mathematical Approaches to Culture Change*, edited by Colin Renfrew and K. L. Cooke, pp. 221–236. Academic Press. New York.
  1980. Explaining Culture Change in the Hohokam Preclassic. In *Current Issues in Hohokam Prehistory*, edited by D. E. Doyel and F. T. Plog, pp. 4–22. ASUAP, No. 23.
  1983. Political and Economic Alliances on the Colorado Plateaus, A.D. 400–1450. In *Advances in World Archaeology*, Vol. 2, edited by Fred Wendorf and A. Close, pp. 289–330. Academic Press. New York.

Plog, F. T., J. N. Hill, and D. W. Read
  1976. Chevelon Archaeological Research Project. *Monograph II, Archaeological Survey*. Department of Anthropology, University of California, Los Angeles.

Plumet, Patrick
  1979. Thuleen ete Dorsetiens dans L'Ungava (Nouveau-Quebec). In *Thule Eskimo Culture: An Anthropological Retrospective*, edited by A. P. McCartney. NMMMS 88:110–121.

Pohorecky, Z. S.
  1976. Archaeology of the South Coast Ranges of California. CUCARF 34:1–235.

Pokotylo, D. L.
  1978. Lithic Technology and Settlement Patterns in Upper Hat Creek Valley, B.C. PhD dissertation, University of British Columbia, Vancouver.

Pokotylo, D. L., and P. D. Froese
  1983. Archaeological Evidence for Prehistoric Root Gathering in the Southern Interior Plateau of British Columbia: A Case Study from Upper Hat Creek Valley. CJA 7:127–158.

Polhemus, R. R.
  1985. (editor) The Toqua Site—40MR6: A Late Mississippian Dallas Phase Town. RIDAUT, No. 41.

Pond, A. W.
  1937. Wisconsin Joins Ranks of Oldest Inhabited Areas in America. WiA 17(3):51–54.

Pond, G. G.
   1966.   A Painted Kiva near Winslow, Arizona. AAn 31(4):555–558.
Poore, A. V.
   1981.   Survey and Excavations at Pueblo Canyon Cliffs, Los Alamos, New Mexico. Art 19(2):27–54.
Porter, J. W.
   1961.   Hixton Silicified Sandstone: A Unique Lithic Material Used by Prehistoric Cultures. WiA 42(3):78–85.
   1974.   *Cahokia Archaeology as Viewed from the Mitchell Site: A Satellite Community at* A.D. *1150–1200.* PhD dissertation, University of Wisconsin, Madison.
Potter, S. R.
   1982.   *An Analysis of Chicacoan Settlement Patterns.* PhD dissertation, University of North Carolina, Chapel Hill.
   1984.   A New Look at the Accokeek Creek Complex. In *The Prehistoric People of Accokeek Creek* edited by R. L. Stephenson. Alice Ferguson Foundation. Accokeek, Maryland.
Pousson, J. F.
   1983.   Archeological Excavations at the Moore Village Site, Chesapeake and Ohio Canal National Historical Park, Allegany County, Maryland. National Park Service. Washington, D.C.
Powell, Shirley, and G. J. Gumerman
   1987.   *The People of the Mesa: The Archaeology of Black Mesa, Arizona.* Southern Illinois University Press. Carbondale and Edwardsville.
Powers, R. P., W. B. Gillespie, and S. H. Lekson
   1983.   *The Outlier Survey.* U.S. Department of the Interior. Albuquerque, New Mexico.
Powers, W. R., and T. D. Hamilton
   1978.   Dry Creek: A Late Pleistocene Human Occupation in Central Alaska. In *Early Man in America,* edited by A. L. Bryan, pp. 72–77. Archaeological Researches International. Edmonton, Alberta.
Powers, W. R., R. D. Guthrie, and J. F. Hoffecker
   n.d.   Dry Creek: Archaeology and Paleoecology of a Late Pleistocene Alaska Hunting Camp. Report on file at the University of Alaska, Fairbanks.
Prahl, E. J.
   1966.   The Muskegon River Survey: 1965–1966. MiA 12(4):183–212.
   1970.   *The Middle Woodland Period of the Lower Muskegon Valley and the Northern Hopewell Frontier.* PhD dissertation, University of Michigan, Ann Arbor.
Prentice, Guy, and M. W. Mehrer
   1981.   The Lab Woofie Site (11-S-346): An Upland Mississippian Site in the American Bottom Region of Illinois. MJA 6:35–53.
Preston, N. E.
   1969.   The McCann Site. BTAS 40:167–192.
Prewitt, E. R.
   1966.   A Preliminary Report on the Devils Rockshelter Site, Val Verde County, Texas. TJS 18(2):206–224.

1974a. Upper Navasota Reservoir: An Archeological Assessment. RRTAS, No. 47.

1974b. Archeological Investigations at the Loeve-Fox Site, Williamson County, Texas. RRTAS, No. 49.

1974c. Preliminary Archeological Investigations of the Rio Grande Delta of Texas. BTAS 45:55–66.

1976. The Rogers Spring Site: 1974 Investigations. RRTAS, No. 54.

1981. Cultural Chronology in Central Texas. BTAS 52:65–89.

1982a. Archeological Investigations at the Loeve-Fox, Loeve, and Tombstone Bluff Sites in the Granger Lake District of Central Texas. In *Archaeological Investigations at the San Gabriel Reservoir Districts, Central Texas*, Vol. 4, edited by T. R. Hays. Institute of Applied Sciences, North Texas State University. Denton.

1982b. The 1982 TAS Field School, Rowe Valley, Texas. TAr 26(3):2–5.

1983a. Andice: An Early Archaic Dart Point Type. LT 10(3):1–6.

1983b. Rowe Valley Revisited: The 1983 TAS Field School. TAr 27(3):2–4.

1984. Third Time Charm: The 1984 TAS Field School at Rowe Valley (41WM437). TAr 28(3):5–6.

1985. From Circleville to Toyah: Comments on Central Texas Chronology. BTAS 54:201–238.

n.d. Field notes, Bayou Loco. On file at the Texas Archeological Research Laboratory, The University of Texas, Austin.

Price, T. D., and J. A. Brown

1985. (editors) *Prehistoric Hunters-Gatherers: The Emergence of Cultural Complexity*. Academic Press. New York.

Prufer, O. H.

1964. The Hopewell Complex of Ohio. In *Hopewellian Studies*, edited by J. R. Caldwell and Robert Hall, pp. 35–84. SP, No. 12.

1968. Ohio Hopewell Ceramics: An Analysis of the Extant Collections. UM-MAAP, No. 33.

1975. Chesser Cave: A Late Woodland Phase Site in Southeastern Ohio. In *Studies in Ohio Archaeology*, revised edition, edited by O. H. Prufer and D. H. McKenzie, pp. 1–62. Kent State University Press. Kent, Ohio.

Prufer, O. H., and R. S. Baby

1963. *Paleo-Indians of Ohio*. Ohio Historical Society. Columbus.

Prufer, O. H., and O. C. Shane III

1970. *Blain Village and the Fort Ancient Tradition in Ohio*. Kent State University Press. Kent, Ohio.

Prufer, O.H., D.H. McKenzie, O. Pi-Sunyer, H. C. Cutler, R. A. Yarnell, P. W. Parmalee, and D. H. Stansbery

1965. The McGraw Site: A Study in Hopewellian Dynamics. SPu (n.s.) 4(1).

Purrington, B. L.

1971. *The Prehistory of Delaware County, Oklahoma: Cultural Continuity and Change on the Western Ozark Periphery*. University Microfilms. Ann Arbor, Michigan.

Putnam, F. W.

1882. Notes on the Copper Objects from North America and South America, Contained in the Collections of the Peabody Museum. PMR 3(2):83–148.

1885. Exploration of the Harness Mounds in the Scioto Valley, Ohio. PMR 3(4,5):401–418.

1886. The Marriott Mound, No. 1, and Its Contents. PMR 3(5,6):449–466.

1890. The Serpent Mound of Ohio. CM 39:871–888.

1906. Evidence of the Work of Man on Objects from Quaternary Caves in California. AA 8:229–235.

Quimby, G. I.

1941a. The Goodall Focus: An Analysis of Ten Hopewellian Components in Michigan and Indiana. PRS 2(2):63–161.

1941b. Hopewellian Pottery Types in Michigan. PMAS 26:489–495.

1943. The Ceramic Sequence within the Goodall Focus. PMAS 28:543–548.

1944. Some New Data on the Good all Focus. PMAS 29:419–423.

1951. The Medora Site, West Baton Rouge Parish, Louisiana. FMNHAS 24(2).

1952. The Archaeology of the Upper Great Lakes Area. In *Archaeology of Eastern United States*, edited by J. B. Griffin, pp. 99–107. University of Chicago Press. Chicago.

1957. The Old Copper Culture and the Keweenaw Waterway. F:A 36(8):189–201.

1960. *Indian Life in the Upper Great Lakes*. University of Chicago Press. Chicago.

1966a. The Dumaw Creek Site, a Seventeenth Century Prehistoric Indian Village and Cemetery in Oceana County, Michigan. F 56(1):1–91.

1966b. *Indian Culture and European Trade Goods*. University of Wisconsin Press. Madison.

Quimby, G. I., and A. C. Spaulding

1957. The Old Copper Culture and the Keweenaw Waterway. F:A 36(8):189–201.

Ragir, S. R.

1972. The Early Horizon in Central California Prehistory. CUCARF, No. 15.

Rainey, F. G.

1939. Archaeology in Central Alaska. APAMNH 36(4):351–405.

1941. The Okvik Site on the Punuk Islands. APAMNH 37(4).

1971. Excavations at Point Hope. In *McCaleb Module B*. Addison-Wesley Modular Publications. Reading, Massachusetts.

Rajnovich, Grace

1984. A Study of Possible Prehistoric Wild Rice Gathering on Lake of the Woods, Ontario. NAA 5(3):197–215.

Rathbun, T. A.

1984a. Current Research—University of South Carolina. CN 5(3):4.

1984b. Current Research—University of South Carolina. CN 5(4):3–4.

1985. Current Research—University of South Carolina. CN 6(1):7.

Rausch, Robert

1951. Notes on the Nunamiut Eskimo and Mammals of the Anaktuvuk Pass Region, Brooks Range, Alaska. Arc 4(3):146–195.

Ray, C. N.

1938. The Clear Fork Culture Complex. BTAPS 10:193–207.

1948. The Facts Concerning the Clear Fork Culture. AAn 13:320–322.

Ray, V. F.
1939. Cultural Relations in the Plateau of North America. PFWH, No. 3.
Rector, C. H., J. D. Swenson, and P. J. Wilke
1983. *Archaeological Studies at Oro Grande, Mojave Desert, California*. San Bernardino County Museum Association. Redlands, California.
Redman, C. L., and J. W. Hohmann
1986. Small Site Variability in the Payson Region: The Flex Land Exchange. AFS, No. 11.
Reed, E. K.
1937. Excavation of Room 7, Wupatki. SMSR, No. 13.
1942. Kwaika'a in the Historic Period. AAn 8(1):119–120.
1946. The Distinctive Features and Distribution of San Juan Anasazi Culture. SJA 2:295–305.
1948. The Western Pueblo Archaeological Complex. EP 55(1):9–15.
1950. East-central Arizona in Relation to the Western Pueblos. SJA 6:120–138.
1956. Types of Village-plan Layouts in the Southwest. *In Prehistoric Settlement Patterns in the New World*, edited by G. R. Willey, pp. 11–17. VFPA, No. 23.
1958. Excavations in Mancos Canyon, Colorado. UUAP, No. 35.
1967. An Unusual Human Skull from near Lovelock, Nevada. UUAP, 89:63–69.
n.d. Special Report on Preliminary Study of Pottery of Room 7, Wupatka Peublo. Manuscript on file at National Park Service, Southwestern Region. Sante Fe, New Mexico.
Reed, N. A., J. W. Bennett, and J. W. Porter
1968. Solid Core Drilling of Monks Mound: Technique and Findings. AAn 33(2):137–148.
Reeves, B. O. K.
1983. Culture Change in the Northern Plains, 1000 B.C.–A.D. 1000. ASAOP, No. 20.
Reeves, Dache
1936. A Newly Discovered Extension of the Newark Works. OAHSQ 45:187–193.
Regensburg, R. A.
1970. The Savitch Farm Site: A Preliminary Report. BMAS 32(1–2):20–23
Reher, C. A.
1977. *Settlement and Subsistence along the Lower Chaco River: The CGP Survey*. University of New Mexico Press. Albuquerque.
Reid, J. J.
1965. A Comparative Statement of Ceramics from the Hollywood and Town Creek Mounds. SIS 17:13–25.
1967. *Pee Dee Pottery from the Mound at Town Creek*. MA thesis, University of North Carolina, Chapel Hill.
1974. Behavioral Archaeology at the Grasshopper Ruin. K 40(1–2).
Reid, J. J., and S. M. Whittlesey
1982. Households at Grasshopper Pueblo. ABS 25(6):687–703.
Reid, Kenneth
1984a. Nebo Hill and Late Archaic Prehistory on the Southern Prairie Peninsula. UKPA, No. 15.

1984b. Fire and Ice: New Evidence for the Production and Preservation of Fiber-tempered Pottery in the Middle Latitude Lowlands. AA 49(1):55–76.

Reinhart, T. R.
1967a. The Alameda Phase: An Early Basketmaker III Culture in the Middle Rio Grande Valley, New Mexico. SL 33(1):24–32.
1967b. The Rio Rancho Phase: A Preliminary Report on Early Basketmaker Culture in the Middle Rio Grande Valley, New Mexico. AAn 32(4):458–470.

Reiter, Paul
1938. The Jemez Pueblo of Unshagi, New Mexico, 2 vols. UNMAS 3(3).

Reiter, Paul, W. T. Mulloy, and E. H. Blumenthal, Jr.
1940. Preliminary Report of the Jemez Excavations at Nanishagi. UNMAS 3(3).

Renaud, E. B.
1942. Reconnaissance Work in the Upper Rio Grande Valley, Colorado and New Mexico. ASUD, No. 6.

Reyman, J. E.
1978. Pochteca Burials at Anasazi Sites? In *Across the Chichimec Sea: Papers in Honor of J. Charles Kelley,* edited by C. L. Riley and B. C. Hedrick, pp. 242–259. Southern Illinois University Press. Carbondale.

Reynolds, E. R.
1883. On the Aboriginal Shell-Heaps at Pope's Creek, Maryland. Abstracts of Transactions of the Anthropological Society of Washington, D.C. SMC XXV.

Reynolds, J. D
1979. The Grasshopper Falls Phase of the Plains Woodland. ASKSHS, No. 7.
1981. The Grasshopper Falls Phase: A Newly Defined Plains Woodland Cul-tural-Historical Integration Phase in the Central Plains. MA 42:85–95.

Rice, D. G.
1972. The Windust Phase in Lower Snake River Prehistory. RIWSU, No. 50.

Rice, H. S.
1965. *The Culture Sequence at Windust Caves.* MS thesis, Washington State University, Pullman.

Richards, D. D.
1956. Petroglyphs of Kansas and Colorado. KAAN 1(9).Riddell, F. A.

Riddell, F. A.
1951. The Archaeology of a Paiute Village Site in Owens Valley. UCASR, 12:14–28.
1960. The Archaeology of the Karlo Site (Las–7), California. UCASR, No. 53.

Riddell, F. A., and W. H. Olsen
1969. An Early Man Site in the San Joaquin Valley. AAn 34(2):121–130.

Rinaldo, J. B.
1959. Foote Canyon Pueblo, Western New Mexico. F:A 49(2).

Ritche, W. A.
1932. The Lamoka Lake Site: The Type Station of the Archaic Algonkin Period in New York. RT 7(4).
1945. An Early Site in Cayuga County, New York. RRRM 7:8.
1953. A Probable Paleo-Indian Site in Vermont. AAn 18(3):249–258.
1961. A Typology and Nomenclature for New York State Projectile Points. NYSMSB 384:42–53.

1965.   *The Archaeology of New York State*. Natural History Press. Garden City, New York.

1969.   *The Archaeology of New York State*. (revised edition). American Museum of Natural History. New York.

1980.   *The Archaeology of New York State*. (revised edition). Harbor Hill Books. Harrison, New York.

Ritter, E. W., B. W. Hatoff, and L. A. Payen

1976.   Chronology of the Farmington Complex. AAn 41(3):334–341.

Ritzenthaler, R. E.

1946.   The Osceola Site: An "Old Copper" Site near Potosi, Wisconsin. WiA (n.s.) 27(3):53–70.

1950.   Wisconsin Petroglyphs and Pictographs. WiA 31(4):83–125.

1953.   The Potawatomi Indians of Wisconsin. BPMCM 19(3):99–174.

1957a. The Osceola Site: An "Old Copper" Site near Potosi, Wisconsin. WiA 38(4):186–203.

1957b. The Old Copper Culture of Wisconsin. WiA 38(4):183–332.

1964.   The Riddle of the Spencer Lake Horse Skull. WiA 31(4):115–123.

1967.   A Guide to Wisconsin Indian Projectile Point Types. Milwaukee Public Museum. Milwaukee.

Ritzenthaler, R. E., and G. I. Quimby

1962.   The Red Ocher Culture of the Upper Great Lakes and Adjacent States. F:A 36(11):243–275.

Ritzenthaler, R. E., and W. L. Wittry

1957.   The Oconto Site—An Old Copper Manifestation. WiA 38(4):222–243.

Roberts, F. H. H., Jr.

1922.   Report on the Work of the 1922 Season in the Piedra Parada Archaeological Field. UDB 23(9).

1925.   Report on Archaeological Reconnaissance in Southwestern Colorado in the Summer of 1923. CoM 2(2):3–80.

1929a. Certain Early Pueblo Villages in Southwestern Colorado. In *Explorations and Field Work of the Smithsonian Institution in 1928*, pp. 161–168. Smithsonian Institution.

1929b. Shabik'eshchee Village: A Late Basket Maker Site in the Chaco Canyon, New Mexico. BAEB, No. 92.

1930.   Early Pueblo Ruins in the Piedra District, Southwestern Colorado. BAEB, No. 96.

1931.   The Ruins of Kiatuthlanna, Eastern Arizona. BAEB, No. 100.

1932.   The Village of the Great Kivas on the Zuni Reservation, New Mexico BAEB, No. 111.

1935a. A Folsom Camp Site and Workshop. In *Explorations and Field Work of the Smithsonian Institution in 1934*, pp. 61–64. Smithsonian Institution. Washington, D.C.

1935b. A Survey of Southwestern Archaeology. AA 37(1):1–35.

1935c. A Folsom Complex: Preliminary Report on the Investigations at the Lindenmeier Site in Northern Colorado. SMC 94(4).

1939a. The Folsom Problem in American Archeology. In *Smithsonian Institution Annual Report for 1938*, pp. 531–546. Smithsonian Institution, Washington, D.C.

1936b.   Archeological Remains in the Whitewater District, Eastern Arizona. Part I: House Types. BAEB, No. 121.

1940.   Developments in the Problem of the North American Paleo-Indian. SMC 100:51–116.

1943.   A New Site. AAn 8:300.

1945.   The New World Paleo-Indian. In *Annual Report of the Smithsonian Institution for 1944*, pp. 403:433. Smithsonian Institution. Washington, D.C.

1961.   The River Basin Salvage Program after 15 Years. In *Annual Report of the Smithsonian Institution for 1960*, pp. 523–549. Smithsonian Institution. Washington, D.C.

Roberts, R. L.

1978.   *The Archaeology of the Kansas Monument Site*. MA thesis, University of Kansas, Lawrence.

Robertson, J. A.

1986.   Fort Ancient and the Persistence of Blade Core Industries. PnA 56(1–2):29–36.

Robinson, H. H.

1913.   The San Franciscan Volcanic Field, Arizona. USGSPP, No. 76.

Robinson, W. J., J. W. Hannah, and B. G. Harrill

1972.   *Tree-Ring Dates from New Mexico I.O.U.: Central Rio Grande Area.* Laboratory of Tree-Ring Research, University of Arizona. Tucson.

Rodgers, C. L.

1968.   The Habron Site, Warren County, Virginia. ASVQB (23)2:90–98.

Rogers, D. B.

1929.   *Prehistoric Man of the Santa Barbara Coast*. Santa Barbara Museum of Natural History. Santa Barbara, California.

Rogers, J. D.

1982.   Spiro Archaeology: 1980 Research. SOP, No. 9.

Rogers, M. B.

1972.   The 46th Street Site and the Occurrences of Allegan Ware in Southwestern Michigan. MiA 18(2):47–108.

Rogers, M. J.

1929.   The Stone Art of the San Dieguito Plateau. AA 31(3):454–467.

1939.   Early Lithic Industries of the Lower Basin of the Colorado River and Adjacent Desert Areas. SDMP, No. 3.

1945.   An Outline of Yuman Prehistory. SJA 1(2).

Rogers, M. J., H. M. Wormington, E. L. Davis, and C. W. Brott

1966.   *Ancient Hunters of the Far West*. Union Tribune Publishing Co. San Diego, California.

Rogers, R. A., and L. D. Martin

1984.   The 12 Mile Creek Site: A Reinvestigation. AAn 49(4):757–764.

Rogers, S. L.

1974.   An Ancient Human Skeleton Found at Del Mar, California. SDMP, No. 7.

Rohrbaugh, C. L.

1982.   *Spiro and Fort Coffee Phases: Changing Cultural Complexes of the Caddoan Area*. PhD dissertation, University of Wisconsin, Madison.

1984. Arkansas Valley Caddoan: Fort Coffee and Neosho Foci. In *Prehistory of Oklahoma*, edited by R. E. Bell. Academic Press. New York.

Rolingson, M. A.
1982. (editor) Emerging Patterns of Plum Bayou Culture: Preliminary Investigations of the Toltec Mounds Research Project. AASRS, No. 18.

Rolingson, M. A, and F. F. Schambach
1981. The Shallow Lake Site (3UN9/52) and Its Place in Regional Prehistory. AASRS, No. 12.

Roll, T. E., and Ken Deaver
1980. The Bootlegger Trail Site, A Late Prehistoric Spring Bison Kill. IR.

Roosa, W. B.
1965. Some Great Lakes Fluted Point Types. MiA 11(3–4):89–102.
1966. The Warner School Site. MiA 12(1):25–34.

Root, M. J.
1981. *The Milbourn Site: Late Archaic Settlement in the Southern Flint Hills of Kansas*. MA thesis, University of Kansas, Lawrence.

Ross, R. E.
1965. The Archeology of Eagle Cave. PTASP, No. 7.

Rouse, Irving
1958. The Inference of Migrations from Anthropological Evidence. In *Migrations in New World Culture History*, edited by R. H. Thompson. UASSB, No. 27.

Rousseau, M. K., and Thomas Richards
1986. A Culture-Historical Sequence for the South Thompson River—Western Shuswap Lakes Region of British Columbia: The Last 4000 Years. NARN 19(1):1–32.

Rowe, Chandler
1956. The Effigy Mound Culture of Wisconsin. MPMPA, No. 3.

Rowley, G. W.
1940. The Dorset Culture of the Eastern Arctic. AA 42:490–499.

Rowlison, D. D.
n.d.a. A Report of Archeological Investigations at the Big Hill Lake Project, Southeastern Kansas. Report on file at the Kansas State Historical Society, Topeka.
n.d.b. The 1978 Archeological Investigations at Big Hill Lake, Kansas. Report on file at the Kansas State Historical Society, Topeka.

Rozaire, C. E.
1974. Analysis of Woven Materials from Seven Caves in the Lake Winnemucca Area, Pershing County, Nevada. NSMAP, No. 16.

Ruebelmann, G. N.
1978. The Weis Rockshelter: A Problem in Southeastern Plateau Chronology. NARN 12(1):9–16.

Ruegamer, Lana
1980. *A History of the Indiana Historical Society 1830–1980*. Indiana Historical Society. Indianapolis.

Ruppe, R. J.
1955. Cherokee and Turin, Iowa: Archaeological Excavations Reveal More Knowledge about Prehistoric Man. SUISM, Nov:16–20, 30–31.

1956. Archaeological Investigations of the Mill Creek Culture of Northwestern Iowa. In *American Philosophical Society Year Book, 1955*, pp. 335–339. American Philosophical Society. Philadelphia.

Rusco, M. K.

1960. The White Rock Aspect. NB, No. 4.

Ryan, T. M.

1972a. Archeological Survey of the Columbia Zoological Park, Richland and Lexington Counties, South Carolina. SN 4:141–186.

1972b. Test Excavations at the McCollum Site, 38CS2, July 12–30, 1971. SN 4:104–110.

Sabo, Debby, and George Sabo III

1978. A Possible Thule Carving of a Viking from Baffin Island, N.W.T. CJA 2:3–42.

Sabo, George III

1981. *Thule Culture Adaptations on the South Coast of Baffin Island, N.W.T.* PhD dissertation, Michigan State University, East Lansing.

1986. Contributions to Ozark Prehistory. AASRS, No. 27.

Salzer, R. J.

1969. *The Archaeology of Northern Wisconsin.* PhD dissertation, Southern Illinois University, Carbondale.

n.d.a. The Waukesha Focus: Hopewell in Southeastern Wisconsin. Manuscript on file at Logan Museum of Anthropology, Beloit College, Beloit, Wisconsin.

n.d.b. Gotschall Rockshelter Fieldnotes. On file at Logan Museum of Anthropology, Beloit College, Beloit, Wisconsin.

Sampson, C. G.

1985. Nightfire Island: Later Holocene Lakemarsh Adaptation on the Western Edge of the Great Basin. UOAP, No. 33.

Samuels, S. R.

1983. *Spatial Patterns and Cultural Processes in Three Northwest Coast Longhouse Floor Middens from Ozette.* PhD dissertation, Washington State University, Pullman.

Sando, J. S.

1979. Jemez Pueblo. In *Handbook of North American Indians:Southwest*, Vol. 9, edited by W. C. Sturtevant and A. A. Ortiz, pp. 418–429. Smithsonian Institution. Washington, D.C.

1982. *Nee Hamish: A History of Jemez Pueblo.* University of New Mexico Press. Albuquerque.

Sanford, P. R.

1983. *An Analysis of Megascopic Plant Remains and Pollen from Dirty Shame Rockshelter, Southeastern Oregon.* PhD dissertation, University of Oregon, Eugene.

Sanger, David

1968a. The Chase Burial Site in British Columbia. NMCB 224:86–185.

1968b. Prepared Core and Blade Traditions in the Pacific Northwest. ArcA 5:92–120.

1969. Cultural Traditions in the Interior of British Columbia. Sy 2:189–200.

1970. The Archaeology of the Lochnore-Nesikep Locality, British Columbia. Sy 3 (supplement 1).

Sanger, David, R. G. MacKay, and H. W. Borns, Jr.
  1977. The Hirundo Archaeological Project: An Interdisciplinary Approach to
        Central Maine Prehistory. In *Amerinds and their Paleoenvironments in
        Northeastern North America.* ANYAS 288–457–471.
Santini, J. D.
  1974. A Preliminary Report on the Analysis of Incised Stones from Central
        Nevada. NVA 2(1):4–15.
Sassaman, K. E.
  1983. Stratigraphic Description and Interpretation of the Mulberry Mound Site,
        Kershaw County, South Carolina. SCRA, No. 1.
Sauer, Carl, and Donald Brand
  1931. Prehistoric Settlements of Sonora with Special Reference to Cerros de
        Trincheras. UCPG 5:67–148.
Sayles, E. B.
  1936. Some Southwestern Pottery Types, Series V. MP, No. 21.
  1945. The San Simon Branch: Excavations at Cave Creek and in the San Simon
        Valley. I: Material Culture. MP, No. 34.
  1983. The Cochise Cultural Sequence in Southeastern Arizona. APUAr, No. 42.
Sales. E. B. and Ernst Anters
  1941. The Cochise Culture. MP, No. 29.
Scantling, F. H.
  1939. Jackrabbit Ruin. K 5(3):9–12.
Scarry, J. F.
  1980. The Chronology of Fort Walton Development in the Upper Apalachicola
        Valley, Florida. SACB 22:38–45.
  1981. Fort Walton Culture: A Redefinition. SACB 24:18–21.
  1984. *Fort Walton Development: Mississippian Chiefdoms in the Lower South-
        east.* PhD dissertation, Case Western Reserve University, Cleveland, Ohio.
Schaafsma, Polly
  1963. Rock Art in the Navajo Reservoir District. MNMPA, No. 7.
Schaeffer, J. B.
  1958. The Alibates Flint Quarry, Texas. AAn 24(2):189–191.
Schambach, F. F.
  1970. *Pre-Caddoan Cultures in the Trans-Mississippi South: A Beginning Se-
        quence.* PhD dissertation, Harvard University, Cambridge, Massachusetts.
  1982a. An Outline of Fourche Maline Culture in Southwest Arkansas. In *Ar-
        kansas Archeology in Review,* edited by N. L. Trubowitz and M. D. Jeter.
        AASRS, 17(7).
  1982b. The Archeology of the Great Bend Region in Arkansas. In *Contributions
        to the Archeology of the Great Bend Region,* edited by F. F. Schambach and
        Frank Rackerby. AASRS 22:1–11.
Schambach, F. F., A. M. Early, E. T. Hemmings, David Kelley, and Michael Swanda
  1982. Southwest Arkansas. In *A State Plan for Conservation of Archeological
        Resources in Arkansas,* edited by H. A. Davis. AASRS, No. 21.
Schambach, F. F., and J. E. Miller
  1984. A Description and Analysis of the Ceramics. In *Cedar Grove,* edited by
        N. L. Trubowitz. AASRS, No. 23.

Schambach and Frank Rackerby.
   n.d.   The Trans-Mississippi South: The Case for a New Natural Area West of the Lower Mississippi Valley and East of the Plains. Arkansas Archaeological Survey, Southern Arkansas University, Magnolia.
Scheidegger, Edward
   1962.   The Crib Mound. CSAJ 9(1):4–14.
   1965.   Crib Mound Banner Stones. CSAJ 12(3):96–103.
   1968.   The Crib Mound Cache Blades. CSAJ 15(4):144–147.
Schellbach, Louis III
   1926.   An Unusual Burial in Mesa House Ruin, Overton, Clark County, Nevada. SMP 4:93–105.
Schiffer, M. B.
   1982.   Hohokam Chronology: An Essay on History and Method. In *Hohokam and Patayan: Prehistory of Southwestern Arizona*, pp. 299–344. Academic Press. New York.
Schledermann, Peter
   1975.   Thule Eskimo Prehistory of Cumberland Sound, Baffin Island, Canada. NMMMS, No. 38.
   1978a.   Prehistoric Demographic Trends in the Canadian High Arctic. CJA 2:43–58.
   1978b.   Preliminary Results of Archaeological Investigations in the Bache Peninsula Region, Ellesmere Island, N.W.T. Arc 31:459–474.
   1981.   Eskimo and Viking Finds in the High Arctic. NG 159:575–601.
Schmits, L. J.
   1978.   The Coffey Site: Environment and Cultural Adaptation at a Prairie Plains Archaic Site. MJASP, No. 1.
   1980a.   The Williamson Site. ASKSHS, No. 8.
   1980b.   Salvage Archeology of the John Redmond Lake, Kansas (edited by T. A. Witty, Jr). ASKSHS, No. 8.
Schmitt, Karl, Jr.
   1952.   Archaeological Chronology of the Middle Atlantic States. In *Archaeology of Eastern United States*, edited by J. B. Griffin, pp. 59–70. University of Chicago Press. Chicago.
   1965.   Patawomeke: An Historic Algonkian Site. ASVQB 20(1):1–36.
Schnell, G. S.
   1981.   A Preliminary Political Model for the Rood Phase. SACB 24:23–24.
Schnell, F. T., V. J. Knight, Jr., and G. S. Schnell
   1981.   *Cemochechabee: Archaeology of a Mississippian Ceremonial Center on the Chattahoochee River*. RBMAH, No. 3.
Schoenbeck, Ethel
   1940.   Prehistoric Aboriginal Pottery of the Peoria Region. TIAS, No. 33.
   1941.   Cultural Objects of Clear Lake Village Site. TIAS, No. 34.
   1942.   Additional Clear Lake Village Material. TIAS, No. 35.
   1943.   Some Data on Clear Lake Village Cultural Objects. TIAS, No. 36.
   1944.   More Data on Clear Lake Village. TIAS 37:45–50.
   1946.   Cord-decorated Pottery in the General Peoria Region. TIAS, No. 39.
   1947.   A Seven-Pound Copper Axe among 1946 Hopewell Discoveries. TIAS 40:32–42.

1948. Steuben Village Site, a Hopewell Village of Central Illinois. TIAS 41:19–20.

1949. More Data on Hopewell Sites in Peoria Region. TIAS 42:41–46.

Schoenwetter, James, and F. W. Eddy

1964. Alluvial and Palynological Reconstruction of Environments, Navajo Reservoir District. MNMPA, No. 13.

Scholes, F. V., and H. P. Mera

1940. Some Aspects of the Jumano Problem. CIWP, No. 523.

Scholtz, S. C.

1975. Prehistoric Plies: A Structural and Comparative Analysis of Cordage, Netting, Basketry, and Fabric from Ozark Bluff Shelters. AASRS, No. 9.

Schorsch, R. L.

1962. A Basketmaker Pit House near Albuquerque. EP 69(2):114–118.

Schreiber, J. P., and W. J. Breed

1971. Obsidian Localities in the San Francisco Volcanic Field, Arizona. P 43(3):115–119.

Schroeder, A. H.

1940. A Stratigraphic Survey of Pre-Spanish Trash Mounds of the Salt River Valley, Arizona. MA thesis, University of Arizona, Tucson.

1947. Did the Sinagua of the Verde Valley Settle in the Salt River Valley? SJA 3(3):230–246.

1949. Cultural Implications of the Ball Courts in Arizona. SJA 5(1):28–36.

1952. *A Brief Survey of the Lower Colorado River from Davis Dam to the International Border.* Bureau of Reclamation. Boulder City, Nevada.

1954. Four Prehistoric Sites near Mayer, Arizona Which Suggest a New Focus. P 26(1).

1955. Archaeology of Zion National Park. UUAP, No. 22.

1960. The Hohokam, Sinagua and Hakataya. SAAAA, No. 5.

1961a. An Archaeological Survey of the Painted Rocks Reservoir, Western Arizona. K 27:1–28.

1961b. The Archeological Excavations at Willow Beach, Arizona, 1950. UUAP, No. 50.

1961c. The Pre-Eruptive and Post-Eruptive Sinagua Patterns. P 34(2):60–66.

1963. Diffusion North out of South Central Arizona. EP 70:13–24.

1972. Rio Grande Ethnohistory. In *New Perspectives on the Pueblos.* School of American Research, University of New Mexico. Albuquerque.

1974. A Brief History of Picuris Pueblo, a Tiwa Indian Group in North Central New Mexico. ASCSA, No. 2.

1975. The Hohokam, Sinagua, and the Hakataya. IVCOP, No. 3.

1977. *Of Men and Volcanoes: The Sinagua of Northern Arizona.* Southwest Park and Monuments Association. Globe, Arizona.

1979. Prehistory: Hakataya. In *Handbook of North American Indians:Southwest*, Vol. 9, edited by W. C. Sturtevant and A. A. Ortiz, pp. 100–107. Smithsonian Institution. Washington, D.C.

1985. Aspects of Continuity, Change, and Cultural Identity in Prehistoric Arizona. In *Proceedings of the 1983 Hohokam Symposium*, Pt. 1, pp. 157–180. AASOP, No. 2.

in press. The Hakataya Concept and Origins of Its Groups. P.

Schroedl, G. F.
  1965. Unregulated Diffusion from Mexico into the Southwest Prior to A.D. 700. AAn 30(3):297–309.
  1966. Pattern Diffusion from Mexico into the Southwest after A.D. 600. AAn 31(5):683–704.
  1982. Overhill Cherokee Archaeology at Chota-Tanasee. RIDAUT, No. 38.
Schroedl, G. F., R. P. Stephen Davis, Jr., and C. C. Boyd, Jr.
  1985. Archaeological Contexts and Assemblages at Martin Farm. RIDAUT, No. 39; PATVA, No. 37.
Schuilling, W. C.
  1979. (editor) *Pleistocene Man at Calico*, 2nd ed. San Bernardino County Museum Association. Redlands, California.
Schultz, C. B.
  1943. Some Artifact Sites of Early Man in the Great Plains and Adjacent Areas. AAn 8:242–49.
Schultz, Floyd, and A. C. Spaulding
  1948. A Hopewellian Burial Site in the Lower Republican Valley, Kansas. AAn 13(4):306–313.
Schwartz, D. W., and R. W. Lang
  1973. *Archaeological Investigations at the Arroyo Hondo Site: Third Field Report—1972*. School of American Research. Sante Fe, New Mexico.
Schwartz, D. W., R. C. Chapman, and Jane Kepp
  1980. Archaeology of the Grand Canyon: Unkar Delta. GCAS, No. 2.
Schwartz, D. W., Jane Kepp, and R. C. Chapman
  1981. Archaeology of the Grand Canyon: The Walhalla Plateau. GCAS, No. 3.
Sciscenti, J. V., and H. C. Greminger
  1962. Archaeology of the Four Corners Power Projects. MNMPA, No. 5.
Sciscenti, J. V., A. E. Dittert, Jr., and B. Dickey
  1963. Excavations at the Railroad Site, LA 4103. In *Pueblo Period Sites in the Piedra River Section, Navajo Reservoir District*, assembled by A. E. Dittert, Jr., and F. W. Eddy, Ch. 4. MNMPA, No. 10.
Scurlock, J. D.
  1962. The Culpepper Site: A Late Fulton Aspect Site in Northeastern Texas. BTAS 32:285–316.
Scurry, J. D., J. W. Joseph, and Fritz Hamer
  1980. Initial Archeological Investigations at Silver Bluff Plantation, Aiken County, South Carolina. RMS, No. 168.
Sears, Elsie, and W. H. Sears
  1976. Preliminary Report on Prehistoric Corn Pollen from Fort Center, Florida. SACB 19:53–56.
Sears, W. H.
  1956. Excavations at Kolomoki, Final Report. UGSA, No. 5.
  1962. The Hopewellian Affiliations of Certain Sites on the Gulf Coast of Florida. AAn 28:5–18.
  1967. The Tierra Verde Burial Mound. FA 20:25–73.
  1971. Food Production and Village Life in Prehistoric Southeastern United States. Ar 24:93–102.

1974. Archaeological Perspectives on Prehistoric Environment in the Okeechobee Basin Savannah. In *Environments in South Florida: Present and Past*,
edited by P. J. Gleason, pp. 347–351. MGSM, No. 2.

1982. *Fort Center: An Archaeological Site in the Lake Okeechobee Basin*. University Presses of Florida. Gainesville.

Seeman, M. F.

1975. The Prehistoric Chert Quarries and Workshops of Harrison County, Indiana. IAB 1(3):47–61.

1979. The Hopewell Interaction Sphere: The Evidence for Interregional Trade
and Structural Complexity. PRS 5(2).

Seeman, M. F., and O. H. Prufer

1982. An Updated Discussion of Ohio Fluted Points. MJA 7:155–169.

1984. The Effects of Cultivation and Collecting on Ohio Fluted Point Finds: A
Cautionary Note. MJA 9:227–233.

Seeman, M. F., and Frank Soday

1980. The Russell Brown Mounds: Three Hopewell Mounds in Ross County,
Ohio. MJA 5(1):73–116.

Segall, A. L.

1981. *The Red Hill Site (44CH7): An Analysis of the Feature Fill*. Senior thesis,
College of William and Mary, Williamsburg, Virginia.

Sellards, E. H.

1938. Artifacts Associated with Fossil Elephant. GSAB 49:999–1009.

1952. *Early Man in America*. University of Texas Press. Austin.

Sellards, E. H., G. L. Evans, and G. E. Meade

1947. Fossil Bison and Associated Artifacts from Plainview, Texas. GSAB
58:927–954.

Sellars, G. E.

1877. Aboriginal Pottery of the Salt Spring. PSM 11:573–585.

Setzler, F. M., and J. D. Jennings

1941. Peachtree Mound and Village Site, Cherokee County, North Carolina.
BAEB, No. 131.

Shaeffer, J. B.

1958. The Alibates Flint Quarry, Texas. AAn 24(2):189–191.

Shafer, H. J.

1963. Test Excavations at the Youngsport Site: A Stratified Terrace Site in Bell
County, Texas. BTAS 34:57–81.

1974. Archaeology and Indians of Southeast Texas. In *Participants Handbook,
The Big Thicket* (Contemporary Science Seminar). University of Houston and
Houston Museum of Natural Science, Houston, Texas.

1975. Comments on Woodland Cultures of East Texas. BTAS 46:249–254.

1977. Art and Territoriality in the Lower Pecos Archaic. PA 19:228–230.

Shafer, H. J, and V. M. Bryant, Jr.

1977. Archaeological and Botanical Studies at Hinds Cave, Val Verde County,
Texas. ALSS, No. 1.

Shane, O. C. III

1975. The Leimbach Site: An Early Woodland Village in Erie County, Ohio. In
Studies in Ohio Archaeology, revised edition, edited by O. H. Prufer and
D. H. McKenzie, pp. 98–120. Kent State University Press. Kent, Ohio.

Shaw, Robert, and C. E. Holmes
  1982. (editors) The Norton Interaction Sphere: Selected Papers from a Symposium. ArcA 19.
Shay, C. T.
  1971. The Itasca Bison Kill Site: An Ecological Analysis. MPS, No. 6.
Sheldon, C. T.
  1974. The Mississippian-Historic Transition in Central Alabama. PhD dissertation, University of Oregon, Eugene.
Shepard, A. O.
  1942. Rio Grande Glaze Point Ware: A Study Illustrating the Place of Ceramic Technological Analysis in Archaeological Research. CAAH, No. 39.
Shetrone, H.:C.
  1920. The Culture Problem in Ohio Archaeology. AA (n.s.) 22:144–172.
  1924. Exploration of the Wright Group of Pre-historic Earthworks. OAHSQ 33:341–358.
  1925. Explorations of the Hopewell Mound; the Miese Mound. OAHSQ 34:154–168.
  1926. Explorations of the Hopewell Group of Prehistoric Earthworks. OAHSQ 35:1–227.
  1930. The Mound-Builders. Appleton-Century. New York.
Shetrone, H.:C., and Emerson Greenman
  1931. Explorations of the Seip Group of Prehistoric Earthworks. OAHSQ 40:343–509.
Shields, H. M.
  1977. Salvage Archaeology in Katmai National Monument, 1974. OPUA, No. 2.
Shiner, J. L.
  1961. The McNary Reservoir: A Study in Plateau Archaeology. RBSP, No. 23; BAEB, 1979:149–266.
Shippee, J. M.
  1948. Nebo Hill, A Lithic Complex in Western Missouri. AA 14:29–32.
  1972. Archaeological Remains in the Kansas City Area. MASRS, No. 9.
Shoemaker, E. M.
  1977. Eruption History of Sunset Crater, Arizona: Investigator's Annual Report. Report on file at Wupatka–Sunset Crater National Monument, Flagstaff, Arizona.
Shoemaker, E. M., and S. W. Kieffer
  1974. Guidebook to the Geology of Meteor Crater, Arizona. 37th Annual Meeting of the Meteoritical Society, Publication No. 17. Arizona State University Tempe.
Shutler, Richard, Jr.
  1951. Two Pueblo Ruins in the Verde Valley, Arizona. P. 24(1).
  1961. Lost City: Pueblo Grande de Nevada. NSMAP, No. 5.
  1983. (editor) Early Man in the New World. Sage Publications. Beverly Hills, California.
Shutler, Richard, Jr., and W. Y. Adams
  n.d. Tuzigoot Black-on-brown: New Type. In The Dry Creek Site: A Nonceramic Lithic Horizon and Two Small Pueblo Ruins in the Upper Verde Valley, Arizona, p. 126. Manuscript on file at Department of Anthropology, Museum of Northern Arizona, Flagstaff.

Simmons, A. H.
  1986. New Evidence for the Early Use of Cultigens in the Southwest. AAn
    51(1):73–89.
Simpson, R. D.
  1958. The Manix Lake Archaeological Survey. M 32(1):4–10.
Sinclair, J. L.
  1951. The Story of the Pueblo of Kuaua. EP 58(7):206–214.
Sinclair, W. J.
  1904. The Exploration of the Potter Creek Cave. UCPAE 2:1–27.
  1908. Recent Investigations Bearing on the Question of the Occurrence of Neo-
    cene Man in the Auriferous Gravels of the Sierra Nevada. UCPAE 7(2):107–
    131.
Skinner, S. A.
  1965. The Sedillo Site: A Pit House Village in Albuquerque. EP 72(1):5–24.
Skinner, S. A., R. K. Harris, and K. M. Anderson
  1969. (editors) Archaeological Investigations at the Sam Kaufman Site, Red
    River County, Texas. SMUCA, No. 5.
Skinner, S. A., Chester Shaw, Carol Carter, Maynard Cliff, and Carol Heathington
  1980. Archaeological Investigations at Nambe Falls, ARPRR, No. 121.
Slattery, R. G
  1946. A Prehistoric Indian Site on Selden Island, Montgomery County, Mary-
    land. AAn 36(8):262–266.
Slattery, R. G., W. A. Tidwell, and D. E. Woodward
  1966. The Montgomery Focus. ASVQB 21(2):49–51.
Smart, T. L., and R. I. Ford
  1983. Plant Remains. In *Recent Excavations at the Edwin Harness Mound,
    Liberty Earthworks, Ross County, Ohio*, edited by N'omi Greber. MJASP,
    No. 5.
Smiley, T. L.
  1952. Four Late Prehistoric Kivas at Point of Pines, Arizona. SSB, No. 21.
  1958. The Geology and Dating of Sunset Crater, Flagstaff, Arizona. In *Guide-
    book of the Black Mesa Basin, Northeastern Arizona*, pp. 186–190. New
    Mexico Geological Society, Ninth Field Conference. Albuquerque.
Smith, B. A.
  1979. The Hopewell Connection in Southwest Georgia. In *Hopewell Archae-
    ology: The Chillicothe Conference*, edited by D. S. Brose and N'omi Greber,
    pp. 181–187. Kent State University Press, Kent, Ohio.
Smith, B. D.
  1985. Mississippian Patterns of Subsistence and Settlement. In *Alabama and the
    Borderlands*, edited by R. R. Badger and L. A. Clayton. University of Ala-
    bama Press. University.
Smith, C. F, and Myrtle Smith
  1960. Projectile Point Cache. JAA 6(2):84–86.
Smith, C. S.
  1949. Archaeological Investigations in Ellsworth and Rice Counties, Kansas.
    AAn 14(4):292–300.
  1950. European Trade Material from the Kansas Monument Site. PACN 3(2).
  1960. The Temporal Relationships of Coalescent Village Sites in Fort Randall
    Reservoir, South Dakota. *Actas del XXXIII Congreso Interacional de Amer-
    icanistas* 2:111–123.

1963. Time Perspective within the Coalescent Tradition in South Dakota. AAn 28(4):489–495.

1977. The Talking Crow Site, a Multi-Component Earthlodge Village in the Big Bend Region, South Dakota. UKPA, No. 9.

Smith, C. S., and R. T. Grange, Jr.

1958. The Spain Site (39LM301), a Winter Village in Fort Randall Reservoir, South Dakota. RBSP, No. 11; BAEB, No. 169.

Smith, C. S., and A. E. Johnson

1968. The Two Teeth Site. RBSPSA, No. 8.

Smith, G. A.

1963. Split-Twig Figurines from San Bernardino County, California. M 37(3):86–90.

Smith, G. H.

1972. Like-A-Fishhook Village and Fort Berthold, Garrison Reservoir. APNPS, No. 2.

Smith, G, P.

1971. *Protohistoric Sociopolitical Organizations of the Nottoway in the Chesapeake Bay—Carolina Sounds Region.* PhD dissertation, University of Missouri, Columbia.

1984. The Hand Site, Southampton County, Virginia. ASVSP, No. 11.

Smith, H. G.

1951a. Crystal River Revisited, Revisited, Revisited. AAn 17:143–44.

1951b. The Crable Site, Fulton County, Illinois. UMMAAP, No. 7.

Smith, H. I.

1899. Archaeology of Lytton, British Columbia. PJNPE 1:129–161.

1900. Archaeology of the Thompson River Region. PJNPE 1:401–442.

1903. Shell-Heaps of the Lower Fraser. PJNPE 2:133–191.

1907. Archaeology of the Gulf of Georgia and Puget Sound. PJNPE 2:301–441.

Smith, H. I., and Gerard Fowke

1901. Cairns of British Columbia and Washington. PJNPE 2:55–75.

Smith, Watson

1952a. Excavations in Big Hawk Valley, Wupatki National Monument, Arizona. MNAB, No. 24.

1952b. Kiva Mural Decorations at Awatovi and Kwaika'a, with a Survey of Other Wall Paintings in the Pueblo Southwest. PPM, No. 37.

1971. Painted Ceramics of the Western Mound at Awatovi. PPM, No. 38.

1972. Prehistoric Kivas of Antelope Mesa. PPM, No. 39.

Snow, D. H.

1976. Archaeological Excavations at Pueblo del Encierro, LA 70, Cochiti Dam Salvage Project, Cochiti, New Mexico: Final Report of the 1964–1965 Seasons. LAN, No. 98.

Snow, D. R.

1980. *The Archaeology of New England.* Academic Press. New York.

Snyder, K. A., and A. M. Fehr

1971a. Painted Ceramics of the Western Mound at Awatovi. PPM, No. 38.

1971b. Excavations at Cochiti Dam, New Mexico, 1964–1966 Seasons, Vol. 1: LA 272, LA 9154, LA 34. LAN, No. 79.

1972. Prehistoric Kivas of Antelope Mesa. PPM 39(1).

1984. *Data Recovery Excavations at 44WR3, 44WR299, 44WR300, and 44WR301*. Thunderbird Research Corporation. Front Royal, Virginia.

Soday, F. J.
1954. The Quad Site, a Paleo-Indian Village in Northern Alabama. TA 10(1):1–20.

Soil Systems
n.d. A Long Term Management Plan for Significant Sites in the Vicinity of Winslow, Arizona. Report on file at Arizona State Land Department, Phoenix.

Solberger, J. B.
1967. A New Type of Arrow Point with Speculations as to Its Origins. TRec 23(3):12–22.

Sorrow, W. M.
1968. The Devils Mouth Site: The Third Season—1967. PTASP, No. 14.
1969. Archeological Investigations at the John Ischy Site: A Burnt Rock Midden in Williamson County, Texas. PTASP, No. 18.

Sorrow, W. M., H. J. Shafer, and R.E. Ross
1967. Excavations at Stillhouse Hollow Reservoir. PTASP, No. 11.

South, Stanley
1959. *A Study of the Prehistory of the Roanoke Rapids Basin*. MA thesis, University of North Carolina, Chapel Hill.
1960. An Archaeological Survey of Southeastern North Carolina. Manuscript on file at Research Laboratories of Anthropology, University of North Carolina, Chapel Hill.
1970. A Ceremonial Center at the Charles Towne Site. SN 2(6–7):3–5.
1971. Archaeology at the Charles Towne Site (38CH1) on Albermarle Point in South Carolina. RMS, No. 10.
1976. An Archaeological Survey of Southeastern North Carolina. USCIN, No. 8.
n.d. An Archaeological Survey of Two Islands in the White Oak River near Swansboro, North Carolina. Report on file at North Carolina Department of Archives and History. Raleigh.

Souther, J. G.
1970. Recent Volcanism and Its Influence on Early Native Cultures of Northwestern British Columbia. In *Early Man and Environments in Northwest North America*, edited by R. A. Smith and J. W. Smith, pp. 53–64. University of Calgary Archaeological Association, Calgary, Alberta.

Spaulding, A. C.
1956. The Arzberger Site, Hughes County, South Dakota. UMMAOC, No. 16.

Spector, J. D.
1975. Crabapple Point (JE93): An Historic Winnebago Indian Site in Jefferson County, Wisconsin. WiA 56(4):270–345.

Spence, M. W.
1978. A Cultural Sequence from the Sierra Madre of Durango, Mexico. In *Across the Chichimec Sea: Papers in Honor of J. Charles Kelley*, edited by C. L. Riley and B. C. Hedrick, pp. 165–189. Southern Illinois University Press. Carbondale.

Spencer, R. F., and J. D. Jennings et al.
1965. *The Native Americans*. Harper and Row. New York.

Sperry, J. E.
   1968.   The Shermer Site, 32EM10. PAM, No. 5.
Spicer, E. H.
   1936.   The King's Ruin. In *Two Pueblo Ruins in West Central Arizona*, by E. H.
           Spicer and L. P. Caywood. UASSB, No. 10.
Spoerl, P. M., and G. J. Gumerman
   1984.   Prehistoric Cultural Development in Central Arizona: Archaeology of the
           Upper New River Region. OPCAI, No. 5.
Sprague, R., and A. Signori
   1963.   Inventory of Prehistoric Southwestern Copper Bells. K 28(4).
Squier, E. G.
   1849.   Aboriginal Monuments of New York. SCK, No. 2.
Squier, E. G., and E. H. Davis
   1848.   Ancient Monuments of the Mississippi Valley. SCK, No. 1.
Squier, G. H.
   1905.   Certain Archaeological Features of Western Wisconsin. WiA (o.s.)
           4(2):25–34.
St. John, Harold
   1963.   *Flora of Southeastern Washington*. Outdoor Pictures. Escondido,
           California.
Stafford, B. D, and M. B. Sant
   1985.   (editors) The Smiling Dan Site: Structure and Function at a Middle Wood-
           land Settlement in the Illinois Valley. KACRS, No. 2.
Stafford, T. W., Jr, et al.
   1984.   Holocene Age of the Yuha Burial: Direct Radiocarbon Determinations
           by Accelerator Mass Spectometry. N 308:446–447.
Stallings, W. S.
   1931.   El Paso Polychrome. LATSB, No. 2.
Stanford, D. J.
   1976.   The Walakpa Site, Alaska: Its Place in the Birnirk and Thule Cultures.
           SCA, No. 20.
Stanford, Dennis
   1978.   The Jones-Miller Site: An Example of Hell Gap Bison Procurement Strat-
           egy. In *Bison Procurement and Utilization: A Symposium*, edited by L. B.
           Davis and Michael Wilson. PAM, No. 14.
   1983.   Pre-Clovis Occupation South of the Ice Sheets. In *Early Man in the New
           World*, edited by Richard Shutler, Jr., pp. 65–72. Sage Publications. Beverly
           Hills, California.
Stanislawski, M. B.
   1963a. Extended Burials in the Prehistoric Southwest. AAn 28(3):308–319.
   1963b. *Wupatki Pueblo: A Study in Cultural Fusion and Change in Sinagua
           and Hopi Prehistory*. PhD dissertation, University of Arizona, Tucson.
   1978.   If Pots Were Mortal. In *Explorations in Ethnoarchaeology*, edited by R. E.
           Gould, pp. 201–227. School of American Research/University of New Mex-
           ico Press. Albuquerque.
   1979.   Hopi-Tewa. In *Handbook of North American Indians: Southwest*, edited
           by C. W. Sturtevant and A. A. Ortiz, Vol. 9:587–602. Smithsonian Institu-
           tion. Washington, D.C.

Statham, D. S.
  1982.   Camas and the Northern Shoshoni. ARBSU, No. 10.
Stearns, R. E.
  1940.   The Hughes Site: An Aboriginal Village Site on the Potomac River in
          Montgomery County, Maryland. PNHSM, No. 6.
  1943.   Some Indian Village Sites of Tidewater, Maryland. PNHSM, No. 9.
Steen, C. R.
  1977.   *Pajarito Plateau Archaeological Surveys and Excavations*. Los Alamos
          Scientific Laboratory. Los Alamos, New Mexico.
  1982.   *Pajarito Plateau Archaeological Surveys and Excavations—II*. Los Alamos
          Scientific Laboratory. Los Alamos, New Mexico.
Steen, C. R., L. M. Pierson, V. L. Bohrer, and K. P. Kent
  1962.   Archaeological Studies at Tonto National Monument, Arizona. SMATS
          No. 2.
Steensby, H. P.
  1917.   An Anthropogeographical Study of the Origin of Eskimo Culture. MG
          53:39–288.
Steinbring, Jack
  1974.   The Preceramic Archaeology of Northern Minnesota. MPS 11:64–73.
Stenton, Douglas
  1983.   *An Analysis of Faunal Remains from the Peale Point Site (KkDo–1) Baffin
          Island, N.W.T.* MA thesis, Trent University, Peterborough, Ontario.
Stephenson, R. L.
  1952.   The Hogge Bridge Site and the Wylie Focus. AAn 17(4):299–312.
  1954.   Taxonomy and Chronology in the Central Plains—Middle Missouri Area.
          PA 1:15–21.
  1969.   Archeology at Charles Towne. SCIAN 1(11):9–13.
Stephenson, R. L., A. L. L. Ferguson, and H. G. Ferguson
  1963.   The Accokeek Creek Site: A Middle Atlantic Seaboard Culture Sequence.
          UMMAAP, No. 20.
Steponaitis, L. C.
  1969.   Archeology at Charles Towne. SN 1 (11):9–13.
  1980.   A Survey of Artifact Collections from the Patuxent River Drainage, Mary-
          land. MHTMS, No. 1.
Steward, J. H.
  1933.   Ethnography of the Owens Valley Paiute. UCPAE 33(3):233–350.
  1938.   Basin-Plateau Aboriginal Sociopolitical Groups. BAEB, No. 120.
Stewart, Hilary
  1973.   *Artifacts of the Northwest Coast Indians*. Hancock House. Saanichton,
          British Columbia.
Stewart, R. M.
  1982.   Prehistoric Ceramics of the Great Valley of Maryland. AENA 10:69–94.
Stewart, T. D.
  1939.   Excavating the Indian Village of Patawomeke (Potomac). In *Explorations
          and Field-Work of the Smithsonian Institution in 1938*, pp. 87–90. Smith-
          sonian Institution. Washington, D.C.

n.d.   Report on the Excavation of an Indian Site on Potomac Creek in Stafford County, Virginia, Possibly the Site of the Town of Patawomeke Visited by Captain John Smith in 1608. Report on file at the Department of Anthropology, Smithsonian Institution, Washington, D.C.

Stokes, J. S.
1985.   *Cultural Resources Management Plan, Wallisville Lake Project, Chambers and Liberty Counties, Texas*. MA thesis, The University of Texas, Austin.

Stoltman, J. B.
1962.   *A Proposed Method of Systematizing the Modal Analysis of Pottery and Its Application to the Laurel Focus*. MA thesis, University of Minnesota, Minneapolis.
1966.   New Radiocarbon Dates for Southeastern Fiber-Tempered Pottery. AAn 31:872–874.
1973.   The Laurel Culture in Minnesota. MPS, No. 8.
1974a.   Groton Plantation: An Archaeological Study of a South Carolina Locality. MPM, No. 1.
1974b.   An Examination of Within-Laurel Cultural Variability in Northern Minnesota. MPS 11:74–89.
1979.   Middle Woodland Stage Communities of Southwestern Wisconsin. In *Hopewell Archaeology: The Chillicothe Conference*, edited by D. S. Brose and N. Greber, pp. 122–139. Kent State University Press. Kent, Ohio.

Stoltman, J. B., J. Behm, and H. A. Palmer
1984.   The Bass Site: A Hardin Quarry/Workshop in Southwestern Wisconsin. In *Prehistoric Chert Exploitation: Studies from the Midcontinent*, edited by B. M. Butler and E. E. May. OPCAI, No. 2.

Stone, L. M.
1972.   Archaeological Investigation of the Marquette Mission Site, St. Ignace, Michigan, 1971: A Preliminary Report. RMHA, No. 1.
1974.   Fort Michilimackinac 1715–1781. ASMSU, No. 2.

Story, D. A.
1968.   Archeological Investigations at Two Central Texas Gulf Coast Sties. TBAP, No. 13.
1981.   An Overview of the Archaeology of East Texas. PA 26:139–156.
1982.   (editor) The Deshazo Site, Nacogdoches County, Texas. TAPSR 7, Vol. 1.

Story, D. A., and D. G. Creel
1982.   The Cultural Setting. In *The Deshazo Site, Nacogdoches County, Texas*. TAPSR 7, Vol. 1.

Story, D. A., and Salvatore Valastro, Jr.
1977.   Radiocarbon Dating and the George C. Davis Site, Texas. JFA 4:63–89.

Stothers, D. M.
1975.   The Western Basin Tradition: A Preliminary Note. TARB 4:44–48.

Stothers, D. M., G. M. Pratt, and O. C. Shane III
1979.   The Western Basin Middle Woodland: Non-Hopewellians in a Hopewellian World. In *Hopewell Archaeology: The Chillicothe Conference*, edited by D. S. Brose and N'omi Greber, pp. 47–58. Kent State University Press. Kent, Ohio.

Stout, Wilbur, and R. A. Schoenlaub
1946. The Occurrence of Flint in Ohio. GSOB, No. 46.
Strong, W. D.
1935. An Introduction to Nebraska Archaeology. SMC 93(10).
1940. From History to Prehistory in the Northern Great Plains. SMC 100:370–376.
Strong, W. D, W. E. Schenck, and Julian Steward
1930. Archaeology of the Dalles-Deschutes Region. PAAE 29(1):1–154.
Struever, Stuart
1968. Woodland Subsistence-Settlement Systems in the Lower Illinois River Valley. In *New Perspectives in Archaeology*, edited by S. R. Binford and L. R. Binford, pp. 285–312. Aldine Publishing Co. Chicago.
Struever, Stuart, and G. L. Houart
1972. An Analysis of the Hopewell Interaction Sphere. In *Social Exchange and Interaction*, edited by E. N. Wilmsen, pp. 47–79. UMMAAP, No. 46.
Stuart, D. A., and R. P. Gauthier
1981. *Prehistoric New Mexico: Background for Survey*. Historic Preservation Bureau. Sante Fe, New Mexico.
Stuart, G. E.
1975. *The Post-Archaic Occupation of Central South Carolina*. PhD dissertation, University of North Carolina, Chapel Hill.
Stubbs, S. A.
1954. Summary Report on an Early Pueblo Site in the Tesuque Valley, New Mexico. EP 61(2):43–45.
Stubbs, S. A., and W. S. Stallings, Jr.
1953. The Excavation of Pindi Pueblo, New Mexico. MSAR, No. 18.
1959. "New" Old Churches Found at Quarai and Tabira. EP 66(5).
Styles, B. W., S. R. Ahler, and M. L. Fowler
1983. Modoc Rock Shelter Revisited. In *Archaic Hunters and Gatherers in the American Midwest*, edited by J. L. Phillips and J. A. Brown, pp. 261–297. Academic Press. New York.
Styles, T. R.
1985. Holocene and Late Pleistocene Geology of the Napoleon Hollow Site in the Lower Illinois Valley. KACRS, No. 5.
Suhm, D. A.
1957. Excavations at the Smith Rockshelter, Travis County, Texas. TJS 9:26–58.
1958. A Review of Central Texas Archeology. BTAS 29:63–107.
1959. The Williams Site and Central Texas Archeology. TJS 11:218–250.
Suhm, D. A., A. D. Krieger, and E. B. Jelks
1954. An Introductory Handbook of Texas Archeology. BTAS, No. 25.
Suhm, D. A., and E. B. Jelks
1962. Handbook of Texas Archeology: Type Descriptions. TASSP, No. 1; TMMB, No. 4.
Sutherland, Donald
1973. Preliminary Analysis of Ceramic Materials Recovered from the Spanish Mount Site, Edisto Island, S.C. SCAn 5(2):46–50.

1974.   Excavations at the Spanish Mount Shell Midden, Edisto Island, S.C. SCAn 6(1):25–36.

Sutherland, P. D.
1974.   Archaeological Investigations at Blue Jackets Creek, F1Ua 4, Queen Charlotte Islands, British Columbia. CAAB, 6:163–205.
n.d.   Archaeological Survey on Northern Ellesmere Island and Eastern Axel Heiberg Island (Summer 1981). Report on file at Archaeological Survey of Canada, Ottawa, Ontario.

Swanson, E. H., Jr.
1962.   The Emergence of Plateau Culture. OPISCM, No. 8.
1966.   The Geographic Foundations of Desert Culture. In *Current Status of Anthropological Research in the Great Basin: 1964*, edited by W. L. d'Azevedo. DRITS, 5–11: 137–146.

Swanton, J. R.
1946.   The Indians of the Southeastern United States. BAEB, No. 137.

Swartz, B. K., Jr.
1971.   *Adena: The Seeking of an Identity*. Ball State University. Muncie, Indiana.
1976.   The New Castle Site: A Hopewell Ceremonial Complex in East Central Indiana. CAH, No. 2.

Syms, E. L.
1977.   Cultural Ecology and Ecological Dynamics of the Ceramic Period in Southwestern Manitoba. PAM, No. 12.

Szuter, C. R.
1979.   *The Schlemmer Site: A Late Woodland-Mississippian Site in the American Bottom*. MA thesis, Loyola University, Chicago.
1982.   The Arvilla Burial Complex: A Re-assessment. JNDA 1:135–166.

Taggart, D. W.
1967.   Seasonal Patterns in Settlement Subsistence and Industries in the Late Archaic. MiA 13(4):153–170.
n.d.   The Feeheley Site: A Late Archaic Site in the Saginaw Valley. Manuscript on file at the Museum of Anthroplogy, University of Michigan, Ann Arbor.

Tainter, J. A.
1975.   *The Archaeological Study of Social Change: Woodland Systems in West Central Illinois*. PhD dissertation, Northwestern University, Evanston, Illinois.
1977.   Woodland Social Change in West Central Illinois. MJA 2:67–98.

Tainter, J. A., and D. A. Gillio
1980.   *Cultural Resources Overview: Mt. Taylor Area, New Mexico*. U.S. Forest Services, and Bureau of Land Management. Albuquerque, New Mexico.

Tankersley, K. B., C. A. Munson, P. J. Munson, N. R. Shaffer, and R. K. Leininger
in press. The Mineralogy of Wyandotte Cave and Its Archaeological Significance. In *The Archaeological Geology of North America*, Centennial Volume edited by Jack Donahue. Geological Society of America. Washington, D.C.

Taylor, R. E., Jr.
1978.   Radiocarbon Dating: An Archaeological Perspective. In *Archaeological Chemistry II*, edited by J. B. Lambert, pp. 33–69. American Chemical Society. Washington, D.C.

Taylor, R. E., and L. A. Payen
  1979. The Role of Archaeometry in American Archaeology: Approaches to the
         Evaluation of the Antiquity of *Homo sapiens* in California. In *Advances in
         Archaeological Method and Theory*, edited by M. B. Schiffer 2:239–283.
         Academic Press. New York.
Taylor, R. E., Jr., L. A. Payern, Bert Saraw, D. J. Donohue, T. H. Zabel, A. J. T.
         Jull, and P. E. Damon
  1983. Middle Holocene Age of the Sunnyvale Human Skeleton. S 220:1271–
         173.
Taylor, R. E., L. A. Payen, C. A. Prior, P. J. Slota, Jr., R. Gillespie, J. A. J. Gowlett,
         R. E. M. Hedges, A. J. T.Tull, T. H. Zabel, D. J. Donahue, and R. Berger
  1985. Major Revisions in the Pleistocene Age Assignments for North American
         Human Skeletons by C–14 Accelerator Mass Spectrometry: None Older than
         11,000 C–14 Years B.P. AAn 50(1):136–140.
Taylor, W. E., Jr.
  1960. A Description of Sadlermiut Houses Excavated at Native Point, South-
         ampton Island, N.W.T. NMCB 62:53–99.
  1962. Pre-Dorset Occupations at Ivugivik in Northwestern Ungava. In *Prehis-
         toric Cultural Relations Between the Arctic and Temperate Zones of North
         America*, edited by J. M. Campbell. AINATP, No. 11.
  1967. Summary of Archaeological Field Work on Banks and Victoria Islands,
         Arctic Canada, 1965. ArcA 4:221–243.
  1968. The Arnapik and Tyara Sites: An Archaeological Study of Dorset Culture
         Origins. MSAA, No. 22.
  1972. An Archaeological Survey Between Cape Parry and Cambridge Bay,
         N.W.T. NMMMS 1.
Taylor, W. W.
  1948. A Study of Archaeology. MAAA, No. 69.
  1956. Some Implications of the Carbon–14 Dates from a Cave in Coahuila,
         Mexico. BTAS 27:215–234.
  1966. Archaic Cultures Adjacent to the Northeastern Frontiers of Mesoamerica.
         In *Handbook of Middle American Indians*, edited by Robert Wauchope, G. F.
         Ekholm, and G. R. Willey, Vol. 4, pp. 59–94. University of Texas Press.
         Austin.
Teague, G. A.
  1972. An Archaic-Woodland Site (38CL4) in Calhoun County, South Carolina.
         SN 4:131–133.
Teit, James
  1900. The Thompson Indians of British Columbia. AMNHM 2(2):163–392.
Texas Archeological Survey Staff
  1981. Phase III: Prehistoric Archeological Research within Palmetto Bend Res-
         ervoir, Jackson County, Texas. RRTAS, No. 82.
Thies, R. M.
  n.d.   Archeological Investigations at Big Hill Lake, Southeastern Kansas, 1980.
         Report on file at the Kansas State Historical Society, Topeka.
Thomas, Cyrus
  1889. The Circular, Square, and Octagonal Earthworks of Ohio. BAEB, No.
         10.

1891.   Catalogue of Prehistoric Works East of the Rocky Mountains. BAEB, No. 12.

1894.   Report on Mound Explorations of the Bureau of American Ethnology. *Twelfth Annual Report of the Bureau of American Ethnology, 1890–1891.* Smithsonian Institution. Washington, D.C.

1898.   *Introduction to the Study of North American Archaeology.* Robert Clarke Co. Cincinnati, Ohio.

Thomas, D. H.

1981.   How to Classify the Projectile Points from Monitor Valley, Nevada. JCGBA 3(1):7–43.

1982.   *The 1981 Alta Toquima Village Project: A Preliminary Report.* Desert Research Institute, University of Nevada. Reno.

1983.   The Archaeology of Monitor Valley, 2: Gatecliff Shelter. APAMNH59(1).

1985.   The Archaeology of Hidden Cave. APAMNH 61(1).

Thomas, D. H., and C. S. Larsen

1979.   The Anthropology of St. Catherines Island, 2: The Refuge-Deptford Mortuary Complex. APAMNH 56(1).

Thomas, P. M., Jr.

1980.   Cultural Resources Investigations at Redstone Arsenal, Madison County, Alabama. NWRRI, No. 35.

Thomas, P. M., Jr., L. J. Campbell, and S. R. Ahler

1980.   The Hanna Site: An Alto Focus Village in Red River Parish. LA, No. 5.

Thomas, R. A.

1969.   *Breckenridge: A Stratified Shelter in Northwest Arkansas.* MA thesis, University of Arkansas, Fayetteville.

1970.   Adena Influence in the Middle Atlantic Coast. In *Adena: The Seeking of an Identity,* edited by B. K. Swartz, pp. 56–87. Ball State University. Muncie, Indiana.

1974.   A Brief Survey of Prehistoric Man on the Delmarva Peninsula. TDAS 5:119–140.

1976.   A Re-evaluation of the St. Jones River Site. AENA 4:89–110.

Thomas, R. A., and N. Warren

1970.   A Middle Woodland Cemetery in Central Delaware: Excavations at the Island Field Site. BASD: 8:1–33, 56–87.

Thomas, Trudy

1983.   The Visual Symbolism of Gatecliff Shelter. APAMNH 59(1):246–278.

Thompson, R. G.

1985.   The Natwick, Warner, and Slininger Habitations: Their Relationship with the Arvilla Complex and the Late Woodland Period on the Northeastern Plains. MinA 44(1):18–28.

Thomson, Callum

1981.   Preliminary Archaeological Finds from Shuldham Island, Labrador, 1980. In *Archaeology in Newfoundland and Labrador, 1980,* edited by J. Sproull-Thomson and B. Ransom, *Historic Resources Division, Government of Newfoundland and Labrador, Annual Report 1.*

1982.   Archaeological Finds from Saglek Bay, 1981. In *Archaeology in Newfoundland and Labrador, 1981,* edited by J. Sproull-Thomson and Callum Thomson, *Historic Resources Division, Government of Newfoundland and Labrador, Annual Report 2.*

Thruston, G. P.
  1897. *The Antiquities of Tennessee*. Robert Clarke Co. Cincinnati, Ohio.
Thurmond, J. P., II
  1981. *Archaeology of the Cypress Creek Basin, Northeastern Texas and North-western Louisiana*. MA thesis, The University of Texas, Austin.
Tiffany, J. A.
  1982. Chan-ya-ta: a Mill Creek Village. OSAIR, No. 15.
Titiev, Mischa
  1944. Old Oraibi, a Study of the Hopi Indians of Third Mesa. PPM 22(1).
Tjaden, Rex
  1974. The Cogan Mounds, 23PL125, Platte County, Missouri. MASN, No. 269.
Toll, H. W.
  1985. *Pottery Production, Public Architecture, and the Chaco Anasazi System*, PhD dissertation, University of Colorado, Boulder.
Toll, H. W., and P. J. McKenna
  1987. The Ceramography of Pueblo Alto. In *Investigations at the Pueblo Alto Complex*, Vol. 2. NPSPA, No. 18F.
Tomak, C. H.
  1979. Alton: A Paleo-Indian Site in Southern Indiana. PIAS 89:84–90.
Tordorff, Judith
  1983. *An Archaeological Perspective on the Fur Trade in Eighteenth Century New France*. PhD dissertation, Michigan State University, East Lansing.
Toth, E. A.
  1974. Archaeology and Ceramics of the Marksville Site. UMMAAP, No. 56.
Toulouse, J. H., Jr.
  1949. The Mission of San Gregorio de Abo. MSAR, No. 13.
Toulouse, J. H., Jr., and R. L. Stephenson
  1960. Excavations at Pueblo Pardo. MNMPA, No. 2.
Trace, Andrew
  1981. *An Examination of the Locarno Beach Phase as Represented at the Crescent Beach Site, DgRr1*. MA thesis, Simon Fraser University, Burnaby, British Columbia.
Treganza, A. E., and A. Bierman
  1958. The Topanga Culture: Final Report on Excavations, 1948. UCAR 20(2):45–86.
Treganza, A. E., and R. F. Heizer
  1953. Additional Data on the Farmington Complex, a Stone Implement Assemblage of Probable Early Postglacial Date from Central California. UCASR 22:28–41.
Treganza, A. E., and C. G. Malamud
  1950. The Topanga Culture: First Season's Excavation of the Tank Site, 1947. UCAR 12(4):129–157.
Trinkley, Michael
  1974. Report of Archaeological Testing at the Love Site (SoC 240), South Carolina. SIS 26:3–18.
  1976a. Excavations at Thom's Creek. SN 1(11):2–16.
  1976b. *A Typology of Thom's Creek Pottery for the South Carolina Coast*. MA thesis, University of North Carolina, Chapel Hill.

1980a. A Typology of Thom's Creek Pottery for the South Carolina Coast. SCAn 12:1–35.

1980b. *Investigation of the Woodland Period along the South Carolina Coast.* PhD dissertation, University of North Carolina, Chapel Hill.

1980c. *Additional Investigations at Site 38LX5.* South Carolina Department of Highways and Public Transportation. Columbia.

1981a. *Studies of Three Woodland Period Sites in Beaufort County, South Carolina.* South Carolina Department of Highways and Public Transportation. Columbia.

1981b. *Archaeological Testing of the Awendaw Shell Midden (38CH300), Located in the Wambaw District, Francis Marion National Forest, Charleston, S.C.* U.S. Forest Service. Columbia, South Carolina.

1981c. *Archaeological Testing of the Walnut Grove Shell Midden (38CH260), Charleston County.* U.S. Forest Service. Columbia, South Carolina.

1982. *A Summary Report on the Excavations at Alligator Creek, Charleston County, S.C.* U.S. Forest Service. Columbia, South Carolina.

1985. The Form and Function of South Carolina's Early Woodland Shell Rings. In *Structure and Process in Southeastern Archaeology,* edited by R. S. Dickens and H. T. Ward, pp. 102–118. University of Alabama Press. University.

1986. (editor) Indian and Freedman Occupation at the Fish Haul Site (38BU805), Beaufort County, South Carolina. RSCF, No. 7.

Trinkley, Michael, and Martha Zierden
1983. *The Archaeology of Fish Haul Creek, Hilton Head Island, Beaufort County, South Carolina: A Preliminary Statement and Recommendations.* Charleston Museum. Charleston, South Carolina.

Trinkley, Michael, Jeanne Calhoun, and Debi Hacker-Norton
1985. *Archaeological and Historical Investigation of 38SU81, 38SU82, 38SU83, and 38SU86.* South Carolina Department of Highways and Public Transportation. Columbia.

Trinkley, Michael, S. H. Hogue, Martha Zierden, and J. H. Wilson, Jr.
1983. Test Excavations at the Wachesaw Landing Site, Georgetown County, South Carolina. NCACP, No. 20.

Truell, Marcia
1975. *1972 Archaeological Explorations at the Ravine Site, Chimney Rock, Colorado.* MA thesis, University of Colorado, Boulder.

Tuck, J. A.
1975. Prehistory of Saglek Bay, Labrador: Archaic and Palaeo-Eskimo Occupations. NMMMS, No. 32.

1976. Newfoundland and Labrador Prehistory, Canada. NMMMS, ASCP, No. 32.

1978. Regional Cultural Development, 300 B.C. to A.D. 1000. In *Handbook of North American Indians: Northeast* edited by W. C. Sturtevant and B. G. Trigger, Vol. 15:28–43. Smithsonian Institution. Washington, D.C.

Tucker, G. C.
1981. *The Prehistoric Settlement System on Chimney Rock Mesa, South-central Colorado,* A.D. *925–1125.* PhD dissertation, University of Colorado, Boulder.

Tunnell, C. D.
1977. Fluted Projectile Point Reduction as Revealed by Lithic Specimens from the Adair-Steadman Site in Northwest Texas. TTUMJ, 17:140–168.

Tuohy, D. R.
1968.   Some Early Lithic Sites in Western Nevada. ENMUCA 1:27–39.
1981.   A Brief History of the Discovery and Exploration of Pebble Mounds, Boulder Cairns, and Other Rock Features at the Sadmat Site, Churchill County, Nevada. NVA 3(1):4–16.

Turnbull, C. J.
1976.   The Augustine Site: A Mound from the Maritimes. AENA, Vol. 4:50–62.

Turner, C. G., II, J. S. Aigner, and L. R. Richards
1974.   Chaluka Stratigraphy, Umnak Island, Alaska. ArcA 11(suppl).):125–142.

Turner, E. R. III
1983.   Recent VRCA Research at the Conover Paleo-Indian Site in Dinwiddie County, Virginia. In Piedmont Archaeology, edited by J. M. Wittkofski and L. E. Browning. ASVSP 10:109–117.

Turner, E. S., and T. R. Hester
1985.   A Field Guide to Stone Artifacts of Texas Indians. Texas Monthly Press. Austin.

Turner, R. L., Jr.
1978.   The Tuck Carpenter Site and Its Relation to Other Sites within the Titus Focus. BTAS 49:1–110.

Turpin, S. A.
1982.   Seminole Canyon: The Art and the Archeology, Val Verde County, Texas. RRTAS, No. 83.

Ubelaker, D. H.
1974.   Reconstruction of Demographic Profiles from Ossuary Skeletal Samples. SCA, No. 18.

Uhle, Max
1907.   The Emeryville Shellmound. UCPAE 7(1):1–106.

United States Geological Survey
1958.   Surface Water Supply of the United States, Part 9: Colorado River Basin. WSP, No. 1443.

Upham, Steadman
1982.   Politics and Power, An Economic and Political History of the Western Pueblo. Academic Press. New York.
n.d.   Final Report on Investigations at Chavez Pass Ruin, Coconino National Forest, Arizona: The 1978 Field Season. Report on file at Department of Anthropology, Arizona State University, Tempe.

Valentine, E. P.
1903.   Report of the Exploration of the Hayes' Creek Mound, Rockbridge County, Virginia. Valentine Museum. Richmond, Virginia.

Vancouver Art, Historical and Scientific Association
1948.   The Great Fraser Midden. Vancouver, British Columbia.

VanStone, J. W, and J. B. Townsend
1970.   Kijik: An Historic Tanaina Indian Settlement. F:A 59.

Vickery, K. D.
1979.   "Reluctant" or "Avant-Garde" Hopewell?: Suggestions of Middle Woodland Culture Change in East-central Indiana and South-central Ohio. In Hopewell Archaeology: The Chillicothe Connection, edited by D. S. Brose and N'omi Greber, pp. 59–63. The Kent State Press. Kent, Ohio.

Vivian, R. Gordon
1934. The Excavation of Bandelier's Puaray. EP 37(19–20):153–161.
1959. The Hubbard Site and Other Tri-Structures in New Mexico and Colorado. ARS, No. 5.
1962. *Prehistoric Ruins Stabilization Handbook*. Revised from 1949 edition. National Park Service. Washington, D.C.
1964. Gran Quivira: Excavations in a 17th Century Jumano Pueblo. ARS, No. 8.
Vivian, R. Gordon, and T. W. Mathews
1965. Kin Kletso, A Pueblo III Community in Chaco Canyon, New Mexico. SMATS 6(1).
Vivian, R. Gordon, and Paul Reiter
1965. The Great Kivas of Chaco Canyon and Their Relationships. MSAR, No. 22.
Vivian, R. Gwinn, D. N. Dodgen, and G. H. Hartmann
1978. Wooden Ritual Artifacts from Chaco Canyon, New Mexico: The Chetro Ketl Collection. APUAr, No. 22.
Vytlacil, Natalie, and J. J. Brody
1958. Two Pit Houses near Zia Pueblo. EP 65(5):174–184.
Wainwright, R. D.
n.d. Letters dated 5 January 1914 and 1 September 1915, on file at the Bureau of American Ethnology, Smithsonian Institution, Washington, D.C.
Walker, E. F.
1951. Five Prehistoric Sites in Los Angeles County, California. PFWH, No. 6.
Walker, John
1971. *Excavation of the Arkansas Post Branch of the Bank of the State of Arkansas*. Southeast Archeological Center, National Park Service. Tallahassee, Florida.
Walker, S. T.
1885. Mounds and Shell Heaps on the West Coast of Florida. ARSI, 1883 pp. 854–868.
Walker, W. M.
1936. The Troyville Mounds, Catahoula Parish, Louisiana. BAEB, No. 113.
Wallace, W. J.
1951. The Mortuary Caves of Calaveras County, California. Ar 4:199–203.
1955. A Suggested Chronology for Southern California Coastal Archaeology. SJA 11:214–230.
1962. Prehistoric Cultural Development in Southern California Deserts. AAn 28(2):172–180.
Walthall, J. A.
1973. *Copena: A Tennessee Valley Middle Woodland Culture*. PhD dissertation, University of North Carolina, Chapel Hill.
1979. Hopewell and the Southern Heartland. In *Hopewell Archaeology: The Chillicothe Coference*, edited by D. S. Brose and N. M. B. Greber. Kent State University Press. Kent, Ohio.
1980. *Prehistoric Indians of the Southeast*. University of Alabama Press, University.
1981. Monumental Moundville. EM 3(4):12–22.

Walthall, J. A., and N. J. Jenkins
  1976. The Gulf Formational Stage in Southeastern Prehistory. SACB, No. 19.
Ward, H. T.
  1980. *The Spatial Analysis of the Plow Zone Artifact Distributions from Two Village Sites in North Carolina*. PhD dissertation, University of North Carolina, Chapel Hill.
  1983. A Review of Archaeology in the North Carolina Piedmont: A Study of Change. In *The Prehistory of North Carolina: An Archaeological Symposium*, edited by M. A. Mathis and J. J. Crow, pp. 53–81. North Carolina Division of Archives and History, Department of Cultural Resources. Raleigh.
Waring, A. J.
  1968. The Refuge Site, Jasper County, South Carolina. In *The Waring Papers: The Collected Works of Antonio J. Waring, Jr.*, edited by Stephen Williams, pp. 198–208. PPM, No. 58.
Waring, A. J., and Preston Holder
  1945. A Prehistoric Ceremonial Complex in the Southeastern United States. AA 47(1):1–34.
Warren, A. H.
  1979. The Glaze Paint Wares of the Upper Middle Rio Grande. In *Archaeological Investigations in Cochiti Reservoir, New Mexico, Vol. 4: Adaptive Change in the Northern Rio Grande Valley*, edited by J. V. Biella and R. C. Chapman, pp. 187–216. Office of Contract Archaeology, University of New Mexico. Albuquerque.
Warren, C. N.
  1966. (editor) The San Dieguito Type Site: M. J. Rogers' 1938 Excavation on the San Dieguito River. SDMP, No. 5.
  1967. The San Dieguito Complex: A Review and Hypothesis. AAn 32(2):168–185.
  1968. Cultural Tradition and Ecological Adaption on the Southern California Coast. In *Archaic Prehistory in the Western United States*, edited by Cynthia Irwin-Williams, pp. 1–14. ENMUCA, No. 1.
  1984. The Desert Region. In *California Archaeology*, by M. J. Moratto, pp. 339–430. Academic Press. Orlando, Florida.
Warren, C. N., and D. L. True
  1961. The San Dieguito Complex and Its Place in California Prehistory. *University of California Archaeological Survey Annual Report, 1960–1961*, pp. 246–338. University of California, Berkeley.
Waselkov, G. A.
  1982. *Shellfish Gathering and Shell Midden Archeology*. PhD dissertation, University of North Carolina, Chapel Hill.
  1985. Shell Midden Archaeology: Coastal Adaptation in the Lower Potomac Valley. RRNGS 20:835–840.
Washburn, D. K.
  1974. Nearest Neighbor Analysis of Pueblo I-III Settlement Patterns along the Rio Puerco of the East, New Mexico. AAn 39:315–335.
Wasley, W. W, and A. E. Johnson
  1963. The Trincheras Culture of Northern Sonora. AAn 29:174–186.

1965. Salvage Archaeology in Painted Rocks Reservoir, Western Arizona. UAAP, No. 9.

Watson, Virginia
1950. The Optima Focus of the Panhandle Aspect: Description and Analysis. BTAPS 21:7–68.

Wauchope, Robert
1966. Archaeological Survey of Northern Georgia with a Test of Some Cultural Hypotheses. MSAA, No. 21.

Weaver. D. E.
1974. Archaeological Investigations at the Westwing Site, Az. T:7:27(ASU), Agua Fria Valley, Arizona. ASUAP, No. 7.

Weaver, D. E., Jr., S. G. Dosh, and K. E. Miller
n.d. An Archaeological Assessment of Homolovi II Ruin. Report on file at Museum of Northern Arizona, Flagstaff.

Webb, C. H.
1945. A Second Historic Caddo Site at Natchitoches, Louisiana. BTAPS 16:52–83.

1946. Two Unusual Types of Chipped Stone Artifacts from Northwest Louisiana. BTAPS 17:9–17.

1948. Caddoan Prehistory: The Bossier Focus. BTAPS 19:100–147.

1959. The Belcher Mound, a Stratified Caddoan Site in Caddo Parish, Louisiana. MSAA, No. 16.

1961. Relationships between the Caddoan Area and Central Louisiana Cultural Sequences. BTAS 31:11–25.

1968. The Extent and Content of Poverty Point Culture. AAn 33(3):297–32.

1977. The Poverty Point Culture. GM, No. 17.

1982. The Poverty Point Culture. Revised edition. GM, No. 22.

1983. The Bossier Focus Revisited: Montgomery, Werner and Other Unicomponent Sites. In Southeastern Natives and Their Pasts, edited by D. G. Wyckoff and J. L. Hofman. OASOP, No. 11.

Webb, C. H., and M. E. Dodd, Jr.
1939. Further Excavations of the Gahagan Mound. BTAPS 11:92–126.

Webb, C. H., and R. R. McKinney
1975. Mounds Plantation (16CD12), Caddo Parish, Louisiana. LA 2:39–127.

Webb, C. H., J. L. Shiner, and E. W. Roberts
1971. The John Pearce Site (16CD56): A San Patrice Site in Caddo Parish, Louisiana. BTAS 42:1–49.

Webb, C. H., F. E. Murphey, W. G. Ellis, and H. R. Green
1969. The Resch Site, 41HS16, Harrison County, Texas. BTAS 40:3–106.

Webb, W. S.
1939. An Archaeological Survey of Wheeler Basin on the Tennessee River in Northern Alabama. BAEB, No. 122.

1946. Indian Knoll, Site Oh 2, Ohio County, Kentucky. RAA 4(3).

Webb, W. S., and R. S. Baby
1957. The Adena People—No. 2. The Ohio State University Press. Columbus.

Webb, W. S., and C. E. Snow
1945. The Adena People. PDAA, No. 6.

Webb, W. S., and D. L. DeJarnette
1942. Archeological Survey of Pickwick Basin. BAEB, No. 129.
Weber, R. H.
1973. *Geology of the Mockingbird Gap Site in Central New Mexico.* Abstracts with Program, 1973 Annual Meeting of the Geological Society of America 7:857–858.
Weber, R. H., and G. A. Agogino
n.d.a. The Mockingbird Gap Site: A Clovis Site with Possible Transitional Folsom Characteristics. Unpublished manuscript. Department of Anthropology, Eastern New Mexico University, Portales, New Mexico.
n.d.b. Mockingbird Gap Paleo-Indian Site: Excavations in 1967. Unpublished manuscript. Department of Anthropology, Eastern New Mexico University, Portales, New Mexico.
Webster, D. L.
1967. *Mounds of the Rainy River: An Examination of the Laurel Focus of Minnesota.* MA thesis, University of Minnesota, Minneapolis.
Webster, L. D.
n.d. An Archaeological Survey of the West Rim of the Piedra River. Report on file at the San Juan National Forest, Durango, Colorado.
Wedel, W. R.
1936. An Introduction to Pawnee Archeology. BAEB, No. 112.
1941. Archeological Investigations at Buena Vista Lake, Kern County, California. BAEB, No. 130.
1943. Archeological Investigations in Platte and Clay Counties, Missouri. USNMB, No. 183.
1951. Archeological Reconnaissance near Saltville, Virginia in 1940. ASVQB (5)4.
1959. An Introduction to Kansas Archaeology. BAEB, No. 174.
1961. *Prehistoric Man on the Great Plains.* University of Oklahoma Press. Norman.
1967. The Council Circles of Central Kansas: Were They Solstice Registers? AAn 32(1):54–63.
1979. House Floors and Native Settlement Population in the Central Plains. PA 24(84, pt. 1):85–94.
1985. *Central Plains Prehistory.* University of Nebraska Press. Lincoln.
Wedel, W. R., Wilfred Husted, and John Moss
1968. Mummy Cave: Prehistoric Record from the Rocky Mountains of Wyoming. S 160:184–186.
Weide, M. L.
1968. *Cultural Ecology of Lakeside Adaptation in the Western Great Basin.* PhD dissertation, University of California, Los Angeles.
1974. North Warner Subsistence Network: A Prehistoric Band Territory. NASRP 5:62–79.
Weir, Frank A.
1976. *The Central Texas Archaic.* PhD dissertation, Washington State University, Pullman.
1979. Greenhaw: An Archaic Site in Central Texas. BTAS 50:5–67.

Wells, S. J.
  1981.   *An Archaeological Survey of the Bald Hill Locality, Mogollon Rim, North Central Arizona.* MA thesis, University of Arizona, Tucson.
Wendorf, Fred
  1953.   Salvage Excavations in the Chama Valley. MSAR, No. 17.
Wendorf, Fred, A. D. Krieger, C. C. Albritton, and T. D. Stewart
  1955.   *The Midland Discovery.* University of Texas Press. Austin.
Wendorf, Fred, and J. P. Miller
  1959.   Artifacts from High Mountain Sites in the Sangre de Cristo Range. EP 66(2):37–52.
Wendorf, Fred, and E. K. Reed
  1955.   An Alternative Reconstruction of Northern Rio Grande Prehistory. EP 62(5–6):131–173.
Weslager, C. A.
  1968.   *Delaware's Buried Past,* second edition. Rutgers University Press. New Brunswick, New Jersey.
Wessen, G. C.
  1982.   *Shell Middens as Cultural Deposits: A Case Study from Ozette.* PhD dissertation, Washington State University, Pullman.
Wesolowsky, A. B., T. R. Hester, and D. R. Brown
  1976.   Archeological Investigations at the Jetta Court Site (41TV151), Travis County, Texas. BTAS 47:25–87.
Westbrook, K. C.
  1982.   Caddo Pottery. In *Legacy in Clay: Prehistoric Ceramic Art of Arkansas,* edited by K. C. Westbrook. Arkansas Art Center. Little Rock.
Weston, Donald
  1975.   The Indian Rock Art Tradition in Michigan. GLIMH. Ser. 1, No. 5.
Westover, A. R.
  1984.   *A History of the Excavations at Starved Rock, Illinois.* MA thesis, Illinois State University, Norman.
Wetherington, R. K.
  1968.   Excavations at Pot Creek Pueblo. FBRC, No. 6.
Wettlaufer, Boyd
  1955.   The Mortlach Site at the Besant Valley of Saskatchewan. ASSDNR, No. 1.
Wettlaufer, Boyd, and W. J. Mayer-Oakes
  1960.   The Long Creek Site. ASSDNR, No. 2.
Weyer, E. M.
  1930.   Archaeological Material from the Village Site at Hot Springs, Port Moller, Alaska. APAMNH 31(3):243–277.
Whalen, M. E.
  1981.   Origin and Evolution of Ceramics in Western Texas. BTAS 52:215–229.
Whalen, N. B.
  1971.   *Cochise Culture Sites in the Central San Pedro Drainage, Arizona.* PhD dissertation, University of Arizona, Tucson.
Whallon, R. E., and J. A. Brown
  1982.   (editors) *Essays on Archaeological Typology.* Center for American Archaeology. Evanston, Illinois.

Wheat, J. B.
   1953.   An Archaeological Survey of the Addicks Dam Basin, Southeast Texas.
           BAEB 154:143–252.
   1955.   Mogollon Culture Prior to A.D. 1000. MSAA, No. 10; MSAA, 57(2)3.
   1972.   The Olsen-Chubbuck Site, A Paleo-Indian Bison Kill. MSAA, No. 26.
   1979.   The Jurgens Site. PAM, No. 15.
Wheeler, M.E., and D. W. Clark
   1977.   Elemental Chracterization of Obsidian from the Koyukuk River, Alaska,
           by Atomic Absorption Spectrophotometry. Arch 19(1):15–31.
Whiteford, G. L.
   1941.   *Indian Archeology in Saline County, Kansas.* Salina, Kansas.
Whitney, J. D.
   1897.   The Auriferous Gravels of the Sierra Nevada of California. MHMCA,
           No. 6.
Whittlesey, Charles
   1851.   Descriptions of Ancient Works in Ohio. SCK 3:Art. 7.
   1871.   Ancient Earthforts of the Cuyahoga Valley, Ohio. Tr, No. 5.
Wiant, M. D., and C. R. McGimsey
   1986.   The Woodland Period Occupations of the Napoleon Hollow Site. KACRS,
           No. 6.
Wiant, M. D, E. R. Hajic, and T. R. Styles
   1983.   Napoleon Hollow and Koster Site Stratigraphy: Implications for Holocene
           Landscape Evolution and Studies of Archaic Period Settlement Patterns in
           the Lower Illinois River Valley. In *Archaic Hunters and Gatherers in the
           American Midwest,* edited by J. L. Phillips and J. A. Brown, pp. 147–165.
           Academic Press. New York.
Wigand, P. E.
   1985.   *Diamond Pond, Harney County, Oregon: Man and Marsh in the Eastern
           Oregon Desert.* PhD dissertation, Washington State University, Pullman.
Wilcox, D. R, and D. E. Doyel
   1987.   Site Structure and Maximum Extent of the Pueblo Grande Site. PGMAP,
           No. 1.
Wilcox, D. R., and L. O. Shenk
   1977.   The Architecture of the Casa Grande and Its Interpretation. ASMAS, No.
           115.
Wilcox, D. R., and Charles Sternberg
   1983.   Hohokam Ballcourts and Their Interpretation. ASMAS, No. 160.
Wilcox, D. R., T. R. McGuire, and Charles Sternberg
   1981.   Snaketown Revisited. ASMAS, No. 155.
Wilde, J. D.
   1985.   *Prehistoric Settlements in the Northern Great Basin: Excavations and
           Collections Analysis in the Steens Mountain Area, Southeastern Oregon.* PhD
           dissertation, University of Oregon.
Wilford, L. A.
   1937.   *Minnesota Archaeology with Special Reference to the Mound Area.* PhD
           dissertation, Harvard University, Cambridge, Massachusetts.
   1941.   A Tentative Classification of the Prehistoric Cultures of Minnesota. AAn
           6(3):238–240.

1942.   Minnesota Archaeology: Current Explorations and Concepts. PRMAS 10:20–26.

1944.   The Prehistoric Indians of Minnesota: The Mille Lacs Aspect. MH 25(4):329–341.

1945a.   The Prehistoric Indians of Minnesota: The Headwaters Lakes Aspect. MH 26(4):312–329.

1945b.   Three Village Sites of the Mississippi Pattern in Minnesota. AAn 11(1):32–40.

1950a.   The Prehistoric Indians of Minnesota: Some Mounds of the Rainy River Aspect. MH 31(3):163–167.

1950b.   The Prehistoric Indians of Minnesota: The McKinstry Mounds of the Rainy River Aspect. MH 31(3):231–237.

1954.   Archaeological Method in the Eastern United States. In *Method and Perspective in Anthropology: Papers in Honor of Wilson D. Wallace*, edited by R. F. Spencer, pp. 171–191. University of Minnesota Press. Minneapolis.

1955.   A Revised Classification of the Prehistoric Cultures of Minnesota. AAn 21(2):130–142.

1970.   Burial Mounds of the Red River Headwaters. MPS, No. 5.

n.d.a.   The Shocker Village Site. Report on file at the Department of Anthropology, University of Minnesota, Minneapolis.

n.d.b.   The Osufsen Mound. Report on file at the Department of Anthropology, University of Minnesota, Minneapolis.

n.d.c.   Howard Lake Mounds. Report on file at the Department of Anthropology, University of Minnesota, Minneapolis.

n.d.d.   The Sheffield Site. Report on file at the Department of Anthropology, University of Minnesota, Minneapolis.

Wilford, L. A., Elden Johnson, and Joan Vicinus

1969.   Burial Mounds of Central Minnesota. MPS, No. 1.

Wilkins, E. S., Jr.

1962.   A Preliminary Report on the Harlan Mill Steatite Quarry (18CE5). BASD (n.s.) 2:1–11.

1964.   The Harlan Mill Steatite Quarry, Cecil County, Maryland. ESAFB, No. 23.

1970.   Harlan Mill Steatite Quarry. I 16(2):2–3.

Willey, G. R.

1945.   The Weeden Island Culture: A Preliminary Definition. AAn 10:225–254.

1949a.   Archaeology of the Florida Gulf Coast. SMC, No. 113.

1949b.   Crystal River Florida: A 1949 Visit. FA 2:41–46.

1949c.   Excavations in Southeast Florida. YUPA, No. 42.

1966.   *An Introduction to American Archaeology,*, Vol. 1: *North and Middle America*. Prentice Hall. Englewood Cliffs, New Jersey.

Willey, G. R., and R. B. Woodbury

1942.   A Chronological Outline for the Northwest Florida Coast. AAn 7:232–254.

Williams, J. A.

1978.   *44CP1 The Onion Field Site 'Dan River Focus.'* Senior thesis, College of William and Mary, Williamsburg, Virginia.

1982. The Inkster Burial, 32GF19: Skeletal Biology of a Northeastern Plains Woodland Population. JNDA 1:181–215.

Williams, Stephen, and J. P. Brain
1983. Excavations at the Lake George Site, Yazoo County, Mississippi, 1958–1960. PPM, No. 74.

Williams, Stephen, and J. M. Goggin
1965. The Long-Nosed God in the Eastern United States. MA 18(3):1–72.

Williams-Dean, Glenna
1978. *Ethnobotany and Cultural Ecology of Prehistoric Man in Southwest Texas.* PhD dissertation, Texas A&M University, College Station.

Williston, S. W.
1879. Indian Figures in Western Kansas. KCRSI 3(1).
1899. Some Prehistoric Ruins in Scott County, Kansas. KUQ, Series B 7(4).
1902. An Arrow-Head Found with Bones of *Bison occidentalis* Lucas, in Western Kansas. AG 30:312–315.

Willoughby, C. C.
1917. The Art of the Great Earthwork Builders of Ohio. ARSI (for 1916):489–500.
1919. The Serpent Mound of Adams County, Ohio. AA 21:153–164.

Willoughby, C. C., and E. A. Hooton
1922. The Turner Group of Earthworks, Hamilton County, Ohio, PPM 8(3).

Wilmeth, Roscoe
1970. Excavations in the Pomona Reservoir. ASKSHS, No. 5.

Wilmsen, E. N., and F. H. H. Roberts, Jr.
1978. Lindenmeier 1934–1974: Concluding Report of Investigations. SCA, No. 24.

Wilson, J. P.
1969. *The Sinagua and Their Neighbors.* PhD dissertation, Harvard University, Cambridge, Massachusetts.
1973. Quarai, Living Mission to Monument. EP 78(4):14–26.

Wilson, Mrs. L. L. W.
1916. Excavations at Otowi. EP 3(2):29–36.

Wilson, R. L., and C. Carlson
1980. The Archaeology of Kamloops. DASFUP, No. 7.

Wimberly, S. B.
1960. Indian Pottery from Clarke County and Mobile County, Southern Alabama. GSAMP, No. 36.

Windes, T. C.
1977. Typology and Technology of Anasazi Ceramics. In *Settlement and Subsistence along the Lower Chaco River.* University of New Mexico Press. Albuquerque.
1984. A View of Cibola Whiteware from Chaco Canyon. In *Regional Analysis of Prehistoric Ceramic Variation: Contemporary Studies of the Cibola Whitewares.* ASUAP, No. 31.
1986. Chaco-McElmo Black-on-white from Chaco Canyon with an Emphasis on the Pueblo del Arroyo Collection. In *Prehistory and History in the Southwest: Collected Papers in Honor of Alden C. Hayes.* Archaeological Society of New Mexico. Santa Fe.

1987.   Investigations at the Pueblo Alto Complex, Chaco Canyon, New Mexico. NPSPA, No. 18F, Vols. 1, 2.

Winfree, R. W.
1969.   Newington, King and Queen County. ASVQB (23)4:160–224.
1972.   Monacan Farm, Powhatan County, Virginia. ASVQB (27)2:65–93.

Winters, H. D.
1963.   An Archaeological Survey of the Wabash Valley in Illinois. RIISM, No. 10.
1969.   *The Riverton Culture*. ISMRI, No. 13.

Wiseman, R. N., and J. A. Darling
n.d.   The Bronze Trail Site Group: More Evidence for a Cerrillos-Chaco Turquoise Connection. Manuscript on file at Laboratory of Anthropology, Museum of New Mexico, Santa Fe.

Wiseman, R. N., M. Y. El Najjar, J. S. Bruder, M. Heller, and R. I. Ford
1976.   Multi-Disciplinary Investigations at the Smokey Bear Ruin (LA 2112), Lincoln County, New Mexico, CPRM, No. 4.

Withers, Arnold
1954.   University of Denver Archaeological Fieldwork. SL 19(4):1–3.
1973.   Excavations at Valshni Village, Arizona. AAr 7.

Witthoft, John
1952.   *A Paleo-Indian Site in Eastern Pennyslvania: An Early Hunting Culture.* PAPS 96(4):464–495.
1953.   Broad Spearpoints and the Transitional Period Cultures. PnA 23(1):4–31.

Wittry, W. L.
1959a.   The Raddatz Rockshelter (Sk-5), Sauk County, Wisconsin. WiA 40(2):33–69.
1959b.   Archaeological Studies of Four Wisconsin Rockshelters. WiA 40(4):137–267.
1963.   The Bell Site, Wn 9: An Early Historic Fox Village. WiA 44(1):1–58.
1969.   The American Woodhenge. In *Explorations into Cahokia Archaeology.* IASB 7:43–48.

Witty, T. A., Jr.
1962a.   *The Anoka Focus.* MA thesis, University of Nebraska, Lincoln.
1962b.   Archeological Investigations of the Hell Creek Valley in the Wilson Reservoir, Russell and Lincoln Counties, Kansas. ASKSHS, No. 1.
1967.   The Pomona Focus. KAAN 12(9):1–5.
1968.   The Pawnee Indian Village Museum Project. KAAN 13(5).
1969.   The Caldwell Dig. KAAN 15(2).
1978a.   The Penokee Store Indian. KAAN 23(16).
1978b.   Along the Southern Edge: The Central Plains Tradition in Kansas. In *The Central Plains Tradition*, edited by D. J. Blakeslee. OSAIR, No. 11.
1981.   The Pomona Focus, Known and Unknown. MA 42:77–83.
1982.   The Slough Creek, Two Dog and William Young Sites, Council Grove Lake, Kansas. ASKSHS, No. 10.
1983.   An Archaeological Review of the Scott County Pueblo. OASB 32:99–106.

Wood, E. F.
   1936.   A Central Basin Manifestation in Eastern Wisconsin. AAn 1:215–219.
Wood, W. R.
   1961.   The Square Earth Lodges of the Central Great Plains. PACN 5:5–17.
   1963.   Breckenridge Shelter—3CR2. An Archeological Chronicle in the Beaver Reservoir Area. ArA 1962:68–96.
   1965.   The Redbird Focus and the Problem of Ponca Prehistory. PAM No. 2.
   1967.   An Interpretation of Mandan Culture History. BAEB, No. 198.
   1971.   Biesterfeldt: A Post-Contact Coalescent Site on the Northeastern Plains. SCA, No. 15.
   1976.   (editor) Fay Tolton and the Initial Middle Missouri Variant. MASRS, No. 13.
   1986.   *The Origins of the Hidatsa Indians: A Review of the Ethnohistorical and Traditional Data.* J & L Reprint Co. Lincoln, Nebraska.
Wood, W. R., and R. B. McMillan
   1976.   *Prehistoric Man and His Enviroments: A Case Study in the Ozark Highland.* Academic Press. New York.
Woodall, J. N.
   1984.   The Donnaha Site: 1973, 1975 Excavations. NCACP, No. 22.
Woodbury, R. B.
   1954.   Prehistoric Stone Implements of Northeastern Arizona. PPM, No. 34.
   1961.   Prehistoric Agriculture at Point of Pines. MSAA, No. 17.
Woodward, Arthur
   1931.   The Grewe Site. OPLAM, No. 1.
Woosley, A. I.
   1980.   *Taos Archaeology.* Fort Burgwin Research Center, Southern Methodist University. Dallas.
Word, J. H., and C. L. Douglas
   1970.   Excavations at Baker Cave, Val Verde County, Texas. BTMM, No. 16.
Workman. W. B.
   1966.   Prehistory at Port Moller, Alaska Peninsula, in Light of Fieldwork in 1960. ArcA 3(2).
   1974.   First Dated Traces of Early Holocene Man in the Southwest Yukon Territory, Canada. ArcA 11(suppl.):94–103.
   1978.   Prehistory of the Aishihik-Kluane Area, Southwest Yukon Territory. NMMMS, No. 74.
Workman, W. B., K. K. Werlemang, and J. E. Lobdell
   1980.   Recent Archaeological Work in Kachemak Bay. Arc 33(31):385–399.
Worman. F. C. V.
   1967.   *Archaeological Salvage Excavations in the Mesita del Buey, Los Alamos County, New Mexico.* Los Alamos Scientific Laboratory. Los Alamos, New Mexico.
Wormington, H. M.
   1955.   A Reappraisal of the Fremont Culture. DMP, No. 1.
   1957.   Ancient Man in North America. DMPS, No. 4.
Wormington, H. M., and R. G. Forbis
   1965.   An Introduction to the Archaeology of Alberta, Canada. DMP, No. 11.

Wray, D. E., and R. S. MacNeish
   1961.   The Hopewellian and Weaver Occupations of the Weaver Site, Fulton
           County, Illinois, edited by W. L. Wittry. ISMSP 7(2).
Wright, H. T.
   1973.   An Archeological Sequence in the Middle Chesapeake Region, Maryland.
           ArS, No. 1.
Wright, H. T, and W. B. Roosa
   1966.   The Barnes Site: A Fluted Point Assemblage from the Great Lakes Region.
           AAn 31 (6):850–860.
Wright, J. V.
   1967.   The Laurel Tradition and the Middle Woodland Period. NMCB, No. 217.
   1972a. *Ontario Prehistory.* Archaeological Survey, National Museum of Man.
           Ottawa. Ontario.
   1972b. The Aberdeen Site, Keewatin District, N.W.T. NMMMS, No. 2.
Wyantt, H.
   n.d.   Pennsylvania Jasper Quarries. Report on file at the Island Field Museum,
           South Bowers, Delaware.
Wyckoff, D. G.
   1970.   Archaeological and Historical Assessment of the Red River Basin in Okla-
           homa. In *Archaeological and Historical Resources of the Red River Basin,*
           edited by H. A. Davis. AASRS 1:67–134.
   1971.   *The Caddoan Culture Area: An Archaeological Perspective.* Oklahoma
           Archaeological Survey. Norman.
   1974.   The Caddoan Culture Area: An Archaeological Perspective. In *Caddoan
           Indians,* Vol. 1:25–279. Garland Publishing, Inc., New York.
Wyckoff, L. M.
   1981.   The Physical Anthropology of the Sand Point Site (20-BG14). MiA 27(1–
           2):5–30.
Yarnell, R. A.
   1964.   Aboriginal Relationship between Culture and Plant Life in the Upper
           Great Lakes Region. UMMAAP, No. 23.
Yates, L. G.
   1889.   Charm Stones or "Plummets" from California. *Annual Report of the
           United States National Museum for 1886,* pp. 296–305. Smithsonian Insti-
           tution. Washington, D.C.
Yent, M. E.
   1976.   *The Cultural Sequence at Wawawai (45WT39), Lower Snake River Re-
           gion, Southeastern Washington.* MA thesis, Washington State University,
           Pullman.
Young, W. C.
   1985.   Archaeological Excavations at Site 41BT6, Burnet County, Texas.
           TDHPA, No. 28.
Yourd, W. J.
   n.d.   An Archaeological Assessment Study of Proposed MnDOT Project S.P.
           3604–44, T.H. 11: Reconnaissance and Evaluation Phase of the McKinstry
           Site, Koochiching County, Minnesota. Report on file at the Minnesota His-
           torical Society, Fort Snelling.

Zimmerman, L. J.
  1977. Prehistoric Locational Behavior: A Computer Simulation. OSAIR, No.
    10.
Zimmerman, L. J., T. Emerson, P. Willey, M. Swegle, J. Gregg, P. Gregg, E. White,
    C. Smith, T. Haberman, and M. Bumsted
  1981. *The Crow Creek Site (39BF11) Massacre: A Preliminary Report.* U.S.
    Army Corps of Engineers, Omaha District. Omaha, Nebraska.

Index

The page numbers of actual entries appear in **boldface**.

Hayes, A. C., 188, 446
Hayes' Creek Mound, 204
Hayes Site, 119
Haynes, C. V., 52
Healy Lake locality, 204, 337
Heart River Phase, 204
Heins Creek Culture, 205
Heins Creek Site, 204–5; similarities to, 258
Heins Creek Ware, 205
Heizer, R. F., 145, 246, 263, 280, 303, 510, 531
Helena Mounds, 205
Helena Phase, type site, 205
Hellebaek Site, 205
Hell Gap Complex, 205; components, 5, 73, 79, 205, 235, 488; subsumed within Plano Culture, 378
Hell Gap point, 79, 90, 235, 408, 452, 488
Hell Gap Site, 5, 205–6; Goshen Complex defined from, 186
Helmer, J. W., 241–42
Helton Phase, 206; successors of, 328
Hemenway Southwest Expedition, 394
Hemmings, E. T., 161, 280
Henning, D. R., 117
Henrietta Focus, 206
Hercules Ware, 206
Hesquiat Harbour Sequence, 206–7
Hester, J. J., 46, 658
Heuguenot settlement, 315
Hewett, E. L., 91, 188, 395, 398, 485, 503
Heye, G. G., 178
Hibben, F. C., 84, 304, 334, 386, 430, 508
Hickory pottery, 11
Hidatsa-Fall River Culture, components, 277
Hidatsa Indians, 107, 197, 348; acculturation of, 384; villages, 269, 333, 448, 486
Hidden Cave, 207
Hidden Falls Site, 207
Hidden Valley Phase, 180
Higgins Flat Pueblo, 207–8
Hill, A. T., 22, 511

Hillside sites, 178
Hinds Cave, 208
Hirsh Mound Site, 208
Hirundo Site, 208
Hisatsinom Phase, 44
Historic Contact Phase, 329, 487; components, 344
Historic Pueblo, 460, 482
Hiwassie Island Culture, 208
Hiwassee Island Site, 129, 208–9
Hixon Site, 129
Hixton Silicified Sandstone, 470
Hixton Site, 209
Hochelaga, 209
Hoffman, W. J., 358
Hoge Site, 209
Hogup Cave, 173, 209
Hohokam core area, 370
Hohokam Culture, 5, 14, 105, 209–11, 361; architecture, 533; ball courts, 32; campsites of, 512; check dams, 90; colonies of, 513; components, 73, 394, 456; contacts with, 261; contrasts to, 423; elements in East Verde Province, 146; glycymeris bracelets, 184; influence of, 197, 213, 452; migrations, 15, 198, 336, 533; outposts, 534; periods, 111, 375, 443; pottery 69, 105–6, 219, 405, 407, 436; provinces, 181, 417, 436, 496, 513; relations to, 100, 109, 162; similarities to, 494; trade with, 149, 316, 429
Hoko River Site, 274
Holbrook, S. J., 261
Holbrook Black-on-white pottery, 211, 271
Holbrook Focus, 211, 534
Holcombe Site, 211
Holden, W. C., 21
Holder, Patricia, 376
Holder, Preston, 134, 458
Holiday Site, 211
Holland, C. G., 97, 200, 208, 225, 234, 267, 399, 403, 441, 494, 533
Holly pottery, 11, 175
Hollywood Site, 211
Holmes, B. E., 199, 450